The Critical Idiom

General Editor: JOHN D. JUMP

29 Expressionism

In the same series

Expressionism/*R. S. Furness*

Methuen & Co Ltd

First published 1973
by Methuen & Co Ltd
11 New Fetter Lane London EC4
© 1973 R. S. Furness
Printed in Great Britain
by Cox & Wyman Ltd, Fakenham, Norfolk

ISBN 0 416 75660 3 Hardback
ISBN 0 416 75670 0 Paperback

Distributed in the U.S.A. by

HARPER & ROW PUBLISHERS, INC.
BARNES & NOBLE IMPORT DIVISION

Contents

General Editor's Preface

The volumes composing the Critical Idiom deal with a wide variety of key terms in our critical vocabulary. The purpose of the series differs from that served by the standard glossaries of literary terms. Many terms are adequately defined for the needs of students by the brief entries in these glossaries, and such terms do not call for attention in the present series. But there are other terms which cannot be made familiar by means of compact definitions. Students need to grow accustomed to them through simple and straightforward but reasonably full discussions. The purpose of this series is to provide such discussions.

Many critics have borrowed methods and criteria from currently influential bodies of knowledge or belief that have developed without particular reference to literature. In our own century, some of them have drawn on art-history, psychology, or sociology. Others, strong in a comprehensive faith, have looked at literature and literary criticism from a Marxist or a Christian or some other sharply defined point of view. The result has been the importation into literary criticism of terms from the vocabularies of these sciences and creeds. Discussions of such bodies of knowledge and belief in their bearing upon literature and literary criticism form a natural extension of the initial aim of the Critical Idiom.

Because of their diversity of subject-matter, the studies in the series vary considerably in structure. But all authors have tried to give as full illustrative quotation as possible, to make reference whenever appropriate to more than one literature, and to write in such a way as to guide readers towards the short bibliographies in which they have made suggestions for further reading.

John D. Jump

University of Manchester

I
Origins

PROBLEMS OF DEFINITION

'Expressionism' is a descriptive term which has to cover so many disparate cultural manifestations as to be virtually meaningless: of all the 'isms' in literature and art it seems the one most difficult to define, partly because it has a general, as well as a specific application, and partly because it overlaps to a great extent with what can be called 'modernism', as well as having antecedents in Baroque dynamism and Gothic distortion. The situation is summed up with admirable clarity by Malcolm Pasley, who writes in *Germany, A Companion to German Studies*: 'Whether we want to attach this label (i.e. expressionism) to a particular author or work depends on the importance we allow to the following: (i) the use of various anti-naturalistic or "abstracting" devices, such as syntactical compression or symbolic picture-sequences, (ii) the assault on the sacred cows of the Wilhelmine bourgeoisie from a left-wing internationalist position, (iii) the choice of the theme of spiritual regeneration or renewal and (iv) the adoption of a fervent declamatory tone.' (p. 579.) The first point refers to an international tendency in the arts, while the other three denote a more German pre-occupation and, unfortunately, the word 'expressionism' has to cover both these meanings.

What this present study will attempt to do is to describe both that which is called expressionism in general and also what is called German Expressionism; it will take as its starting point the cultural situation in Europe at the end of the nineteenth century to see how the movement known as expressionism arose, particularly in lyric poetry, the theatre and the plastic arts. An analysis of what is called German Expressionism will then follow, and we shall look at the links between that particular tendency and the more general outlook prevailing elsewhere; finally we shall take stock of the situation after the waning of the German movement, to see what expressionistic features may have survived. The Germans were not the innovators, but the catalysts; although this study will focus upon Germany, the expressionistic precursors and developments elsewhere will be of equal importance.

PRECURSORS

The transition from the nineteenth to the twentieth century in Europe is characterized by a plethora of artistic styles and movements, a rich confusion with no clear-cut tendency or direction. The various 'isms' follow each other, or exist side by side, or overlap: naturalism, impressionism, symbolism, neo-romanticism, art-nouveau, then futurism and expressionism – these are the labels which, frequently unsatisfactorily, adhere to the conflicting ways of thought and feeling which crystallized between the late 1880s and the early 1920s, and which betray a profound uncertainty in man's imaginative response to the world around him.

A certain degree of over-simplification is perhaps inevitable during a discussion of literary movements and their aims. But a tendency which becomes increasingly apparent in these years is what might be called anti-naturalism. It would be false to see in symbolism a 'reaction' here, for the two schools, both stemming from France, exist side by side: neither is it correct to see impressionism as a movement away from naturalism, for the two schools have much in common; it would be closer to the truth to see, on the one hand, a naturalist-impressionist tendency and, on the other, a symbolist-neoromantic attitude in literature and the arts. The former movement would contain the names of the French novelists such as Zola, Maupassant and the Goncourts, also the French painters who conveyed the tactile essence of reality on their canvasses and, in the theatre, the names of Ibsen and Gerhart Hauptmann; the latter movement would claim Mallarmé and Verlaine, Huysmans and Maeterlinck, Stefan George, early Rilke and Hofmannsthal. The naturalist-impressionist tendency found in life material which was worthy of description and comment; the symbolist-neoromantic attitude was one of flight from the world towards the creation of artificial paradises and rarefied beauty.

It became apparent, however, that both these attitudes failed to satisfy on a profound level. For naturalism and impressionism remained too near the surface of things, while symbolism and neoromanticism, in their flight towards the rarefied and the refined, became ultra-precious, decadent and jejune: a new vision, a new energy and a new restlessness were needed. It is not simply that a more 'modern' way of thinking and feeling was felt to be lacking, for the naturalists had prided themselves on their modernity, but art seemed to have reached an impasse: a new passion was needed, a new pathos, the expression of a subjective vision regardless of mimesis, a concern for human life, a concern for man crushed by pitiless machinery and ruthless cities which was far more intense and poignant than the naturalist's description of social conditions. Likewise the emphasis on inner vision, on the creative powers, on the imagination above all, was to exceed the symbolist cult of the soul. More vital emotions, more dynamic powers of description were extolled, a creation from within, an intense subjectivity which had no reluctance in destroying the conventional picture of reality in order that the expression be more powerful: this is the new tendency. And if distortion and aggressive expression of emotion were found in earlier works of art, then these works were extolled as forerunners of the new outlook.

Like so many titles used to designate the various literary movements, the term 'expressionism' originated in painting, and only later came to describe a literary phenomenon. John Willett finds the terms used as early as 1850 to describe 'modern' painting; he also quotes it (in *Expressionism*, Weidenfeld and Nicolson, London, 1970, p. 25) as having been used in Manchester in 1880 to describe 'those who undertake to express special emotions or passions'. Many critics point to the use of the word 'expressionist' to designate the particular intensity of the work of those painters who strove to go beyond impressionism, beyond the passive registration of impressions towards a more violent, hectic, energetic creativity such as is found above all in Van Gogh. The dissolution of conventional form, the abstract use of colour, the primacy of powerful emotion – above all the turning away from mimesis herald a new consciousness and a new approach in painting, which literature was to follow. The growing independence of the image, the absolute metaphor, the intense subjectivity of the writer and the probing of extreme psychological states – above all the artist as creator, as passionate centre of a whirling vortex: all this becomes more and more apparent, as both the objectivity of the naturalists and the *l'art pour l'art* aspect of symbolism are left far behind.

A most interesting letter which demonstrates the reservations felt by Zola when confronted by the new direction in the theatre is that which he wrote to Strindberg on December 14th, 1887, to comment on the latter's play *The Father*. Zola objected to the schematic nature of Strindberg's characters, their lack of reality, and to the Captain particularly, 'who does not even have a name . . .'. Zola felt estranged from the new direction that Strindberg's drama was taking, a path towards abstraction, to the use of types rather than individuals and a lack of concern for naturalistic plausibility; here was no 'coin de la nature vu à travers un tempéra-ment' ('segment of nature seen through the eyes of a certain temperament'), but life flowing through a soul, a universalization of autobiographical material. *The Dance of Death* (1900) would, surely, also have met with Zola's strictures, with its effect almost of pantomime, its two primitive creatures locked in a love-hate embrace using a contrapuntal dialogue on their claustrophobic island.

It is, however, not until *To Damascus* (1898–1901) that a work is encountered which definitely marks the end of naturalist drama for Strindberg; it has been called the first expressionist play, where all the characters are emanations of a soul, symbolizing powers with whom the Unknown One is in combat. The canons of naturalism, the demand for plausibility and inner logic are totally ignored: an intense subjectivity prevails. The beggar, the woman, the doctor and the madman Caesar all represent aspects of the Unknown One's psyche, and move before him during his journey of self-discovery. They can be called symbols: the beggar is that degradation which the arrogant protagonist fears, yet which is necessary for his rebirth; he is the embodiment of the Unknown One's repressed thoughts, a reminder of a possibility of existence towards which the hero must move. Walter Sokel, in *The Writer in Extremis* (Stanford, 1959, p. 35) calls him 'the literal embodiment of a leitmotiv, an aesthetic attribute in the disguise of a human shape, a function of the dramatic idea'. The woman would be the link with life, a fusion of the sexual and the sublime which torments and inspires; the Doctor represents the Unknown One's guilt, while Caesar the madman would be a caricature of the protagonist's arrogance and pride. The complex trilogy portrays a gradual process of self-awareness, a Road to Damascus both painful and necessary, a Passion marked by the stations of the cross. The Christian terminology used here is appropriate, for the concern with the soul, with the inner life and the birth of a new man, betray an undeniably religious concern which will characterize many expressionist writers: the ego is seen as a magic crystal in which the Absolute is in constant play.

It may be of interest here to mention briefly a remarkable piece of dramatic writing which anticipates Strindberg's method by over three hundred years. This is Act Three of *King Lear*, in which, in scenes iv and vi, both the natural elements and the characters may be regarded as manifestations of Lear's tormented condition. The spectator enters into Lear's mind by seeing him grouped with three other characters, each of whom is a projection of some part of that mind. Through the Fool, Lear's repressed self-reproach rises to consciousness; Kent, as the loyal servant, recalls those supposedly 'natural' relationships of King and subject, master and servant, parent and child, which sustained Lear in the role that was his early in the play; Poor Tom (who is really Edgar, but for the time being Edgar is lost in Poor Tom) is Lear's vision of man deprived of those relationships and of all other removable supports, in short, 'unaccommodated man'. Lear's discovery of truths about himself and about the life around him is communicated to us through the movements, gestures and speeches of this group of characters.

With *A Dream Play* (1901–1902) Strindberg approached an almost neo-romantic mystery play such as Hofmannsthal might have written (with the description of the castle of life, for instance, from which the crysanthemum-soul arises), but that which might be called the expressionist element is seen in the way in which the characters appear as symbols or fragments of a dreaming mentality. In the 'Reminder' which Strindberg desired to have printed on the programme he wrote: 'The characters split, double, multiply, vanish, solidify, blur, clarify. But one consciousness reigns above them all – that of the dreamer; and before it there are no secrets, no incongruities, no scruples, no laws. There is neither judgement nor exoneration, but merely narration.' (See C. L. Dahlström, *Strindberg's Dramatic Expressionism*, Ann Arbor, 1930, p. 177.) The concentration on a dream-reality, of course, looks forward to surrealism, but it also exemplifies a growing tendency of expressionism to admit, and extol, the mystical, quasi-religious yearnings of the human soul. It is obvious that Strindberg is of great importance in any inquiry into the roots of the anti-naturalist tendency in the theatre: between 1913 and 1915 there were one thousand and thirty-five performances of twenty-four different Strindberg plays in Germany alone, and it was in Germany above all, as we shall later see, that Strindberg's expressionist tendency was to be developed and modified.

If *To Damascus* portrays the soul's struggles to find and transcend itself, then a writer must be mentioned who is of crucial importance at this time, and who may well be seen caricatured as Caesar in Strindberg's play. This is Friedrich Nietzsche, with whom Strindberg corresponded briefly before and at the time of Nietzsche's mental collapse (Nietzsche's letter of 7 December 1888 congratulated Strindberg on his own translation into French of *The Father*, and suggested that Strindberg might undertake the translation of *Ecce Homo*). A discussion of Nietzsche is vital in any description of the precursors of expressionism: he is a European, rather than simply a German, phenomenon and, for good or for ill, stands behind so many developments in twentieth-century art and thought. The dithyrambic ecstasy of *Thus Spake Zarathustra* reverberated through literature and music before the First World War; a perverse distortion of his thinking also became apparent in the Third Reich. It was Nietzsche's emphasis on self-awareness, self-mastery and passionate self-fulfilment that gave the expressionist mode of thought its keenest impetus. The naturalists may have applauded Nietzsche's attack on bourgeois complacency, and the symbolists have thrilled to his vision of the poet-prophet remote in azure loneliness: it was the expressionist generation, however, which was overwhelmed by his daring pathos, his insistence on the destruction of the old and moribund, and his emphasis upon daring and vision. 'Develop each of your powers – but this means: develop anarchy! Perish!' 'Where is the lightning to lick you with its tongue? Where is the madness with which you should be filled?' 'My brothers, destroy, destroy the ancient tablets!' Nietzsche's imperious apostacy thrilled a whole generation of poets and thinkers; his emphasis upon idealism, upon the will and upon passionate ecstasy found its counterpart in the intense subjectivity of many of the expressionists, and their demand for a New Man, whose features often bore a distinct resemblance to those of Zarathustra. Above all it was Nietzsche's worship of creativity and the life-force which struck the deepest roots in the new mentality.

But the movement, or mentality, known as expressionism is complex, and contains many divergent tendencies and contradictions which are to be found at the heart of Nietzsche himself. Beneath the passionate proclamations and the dithyrambic ecstasies a softer tone is heard in Nietzsche, a voice full of disquiet and foreboding. The madman who appears on the market-place (see Book Three of *The Gay Science*) flings his lantern to the ground and cannot hold back his fearful knowledge that, after God's death, man is plunging into icy nihilism. 'Where are we moving? Away from all suns? Are we not staggering, backwards, forwards, sideways, in all directions? Is there an Above, a Below? Are we not wandering through an eternal nothingness? Does not empty space breathe at us? Has it not grown colder? . . .' Can man indeed fill the void of God's absence, or is man not destroyed by the enormity of the crime of deicide? Is man striding forward to a new vision, glorious in his beauty and power, or is the world moving into anarchy and disintegration? Nietzsche's own uncertainty was reflected in the different emphases of the expressionist writers, some of whom glory in spiritual and political visions of Utopia while others are unable to banish the spectre of nihilism and anticipations of a universal dread. The tensions in expressionism, particularly in Germany, do not simply result from the hopes and terrors brought about by the First World War: they go back to Nietzsche, but are also, of course, the positive and negative poles of the human psyche; the expressionist writers, however, with their predilection for extreme states of tension, ecstatic or desperate, seem more prone to hyperbole. The cry or shriek, so often met with in expressionist art, need not necessarily be one of joy: Edvard Munch showed in his famous lithograph of 1894 that it may also be a scream of existential terror.

The soul under stress, racked and burning in fearful incandescence – this preoccupation may be called expressionist. It brings Nietzsche very much to mind, also Dostoevsky, the only psychologist, Nietzsche explained, from whom he had anything to learn. As in the case of Strindberg, Nietzsche came to Dostoevsky late in his creative life, but immediately sensed that here was a writer whose psychological finesse and fearless probing of the darker corners of the psyche were to be admired. It is interesting to observe the fascination that Dostoevsky held for a great many writers, particularly in Germany, between 1900 and 1925. The naturalists had praised him as a 'realist' because of his descriptions of poverty and social outcasts: *Crime and Punishment* was the great impetus here. But later the emphasis shifted to Dostoevsky as an explorer of pathological conditions, as the psychologist of crime, and in the expressionist period it was the irrational and the pseudo-religious aspects of the writer which came to the fore. The dominating influence in the Dostoevsky cult in Germany was above all Moeller van den Bruck who edited, with Dmitri Mereschkowski and others, the great Piper edition of Dostoevsky's work, commenced in 1906. Moeller van den Bruck wrote prefaces to several of the volumes in this edition, and propagated his own views on art and society through the mouthpiece of the Russian novelist: between 1908 and 1923 Piper Verlag printed 65,000 copies of *The Brothers Karamazov*; in the twenty years between 1914 and 1934 the *Legend of the Grand Inquisitor* reached 110,000 copies in the Insel edition alone. But the peak of the cult coincided with the climax of German Expressionism: between 1920 and 1922 there were nearly half a million copies of the works of Dostoevsky published and translated in the Piper edition: Dostoevsky's reactionary mysticism, his anti-Westernism and fervent patriotism undoubtedly inspired Moeller van den Bruck's own work *Das dritte Reich*. It is false to equate the expressionist mentality with radical left-wing attitudes; although many of the German Expressionists, particularly during the First World War, did join the socialist and communist parties, the burning idealism unleashed could and frequently did express itself in right-wing politics. The emphasis on the subjective, the flirtation with the irrational, the desire for a New Man did find an outlet, as we shall see, in National Socialism, and Dostoevsky's idea of the 'conservative revolution' also appealed directly to a writer like Thomas Mann, who acknowledges this in his *Meditations of a Non-Political Man*; it is interesting, however, that the left-wingers Kurt Eisner and Rosa Luxemburg should have found his influence pernicious.

Dostoevsky's contribution to the expressionist mentality is considerable. He shares with Nietzsche and Strindberg an emphasis on extreme, often pathological psychological states, on the rejection of 'normal' canons of thinking and feeling, on the need for a daring transvaluation of values. Both Nietzsche and Dostoevsky stress the need for a spiritual revival, a New Man born of suffering and passion. As Zarathustra destroyed the tablets of the law, so Dostoevsky seemed to stand beyond good and evil, a frightening, and yet liberating visionary: the fervent, even febrile quality of his writing was worshipped by a generation grown tired of naturalistic dullness and neoromantic velleities.

In Russia, Sweden and Germany, and also in America, the precursors of the expressionist mentality are to be found. A most potent force was the poetry of Walt Whitman, who has much in common with Nietzsche, and whose vitalism later found an undeniable echo in expressionist rhapsodic utopianism. The following lines from *The Mystic Trumpeter* could well be taken from the German Expressionist Franz Werfel:

> A reborn race appears – a perfect world, all joy!
> Women and men in wisdom innocence and health – all joy!
> Riotous laughing bacchanals filled with joy!
> War, sorrow, suffering gone – the rank earth purged – nothing
>   but joy left!
> The ocean filled with joy – the atmosphere all joy!
> Joy! joy! in freedom, worship, love! joy in the ecstasy of life!
> Enough to merely be! enough to breathe!
> Joy! joy! all over joy!

And Dostoevsky's *From the House of the Dead* seems very close in spirit to the sentiment expressed in the lines from *You Felons on Trial in Courts*:

> Lust and wickedness are acceptable to me,
> I walk with delinquents with passionate love,
> I feel I am of them – I belong to those convicts and
>   prostitutes myself,
> And henceforth I will not deny them – for how can I deny myself?

It is Zarathustra who is adumbrated in the following lines:

> Dazzling and tremendous how quick the sunrise would kill me,
> If I could not now and always send sun-rise out of me . . .
> (Song of Myself)

and Nietzsche himself here:

> Do I contradict myself?
> Very well then I contradict myself,
> (I am large, I contain multitudes.)
> (Song of Myself)

And Whitman, addressing the creative potential of the New World, strikingly anticipates the emphasis on the modern which will also play a considerable role in the expressionist outlook:

B

Brain of the New World, what a task is thine,
To formulate the Modern – out of the peerless grandeur of the
    modern,
Out of thyself, comprising science, to recast poems, churches, ar\
(Recast, maybe discard them, end them – maybe their work is
    done, who knows?)
By vision, hand, conception, on the background of the mighty
    past, the dead,
To limn with absolute faith the mighty living present.

(Thou Mother with thy Equal Brood)

Here an Italian, Filippo Marinetti, must be mentioned, author
of the *Futurist Manifesto* (1909), which extolled in rhapsodic
admiration the age of the machine. 'We shall sing of great crowds
in the excitement of Labour, Pleasure or Rebellion; of the nocturnal
vibration of arsenals and work-shops beneath their electric moons;
of greedy stations swallowing smoking snakes; of adventurous
liners scenting the horizon; of broadchested locomotives galloping
on rails . . .'. The most famous statement of Marinetti, however,
is the following: 'We maintain that the splendour of the world
has been enriched by a new beauty: the beauty of speed. A racing-
car decorated with exhaust-pipes like snakes spitting fire, a
menacing racing-car which roars into the distance like a burst of
machine-gun fire is more beautiful than the Winged Victory of
Samothrace . . .' (see the introduction to *The Penguin Book of
French Verse*, ed. Anthony Hartley, p. xxxix, also the article on
'Expressionismus und Technik' in *Expressionismus als Literatur*,
ed. Rothe, 1969, p. 173). His novel *Mafarka le Futuriste* (1909)
depicts a mechanical superman who flies and eventually conquers
space; his novels were translated into German and his lecture in
Berlin in 1913 had a profound effect. Marinetti and the group
associated with him were bent upon the destruction of symbolism:
the desire to 'murder the moonlight' was an attempt to rid
literature of the subtleties and exquisite shadings of the symbolist
school. Futurist art was above all an attempted identification with

modern life, with speed and the machine, and in their movement away from the embodiment to the idea they anticipated the idea of conceptual art. Wyndham Lewis, as we shall later see, came to terms with Marinetti and futurism in the first number of *Blast*.

There seems to be a paradox here: how can the praise of the aggressively technological be reconciled with the desire to preserve human imagination and creative expression? Does not the machine stunt and maim? Later it will be Georg Kaiser and Ernst Toller in Germany, also Eugene O'Neill and Elmer Rice in America, who portray the juggernaut in all its ferocity. But the machine could also be extolled as an expression of the human will, of human power and inventiveness: the futurist-expressionist looked upon man as the modern Prometheus, the machine (train, aeroplane or motor-car) as guarantor of freedom and escape. As a manifestation of man's creative vision the machine was worthy of praise: as an exemplification of modernity it was accepted by all those who longed to cast aside tradition and set forth into the unknown. Whitman himself had had his vision, the 'new race dominating previous ones, and greater far, with new contests,/ New politics, new literatures and religions, new inventions and arts' (*Starting from Paumanok*); he summed up so well the need to affirm all, man and machine, in a fervent pantheistic embrace:

As for me, (torn, stormy, amid these vehement days,)
I have the idea of all, and am all and believe in all,
I believe materialism is true and spiritualism is true, I reject no
    part . . .

(With Antecedents)

To conclude: the movement, or tendency, or mentality known as expressionism emerged in Europe from an intellectual climate consisting of diverse features, amongst which Nietzsche's vitalism, Marinetti's futurism, Whitman's pantheism and Dostoevsky's psychological probing into sub-rational darkness play an important part. A further impetus came from Bergson, whose description, in *Essai sur les données immédiates de la conscience* (1889) of 'le moi d'en bas qui remonte à la surface' ('the subterranean ego which rises to the surface') and 'la croûte extérieure qui éclate, cédant à une irrésistible poussée' ('the outer crust which bursts, giving way to an irresistible force') is a further emphasis on subjective force and radical change. Everywhere the call is for self-expression, creativity, ecstatic fervour and a ruthless denial of tradition: the arts are ready for a new beginning, a new departure or *Aufbruch*, and expressionism, in its vitalism and forcefulness, seems a fitting herald for the new century.

2

Formal Innovations: expressionism and modernity

Whether it was Paul Cassirer, the art-dealer, in the presence of a selection committee looking at a painting by Max Pechstein, or the *Figaro* critic Louis Vauxcelles, or Wilhelm Worringer, the art historian, in his work *Abstraktion und Einfühlung* who first brought the term 'expressionism' into common usage is unknown and ultimately unimportant: what is of interest is that it was the world of painting, as was mentioned in the first section, which first demonstrated the new expressive force, the anti-mimetic tendency, the movement towards abstraction. In France it was the cubists and the fauves who reacted against impressionism; the famous Salon d'Automne exhibition of *fauvisme* in 1905 brought a new and disturbing world before the public gaze. In Germany the modern, expressionist painters formed two schools, firstly *Die Brücke* in Dresden in 1905 (amongst them Heckel, and Schmidt-Rottluff), and then *Der blaue Reiter* in Munich in 1912, including such famous names as Franz Marc, August Macke and, above all, Kandinsky. It is enlightening to look briefly at the art world to see the tendencies which will become apparent likewise within the new poetry: this is also permissible as many of the expressionists, rather like the German romantics a century before, had stressed the ultimate union of all the arts and, perhaps with more success, had demonstrated this in their achievements: Schoenberg was both musician and painter (his remarkable pictures, when exhibited in Vienna in 1910, created much the same *succès de scandale* as the 'Five Orchestral Pieces'); Kokoschka was painter and playwright, Ernst Barlach drew and sculpted and wrote plays of outstanding quality, and Kandinsky was a lyric poet and a dramatist as well as being an important innovator in painting.

An expressionist canvas makes an almost physical attack on the observer, and it was Van Gogh with his violent brushwork and unrealistic colours who was one of the first to concentrate on the expression of disturbing and emotional experiences, conveying, in *L'Arlésienne*, with red and yellow the frightening passions of man. In Van Gogh it becomes more and more apparent that colour attains increasing independence as a carrying force of emotion; it arouses a response without the help of conventional form. This abstracting of colour from traditional composition is also seen in expressionist poetry, particularly in the work of the Austrian poet Georg Trakl (1887–1914): the problem concerning the abstracted or 'autotelic' (or independent) image is of interest here, the image not as a projection of reality but an inner truth told in line and colour, or in a manipulation of words. An important work in this context is Kandinsky's *Über das Geistige in der Kunst (Concerning the Spiritual in Art)* (1912), which, quickly translated, reached a wide audience in many countries. Art, for Kandinsky, was neither decoration, nor entertainment, nor a mere mirror of nature: each work of art was to be the manifestation of a creative vision, and each colour was to transmit an emotional state. Of the artist Kandinsky wrote: 'Sein offenes Auge soll auf sein inneres Leben gerichtet werden und sein Ohr soll dem Munde der inneren Notwendigkeit stets zugewendet sein . . . (p. 84). Der Künstler ist nicht nur berechtigt, sondern verpflichtet, mit den Formen so umzugehen wie es für seine Zwecke notwendig ist' (p. 133). ('His open eye should be fixed upon his inner life, and his ear should always be turned to the mouth of his inner necessity . . . The artist is not only justified in treating form in any way that is necessary for his purpose, but is obliged to do this.') An extreme subjectivity is underlined here, with the artist as creator, driven by an inner necessity. 'Das ist schön, was einer inneren seelischen Notwendigkeit entspringt. Das ist schön, was innerlich schön ist' (p. 137). ('Beautiful is that which springs from an inner necessity; beautiful is that which is inwardly beautiful.') (The quotations are taken from the 8th edition, Berne, Benteli, 1965.) Kandinsky also stressed a mingling of the senses and of the art-forms, a visual mysticism in the manner of Rudolf Steiner and a synaesthesia which recalls Rimbaud and Scriabin; this is seen in his experimental stage works *Der gelbe Klang* of 1909 and *Violett* in 1911, also in the abstract woodcuts *Klänge*.

Abstraction of colour, inner necessity, the artist as sole legislator and creator of a new reality – these ideas become translated more and more into writing, particularly poetry. Walter Sokel has described very clearly the philosophical foundation of modernism to be found in Kant, who shattered the formulation of art as mimesis by insisting that nature does not exist outside the mind, and hence the imitation of nature would become a somewhat dubious affair. Sokel discusses Kant's concept of the 'aesthetic idea' and his recognition of the metaphor as an 'aesthetic attribute' of language which reveals a reality surpassing the logical: this is linked to Mallarmé's 'la parole essentielle', an aesthetic phenomenon used to produce emotional effects and symbolic worlds. He also describes the use of emotional, aesthetic attributes, or symbols, in nineteenth-century realism, for example, in Flaubert, where, in *Madame Bovary*, the blind, deformed beggar, although enjoying a fair degree of plausibility, of 'reality', also becomes a symbol, or 'metaphor', being a demonstration of the heroine's inner condition, and a foreshadowing of what is to come. Flaubert here expresses the main character's repressed, even unknown, feelings by embodying them in another character, this symbolic character becoming an objective correlative for certain inner states. This tendency became important in Strindberg, as was seen, and will be seen in the plays of German Expressionism; it will be found in the Nighttown section of Joyce's *Ulysses* and also in Kafka, where metaphor is treated as actual fact (in *Die Verwandlung*): instead of quality becoming attached to a substantive, substance becomes a function of quality. As Kandinsky created pure compositions of colour and line, so many expressionist poets created pure composition of autonomous metaphors which stand as abstracted and powerful nuclei of feeling.

The problem of the metaphor is central to expressionism. It seems a characteristic of poetry since, roughly speaking, the beginning of the century, that the metaphor has become more complex in that the link or point of comparison between the two worlds has become less evident, more personal, laconic or esoteric. Ezra Pound's lines, 'In a station of the Metro', are a useful example: 'The apparition of these faces in the crowd:/Petals, on a wet, black bough', where the appearance of wet petals against the darkness suggests faces glimpsed in the Underground, the condition belonging to both worlds being, probably, hopelessness and vulnerability. T. S. Eliot's 'The yellow fog that rubs its back upon the window panes' (in *Prufrock*) is a most effective picture: the dirty fog partakes of the furtiveness and stealth of a tomcat. But it is obvious that a gradual dissociation of the two realms (the situation and the referent) is undeniable: in Pound's case the link petals/faces is still acceptable, whereas in Eliot's case fog/cat is more tenuous. And the tendency for the metaphor to become more and more independent and increasingly 'absolute' is one of the hallmarks of modern poetry. The absolute metaphor would be one in which the original situation, the experience which should call to mind the comparison, no longer appears. A concrete situation fades behind a weight of metaphorical associations: it is as though a noun were lost behind its attributive adjectives (a situation prevalent in the poetry of the Austrian Georg Trakl). An extreme subjectivity would result here, where the poet's metaphors (or epithets) replace the actual existing situation or object; the metaphor would then exist in its own right *as an image*, often juxtaposed with other images to create a world remote from the real. The metaphor (or image) becomes *expressive* rather than imitative, existing as a powerful, autonomous figure of speech from which radiate a host of evocative meanings. An example often quoted here is the last line of Guillaume Apollinaire's 'Zone' (from the collection *Alcools*): 'Adieu adieu/Soleil cou coupé', where the link between sun and cut throat is indeed tenuous, and it is for the reader to grasp the point of comparison – the idea of termination, finality, sunset, redness and blood.

An absolute or autotelic metaphor may also be called an image, an image being defined as a simile, metaphor or figure of speech, an objectification or re-enactment of an inner experience. It may also be said that, in modern poetry, images become autotelic in the sense that they become increasingly divorced from the object and exist as evocative forces. It was Ezra Pound again who attempted to define the image as he saw it in modern poetry: 'An "image" is that which presents an intellectual and emotional complex in an instant of time' (*Poetry*, March 1913), and again: 'The image is not an idea. It is a radiant node or cluster; it is ... a VORTEX, from which, and through which, and into which, ideas are constantly rushing' (*Gaudier-Brzeska. A Memoir*, p. 106). An imagist would be he who seeks clarity of expression through the use of precise images, but 'precise' not in any naturalist or impressionist sense, but rather meaning effective, disturbing (possibly shocking) and expressive. Imagist poets, writes Michael Hamburger, 'deal with bare phenomena in the form of images, not as an ornament added to what they have to say, nor as a means of illustrating a metaphysical statement, but as an end in itself. The mere existence of phenomena is their justification: and to understand their Being is to understand their significance. The poetic image, then, becomes autonomous and "autotelic", or as nearly so as the medium of words permits . . .' (*Reason and Energy*, London, 1957, pp. 239–40).

The links between what might be called imagism and expressionism are very close. It is the condensation of juxtaposed images that characterizes the new poetry, particularly in Germany, where the names of Georg Trakl (1887–1914), Georg Heym (1887–1912) and Ernst Stadler (1883–1914) spring to mind. An impressionist poet would feel fascinated by the tactile, sensuous aspects of phenomena, whereas the expressionist (sharing much in common with the symbolist here) feels the need to point beyond, or to indicate by the sensitive use of images and symbols that the ultimate meaning of the world might lie beyond its purely external appearance. What is puzzling in much twentieth-century poetry is the fact that the same image might be used for different purposes, sometimes descriptive, sometimes symbolic; a symbolic extension of an image may sometimes be assumed.

For our present purposes it can safely be argued that the predominance of the image, with frequent symbolic overtones, *is* a characteristic of expressionism; the expressionist poet feels the need to use an image not merely as a mirror of external reality but as a crucial centre of meaning (Pound's vortex); it becomes independent, and is used to set up a host of echoes within the reader, to act as an impulse to his imagination or as a catalyst to his reactions. A skilful manipulation of images may not necessarily describe reality, but weave an incantatory spell which should induce the reader to discover for himself what the poet has experienced and wishes to express. Both image and symbol express an inner world of meaning, and are abstracted from common experience: image-as-metaphor and image-as-symbol move beyond mimesis, accumulate heightened meanings in a re-interpretation of the world. 'An "image" may be invoked once as a metaphor, but if it persistently recurs, both as presentation and representation, it becomes a symbol, may even become part of a symbolic (or mythic) system' (Wellek and Warren, *Theory of Literature*, London, 1949, p. 193).

To sum up the argument so far: the outlook known as expressionism combines the following: a movement towards abstraction, towards autonomous colour and metaphor, away from plausibility and imitation; a fervent desire to express and create regardless of formal canons; a concern for the typical and essential rather than the purely personal and individual; a predilection for ecstasy and despair and hence a tendency towards the inflated and the grotesque; a mystical, even religious element with frequent apocalyptic overtones; an urgent sense of the here and now, the city and the machine seen not from any naturalistic point of view but *sub specie aeternitatis*; a desire for revolt against tradition and a longing for the new and the strange. The revolutionary fervour will later assume positive political direction, towards either communism or fascism (National Socialism). Expressionism will have much of the Baroque in it (its dynamic sweep and restlessness, also its *memento mori*) yet more of the Gothic (the distortion, abstraction and mystical ecstasy); artists of earlier centuries who had deliberately used distortion to obtain a greater degree of expressiveness were hailed as forerunners. In expressionism there is an undeniable tendency away from the natural, the plausible and the normal towards the primitive, the abstract, the passionate and the shrill; it is in the theatre and in the lyric that the tendencies are most marked, rather than in the novel, which remained closer to its nineteenth-century models. In its restlessness and its tendency towards the extreme the expressionist movement seems quintessentially German, rather than simply modernist, and it is therefore at German Expressionism that we shall now look.

3
The German Situation
1900-1914

In Germany the decade immediately preceding the outbreak of the First World War is more memorable for the intensity and vehemence of the critics than for the convictions of the defenders of the existing order: every artist of note took up arms against the stifling pomposity of Wilhelmine institutions, the complacency and hypocrisy of bourgeois *moeurs* and the arrogance of a militaristic caste. The attitude of revolt in Germany was more extreme than in any other European country because of the more pronounced philistinism of the established society and the traditional feeling of isolation and vulnerability of the artist in Germany; the theatre, particularly, anticipated by fifty years anything that the British stage dared or deigned to consider. What the German Expressionist playwrights portrayed with passionate earnestness shortly before and after the war was already there, albeit in an ironic and often cynical vein, in the plays of Frank Wedekind (1864–1918).

To extol the power of sex and to attack a hypocritical, stultifying society – these were Wedekind's main aims. He seems to derive much from Nietzsche and Strindberg (whose second wife became his mistress), also from the cabaret tradition: he performed on his guitar in the Munich cabaret 'Die elf Scharfrichter', collaborated on the satirical journal *Simplizissimus* and served a spell of imprisonment at the very beginning of the new century for *lèse-majesté*. His first play, *Frühlings Erwachen (Spring Awakening)* was begun in 1890 and received its first public performance in

1906: the attack on bourgeois morality is ruthless, and the school atmosphere particularly is singled out for bitter criticism. Yet here is no naturalist drama à la Hauptmann: a grotesque element is undeniable in the use of caricature, and the last scene, in a churchyard, completely abandons any attempt at realism. As the hero stands by the dead girl's grave (the stated cause of death being 'anaemia', the actual cause an attempted abortion) he is tempted by the headless ghost of a school friend (who had committed suicide after failing his examinations) to kill himself; as he is about to yield a 'masked gentleman' in evening dress (frequently played by Wedekind himself) steps from behind the tombs and persuades him to chose life instead. But there is no rhetoric or bombast: the representative of 'life' – Wedekind – seems a cynical *roué* and by no means a devout advocate of the virtues of living. Yet the farce of the staffroom scenes (the absurd names, the interminable wrangling about whether or not to open the window) and the grotesque ending do conceal a serious purpose: to praise the life-force and healthy sexuality as opposed to deceit, complacency and dull respectability.

The desire to shock is seen even more clearly in his two most famous plays, *Erdgeist* (*Earth Spirit*) and *Die Büchse der Pandora* (*Pandora's Box*), dating from the period 1895–1904. The Lulu-figure is both fascinating and revolting, a personification of woman which both Strindberg and Nietzsche would have endorsed, tempting, cunning, cruel and destructive. Does Wedekind glorify sex in these plays, is it a salvation from the drabness of life? Do we admire Lulu for her courage and ultimate integrity? Or is the story a moral one, showing how Lulu sinks to a sordid and fearful end – a victim of Jack the Ripper? Wedekind proclaims that he will show us 'das wahre Tier, das wilde, schöne Tier' ('the true animal, the wild, beautiful animal') in an almost Nietzschean way, but also prevents too close an involvement with the issues by the circus technique, the deliberate theatricality of the whole thing, and the element of farce and absurdity. The alienation techniques look forward to Brecht, a great admirer of Wedekind, and it is Wedekind who shares with later German Expressionist writers the aggressive attack on Wilhelmine society (in the novel it would be Heinrich Mann who comes to mind), the praising of life and energy, the use of distortion and caricature and the overt rejection of naturalism (see the circus-master's contemptuous rejection of various Hauptmann 'heroes' in the prologue to *Erdgeist*). But Wedekind ultimately defies classification: his cynicism, self-travesty and satirical moralizing are far removed from the extravagant hyperbole of many German Expressionist playwrights.

The attack against red plush, potted plants and *bric-à-brac* is heightened and sharpened to ruthless precision in the plays of Carl Sternheim (1878–1942), whose comedies, entitled *Aus dem bürgerlichen Heldenleben (From the Heroic Life of the Middle-class)*, earned him the name of the modern Molière. If Wedekind is the cynical moralist, Sternheim is satirist pure and simple, aloof yet dedicated to a merciless attack; that which he shares with Wedekind is the anti-naturalist tendency, seen in the frequency with which Sternheim reduces his characters to types, and the deliberate artificiality of the language. He strove to break through the 'genteel' in the German language, to cut away sentimentality and platitudes: the foreshortening of language and syntax is highly self-conscious and very effective. This 'telegraphic' style could be an anticipation of the 'Neue Sachlichkeit' tendency of the later twenties, but can also be called expressionistic as it tends towards concentration, abstraction and extreme intensity. The synthetic curtness will appear very much to the fore in the plays of Georg Kaiser: in Sternheim it does not have the steely quality of Kaiser, but rather the deliberate quirkiness and unreality which alienates and yet fascinates the reader.

The deliberate flouting of Wilhelmine tabus is seen in the very title of the play *Die Hose* (*Knickers*) of 1911, where the attractive wife of a small clerk loses this garment in the street just as the Emperor passes by; the husband, Theobald Maske, exploits this incident and uses his wife as bait to lure in lodgers. Maske verges on the grotesque throughout, yet it is difficult to know if he is simply a monster of selfishness or a man to be admired: the pusillanimous and prurient lodgers cut very sorry figures indeed beside him. In the next play, *Der Snob* (1914) Sternheim traces the fortunes of Maske's son Christian, and its successor, *1913* (1915), is the most expressionistic of the three in that it portrays a world ripe for destruction, where Maske's grandchildren, effete, brutal and opportunist, blindly pursue their aims on the very edge of the abyss. 'Nach uns Zusammenbruch! Wir sind reif!' ('After us the deluge! We're ripe for it!') calls Christian, and the play ends with the lights extinguished, and the wind blowing the curtains into the room. The play is dedicated to the memory of Ernst Stadler, one of the most talented of the early German Expressionist poets, who was killed in France early in September 1914. Albeit ironic, the idea of the need for a New Man seems also present in Sternheim here, and the tentative hope is expressed that something better might emerge from the holocaust. And although both Wedekind and Sternheim stand apart from many of the new tendencies in the theatre at this time, they nevertheless make their contribution to the new outlook.

The truly revolutionary features of the theatre are seen in a number of plays written by Kokoschka between 1907 and 1918, which incensed the theatre-going public on their appearance. As was pointed out in Chapter 2, the arts were closer together during expressionism than they had been in any other preceding movement in the nineteenth century, and although Kokoschka's plays do not possess the same important proportions in his output as those of Barlach do in his, they are nevertheless organically related to his painting and graphic work of the period and, both as regards content and technique, they foreshadow some typical aspects of German Expressionist drama.

Kokoschka's first literary work was a lyrical monologue *Die träumenden Knaben* (*The Dreaming Boys*); dedicated to Gustav Klimt it is an erotic, *fin-de-siècle* reverie, a German *L'Après-midi d'un faune* with moments of original poetic invention. It could be called a typical piece of *Wiener Sezession*, but with his first play, *Mörder Hoffnung der Frauen* (*Murderer, the Hope of Women*), Kokoschka turns to the sombre and the violent in his treatment of the theme of the gulf between the sexes. It was written in 1907, a year after the important Van Gogh exhibition in Vienna and a performance there of Strindberg's *Dance of Death*.

In *Mörder Hoffnung der Frauen* (see *Die deutsche Literatur VII*, ed. Killy, Munich, Beck, 1967, pp. 661–4) the presentation of the fight between the sexes is febrile and nightmarish in its intensity. Like *Der brennende Dornbusch* (*The Burning Bush*) of 1911 it is simply a sequence of highly charged utterances, outbursts from the subconscious of the two antagonists, Man and Woman, which vary between attraction and repulsion. There can be no talk of plot here; it is a psychodrama, predominantly irrational, full of surging and ebbing emotions. The utterances are elliptical: lighting and lengthy stage directions emphasize the symbolic atmosphere of the whole. Heinrich von Kleist's *Penthesilea* seems to have provided the impetus here, with its murderous combat between hero and heroine: Nietzsche and Freud are also brought to mind. The Man and his followers are 'Bestürmer verschlossener Festungen' ('Besiegers of sealed fortresses'), whilst the Woman exults: 'Mit meinem Atem erflackert die blonde Scheibe der Sonne' ('At my breath the blond disc of the sun flares up'). There is both tenderness and brutality, but the sexual images of futile, senseless 'whirling' predominate, as the Man chants: 'Sinnlose Begehr von Grauen zu Grauen, unstillbares Kreisen im Leeren.

Gebären ohne Geburt, Sonnensturz, wankender Raum . . .'
('Senseless desire, from horror to horror, insatiable whirling in
emptiness, baring, but no birth, sun-plunge, staggering space . . .').
And the woman's followers proclaim: 'Der Streit ist unverständ-
lich und dauert eine Ewigkeit' ('The battle is incomprehensible,
and lasts an eternity'); finally the woman recoils, fearing that the
Man will dominate. In a furious outburst the Man kills the Woman,
and flees. Is the man an inadequate partner? Can he only assert
himself in a fit of gratuitous violence? There are echoes of the
Lulu tragedy here, also anticipations of Schoenberg's *Die glückliche Hand* (*The Fortunate Hand*), a short opera with a similar
theme, complex use of lighting and colour and the idea again of
the impossibility of true communion between man and woman,
the man being too cerebral, the woman too natural. But the
Kokoschka play (transposed into an opera in 1920 by Hindemith)
cannot be given a satisfactory interpretation: it is a violent eruption
which overwhelms, appals and amazes.

An amusing contrast is *Sphinx und Strohmann*, written in the
same year and described as a *curiosum*. It anticipates, if anything,
the Dadaist antics of the war years and was, in fact, staged by
them in 1917; it transposes into the absurd the fears of Strindberg's
Captain in *The Dance of Death*. Herr Firdusi's large straw head
is turned so that he cannot see his wife Anima, a sensual, Lulu-
like woman, who is fascinated by Herr Kautschukmann, an evil
scientist; as Herr Kautschukmann desires Anima he explains that
fear of a wife's adultery brings about death, and Herr Firdusi
dies, horns sprouting from his head. Nonsensical aphorisms are
shouted by an actor who sticks his head from the backdrop as
Herr Kautschukmann and Anima exult; in the 1917 performance
in Zurich Hugo Ball played Firdusi and Emmy Hennings Anima,
while Tristan Tzara played the parrot and provided the thunder
effects with reckless abandon.

It is interesting that when Kokoschka chose to illustrate Bach's

c

cantata no. 60, *O Ewigkeit, du Donnerwort* he saw the basic situation of the work (the long, troubled dialogue between Fear and Hope) in the same sombre terms as in his dramas; there is no harmony for him as there was in Bach. The gulf is still evident in the famous painting *Die Windsbraut* of 1914; there is the whirling turmoil, the man and woman who lie close, yet who are separated by immeasurable distances, the woman serene, the man tense, preoccupied and remote. The Austrian poet Georg Trakl saw this canvas; although he resorted to the mystical notion of androgyny in certain of his poems there is no such solution in Kokoschka.

The sex problem, then, looms large in the works of artists who may be described as early expressionists: a more important theme, however, is the relationship between father and son. The German playwrights, between 1900 and the war years, portrayed with incredible intensity and violence the clash between generations, in which incest and murder play an important part. This seems a common German theme in literature: the antecedents may be found in the *Sturm und Drang*, in early Schiller particularly. The father-figure becomes a symbol for authority, and the rebellion against this image reaches feverish and strident proportions. Reinhard Sorge prepared the way with his play *Der Bettler* (*The Beggar*) written in 1912, although not performed until five years later. The protagonist is a poet, an incarnation of pure feeling, who pioneers a new drama which will sweep away outmoded conventions, and bring spiritual illumination to the masses: he describes his vision thus:

> Das Werk! das Werk! und nur das Werk war Herr!
> Wie soll ich reden . . . Ich will Ihnen Bilder
> Der Zukünfte erzählen, die in mir
> Mit Pracht sich aufgerichtet haben . . .
> Hören Sie doch: es wird
> Das Herz der Kunst: aus allen Ländern strömen

Die Menschen alle an die heilende Stätte
Zur Heiligung, nicht nur ein kleines Häuflein
Erlesener! . . . Massen der Arbeiter
Schwemmt an die Ahnung ihres höheren Lebens
In großen Wogen . . .

(The work! the work! only the work was master! How shall I speak
. . . I will show you visions of future times, which splendidly have
risen within me. Listen! My work shall be the very heart of art:
from all the lands there stream men, men towards the holy place to
be redeemed – not just a little group of chosen ones! Masses of
workers feel in waves, tumultuous, a vision now of higher life. . . .)

The poet strides through various stations and experiences, including the murder of his parents, to a realization, ecstatic and
yet desperate, of the meaning of his life, of his love and his
mission:

Laß sinnen . . . sinnen . . . Symbole . . . (Jäh empor, mit Händen
aufwärts): O Trost des
Blitzes . . . Erleuchtung . . . Schmerztrost des Blitzes . . .
Symbole der Ewigkeit . . .
Ende! Ende! Ziel und Ende! . . .
Durch Symbole der Ewigkeit zu reden . . .
(Let me think . . . think . . . (Leaps up, his hands outstretched):
Oh consolation of
Lightning . . . Illumination . . . Pain-consolation of lightning . . .
Symbols of eternity . . .
The end! the end! The goal and the end!
To speak through symbols of eternity . . .)

He struggles towards self-knowledge: even murder is necessary.
In this play the conflict between father and son is occasioned by
the father's insanity and monstrous engineering visions; the
scientific interpretation of life is rejected and superseded by the
struggle towards spiritual regeneration. The form of *Der Bettler*
owes much to Strindberg: the characters are nameless, the scene
with the pilots and the prostitutes verges upon a nightmare. The
chorus-like chanting, the harsh spotlighting and grouping of

characters deliberately stress the movement away from naturalist drama.

But the play which became the central expression of revolt in the theatre was Hasenclever's *Der Sohn* (*The Son*), written after Sorge's play but performed one year earlier, in 1916. Like *Der Bettler*, Hasenclever's play is constructed formally along traditional lines, but the mixture of dramatic prose and blank verse reflects an intensely-expressed vision, an emphasis on fervour and hyperbole. Again the characters are not named: we learn of the Son who is tyrannized by the Father, of the Friend who lures him into life, and the Governess who watches his revolt with trepidation and hope. 'Man lebt nur in der Ekstase, die Wirklichkeit würde einen verlegen machen' ('We only live in ecstasy, reality would embarrass us!') cries the young man, full of Nietzschean *Pathos* and Faustian desires; rescued by his friends (to the strains of Beethoven's Ninth Symphony) he joins a revolutionary organization demanding the death of fathers, the brutalization of the ego, and a Dionysian frenzy. The Friend gives him a revolver to commit parricide: the final confrontation between father and son is one of extreme tension, but the actual act of murder is spared by the father's death of a stroke. In another play, however, Arnolt Bronnen's *Vatermord* (*Parricide*) (written in 1915 and performed in uproar in 1922) the act of murder is perpetrated in a paroxysm of hatred; the theme of incest also plays an important part. Further violence is rife in Paul Kornfeld's *Die Verführung* (*The Seduction*), written in 1913, which, in exalted prose, shows how the rebellious youth murders a man he has never met before simply because he seems to embody the oppressive spirit of the age. The intensity of the revolt is also seen in Hanns Johst's *Der junge Mensch. Ein ekstatisches Szenarium* (*The Young Man: An ecstatic scenario*) which bears the motto: 'Es ist eine rasende Wollust: jung sein und um die Verzückung des Todes wissen' ('This is raving voluptuousness – to be young, and to know of the raptures of death'). Wedekind is very much in evidence in this play, particularly in the classroom scenes and in the ending in the cemetery where the Young Man, dead and buried, leaps across the cemetery wall at the audience, reborn and emerging from the old self. Much influenced by Hasenclever's *Der Sohn* is Anton Wildgans's *Dies Irae* (written in 1918), which culminates in the suicide of the young hero, whose fatal conflict with his father finally destroyed his life; act five, the 'Actus quintus fantasticus', consists of a 'chorus puerorum et adolescentium', where the Friend, as 'choragetes', summons the father to a final judgement. The hymn-like pathos comes to a climax in a blaze of frenzy at the end: 'O die den Menschen zeugen/Nicht um des Menschen willen,/Ihrer die Schuld!! Weh! Weh! Weh!' ('They who create Man, not for the sake of Man, they are the guilty ones!! Woe! Woe! Woe!') A 'Vox patrise tenebris infimis' proclaims 'Posaunen! Posaunen! Posaunen!' ('The last trump! The last trump! The last trump!') and 'Voces apocalypticae de coelis cantantes' declaim the 'Dies irae, dies illa'.

In so many of these plays the father represents authority, discipline and order, an order which is stultifying and ultimately destructive, for it stifles the passionate life of the young man who longs to hold all in a passionate embrace. Criticism of parental authority implied also the criticism of military academies and educational establishments: Gottfried Benn's short play *Ithaka*, published in the periodical *Die weißen Blätter* in Leipzig, 1914, ends with the students seizing the professor by the throat, beating him about the head, and shouting: 'Wir wollen den Traum. Wir wollen den Rausch. Wir rufen Dionysos und Ithaka!' ('We want dream, we want ecstasy, we call upon Dionysus and Ithaca!'). But the revolt portrayed in so many of these works has virtually no constructive motives: it is pure self-expression. The feverish desire for life is akin to a death-intoxication: vitalism is not necessarily a sign of health, but can spring from deep uncertainty, even neuroses. There is an undeniable atavism about much of this attitude, a primitivism and dangerous instability which became more and more apparent in German history. As well as irrational violence there is also in many of the works of this time an almost religious fervour, seen at the end of *Dies Irae* and also Kornfeld's *Himmel und Hölle* (1919), an operatic drama where the temptation of nihilism is overcome by a vision of love and self-sacrifice for humanity. An element of mysticism emerges, which lies at the heart of expressionism, with its emphasis on fervour and subjectivity: the religious quality is seen at its purest in the plays of Ernst Barlach (whose sculpture 'Der Ekstatiker' is as quintessentially expressionist as is Munch's 'The Shriek'). In 1912 Barlach wrote *Der tote Tag* (*The Dead Day*), a ghostly, mythical work, a dramatic exploration of the interaction of supernatural forces, some grotesque and menacing, others benign. Here it is the Father-principle which is divine and free: the boy's longing for the Father, for transcendence, is thwarted by the Mother, who represents the earth-bound and the immanent. In Barlach's mystical world of goblins, mist and nightmares the Son must assert himself and seek the Father: although he perishes the knowledge is gained that God is the Father of man. In his next play, *Der arme Vetter* (*The Poor Cousin*) (1918), Barlach starts with a realistic milieu, but moves towards mystery and ultimate redemption with his portrayal of 'die wachsende Ex-karnation des wesenhaften Menschen', 'the growing excarnation of essential man'.

The German stage, then, with its treatment of revolt, violence and mysticism, clearly demonstrated, even before the outbreak of the First World War, the new outlook which can be called expressionist. But another art-form, even more suitable for the expression of turbulent emotion, disquiet and unreality, was the lyric, and an important name here is Herwarth Walden (i.e. Georg Levin), editor of the vitally important periodical *Der*

Sturm. Founded as a weekly in Berlin in 1910, this journal played a major role in pioneering the new outlook: in that year it published Kokoschka's drawings and in the following year it printed Marinetti's *Futurist Manifesto*. In March 1912 Walden opened the journal's own gallery, and his interest shifted increasingly towards the visual arts, although Guillaume Apollinaire contributed 'Zone' in French, and the poet August Stramm (1874–1915) proved a major literary discovery. The *Sturm* circle in Berlin also inspired similar ventures: in 1910 Kurt Hiller founded his *Neopathetisches Cabaret*, with which were associated the poets Blass (1890–1939), Lichtenstein (1889–1914) and Jakob van Hoddis (1887–1942?). It has been claimed that German literary Expressionism began with the publication in a further journal, *Die Aktion* (founded in Berlin by Franz Pfemfert in 1911), of the poem 'Weltende' ('End of the World') by van Hoddis, followed soon after by Alfred Lichtenstein's 'Die Dämmerung' ('The Twilight').

These two poems are good examples of the poetic modernity described in Chapter 2; Michael Hamburger describes them thus: 'What was new about them is that they consisted of nothing more than an arbitrary concatenation of images derived from contemporary life; they presented a picture, but not a realistic one . . . They were a kind of *collage* . . .' (*Reason and Energy*, p. 222). They do not attempt to reflect a meaningful order, but *express* the poet's sense of the vulnerability and disharmony in the world. The poems are formally quite conventional, but convey a disturbing sense of *malaise* which borders upon the bizarre: the tension between regular metres and irregular vision is most effective.

Weltende reads as follows:

> Dem Bürger fliegt vom spitzen Kopf der Hut,
> In allen Lüften hallt es wie Geschrei,
> Dachdecker stürzen ab und gehn entzwei
> Und an den Küsten – liest man – steigt die Flut.

> Der Sturm ist da, die wilden Meere hupfen
> An Land, um dicke Dämme zu zerdrücken.
> Die meisten Menschen haben einen Schnupfen.
> Die Eisenbahnen fallen von den Brücken.

(The hat flies from the burgher's pointed head,/In all the skies there seems a fearful scream,/The tilers fall from roofs and break in half,/ And at the coast – we read – the tide is high./The storm is here, the wild seas bound/On to the land, to break the solid dams./Most people have a cold./The railway lines fall from the bridges.)

> and 'Die Dämmerung' is similar:

> Ein dicker Junge spielt mit einem Teich.
> Der Wind hat sich in einem Baum gefangen.
> Der Himmel sieht verbummelt aus und bleich,
> Als wäre ihm die Schminke ausgegangen.

> Auf lange Krücken schief herabgebückt
> Und schwatzend kriechen auf dem Feld zwei Lahme.
> Ein blonder Dichter wird vielleicht verrückt.
> Ein Pferdchen stolpert über eine Dame.

> An einem Fenster klebt ein fetter Mann.
> Ein Jüngling will ein weiches Weib besuchen.
> Ein grauer Clown zieht sich die Stiefel an.
> Ein Kinderwagen schreit und Hunde fluchen.

(A fat boy is playing with a pond./The wind has become tangled in a tree./ The sky looks pale and debauched/As though its make-up had run out./On long crutches, crookedly bent, and chatting,/Two cripples crawl about a field./Perhaps a fair poet will become insane./ A pony stumbles over a lady./A fat man is sticking to a window./ A youth wishes to visit a soft woman./A grey clown pulls on his boots./A pram screams, and dogs curse.)

The syntactical compression, sense of the bizarre and dream logic of these two poems is one aspect of expressionism; the caricature-apocalypse à la Hoddis and the more ironic urban sense of discomfort adumbrated by Lichtenstein gave way gradually to a general sense of doom in many poets. The famous anthology of

German Expressionist verse, *Menschheitsdämmerung*, (*Dawn* [*or dusk?*] *of Mankind*), which was edited by Kurt Pinthus and which appeared in 1920, seemed to prophesy a new millennium, but the chiliastic overtones are very much apparent. A further sense of disaster is apparent in the poetry of Georg Heym who died in a skating accident in 1912 at the age of twenty-four. Again, in Heym's case the syntax is conventional, but the dynamic imagery has an expressive power which transcends mere description; the poems 'Der Gott der Stadt' ('The God of the City'), 'Die Dämonen der Städte' ('The Demons of the Cities') and 'Umbra Vitae' portray in hyperbolic images the monstrous horror of life in great cities, where sickness, deformity and death are all that man can know. At this time the city of Berlin came more and more to amaze and horrify several of the young German Expressionist poets, with its size and fearful indifference to suffering. A writer such as Gottfried Benn was cynical in his view of man and his modernity (Georg Grosz well illustrated many of Benn's themes), and Bert Brecht frequently followed Marinetti in his admiration for the machine and the technology of the cities. But Georg Heym and, to a lesser extent Georg Trakl, were filled with dread at the plight of man trapped within the asphalt labyrinth. Heym's tendency to mythologize is seen very clearly in his town poetry, but is probably most effective of all in the apocalyptic and prophetic *Der Krieg* ('War'), written in 1912, whose first three stanzas run as follows:

> Aufgestanden ist er, welcher lange schlief,
> Aufgestanden unten aus Gewölben tief.
> In der Dämmerung steht er, groß und unbekannt,
> Und den Mond zerdrückt er in der schwarzen Hand.
>
> In den Abendlärm der Städte fällt es weit,
> Frost und Schatten einer fremden Dunkelheit.
> Und der Märkte runder Wirbel stockt zu Eis.
> Es wird still. Sie sehn sich um. Und keiner weiß.

In den Gassen faßt es ihre Schulter leicht.
Eine Frange. Keine Antwort. Ein Gesicht erbleicht.
In der Ferne zittert ein Geläute dünn,
Und die Bärte zittern um ihr spitzes Kinn . . .

(He has arisen, the one who has slept long,/He has arisen from deep
vaults below./He stands in the dusk, large, unknown/And he crushes
the moon in his black hand./Far into the evening noise of the town
there falls/The frost and shadow of a strange darkness./The round
whirling of the markets freezes to ice./It becomes still. They look
around. And no one knows./In the narrow streets it lightly touches
their shoulders./A question. No answer. A face grows pale./In the
distance there is a thin, tremulous ringing,/And their beards tremble
round their pointed chins . . .)

The first stanza of this poem has become famous in anthologies of
German Expressionist verse, with its dynamic verb at the beginning of the sentence and the powerful image of War 'crushing
the moon in his black hand'. The expressionist tendency to see
through the surface of things to behold a mythical, archetypal
vision is well represented here; a statement by the writer Kasimir
Edschmid (i.e. Eduard Schmid) in 1917 explains that, although
the expressionist may take the same themes as the naturalist,
there is a vast difference; 'So wird der Raum des expression-
istischen Künstlers Vision. Er sieht nicht, er schaut. Er schildert
nicht, er erlebt. Er gibt nicht wieder, er gestaltet. Er nimmt
nicht, er sucht. Nun gibt es nicht mehr die Kette der Tatsachen:
Fabriken, Häuser, Krankheit, Huren, Geschrei und Hunger. Nun
gibt es die Vision davon' (*Expressionismus*, dtv, p. 96): ('The
space of the expressionist artist, then, becomes vision. He does
not see, he looks. He does not describe, he experiences. He does
not reproduce, he forms. There is no longer the chain of facts:
factories, houses, sickness, whores, screams, and hunger. Now
there is the vision of this'). The expressionists, Edschmid suc-
cinctly comments, do not take photographs, but have visions;

imitation of nature is totally rejected in favour of fervent subjectivity.

In Heym the vision is eschatological; in a poet like Ernst Stadler, killed in 1914, there is a vitalism akin to that of Walt Whitman. Stadler's surging lines of poetry and his rushing sweep of self-generating images also betray a dithyrambic passion akin to Nietzsche's; there is also, however, a humanitarian concern in his poetry, not as rhapsodic as Werfel's, but nevertheless moving and sincere. (His excursions into the East End of London filled him with horror and his poem 'Ballhaus' portrays the dawn and the new, ringing song of the workers which cuts through the stale air of the degenerate ballroom.) His masterpiece is indubitably 'Fahrt über die Kölner Rheinbrücke bei Nacht' ('Night-journey across the Rhine bridge at Cologne'), a poem whose imagery is realistic, yet which is shot through with a subjective passion which gives a vast extension to its meaning. There is an ecstasy, yet also a movement towards dissolution, a soaring flight of the imagination which culminates in a vision of the sea, the flux and turmoil of existence itself. Regular syntax is abandoned here, and the lines swell to an almost Klopstock-like splendour:

> Der Schnellzug tastet sich und stößt die Dunkelheit entlang.
> Kein Stern will vor. Die ganze Welt ist nur ein enger,
>   nachtumschienter Minengang,
> Darein zuweilen Förderstellen blauen Lichtes jähe Horizonte
>   reißen: Feuerkreis
> Von Kugellampen, Dächern, Schloten, dampfend, strömend . . .
>   nur sekundenweis . . .
> Und wieder alles schwarz. Als führen wir ins Eingeweid der
>   Nacht zur Schicht.
> Nun taumeln Lichter her . . . verirrt, trostlos vereinsamt . . .
>   mehr . . . und sammeln sich . . . und werden dicht.
> Gerippe grauer Häuserfronten liegen bloß, im Zwielicht bleichend,
>   tot – etwas muß kommen . . . o, ich fühl es schwer

Im Hirn. Eine Beklemmung singt im Blut. Dann dröhnt der Boden
plötzlich wie ein Meer:
Wir fliegen, aufgehoben, königlich durch nachtentrißne Luft, hoch
übern Strom. O Biegung der Millionen Lichter, stumme Wacht,
Vor deren blitzender Parade schwer die Wasser abwärts rollen.
Endloses Spalier, zum Gruß gestellt bei Nacht!
Wie Fackeln stürmend! Freudiges! Salut von Schiffen über blauer
See! Bestirntes Fest!
Wimmelnd, mit hellen Augen hingedrängt! Bis wo die Stadt mit
letzten Häusern ihren Gast entläßt.
Und dann die langen Einsamkeiten. Nackte Ufer. Stille. Nacht.
Besinnung. Einkehr. Kommunion. Und Glut und Drang
Zum Letzten, Segnenden. Zum Zeugungsfest. Zur Wollust.
Zum Gebet. Zum Meer. Zum Untergang.

(The express train gropes and pushes along the darkness. No star
wishes to come. The whole world is only a narrow mine-gallery,
railed in by night, into which sudden skylines are torn by hauling-
shafts of blue light; a fiery circle of light-globes, roofs, chimneys,
smoking, streaming, only for moments . . . then all is black again.
As though we were off on our shift into the very bowels of night.
Now lights stagger towards us . . . lost, inconsolable, isolated . . .
more . . . and gather . . . and grow dense. Skeletons of grey house-
fronts are exposed, pallid in the half-light, dead — something must
come . . . oh, I feel it, pressing, in my brain. An oppression sings in
my blood. Then the ground booms suddenly like the sea: we are
flying, suspended, king-like through air torn from the night, high
above the river. Oh the curving of millions of lights, the silent sentry
before whose glittering parade the waters roll heavily downwards . . .
Endless cordon, posted as a greeting by the night! Rushing like
torches! Joyful being! The salute of ships across the blue sea! A
festival of stars! Teeming, pushed onwards with bright eyes! Until
where the city with its last houses leaves its guest. And then the long
stretches of loneliness. Bare shores. Silence. Night. Reflection.
Return. Communion. And the glow, the urge towards the ultimate,
the blessing one. To the feast of creation. To ecstasy. To prayer. To
the sea. To extinction.)

As Michael Hamburger explains: 'Because of their extreme dynamism, his [Stadler's] poems have a rhetorical effect; but it is private rhetoric, as it were, not aimed at the reader in the manner of Werfel and many of the later Expressionists. Only his excellent craftsmanship saved Stadler from other dangers. Few poets would have got away with the long succession of a-syntactic words – most of them abstract and general – in the last two lines . . . Stadler brings off these verbal and mental leaps, just as he manages to keep his long line from spilling over into prose, and makes his rhymes all the more effective for being delayed' (*Reason and Energy*, p. 230). The poem 'Anrede' ('Salutation') uses a Nietzschean imagery (flame, thirst, scream and fire) which later became debased in the hands of less skilful poets; the most effective 'Form ist Wollust' ('Form is Rapture') is more conventional in form than the 'Fahrt über die Kölner Rheinbrücke', but is an exact statement of Stadler's belief, an expressionist creed *in nucleo*:

> Form und Riegel mußten erst zerspringen,
> Welt durch aufgeschloßne Röhren dringen:
> Form ist Wollust, Friede, himmlisches Genügen,
> Doch mich reißt es, Ackerschollen umzupflügen.
> Form will mich verschnüren und verengen,
> Doch ich will mein Sein in alle Weiten drängen –
> Form ist klare Härte ohn' Erbarmen,
> Doch mich treibt es zu den Dumpfen, zu den Armen,
> Und in grenzenlosem Michverschenken
> Will mich Leben mit Erfüllung tränken.

(Form and bolt had to burst, world had to force its way through opened pipes; form is ecstasy, peace, divine contentment, yet I feel I must plough up the clods of earth. Form wants to strangle, to contain me, yet I want to force my being in all directions – form is clear hardness without pity, yet I am driven to the dull, the poor, and in the limitless giving of myself life will fill me with fulfilment.)

It is also Stadler's 'Der Spruch' ('The Motto') which contains the quintessential line 'Mensch, werde wesentlich!' – virtually untranslatable, but which has the meaning: Man, know your essence and live it to the full!

The poetry of Ernst Stadler exhibits one aspect of expressionist verse, which may be called the dithyrambic-rhetorical method: that of August Stramm, killed in 1915, is at the other pole, that of intense concentration. A subjective, inner state is expressed in a form of words which approximate to an abstract picture; neologisms intensify the impression of an unreality which paradoxically conveys a powerful truth. Stramm seems concerned to express absolute essence: adjectives and visual images are superfluous to this. 'Trieb' ('Urge') and 'Schwermut' ('Melancholy') are good examples of his experiments:

> Schrecken Sträuben
> Wehren Ringen
> Ächzen Schluchzen
> Stürzen
> du!
> Grellen Gehren
> Winden Klammern
> Hitzen Schwächen
> ich und du!
> Lösen Gleiten
> Stöhnen Wellen
> Schwinden Finden
> ich
> dich
> du!

(Frightening struggling/Protecting wrestling/Groaning sobbing/ Plunging/you!/Piercing lusting/Writhing clutching/Heats weakenings/I and you!/Loosening, gliding/Moaning waves/Fading finding/ I/you/you!)

> Schreiten Streben
> Leben sehnt
> Schauern Stehen
> Blicke suchen
> Sterben wächst
> Das Kommen
> Schreit!
> Tief
> Stummen
> Wir.

(Striding striving/Living longs/Shuddering standing/Glances seek/ Dying grows/The coming/Screams!/Deep/Dumb are/We.)

The intensity and sincerity of Stramm's method may not be doubted, but the dangers are obvious: in the hands of lesser poets such stammering concentration could, and did, become pretentious and ludicrous, particularly when such words as God, Man, Chaos, Death, Goodness and Spirit are used indiscriminately. Later it was the Dadaist poets who used this method and deliberately reduced all to absurdity, and perhaps this is preferable to its use by an earnest but mediocre poetaster.

Both Stadler and Stramm are innovators, the latter being particularly extreme in his rejection of conventional verse forms; compared with their poetry, that of the Austrian Georg Trakl, who committed suicide in 1914, appears traditional, with its frequent use of the sonnet. But Trakl's moonlit, autumnal death-landscapes of the soul betray a most original use of metaphor and image, whose expressive powers are remarkable. Walter Sokel explains: 'The Austrian poet Georg Trakl represents in Expressionist poetry an equivalent to Kandinsky's role in Expressionist painting. Just as Kandinsky creates pure compositions of colors and lines, so Trakl creates pure compositions of autonomous metaphors . . . Trakl's poetry is not a system of communication of ideas, but a flight of images, or autonomous metaphors, resembling an incoherent dream' (*Writer in Extremis*, p. 49). Trakl's poetry most effectively marks the transition from the passive receptivity of impressionism to a more dynamic, expressive use of metaphor: description gives way to expression. The juxtaposition of apparently disparate images is the characteristic of Trakl's poetry which fascinates, puzzles and alienates the reader, as does the ambiguity between image-as-metaphor and image-as-symbol. Similarly the use of colour-epithets makes understanding difficult: are the colours symbolic or merely evocative? The poem 'Siebengesang des Todes' ('The Sevenfold Song of Death') is a good example of his art:

> Bläulich dämmert der Frühling; unter saugenden Bäumen
> Wandert ein Dunkles in Abend und Untergang,
> Lauschend der sanften Klage der Amsel.
> Schweigend erscheint die Nacht, ein blutendes Wild,
> Das langsam hinstirbt am Hügel.

> In feuchter Luft schwankt blühendes Apfelgezweig,
> Löst silbern sich Verschlungenes,
> Hinsterbend aus nächtigen Augen; fallende Sterne;
> Sanfter Gesang der Kindheit.

> Erscheinender stieg der Schläfer den schwarzen Wald hinab,
> Und es rauschte ein blauer Quell im Grund,
> Daß jener leise die bleichen Lider aufhob
> Über sein schneeiges Antlitz;

> Und es jagte der Mond ein rotes Tier
> Aus seiner Höhle;
> Und es starb in Seufzern die dunkle Klage der Frauen.

> Strahlender hob die Hände zu seinem Stern
> Der weiße Fremdling;
> Schweigend verläßt ein Totes das verfallene Haus.

> O des Menschen verweste Gestalt: gefügt aus kalten Metallen,
> Nacht und Schrecken versunkener Wälder
> Und der sengenden Wildnis des Tiers;
> Windesstille der Seele.

Auf schwärzlichem Kahn fuhr jener schimmernde Ströme hinab,
Purpurner Sterne voll, und es sank
Friedlich das ergrünte Gezweig auf ihn,
Mohn aus silberner Wolke.

(Bluish the Spring grows dusk; beneath sighing trees a dark one
wanders into evening and decline, listening to the soft lament of the
blackbird. Silent appears the night, a bleeding wild animal, that
slowly dies along the hill. In moist air sway blossoming apple
branches; that which is tangled separates silverly, dying away from
nocturnal eyes; falling stars; the gentle song of childhood. The
sleeper appears more radiant along the dark forest, and a blue spring
rushes in the hollow, that one should raise his pale eye-lids above
his snow-like countenance. And the moon drove a red beast from its
cave, and the dark lament of women dies into sighs. The white
stranger, more gleaming, lifted his hands to his star; silently a dead
thing left the derelict house. Oh the putrified form of man; forged
from cold metals, night, and the terrors of sunken forests, and the
singeing wildness of the beast; doldrums of the soul. On a black
canoe that one sailed down shimmering streams, full of purple stars,
and the green branches sank peacefully on to him, poppy from a
silver cloud.)

The remote, luminous world portrayed here, the shadowy
neutral substantives and the hermetic correspondences are akin to
the world of the symbolist; the use of colours and powerful images,
however, places Trakl without doubt among the expressionist
poets. There is no bombast, no rhetoric, but a haunting euphony
in almost all that he wrote: the problem of the big city is only
occasionally found. But a sense of evil links him with Heym, and
the apocalyptic note breaks through in the last poems, in jagged,
terrible visions:

> Dich sing ich wilde Zerklüftung,
> Im Nachtsturm
> Aufgetürmtes Gebirge;
> Ihr grauen Türme

> Überfließend von höllischen Fratzen,
> Feurigem Getier,
> Rauhen Farnen, Fichten,
> Kristallnen Blumen.
> Unendliche Qual,
> Daß du Gott erjagtest
> Sanfter Geist,
> Aufseufzend im Wassersturz,
> In wogenden Föhren.
>
> Golden lodern die Feuer
> Der Völker rings.
> Über schwärzliche Klippen
> Stürzt todestrunken
> Die erglühende Windsbraut,
> Die blaue Woge
> Des Gletschers
> Und es dröhnt
> Gewaltig die Glocke im Tal:
> Flammen, Flüche
> Und die dunklen
> Spiele der Wollust,
> Stürmt den Himmel
> Ein versteinertes Haupt.

(Wild fragmentation, I sing you, in nocturnal storm, in piled up mountains; you grey towers bursting with hellish faces, fiery beasts, rough ferns, pines, crystal flowers. Unending torment, that you should hunt down God, gentle spirit, sighing in the water-fall, in waving pines. Gold gleam the fires of peoples round about, over blackish cliffs, drunk with death, rushed the glowing storm, the blue wave of the glacier, and the bell hammers powerfully in the valley; flames, curses, and the dark games of lust; a petrified head storms heaven.)

And that which Trakl and Heym had foreseen came to pass: On 28 July Austro-Hungary declared war on Serbia, and within a week the whole of Europe was in arms.

*   *   *

From this brief account of the German cultural condition before 1914 it must be apparent that both the theatre and lyric poetry moved away from nineteenth-century models towards a more dynamic, unstable and intensely subjective mode of expression. The novel was less obviously involved in the new ferment: the stream of consciousness technique which marks the new direction in that genre owes much to the *Sekundenstil* of the Naturalists and often seems a continuation of impressionist (or 'pointilliste') practice. If 'expressionism', as Malcolm Pasley has written, also refers to the predilection for attack against Wilhelmine society, then the novels of Heinrich Mann would qualify from the point of view of subject matter, although their form is mostly conventional; the abnormal intensity of many of the characters in the work of Jakob Wassermann seems reminiscent of the Dostoevsky-quality of much expressionist writing, and hence are worthy of mention. But unlike Naturalism, where the novel was of paramount importance, the expressionist mentality found a more appropriate outlet in other forms.

Developments in literature and painting ran parallel: Kandinsky and Kokoschka demonstrated how closely linked the two arts were at this time. There were also close ties between Schoenberg and the *Blaue Reiter* group; Kandinsky discussed Schoenberg's paintings and in 1912 published his 'Arnold Schönberg in höchster Verehrung' ('Homage to Arnold Schoenberg'). In 1909 Schoenberg composed his *Erwartung (Expectation)*, a sombre monodrama full of hallucinatory violence, an eruption from the subconscious; his *Die glückliche Hand (The Fortunate Hand)*, finished in 1913, with its Man, Woman, Gentleman and chorus, together with the symbolic use of colours and lighting, seems to stem from Strindberg and Kokoschka: the struggle of the artist to free himself from woman and society is a worthy expressionist theme. Other links between music and literature are found in Berg's setting of Trakl's poems and particularly in his two operas *Wozzeck* and

Lulu, the former being recognized as the standard work of musical expressionism, a fiercely dramatic portrayal of a tormented soul. This was not put on until 1925, but Büchner's haunting work had occupied Berg for many years. *Lulu* was likewise not started until 1928, although Berg had seen Wedekind's play *Pandora's Box* in 1905. The same year saw the performance of Richard Strauss's *Salomé* in Dresden, followed four years later by *Elektra*, two operas which push tonal expressiveness towards an undreamt-of intensity. Music, painting and literature were moving forward to a new energy, a new aggressiveness even, and German Expressionism was in the vanguard.

4
The German Situation between 1914 and the Mid-Twenties

It is often mistakenly believed that expressionism, in St John Ervine's words [Willet, p. 173], was simply 'the despair and neurosis of a defeated people', a movement of intellectual crisis originating during the First World War and its aftermath. This is an unsatisfactory definition, as it has been shown that anti-naturalistic devices, attacks against society, and rhapsodic, expressive forms of writing were found in Germany and elsewhere long before 1914. But it is also true that the war did bring to a head certain latent predispositions and characteristics which lent German Expressionism its particular intensity and dimension, and in the early twenties the expressionist tendencies in Germany reached an unusual and often febrile proportion.

Before 1914 the young German writers who may be called Expressionists frequently portrayed an isolated individual struggling to give expression to the life force within him: this may be termed the Nietzschean element. The highest form of existence is glimpsed in glowing incandescence, whilst the meaninglessness of modern life is to be rejected as mere dross. The political orientation of this fervour was not yet apparent, although 1913 saw the appearance of the periodical *Revolution*, in which the poet Erich Mühsam proclaimed:

> Alle Revolution ist aktiv, singulär, plötzlich und ihre Ursachen
>   entwurzelnd . . . Einige Formen der Revolution: Tyrannenmord,
> Absetzung einer Herrschergestalt, Etablierung einer Religion,

Zerbrechen alter Tafeln (in Konvention und Kunst), Schaffen eines Kunstwerks, der Geschlechtsakt.

Einige Synonyma für Revolution: Gott, Leben, Brunst, Rausch, Chaos.

Laßt uns chaotisch sein!

(All revolution is active, singular, sudden, uprooting its causes . . . Some forms of revolution: tyrannicide, deposition of a ruling figure, the establishment of a religion, the destruction of the old tablets (in convention and art), the creation of an art-work, the sexual act. A few synonyms for revolution: God, Life, Lust, Intoxication, Chaos. Let us be chaotic!)

But the desire to be chaotic frequently seemed to bring with it an apocalyptic sense of disaster, and crisis is never far from the scene: the expressionist shriek, as was earlier explained, is one of ecstasy *and* despair. In his *Expressionismus*, finished in 1914 and published two years later, the Austrian Hermann Bahr summed up the situation thus: 'Der Mensch schreit aus seiner Seele, die ganze Epoche wird ein einziger, dringender Schrei. Die Kunst schreit auch, in die tiefe Finsternis, schreit nach Hilfe, schreit nach dem Geist. Das ist Expressionismus' ('Man screams from the depths of his soul, the whole age becomes one single, piercing shriek. Art screams too, into the deep darkness, screams for help, for the spirit. That is expressionism').

The need for a New Vision, a New Reality, a New Man – these are the watchwords. Yet the European nations were locked in bloody strife, and the losses were appalling: in 1914 alone Stadler, Lichtenstein, the poet Ernst Lotz and August Macke were killed, and Trakl committed suicide after seeing the carnage at Grodek; August Stramm was killed in 1915; in 1916 Franz Marc, Reinhard Sorge and the writer Gustav Sack fell; in 1918 the poet Gerrit Engelke died shortly before the armistice. The intellectuals who survived the war or who fled to Switzerland realized that the Wilhelmine order in Germany had to be overthrown before a new world could emerge; suffering was the crucible in which a new sense of brotherhood and solidarity was to be formed. A spiritual feeling of brotherhood seized many of the younger writers, and prepared the way for the political activism which rose to the surface at the end of the war.

The name of Franz Werfel emerges here, whose rhapsodic style, tending towards bombast, exemplified the fervent poetry written at this time. His anthology *Der Weltfreund* (*Friend of the World*) had, in fact, appeared in 1911, but was read widely during the war and reissued in 1920. The poem 'An den Leser' well expresses the new mentality:

> Mein einziger Wunsch ist, Dir, o Mensch verwandt zu sein!
> Bist Du Neger, Akrobat, oder ruhst Du noch in tiefer Mutterhut,
> Klingt Dein Mädchenlied über den Hof, lenkst Du Dein Floß im
>   Abendschein,
> Bist Du Soldat, oder Aviatiker voll Ausdauer und Mut . . .
> Denn ich habe alle Schicksale durchgemacht . . .
> So gehöre ich Dir und allen!
> Wolle mir, bitte, nicht widerstehn!
> O, könnte es einmal geschehn,
> Daß wir uns, Bruder, in die Arme fallen!

> (My only desire, oh Man, is to be related to you! Whether you are a negro, an acrobat, or whether you are still resting deep in a mother's womb, whether your maiden's song echoes across the yard, whether you are steering your raft in the evening sunshine, whether you are a soldier, or airman, full of stamina and courage . . . For I have experienced all the destinies . . . So I belong to you, and to all! Please, do not refuse me! Oh, could it but once happen that, Brother, we fall into each other's arms!)

A hymn to Man, 'Lächeln Atmen Schreiten' ('Smiling Breathing Striding') was published in 1916 and proclaims that Man is the Creator of all, that the human spirit is the ultimate essence and meaning of all existence; another good example of

Werfel's verse is 'Veni creator spiritus', a plea for ecstasy and rapture that will destroy all limitations and drive all men into a joyous embrace:

> Komm, heiliger Geist, Du schöpferisch!
> Den Marmor unsrer Form zerbrich!
> Daß nicht mehr Mauer krank und hart
> Den Brunnen dieser Welt umstarrt,
> Daß wir gemeinsam und nach oben
> Wie Flammen ineinander toben!
> . . .
> Daß tränenhaft und gut und gut
> Aufsiede die entzückte Flut,
> Daß nicht mehr fern und unerreicht
> Ein Wesen um das andre schleicht,
> Daß jauchzend wir in Blick, Hand, Mund und Haaren,
> Und in uns selbst Dein Attribut erfahren!
>
> Daß, wer dem Bruder in die Arme fällt,
> Dein tiefes Schlagen süß am Herzen hält,
> Daß, wer des armen Hundes Schaun empfängt,
> Von Deinem weisen Blicke wird beschenkt,
> Daß alle wir in Küssens Überflüssen
> Nur Deine reine heilige Lippe küssen!

(Come, Holy Ghost, creative spirit! Shatter the marble of our form, that a sick, hard wall should no longer stand rigid around the well of this world, that together, upwards, we may rush like flames into each other! . . . That tearfully and good, good, the ecstatic flood may seethe upwards, so that no longer beings should creep around each other, far and isolated, so that joyfully with looks, hand, mouth and hair we should recognize your attributes! So that who ever falls into a brother's arms may feel your sweet beating against his heart, so that whoever catches the look of some poor dog also receives the wisdom of your glance, so that all of us, in a profusion of kisses, may only kiss your pure, holy lips!)

Such windy rhetoric can easily degenerate into bathos; the more jubilant the shouts of ecstasy become, the more unreadable becomes the poetry. Johannes Becher, later to become Minister of Culture in East Germany, became famous for such chaotic outbursts as 'Der Mensch steht auf!' ('Man arises!'):

Verfluchtes Jahrhundert! Chaotisch! Gesanglos! Ausgehängt du
  Mensch, magerster der Köder, zwishen Qual Nebel-Wahn Blitz.
Geblendet. Ein Knecht. Durchfurcht. Tobsüchtig. Aussatz und
  Säure.
Mit entzündetem Aug. Tollwut im Eckzahn. Pfeifenden Fieberhorns.
Aber
Über dem Kreuz im Genick wogt mild unendlicher Äther.
Heraus aus Gräben Betrieben Asylen Kloaken, der höllischen
  Spelunke!
Sonnen-Chöre rufen hymnisch auf die Höhlen-Blinden.
Und
Über der blutigen Untiefe der Schlachten-Gewässer
Sprüht ewig unwandelbar Gottes magischer Stern.
. . .
Sage mir, o Bruder Mensch, wer bist du?!
Wüter. Würger. Schuft und Scherge.
Lauer-Blick am gilben Knochen deines Nächsten.
König Kaiser General.
Gold-Fraß. Babels Hure und Verfall.
Haßgröhlender Rachen. Praller Beutel und Diplomat.
Oder oder
Gottes Kind!!??
. . .
Noch noch ist's Zeit!
Zur Sammlung! Zum Aufbruch! Zum Marsch!
Zum Schritt zum Flug zum Sprung aus kananitischer Nacht!!!
Noch ist's Zeit –
Mensch Mensch Mensch stehe auf stehe auf!!!

(Cursed century! Chaotic! Songless! You, Man, most wretched of baits, suspended between torment fog-madness lightning. Blinded. A serf. Lacerated. Leprosy and acid. With enflamed eye. Rabies in the fang. Whistling fever-horn. But – above the cross in the neck there wafts a mild and infinite aether. Come – out of the graves the offices the institutions the cess-pits, the hellish dens! Sun choruses call hymn-like to the cave-blinded. And – above the bloody depths of the battle-waters there sparkles eternal and unchangeable God's magic star . . . Tell me, brother man, what are you? Raving one. Murderer. Wretch and hangman. A lurking glance at the yellowed bone of your neighbour. King Emperor General. Gold devourer. Whore of Babylon. Decay. With throat of growling hatred, money-bag, diplomat. Or – or – *Child of God*!!?? There is still time! To the meeting, the departure, the march! To the step, the flight, the leap from the night of Canaan! There is still time! Man, man, man, arise, arise!!!)

The sentiments may be admirable, but the poetry is execrable: the exclamation marks proliferate and the stammering formlessness and hyperbolic declamation lapse into the absurd. But Becher is by no means alone in his visionary fervour and his proclamation of the greatness of man; as the war came to its end the atmosphere of millennial expectancy and revolutionary rapture grew to white heat. Becher may represent German Expressionist longing at its most pretentious and inflated, but an infinitely greater craftsman, Georg Kaiser, was, on the German stage, working out his vision of the New Man in a language which was a remarkable fusion of the cerebral and the passionate. There is no 'Oh Man!' pathos in Kaiser, but a zealous fervour contained within lucid, mathematical precision.

Georg Kaiser is a remarkable phenomenon in theatrical history. At the height of his creative power, and during the climax of German Expressionism, that is, between 1917 and 1923, twenty-four plays by him were performed on the German stage. His plays are above all plays of ideas, of dialectical progression: his compressed, staccato language is a perfect tool to describe the clash of concepts. Kaiser, the *Denkspieler*, sat at his steel writing desk and worked out with ruthless and brilliant logic a dramatic dialogue which thrills the listener with the exhilaration of logical clash and resolution. To write drama, for Kaiser, is to follow a thought to its conclusion, yet thinking is also, for him, full of passion and vitality: his intense idealism was directed towards one vision – the Regeneration of Man. Seeing the dangers of bombast and rodomontade he insisted upon clarity, upon a steely yet flexible beauty; there is nothing nebulous or specious in his work. The famous *Telegramstil* reduces argument to bare essentials, to absolute essence, yet a cold fire burns beneath the surface, a conviction of the ultimate necessity for man's redemption. In 1918 he wrote:

> Gefährlich versucht die Vision: – Leidenschaft stachelt sie – die erstickt die Stimme, die reden soll, um gehört zu sein. Furchtbar schwingt dieser Kampf zwischen Schrei und Stimme. Im Schrei will es sich aus dem Munde reißen – Aufschrei aus Entsetzen und Zorn! – zur Stimme muß er herabsinken, um wirkend zu werden. Kühle Rede rollt leidenschaftlicher Bewegtheit entgegen – das Heißflüssige muß in Form starr werden! – und härter und kälter die Sprache, je flutendüberflutender Empfindung bedrängt.
>
> Von welcher Art ist die Vision?
> Es gibt nur eine: die von der Erneuerung des Menschen.

(Dangerously the vision tempts: passion goads it onwards – this stifles the voice that should speak to be heard. Fearful is this fight between cry and voice. It wishes to burst from the mouth as a shriek – a scream of horror and anger! – it must become a voice in order to be effective. Cool speech rolls towards passionate agitation – the molten must become rigid in form! – and the colder and harder the language is, the more turbulent and moving the emotion will be.

What is the nature of this vision?
There is only one: the Renewal of Man.)

In Kaiser the idea of social reform is only of secondary importance: a Nietzschean self-overcoming, a spiritual regeneration must come first before society can be changed. It is false to refer his plays solely to the conditions prevailing in Germany at the end of the war, as Kaiser's idealism is universally valid, but a certain relevance is undeniable. His famous play *Die Bürger von Calais* (*The Burghers of Calais*) was written in 1913 and published the following year; it is an argued condemnation of war and received its first performance in Frankfurt am Main in 1917. The clash between Duguesclins, Constable of France, who demands resistance to the English, the salvation of honour and the fight to the death, and Eustache de Saint-Pierre, who sees that surrender and preservation of the work of generations is far more valuable, has a fascinating dramatic impetus: thesis and argument are rigidly controlled, and the white-heat of intellectual passion is compressed and concentrated until an intolerable tension is achieved. Eustache de Saint-Pierre demands an absolute self-purification, a dedication to the noblest vision – self-sacrifice and the preservation of the city with its new harbour. Military glory, he exclaims, is a worthless idea, and he who longs for it is as debased as the enemy:

> Wir sahen die Küste, die steil ragt – wir sahen das Meer, das wild stürmt – wir suchten den Ruhm Frankreichs nicht. Wir suchten das Werk unserer Hände! – Einer kommt, den spornt die Wut. Die Wut entzündet die Gier. Mit wütender Gier greift er an – und rafft auf, was er auf seinem Wege findet. Er häuft es zu einem Hügel von Scherben – höher und höher – und auf seinem äußersten Gipfel stellt er sich dar; – lodernd in seinem Fieber – starr in seinem Krampf – übrig in der Zerstörung! – Wer ist das? Empfangt ihr von ihm das Maß eures Wertes – die Frist eurer Dauer? – den heute die Gier anfaßt, die morgen mit ihm verwest?

> (We saw the coast, rising steep – we saw the sea, storming wild – we sought not the fame of France. We sought the work of our hands! One comes, goaded by rage. Rage kindles greed. With raging greed he attacks – and seizes what he finds in his path. He piles it to a heap of rubble – higher and higher – and on its highest peak he stands himself – burning in his fever – rigid in his convulsion – left in the destruction! Who is this? Did you receive from him the measure

of your worth, the length of your duration? – the one whom greed grips today, which perishes with him tomorrow?)

Seven come forward (this is Kaiser's original alteration to the traditional account); six are needed to humiliate themselves before the English king. Eustache de Saint-Pierre knows that they are not yet ready for the need of self-sacrifice, that they all secretly desire life and that they all long to draw the lot which will determine who shall be spared. He ruthlessly admonishes them to transcend human weakness, and the final scene of Act Two is a strange fusion of Christian communion and Nietzschean imperiousness:

Seid ihr reif – für eure neue Tat? . . . Ihr buhlt um diese Tat – vor ihr streift ihr eure Schuhe und Gewänder ab. Sie fordert euch nackt und neu. Um sie klirrt kein Streit – schwillt kein Brand – gellt kein Schrei. An eurer Brunst und wütenden Begierde entzündet ihr sie nicht. Eine klare Flamme ohne Rauch brennt sie – kalt in ihrer Hitze – milde in ihrem Blenden. So ragt sie hinaus – so geht ihr den Gang – so nimmt sie euch an: – ohne Halt und ohne Hast – kühl und hell in euch – ihr froh ohne Rausch – ihr kühn ohne Taumel – ihr willig ohne Wut – ihr neuerol Täter der neuen Tat!

(Are you yet ripe – for your new deed? You woo this deed, you take off shoe and clothing before it. It demands you naked and new. No battle rattles around it, no fire leaps, no cry shrills. Your lust and raving gestures do not ignite this deed. It burns as a clear flame without smoke – cold in its heat – mild in its gleam. Thus it rears up – thus you should go – so it accepts you – without stop or haste – cool and clear in you – happy without wild ecstasy, brave without frenzy – you who are willing without rage – you new perpetrators of the new deed!)

In the final act Eustache de Saint-Pierre commits suicide that he may go on before the six into death and show the way; his father brings the body and speaks as a prophet to the waiting citizens:

'Ich komme aus dieser Nacht – und gehe in keine Nacht mehr. Meine Augen sind offen – ich schließe sie nicht mehr. Meine blinden Augen sind gut, um es nicht mehr zu verlieren: – ich habe den neuen Menschen gesehen – in dieser Nacht ist er geboren!' ('I come from night, and go no longer into night. Mine eyes are open, I close them no more. Mine eyes are good, to lose this never: I have seen the new man, he is born in this night!'). The body of his son is carried into the church and laid upon the altar, so that the English king, who has spared the lives of the six because of the birth of a son, and who wishes to offer thanks to God, must kneel before his spiritual conqueror. The final tableau, assisted by the lighting, emphasizes the Christ-like sublimity of the moral victor, showing resurrection and ascension.

Three months later, in the same year, Kaiser's most famous play, *Von morgens bis mitternachts* (*From Morn till Midnight*) was staged in Munich (it was, in fact, his thirtieth play, written in 1912, shortly before *Die Bürger von Calais*). It was this play more than any other that seemed to be the quintessence of German Expressionist theatre, and made Kaiser's name and method famous outside Germany; after the war it was staged in London and New York, and also made into a film by Karlheinz Martin. A nameless bank cashier passes through several stations in a process of self-exploration; he revolts against his meaningless life, steals 60,000 marks and sets off ('bricht auf') in search of frenzied excitement. The concentration is extreme: the opening scene in the bank has a deliberately jerky quality, as though the actors were in fact puppets, and in each 'station' the grotesque element becomes more and more apparent. The action becomes barely causal; the cashier indulges in the pleasures of the flesh in a scene which is very reminiscent of the prostitute scene in Sorge's *Der Bettler*, and with an undeniable sadism exults in the frenzy of a six-day cycle race. Finally, in a Salvation Army Hall, he realizes the worthlessness of money and hurls it amongst the audience, who fight like wild beasts for it; betrayed by the Girl he shoots himself before a crucifix: his dying words sounding like 'Ecce Homo'. He had hoped to live life to the full, to cast off an inauthentic existence, but was corrupted from the start by his crime; reliance on capitalist gain was not the premise for the overcoming of mechanical, materialist society.

Kaiser does not attempt to create rounded characters of flesh and blood: psychological naturalism was of no interest to him. The characters are stripped to bare essentials, they are frequently abstractions, types who point out the main tenets of the argument. The Salvation Army penitents could well be emanations from the protagonist's mind, as in Strindberg; the symbol of death – the skeleton in the wintry trees, and finally in the wires holding the chandelier – is a warning and a projection of the cashier's dread. The blasts on the trumpet which intersperse his final peroration seem to herald a last judgement. The deliberate un-reality of the play, the jerkiness, frenzy, self-laceration and almost flippant awareness of the worthlessness of life were well captured in the film, made in 1920 and presumed lost, until finally discovered in archives in Japan.

After *Die Bürger von Calais* and *Von morgens bis mitternachts* it is the *Gas* trilogy which established Kaiser's reputation. The first part, *Die Koralle* (*The Coral*), was staged in Frankfurt am Main and Munich in 1917; in it Kaiser shows himself to be highly critical of capitalist ruthlessness, for although the Millionaire domin-ates the play, both his son and his daughter represent a rejection of bourgeois complacency and a criticism of social inequality. The son particularly identifies himself with the oppressed masses and, in Act Three, is on the point of shooting his father before he joins the workers: it is he who will be the hero of *Gas I*. Connected with the idea of the emergence of the New Man is a theme which is common in Kaiser – the exchange of a man's identity to gain a new lease of life: this the Millionaire attempts to do, assuming the role of his murdered secretary, and living vicariously through his son.

It is, however, the second play of the trilogy, *Gas I*, which made Kaiser a European name. It was performed a few days after the armistice, and, with its idea of the regeneration of society at large, it seemed again, like *Die Bürger von Calais*, to have a meaning especially relevant to the German situation at that time. Gas, the driving force behind all modern machines, is the symbol or essence of the new industrial age. At the factory which produces gas the Millionaire's son rules with a devoted idealism, but he cannot prevent the immense explosion which reduces the factory to rubble. A Strindbergian touch is 'der weiße Herr' who is an embodiment of a premonition of disaster, the white terror which obliterates all. After the catastrophe the Millionaire's son sees the chance for a new life: he will resettle his workers on the land, and restore them to health and joy. Act Four is the brilliant dialectical clash between the Millionaire's son and the Engineer, who represents ruthless technology; the workers are swayed back and forth between the two opposing theses:

> INGENIEUR: Helden seid ihr – in Ruß und Schweiß! Helden seid ihr am Hebel – vorm Sichtglas – am Schaltblock! Reglos harrt ihr aus im Treiben der Riemen und mitten im Donner der polternden Kolben! – Und noch das Schwerste stößt in euch kein langes Erschrecken: – die Explosion!
>
> MILLIARDÄRSOHN: Kommt aus der Halle!
>
> . . .
>
> INGENIEUR: Herrscher seid ihr hier – im Werk von allmächtiger Leistung – ihr schafft Gas! . . . Herrscher seid ihr hier – da seid ihr: – Bauern!!
>
> EINE STIMME (*schreit*): Bauern!
>
> ANDERE STIMMEN: Bauern!!
>
> NEUE STIMMEN: Bauern!!!

ALLE MÄNNER UND FRAUEN (*Brandung von Schreien und Fäuste auf*): Bauern!!!!

MILLIARDÄRSOHN (*auf Stufen der Tribüne*): Hört ihr auf mich – oder ihn?

ALLE MÄNNER UND ALLE FRAUEN: Der Ingenieur!!!!

. . .

MILLIARDÄRSOHN: . . . Kommt nun heraus!! Ihr seid Helden – die keinen Versuch unterschlagen! Bis ans Ende des Wegs dringt ihr kühn – kein Schrecken fällt in euren Schritt! – Der Weg ist zu Ende – *ein* Weg ist wieder zu Ende – lobt euren Mut mit neuem Mut: – der Mensch ist da!!!!

. . .

ALLE MÄNNER UND FRAUEN: Der Ingenieur soll uns führen!!!!

INGENIEUR: Kommt aus der Halle!! – ins Werk!! – von Explosion zu Explosion!! – Gas!!

ALLE FRAUEN UND ALLE MÄNNER: Gas!!!!

(ENGINEER: You are heroes – in soot and sweat! You are heroes at the lever, before the gauge, at the gear-switch! Motionless you stand in the whirring of the belts and in the thunder of the crashing pistons! And even the most fearful event causes you no lasting fear – the explosion!

MILLIONAIRE'S SON: Come out of the hall!

. . .

ENGINEER: You are rulers here, in the work of all-powerful production – you make gas! . . . Here you are rulers – there you are – peasants!!

A VOICE (*cries*): Peasants!

OTHER VOICES: Peasants!!

NEW VOICES: Peasants!!!

ALL THE MEN AND WOMEN: Peasants!!!!

MILLIONAIRE'S SON (*on the steps of the tribune*): Do you listen to me – or to him?

ALL THE MEN AND WOMEN: The Engineer!!!!

. . .

MILLIONAIRE'S SON: . . . Come away!! You are heroes, who fear no trial! You carry on without fear to the end of the road – no terror makes you falter in your stride! The road has ended – *one*

> road has ended again – praise your courage with fresh courage –
> Man is there!!!!
>
> . . .
>
> ALL THE MEN AND WOMEN: The engineer shall lead us!!!!
>
> ENGINEER: Come out of the hall – back to work!! – From explosion
> to explosion!! – Gas!!
>
> ALL THE MEN AND WOMEN: Gas!!!!)

The mass of workers, unregenerate, pour back into the factory
after the Engineer: the vision of the Millionaire's Son is not
realized. In the final act representatives of big business, as well
as the army, seize the works to ensure the production of gas:
ruthless egotism and mechanization rule triumphant. But the
Millionaire's Son cannot forget his ideal:

> MILLIARDÄRSOHN: Sage es mir: wo ist der Mensch? Wann tritt
> er auf – und ruft sich mit Namen: – Mensch? . . . Muß er nicht
> ankommen – morgen und morgen – und in stündlicher Frist?! –
> Bin ich nicht Zeuge für ihn – und für seine Herkunft und Ankunft?
> – ist er mir nicht bekannt mit starkem Gesicht?! – Soll ich noch
> zweifeln?!!
>
> TOCHTER (*nieder in Knie*): Ich will ihn gebären!
>
> (MILLIONAIRE'S SON: Tell me – where is Man? When will he
> appear, and call himself by name: Man? . . . Must he not arrive –
> tomorrow, and tomorrow, and in the space of an hour?! Am I
> not a witness to him – his origin and advent – is he not known to me
> with his face of strength?! Must I still doubt?!!
>
> HIS DAUGHTER (*kneeling*): I shall give him birth!)

There is hope, then, for the future. But *Gas II*, performed two
years later, is a portrayal of apocalyptic doom. The Millionaire's
grandson has remained true to humanitarian ideals: he is now the
Millionaire-Worker. His antagonist is the Engineer, now Chief-
Engineer, who is virtually an automaton: the mechanical regularity
of his movements mirrors the machinery around him, and the
total abstract soullessness of modern technology. Gas is in even
greater demand since the outbreak of war, and the workers are

reduced to machinery themselves: the Millionaire-Worker, however, suggests that the workers should unite with their fellowmen on the enemy's side, that a call for peace and mutual love be radioed across the world. But he is greeted only with silence and the destructive savagery of the Chief-Engineer, who tells of the production of *Giftgas* – poison gas which eats away the living flesh. The clash between Millionaire-Worker and Chief-Engineer reaches a fearful intensity:

MILLIADÄR-ARBEITER: Gründet das Reich!!
GROSSINGENIEUR: Zündet das Giftgas!!!
ARBEITER: Giftgas!!!!

(MILLIONAIRE-WORKER: Found the new Kingdom!!
CHIEF-ENGINEER: Set off the Poison Gas!!!
WORKERS: Poison Gas!!!!)

In a climax of horror the Millionaire-Worker realizes that his ideal is totally unrealizable, and, in bitterness and disillusionment, he smashes the glass of poison gas on the floor, whilst the enemy bombardment starts outside. A Yellow Figure, one of the enemy soldiers, sees the shattered building, the concrete slabs lying on top of each other like gravestones, beneath which are lying the skeletons of those whose flesh the gas has destroyed. He reports back to his troops, crazed and demented, for he has seen the Day of Judgement: 'Kehrt die Geschütze gegen euch und vernichtet euch – die Toten drängen aus den Gräbern – jüngster Tag – dies irae – solvet – in favil . . .' (er zerschießt den Rest in den Mund) . . . ('Turn the guns against yourselves and destroy yourselves – the dead are bursting from the graves . . . judgement day – dies irae – solvet – in favil . . . (He shoots the rest in his mouth, . . .'). The final stage direction explains: 'In the hazy distance clusters of fire-balls hurtle against each other – clearly in self-destruction'. In this startling work Kaiser shows what war means in an age which can produce weapons of mass destruction;

he has seen how the demagogue seizes power over others and how, finally, man can destroy himself in a paroxysm of self-hatred. Man devotes his energies ultimately to suicide: the self-annihilation of civilization is at hand.

What, then, of the New Man? Will the potential in man for goodness and love be realized, or is man bent on destroying the world and himself? A play written between *Gas I* and *Gas II*, *Hölle Weg Erde* (*Hell Way Earth*) describes in almost religious terms a journey made by 'Spazierer' (the 'Walker') out of the hell of modern capitalism to the heaven-on-earth of universal brotherhood: light floods the stage at the end as men struggle towards true communion. But is it achieved? And the question must be asked: is there not in Kaiser a ruthless, almost cruel element, a narcissistic sense of power which contradicts the altruism of the vision of the New Man? One remembers the hectic selfishness of the Bank Cashier in *Von morgens bis mitternachts*, the deliberate, almost sadistic prolongation of suffering deemed necessary by Eustache de Saint-Pierre in *Die Bürger von Calais*; there is the violence used in *Hölle Weg Erde* and other plays (*Kanzlist Krehler* and *Zweimal Oliver*) and the hideous carnage of *Gas II*. The obsession of Kaiser with certain themes, the almost monomaniacal dedication of many of his characters, the reduction of men to automata, the abstract stage settings, the steel constructions and harsh lighting reflect a cruelty and bleakness which is not altogether expelled by an ideal which seems frequently Nietzschean rather than Christian. It must, however, be remembered that the plays Kaiser wrote between 1917 and 1923 were created whilst Germany was in the grip of defeat, collapse, revolution and disillusionment; the country was tremulous with hopes for a better future, yet shot through with brutality and civil strife.

Before the end of the fighting in 1918 two further plays appeared on the German stage (albeit in restricted performances) which showed the senselessness of war and its brutalizing effect on men: Fritz von Unruh's *Ein Geschlecht* (*A Stock*) and Reinhard Goering's *Seeschlacht* (*Naval Battle*). Fritz von Unruh (1885–1970) was a Prussian officer, formerly a page at the Imperial Court, who had devoted himself to literature at the age of twenty-seven, modelling himself upon Heinrich von Kleist. His earlier plays, *Offiziere* and *Prinz Louis Ferdinand* had extolled the Prussian military traditions, and were full of patriotic fervour and panache, but direct experience in the fighting of 1914 had convinced von Unruh of the horror and degradation of modern warfare. His dramatic poem *Vor der Entscheidung* (*Before the Decision*) describes the change of heart, the rejection of Heinrich von Kleist and his hectic and morbid nationalism, and the debt to Shakespeare, the writer who loved mankind in all its forms. Kleist may tempt to death, but von Unruh does not heed him: he recognizes and abominates the life-destroying cult of militarism and glory and turns his back upon his birth, upbringing and traditions. *Ein Geschlecht* was written in 1916: its blank verse is modelled upon that of Kleist and the lofty grandeur of the language looks back to Schiller, but the violence and extremity of the emotions expressed place von Unruh very much within the German Expressionist fold.

The scene is a nocturnal cemetery, where the Mother, the Daughter and the Youngest Son have buried a favourite son who died a hero in battle. Suddenly the two remaining sons are brought to them in chains, one guilty of cowardice, the other of brutal insubordination. This latter is the Eldest Son and he is the protagonist, a figure exemplifying amoral energy and radical nihilism. Brutalized by the war, he turns his violence against the Mother and Daughter, his sexual urges lusting for an incestuous relationship with his sister. Von Unruh sees clearly that nationalism liberates aggressiveness which it cannot ultimately control (the Eldest Son had been found guilty of rape), and yet which it obtusely expects to keep within limits; frustrated and racked with violent torment the Eldest Son curses the Mother for giving him life which brings death with it. He cannot control his murderous impulses which were formerly approved by the State: his vitalism, perverted, turns to self-destruction, and he jumps from the cemetery wall. The Mother, spiritually transformed, calls upon the mothers of the world to stop the madness of war, and proclaims a message of hope and love. Although she is killed by the Commander, the Youngest Son is inspired by her vision and leads the soldiers to rebellion down on the plains; the dawn proclaims a new day for mankind.

This is a most remarkable play, a concentrated expression of explosive power. It is obviously an anti-war play, in that the Mother seizes the staff of power and calls for a halt to the killing; although she perishes her ideal will ultimately triumph. But the work also touches on the theme of the proximity of lust and violence and also contains a deep conviction of the absurdity of life (the Eldest Son's condemnation of birth which contains death already within it), as well as a proclamation of matriarchal triumph. It is quintessentially expressionistic in that it is an outburst (albeit in traditional verse form) of pent-up, lava-like emotions: it combines an optimistic humanitarian ideal with a shrill, hectic sadism which is only just dispelled.

Reinhard Goering (1887–1936) wrote his play in a Davos sanatorium during convalescence; although not as powerful as *Ein Geschlecht* and more closely linked to a particular situation (the Battle of Jutland) it has a gripping, fatalistic quality at times reminiscent of ancient tragedy. The action takes place in a gun-turret of a battleship, dominated by a huge gun: the seven sailors are nameless and, after donning their gasmasks, faceless. The language is clipped and jagged, swelling at times to a rhythmic pathos; memories and visions give way to fervour and a sombre ecstasy:

DER ERSTE MATROSE (*an der Luke*): Skagerrak! Skagerrak! Letzter Mai! Siegestag! Jammertag! Lebt wohl Heimat, Land, alles, alles . . .
DER ZWEITE MATROSE: Komm mit uns, Bruder! Komm! Lebe!
DER DRITTE MATROSE: Komm mit uns, Bruder! Komm! Siege!
DER VIERTE MATROSE: Komm einfach mit uns sterben, Junge!

(FIRST SAILOR (*at the lookout*): Jutland! Jutland! Last day of May! Day of Victory! Day of Woe! Farewell Fatherland, home, everything, everything . . .
SECOND SAILOR: Come with us, brother! Come! Live!
THIRD SAILOR: Come with us, brother! Come! Triumph!
FOURTH SAILOR: Come with us, lad, simply – to die . . .)

The problems of obedience and the possibility of mutiny are touched upon; what meaning has their sacrifice?

STIMME: Vaterland, Vaterland, o lieb Vaterland. Wir sind Schweine, die auf den Metzger warten. Wir sind Kälber, die abgestochen werden. Unser Blut färbt die Fische! Vaterland, siehe, sieh, sieh! Schweine, die gemetzt werden, Kälber, die abgestochen werden! Herde, die der Blitz zerschmeißt. Der Schlag, der Schlag, wann kommt er uns? Vaterland, Vaterland, was hast du mit uns noch vor?

(VOICE: Fatherland, Fatherland, oh dear Fatherland. We are pigs waiting for the butcher, we are calves waiting to be slaughtered. Our blood dyes the fishes! Fatherland, look, look, look! Pigs to be butchered, calves to be slaughtered. A herd, shattered by the lightning. The blow, the blow, the blow, when will it strike us! Fatherland, Fatherland! What have you left for us?)

But a death-filled rapture triumphs:

STIMMEN: Vaterland, Vaterland, was noch von uns! Vaterland, Vaterland, Tod frißt uns wie Reis. Sieh uns hier liegen, Vaterland. Gib uns Tod, Tod! Tod! Gib uns Tod! Tod!

(VOICES: Fatherland, Fatherland, what more from us! Fatherland, Fatherland, death eats us like rice. See us lying here, Fatherland. Give us death, death, death! Give us death, death!)

The final explosion kills all: the fifth sailor, the most rebellious, recognizes before his death that dedication finally conquered the thought of insurrection. But Goering is not simply a 'patriotic' playwright here: he portrays men under stress, going ineluctably to their doom and reacting with expressive intensity to their predicament. His *Scapa Flow*, however, which appeared in the following year, is a much more conventional and less distinguished work.

The collapse of Germany, the establishment of the Weimar Republic, the turmoil of violence unleashed upon the streets during the fighting between extremist factions, the feverish and hectic optimism and the strident call for brotherhood created an atmosphere without parallel anywhere else in Europe. Would the New Man now emerge? Could mankind transcend its baseness and rise to spiritual sublimity? In the famous anthology of many of the younger poets already quoted, *Menschheitsdämmerung (The Dawn of Humanity)*, which was published in 1920, the editor, Kurt Pinthus, wrote: 'Und immer wieder muß gesagt werden, daß die Qualität dieser Dichtung in ihrer Intensität beruht. Niemals in der Weltdichtung erscholl so laut, zerreißend und aufrüttelnd der Schrei, Sturz und Sehnsucht einer Zeit, wie aus dem wilden Zuge dieser Vorläufer und Märtyrer' ('It must be said, again and again, that the quality of this poetry resides in its intensity. Never before in world poetry was the cry so loud, so piercing and convulsing, this cry, the plunging and yearning of the time, as it was from the wild procession of these precursors and martyrs'). In the same year Karl Bröger, in his collection of poems *Flamme*, greeted the new Utopia, whose advent was inevitable; the novelist Leonhard Frank, in his book *Der Mensch is gut (Man is Good)* announced the new era, the epoch of brotherhood and love. But the supreme example of German Expressionist fervour, of the expression of hope for the transfiguration and redemption of man, is Ernst Toller's play *Die Wandlung (The*

Transformation), performed in Berlin in 1919 and possibly the greatest product of the German theatre at this time.

Toller (1893–1939) had joined the army in 1914: at the front line he underwent a complete transformation, and suffered a spiritual and physical collapse. In Munich he joined the extreme Left, and was imprisoned for his pacifist views; there, in prison, between 1917 and 1918, he wrote *Die Wandlung*, subtitled *Das Ringen eines Menschen* (*A Man's Struggle*), a station-drama moving on two planes, realistic and symbolic, which demonstrates the conversion of the hero from an unthinking patriot to a fervent revolutionary leader.

A nightmare vision opens the play, where skeletons climb from their graves and roll their heads by numbers: a universal death prevails. The first station shows the hero, Friedrich, in opposition to his parental home (one thinks of Hasenclever here): he longs for release and freedom and joins the army to fight in the colonies. The realistic scenes alternate with dream-like visions which could be interpreted as the workings of his subconscious mind, and are frequently anticipations of what the realistic pictures later bring. The train carrying soldiers to their death precedes his awareness of the futility of war; the ghastly scene of the skeletons crawling from the barbed wire entanglements are a premonition of his own wounding and convalescence. A debt to Büchner, particularly *Woyzeck*, is evident in the scene with the medical Professor and the hideously mutilated patients: this will also be found in Toller's later play *Hinkemann*. After the war Friedrich, as a sculptor, is at work on a colossal statue of Victory, but the sight of two wretched war-invalids overwhelms him; he shatters the statue and, after a mental crisis bordering upon suicide, strides forth to join the masses:

Sonne umwogt mich,
Freiheit durchströmt mich,

Meine Augen schauen den Weg . . . (Schreitet ekstatisch zur Tür
hinaus)

(Sun flows around me,
Freedom suffuses me,
My eyes see the way. . . . He strides ecstatically through the
door)

His task is to move amongst men and inspire them with his ideal
of brotherhood and peace. He sees the wretchedness of slums,
the sufferings of the oppressed, the indifference and cruelty of
the authorities; but there is joy at the birth of a child, even amidst
the squalor of prison. Friedrich attends a political gathering,
and clashes with the Agitator who preaches revolution and
yet has no love in his soul; he foretells the new hope, the new
vision, the spiritual rebirth of men in almost Nietzschean terms:

Nun öffnet sich, aus Weltenschoß geboren
Das hochgewölbte Tor der Menschheitskathedrale.
Die Jugend aller Völker schreitet flammend
Zum nachtgeahnten Schrein aus leuchtendem Kristall.
Gewaltig schau ich strahlende Visionen.
Kein Elend mehr, nicht Krieg, nicht Haß,
Die Mütter kränzen ihre lichten Knaben
Zum frohen Spiel und fruchtgeweihtem Tanz.
Du Jugend schreite, ewig dich gebärend,
Erstarrtes ewig du zerstörend,
So schaffe Leben gluterfüllt vom Geist. . . .

(Now opens, born from the womb of the world, the high-arched door
of the cathedral of humanity. The youth of all the nations strides
radiant to the shrine of gleaming crystal which was sensed in the
darkness. Powerfully I see gleaming visions, no more misery, no
more war, no more hatred; mothers crown their shining boys for
the game of joy and the fruitful dance. Youth, stride, eternally
propagating yourself, eternally destroying that which is petrified,
and create, create life passionately filled with spirit. . . .)

The *Zarathustra* imagery intensifies: Friedrich becomes Leader, *Führer*, and, in the symbolic mountain scene, leaves the friend who cannot follow. Finally, on the market place, a message of love is preached which stresses the god-like qualities of man and the need for the realization of man's highest potentialities. The prerequisite for this is revolution, glorious, but bloodless:

> FRIEDRICH: Nun, ihr Brüder, rufe ich euch zu: Marschiert! Marschiert am lichten Tag! Nun geht hin zu den Machthabern und kündet ihnen mit brausenden Orgelstimmen, daß ihre Macht ein Truggebilde sei. Geht hin zu den Soldaten, sie sollen ihre Schwerter zu Pflugscharen schmieden. Geht hin zu den Reichen und zeigt ihnen ihr Herz, das ein Schutthaufen ward. Doch seid gütig zu ihnen, denn auch sie sind Arme, Verirrte. Aber zertrümmert die Burgen, zertrümmert lachend die falschen Burgen, gebaut aus Schlacke, aus ausgedörrter Schlacke. Marschiert – marschiert am lichten Tag. Brüder, recket zermarterte Hand/Flammender freudiger Ton!/Schreite durch unser freies Land/Revolution! Revolution!

> (FREDERICK: Now, brothers, I call to you: March! March in the brightness of day! Now go to the rulers and announce with the rushing voice of the organ that their power is only a deception. Go to the soldiers, tell them to beat their swords into ploughshares. Go to the rich and show them their hearts, which have become heaps of rubble. But be kind to them, for they too are poor, are lost. But destroy the palaces, laugh while you destroy the false palaces, built of slack, nothing but dried slack. March – march in the brightness of day. Brothers, lift up your broken hands, a flaming, joyful tone! Stride through our free land, Revolution! Revolution!)

The workers join hands and stride forth with Friedrich, joining in the chorus with him; a revolution, political and spiritual, is greeted with an almost religious ecstasy, for it is the God in Man that must be released for the New Millennium to dawn.

This play represents a supreme example of what may be called expressionist political activism: the revolt and aggressive egotism of the writers of the pre-war years have been channelled into an overtly political direction. But the idealism and spiritual foundation of Toller's political engagement was of such an intensity that disillusionment with the actual historical events around him was perhaps inevitable. The soviet republic set up in Munich in the early weeks of 1919 seemed to Toller the promise of a new world, but its ruthless suppression put an end to the Utopian hopes. And not only the Right-wing troops, but the Communists themselves, before Toller's eyes, committed acts of outrage. Poets and writers such as Johannes Becher, Leonhard Frank and Ludwig Rubiner embraced Communism: Toller could not reconcile the violence and brutality of the Communists with their pacifist ideals. His next play, *Masse Mensch* (*Masses Man*), written in 1919 and performed in 1921, is the working out of a conflict between the intellectual and the mob who are not yet ripe for his vision: the situation is obviously Toller's own. His further imprisonment, lasting five years, forced him to take stock of his situation and that of his country, and the whole problem of political activity; his play *Hinkemann*, like *Woyzeck*, shows the hard core of suffering at the heart of existence which no social amelioration can improve. The hero of *Hinkemann*, emasculated during the war, returns home to humiliation and degradation; reduced to earning his living by eating live mice, he sees his wife seduced and hears himself ridiculed. In one section reality is transcended and the contemporary world is shown in a sequence of nightmare pictures which are reminiscent of the newspaper-reading scene of *Der Bettler*; Hinkemann, deranged, hangs himself after the suicide of his wife. The later play, *Hoppla, wir leben* (*Hoppla*), written in 1927, again contains Toller's bitter awareness of the futility of political activity: the hero, closely modelled on Toller himself, sees the fading of the old ideals and the re-emergence of reactionary forces in Germany, and Erwin Piscator's influence is seen in the production in the use of film-shots and documentary elucidation of recent history. The suicide of the hero seems a sombre anticipation of Toller's own in 1939.

It was claimed in Chapter 3 that the German Expressionists were first and foremost poets and dramatists, and that the discursive prose form lacked the potentiality for immediate, ecstatic expression. Novelists such as Heinrich Mann could, however, and frequently did share the expressionist attack against established authority. His essay of 1910, *Geist und Tat* (*The Spirit and the Deed*), was a call for a united stand by the writers against the threat of militarism and anti-intellectualism in Germany, and his well known novel *Der Untertan* (*Man of Straw*) bitterly attacked all that Dietrich Hessling stood for. Heinrich Mann's attitude to the young writers who welcomed the new way of writing was ambiguous: he feared the irrational elements of German Expressionism yet prided himself on being, with Frank Wedekind and Carl Sternheim, one of the 'precursors and teachers of the younger generation of writers'. He stressed the great social task of the novel form and condemned self-indulgence in the arts, yet his novel *Der Kopf* (*The Head*) of 1925 with its use of slang, its dislocation of syntax and extreme concentration of language seems to be more 'modern' than he would admit. The novella *Kobes* (1923) also had a strange jerkiness and reduction to essentials characteristic of Georg Kaiser. It is probably in Heinrich Mann's plays, however, that the modernist techniques are most apparent: *Brabach* (1916) is very reminiscent of *Von morgens bis mitternachts*, and *Das gastliche Haus* (*The House of Hospitality*) of 1925 is not far removed from the world of Carl Sternheim.

Another novelist worthy of mention in this context is Alfred Döblin (1878–1957) whose best-known novel, written in 1929, is *Berlin Alexanderplatz*. The epic montage effect of his work is similar to that used in Joyce's *Ulysses*; the theme of the individual and the great city resembles also that of Dos Passos's *Manhattan Transfer*. The novel starts from the real, yet moves towards the surrealistic; its theatrical qualities tend to destroy the traditional novel form, and the grotesque elements overlap with the German Expressionist predilection for the bizarre. Döblin's *Berge Meere und Giganten (Mountains, Seas, Monsters)* of 1924, with its almost science-fiction play of the imagination and its asyntactical accumulation of dynamic verbs, is a bold fusion of futurism, expressionism and surrealism; in *Wadʒaks Kampf mit der Dampf- urbine (Wadʒaks Struggle against the Steam-Turbine)* of 1918 the theme of protest and the extreme tension of language betray a definite expressionist tendency. It would seem appropriate to claim that a novelist is an 'expressionist' if he was critical of society and pushed language to an extreme tension in an attempt to convey his convictions the more readily: as regards the use of expressionist techniques, Hermann Hesse's *Der Steppenwolf* of 1927 could perhaps be mentioned, particularly the so-called 'Magic Theatre' section, where the hero comes face to face with certain aspects of his own personality which have split off into independent life; but Hesse's work is essentially derivative and lacks the full force of expressive originality.

It is customary to equate German Expressionism with left-wing political movements, particularly in the early twenties: many of the writers did, as has been pointed out, turn to Communism, and this was, after all, one of the reasons why the Nazis banned the movement (another reason was the considerable Jewish element in it). But it should also be remembered that the desire for a new society, a new goal, a New Man also overlaps with the National Socialist programme. The emphasis on vitalism, on the irrational and the visionary, is also found in fascism: the play- wrights Arnolt Bronnen and Hanns Johst, and the poet Gottfried Benn (albeit briefly) embraced the Nazi cause. Goebbels himself wrote a novel *Michael* which has certain expressionist features: his support of the painter Emil Nolde later caused the party certain embarrassment. What is certain is that the atmosphere of febrile fervour, of hysteria and intoxication which characterized the work of so many German Expressionists betrays a restlessness and a tendency to the extreme which cannot be considered healthy. (On the other hand, Kafka's contention, *à propos* a discussion on Hasenclever's *Der Sohn*, that the father–son conflict should be treated as a comedy as Synge does it in *The Playboy of the Western World* comes like a breath of sanity; his views on Ehrenstein and Becher, as reported in the *Conversations with Janouch*, are similarly pertinent and down to earth.) Ronald Gray (in *The German Tradition in Literature 1871–1945*, Cambridge, 1965) describes the situation very well in the following passage:

> Few writers of any nation can have been so intimately concerned with the situation of the day as those of Germany at this time. Yet there is a disturbing quality about their plays, something melo-dramatic about the ghastlinesses they portray, and an excess of emotional language. Skeletons go on parade as soldiers and roll skulls by numbers; a severed head in a sack converses with its former owner; a woman bleats her Dionysiac love to a billy-goat; a father horsewhips his son, a son chases lustfully round the table after his mother, a society is formed for the Brutalization of the Ego. A man earns his living by eating live mice; a crowd of spectators exults pitilessly over the exhausted riders in a seven-day cycle race; the shades of Shakespeare and Kleist stalk over the battlefields; the German navy sinks in ecstatic and apocalyptic splendour in Scapa Flow. Too often there emerges from such scenes a radiant sun flooding the landscape with light while bands of pilgrims rejoice in a new-found freedom or some similar note of boundless optimism is struck. A crowd of dancers press orgiastically together, groaning their self-discovered divinity – this time, no doubt, as objects of satire, although one may ask what kind of society called for such satirizing. A bank-cashier stands with arms outstretched in front of a crucifix, his dying gasps accidentally suggesting the words

'Ecce Homo'. An atmosphere of painful contrivance is felt everywhere, a hysterical abandonment to the wildest hopes and the
unlikeliest despair . . . (pp. 48–9).

The same may equally be said of the lyric, with its distracted,
feverish, millennial hopes, and even more so of the new art-form
of the cinema, with its emphasis on distortion, automata, cruelty
and vampirism. The classic here, of course, is *The Cabinet of Dr.
Caligari*, made in 1919 with its première in February 1920; the
bizarre atmosphere is brilliantly caught in Walter Reimann's
sets, with their distortion and tortuous, labyrinthine quality,
through which the somnambulist (Conrad Veidt) and the maniac
doctor (Werner Krauss) move in a nightmare progression. Two
versions of *Der Golem* (1912 and 1916) captured the mysterious
atmosphere of Prague, the twisting streets and ghostly shadows;
in 1920 the famous *Von morgens bis mitternachts* was filmed, and
three years later Robert Wiene, responsible for *Caligari*, made his
Raskolnikoff. Fritz Lang's famous *Metropolis* (1926) owes an
obvious debt to the *Gas* trilogy, particularly in the portrayal of
the clash between father and son, and the fearful 'Moloch' scene.
The interest taken by many writers in the cinema is seen in the
Kinobuch edited by Kurt Pinthus which contained film scenarios
by Hasenclever, Else Lasker-Schüler (at one time Herwarth
Walden's wife), Max Brod (friend of Franz Kafka) and the minor
Expressionists Albert Ehrenstein, Ludwig Rubiner and Paul
Zech. The weirdness and atmosphere of menace and dread
conveyed by so many of the German Expressionist films led one
critic, Siegfried Kracauer, to claim that, after 1933, Germany
carried out what had been anticipated by her cinema from the
beginning.

German Expressionism, however, was too modernist, too anti-
authoritarian and enjoyed too many links with the international
world to survive under a dictatorship: the works of nearly all the
writers mentioned in this section were either burnt or banned,

and the notorious exhibition of 'Entartete Kunst' ('Degenerate Art') held in Munich in 1937 branded the painters with ignominy. It is ironic that the Nazi party, in stamping out German Expressionism, should have been bent on destroying what was probably Germany's most original contribution to the arts since the Middle Ages. Yet it must also be realized that almost ten years before the Nazis came to power the movement was waning and losing its force. The rhetoric and bombast had overstepped themselves: a reaction was inevitable. The middle years of the Weimar Republic had marked a return to a more normal way of life in Germany, without the hectic fever of the earlier years: a new sobriety, a nonchalance even began to supersede the hyperbolic visions. Brecht's *Baal*, although containing certain expressionist elements, is an attempt to write a better play than Hanns Johst's *Der Einsame (The Lonely One)*; Brecht's second play, *Trommeln in der Nacht (Drums in the Night)* deflates the whole idea of revolutionary fervour. His alienation techniques, together with the functionalism of the Bauhaus, and the new classicism in music demonstrate a desire for a more intellectual, sparser, less emotional attitude in the arts. But before attempting to describe the possible demise of expressionist tendencies we shall look at Europe as a whole to see if a similar pattern is observable outside Germany.

5
Wider Horizons: Europe and North America

It is frequently argued that expressionism is as typically German a phenomenon as impressionism is a French one: the formlessness and turbulence of the movement, as well as its intensity and abstraction, are looked upon as being somehow *urdeutsch*, and the origins are traced back to the *Sturm und Drang* of the eighteenth century, to Baroque dynamism and even Gothic distortion. But it can also be argued that Expressionism is simply the name given to that form which modernism took in Germany (see Patrick Bridgwater's introduction to *Twentieth Century German Verse*), and if this is the case then the expressionist debt to France is considerable, for it was in that country that virtually all the new movements in the arts originated.

Expressionism has been looked upon as a reaction against naturalism and symbolism, literary movements exemplified above all by Zola and Mallarmé. But upon closer consideration it would seem that Zola's famous dictum concerning the work of art, that it should be 'un coin de la nature vu à travers un tempérament' admits the necessity for subjectivity, a *tempérament*, which is not far removed from the expressionist position. Likewise the naturalist *Sekundenstil* and the pointilliste techniques of the impressionists both tend towards a dissolution of conventionally understood reality into fragments, which is surely an approximation to distortion and abstraction. On a more obvious level the political-activist concerns of Zola would link his name with those of certain German Expressionist writers whilst, at the other extreme, the emphasis on abstraction, inwardness and the powerful radiance of the symbol as advocated by Mallarmé would also be meaningful for many expressionist writers. The name of Bergson was also mentioned amongst the precursors of the movement, but the French writer who comes very close to expressionist vitalism, and whose poetry, in fact, predates much of the German writing, is Arthur Rimbaud (1854–1891).

French poetry, of course, had begun to be 'modern' with Baudelaire: poets such as Eliot and Pound in England found in him, and Laforgue and Rimbaud, the modernity for which they were looking. There were no sweeping innovations in twentieth-century French poetry to compare with what Eliot and Pound were doing between 1914 and 1920 in England because it had been done decades before: as early as 1870 Rimbaud had proclaimed that 'il faut être absolument moderne'. And Rimbaud particularly was the guiding spirit of many of the young German writers at the beginning of the century, especially after the K. L. Ammer translations of his poetry in 1907: 'Le bâteau ivre' became the most famous poem in the French language. Theodor Däubler translated it masterfully; Paul Zech wrote a stage-version (produced by Piscator in 1927); Bert Brecht appropriated much of its imagery in *Baal*; Oskar Loerke's 'Pansmusik' is full of echoes of Rimbaud. In November 1910 George Heym described in his diary how Rimbaud was a seer, a prophet, a god, and the poetry of Georg Trakl bears witness to the presence of this deity. The splendid rhetoric of the poem, the virtuosity of the seventeen-year-old author, the masterful coinage of imagery, the use of rare words and neologisms – above all the sense of revolt, the plunge into the elements, the drunken boat as a symbol for total liberation: these features were to make a great impact on German Expressionism. 'Les haleurs' (the towmen) – order and authority – have been destroyed: chaos is unleashed again. The tempestuous violence and the yearning for joyous pantheistic union with the sea carry the poem forward in coruscating images; the drowned corpse forestalls the predilection for the Ophelia theme in Heym, Benn and Brecht. The vitalism in Rimbaud is so intense that it is almost akin to a deathwish; this ambiguity which lies at the very heart of Nietzschean affirmation is an important element in German Expressionism also.

The fusion of mysticism and primitivism in Rimbaud, as well as his insistence that the poet should be *voyant* (in the famous letter to Izambard) have obvious parallels with the work and aspirations of many of the young German writers under scrutiny. A further French poet whose impact was not as great as Rimbaud's but who nevertheless has much in common with the Germans is Guillaume Apollinaire (1880–1918), hailed by many in France as 'le prince de l'esprit moderne'. In 1912 Apollinaire visited Herwarth Walden in Berlin and lectured to the *Sturm* circle: in the following year he published 'Alcools', together with his *L'anti-tradition futuriste*, which was based on a consideration of the work of the Italian futurist Severini. Apollinaire's self-perpetuating imagery reminds the reader of Stadler, and his use of metaphor can be compared to that of Trakl. With 'Qu'est-ce qui se passe', however, he seems closer to Lichtenstein, whereas other works (the play *Les mamelles de Tirésias*) may be called surrealist rather than expressionist, containing echoes of Alfred Jarry, a writer whom Apollinaire held in high esteem. Iwan Goll's *Paris brennt* (*Paris is Burning*) of 1921 owes much to the cubist montage-effect of Apollinaire, whose poems frequently dissolve into images naturally suited to the cinema, as do those of Blaise Cendrars (1887–1961), the title poem of whose *Prose du Trans-sibérien* (1913) is highly reminiscent of Gottfried Benn and brings to mind George Grosz's illustrations. There is much in Apollinaire that looks back to Laforgue and Baudelaire, but the modernity tinged with fantasy, the strange juxtapositions, discontinuity and simultaneity, also the off-hand flippancy, smack very much of the second decade of this century; 'La chanson du mal-aimé' and 'Vitam impendere amori' are good examples here. 'La jolie rousse', however, together with other war poems of 'Calligrammes', is a moving document of the poet who, 'Ayant vu la guerre dans l'Artillerie et l'Infanterie/Blessé à la tête trépané sous le chloroforme/Ayant perdu ses meilleurs amis dans l'effroyable lutte' ('Having seen the war in the artillery and the infantry, wounded in the head, trepanned under chloroform, having lost his best friends in the terrible struggle') emerges only to suffer the attacks of traditionalists and narrow-minded critics, but who nevertheless knows that his way is right. The poem ends on a note of sadness, almost a crucifixion: 'Mais riez, riez de moi/ Hommes de partout surtout gens d'ici/car il y a tant de choses que je n'ose vous dire/ Tant de choses que vous ne me laisseriez pas dire/Ayez pitié de moi' ('But laugh, laugh at me, men everywhere, especially men from here, for there are so many things that I dare not tell you, so many things that you would not let me say. Have pity on me').

Apollinaire died in 1918 of wounds sustained to the brain. Perhaps France's most outstanding war loss, however, was Charles Péguy (1873–1914). Péguy belonged to that generation of poets who emerged in France after the symbolists, naturalists and the decadents of the 1890s, one of that generation inspired by Whitman, Bergson and Nietzsche. A pantheistic vitalism is evident in his poetry; his atavism, mythomania and anti-rationalism make him seem more German than French. Stadler greatly admired his work and translated his poetry into German; it was rumoured that the two poets met and exchanged greetings in the trenches. The periodical *Die Aktion* paid tribute to Péguy after the news of his death in the October number of 1914 and had a drawing of Péguy by Egon Schiele on the cover (see Willett, p. 106), and in 1915 brought out a special French number in memory of him. There is no fierce urgency in Péguy, but a slow descent into the chthonic, a desire, almost, for obliteration in the eternal rhythms of nature. This longing to lose individuality, to submerge into the primitive and the Dionysian, a yearning ultimately for death (as seen in the constant refrain from 'Les sept contre Paris' – 'Heureux ceux qui sont morts . . .' – 'happy are those who are dead') was seen in Kaiser's *Die Koralle*, also in certain of the poems of Gottfried Benn, and indeed in some aspects of D. H. Lawrence; it is interesting also that Valéry, that most cerebral of poets, should also extol the sea, the flux and turmoil of creative forces, the watery abyss, rather than the solipsism of the sparkling mirror in 'Le cimetière marin'.

'From France', writes Walter Sokel, 'came to the Expressionists not only the vitalist modernism of Rimbaud and Apollinaire, the abstractionist modernism of Mallarmé and the political-activist inspiration of Voltaire, Hugo and Zola, but also the Christian poetry of Charles Péguy and the Christian modernism of Paul Claudel' (p. 147). But if 'French Expressionism' seems a highly dubious literary concept it is because the movement known as surrealism rapidly became a most potent force in French literature. Although surrealism shared with expressionism the need for liberation and regeneration, its roots may be found in a different soil, in Jarry and Freud and in such nineteenth-century precursors as Nerval. Such a claim as 'Le surréalisme n'est pas une forme poétique. Il est un cri de l'esprit qui retourne vers lui-même et est bien décidé à broyer désespérément ses entraves' ('Surrealism is not a poetic form. It is a cry of the spirit which turns in upon itself and is determined to shatter its fetters in despair') sounds as though it might have been taken from an expressionist manifesto, but the emphasis on dreams, irrationality and the subconscious advocated by André Breton and others in the *Manifeste du Surréalisme* of 1924 smacks more of neoromanticism and Dada (Tristan Tzara had collaborated briefly with Breton): political activism and pantheistic yearning seem alien here. But it is perhaps inevitable that the German cultural scene should develop in a way radically different from that of France: the collapse of 1918 and the febrile years of the Weimar Republic described in Chapter 4 fashioned a literary mode of expression unique in Europe.

And what of the links between German and Anglo-American poetry immediately preceding, during, and after the war? It has been traditional to regard English literature preceding the war as an anachronism when compared with the modernist experiments elsewhere; Georgian poetry is generally decried as being unadventurous and remote from fascinating dislocation. But it is, of course, Eliot and Pound who approach, in certain poems and other writing, a position not entirely alien to the German cultural scene. The emergence of autotelic image and absolute metaphor is, as was mentioned in Chapter 2, a modern tendency shared by German and Anglo-American poetry alike; Eliot's early poems 'Preludes' and 'Rhapsody on a Windy Night', and particularly his 'Sweeney Agonistes' would in all probability have qualified for the label of 'expressionist' had they been written in German (see Willett, p. 171). It is also interesting to remember Eliot's kinship with Gottfried Benn, and the debt to that poet which Eliot later acknowledged in the 'Three Voices of Poetry' (one also remembers the theme of retrogression touched upon in 'Prufrock' and evident in Benn and elsewhere). As regards other parallels, a similarity could be found between Joyce's polyglot word-coinages and the experiments of August Stramm, who might also be said to have anticipated the famous 'Stein-stutter' (the phrase is Wyndham Lewis's); J. D. Beresford's *Revolution* (1921) seems an English version of Kaiser's *Gas*, and Stephen Spender's poem 'The Express' (where the train, roaring 'further than Edinburgh or Rome/Beyond the crest of the world . . ./Ah, like a comet through flame . . .') a successor to the Stadler poem discussed in Chapter 3: his 'The Landscape near an Aerodrome', with its oblique, even hysterical description and sense of distortion, seems almost to echo

Georg Heym. But the most remarkable similarity between the German and the English literary scene is to be found in the short-lived movement known as vorticism, centred upon Wyndham Lewis's *Blast* and associated with such names as Ezra Pound, Gaudier-Brzeska, David Bomberg, Jacob Epstein and T. E. Hulme: for a few brief months it seemed as though 'English Expressionism' could be a valid term.

On 20 July 1914 the first edition of *Blast*, the 'puce monster' appeared, with a direct appeal to individualism, energy and creative vision; a few days before the vorticist group had exhibited to-gether at the Doré Gallery in Bond Street, their talents directed against romanticism, cubism and also futurism. At the 1914 exhibition Bomberg had announced: 'I completely abandon *Naturalism* and tradition. I am searching for an intenser expression.' In *Blast I* Wyndham Lewis proclaimed: 'Blast proclaims an art of Individuals . . . The Artist of the modern movement is a savage . . . Shakespeare reflects in his imagination a mysticism, madness and delicacy peculiar to the North. . . . Any great Northern Art will partake of this insidious and volcanic chaos . . .' (see sections III and IV. All references to *Blast* are from the Kraus reprint). The first edition included poems by Pound, also Lewis's dramatic fragment 'Enemy of the Stars'; a discussion of Kandinsky's *Über das Geistige in der Kunst* explains: 'Herr Kandinsky . . . writes of art – not in its relation to the drawing-room or the modern exhibition, but in its relation to the universe and the soul of man. Every artist, as a creator, has to express himself . . .' (p. 119). Lewis attempts to describe the movement in the arts towards abstraction, energy and primitivism, and finally arrives at the concept of the vortex:

> As 'Futurist', in England, does not mean anything more than a painter, either a little, or every much, occupying himself with questions of a renovation of art, and showing a tendency to rebellion against the domination of the Past, it is not necessary to correct it . . .

If Kandinsky had found a better word than 'Expressionist' he might have supplied a useful alternative. Futurism, as preached by Marinetti, is largely Impressionism up-to-date. To this is added his Automobilism and Nietzsche stunt ... Our Vortex is not afraid of the Past: it has forgotten it's (sic) existence. The new Vortex plunges to the heart of the Present ... Our Vortex rushes out like an angry dog at your Impressionistic fuss. Our Vortex is white and abstract with its red-hot swiftness.

> (See the sections 'The Melodrama of Modernity' and
> 'Our Vortex', pp. 143–9.)

Lewis does not like the term 'expressionism' (he assumed that Kandinsky had coined the word), neither does he approve of Marinetti's 'automobilism'. But his emphasis on the mysticism and madness of the North, and on the need for self-expression, together with the attack against impressionism and naturalism, puts him very much in the vanguard of the new cultural movement. The first number of *Blast* closed with Pound's views on the primacy of the image in poetry (containing the famous definition: 'An image is that which presents an intellectual and emotional complex in an instant of time'), and a contribution by Gaudier-Brzeska with the memorable statement: 'Will and consciousness are our VORTEX' (p. 158).

But the war destroyed those energies which might have created a new movement in England: by 1915 T. E. Hulme and Gaudier-Brzeska were killed: the second and last issue of *Blast* contained an announcement of the latter's death. It seemed as though the force and dynamism of the 1914 number of the journal were spent; the 1915 *Blast* contained little that was new, but it is interesting that Wyndham Lewis considered the expressionists 'ethereal, lyrical and cloud-like' (p. 40), and talks of their 'Blavatskyish soul'. The two Eliot poems 'Preludes' and 'Rhapsody on a Windy Night' were also published in this number. Yet although *Blast* did not survive, Ezra Pound published, in

1916, his *Gaudier-Brzeska: A Memoir* which contained the important discussion on imagism and also the statement: 'In the eighties there were symbolists opposed to impressionists, now you have vorticism, which is, roughly speaking, expressionism, neo-cubism and imagism all gathered together in one camp and futurism in the other' (p. 104). The famous description of the image as VORTEX (quoted in section 2) is also found here.

Pound equates expressionism with 'neo-cubism' and imagism: his insistence on the clarity of the image, however, and his hatred of abstractions (see his *Don'ts for Imagists* of 1913) would of necessity have made him reject out of hand the turgid bombast and nebulous effusions of much of the German work discussed in Chapter 4. The problem of tradition, with which he and Eliot were much concerned after the war, would have led him increasingly further from the German literary scene of the early twenties. But a man who lived in the heart of Europe even during the war, and who was keenly aware of the new developments was James Joyce, who arrived in Zurich in June 1915 and on parts of whose work an expressionist influence is undeniable. He met René Schickele (1883–1940), the Alsatian writer who was editor for six years of the journal *Die weißen Blätter*, and who wished Joyce to translate his play *Hans im Schnakenloch*; he attended performances of plays by Wedekind, including *Franziska* (he was much interested in Wedekind and his library included the latter's *Die Zensur*); he also saw Büchner's *Dantons Tod* and Strindberg's *Dance of Death* performed by Max Reinhardt's theatre. But it is above all the 'Nighttown' episode of *Ulysses* which justifies the reference to Joyce in this study, for here his prose assumed a degree of expressiveness and intensity unequalled elsewhere in the novel.

Walter Sokel writes: 'Joyce . . . abandons the verbalizing stream of consciousness for a symbolizing technique close to Expressionism' (p. 44). He sees that Joyce lets Bloom's and Stephen's subconscious fears and desires appear as apparitions and hallucinations much as Strindberg had done in *To Damascus*: a *dramatic* visualization is very much in evidence here. In the Nighttown episode there are sections which might almost be part of an expressionist drama (and 'Nighttown' has, in fact, been dramatized): the hallucinatory scenes project the inner preoccupations and tensions of the two men. The nightmarish and the grotesque elements of 'Nighttown' are also worthy of the German cinema of the twenties, which captured, as was described in Chapter 4, the sinister and disturbing aspects of life. Only a few years separate 'Nighttown' and *Caligari*, and the opening of 'Nighttown' might almost be taken from this film: 'The Mabbot street entrance of nighttown, before which stretches an uncobbled tramsiding set with skeleton tracks, red and green will-o'-the-wisps and danger signals. Rows of flimsy houses with gaping doors . . . A deafmute idiot with goggle eyes, his shapeless mouth dribbling, jerks past, shaken in St. Vitus' dance. . . .' Such a scene is an appropriate setting for the dredgings from the deepest recesses of Bloom's mind particularly: his feelings of inadequacy and passivity being externalized in remarkably vivid forms and possibly showing the influence of Joyce's study of Sacher-Masoch. The father-son relationship, a central problem in German Expressionism (see Chapter 3) also figures prominently in *Ulysses*.

The tendency to split off and personify inner states of soul is indeed reminiscent of Strindberg (although it is diverting to read of Joyce's rejection of that dramatist: 'No drama behind the hysterical raving!'); it is, however, the German Expressionist playwrights who came into their own in England and America after the defeat of 1918. A most important intermediary between the German and the English theatre at this time was Ashley Dukes, who, as a German-speaking officer stationed near Cologne, was in the exceptionally privileged position of being able to see all the new experiments on the German stage. He was immensely impressed by Reinhard Sorge's *Der Bettler*, and describes the play in his reminiscences:

> It was the first expressionist drama, and perhaps the best because it never left the plane of poetry. The subject was modern yet timeless, just one of those German domestic dramas that in prose can be so boring; the verse irregular and strong, seldom lyrical, always dramatic. The staging showed an understanding of the expressionist mind; across the proscenium hung a fine gauze, that now familiar device for preventing the diffusion of light on a subdivided scene. Symbolic arrangements of pieces of furniture and a stove, café seats on a raised terrace, a high window and the shrubs of a garden, formed the sub-division. The lighting moved from one part of this scene to another, leaving all the unlighted part invisible.

(See the article by J. M. Ritchie in *Affinities*, 1971, ed. R. W. Last, p. 99). But the revelation came later in Cologne when Ashley Dukes saw *Von morgens bis mitternachts*, and on his return to England he was determined to translate the play and introduce German theatrical Expressionism into the English theatre.

In 1922 he saw Reinhardt's production of Toller's *Maschinenstürmer* (*The Machine-wreckers*) in Berlin, and arranged a meeting with Toller in prison at Niederschönenfeld to discuss translation. But it was, as J. M. Ritchie has stressed (*Affinities*, p. 103), his version of *From Morn till Midnight* which played a vital role in the little theatre movement in England, particularly the Stage Society and the Gate Theatre: it was at the latter that the famous production with Claude Rains as the Cashier took place in 1925. Financial stringency meant a toning-down of the original Kaiser play, and the element of the grotesque is much less in evidence, but here at last was a chance for the soporific English theatre to see one of the finest examples of Kaiser's craftsmanship. It was, however, in America that the impact made by German Expressionist theatre was most strongly felt, and certain plays of Eugene O'Neill seem to be deeply indebted to it. Although O'Neill had written *The*

Hairy Ape and *The Emperor Jones* before any German Expressionist play had been seen in New York, he had certainly read Kaiser's *Von morgens bis mitternachts* before the 1922 New York production of the Ashley Dukes version. He had also seen *Caligari* in 1921, and the distorted settings reflecting the deranged mind of the protagonist, together with the juxtaposed areas of light and darkness had made a deep impression on him.

O'Neill's remarks to Tennessee Williams on Strindberg demonstrate his admiration for the Swedish writer, but it is interesting that he tended to deny any stimuli from the Germans. 'The point is that *The Hairy Ape* is a direct descendant of *Jones*, written long before I had ever heard of Expressionism, and its form needs no explanation but this' (quoted in B. H. Clark's *Eugene O'Neill*, New York, Dover, 1947, p. 83). *The Emperor Jones* does seem closer to Strindberg in that the distortion is motivated by the character's state of mind, and the 'little formless fears' are externalized as phantom realities, but this tendency is also observable in the case of the Salvation Army penitents in *Von morgens bis mitternachts*. *The Hairy Ape* would seem to stand between *The Emperor Jones* and the plays of Toller and Kaiser in that there is a mixture of realism and stylized elements (O'Neill himself explained that it ran 'the whole gamut from extreme naturalism to extreme expressionism – with more of the latter than the former'). The chorus of stokers, the stylized sets and lighting are certainly reminiscent of Kaiser's *Die Koralle*, as is the descent of Mildred to the nether realm. The Fifth Avenue scene, with the use of automata, has a jerky unreality akin to the films of the twenties. It is also obvious that O'Neill wished to stress the anti-naturalistic aspects of *The Hairy Ape* in the stage directions, where he talks of 'the eight sets, which must be in the Expressionistic method' (see A. and B. Gelb's *O'Neill*, New York, 1962, p. 492), but it is *The Great God Brown* which contains the most expressionistic features of all.

O'Neill's comments on the use of masks are very similar to those of Iwan Goll (see the latter's preface to *Die Unsterblichen* (*The Immortal Ones*)); O'Neill saw how an essential, inner reality may be made more accessible by deliberate distortion and *unreality*. The mask, stylization and ecstatic stammering convey essences far more readily than any attempt at naturalism: the disconnected yet highly suggestive outbursts of Dion in *The Great God Brown* seem to stem directly from German Expressionism: 'I love, you love, we love!... Come! Rest! Relax! Let go your clutch on the world! Dim and dimmer! Fading out in the past behind! Gone! Death! Now! Be born! Awake! Live! Dissolve into dew – into silence – into night – into earth – into space – into peace – into meaning – into joy – into God – into the Great God Pan!' The deliberately unrealistic, declamatory speech reminds the reader of O'Neill's confession that *'Thus Spake Zarathustra* had influenced him more than any other book he had ever read' (see the Gelbs, p. 121); it can be safely claimed that O'Neill's projecting of the states of soul of his characters through distorted settings, masks, and unrealistic, highly expressive speech does suggest a close affinity with German Expressionism: likewise Brown's assumption of his friend's identity after death in the hope of acquiring his talents and success does seem to stem directly from Kaiser's *Die Koralle* again.

The New York stage of the early twenties was aware of German Expressionism as a theatrical force and emulated many of its characteristics. Short scenes took the place of longer ones, the dialogue became staccato, symbolic characters replaced naturalistic ones; scenes became starkly abstract, lighting was used to create an atmosphere of unreality and choral effects were used together with allegorical group chanting. Elmer Rice's *The Adding Machine* (1923) owes an obvious debt to Kaiser with its seven 'stations', its hero closely modelled on Kaiser's Cashier ('Mr. Zero') and its settings of whirling turntables, its walls decorated with numbers and an adding-machine over which men crawl. The adventurous

Theatre Guild had as its first production of the 1922–23 season Karel Čapek's *R.U.R.*, which certainly seemed in keeping with expressionist tendencies with its bizarre and symbolical drama of man and machine; in 1923–24 Strindberg's *Ghost Sonata* was performed and, in April 1924, Toller's *Masse Mensch*, which, however, was far from a success. In 1924–25 Wedekind's *Erdgeist* appeared and a most ambitious attempt at Hasenclever's metaphysical drama *Jenseits (Beyond)*, a truly subjective experience, a passionate, staccato interchange between two symbolic characters, surrounded by hallucinatory effects (dissolving walls, trees growing into windows and looming shadows) and involved in a mystical, nebulous presentation of life and death. This was the most extreme of the German Expressionist plays performed in America: after this it was Franz Werfel who became famous in New York, with productions of his *Bocksgesang (Goat Song)* and *Spiegelmensch (Mirror-man)*, from which O'Neill may have learned more than he cared to admit: *The Great God Brown*, in its treatment of the two central characters William Brown and Dion Anthony, shows striking parallels with both the Werfel plays. In passing it might also be claimed that John Dos Passos's play *The Moon is a Gong* (staged in the 1925–26 season), in which the mourners do a Charleston around the corpse, is highly reminiscent of the Stockbroker's foxtrot around the stock-exchange in Toller's *Masse Mensch*: the dead from the train wreck remind one of the opening scene of *Die Wandlung*, while the grotesquely stylized houses seem to come directly from *Caligari*.

If it seems that the Americans were more open to German Expressionist theatre than the British, then one play must be mentioned which, in part at least, owes much to the German stage. This is Sean O'Casey's *The Silver Tassie*, which was rejected by W. B. Yeats and only put on in the Abbey Theatre in 1935, whereas London saw it in 1929. O'Casey was familiar with the work of Strindberg, Kaiser, Toller and O'Neill, and in the symbolic stagecraft of these dramatists he found a means of projecting, in the second act of his play, the fearful tragedy of battle. The soldiers are almost types from a morality play; a huge howitzer gun dominates the set (very much as the gun does in Goering's *Seeschlacht*), and the use of antiphonal chanting and staccato phrases are further anti-naturalist techniques. A ruined monastery wall has one unbroken stained-glass window of the Virgin: a shattered crucifix with a loosened arm seems to stretch towards her. The flashing light of the guns, the booming organ celebrating mass and the murmuring soldiers accompany the chanting of The Croucher, a deranged figure who chants his distorted version of the passage from Ezekiel on the dry bones. The face of this crazed, demented figure is to be made up as a skull, his hands must be skeletal; he sits somewhere above the group of soldiers and intones his liturgy of death. O'Casey nowhere else indulges in such expressionist devices, but here he seemed to need them, for they conveyed as nothing else could the monstrous nightmare of war.

Other European countries showed the German influence in the theatre: Čapek's *R.U.R.*, reminiscent of Kaiser's *Gas*, has already been mentioned. In the Soviet Union there was initially an acceptance of expressionist practice: Kandinsky and Chagall held official posts, and Meyerhold's productions of Toller proved most successful. But the subjectivity, mysticism and often almost religious concern for the soul of man struggling to free himself not only from the chains of capitalism but even from life itself were obviously alien to a Marxist ideology, and the increasing regimentation and orthodoxy of Soviet cultural life soon drove expressionism from the scene. A word should finally be said about expressionism in the dance: although Germany was the scene of fascinating experiments here the impetus came from Isadora Duncan, who had formulated a new expressiveness in dance, freed from the strictures of classical ballet, and from Mary Wigman, a student of Jacques-

Dalcroze and later collaborator with Rudolf von Laban, who created the dance of absolute abstraction, founded on expressiveness of gesture. The massed choral miming devised by Hanns Niedecken-Gebhard may also have had its origins in Isadora Duncan: his staging of Handel's *Herakles* in Münster (1927), with massed chorus and dance, demonstrated once more the *drama*, the *movement* and the externalization of inner states of soul which lie at the heart of the expressionist mentality.

But the disenchantment adumbrated in Chapter 4 must now be assessed: that particular quality to which the name expressionistic is given emerged in many of the arts of Europe during the twenties but at a time when, paradoxically, its German manifestation was fading. It is probably also true that it carried the seeds of its own demise within itself.

6
Decline?

As early as 1921 the young Alsatian Iwan Goll (who was, incidentally, one of the first to call himself an Expressionist) wrote an article entitled *Expressionismus stirbt* (*Expressionism is dying*); in the following year Brecht's *Trommeln in der Nacht* was performed in Munich. His *Baal*, as was mentioned in section 4, brilliantly parodies and outdoes Johst's play on Grabbe: a new force to be reckoned with now appeared in German theatre. Writing much later in his life, Brecht describes how the 'Oh Man!' plays of his time had appalled him: his youthful aggressiveness, nonchalance and cynicism, and in fact much of his later theatrical method, its spareness, coolness and intellectualism is a deliberate rejection of inflated theatrical expressionism. In Fritz Lang's film *Dr. Mabuse der Spieler* expressionism is rejected as 'a jest, what else?' and in 1925 G. F. Hartlaub organized an exhibition in Mannheim which he termed 'Neue Sachlichkeit' (a term difficult to translate, but meaning, essentially, new realism or matter of factness): a more sober, even disillusioned, attitude was emerging.

Certainly the rhetoric and bombast of German Expressionism faded. But expressionism is a complex phenomenon, and it is true to say that the three main tendencies that superseded it, dadaism, 'Neue Sachlichkeit' and surrealism were all unthinkable without it. The Dadaists' nihilistic antics, their anti-art and deliberate shock-tactics are not far removed from the expressionist urge to formlessness and extreme situations: Hugo Ball, Emmy Hennings and Hans Arp had been closely connected with German Expressionism before the move to Zurich. 'Neue Sachlichkeit' seems very remote from expressionistic hyperbole, but the deliberate modernity and big-city terminology is to be found in Benn and, of course, Marinetti. Willett rightly claims that much early expressionist verse (i.e. that of Lichtenstein and van Hoddis) was far closer to the poetry of the later twenties than to the more symbolic and declamatory writing of the movement's climax. Certain aspects of expressionism were identified with what could be called the modernist spirit, if the term is applied to English literature (for example, Pound's 'Imagism') and an important study of German Expressionism claimed that 'In many respects the Modern Movement in England and America corresponds not only to Expressionism but also to the succeeding German movement, the New Realism ('Neue Sachlichkeit') with its sceptical and disillusioned outlook' (see R. Samuel and R. Hinton Thomas, *Expressionism in German Life, Literature and the Theatre 1910–1924*, Cambridge, 1939, p. 17). And, thirdly, surrealism overlapped to a considerable extent with expressionism, in the emphasis on, in fact, *expressing*, on liberation from restrictions, and on the importance of vision: it was Guillaume Apollinaire (together with Iwan Goll) who invented the term, as well as being closely connected with the literary expressionism of the *Sturm* circle.

It is, then, false to assume that expressionism came to an abrupt end. The Nazis, as has been shown, shared much in common with it. Goebbels's novel stressed the need to 'shape the outside world from within' (Willett, p. 202); the experiments with the 'Thingspiel' were very close to certain manifestations of German Expressionist drama, as was the vast, theatrical staging of the rallies. In Italy, Marinetti's Fascism demonstrated the links between futurism and Mussolini's ambitions, and the perverted vitalism of both Fascism and Nazism seem to spring from tendencies latent within the movement. Neither the burning of the books nor the Degenerate Art exhibition in Munich can quite conceal the parallels.

In England it was questionable, in spite of Ashley Dukes's

valiant efforts, whether theatrical expressionism struck deep roots: already in 1930 James Agate published his *Their Hour upon the Stage. The Case against Expressionism*, and later in *Red Letter Nights* he attacked *Von morgens bis mitternachts* thus: 'I tried with might and main to see the spiritual significance of Mr. Kaiser's bombinations, but all I could see, or rather, hear, was a small cashier talking at enormous length through a very large hat' (*Affinities*, p. 105). Whether or not the Auden/Isherwood *Ascent of F6* might in any ways reflect German Expressionist concerns is debatable: J. B. Priestley's *Johnson over Jordan* seems a very dim reflection of Kaiser. Yet J. M. Ritchie points out that, when Peter Godfrey, in 1944, opened a Gate Theatre in Hollywood, he chose as one of the plays for the opening the indomitable *Von morgens bis mitternachts*, a play which uncannily refuses to pass into obscurity. As far as the English novel is concerned, the obvious debt to the German Expressionist scene is D. H. Lawrence's *Women in Love*, at which he was working during the First World War. The self-expression of Gudrun before the cattle, her Jacques-Dalcroze eurythmics remind one of Laban's expressionistic dance; Wagnerian and Nietzschean elements are much in evidence in the concept of *Blutbrüderschaft* and in Gerald's ascent to a frozen death in the mountains (this scene, in fact, would be very much in keeping in a Hesse novel or an early Leni Riefenstahl film). Lawrence's dithyrambic rhythms in his poetry, his free, essential verse that cuts to the very centre of things, with its obvious debt to Whitman, also bears comparison with Stadler. His openness to the German situation, his awareness of and sensitivity to the atmosphere there in the early twenties makes it not unlikely that German Expressionism was known to him; he could feel in 1924, 'a sense of danger, a queer, bristling feel of uncanny danger', and could describe 'the destructive vortex of Tartary' (Gray, p. 341).

But the nineteen-thirties brought other ways of feeling, other concerns and modes of expression: the 'Pylon' poets, the Spanish

Civil war, the Marxist orientation. The premises seem so different, but expressionism also shared a concern for social issues, and although Stephen Spender, in his review of the Samuel/Thomas study of German Expressionsim which appeared in *The London Mercury* in March 1938, repudiated the suggestion that there may have been expressionist elements in his work, nevertheless his description, in *Poetry since 1939*, of the poetry of the thirties, seems most applicable to expressionism – the emphasis on modernism, on powerful images, on the sense of communal disease and a left-wing inclination. But closer to the more dynamic aspects of expressionism was the so-called 'New Apocalypse' poetry of the early forties, the reaction against the notion of poetry as merely social reporting in favour of an emphasis on individualism and inner vision. The names that spring to mind here are, of course, Dylan Thomas, together with George Barker and David Gascoyne; the rejection of Auden's self-conscious, over-intellectualized manner, the intoxication with words and a love of myth seem very much in the expressionist mode. It is Dylan Thomas particularly who comes closest to the dynamism of much expressionist poetry, with his plethora of self-generating images; he had certainly read, in Vernon Watkins's translations, Novalis, Hölderlin and Rilke, but probably little else of modern German poetry.

AFTER 1945

It is tempting to compare the German situation in 1945 with that in 1918 to see whether or not a form of writing emerged similar to that of post-1918 German Expressionism. But the collapse of 1945 totally paralyzed all cultural life: this was a veritable zero-point as 1918 had never been. The massive physical destruction, the dawning awareness of the full horror of Nazism, and the division of Germany created a completely different set of conditions from those obtaining in the early twenties. But it is interesting that at least one playwright attempted, in 1947, to portray the nihilism, helplessness and despair of those years in an almost German Expressionist way: this was Wolfgang Borchert, whose play *Draußen vor der Tür* (*The Man Outside*) might almost have been written by Ernst Toller. The stylized characters – the Girl, the Man, an Undertaker (Death), an Old Man (God), also the River Elbe – the short scenes and above all the element of the grotesque, would not have been out of keeping twenty-five years earlier. But Borchert was soon forgotten: the *enfant terrible* of the twenties, Bert Brecht, returned to the Schiffbauerdamm Theatre to dominate, paradoxically, the West German Stage.

What, then, remains? The modernist techniques associated with early expressionism have become part of the stock-in-trade of modern writing, although it would seem that the frenzied pathos and the hyperbole are gone forever. Yet expressionism is, ultimately, an attitude of mind which can emerge at any time, a particular kind of response to a given number of factors. Self-expression, religious fervour, the predilection for the irrational and the occult, also political activism and total disregard for authority are, as Willett quite correctly points out (p. 244), very much part of the cultural scene today, and although the word 'expressionism' is now rarely used (yet did not the fifties talk of 'Abstract Expressionism' in painting?), the frame of mind and emotional state the term signifies are timeless conditions. If the term, one of Herbert Read's 'necessary' words like idealism and realism, designates the right to dream (to have nightmares even), the right to instinctive freedom and to revolt against automatism and stultifying restrictions – above all the right to express and create – then it is a positive attitude to life, for these are precious privileges; the tendency towards the extreme, with its own dangerous fascination, is a necessary concomitant.

Bibliography

I. GENERAL ACCOUNTS

ARNOLD, A., *Die Literatur des Expressionismus*, Stuttgart, 1966.
A very useful account of the movement's origins.

EDSCHMID, K., *Frühe Manifeste*, Hamburg, 1957.

FRIEDMANN, H. and MANN, O. (editors), *Expressionismus. Gestalten einer literarischen Bewegung*, Heidelberg, 1956.
A collection of essays of unequal merit.

KRISPYN, E., *Style and Society in German Literary Expressionism*, University of Florida, 1964.

MARTINI, F., *Was war Expressionismus?* Urach, 1948.

MYERS, B. S., *The German Expressionists*, New York, 1957.

PÖRTNER, P., *Literatur-Revolution 1910–1925*, Darmstadt, 1961.
Two volumes of documents, manifestoes and programmes.

RAABE, P. (editor), *Expressionismus. Literatur und Kunst 1910–1923*, Munich, 1960.
A most informative catalogue of the Schiller Nationalmuseum Exhibition.

RAABE, P. (editor), *Die Zeitschriften und Sammlungen des literarischen Expressionismus*, Stuttgart, 1964.
An indispensable bibliography.

RAABE, P. (editor), *Expressionismus. Aufzeichnungen und Erinnerungen der Zeitgenossen*, Olten, 1964.

RAABE, P. (editor), *Expressionismus. Der Kampf um eine literarische Bewegung*, Munich, 1965.
A very useful selection in paperback (Deutscher Taschenbuch Verlag) of writings and manifestoes by several German Expressionists.

ROTHE, W. (editor), *Expressionismus als Literatur*, Berne, 1969.
A good selection of essays on various writers, plus bibliographies and biographical notes.

MUSCHG, W., *Von Trakl zu Brecht*, Munich, 1961.

SAMUEL, R. and HINTON THOMAS, R., *Expressionism in German Life, Literature and the Theatre 1910–1924*, Cambridge, 1939.
The first serious account of the movement in English, and still a most useful study.

SOERGEL, A. and HOHOFF, C., *Dichtung und Dichter der Zeit*. Vom Naturalismus bis zur Gegenwart. 2 vols., Düsseldorf, 1961 and 1963.
A general, but perceptive, study of the period.

SOKEL, WALTER, *The Writer in Extremis*. Expressionism in Twentieth Century German Literature. Stanford, 1959.
An indispensable study of expressionism and 'modernism'.

WILLETT, J., *Expressionism*, Weidenfeld and Nicolson, 1970.
The fullest account in English of the movement in all its various manifestations.

2. STUDIES OF SPECIFIC GENRES

L'Expressionnisme dans le théâtre européen. (Edition du centre national de la recherche scientifique), Paris, 1971.
Various papers from a colloquium held in Strasbourg in 1968.

BAULAND, P., *The Hooded Eagle*. Modern German Drama on the New York Stage. Syracuse, 1968.
Contains a useful account of the impact made by German Expressionist drama in America.

DIEBOLD, B., *Anarchie im Drama*, Frankfurt/M., 1921.
An excellent early description of German Expressionist drama.

DENKLER, H., *Drama des Expressionismus*, Munich, 1967.

EISNER, LOTTE, *The Haunted Screen*, London, 1969.
A study of German Expressionist cinema.

GARTEN, H. F., *Modern German Drama*, London, 1959.

HAMBURGER, M. and MIDDLETON, C. (eds.), *Modern German Poetry 1910–1960*, London, 1963.

HILL, C. and LEY, R., *The Drama of German Expressionism*. A German-English Bibliography, University of North Carolina Press, 1960.

KRACAUER, S., *From Caligari to Hitler*, Princeton and London, 1947.
A fascinating account of expressionist cinema and the social background.

PINTHUS, K., *Menschheitsdämmerung*, Hamburg, 1957.
A reprint of the most representative anthology of German Expressionist poetry.

RÜHLE, G. *Theater für die Republik 1917–1933*, Frankfurt/M., 1967.
A judicious selection of excerpts from contemporary criticism of the German theatre at that time.

SCHNEIDER, K. L., *Zerbrochene Formen*. Wort und Bild im Expressionismus. Hamburg, 1967.

WALDEN, N. and SCHREYER, L. (editors), *Der Sturm*. Ein Erinnerungsbuch an Herwarth Walden und die Künstler aus dem Sturmkreis. Baden-Baden, 1954.
Reminiscences of the Berlin *Sturm* circle around Herwarth Walden.

3. STUDIES OF PARTICULAR WRITERS

CLARK, B. H., *Eugene O'Neill*. The Man and his Plays. New York, 1947.
Contains an account of O'Neill's attitude to German Expressionist drama.

DAHLSTRÖM, C. W. L., *Strindberg's Dramatic Expressionism*, Ann Arbor, 1930.

EYKMAN, C., *Die Funktion des Häßlichen in der Lyrik Georg Heyms, Georg Trakls und Gottfried Benns*, 1965.

HOFFMANN, E., *Kokoschka. Life and Work*, London, no date.

KENWORTHY, B. J., *Georg Kaiser*, Oxford, 1957.
The fullest study in English of this prolific playwright.

KRAUSE, D., *Sean O'Casey. The Man and his Work*, London, 1960.
Contains a discussion of expressionistic elements in O'Casey.

HELLER, P., 'The Masochistic Rebel in Recent German Literature' in *Journal of Aesthetics and Art Criticism*, 11, 1952/53.
Contains a discussion of Ernst Toller.

HINTON THOMAS, R., 'Notes on some unpublished papers of Reinhard Sorge' in *The Modern Language Review*, 1937.

PAULSEN, W., *Georg Kaiser*, 1960.

PINTHUS, K., 'Walter Hasenclever. Leben und Werk'. An introduction to Hasenclever's *Gedichte, Dramen, Prosa*, 1963.

PIPER, R., *Vormittag. Erinnerungen eines Verlegers*, Munich, 1947.
An account by the publisher of the reception of Dostoevsky in Germany during the time of Expressionism.

RÖLLEKE, H., *Die Stadt bei Stadler, Heym und Trakl*, Berlin, 1966.

SCHNEIDER, K. L., *Der bildhafte Ausdruck in den Dichtungen Georg Heyms, Georg Trakls und Ernst Stadlers*, Heidelberg, 1954.
An excellent analysis of the use of imagery and metaphor in the work of these three poets.

VALGEMAE, M., 'O'Neill and German Expressionism' in *Modern Drama*, 10, 2, September 1967.

Volumes 2 and 3 of the 'German Men of Letters' series (Oswald Wolff, London) contain essays of varying quality on the main figures of German Expressionism. The essay on the movement by Hector Maclean in *Periods in German Literature* (ed. J. M. Ritchie) is a perspicacious one. Professor Ritchie also edits a series of translations of German Expressionist plays for Calder and Boyars: *Seven Expressionist Plays* (including Kokoschka's *Murderer Hope of Womankind*); *Vision and Aftermath* (consisting of four war plays and including Goering's *Naval Encounter*); *Five Plays* of Georg Kaiser (that is, *From Morning to Midnight, The Burghers of Calais* and the *Gas* trilogy) and lastly *Scenes from the Heroic Life of the Middle Classes* by Carl Sternheim. Professor Ritchie has recently written a useful monograph on *Gottfried Benn* (Oswald Wolff, 1972), which contains a translation of *Ithaca* and the *Confession of Faith in Expressionism.*

Index

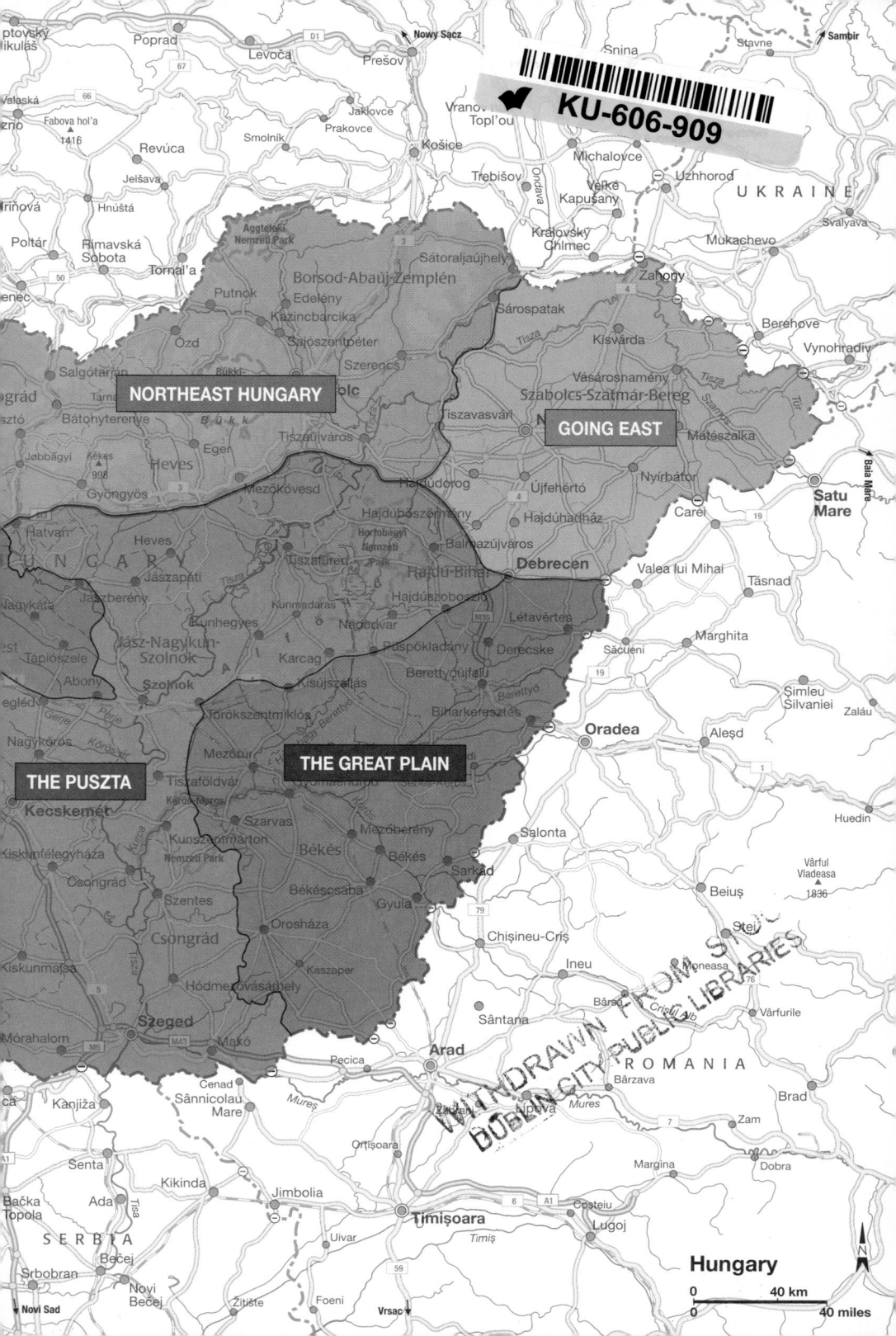

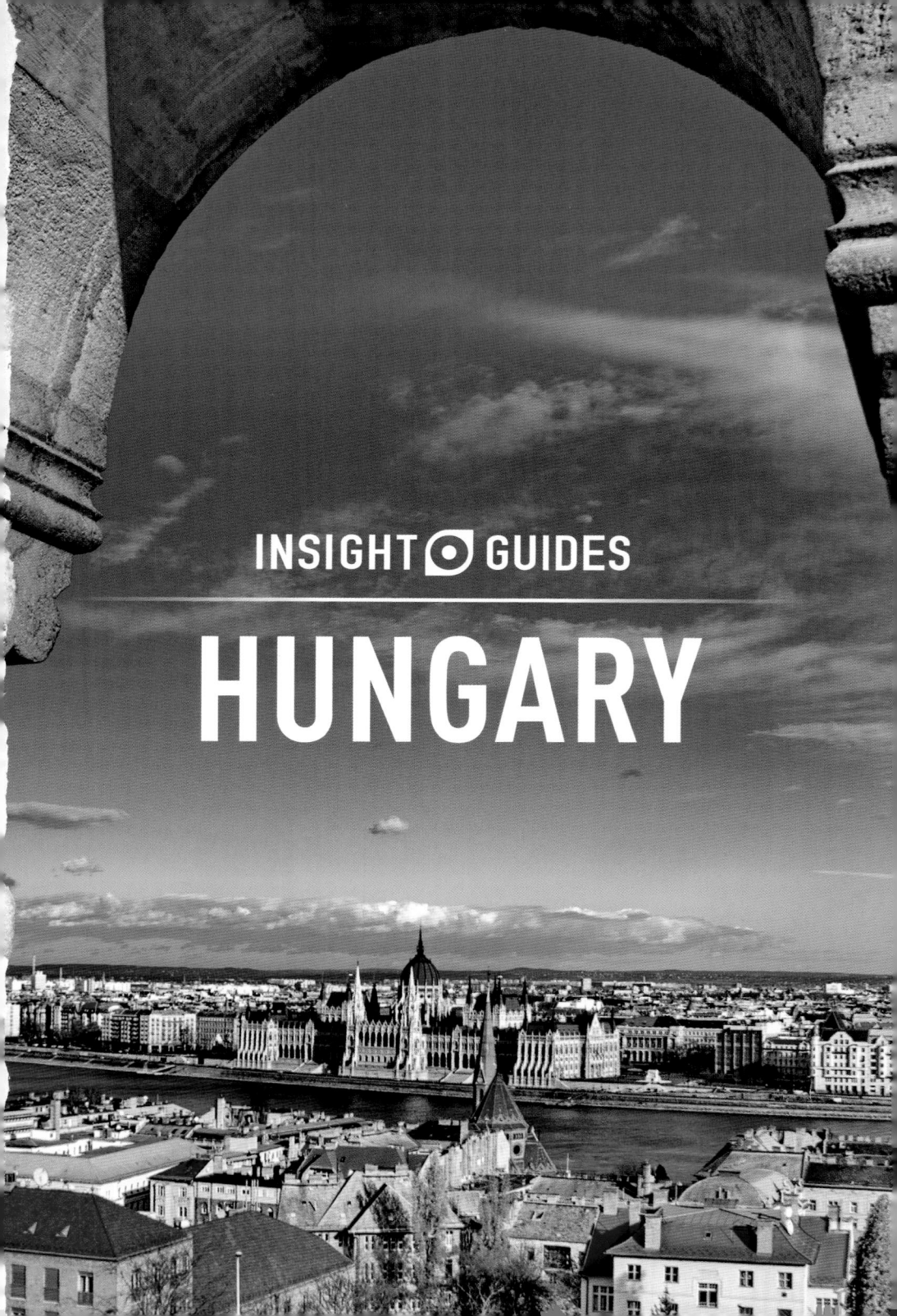

INSIGHT ◎ GUIDES

HUNGARY

PLAN & BOOK
YOUR TAILOR-MADE TRIP

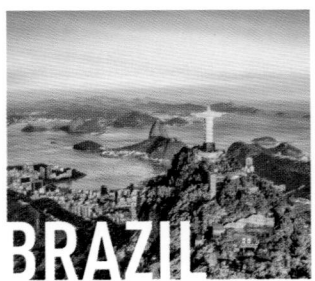 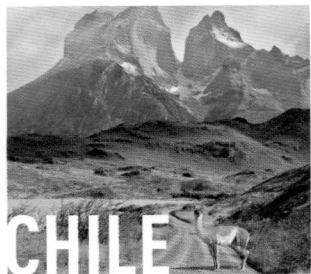 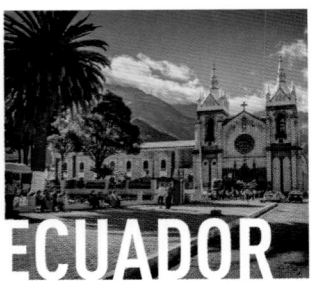

BRAZIL **CHILE** **ECUADOR**

TAILOR-MADE TRIPS & UNIQUE EXPERIENCES CREATED BY LOCAL TRAVEL EXPERTS AT INSIGHTGUIDES.COM/HOLIDAYS

Insight Guides has been inspiring travellers with high-quality travel content for over 45 years. As well as our popular guidebooks, we now offer the opportunity to book tailor-made private trips completely personalised to your needs and interests. By connecting with one of our local experts, you will directly benefit from their expertise and local know-how, helping you create memories that will last a lifetime.

HOW INSIGHTGUIDES.COM/HOLIDAYS WORKS

STEP 1

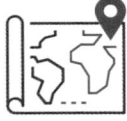

Pick your dream destination and submit an enquiry, or modify an existing itinerary if you prefer.

STEP 2

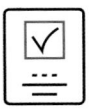

Fill in a short form, sharing details of your travel plans and preferences with a local expert.

STEP 3

Your local expert will create your personalised itinerary, which you can amend until you are completely satisfied.

STEP 4

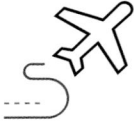

Book securely online. Pack your bags and enjoy your holiday! Your local expert will be available to answer questions during your trip.

BENEFITS OF PLANNING & BOOKING AT
INSIGHTGUIDES.COM/HOLIDAYS

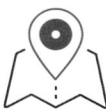

PLANNED BY LOCAL EXPERTS

The Insight Guides local experts are hand-picked, based on their experience in the travel industry and their impeccable standards of customer service.

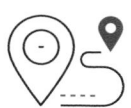

SAVE TIME & MONEY

When a local expert plans your trip, you save time and money when you book, even during high season. You won't be charged for using a credit card either.

TAILOR-MADE TRIPS

Book with Insight Guides, and you will be in complete control of the planning process, from the initial selections to amending your final itinerary.

BOOK & TRAVEL STRESS-FREE

Enjoy stress-free travel when you use the Insight Guides secure online booking platform. All bookings come with a money-back guarantee.

WHAT OTHER TRAVELLERS THINK ABOUT TRIPS BOOKED AT
INSIGHTGUIDES.COM/HOLIDAYS

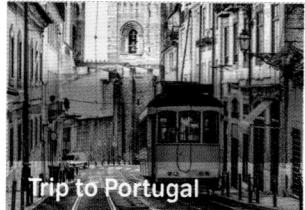

Trip to Portugal

Every step of the planning process and the trip itself was effortless and exceptional. Our special interests, preferences and requests were accommodated resulting in a trip that exceeded our expectations.

Corinne, USA ★★★★★

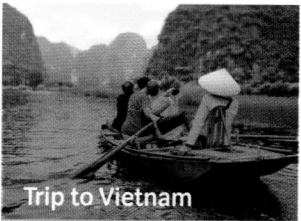

Trip to Vietnam

The organization was superb, the drivers professional, and accommodation quite comfortable. I was well taken care of! My thanks to your colleagues who helped make my trip to Vietnam such a great experience. My only regret is that I couldn't spend more time in the country.

Heather ★★★★★

CONTENTS

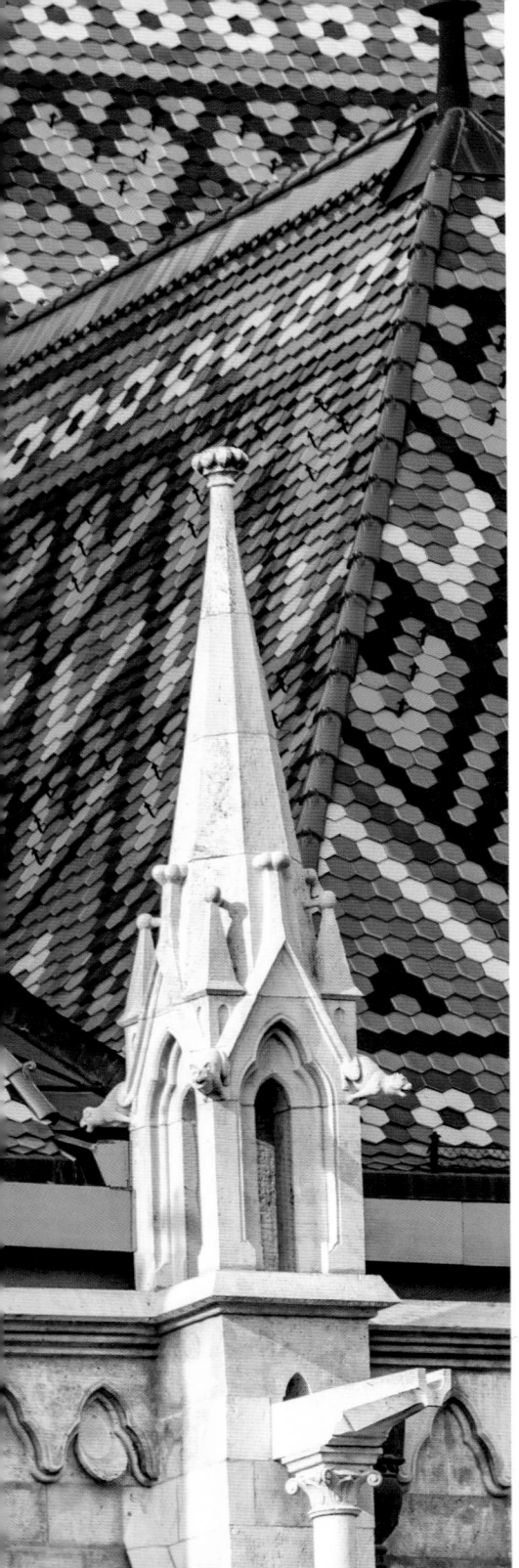

LEGEND
♀ Insight on
◎ Photo story

THE BEST OF HUNGARY: TOP ATTRACTIONS

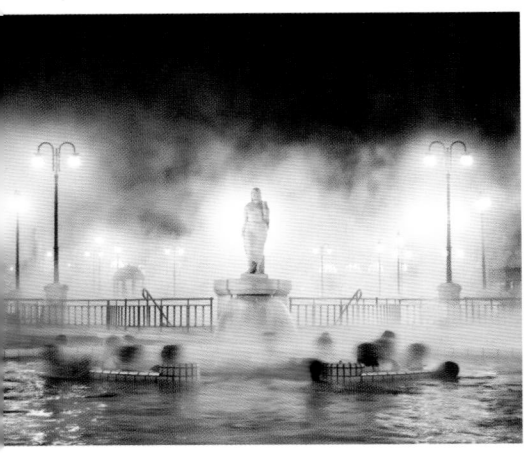

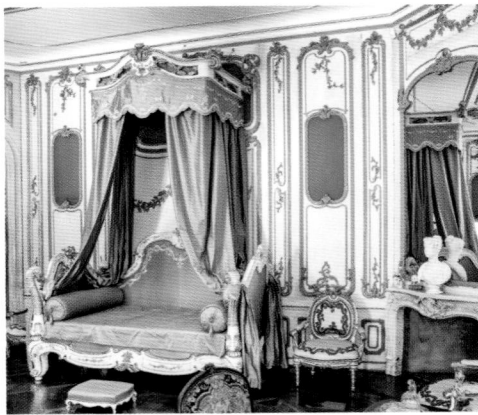

△ **Budapest**. Straddling the Danube and essentially two cities in one, Budapest has something for everyone, including Turkish baths, Art Nouveau architecture, river islands, top-drawer restaurants and exciting nightlife. See page 143.

▽ **Danube Bend**. One of the most enchanting stretches of the River Danube sweeps its way up from Budapest before dramatically twisting through a forested valley towards Slovakia.See page 173.

△ **Fertod Palace**. Once one of the most opulent palaces in Europe, and one-time home of the Estherházy family, this 18th-century Baroque and Rococo masterpiece remains the most impressive in the country. See page 193.

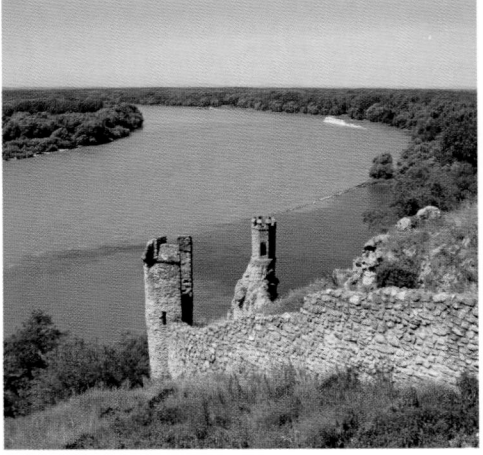

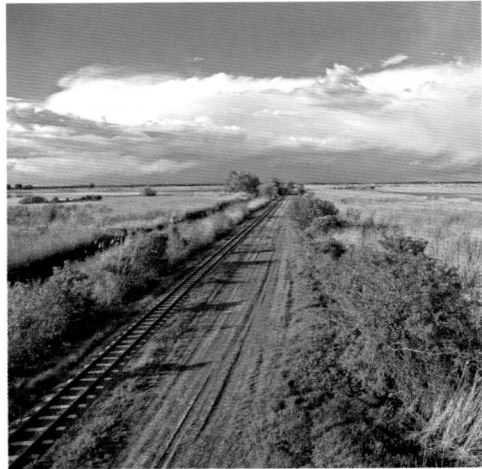

△ **Hortobágy National Park**. Hungary's largest national park and Unesco World Heritage Site, this outstanding natural landscape offers the quintessential *puszta* experience – don't miss the rodeo shows. See page 254.

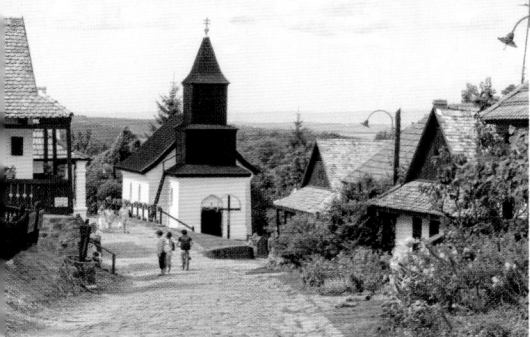

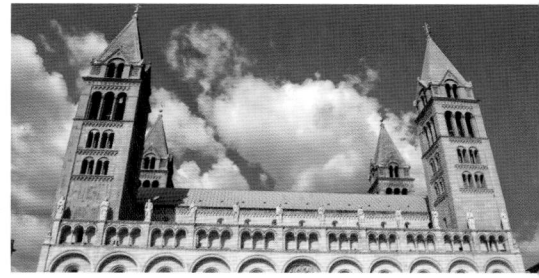

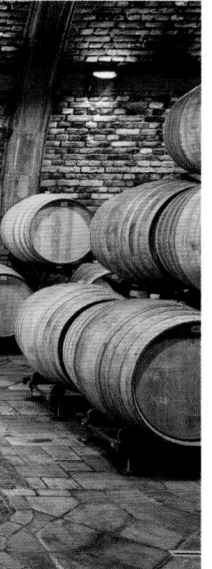

△ **Hollókö**. Nestling in the heart of the Cserhát Hills, a visit to this delightfully preserved village is a must for its vernacular architecture and long-standing folk customs. See page 222.

◁ **Wine cellars**. Don't leave Hungary without visiting one of its famous wine cellars, the best of which are located along the Villány-Siklós wine road and in the Tokaj region. See page 124.

▷ **Folk and gypsy music**. Don't pass up the chance to experience the wild, irrepressible sounds of Hungarian folk and gypsy music, whether that's at a concert in Budapest or a local restaurant. See page 104.

△ **Pécs**. After Budapest, this is Hungary's most appealing city, featuring a magnificent cathedral and packed with one of the most important collections of Turkish buildings in this part of Europe. See page 260.

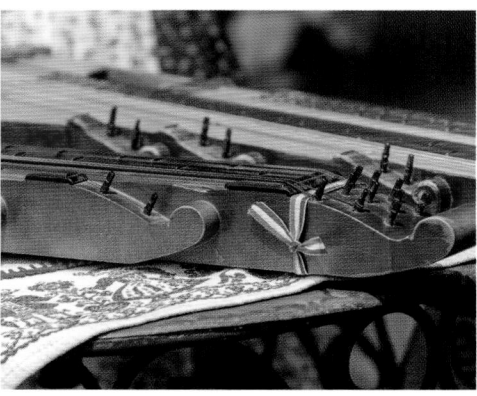

▽ **Pannonhalma Monastery**. Designed in an unusual blend of architectural forms, this grand-looking Benedictine Abbey is Hungary's most impressive monastery; the Empire-style library is a real highlight. See page 190.

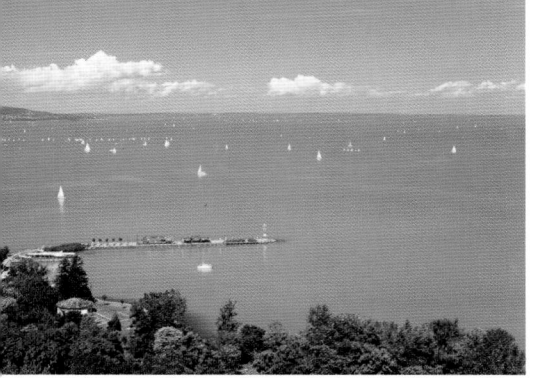

△ **Lake Balaton**. Escape the heat of the city and head to the 'Hungarian Sea', where you can chill on the beach, swim in shallow waters, or try your hand at windsurfing or sailing. See page 201.

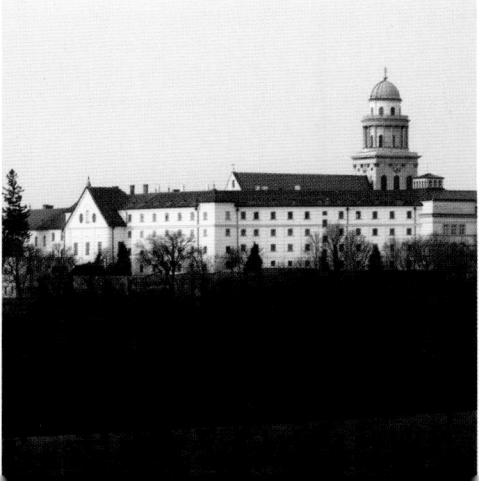

THE BEST OF HUNGARY: EDITOR'S CHOICE

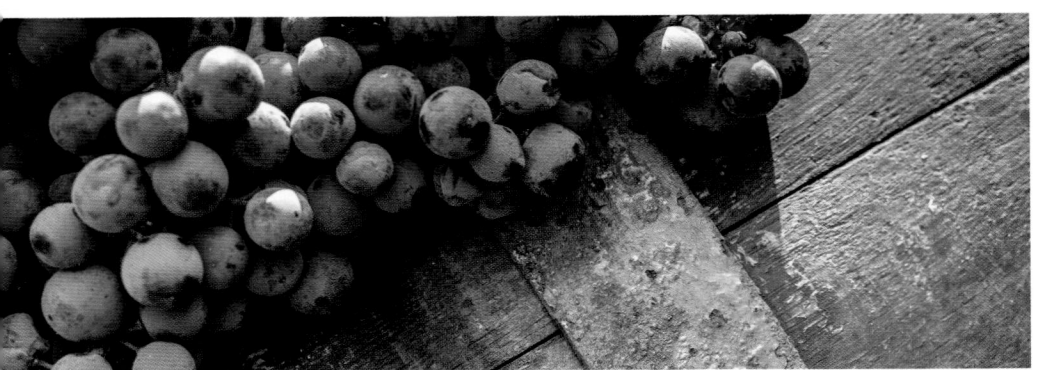

Hungarian grapes.

BEST BATHS

Gellért, Budapest. One of the oldest, and still the most traditional, of the city's bathhouses, the Gellért is the one to head to if time is limited. See page 148.

Hévíz. Bob on the water in rented rubber tubes in Europe's largest outdoor thermal baths, where temperatures never drop below 30°C. See page 212.

Széchenyi, Budapest. The city's largest open-air baths is a maze of hot and cold pools – 16 in fact. See page 154.

Hajdúszoboszló. This vast complex of pools and steam rooms also incorporates Hungary's largest water park – which make this a great place for kids. See page 114.

Király, Budapest. An atmospheric Ottoman bathhouse is distinguished by four copper cupolas and centred on a magnificent octagonal pool. See page 110.

Széchenyi Thermal Bath.

BEST WINE REGIONS

Tokaj. Hungary's most celebrated wine region is known above all else for its sweet Aszù dessert wines, such as the utterly lovely Furmint. See page 229.

Villány-Siklós. Hungary's first wine road consistently yields both fine-quality reds and whites, with the Cabernet Sauvignon and Cabernet France particularly treasured. See page 266.

Balaton. Lake Balaton boasts five different wine regions around its lakeshore, where white varieties dominate; look out for Légli and Szeremley. See page 201.

Eger. One of the biggest wine regions in the north, Eger is famous for its red Egri Bikavér, otherwise known as "Bull's Blood". See page 224.

Szkeszard. It may be one of the country's less heralded wine areas, but the reds are fantastic, especially the Kadarka. See page 260.

Winery in Balaton.

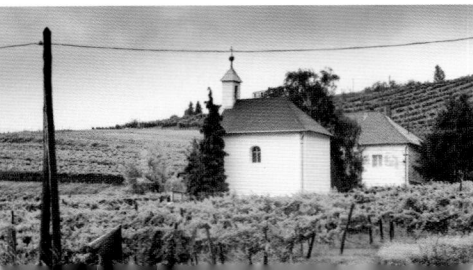

BEST BUDAPEST FOOD AND DRINK TREATS

Great Market Hall. You'll find plenty of cheap, filling and tasty Hungarian food in Budapest's grandest market place – as well as loads of great produce for a picnic. See page 148.

Ruszwurm Pâtisserie. Head to this family-run spot for a traditional sweet treat, served over a 200-year-old cherry wood counter and enjoyed in a 19th-century dining room. See page 147.

New York Café. Majestic Art Nouveau coffee house dating back to 1894 that still doles out some of the city's best coffee and cake today. See pages 126 and 153.

Goulash. This distinctively coloured, famous Hungarian dish is available in different forms from establishments all over the city. See page 121.

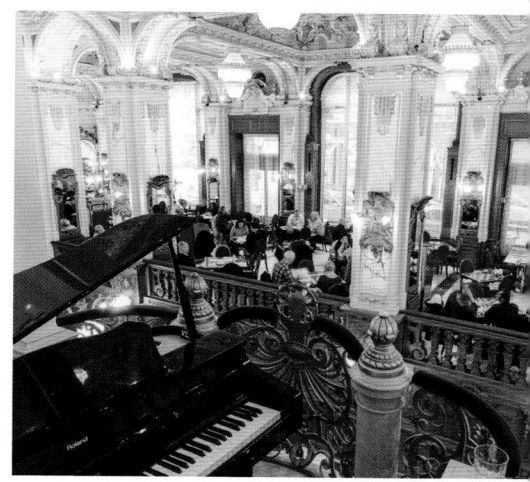

Budapest's New York Café.

BEST BUILDINGS

Cifra Palace, Kecskemét. A wonderful Secessionist building with a gingerbread-house like façade now houses the town's excellent art gallery. See page 235.

Holy Spirit Church, Paks. One of several typically exuberant wooden structures scattered around Hungary designed by the controversial architect Imre Makovecz. See page 179.

Great Synagogue, Budapest. Europe's largest synagogue is an extravagant Byzantine-Moorish designed edifice topped by two gilded onion-domed towers. See page 150.

Matthias Church, Budapest. A Neo-Gothic masterpiece manifesting a dazzling diamond-patterned roof and toothy spires and, inside, richly carved coats-of-arms and colourful frescoes. See page 145.

Festetics Palace, Keszthely. Erstwhile home of the eponymous family, the highlights of this imposing Neo-Baroque pile are the gilt, mirrored ballroom and the beautifully carved Helikon library. See page 210.

The Great Synagogue.

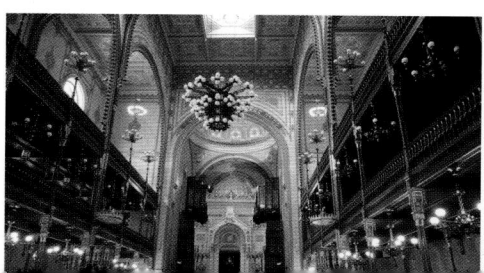

BEST ACTIVITIES

Windsurfing, Lake Balaton. Balaton's breezy shores are perfect for a spot of windsurfing, and there are dozens of places dotted all around the lake where you can hire equipment. See page 211.

Horse-riding. Hungarians have a deep attachment to all things equine, and there's nowhere better to have a go yourself than on the puszta. See page 249.

Hiking, Bükk Hills. These lovely, beech-covered hills in the Northern Uplands offer some of Hungary's best and most varied hiking opportunities with trails to suit walkers of all abilities. See page 226.

Birdwatching. For something a little more sedate, check out some of the country's many fantastic birding spots such as the Hortobágy, the Kiskunság and Lake Tisza. See pages 255 and 238.

Windsurfing, Lake Balaton.

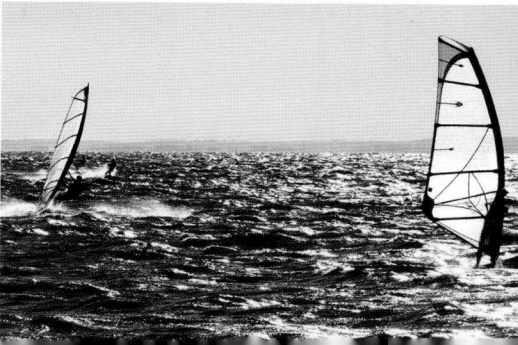

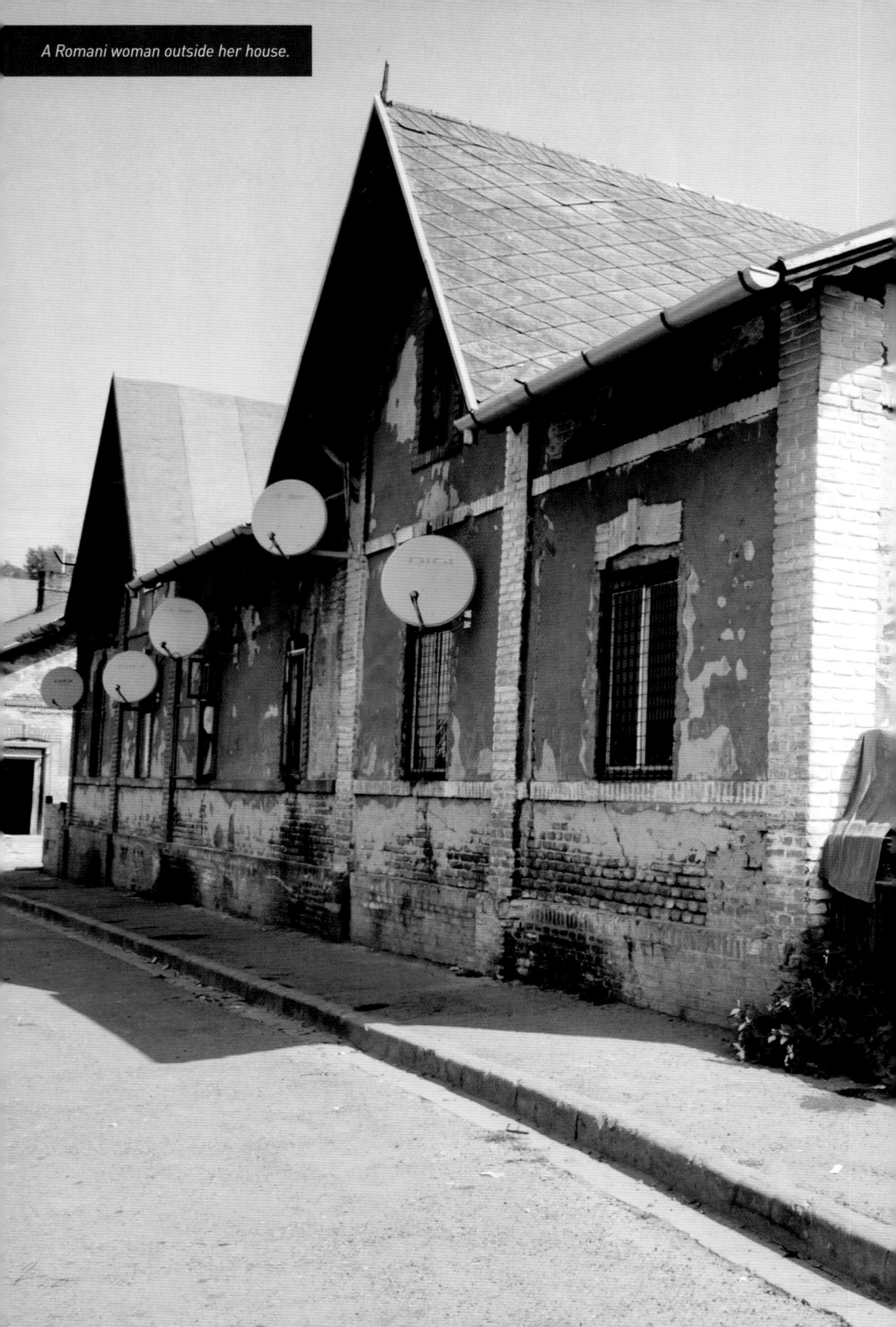

A Romani woman outside her house.

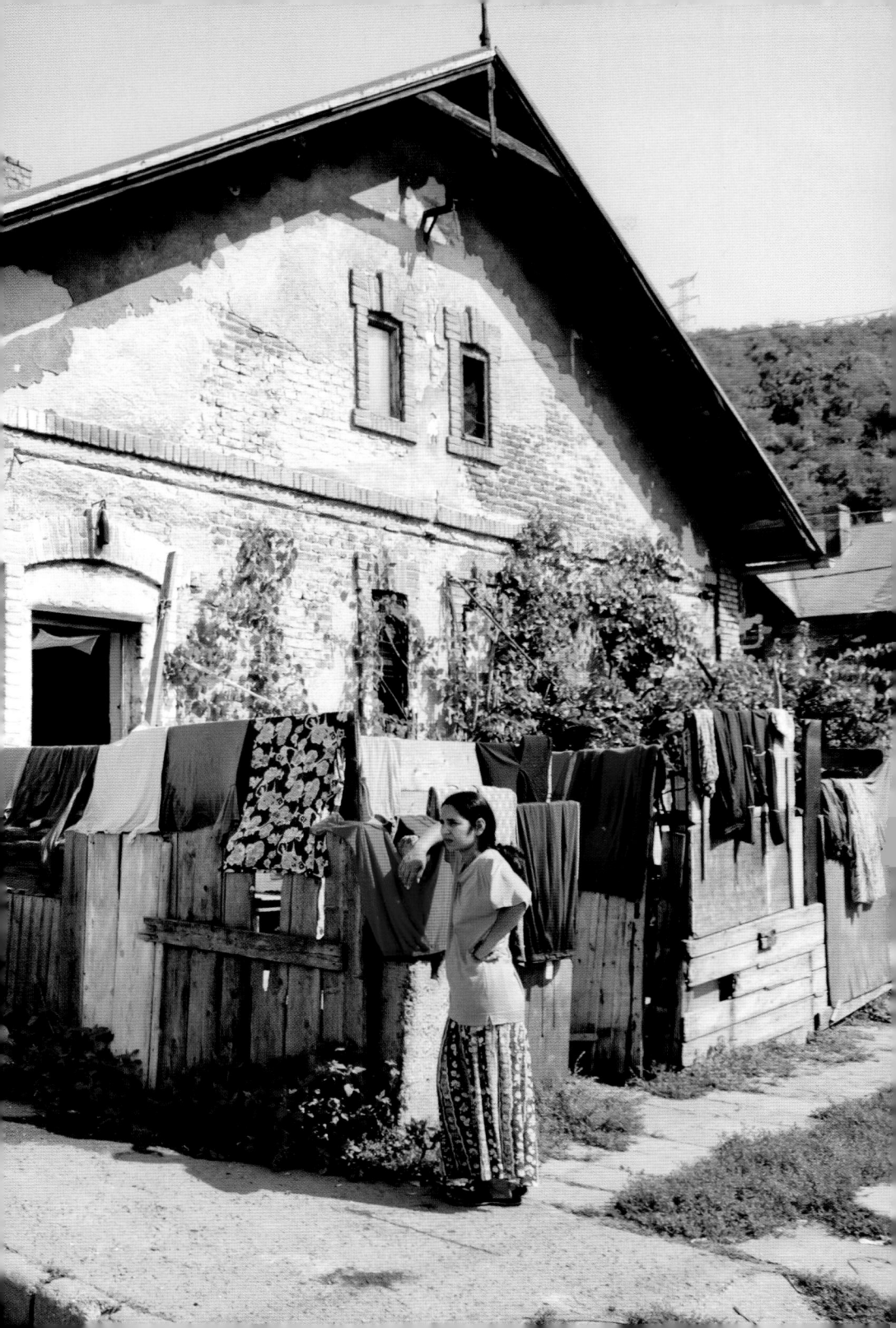

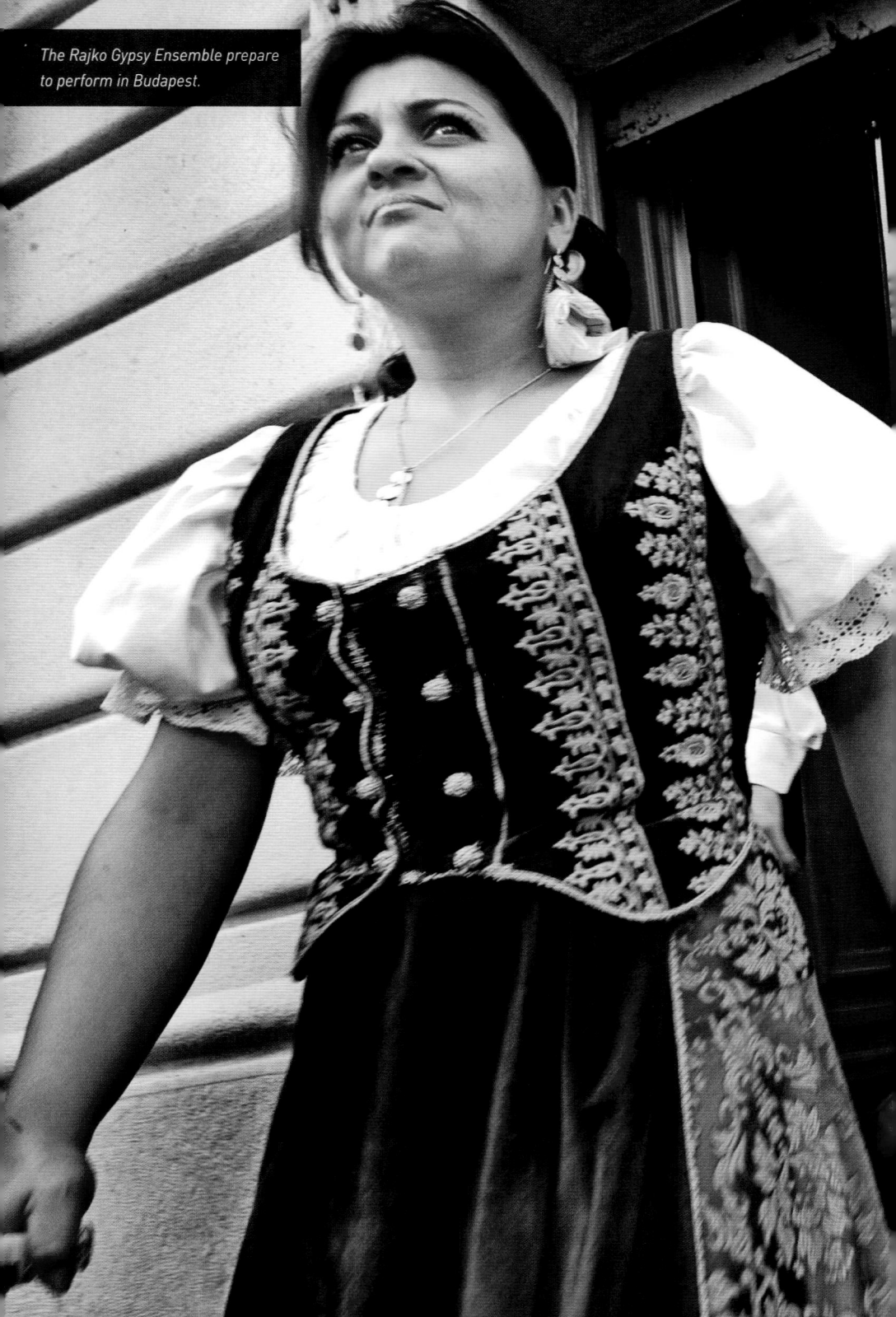
The Rajko Gypsy Ensemble prepare to perform in Budapest.

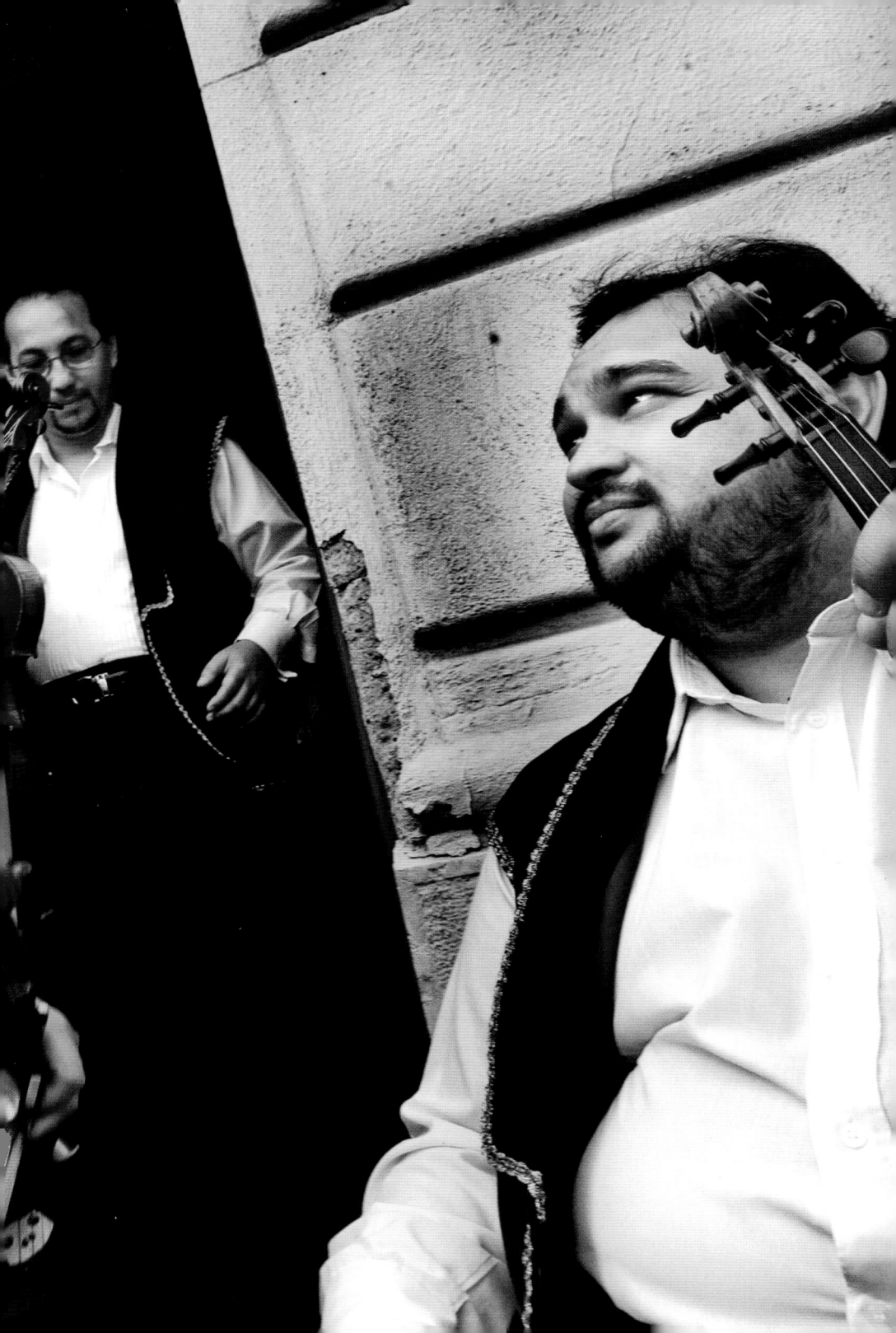

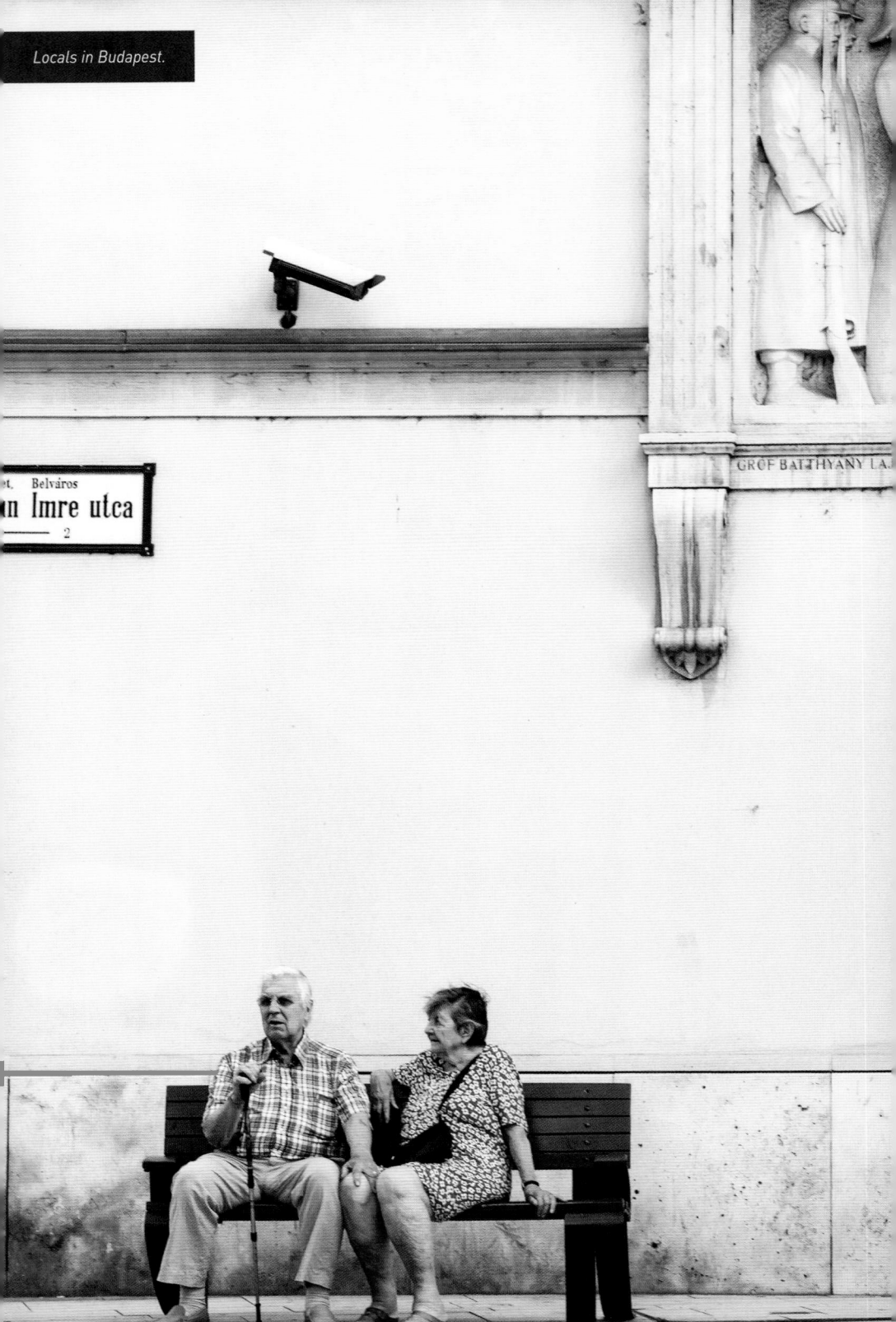

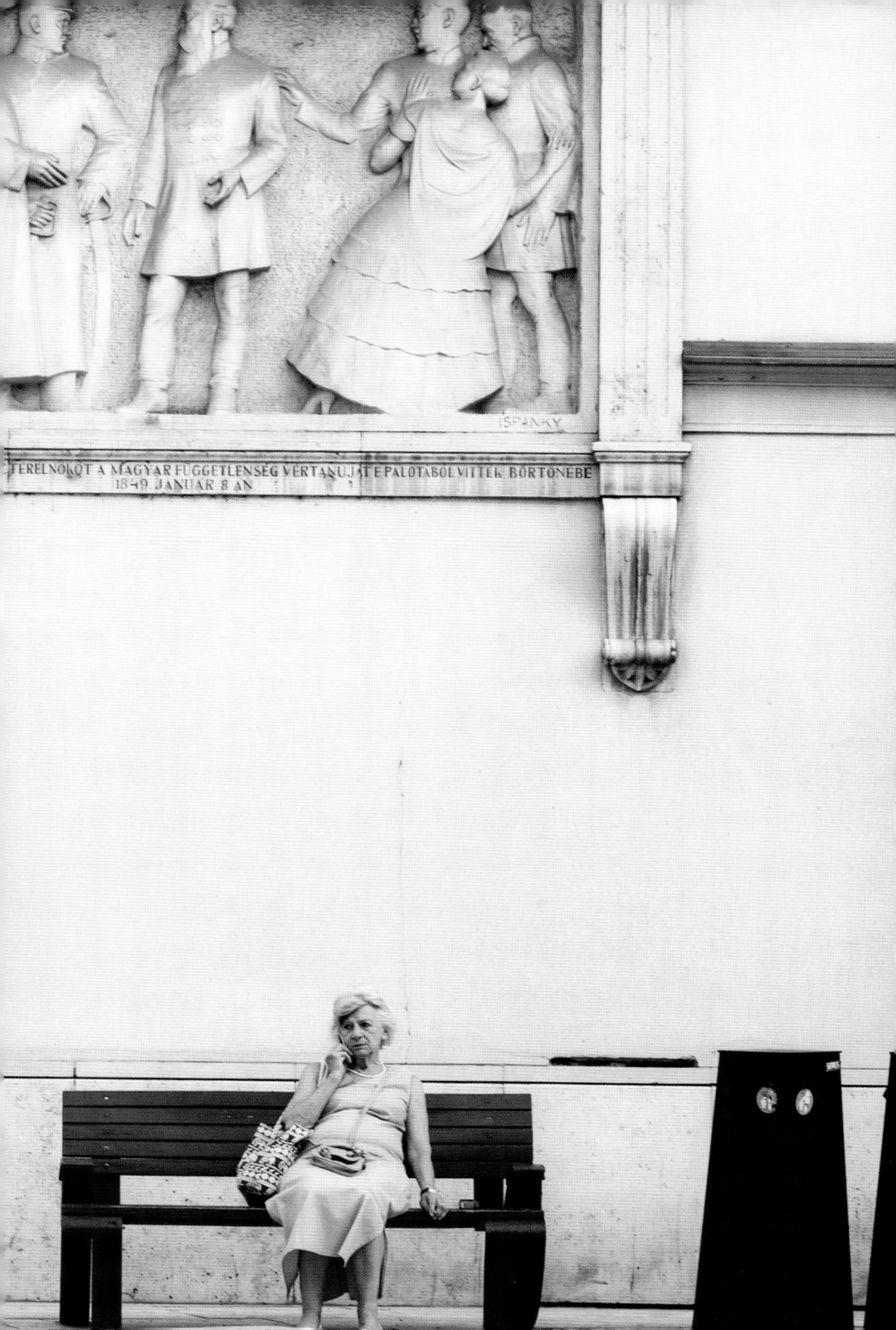

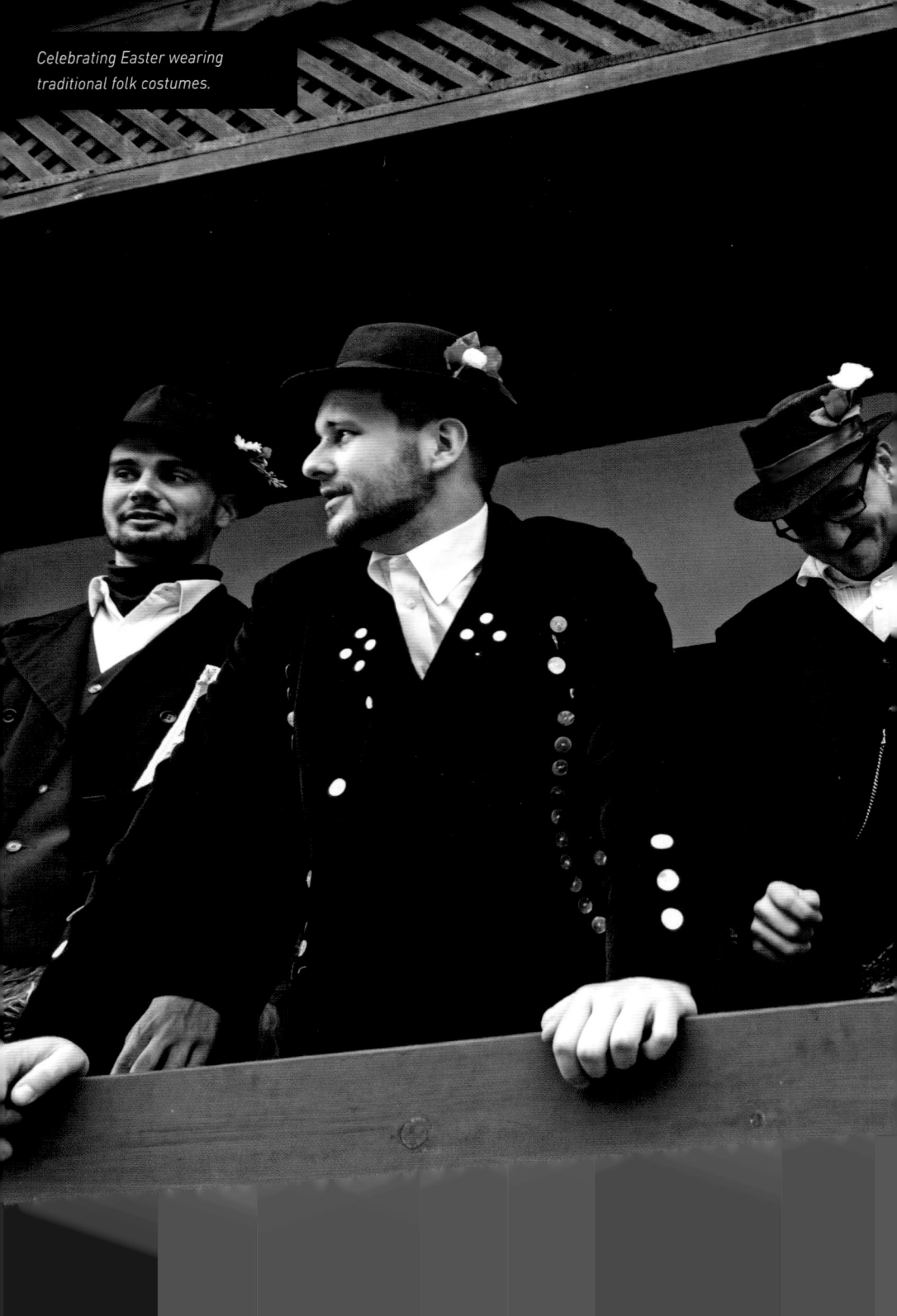

A NATION OF NOMADS

At the crossroads of Europe, Hungary has finally found peace and independence after centuries of foreign domination.

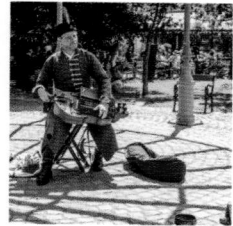

Musician in Budapest.

Hungary and the Hungarians as we know them today were at one time two quite different entities. The land, a large and fertile plain defended in the east and north by the Carpathians and in the west by natural obstacles – swamps, rivers and the foothills of the Alps – served as a haven to tribes before the Magyars came sweeping through in AD 896 and made it their home.

Hungary's subsequent history is relatively short but complex. Survival as an independent nation at the intersection of Western and Eastern Europe and the Balkans demanded a cunning foreign policy not all Hungarian leaders could provide. After becoming a kingdom sanctioned by the Pope in 1001, Hungary acted as a bastion for Western Europe, only to be left to its own devices when the going got rough. Internecine struggles between powerful magnates, nobles, tyrants, monarchs and a galaxy of fine political leaders also sundered the nation from within.

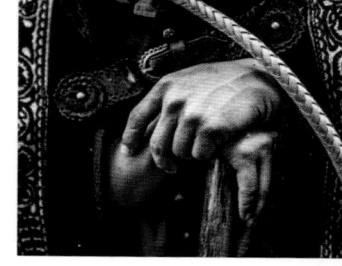

A shepherd's hands.

Hungary's fortunes have waxed and waned with the tides of history. At times it exhibited boundless wealth, which was then coveted by others. Under the Angevin King Lajos I, the realm stretched from the Adriatic to the Black Sea and almost to the Baltic in the north. Domination by the Turks, Habsburgs, Nazis and communists was to follow; all hopes of independence were mercilessly crushed. In the aftermath of World War I, two-thirds of Hungarian territory was carved up and handed out to Romania, Czechoslovakia and Yugoslavia, and one-fifth of its population went with the land. All these events forced Hungarians from their homes, and they continue to be nomads: today, some 30 percent of the "Magyar nation" lives outside Hungary.

Thanks perhaps to their turbulent and often painful history, Hungarians tend to have a melancholy streak, but they can also be a friendly and hospitable people. The visitor travelling the country will also notice the ubiquity of the Hungarian colours, red, white and green (*piros, fehér, zöld*). Patriotism here often takes the form of venerating, celebrating or commemorating one of the country's many tragedies. The Magyar people were (and remain) incurable romantics, confronting their enemies when the odds seem hopeless and earning acclaim for their many gallant defeats.

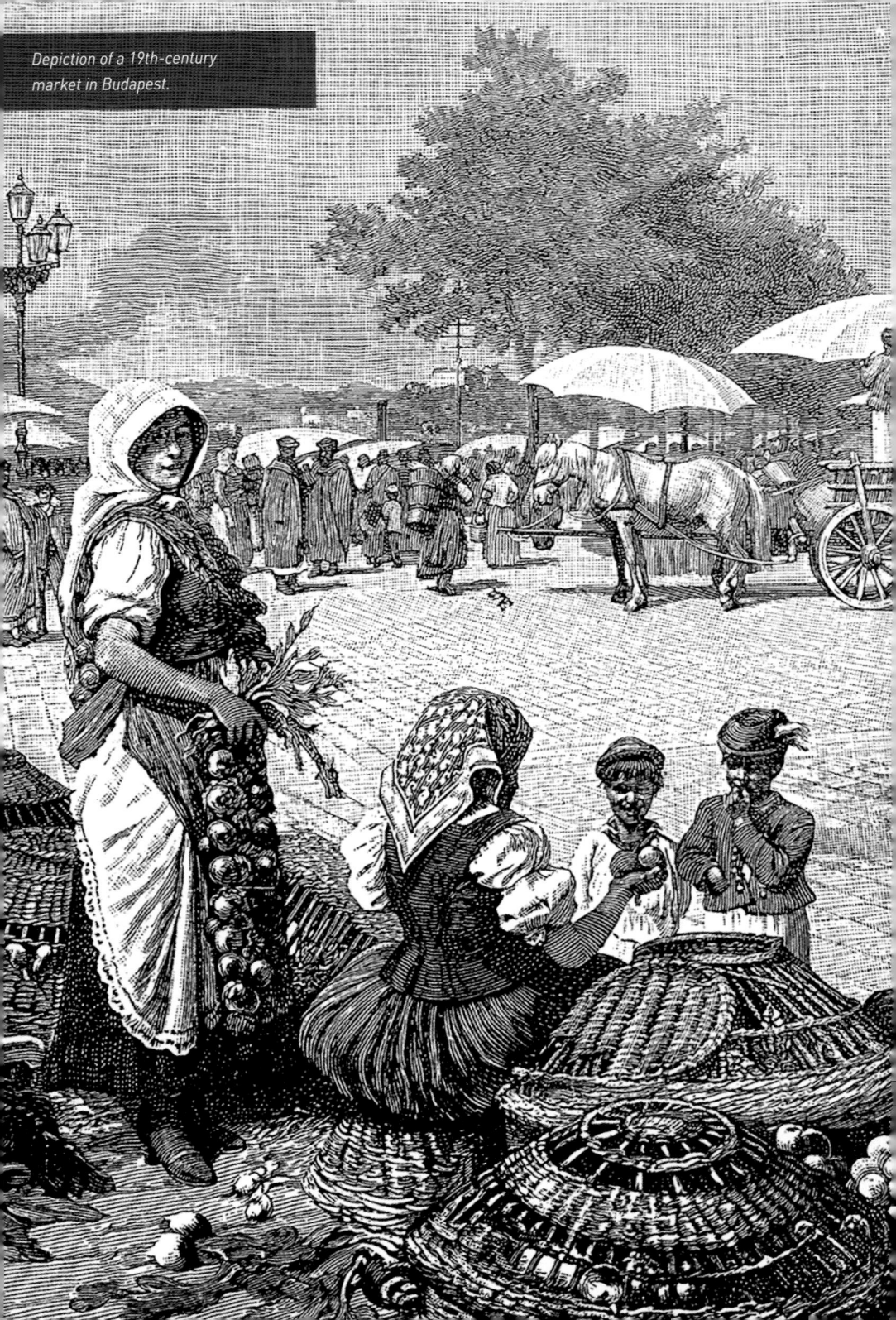

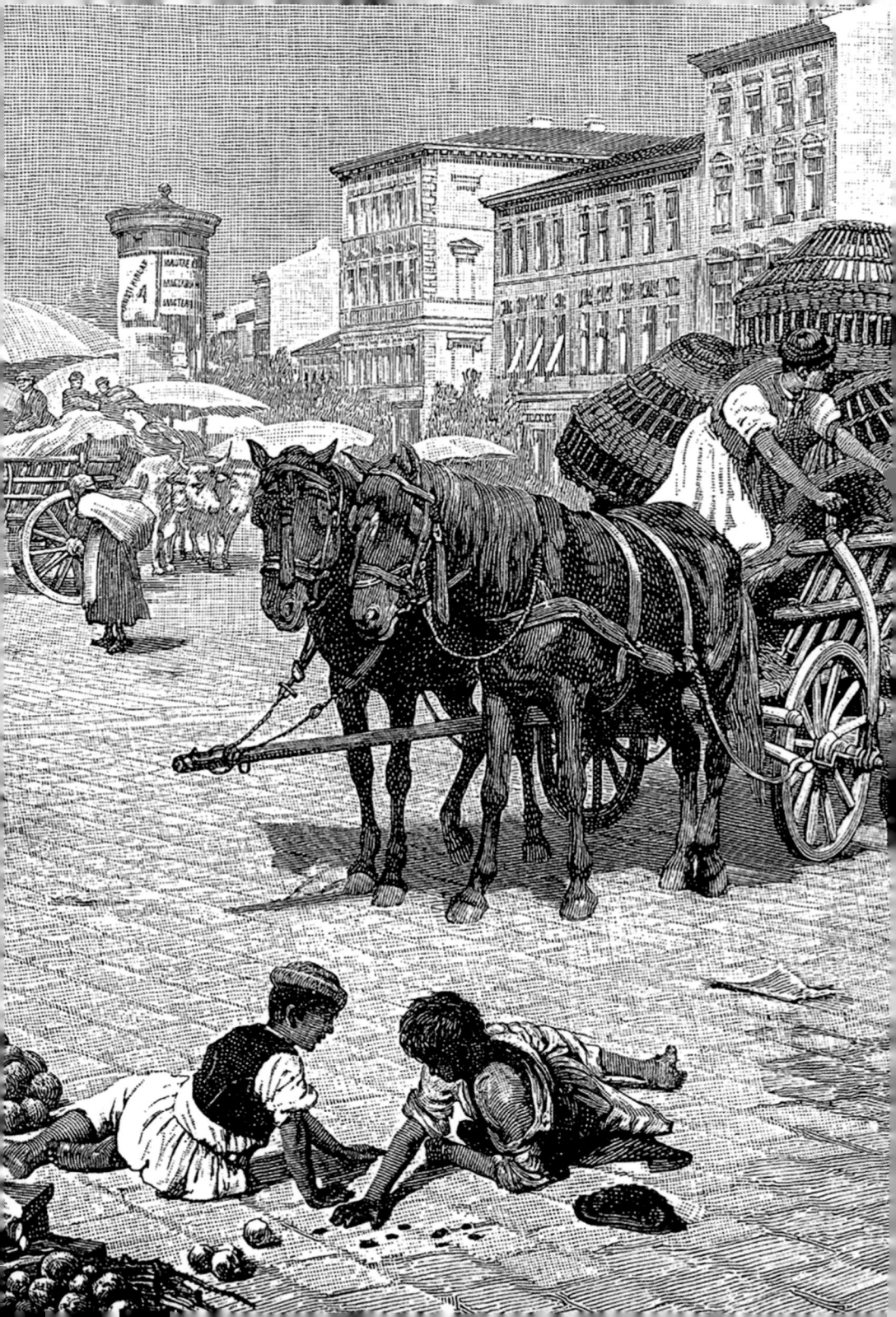

DECISIVE DATES

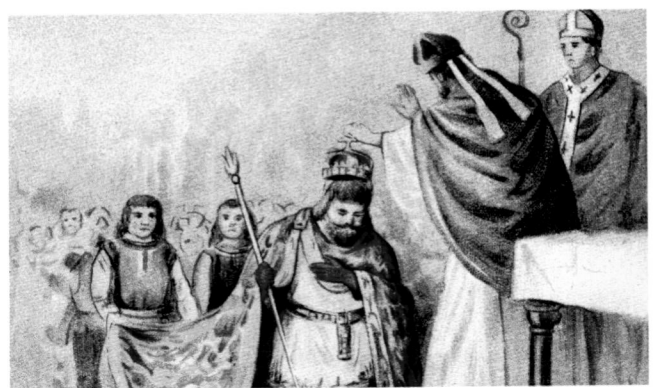

The coronation of King Stephen I on Christmas Day, 1000.

EARLY TIMES

350,000 BC
Earliest remains of peoples living in Danube and Carpathian basins

1st–4th century AD
The Romans conquer the Danube and create the state of Pannonia in western Hungary.

896
Legendary chieftan Árpád leads the Magyars into the Carpathian Basin, and takes control of Pannonia.

955
The Magyar riders, after terrorising Western Europe for decades, are defeated at the Battle of Lechfeld. Prince Géza, the Magyar leader, subsequently allies himself with the West.

THE ÁRPÁD DYNASTY

1000
István (Stephen) I, the founder of the Árpád dynasty, becomes the first Christian king of Hungary. He centralises royal authority, establishes Christianity as the official religion, and divides the country into counties, whose boundaries remain intact today.

1172–96
The reign of Béla III is an orderly, prosperous period in Hungary's history. His scribe, known as Anonymous, writes Gesta Ungarorum, the earliest surviving chronicle of Hungary.

1222
Under the rule of Andrés II, favouritism flourishes and the dispossessed nobles rebel. He is forced to sign the 'Golden Bull', a charter guaranteeing the rights of nobles and fixing the relationship between aristocracy and king.

1241
Mongols invade and defeat the Hungarians at Muhi. King Béla IV evades capture and the Mongols leave in 1242. Most of the great Hungarian fortresses are built at this time in anticipation of another attack.

1301
András III, the last of the Árpád kings, dies.

THE TURKISH THREAT

1308
The barons elect Charles-Robert of Anjou king of Hungary. A shrewd leader, Charles-Robert (Carobert) restores order and consolidates the realm.

1342–82
His successor, Lajos, adopts a policy of conquest, acquiring enough territory to form one of the largest realms in Europe. By the time of his death, the Turks are advancing into the Balkans.

1456
János Hunyadi, the national hero of Hungary, defeats the Turks at the siege of Nándorfehérvár (Belgrade), keeping them out of Hungary for 70 years.

1458
His son Mátyás (Corvinus) is crowned king, ushering in a Golden Age. His Neapolitan wife, Beatrix, introduces the Italian Renaissance to Hungary, creating the greatest Renaissance palace in Europe. Mátyás conquers Moravia, Bohemia and parts of Austria, transforming Hungary into the strongest kingdom in central Europe.

1514
A peasant revolt is brutally crushed and feudal servitude in perpetuity is written into law.

1526

The Hungarian army under Lajos II is crushed by the Turks at the battle of Mohács.

1541

Buda is taken by the Turks. Hungary is divided into three: Royal Hungary, Turkish Hungary and Transylvania. For the next 150 years there is almost continual conflict between Turks, Habsburgs and Hungarians.

1571

István Báthory becomes voivode (governor) of Transylvania, giving the region the status of a European power.

1686–99

Hungary is freed from the Turks by the Habsburg commander Eugene of Savoy.

1703–11

Ferenc Rákóczi II leads the Hungarians in an unsuccessful eight-year war against Habsburg domination. Hungary continues to be little more than a province of the Habsburg Empire.

THE HABSBURGS

1740–80

Maria Theresa ascends the throne, winning the hearts of the Hungarians by establishing peace.

1780–90

Joseph II, a child of the Enlightenment, attempts to modernise Hungary, abolishing serfdom and dissolving all-powerful religious orders. German is made the official language of the Empire.

1789

The French Revolution. Despite revolutionary fervour throughout Europe, the majority of Hungarians remain loyal to Austria.

1815

Resurgence of Hungarian nationalism.

1823

Sándor Petőfi, née Petrovics, Hungary's national poet, is born in Kiskőrös.

1830

Count Széchenyi begins modernising Hungary's

infrastructure, forming the Danube Steamship Company and the Merchant (Kereskedelmi) Bank (1841).

1848–49

The revolution against Austrian supremacy headed by the lawyer Lajos Kossuth ends in failure.

6 October 1849

Revolutionary leaders executed. It remains a day of national mourning in Hungary.

1867

The Great Compromise with Austria creates the Austro-Hungarian Dual Monarchy.

1873

Pest, Buda and Obuda are united, and Budapest is declared the capital.

1890

Hungarian Social Democratic Party is created.

WAR, PEACE AND COMMUNISM

1914–18

World War I marks the end of the Dual Monarchy.

The Austro-Hungarian military, c.1887.

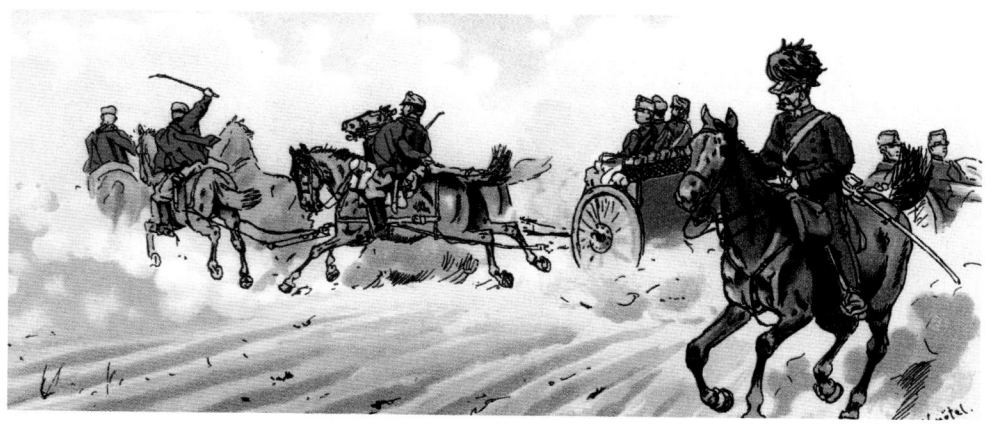

1919
In March, Count Károlyi's Hungarian Democratic Republic fails in the wake of neighbouring states' seizure of Hungarian territory. Béla Kun heads the communist Hungarian Soviet, before fleeing to Austria, unable to cope with foreign intervention and peasant unrest.

1920
Hungary's first free elections are held; Admiral Horthy is appointed regent.

1921
The Treaty of Trianon reduces Hungary's territory by two-thirds.

1938 and 1940
Hitler offers to hand back Slovakia and Transylvania in return for Hungarian cooperation.

1944
The Nazis are given a free hand in Hungary. On 15 October the Hungarian pro-Nazi Arrow Cross Party takes power under Ferenc Szálasi. Several hundred thousand Jews are sent to concentration camps.

1945
The Red Army occupies the country.

1946
The monarchy is abolished and Hungary is declared a republic by the new communist government. The pengö sets a world record for devaluation.

1949
The Soviets take power; the Party is purged of Western influence in show trials. Opponents of the communist regime are sent to labour camps. The head of the Catholic Church in Hungary, József Cardinal Mindszenty, is arrested and sentenced to life imprisonment.

1956
Revolution against the Soviet Union and communist rule is crushed. Hundreds of Hungarians are executed and thousands more flee the country.

Pro-Nazi former Hungarian leader Ferenc Szálasi (centre), moments before his public execution in 1946.

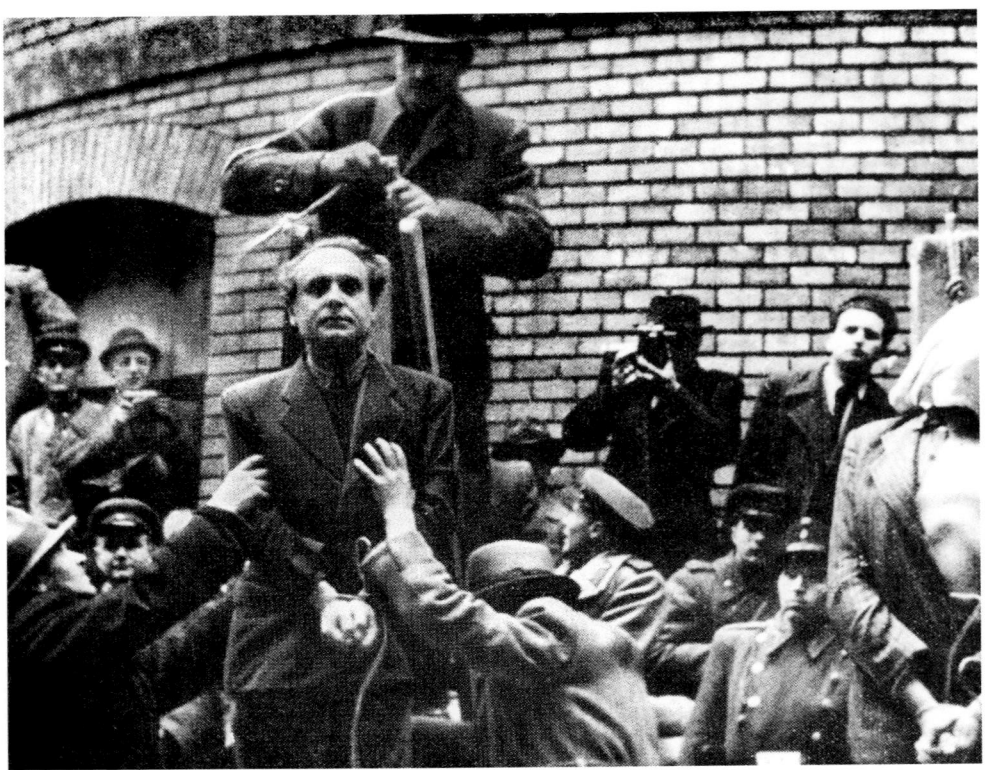

János Kádár becomes premier of a new communist state.

1968
The New Economic Mechanism allows a limited free market to develop.

1970s
Hungary attempts to increase its contact with non-communist countries. Relations with the Catholic Church improve.

1982
Hungary is admitted to the International Monetary Fund, and receives loans from the World Bank.

1989
Hungary opens the Iron Curtain and allows thousands of East European refugees to leave.

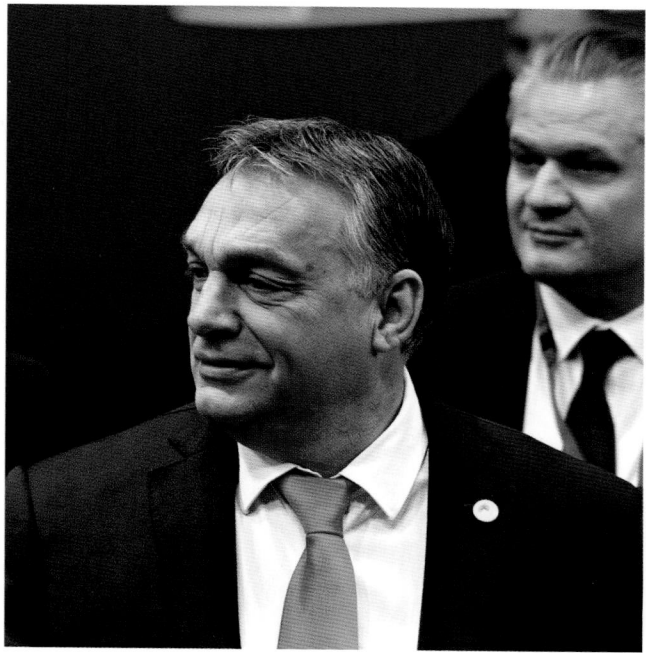

Viktor Orbán, the current Hungarian prime minister.

1990
Free elections are won by the Conservative Democratic Forum.

1990–94
The transition to a market economy sees inflation soar and unemployment increase sharply.

1995
Government reaches agreement with Jewish groups on the restoration of assets seized during World War II.

1996
The World Fair is held in Budapest.

1998
Federation of Young Democrats-Hungarian Civic Party (Fidesz-MPP), Independent Smallholders' Party (FKGP) and the Hungarian Democratic Forum (MDF) form a coalition government.

1999
Hungary, along with the Czech Republic and Poland, joins NATO.

2001
Ferenc Mádl is elected president.

2004
Hungary joins the European Union. The Hungarian Socialist Party ousts Péter Medgyessy as prime minister, replacing him with Ferenc Gyurcsány.

2005
Lászlo Sólyom becomes president.

2006
Widespread riots follow Gyurcsány's admission that his government had lied during the election campaign.

2010
Conservative opposition party Fidesz, led by Victor Orbán, wins landslide parliamentary victory.

2012
Malév, Hungary's state airline, goes bankrupt.

2014
Fidesz returned to power in another sweeping victory.

2016
Orbán's successful anti-refugee campaign results in a fence being built along the country's southern border.

2018
Orbán wins a straight third term as prime minister as concerns are raised within EU circles regarding his increasingly authoritarian measures.

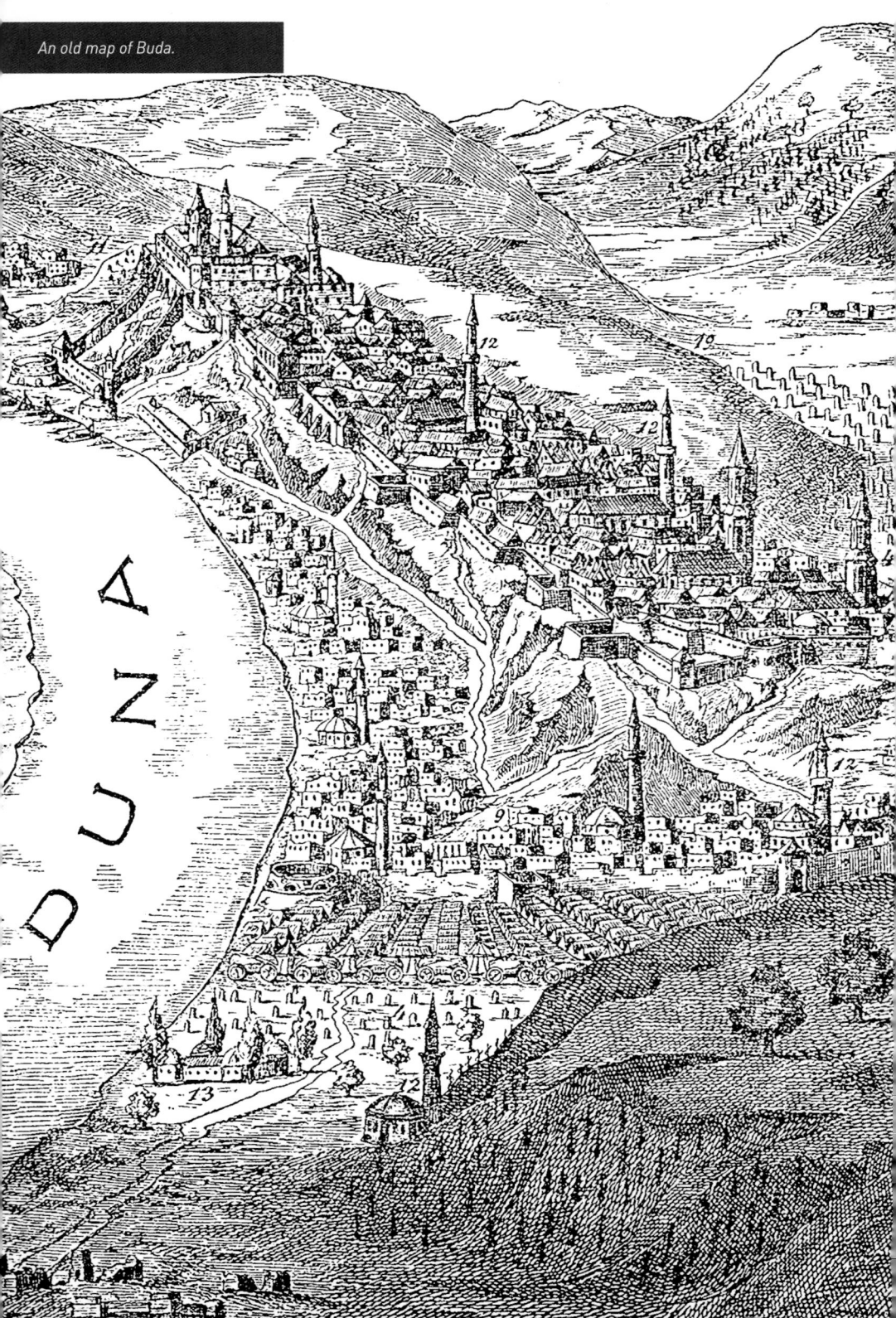

An old map of Buda.

THE MAKING OF A STATE

The Carpathian Basin has been occupied and invaded by countless tribes. In the 9th century the Magyars finally made the land their own.

Archaeological evidence in the form of bone and pottery fragments shows that the Danube and Carpathian basins have been populated by humans since about 350,000 BC. It is thought that the earliest Stone Age inhabitants were hunter-gatherers, living off indigenous fruits and wildlife, mostly reindeer and mammoths. During the Neolithic era (5000 BC), as a result of the climate changes that followed the Ice Age, people began to settle along riverbanks and in valleys, herding animals and cultivating the land.

Around 2000 BC, marauding tribes from the Balkans and the steppes migrated to the area, bringing cattle, horses and copper tools with them. They were followed by a wave of invading tribes. The Scythians from the east introduced iron while the Celts, who arrived in the 3rd century BC, were fine craftsmen who produced glassware and jewellery.

ROMAN OUTPOST

When the Romans arrived in Transdanubia (the area west of the Danube) around 35 BC, it was inhabited by the Illyrians and the Eravisks, who were descendants of the Celts. In 14 BC this region, known as Pannonia, was officially incorporated into the Roman Empire.

In AD 6, angered by Rome's heavy-handed recruitment policies and excessive taxation, the Pannonians joined the Dalmatians in a rebellion that took three years to crush. Emperor Tiberius reacted by setting up various garrison towns and *municipae* (independent cities) – among them Scarbantia (Sopron), Soponiae (Pécs), Arrabona (Győr) and Aquincum (Budapest) where extensive remains can still be seen. Communities grew up around these strongholds: vines were planted, stone houses and thermal baths were constructed, and roads were laid to connect

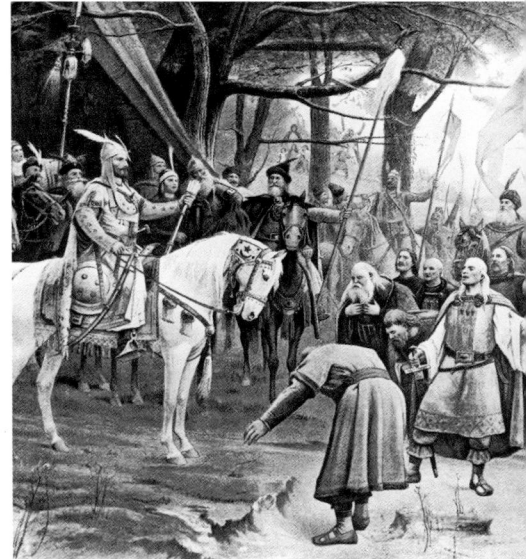

Árpád, head of the Hungarian tribes from c.895–c.907.

this eastern outpost to the heart of the Roman Empire.

Stretched beyond its own human and financial reserves, and pummelled by the continuous onslaught of various tribes of barbarians, the Roman Empire withered away without making further progress east of the Danube. That is where the Huns found them when they came galloping through in the 4th century.

Following the death of Attila the Hun in 453, and the fall of his brief empire, Transdanubia and the Nagyalföld (Hungarian for the Great Plain, the region east of the Danube) were occupied by another succession of invading tribes – Avars, Ostrogoths, Slavs, Bulgars and various Eastern Franks. The Magyars, however, were still on their way.

THE KHAZARS

At some point during the third millennium BC this community dispersed, with one group of tribes migrating westwards. By AD 600 the group consisted of seven tribes living between the Danube, the Don (in the present-day Russian Federation) and the Black Sea, as part of the Kaganate (or kingdom) of the Khazars, a Turkic people commanding a vast empire in Eastern Europe. They led a semi-nomadic existence, moving to rivers in winter and back on to the plains in summer. The Magyars represented the single most powerful tribe in

Riding as mercenaries for various European monarchs took them often into the Nagyalföld (Great Plain), which they soon coveted for its fertile ground and the protective Carpathian Mountains. In addition, a fierce and powerful Turkic tribe, the Pechenegs, had cut a swathe through the dwindling Khazar empire from the east and were threatening the weakly defended Magyar rear. The *gyula* Árpád had begun to move the tribes under his command westward over the Carpathians. He crossed the Verecke Pass (in today's Ukraine) in the spring of 895

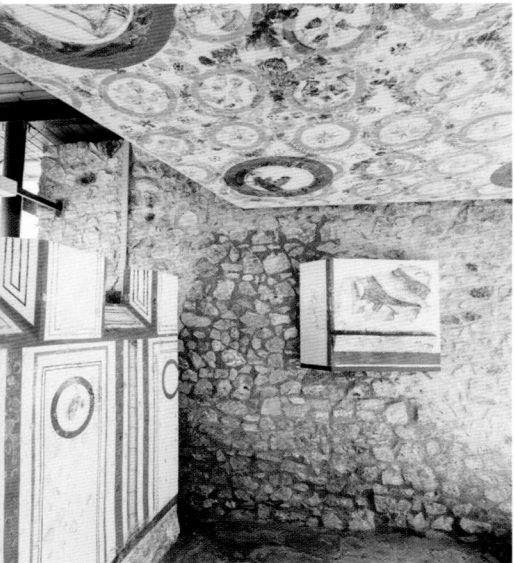

Old Roman murals in the village of Tác.

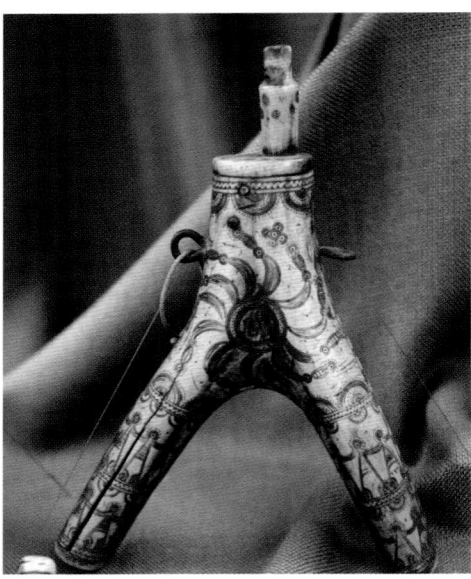

Traditional Hungarian powder horn.

the group, and their name eventually became the eponym for the whole group.

The Magyars rendered important military services to the Khazars and, in return for these, they enjoyed a special status. The Kagan either chose or sanctioned a religious leader *(kende)*, while the tribes elected an executive leader *(gyula)* of their own.

The relationship became understandably strained, however, when the Magyars not only declined to aid the Kagan in quashing a rebellion that had risen in the empire, but also granted asylum to refugee rebels. Since the Kagan was sure to exact revenge, the Magyars began to look westwards for new homelands.

⊘ TRIBAL ORIGINS

The exact origin of the Hungarian people is still hotly debated among historians. The chronicles, usually written centuries after the facts, tend to be unreliable. Some refer to Avars, others to Turkic tribes.

In the 19th century the distinguished Hungarian linguist Antal Reguly researched the languages spoken by the tribes living near the Ural Mountains in central Russia. More linguists followed him and their studies suggest that the Hungarians are descended from a Finno-Ugric-speaking people living near the Ural Mountains.

> *The word 'Hungary' derives from the term Onogur which means '10 arrows', referring to the 10 tribes that made up a larger community linked with the Magyars. Hungary is Magyarország in Hungarian*

and the rest of the tribes had reached the Nagyalföld by 896, completing the conquest of the Carpathian Basin.

knights and defeated them in 933. A repeat performance by the German emperor Otto I in 955 at the Battle of Lechfeld near Augsburg proved decisive. The Magyars ceased their attacks in the west and Otto I was rewarded with the title 'the Great'.

The Augsburg collapse was no accident. Overconfidence and laxity within the Magyar ranks had eroded the fighting will of the riders, and western military organisation finally over-came their turbulent assaults. The Magyars were faced with the choice of either forming a cohesive state of their own or following the Huns into

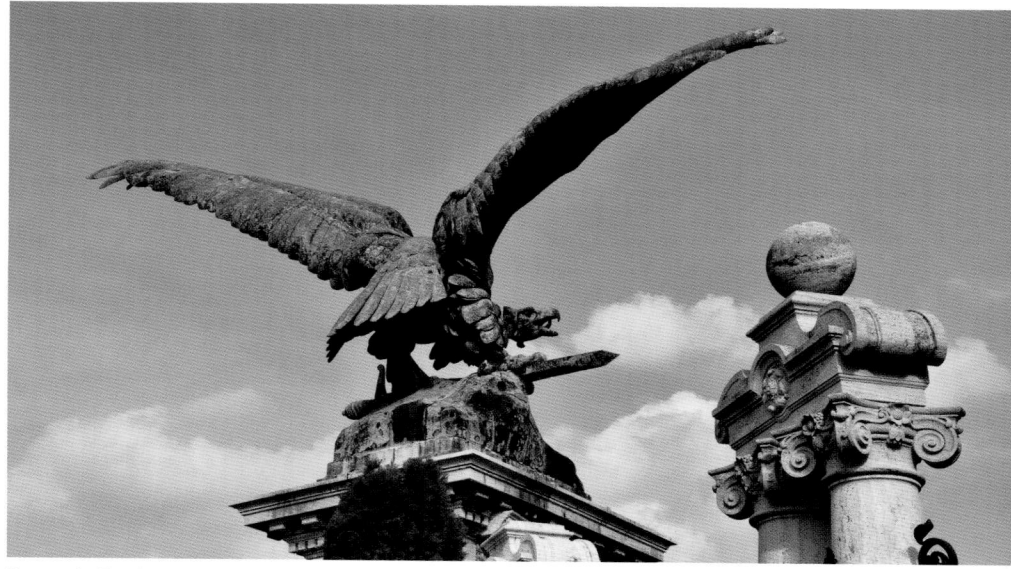

Statue of a Turul, the mythological bird of prey and the national symbol of Hungary.

MARAUDING MAGYARS

The Magyars' new homeland was thinly settled by a mixture of Slavs, Avars and Franks. After establishing their presence, Magyar riders sought out their new country's borders west of the Danube. Initially they met with little resistance as they plundered and pillaged their way through northern Italy and Bavaria. This era is euphemistically referred to by Hungarians as 'The Age of Adventures'. An attempt to rid the Western world of this new Eastern scourge failed miserably on 4 July 907 at the Battle of Bresalauspurc (modern Bratislava).

But the Magyars were not invincible. After staving them off for a time, the Emperor Henry the Fowler organised a division of heavily armed

oblivion. Árpád's great-grandson Prince Géza, leader of the Magyars after 972, read the writing on the wall: integrate or disintegrate. Both Eastern and Western churches were wooing this potentially influential and important ally. Géza opted for Rome. In 975 Géza and his family converted to Christianity. He invited Catholic missionaries to his kingdom and in 996 he married his son István to Gisela of Bavaria, the daughter of Henry II, thus creating an important alliance.

BIRTH OF A NATION

With a little forceful persuasion, many of Géza's subjects also converted. His son, a true believer as well as being a pragmatist, continued the policy of conversion. Named Vajk at first, he was baptised

István (Stephen) after the Bishop of Passau. His teacher – and mentor – was the great Bishop Adalbert of Prague. When he took power, István promptly set about consolidating his kingdom and authority. In AD 1000 he sent envoys to Rome to negotiate official recognition, and in AD 1001, with Pope Sylvester's sanction, he was crowned a Christian king, Stephen I. He later made Esztergom his royal seat.

LAW AND A NEW ORDER

Although István had the support of his large family, the Árpáds, paganism still ruled in many

> *One of King Kálmán's many enlightened laws stated that 'There will be no talk of witches, for they do not exist.'*

Besides consolidating his own power, István also gave Hungary its first set of laws, established a network of bishoprics and ratified the social order. The descendants of the first Magyar tribal chiefs were considered a privileged

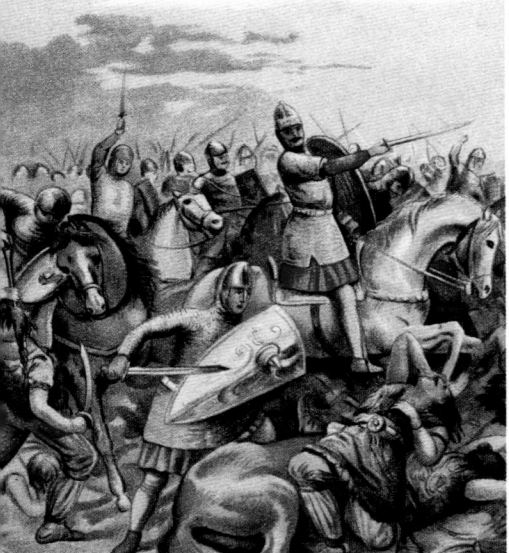

The Battle of Lechfeld, 955.

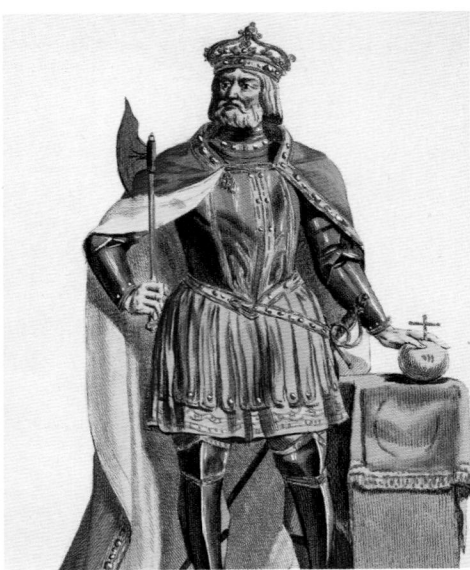

Portrait of László I, King of Hungary from 1077–1095.

parts of the country, and challenged István's rule. Koppány, Prince of Somogy (south of the Balaton), was one such opponent. With the help of his father-in-law's Bavarian knights, István defeated Koppány near Veszprém in 997. Koppány's corpse was cut in four, and the head sent to his refractory uncle, Gyula, who got the message. And for good measure, István confiscated his lands and imprisoned his family. Among his other enemies, Prince Ajtony proved to be particularly resilient. According to legend, István's general, Csanád, was advised by St George when and where to launch an attack, and István's army once more emerged victorious, thus delivering the new Christian nation from the pagan foe.

class because they owned large estates and owed the king only loyalty and military obligation. These magnates gathered in a parliament with advisory rather than executive powers. Whatever land did not belong to them was placed under the control and ownership of the king. A second noble class existed, privileged, serving in the military, and legally free, but not large landowners.

To speed up the conversion process, István ordered a church to be built in one in 10 villages and set up monasteries around the country. He divided Hungary into administrative districts (megye), each led by a royal agent from a fortress (vár). These territorial divisions have remained intact to this day. The royal agents collected taxes from the peasants, and generally maintained small armies of freemen.

Apart from an attempt by Conrad II in 1030 to turn Hungary into a vassal of the Empire, István's rule was peaceful. His only son, Imre, groomed for succession, was killed in a hunting accident in 1031. Suspecting his cousin Vasoly of closet heathenism, István chose his nephew Péter to succeed him. Vasoly was incensed and was suspected of the attempted murder of István. To seal the fate of Vasoly, the king had his eyes gouged, poured molten lead in his ears and

the Holy Roman Empire allowed him to pull strings on both sides. The popes, afraid of new enemies, were willing to overlook the Hungarian church's total subservience to the king and endowed Hungary with its first saints. László I pursued a vigorous foreign policy, pushing into Transylvania and Croatia, and thrashing the aggressive Kumans.

After promising the throne to his younger nephew, the dashing Álmos, László changed his mind and opted for Kálmán, a hunchback bound for the priesthood. The aristocracy was

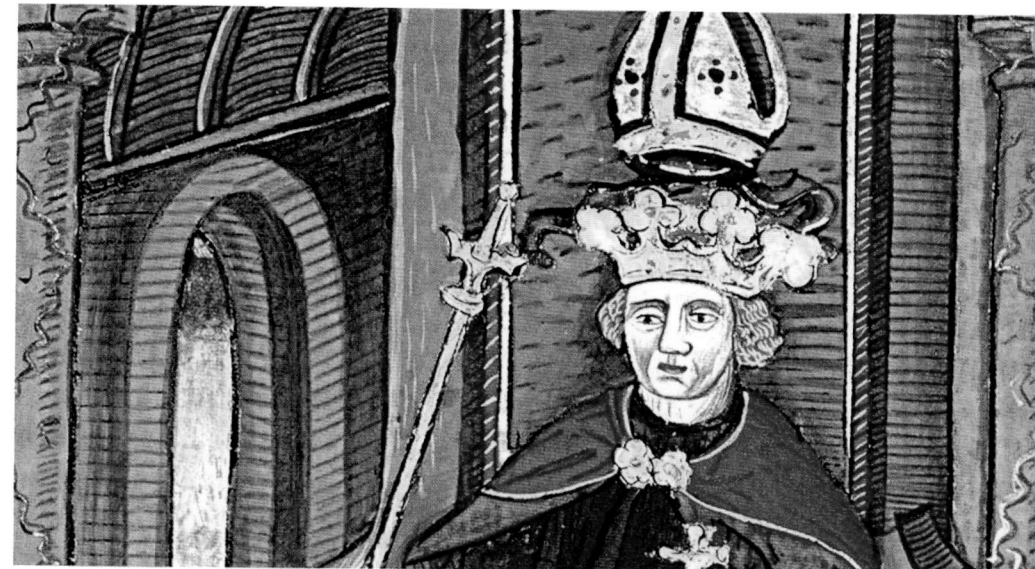

Coloman, King of Hungary from 1095–1116.

banished his three sons from the kingdom.

Fifty tumultuous years followed the death of István in 1038. Péter proved a misfit and was soon overthrown by Sámuel Aba, István's brother-in-law. Henry II, the German emperor, was only too willing to help Péter resume power in exchange for a little vassalage. King followed after king, army followed after army. Vasoly's sons re-emerged to claim their fair share of power and only last-ditch efforts prevented powerful tribes from the east – Pechenegs, Kumans and Uzes – from taking over the frail kingdom.

LÁSZLÓ I AND KÁLMÁN THE BOOKISH

The task of reconstruction fell to László I (1077–95). The struggle raging between the popes and

displeased at the switch, and civil war almost engulfed the nation. But Kálmán proved an able, if at first ruthless, leader. He had Álmos and his son Béla imprisoned and their eyes gouged.

Kálmán, nicknamed 'könyves' (literally, 'beset with books') because of his extensive education, was in many ways an enlightened ruler. The laws he introduced were generally fair and humanitarian for the times, and he promoted literature and the writing of chronicles. He married the daughter of Roger of Sicily, and had his cousin (the daughter of László I) married to the heir to the Byzantine Empire, thus ensuring allies on both sides of the country, and furthered the expansion of Hungary into Dalmatia and Bosnia.

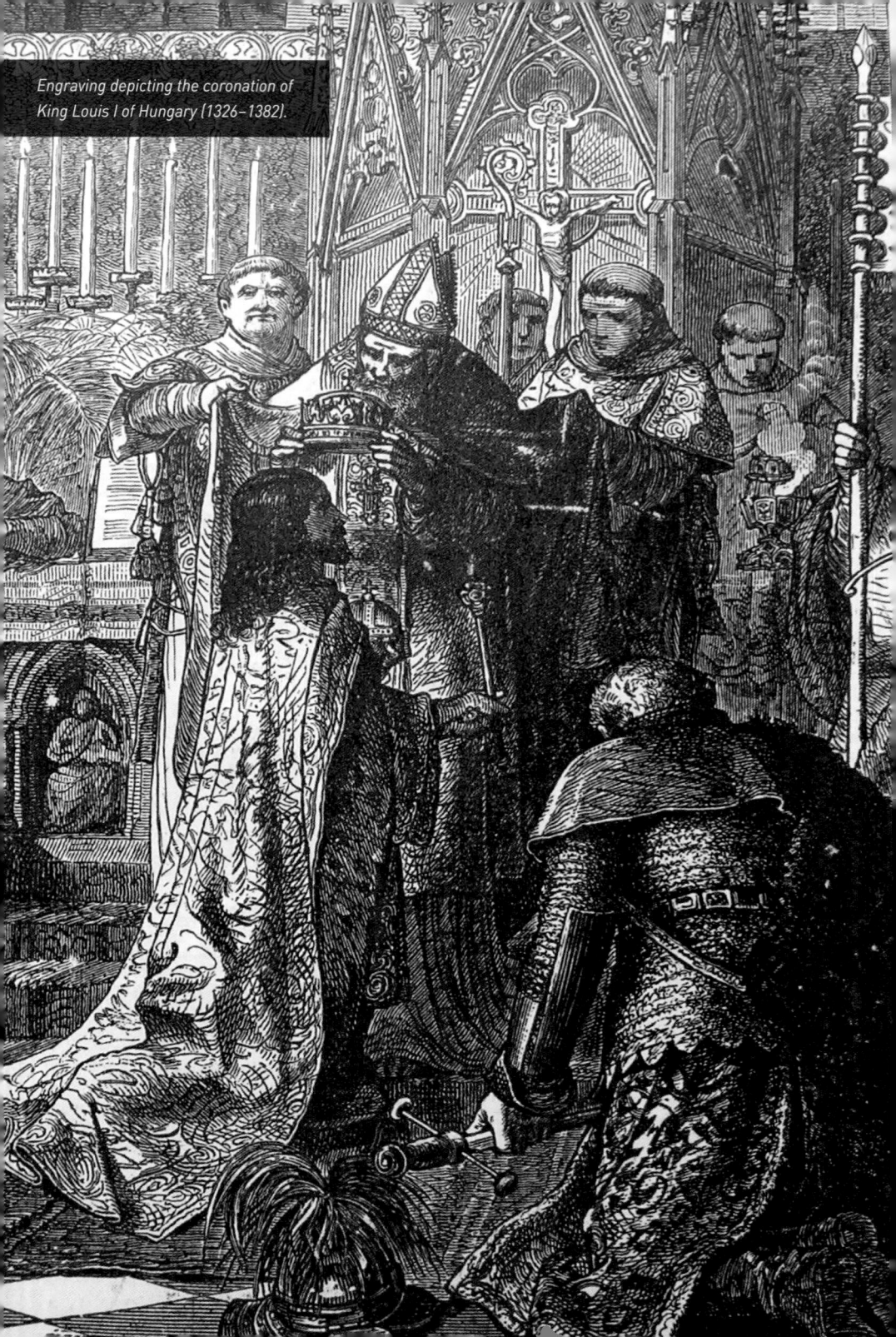

ÁRPÁDS TO ANGEVIN

The Árpád and Angevin dynasties expanded Hungary's territories despite constant internal power struggles and external aggression.

By the Middle Ages, Hungary had become a fairly large country with a cosmopolitan population. Besides the resident Slavs, Magyars and Székelys (another Magyar tribe that lived in the Carpathian basin prior to 896), throngs of Western Europeans had left their crowded homelands to settle and work in the fertile plains of Hungary. The Germanic migrants favoured Transylvania (in present-day Romania), where they applied their skills in developing cities. The Hungarian kings were generous to these settlers; in fact they actively encouraged foreigners to come and live in their country, offering them the status of freemen and the protection of a royal charter.

This open-door policy had two vital bases. King István (St Stephen) had made an explicit point of promoting immigration in his *Exhortations* to his son, a small book outlining his views on how to conduct affairs of state: 'Strangers and foreigners are most useful,' he wrote. 'They bring different values and customs, weaponry and sciences with them. These are all ornaments to a royal court to make it splendid, to the dismay of arrogant foreigners. For a land with one single language and uniform customs is weak and easily shattered.'

The ulterior motive for inviting people to settle on royal lands, however, was that, under the ancient tribal laws, power rested with the man who had the most people working on his land, which meant that it was in the king's interests to maintain the largest estates and the largest number of workers.

THE FIGHT FOR THE THRONE

The death of King Kálmán in 1116 was followed by another long period of instability. Hungary, still a young nation, was weakened by internal

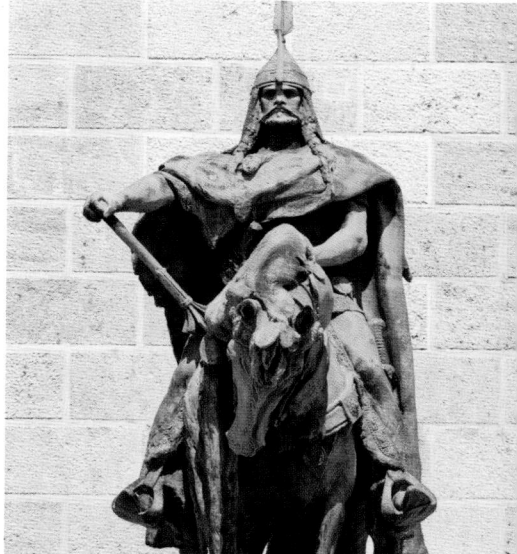
Statue of King Árpád in Budapest.

power struggles between the many pretenders to the throne. When a strong king did emerge, who steered a successful course in his foreign policy and demonstrated his strength to the magnates and nobles, Hungary remained in a position of strength. But given the opportunity of a weak ruler – and there were many – the higher ranks, often venal and corrupt, vied for greater power and possessions. Unfortunately, much royal time and energy was expended in family feuding between uncles, nephews and brothers.

One of the golden periods in Hungarian history was the rule of Béla III (1172–96), who had been raised in Constantinople. He was firm without being tyrannical. He ran a well organised state apparatus, put the finances in order, kept the magnates and the nobles in check and conducted a sound foreign policy. The Byzantine cross was added to the Hungarian emblem, but Béla also relaxed his control of the Catholic Church and made allies through marriage, first to Anne de Chatillon, daughter of the Prince of Antioch and mother of his successor, András II, then to Margaret Capet, widow of Henry Plantagenet, son of the English king Henry II.

Within a few years of his death, however, Béla III's successors brought the country to the brink of ruin. András II (ruled 1202–35) spent most of

and freed the magnates from obligatory participation in foreign ventures.

THE MONGOL INVASION

News of the Mongol invasions of the Russian steppes began seeping through to the west in the 1220s, brought by Russian and Kuman fugitives from the scourge. Béla IV (ruled 1235–70) knew they were heading his way, but stood his ground. The Kumans provided him with 40,000 riders, and he hoped that the western powers and the pope would be able to provide more

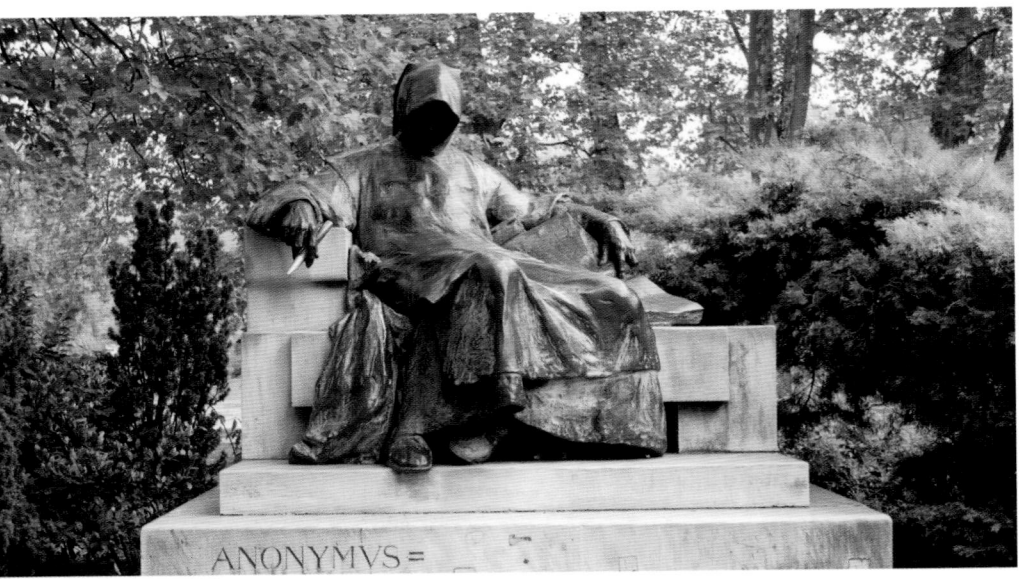

Statue of Anonymus in Budapest.

his reign leading the leisurely, dissipated and bellicose life of the typical *roi fainéant* (idle king). He gave away royal estates to his knights and lords, raised taxes and rented out lands and privileges to the highest bidder. Favouritism flourished and those who did not profit from it – disgruntled magnates, dispossessed nobles, the freemen who served in the army and the church – rebelled.

THE GOLDEN BULL

In 1222 András was forced to promulgate the 'Golden Bull', a kind of Magna Carta, laying down the rights of the nobility and fixing the relationship between aristocracy and king. The charter also permitted resistance to royal actions deemed illegal or harmful to the nation

manpower. Instead of forming a united front, however, Europe fell apart. Emperor Frederick II's lackadaisical attempts to form a coalition of armies were stymied by Pope Gregory IX, who was convinced that the emperor, not the Mongol general Batu Khan, was the Antichrist. The Kumans, meanwhile, were involved in a civil war.

> The Golden Bull was a turning point in the country's history. All subsequent kings had to swear to adhere to it, and it created a social class of freemen and nobles who were to play a major role in the political evolution of the nation.

In 1241 the five-pronged Mongol invasion began in earnest. On 9 April Henry II, Duke of Lower Silesia, thrust himself and 10,000 knights suicidally at one of the prongs near Liegnitz. Two days later, a Hungarian army disintegrated at Muhi, at the confluence of the Hernad and Sajó rivers. The king escaped west over the Danube, which the Mongols did not cross until February 1242, when it was frozen solid. They then continued their devastating progress, sparing only such virtually inaccessible forts as Pannonhalma and Székesfehérvár, which was surrounded by swamps. Less fortunate areas

defences. The people of ravaged Pest were relocated to the hilly west bank of the Danube, where Buda stands today. Béla brought in more foreign settlers to augment the diminished population and help rebuild the country. However, his position was far from secure. He tried to regain control of his lands and reassert his authority, but faced opposition from the magnates and nobles, who had the power to stand their ground, thanks to the dictates of the Golden Bull. In urgent need of support, the king was forced to make concessions and give them land.

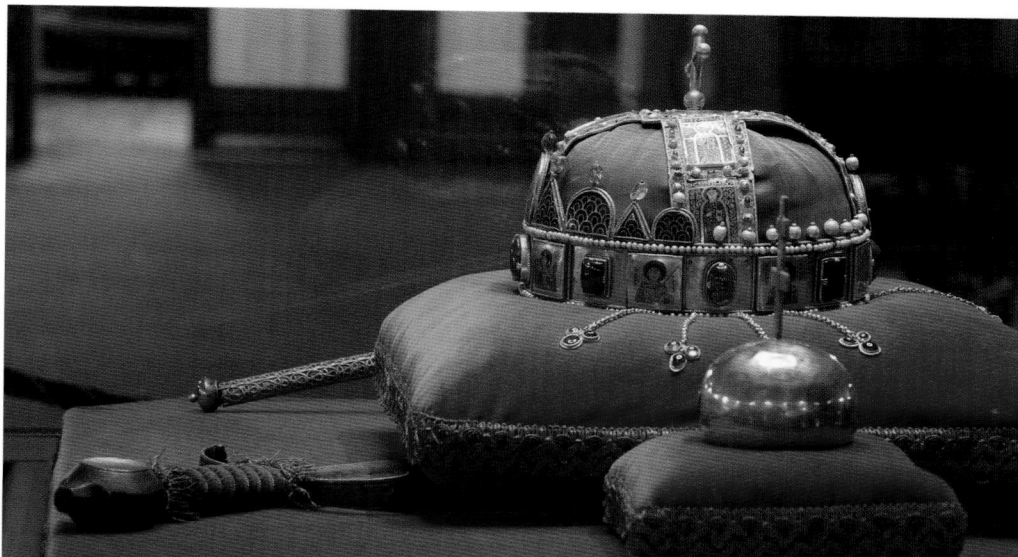

The Hungarian Holy Crown.

were virtually depopulated. The Mongols' principal aim was to capture the king, for according to their rules of warfare (rules interestingly shared by the Hungarians, which is suggestive of the eastern origins of the Magyars), only when the king had been taken prisoner could the country they had invaded be considered conquered. Béla IV managed to avoid capture and was escorted to the safety of an island off the Dalmatian coast.

In 1242 the Mongols disappeared as quickly as they had arrived, leaving the country in ruins. The supreme Khan Ogoday had died and Batu Khan had to return to the Far East to handle the succession. The Mongols had gone forever, but no-one was taking any chances. Béla IV set about building a series of fortresses for future

⊘ THE SPREAD OF CATHOLICISM

During the reign of Louis I, from 1342–82, the Catholic Church in Hungary prospered enormously. Numerous monasteries and religious foundations were set up across the expanding kingdom and the king made sure the bishops appointed to ecclesiastical offices were well educated and thoroughly trained. Several magnificent churches were built in Gross-Mariazell, an important pilgrimage site in neighbouring Styria and at Esztergom, Eger and Nagyvárad in Hungary. In 1381, Louis obtained the relics of St Paul the Hermit from the Venetian Republic and transferred them with much pomp and ceremony to the Pauline monastery near Buda.

LAST OF THE ÁRPÁDS

It was with reluctance that Béla IV married one son to a Kuman, two daughters to Ruthenian princes and a third to a Pole, for the sake of alliances and sources of information in the east. In a letter to Pope Vincent IV, written in 1253, he poured out his heart, regretting in particular the growing influence of the heathen Kumans. 'Further, in the interests of protecting Christianity,' he wrote, 'We married our first born son to a Kuman girl... in order to secure the possibility of converting these people to Christianity...'

The Árpád dynasty was reaching the end of the line. László IV had died childless. His sister, the Queen of Naples, placed her son András III on the throne. In 1301, after a 10-year reign plagued by foreign claims to the throne, András died leaving only a daughter, thus ending the male line of the Árpád dynasty.

Yet another period of struggle for succession followed. With the absence of a central authority, power reverted to the magnates, who had to appoint someone they considered fit to govern. Of course, they could not agree on a successor

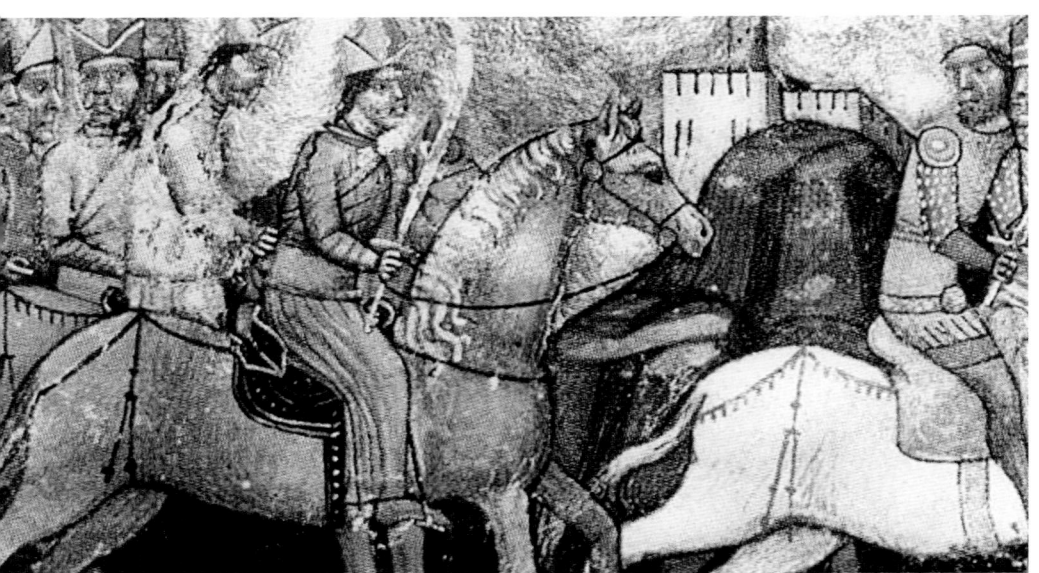

The Mongols in Hungary , c.1241.

That first born, István, died only 2 years after succeeding his father in 1270.

His son László, finally crowned after a troubled period of regency, turned out to be one of the strangest royal figures in the dwindling line of Árpád rulers. He married the Angevin Isabella of Naples, but soon developed a strong, some might say obsessive, attraction to the culture of his mother's people. He threatened to behead the Hungarian bishop, he locked up his wife, he dressed up as a Kuman, took in a string of young Kuman girls as mistresses, adopted various Mongol and Kuman customs, predictably earning himself the nickname 'the Kuman'. Ironically, he was finally murdered by a Kuman, probably in connivance with the exasperated magnates.

and struggles for power continued for another seven years. The three strongest candidates were Wenceslas Premyslid of Bohemia, who spent four years on the throne, Otto of Bavaria, who held on for three and Charles-Robert of Anjou who, with support from the Pope, finally secured the Hungarian crown for the Angevin dynasty of Naples. He reigned as Charles-Robert (Carobert) I (1309–42), and was succeeded by his son Louis (Lajos) I, who became known as Louis the Great; both ruled wisely for many years.

A FIRM HAND

In the absence of royal supervision, the provincial magnates had become accustomed to certain freedoms and Charles-Robert needed to curb their power if he was to keep control. Aided by irate nobles, he soon demonstrated who was boss and immediately set about centralising power (without confiscating too many lands in private ownership), reorganising the army and forging alliances with his neighbours. A new upper class developed, drawn from the ranks of his ministers, all of whom were hand-picked and therefore loyal. No parliament was convened after 1323 and the nobles were left to administer the counties, which they welcomed, since it increased their independence.

The Angevins wanted to establish their headquarters in Naples, and the Hungarian army tried on three occasions to occupy the city but failed each time. Strong resistance came from the Papal States, backed by Venice; the merchant city disapproved of Hungary's designs on the Dalmatian coast of the Adriatic.

In the north, Poland, too, became a Hungarian dominion for a while when Louis I, on the basis of an earlier treaty, acceded to the throne in 1370. But he had little control over the Poles, and even less time to devote to the territory. His

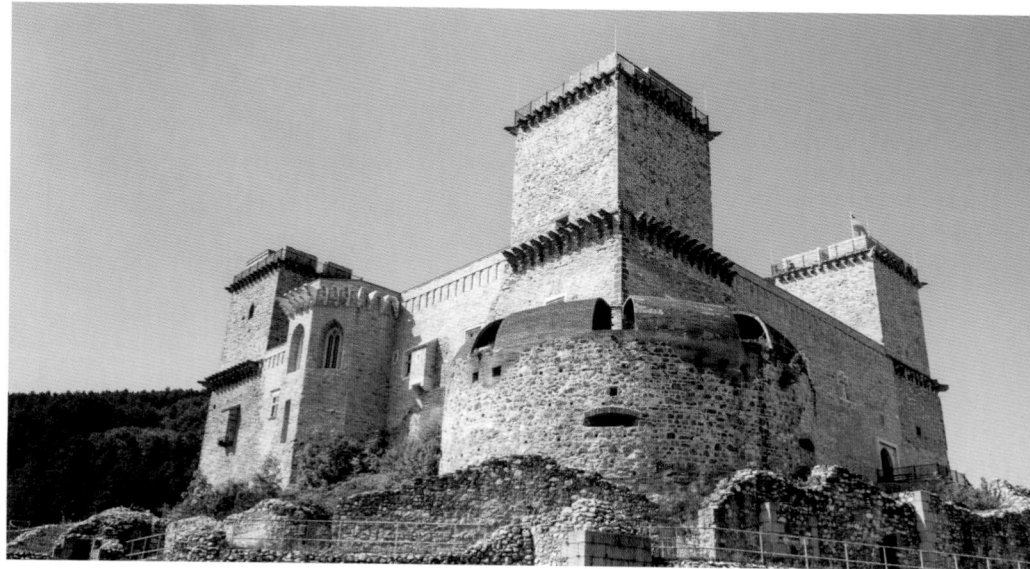

The medieval castle at Diósgyőr.

Liberal mining rights and the introduction of a gold and silver currency increased the country's trading ability. Hungary's mines produced an average of 1,360 kg (3,000 lbs) of gold annually, making it Europe's biggest producer of gold, and therefore one of its richest nations.

Prosperity, in turn, attracted artists, scholars and new settlers, and resulted in a significant population growth in spite of the effects of the Black Death. Most of the pioneers came from the southeast – Ruthenians, Romanians and Wallachians.

TROUBLE ON ALL FRONTS

The complex diplomatic and expansionist manoeuvres of Charles-Robert and his son Louis required military action on several fronts.

attention was, in fact, drawn to the Balkans, where major changes had been taking place.

Bosnia had been annexed to Hungary by marriage, but Serbia had experienced a political renaissance under Stephen Douchan (1331–35) and was flexing its muscles. Rumblings from various nationalities now threatened regional Hungarian control, but even more dangerous was the growing menace of the Ottoman Turks. By the 1350s the boundaries of the Ottoman Empire had reached European soil and the Turkish army was beginning its march on the Balkan states along the lower Danube. In 1377 Louis I defeated the Sultan Murad.

Meanwhile, on Hungary's western flank, the powerful Habsburg dynasty was looking to acquire new territories.

TURKS AND HABSBURGS

King Mátyás expanded and stabilised Hungary, but his reign was followed by 200 years of war and Turkish occupation.

The death of Louis I in 1382 precipitated a crisis in the palace. The Hungarian king had arranged for the elder of his two daughters, Maria, to succeed him in ruling the two kingdoms of Hungary and Poland, but the Poles would recognise only the younger Hedwige as their queen. Moreover, Louis had promised Maria and the crown to Sigismund of Luxembourg, who had been educated at the Hungarian court. The noble estates preferred the Neapolitan Angevins, while the Queen Mother, supported by the court paladin, Miklós Garai, had her eye on Louis of Orléans.

Maria reigned for a time, but it was her husband, Sigismund, who ultimately won the three-way contest.

A EUROPEAN STATESMAN

Despite being deposed on several occasions, Sigismund regained the throne each time, and his long reign (1395–1437) was a period of relative peace and prosperity, during which Hungarian art and architecture flourished. But the king spent little time at home. He was active in European affairs, and fought many campaigns abroad. His long periods of absence caused much resentment, particularly among the peasants, who felt they were not benefiting from the healthy economy, and were still compelled to pay heavy taxes to finance his wars. On the whole, Sigismund neglected Hungary's domestic problems and left the duties of the state in the hands of faithful deputies, so that parliament took on greater responsibilities in governing the country.

Abroad, meanwhile, Sigismund was building power. He managed to acquire the much coveted Bohemian crown and was even made Holy Roman Emperor in 1433. His attempts to halt the Turkish advancement were less successful. In 1396, he led

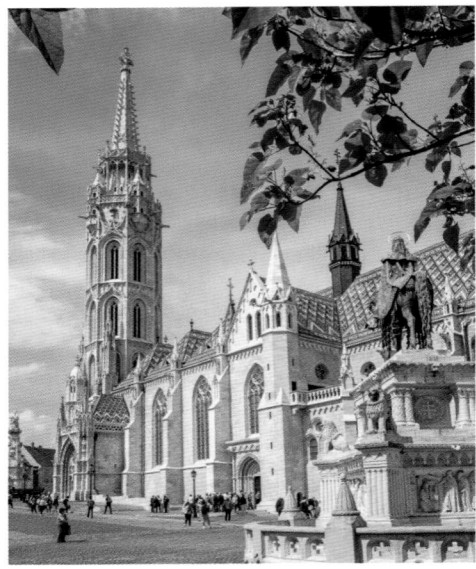

Matthias Church in Budapest.

an ill-fated crusade against the Islamic 'infidel', suffering a crushing defeat at the battle of Nicopolis. In 1417 the Turks reached Wallachia and by the end of Sigismund's reign 20 years later, they had made significant inroads into Hungarian territory.

During his brief reign, Albrecht of Habsburg (1437–39) began work on fortifications for the nation, but he died, leaving a pregnant wife. The estates, in search of some strong ally, selected the young Polish king, Vladislav I Jagiellon, who gallantly charged off to do battle against the Turks at Varna in 1444, where he was killed. Albrecht's wife had in the meantime given birth to László, who was duly elected king, while the regency was entrusted to János Hunyadi, an inspired magnate and skilled soldier.

Other magnates seethed with envy behind his back. Young László's uncle, Ulrik Cillei, Count of Styria, feared for his nephew's crown. The Habsburgs also had to be warded off. Hunyadi's greatest victory was to stem the Ottoman advance at Nándorfehérvár (Belgrade) in 1456. He died soon after, leaving a Hungary once more torn apart by internal strife. Cillei was murdered, and his followers had one of Hunyadi's sons beheaded and the other, Mátyás, imprisoned in Prague. In 1457 László died – possibly poisoned. The magnates had little choice but to recall Mátyás from Prague.

MÁTYÁS CORVINUS

Perhaps the magnates believed a 16-year-old boy could be easily manipulated. Frederick III of Habsburg certainly thought him no threat, as he declared himself king with the support of a few Hungarian nobles. They were all mistaken. Mátyás Corvinus (corvinus is Latin for crow, the bird on his coat of arms), who reigned as Mátyás I, proved to be a tough and autocratic young man, yet one who remained fair in his dealings. By 1463 he had recovered the crown from Frederick III and hammered out a tenuous peace treaty with him.

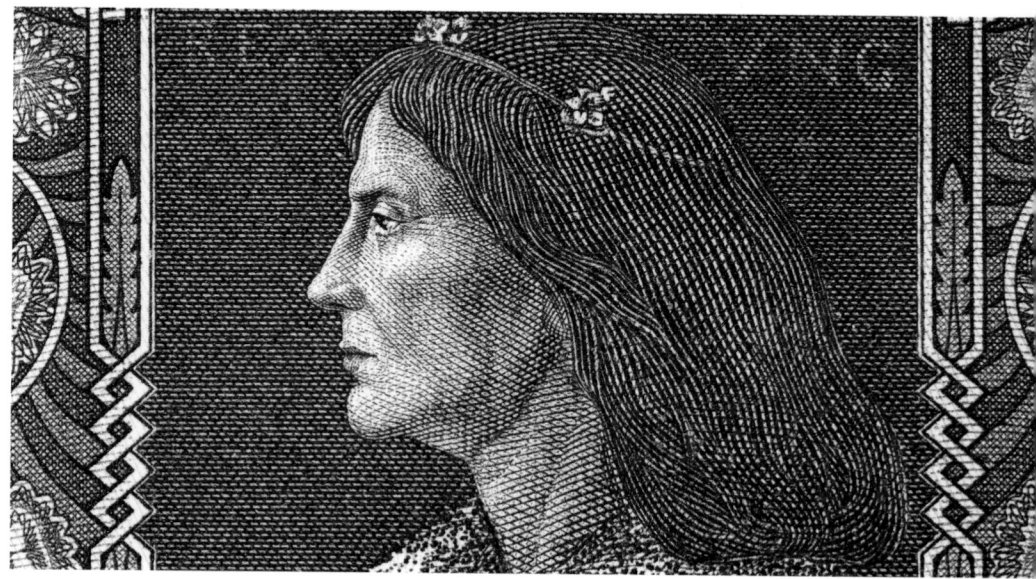

Matthias Corvinus, King of Hungary 1458–1490.

☉ DEFENDER OF CHRISTENDOM AND SCOURGE OF THE TURKS

János Hunyadi is one of Hungary's greatest national heroes, revered for his unceasing efforts to banish the Turks from the country. Born in about 1400, he rose from the minor nobility (although there were rumours that he was the illegitimate son of King Sigismund) to become the richest and most powerful man in the country.

He was a brilliant military strategist and greatly feared by the Turks, who cursed him as a jinx on their crusade to conquer Europe. The campaign against the Turks had the support of the Pope, who saw Hungary as the 'shield of Christendom' after the fall of Constantinople in 1463. His victory in the siege of

Nándorfehérvár (Belgrade) in 1456 succeeded in driving the Turks from Hungary for the next 70 years. When he died of the plague in the same year, the whole of Europe mourned. Even Sultan Mohammed II praised him: 'Although he was my enemy, I feel grief over his death, because the world has never seen such a man.'

On his deathbed, he is said to have uttered these prophetic words: 'Defend, my friends, Christendom and Hungary from all enemies.... Do not quarrel among yourselves. If you should waste your energies in altercations, you will seal your own fate as well as dig the grave of our country.' Failure to heed this advice was to cost Hungary its independence for many years.

In 1466 the two briefly joined forces to fight the Bohemian king, George Poděbrady, a Hussite (follower of the pre-Reformation movement that challenged the authority of the Church). By the end of Mátyás' reign in 1490 Hungary had acquired Lower Austria, Moravia and Silesia.

HUNGARIAN RENAISSANCE

Foreign ventures did not prevent Mátyás from keeping a lid on dissent at home. He operated through hand-picked delegates and the free towns, the large peasant communities and the

Although the first book was printed in Buda in 1473, Mátyás preferred the old handwritten codices, which ultimately made up the famous volume, *Bibliotheca Corviniana*.

When Mátyás died (possibly poisoned) in 1490 it all fell apart. He was greatly mourned, but left no heir. The estates, this time bent on a malleable king, chose Vladislav Jagiellon of Bohemia to succeed him. Affairs of the state, including defence, were left to this mild and incompetent ruler, while the magnates and the lower nobility battled for greater power.

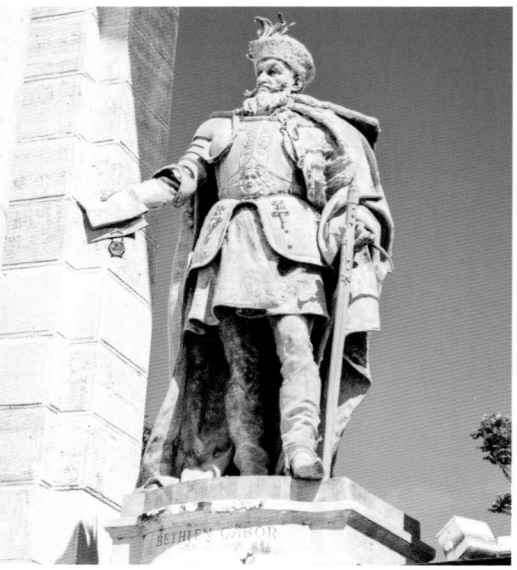

Statue of Gabriel Bethlen at the Millennium Monument, in Budapest.

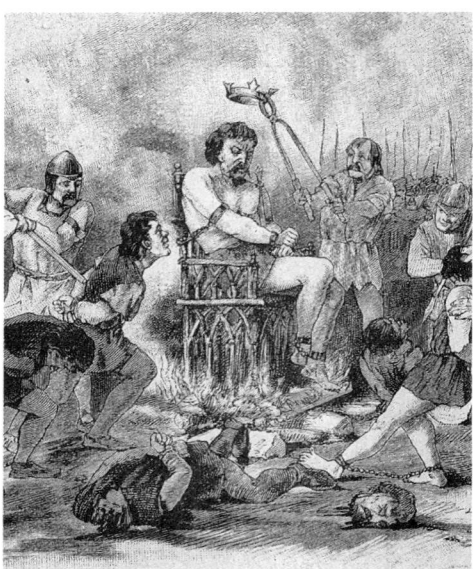

German Peasants' War, 1524–1525.

nobles, setting them against the magnates. He also scraped together a standing army of mercenaries and had a chain of fortresses built along Hungary's vulnerable borders. His reign was stable, secure and organised.

Mátyás was something of a Renaissance man with an eye for Italy. His second wife, the Neapolitan Queen Beatrix, brought artists and humanists over from Italy, and Mátyás raised vast sums to promote the arts and to beautify castles, palaces and churches. The court at Buda was celebrated as the most important centre of Renaissance culture north of the Alps, although thriftier Hungarians felt a little uncomfortable at the lavish expenditure.

In 1514 the court judge, a noble named István Verbőczy, prepared the Tripartium Law, aimed at consolidating the privileges of the nobility and reaffirming their rights over the peasants, who were bound to perpetual serfdom. Friendly relations between the kingdom and the serfs had atrophied. The Reformation, which made headway among the exploited as well as the nobles (as in Western Europe), gave impetus to a violent rebellion among the oppressed peasants in Transylvania, led by the soldier, György Dózsa and spearheaded from Szeged.

The revolt was brutally suppressed: tens of thousands of peasants were tortured and executed and Dózsa was roasted alive. In 1517, the

Diet (assembly) voted for Verbőczy's Law, thus condemning the peasants to 'real and perpetual servitude'. This set of laws, which replaced the 1222 Golden Bull, remained in force (without ever being ratified by parliament) until feudalism vanished in 1848.

DISASTER AT MOHÁCS

While the Reformation was tearing Europe's political and social fabric apart, the Turks, under Sultan Suleiman 'the Magnificent' (ruled 1520–66), were rapidly gaining power and

Courageously, Lajos II placed himself at the head of a small army of some 25,000 men in an attempt to stall the Turkish offensive of 1526. On 29 August the armies clashed at Mohács, a turning point in the nation's history. The Hungarians were outnumbered, outclassed and swiftly defeated. The young king was killed, crushed by his own horse as he tried to retreat across a river.

The Ottoman army moved on to capture Pécs and Buda. They would have penetrated further had they not feared that the Europeans were

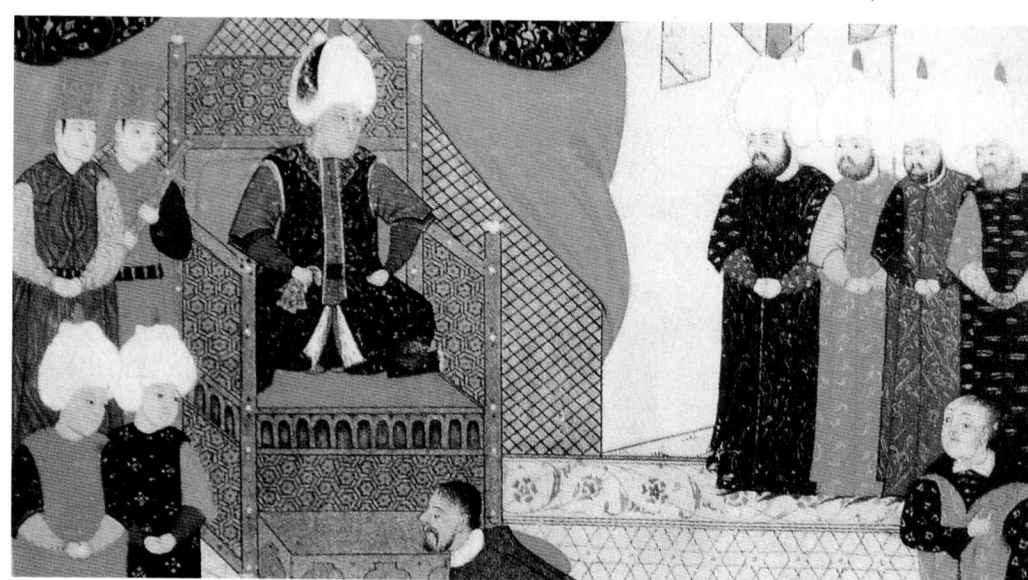

John II Sigismund Zápolya asks Suleiman permission to re-rule Hungary, 1556.

advancing northwards. By the time Verbőczy's Tripartium was passed, most of Mátyás' territorial gains had been lost and his fortifications were in ruins.

The crown in the meantime, had passed to Vladislav's son, Lajos (Louis) II, who had married a Habsburg. Desperately in need of reinforcements, Lajos tried to convince a divided parliament of the need to re-establish the national army of Corvinus. He sought aid from every 'Christian' monarch, including Francis I of France, who was secretly in cahoots with the Turks, in an attempt to surround the Habsburgs. A plea to the magnates of Transylvania and Croatia came too late.

maintaining a secret force more substantial than the pitiful reserve army they defeated with ease at Mohács.

A NATION DIVIDED

But the Hungarians had nothing further up their sleeve. They quickly accepted Ferdinand I of Habsburg's claim to the throne in the vain hope that the Austrians would formulate an assault strategy against the Turks, but apart from a few skirmishes, nothing else happened.

By 1541 the Turks had occupied central Hungary, effectively dividing the country in three – a division that would last for over 150 years. Royal Hungary, a small strip of land in the west with Pozsony (present-day

Bratislava) as its capital, was ruled by the Austrian House of Habsburg, with the help of Hungarian nobles. Transylvania in the east was ruled by János Szápolyai. Elected leader by the nobles, he proved only too willing to make deals with the Turks in return for relative peace in his region.

One heroic figure to shine through this dark age was György Martinuzzi, also known as Friar George, a Dominican monk and cardinal who was in contact with both Szápolyai and Ferdinand I. In 1538, in an attempt to keep the peace whereupon the Turkish army moved in and helped János Sigismund to the throne.

TRANSYLVANIA'S FINEST HOUR

Royal Hungary meanwhile puttered along, a mere latifundium of the Austrian Empire. Its magnates and nobles grew disgruntled, and Protestantism, synonymous at the time with political rebellion, was fast gaining support. Transylvania on the other hand enjoyed a brief period of stability, adopting a more tolerant attitude to racial and religious differences: the

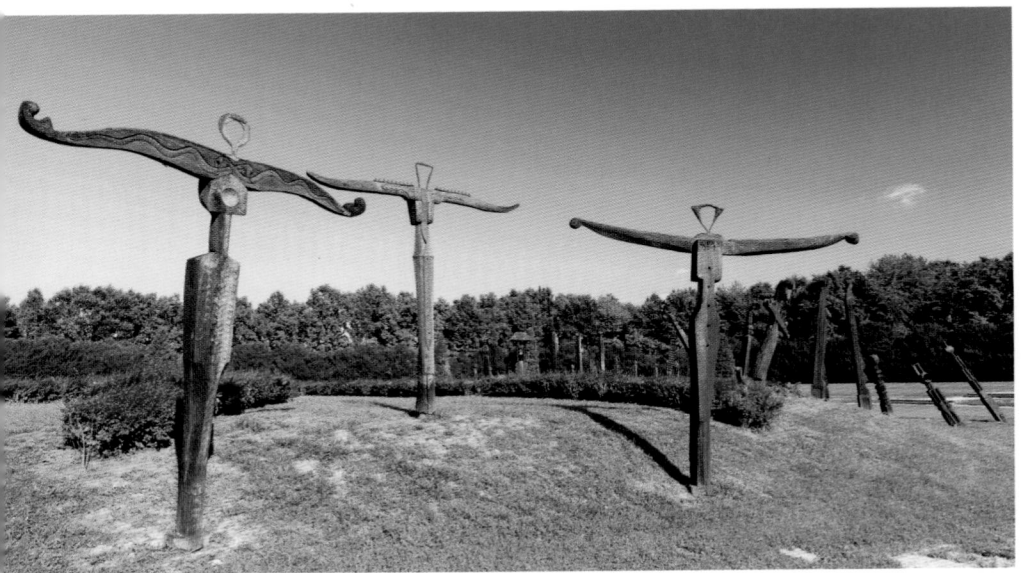

Monument to the Battle of Mohács, which took place in 1526.

and prevent Transylvania from falling into Turkish hands, he concluded a secret agreement between the two rulers that when and if the heirless Szápolyai died first, Ferdinand would be king of Transylvania. Two years later Szápolyai died, leaving an infant son, János Sigismund, to claim the throne. Friar George became regent.

In 1551, during the lull between wars, a small Habsburg army occupied Transylvania, and promised to compensate Szápolyai's heir. Friar George prepared to counter the Turkish wrath at this upset of the balance of power through a number of diplomatic and financial measures. But the Austrian general Castaldo became suspicious and had Friar George assassinated, Saxons opted for Lutheranism, the Székelys remained Catholic, the Hungarian nobles found Calvinism to their liking, while the Romanians remained steadfastly Greek Orthodox.

Although there was constant fighting between Hungary's three divisions, Transylvania's only internal strife at this point came from the Székelys, whose star had been gradually fading through the centuries. Unhappy with the status quo, in 1569 they staged an uprising that Sigismund managed to suppress. Otherwise, as a vassal state, Transylvania remained relatively independent, a status gained on the one hand from paying tribute to the Sultan and allowing him the honour of sanctioning every newly chosen *voivode* (governor) and on the other by officially recognising the Habsburgs through the Treaty of Speyer in 1570.

Transylvania produced a string of brave new leaders who set about retaliating against the Turks and extending their territorial boundaries. In 1571 István (Stephen) Báthory seized power, and not long after was crowned king of Poland. Báthory's son, another Sigismund, distinguished himself by gaining several victories against the Turks. In 1595, after sealing an alliance with Rudolf I of Habsburg, his army under István Bocskai won a major victory at Giurgiu in present-day Romania.

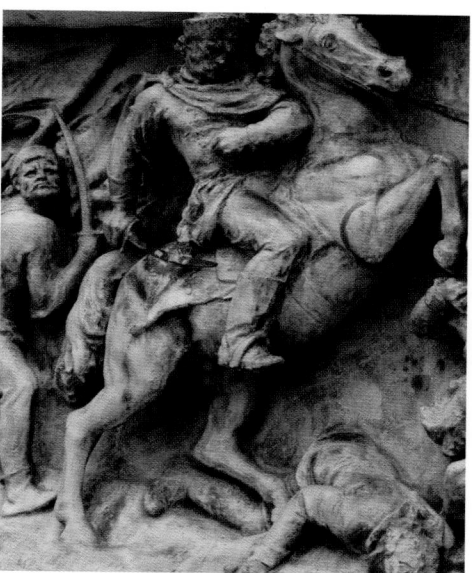

Detail on a statue of Gabriel Bethlen at Budapest's Millennium Monument.

There were further skirmishes and brutal retaliatory expeditions that devastated the outlying areas of Transylvania. After a promising beginning, Sigismund suddenly delivered the principality into the hands of Rudolf I of Habsburg, who sent an army headed by the brutal General Giorgio Basta into Transylvania. The local magnates and nobles suddenly owed total allegiance to the Habsburg emperor, and General Basta began to enforce Catholicism on the tolerant Transylvanians, pushing them past the point of endurance. In 1606, Bocskai gathered together a colourful mercenary army of peasants, brigands, nobles, city-dwellers and discharged soldiers and trounced the Habsburgs led by Basta, then

promptly installed himself on the Transylvanian throne. He quickly restored religious freedom and diplomatic relations with the Ottomans. When he died, it was the Turkish Sultan who proposed his successor, Gábor Bethlen, who ruled as prince of Transylvania from 1613 to 1629.

THE THIRTY YEARS' WAR

The Thirty Years' War (1618–48) began as a conflict between Protestants and Catholics and developed into a territorial war involving most of Europe. Though tolerant towards

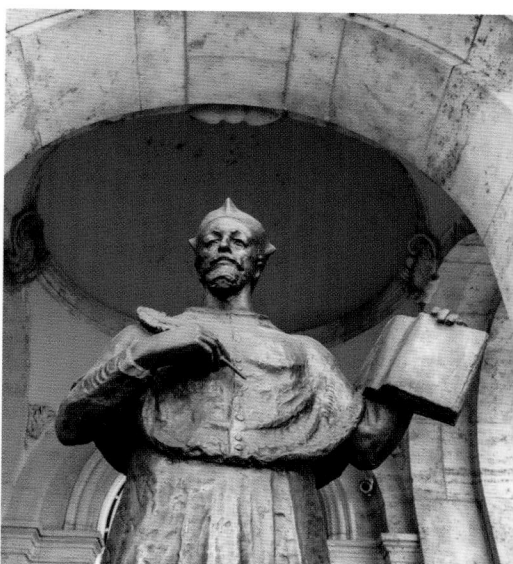

Statue of Cardinal Péter Pázmány, 1570–1637.

all religions, Bethlen, himself a Protestant, looked to Royal Hungary for allies. The Reformation had gained many followers in Hungary in the 16th century and while Transylvania remained tolerant of all religious diversity, the Counter-Reformation in Royal Hungary, under the staunchly Catholic Habsburgs, was gaining momentum. Bethlen extended official protection to all Hungarian Protestants. His wooing of the nobles in Royal Hungary was facilitated by the poor treatment they received from the Habsburgs, and by the atrocious behaviour of the Austrian soldiers while on campaign. Yet his efforts were countered by the brilliant Cardinal Péter Pázmány (1570–1637), who succeeded in reconverting many of the magnates and nobles to Catholicism, and by the plain fact that Transylvania had dealt with the 'infidel'.

In 1621, Bethlen signed the Treaty of Nicolsburg with the Holy Roman Emperor Ferdinand II, renouncing his royal title but retaining control of seven Hungarian provinces as a prince of the empire. He continued to support the Protestant powers and ruled wisely, developing the law, promoting education and the arts and investing huge sums beautifying palaces.

His successor György Rákóczi I pursued policies of expansion and in the Treaty of West-

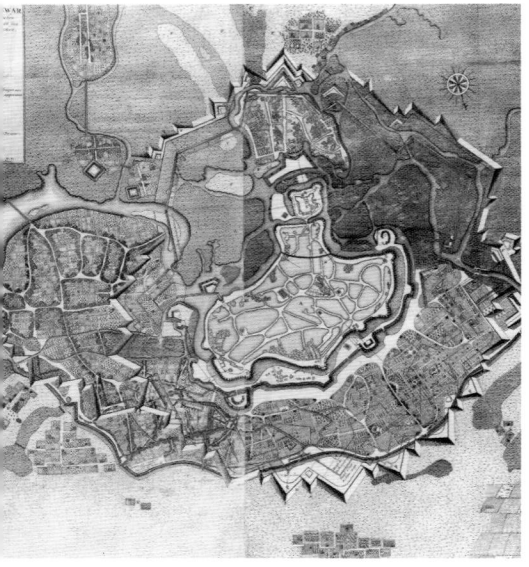

Map of Timișoara, c.1716.

phalia, which marked the end of the Thirty Years' War in 1648, Transylvania was finally recognised as an independent state. Its strength was the result of the weakness of the Habsburgs on the one side and the waning power of the Ottoman Turks on the other.

THE END OF GLORY

The second half of the 17th century was full of highly dramatic events. In 1657 György Rákóczi II joined forces with the Protestant king Karl Gustav of Sweden and attacked Poland without permission from the Turks. The Sultan dispatched an army of Tartars, who put paid to the expedition and invaded Transylvania, effectively putting an end to 150 years of Transylvanian greatness.

Leopold I, the Habsburg emperor, seized the chance to take the initiative away from Transylvania. From then on, the war against the Turks and for the liberation of Hungary rested in the hands of the Austrians. The ensuing conflicts continued until 1663, when the Austrians finally defeated the Turks at Szentgotthárd. Leopold I could hardly wait for the eastern front to be closed to resume his war against the French king Louis XIV, so the treaty signed in nearby Vasvár not only failed to get territorial concessions from the Turks, but it promised them a sweetener of 30,000 gulden to leave Europe alone.

The Hungarian magnates were incensed and hatched an anti-Habsburg conspiracy backed by Louis XIV, but it was soon uncovered and fiercely repressed. Hungarian conspirators were executed, landowners dispossessed and soldiers expelled from the army.

THE OTTOMAN–HABSBURG WAR

Pope Innocent XI, finally putting some money where the Vatican's mouth had been for decades, decided it was time to finance a major operation against the Turks. Counting on support from Hungary's anti-Habsburg rebels, the Kuruzes, the Sultan mounted a counter-offensive in 1683, but the alliance collapsed when the Turks were defeated at the gates of Vienna.

By 1686 Buda had been repossessed and within a few years, most parts of the country, including Transylvania, had been freed of the Turkish yoke. The Peace of Karlóca in 1699 forced the Turks to relinquish power, leaving them only a small section of land between the Maros and the Tisza (ceded to Hungary in 1718), and marking the end of the Ottoman–Habsburg war.

Redistributing the land to its rightful owners and settling various other claims after 150 years of occupation would have been a difficult task under the best possible administration. Now it seemed impossible. Corruption, extortion, high taxes, the sale of land and property to foreign speculators and a violent spate of Counter-Reformation measures quickly brought the Hungarians to the boil. In 1703 Ferenc Rákóczi II initiated a rebellion that was to last until 1711. Fortunately for Rákóczi, the Hungarian military leader of the Austrians, Count Pálffy, offered a settlement. The Peace of Szatmár restored the status quo of 1686 – not ideal, but it did finally bring peace to Hungary.

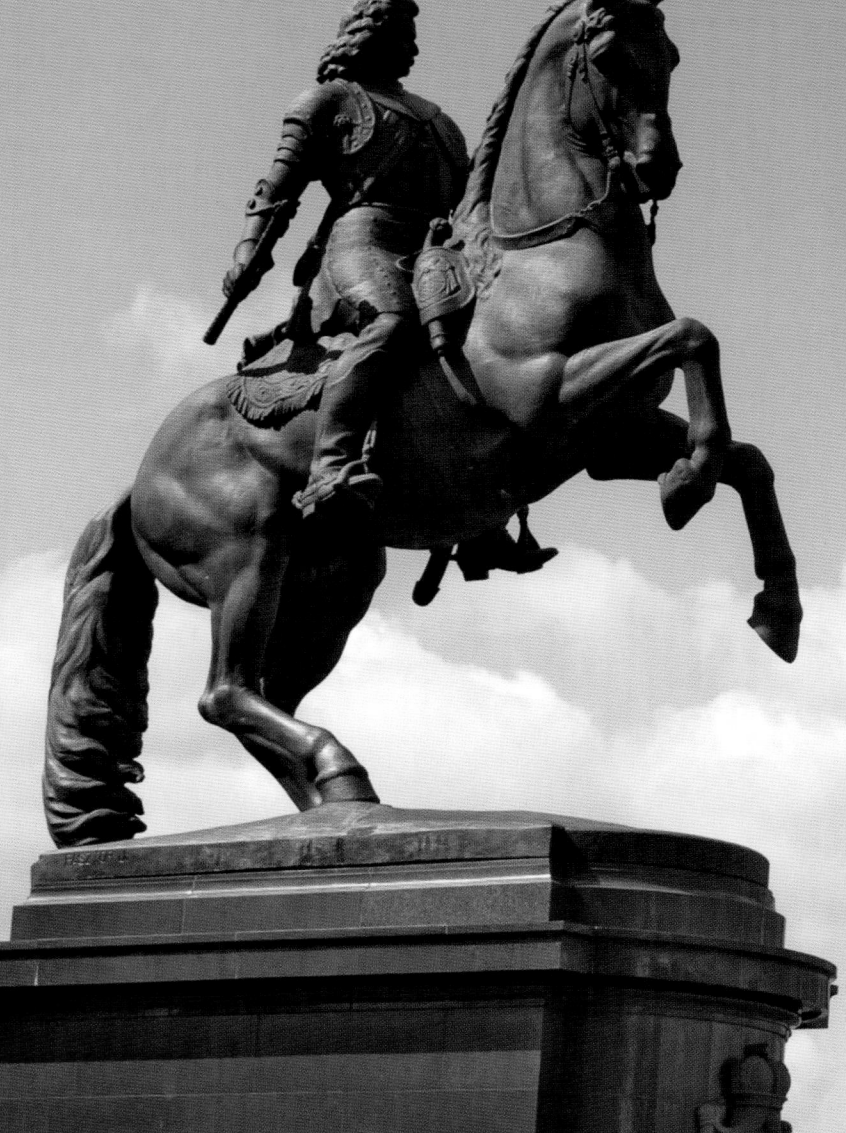

RECRVDESCVNT DIVTINA
INCLYTÆ GENTIS HVNGARÆ
VULNERA

RÁKÓC

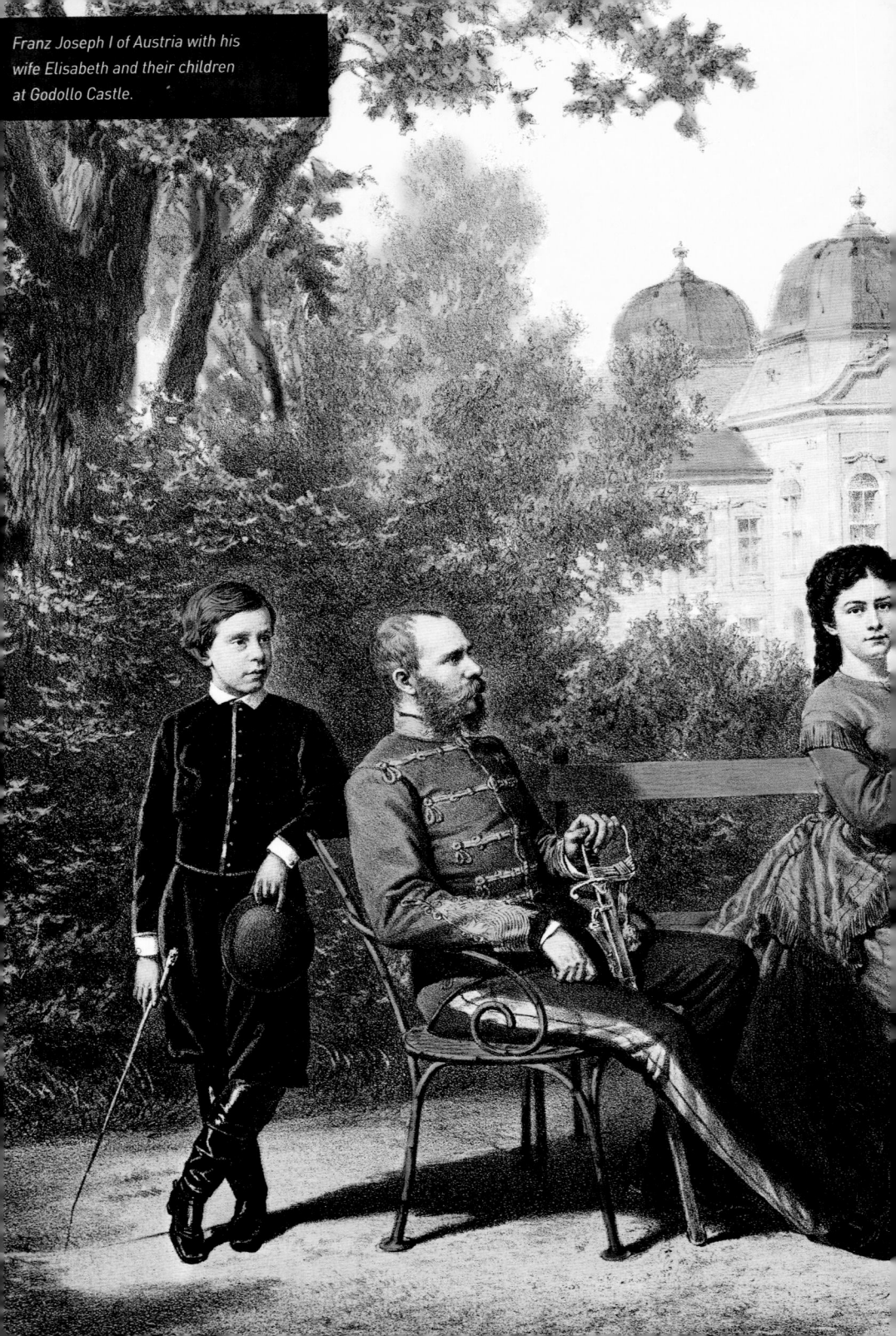

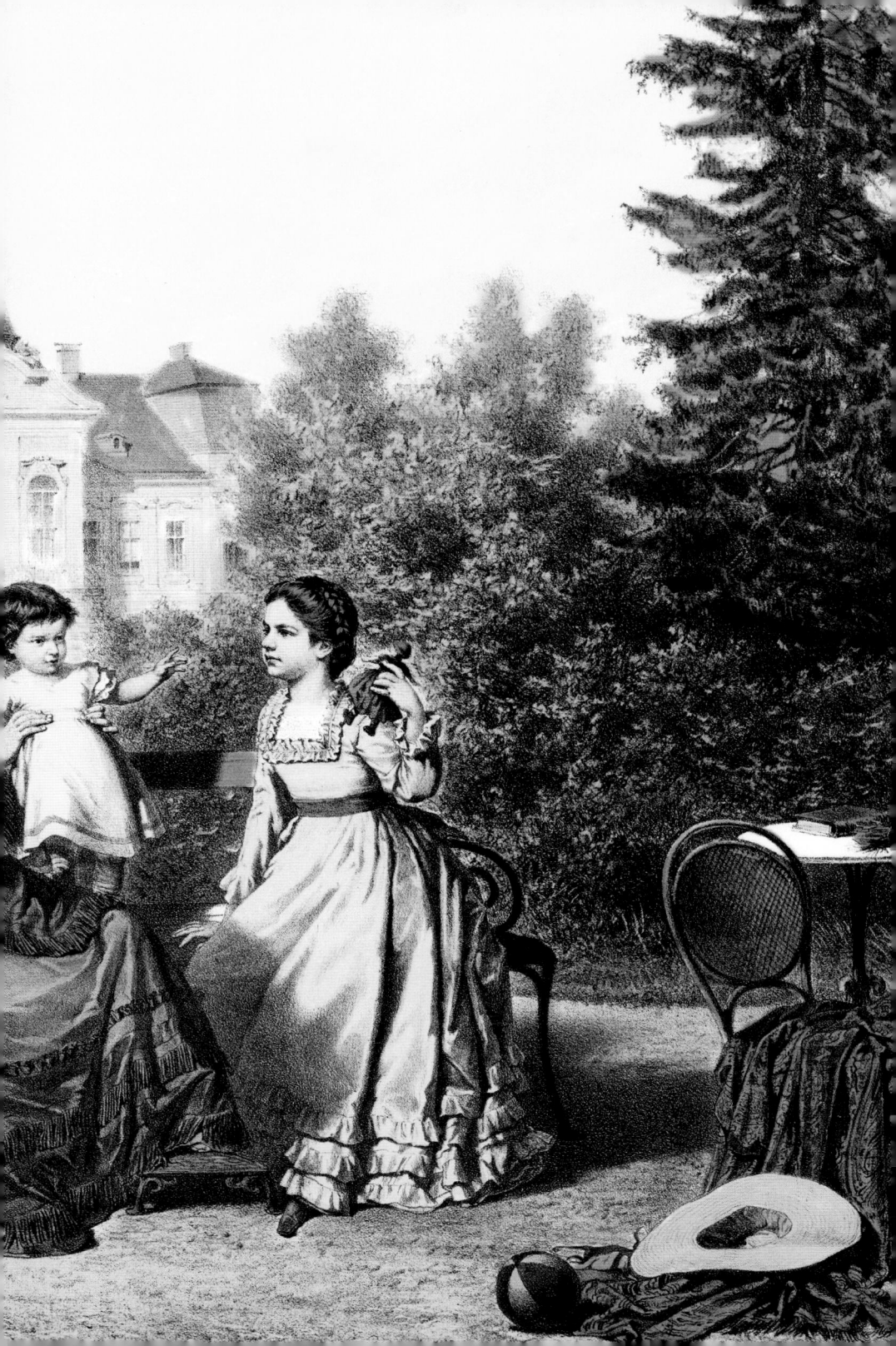

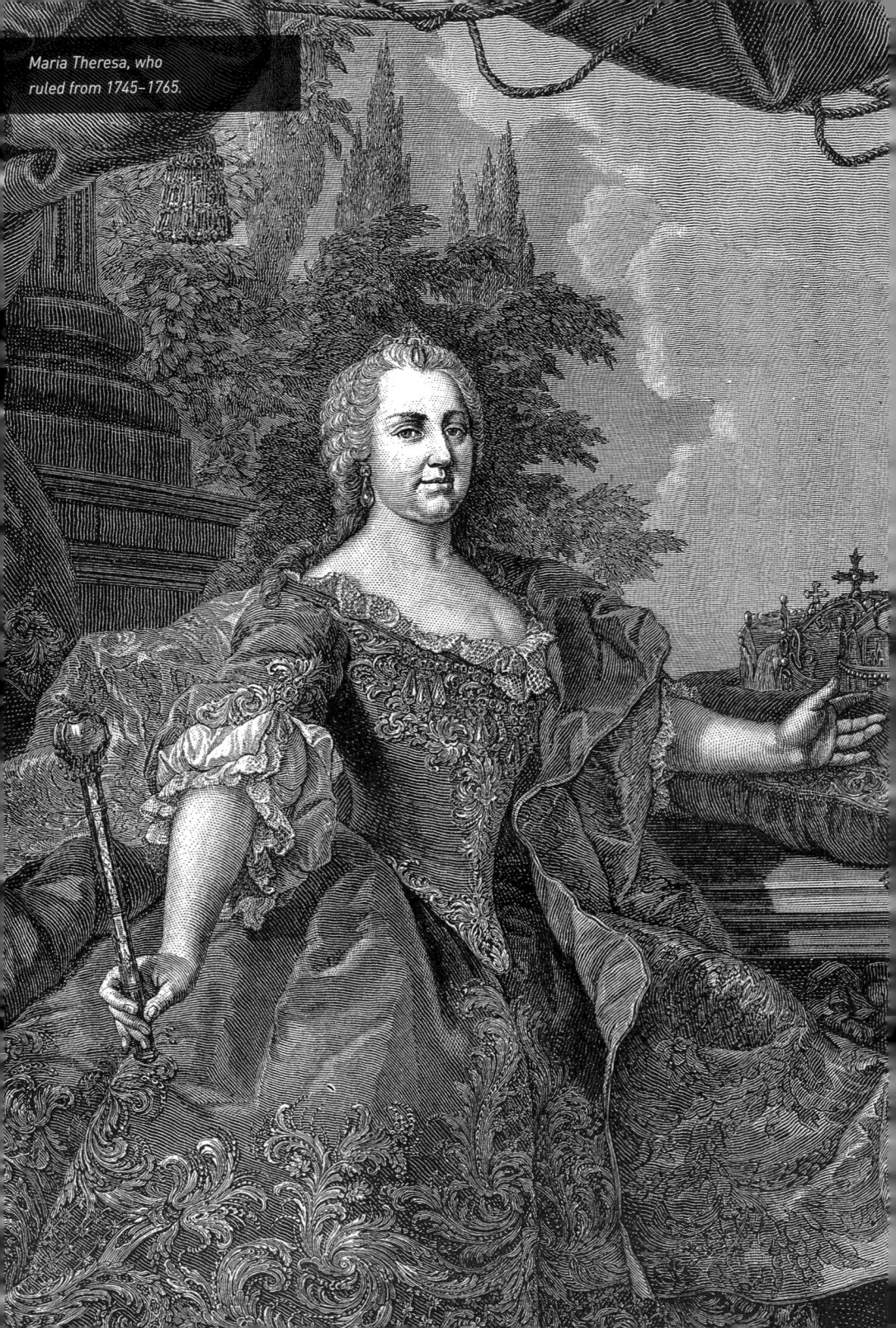

HABSBURG RULE

The Age of Enlightenment reached Hungary, but its dreams of independence were snuffed out by the Habsburg regime.

In 1723 the Hungarian parliament, still seated in Pozsony, ratified the Pragmatic Sanction, an edict issued by the House of Habsburg establishing the legality of female succession and the indivisibility of Habsburg territories. This meant that after the death of Emperor Charles VI in 1740, his daughter, Maria Theresa, was able to succeed him.

In 1741, after Austria's squabble with Prussia developed into a major conflict following the secession of several provinces, she turned to parliament in Pozsony and, dressed in mourning, appealed for help. The chivalrous Hungarian nobles could not resist and in return Maria Theresa did not forget her debt. More importantly, she restored peace and prosperity to a war-torn Hungary and with her persuasive diplomatic style, gained the confidence of both the magnates and the peasants. But the empress could also be tough and autocratic: there were instances when she refused to succumb to parliament when it challenged her policies and, as a fervent Catholic, she 'discouraged' Protestants from working in government service.

During her reign (1740–80) the government and military became more closely linked than ever and the nobles, having pledged their loyalty, continued to enjoy privileges, spending their wealth on building palaces and glorifying their towns. Many Hungarian aristocrats were drawn to the Viennese court. Little changed for the serfs, however, and the issue of freeing them raised by Rákóczi earlier in the century was largely ignored.

Large areas of Hungary that had been depopulated by decades of war were settled by immigrants from across its borders. Swabians occupied the Transdanubia region, and

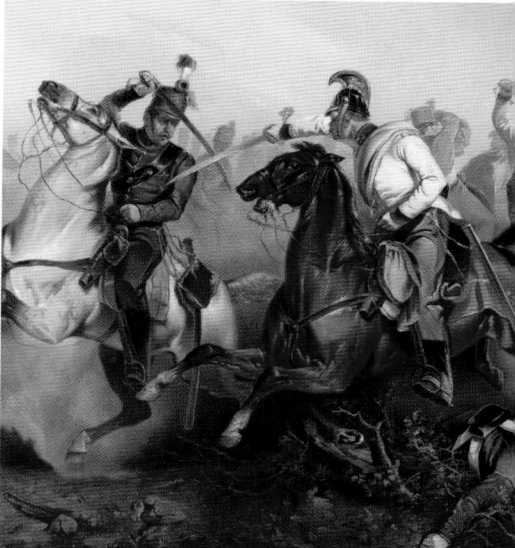

The War of Independence in 1849.

Serbs and Romanians headed for the southern and eastern regions. In 1765, Transylvania was proclaimed a grand principality, and a fortified line drawn between it and Hungary. A large proportion of the Székely population, who felt more Hungarian, migrated across the new border leaving behind a largely Romanian population. On the surface Transylvania was an autonomous region, but in reality its traditional independence was being eroded by Austrian rule.

LIBERALISATION UNDER JOSEF II

On her death in 1780, Maria Theresa was succeeded by her oldest son, Josef II. Born and raised during the Age of Enlightenment, the new emperor was a practical and rational man, and ruled as an enlightened despot.

He believed in central government and made German the empire's official language. He rejected the symbolic power and mythology surrounding the Crown of St Stephen and, instead of wearing it, had it mothballed in Vienna. He tolerated religions in an agnostic fashion, which displeased the Catholic authorities. He turned cloisters into hospitals, regulated church building and practices, conducted a national census, replaced local

Leopold II, whose reign lasted only two years (1790–92), reversed others. Latin was reinstated as the official language, and the nobles were given greater representation. Most importantly, the crown was returned to Buda, and parliament once more officially elected the king.

THE NEW CONSCIOUSNESS

Meanwhile, the effects of the 1789 French Revolution were being felt across Europe. The fall of the monarchy in France sent shock waves

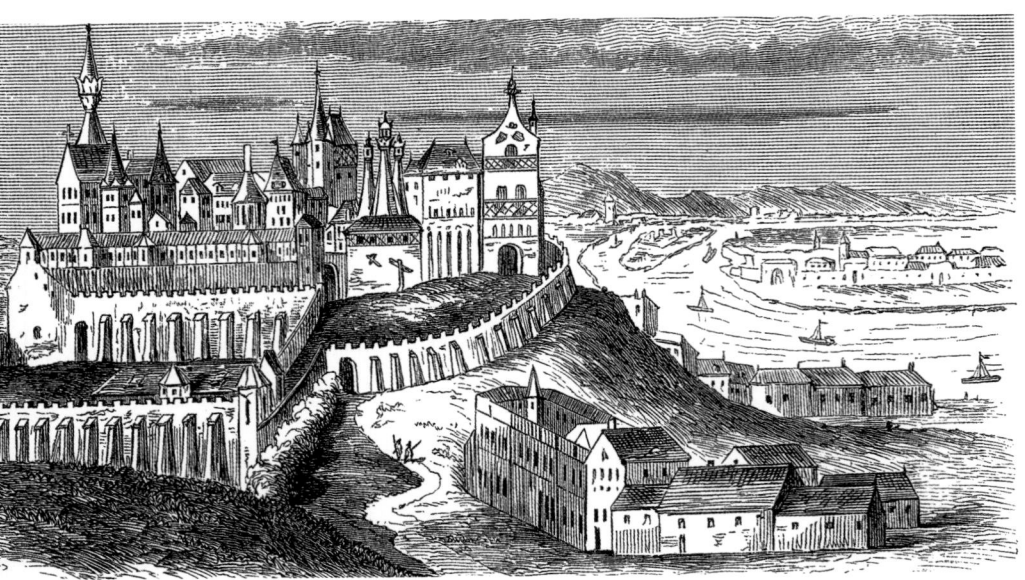

Buda Castle in the late 16th century.

administration with royal delegates and imposed a standard tax according to the area of an estate. He also began to free the serfs from bondage.

By the end of the 1780s the conservative Hungarian nobles stood on the brink of rebellion. Josef II retracted many of his reforms on his deathbed, while his brother

through the Habsburg Empire. After the death of Leopold II, the Assembly ceased to be convened, and a customs barrier was created between Hungary and Austria. Leopold's son and successor, Francis I, looked suspiciously upon the Hungarians. He misunderstood the fundamentally conservative nature of the nobles' historic rebelliousness. The growing tension between Hungary and Austria could only result in an explosion.

REFORM TO REVOLUTION

By the mid-1790s revolutionary Jacobinism from France had gathered a strong following in Hungary and, with the revival of the Magyar language and the enthusiastic

Marie Antoinette, Queen of France, was the daughter of Empress Maria Theresa. She sought Austria's aid against French revolutionaries and in 1793 was tried for treason and guillotined.

promotion of Enlightenment ideals by intellectuals, Hungarian nationalism was finding a voice. The execution of the seven Jacobin conspirators found guilty of plotting against the Habsburgs only fanned the nationalist flames.

One prominent activist was Count István Széchenyi (1791–1860). A passionate patriot with a cosmopolitan background, he called for a Hungarian revival. He promoted the resuscitation of the Magyar language, which had been slowly dying out in the 18th century, and drew

fellow nobles. Among the nationalists to rise to prominence in his wake was the dispossessed landowner and lawyer, Lajos Kossuth, a brilliant orator and cunning statesman.

Vienna's stance towards the troubles brewing in Hungary mutated from tolerance to severe oppression. Kossuth, among others, had to cool his heels in prison for three years.

In February 1848 the French once more overthrew their monarchy. Revolution swept across Europe. Nationalist feeling in Hungary was running high. On 3 March Kossuth addressed the

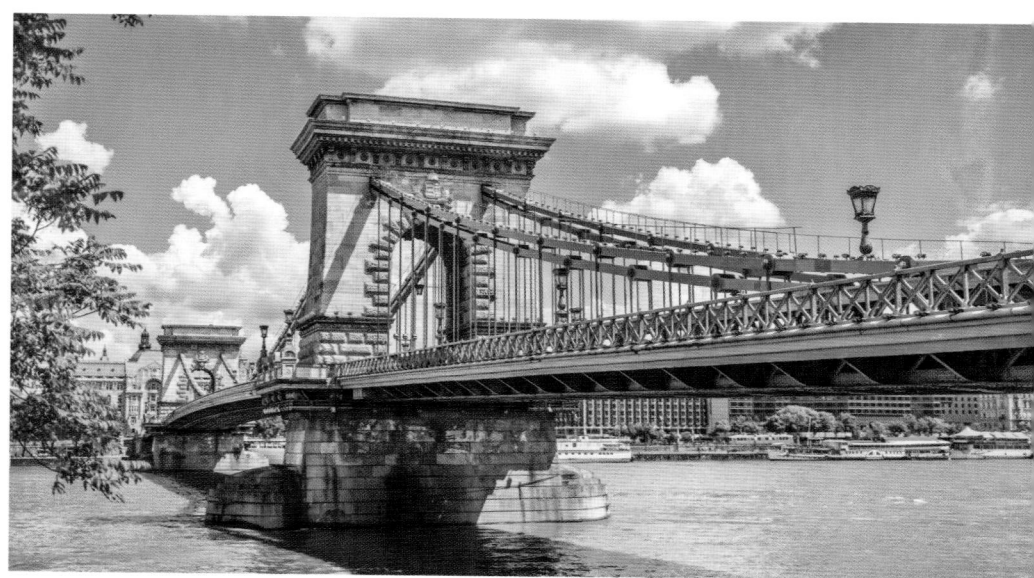

Chain Bridge over the River Danube in Budapest.

up a manifesto for social, political, cultural and industrial modernisation. He advocated a strong work ethic: 'Let us trust our own strength, and never do battle unprepared and administer our forces better; for in the rebirth of a nation... the modest bee and hardworking ant achieve a great deal more than golden rhetoric and the din of enthusiasm.'

Practising what he preached, he busied himself improving the country's infrastructure, building railways and shipyards. His most famous achievement was the construction of the Lanchíd (Chain Bridge) which spans the Danube linking Buda and Pest.

Széchenyi gained widespread support from the working classes he championed and from

Hungarian parliament, demanding the revocation of tax privileges, a constitutional monarchy, extension of the franchise to non-nobles and freedom for peasants – in short, an end to feudalism.

A SHORT-LIVED VICTORY

On 15 March another uprising, led by the poet Sándor Petőfi, took place in Pest. At a stormy session in the Café Pilvax a 12-point manifesto was drawn up reiterating Kossuth's demands and adding freedom of the press, trial by jury and reunification with Transylvania.

The Emperor Ferdinand yielded and agreed to these reforms, which were ratified by the

Hungarian Diet as the 'April Laws'. A new government was formed, and the Diet was dissolved and replaced by the National Assembly. The liberal magnate Count Lajos Batthyány was elected prime minister and assembled an autonomous cabinet, which included some of Hungary's finest minds: Széchenyi, communications and transport; Ferenc Deák, justice; Jozsef Eötvös, education; and Lajos Kossuth, finance.

Resistance to the Hungarian revolution came from another quarter as well, and

Ferdinand passed the imperial throne to his 18-year-old nephew Franz Josef (1848–1916) in December. Kossuth moved his parliament to the relative safety of Debrecen, from where it proclaimed Hungary's independence on 14 April 1849. The Hungarian general Artur Görgey, his ranks swelled by Italian, Polish, Slovak and German patriots from Europe's failed revolutions, routed the Habsburg troops.

But Franz Josef, a more astute leader than his uncle, turned to the Russians for help.

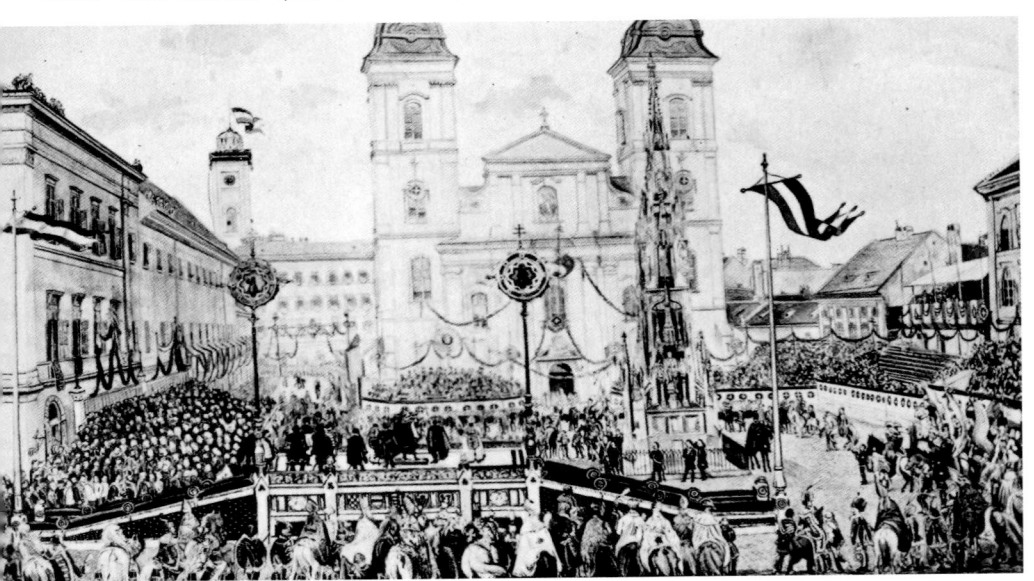

Coronation of Emperor Franz Joseph in Budapest on 8th June 1867.

Vienna knew how to take advantage of it. Swept along by the events, Hungary's ethnic groups – Romanians, Ruthenians, Croats and Slovaks – swamped an unwilling parliament with demands of their own. In June Serbia rebelled. The following month, Kossuth submitted a request to the Assembly for 42 million gulden to strengthen government forces.

Vienna accused the Hungarians of breaking the Pragmatic Sanction and revoked the laws sanctioned in April. Austria and Serbia declared war against Hungary on 11 September. Széchenyi suffered a nervous breakdown (and eventually committed suicide). Batthyány and his cabinet members finally resigned, leaving Kossuth in power.

The Tsar obliged and led his army across the Carpathian basin to fight on the side of the Austrians. The Hungarians were outnumbered, and on 13 August 1849, Görgey surrendered.

Among the casualties was the 26-year-old Sándor Petőfi, his body trampled into some forlorn field during a heroic but hopeless cavalcade. His poetry had given wings to the revolution, and with him went a glorious, tragic period of Hungarian history.

ABSOLUTE RULE

Görgey managed to escape prosecution and lived to the ripe old age of 98. Kossuth reached exile through Turkey. Others were less fortunate.

A wave of imprisonment, exile and execution followed. Batthyány and 13 other leaders of the revolution were shot in Arad (present-day Oradea, Romania).

The truculent General Haynau administered Hungary, once more a mere province of the Habsburg Empire, with an iron hand. All reforms were instantly revoked and Habsburg soldiers were sent round the country to destroy castles and fortification walls. Transylvania, Croatia and Slovenia were cut off from Hungary. Austrian and Czech bureaucrats

flowed between Hungary and Austria. They were counter-balanced by drastic increases in taxes and the shame of having to speak German, the official language, They were as desperate for reform as ever.

While Kossuth's spirit still hovered over Hungary, a new opposition movement formed in the 1850s, made up mostly of conservatives and moderates under the leadership of Ferenc Deák. Two factors were in their favour. They had a powerful ally in Vienna: the Empress Elizabeth who, perhaps roused by the roman-

Lajos Kossuth leads the fight for independence in 1849.

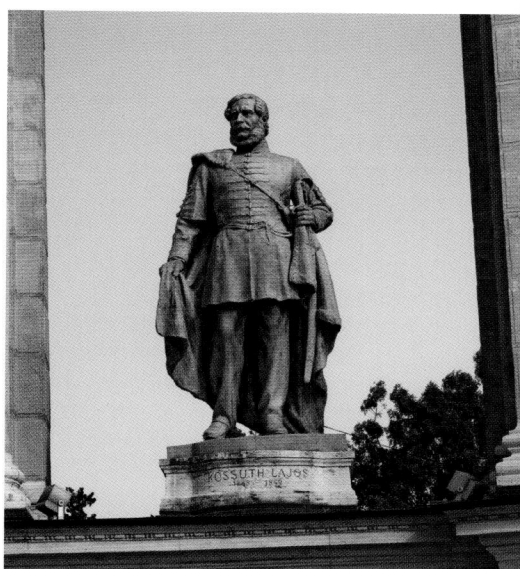

Monument to Lajos Kossuth in Budapest.

rushed in to fill the shoes of Hungarian civil servants.

The return to a repressive, absolutist regime did nothing to pacify the Hungarians. The few concessions to 1848 that were made, such as limited land reform and abolition of trade barriers, failed to wash away the blood that had

tic aspects of the Magyar resistance, often interceded in their favour. In addition, Austria had suffered some disastrous military defeats, not least the loss of Lombardy at the hands of the Italians and the French in 1859. These attacks on the periphery of his empire made Franz Josef more conciliatory.

In the October Diploma of 1860, he proposed a federal relationship between Hungary and Vienna, but the Hungarians refused to give up the idea of full independence. Although Deák wanted a return to the April Laws and more direct involvement in the affairs of state, he bided his time, steering himself into a moderate position from which he would be able to bargain convincingly.

> *After the execution in 1849 of 13 revolutionary leaders, Hungarians swore they would not clink beer glasses for 150 years. In 1999, on the 150th anniversary, the custom was officially reinstated.*

THE GREAT COMPROMISE

The ice thawed in 1865 with the formation of a new cabinet in Vienna. There was talk of a compromise. Then in 1866 came the news of the disastrous Austrian rout in Sadowa at the hands of the Prussians, which forced Franz Josef to the negotiating table. In February 1867 the emperor convened a Hungarian ministry under Count Gyula Andrássy, agreeing to the restoration of the April Laws and the gradual restoration of crown lands (Transylvania had already voted to rejoin Hungary).

Negotiations resulted in the great Austro-Hungarian Compromise (*Ausgleich* in German, meaning 'balance') which established the dual monarchy of Austria-Hungary with two parliaments and two capitals. Foreign, military and financial affairs were decided jointly, but separate constitutions and legislatures were maintained. The agreement was sealed by the crowning of Franz Josef as King of Hungary in the Mátyás Church in Buda on 8 June 1867, which signalled the beginning of an economic and cultural renaissance in Hungary, a golden age that was to last until World War I.

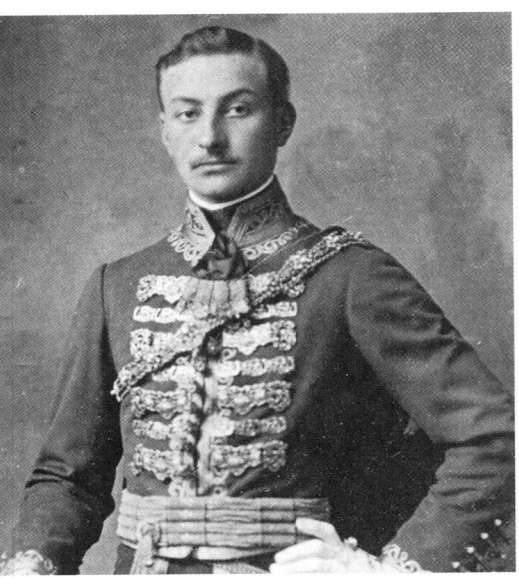

Count Gyula Andrássy in 1908.

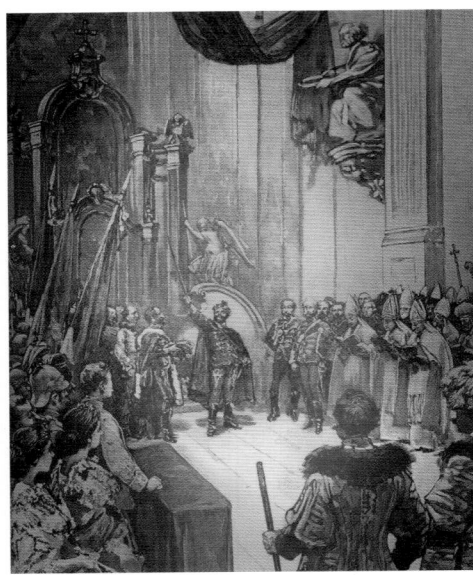

Franz Josef's Coronation as King of Hungary, 1866.

⊘ THE BIRTH OF BUDAPEST

Plans to unite the towns of Pest, Buda and Óbuda, which had officially been on the table since 1849, were finally realised in 1873 when the newly formed municipality of Budapest was declared the capital of Hungary. A city council was elected and Hungarian was subsequently nominated as the city's official language.

An industrial boom was sweeping across the country during this period, with particular emphasis on the processing of agricultural products. Budapest, a centre of this new economic activity, expanded rapidly as a result. Apart from the palaces and apartment houses, the most important

buildings, such as banks, theatres and hotels – intended to rival Vienna – date back to this prosperous period. Between 1850 and 1914, the Hungarian population grew by nearly 60 percent, and eventually reached 19 million.

Despite a growing social awareness among the upper classes, which had been somewhat awakened by recent tumultuous events, not everyone benefited from the economic and cultural boom that was sweeping the country. Slums began to spring up all over Budapest, and in reality, the working classes in the city found that they had few rights and, in reality, not much had changed for the peasants.

Steelworkers protest in Budapest, 1914.

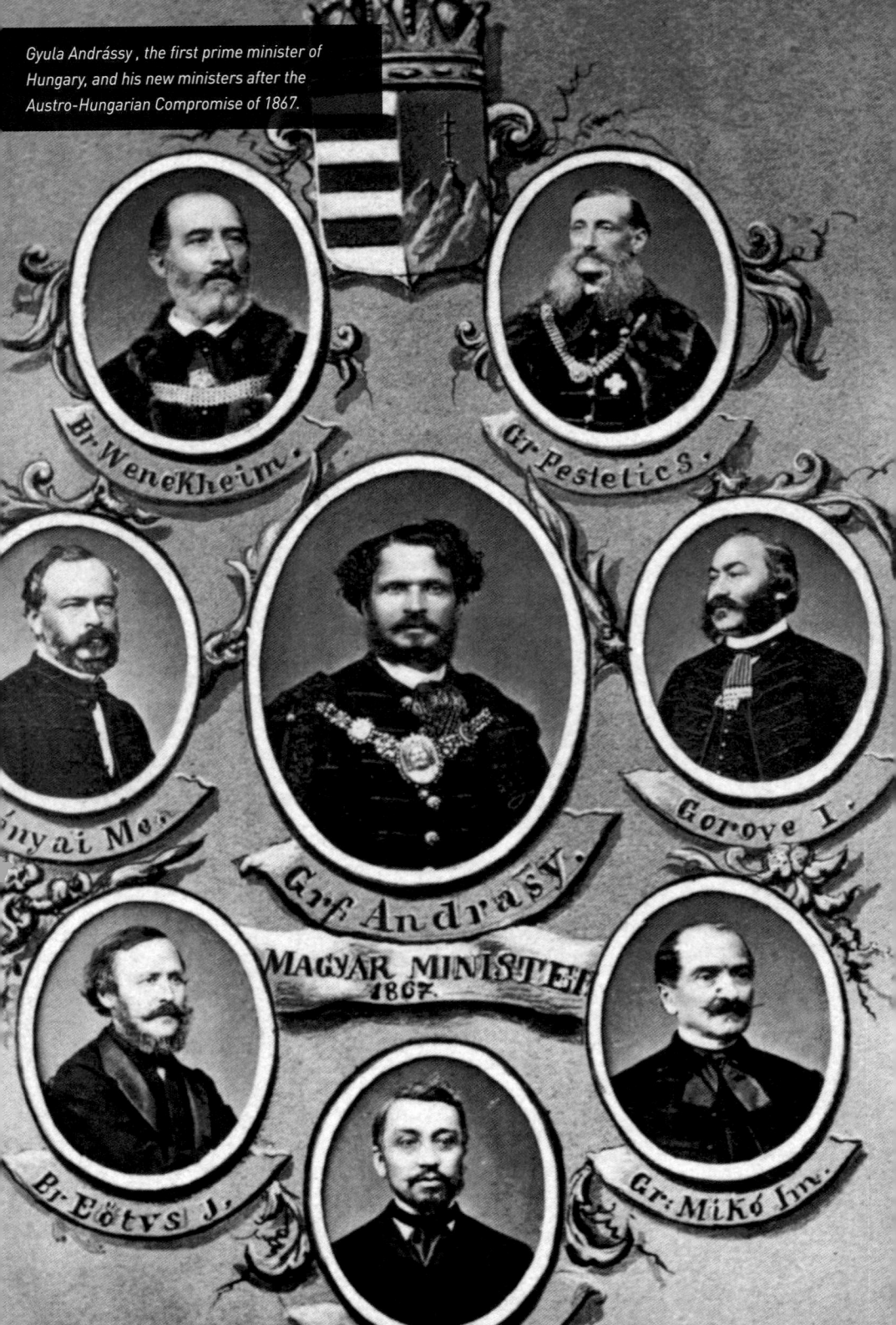

Gyula Andrássy , the first prime minister of Hungary, and his new ministers after the Austro-Hungarian Compromise of 1867.

THE DUAL MONARCHY

The Compromise brought stability until World War I, then the humiliating Treaty of Trianon paved the way for the rise of Nazism.

Under the terms of the Austro-Hungarian Compromise of 1867, Hungary was allowed a sovereign government and its own defensive militia. The ministries of Defence, Foreign Affairs and Finances were shared. The issue of the ethnic minorities was partially resolved by allowing the Croats proportional representation in the Hungarian parliament. The Dual Monarchy was to last until 1918 and, while it heralded a period of economic prosperity, the poor – as ever – did not feel the benefit. Within Hungary, the old status quo remained, with the important landowners (including the Church) oppressing a vast, disenfranchised, poverty-stricken class.

The '67ers' who supported laissez-faire liberal-minded economic and political programmes spent their first 10 years in power splitting hairs on policy and engaging in corrupt deals. A major bone of contention was the degree of compromise with Vienna. Nationalist fires fanned by the exiled Kossuth often threatened the government, which was associated with a partial cave-in to the Habsburgs. The liberals were about to fall apart on this issue when the wily Kálmán Tisza succeeded in forging a brand new liberal coalition, which held power until 1904.

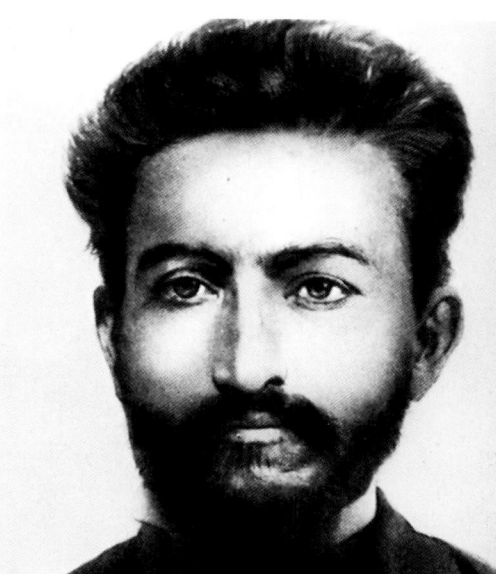

Leo Frankel (1844–1896), a Hungarian revolutionary.

CALL FOR HUMAN RIGHTS

Meanwhile, the strained social conditions in Hungary gave rise to a new political trend. Strikes broke out in 1871, which the government repressed with force. By 1880 Leo Frankel, former minister of the Paris Commune in 1871, had organised the General Workers' Party. Its manifesto called for a 10-hour day, the abolition of child labour, equal pay for men and women and other human rights. Frankel was ultimately arrested, but the movement had developed a life of its own. In 1890 the Hungarian Social Democratic Party came into being.

By the 1890s, government departments and businesses were using Hungarian as their official language, which resulted in strong tendencies towards assimilation of ethnic minorities during the period of urban expansion in the following decades.

The process of 'Magyarisation' was gently imposed on those who wanted to get ahead in life. Jews, for example, who had migrated in large numbers from neighbouring countries, adapted quickly to Hungarian life. Around the middle of the 19th century, the majority had been German-speaking. By 1910, about 75 percent of the Jewish community (which made up 4.5 percent of the population) spoke Hungarian as their first language.

MINORITIES AND NATIONALISTS

Much of the professional middle class was Jewish. On the whole, they were tolerated and their contribution to Hungary's striving for nationhood acknowledged. Nevertheless, a parallel development was that of a deep-seated anti-Semitism which found expression in sporadic violent outbreaks and the creation of an Anti-

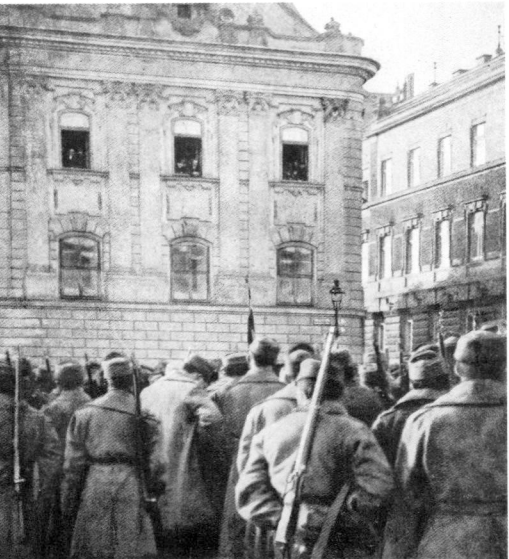

Attempted communist revolution in Budapest, 1919.

Semitic Party under Gyözö Istóczy in 1883.

Hungary's other ethnic minorities were less than pleased with the pressure they were under to 'Magyarise'. Romanians, Slovaks, Serbians, Ruthenians and even the relatively well assimilated Croats reacted strongly against what they saw as oppression and began claiming the right to statehood, fired up by powerful orators and the spirit of the age.

At the same time, the Hungarian nationalists, striving for independence from the Habsburgs, were gaining ground in government. By 1903 they were strong enough to block undesirable parliamentary measures. Parliament was dissolved and the new elections gave a coalition of nationalists the majority, but Franz Josef refused to sanction them until, secretly, they promised to renounce some of their demands. Faced with the threat of an extended suffrage, they agreed to govern in coalition with the liberals.

In 1910 the 'Party of Work', old liberal wine in new bottles, took power. The nation was riddled with tensions, while in Europe the dogs of war were frothing at the mouth. The outbreak of hostilities in 1914 came as a welcome diversion from Hungary's internal strife.

WORLD WAR I

In July 1914, the Dual Monarchy entered the war as allies of the German Empire, one month after the assassination of Archduke Franz Ferdinand, heir to the Habsburg throne. The enthusiasm that initially unified the country against a common enemy quickly faded to disillusionment as news of the first defeats and costly victories reached home. Anger with the strutting but ineffective military leadership – and with national leadership in general – was spreading as the extent of the destruction and the loss of hundreds of thousands of lives gradually became known.

Peace negotiations began as early as July 1916. For Count Mihály Károlyi, head of the new Independence Party, the key issues for Hungary's future were separation from Austria, peace without annexation, major concessions to the ethnic minorities and land reforms. But the already precarious balance of power that had been maintained between Austria and Hungary through half a century of compromise was brought to the brink of collapse with the death of Franz Josef in November 1916. Charles I, his successor, made peace overtures with the Entente powers, but the war had gained its own momentum.

As the war progressed, the discontent of Hungary's ethnic minorities re-emerged in a different form: lacklustre performances in battle, mass desertions from the army and general bitterness in the face of the notion that this was someone else's war.

Throughout 1917 the country was in ferment. In May that year the trades unions in Hungary had already numbered over 200,000 seething members. Charles I's last-minute changes to the leadership did little good.

A wave of strikes and demonstrations swept through Austro-Hungary in January 1918, paralysing several domestic munitions factories. Some months later, a mutiny broke out in Pécs. By the time World War I ended, Hungary was divided along so many boundaries, social, political and ethnic, that only a miracle would have kept it together.

THE LONG APOCALYPSE

Károlyi formed a National Council on 25 October 1918. The war was lost, heavy casualties were incurred, and the great Danube monarchy was going to pieces. In better times, the manifesto hammered out by the brilliant journalist and statesman, Oszkár Jászi, might have provided a solid base upon which a modern state could have been forged out of a political Babylon such as Hungary.

Unfortunately the landowners seemed little inclined to follow the example of Károlyi himself and redistribute their huge holdings. Moreover, the Hungarian ethnic minorities had quite a different understanding of the term 'concessions' from that of the Hungarians. Jászi's efforts, especially with the Romanians, were in vain.

American President Woodrow Wilson went before Congress in January 1918 to put forward the famous Fourteen Points, the last of which would establish 'a general association of nations... affording mutual guarantees of political independence and territorial integrity to great and small states alike'. Unfortunately, the territorial integrity proposed by Wilson turned out to be inapplicable to Hungary. As no clear demarcation line existed at the close of the war, the Czech, Serb, and Romanian armies went about grabbing as much land as they could from the supine Hungarians, while the French army, bivouacked in Szeged, stood by and watched. With the entire economy at a standstill, and with virtually no army to speak of and no hint of an ally anywhere in the world, Károlyi and his cabinet were impotent.

BÉLA KUN AND THE INTER-WAR YEARS

The newly established, very active Communist Party also put the Károlyi government under pressure. Its rank-and-file consisted partly of hordes of dissatisfied, disenfranchised workers

In February 1919, the Entente powers – Britain, France and Russia – decided to create a neutral zone in southeast Hungary and allowed another allied division to enter the country.

and partly of demoralised soldiers returning from Russian POW camps where they had experienced the October Revolution at first hand. The leaders were imprisoned, but a chain reaction

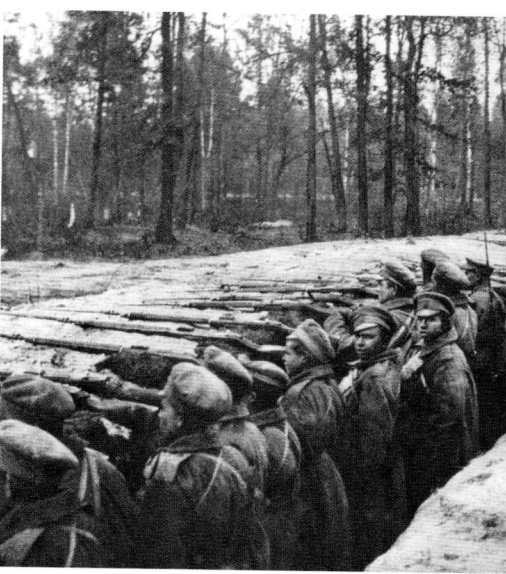

Russian forces fighting near Hungary during World War I.

among their staunch supporters paved the way for their meteoric rise to power.

Unable to control the nation's foreign policy, Károlyi decided to leave power to the Social Democrats, who in turn realised they could only rule with the communists, who might be able to find support and help in Soviet Russia.

On 22 March the Social Democrats capitulated. Béla Kun took power and the Hungarian Soviet was declared. By 25 March Hungary had a Red Army, which occupied the Ministry of Justice and also controlled the police force. The so-called Republic of Councils (*Tanácsköztársaság*) issued edict after edict, nationalising the banks and industries employing more than 20 people, reforming the education system, cutting back the power of the Church and, of course, redistributing the land. Order was temporarily restored, but the price was fierce repression of real and perceived dissent.

CONSERVATIVE REACTION

The pendulum that had swung to the far left was now being pulled back to the right. Conservative forces began forming conspiracies. The Western powers, who had already dispatched troops to fight the Bolsheviks in the Soviet Union, became more worried than ever about the possible

failed. On 3 August, Romanian troops reached Budapest and Hungary's short-lived communist regime came to an end.

Chaos ruled for the remainder of 1919, with the Romanian and Allied delegations playing the role of spectators. The Red Terror gave way to a bloody White Terror as paramilitary bands of ex-soldiers and officers, students and wandering, homeless Magyars chased out of their native lands, dished out summary justice to anyone accused or suspected of connections with the Kun regime. Communists

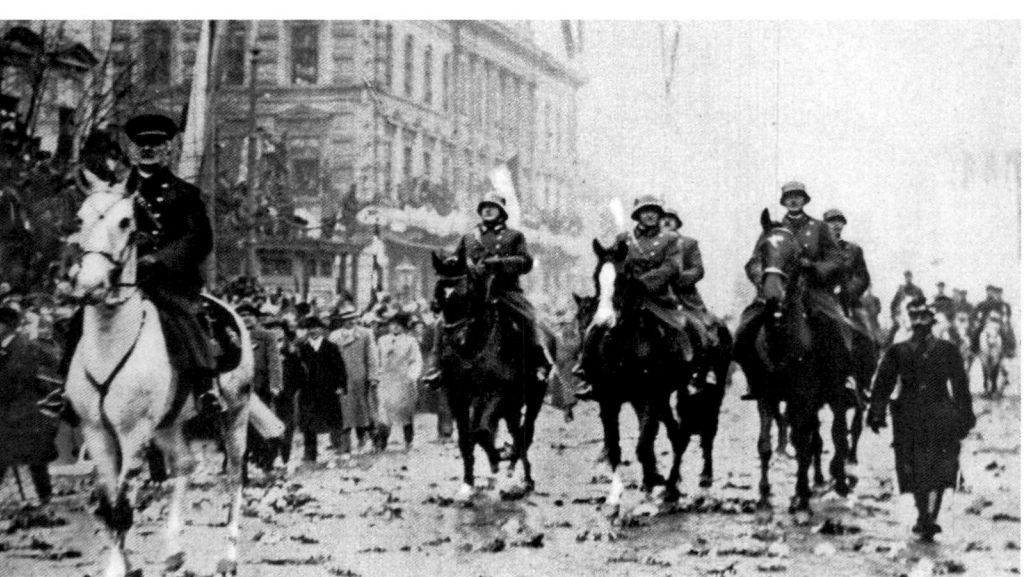

Miklos Horthy, who served as Regent of the Kingdom of Hungary between World War I and II.

emergence of another 'Red' state. Czechs and Romanians saw an opportunity to gain more territory and played quite willingly into the Allies' hands. They attacked Hungary in mid-April, but the Hungarians fought back – and much to everyone's surprise, they did so quite successfully.

Realising that their strategy of pitting the Romanians against the communists had failed, the Allies changed tack. The Hungarians were ordered to cease hostilities and the Romanians were told to return to their original positions east of the Tisza River. Kun accepted, but the Romanians dragged their heels, agreed to the settlement, and waited for the Hungarians to disarm. Kun decided to resume hostilities, but the attack which was launched on 20 July

⊘ BUDAPEST'S BOOM

After World War I, Budapest was bursting at the seams. Following the Treaty of Trianon, the capital had to cope with 325,000 refugees from the ceded areas, while the rural population had shrunk dramatically. With nearly one-eighth of the population now living in the capital, many in appalling conditions, Budapest's housing problems escalated and, as an emergency measure, thousands had to be housed in box railway cars. City officials tried desperately to raise funds abroad for housing projects and so ease social tensions. Between 1920 and 1941 there was a construction boom and the number of buildings in Budapest increased by 50 percent.

and socialists were imprisoned, tortured and executed without trial. Jews were also singled out for retribution as they were seen as a threat to the traditional Hungarian political order that the right-wing movement was seeking to establish. A wave of anti-Semitism swept through the land.

ADMIRAL WITHOUT A NAVY

It took a few months for some form of political stability to return. The Romanians were finally persuaded to leave the capital in November 1919

Terror that still raged in the countryside. The two parties with the most votes were the Independent Smallholders' Party with 40 percent and the Christian National Party with just over 35 percent.

The first issue that caused major dissension involved the status of the monarchy. The Legitimists believed Charles IV (Charles I of Habsburg) to be the rightful heir, while others insisted that a new ruler should be elected. Parliament annulled the Pragmatic Sanction of 1723 and the Compromise of 1867, but rather than elect

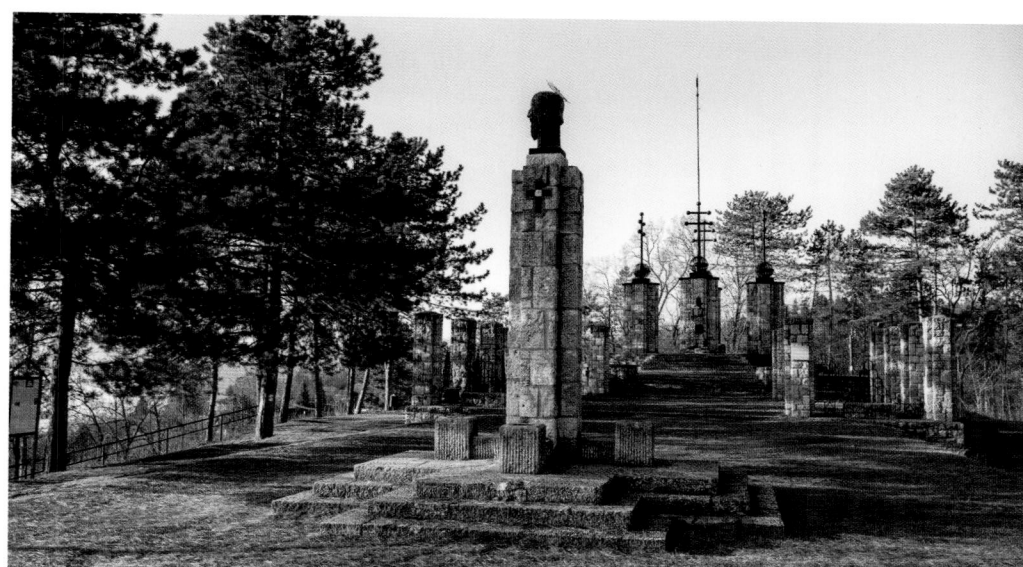

Trianon Memorial in Zebegény, marking the territorial losses forced on Hungary under the Treaty of Trianon.

after the interim Hungarian government (under Gyula Peidl) promised to set up a democratic system following the Western model, with elections by secret ballot. Admiral (a curious title in a country without a navy) Miklós Horthy had distinguished himself as a counter-revolutionary leader and now led an army of 25,000 into the capital, which the Romanians had thoroughly plundered. A new government was established under Károly Huszár to conduct the parliamentary elections.

Hungary's first free elections by secret ballot took place on 25 January 1920. Not all parties were represented; the Communist Party wasn't, of course, and the Social Democrats boycotted the event in protest at the White

a king they finally chose Horthy to be regent of Hungary. He took office on 1 March 1920 and was empowered to command the armed forces, dissolve parliament, veto laws and appoint the prime minister. He chose Pál Teleki to head his right-wing government.

Under the Treaty of Trianon, Hungary didn't just lose people: it was deprived of its outlet to the sea, the majority of its agricultural land, livestock, industry, railways, mineral reserves and forests

TREATY OF TRIANON

Meanwhile, a sword of Damocles was hanging over the nation's destiny. A delegation had been sent to the Paris Conference to see if anything could be salvaged from the wreck of World War I; it failed. On 4 June 1920, to the horror of the entire nation, delegates reluctantly signed the humiliating Treaty of Trianon. Overnight, Hungary's territory shrank by two-thirds from 283,000 sq km (109,270 sq miles) to 93,000 sq km (35,900 sq miles).

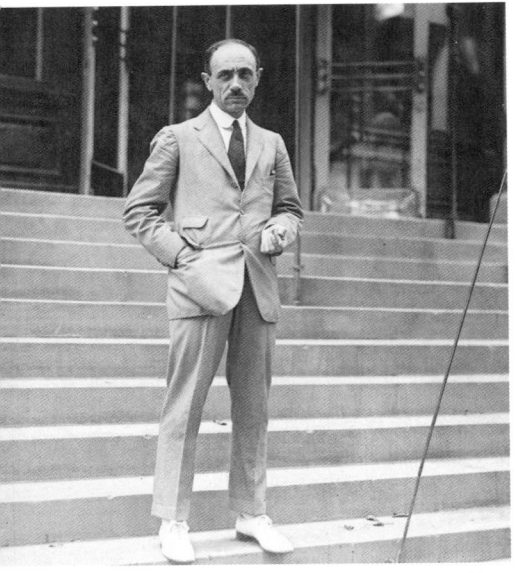

Pál Teleki, prime minister from 1920–21 and 1939–41.

The bulk of the land was ceded to Romania, including the quintessentially Hungarian Transylvania, which was the most devastating loss. (Today, the sovereignty of this region, which has a population of around 2 million Hungarians, is still a live political issue for nationalists and irridentists.)

Of its overall population of about 18 million before the war, post-Trianon Hungary lost approximately 3.4 million Maygars to Romania, Czechoslovakia and Yugoslavia.

To maintain internal order, the nation was allowed a militia of 35,000 men without heavy artillery. The economy was at rock bottom after the war. Frightened investors had hastily transferred their capital out of the country during the Kun months, and the Romanians had taken with them anything that could conceivably be removed. Although Trianon had cut off Hungary from its most important sources of raw materials, the Allies thought it necessary to exact reparations.

Hungarians between the wars had a single slogan to express their opinion of the treaty: *Nem, nem, soha!* (No, no, never!). As was the case with the Treaty of Versailles in Germany, revising a treaty perceived as grossly unjust became an *idée fixe* that helped to fuel the furnace of right-wing nationalism.

THE 1920S

Something had to be done about the economic and social situation. Soon after its assumption of power in July 1920, the cabinet of Pál Teleki introduced a string of land reform measures to mollify the discontented in rural areas. He took steps to break up some of the enormous holdings still in the hands of the old magnate families. On paper and in discussions these measures satisfied the Smallholders' Party, but in practice the reforms were modest and very little was achieved.

The complex issue of the monarchy flared up again in April 1921 when Charles IV, ousted the previous year, made a futile attempt to regain the throne. It precipitated a crisis that split the Christian National Party and led to a new coalition between Anti-Legitimists and Smallholders, called the Unity Party, under Count Bethlen. In October 1921, Charles IV gathered loyal army units and started a second campaign against Budapest. The Allies were not happy with this turn of events, and Horthy and Bethlen mobilised their forces, many from the ranks of the paramilitary organisation led by radical nationalist Gyula Gömbös, to expel the king. Their successful operation in Budaörs on 23 October 1921 finally ended Legitimist clamouring.

Count Bethlen, who led the country for the next decade, combined sagaciousness with political cynicism and a touch of ruthlessness. His aim was to cultivate the international community as a means of restoring Hungary's lost territory and gaining compensation for those Magyars who now found themselves in a foreign land. His success in handling the various factions on the right and left gave Hungary at least the appearance of stability. He struck deals with the Social Democrats to rein in worker and peasant rebelliousness, and some of their members returned from exile abroad. He abolished media censorship, but banned the Communist Party, and pacified members of the radical right, who still engaged in acts of White Terror. In September 1922, Hungary joined the League of Nations, and in the spring of 1924 it obtained from the League a loan of 250 million gulden, which effectively put the brakes on ever increasing inflation and restored investor confidence in the country. In 1927 a new currency, the pengö, was introduced to replace the heavily devalued crown.

With financial stability restored, Bethlen could maintain political stability. Labour unrest was put down with police force. Meanwhile, Gömbös was diligently rallying the forces of the right. His message had nationalist appeal, and was heavily peppered with racism and anti-Semitism. The fall in world wheat prices in 1929 and the financial crisis following the Wall Street Crash took their toll. Capital vanished and Hungary was once again insolvent. Discontent that had lain dormant now erupted. Bethlen chose to resign and, after the brief rule of Gyula Károlyi, Horthy appointed Gyula Gömbös in October 1932.

THE NAZI SPECTRE

The humiliation of the Trianon Treaty made Hungary an ideal candidate for Nazism. Gömbös, a conservative and a populist, dreamt of a Berlin-Budapest-Rome axis – he even coined the famous term – but at the time Mussolini and Hitler were not on friendly terms. The ebbing of the world economic crisis also took some of the wind out of his sails. Moreover, Horthy did not trust Gömbös' supporters, and refused to allow elections until April 1935.

Gömbös' Unity Party garnered over 43 percent of the vote, a comfortable majority. Later that year he visited Berlin, and returned convinced of the need to implement a system patterned on Nazi Germany. Gömbös died in October 1936, just a year before the Berlin-Rome pact, and before he was able to carry out his schemes.

By then, Hungary had already moved to the right and by extension towards Nazi Germany. Hitler courted the Hungarians by investing heavily in their industry and by providing a dumping ground for their agricultural products in the late 1930s. Hungary's rearmament programme depended on German products.

Successive Hungarian governments responded equivocally. There were Hungarians who sympathised with the way Germany had been treated by the Treaty of Versailles in 1919, and yet feared Hitler and his regime.

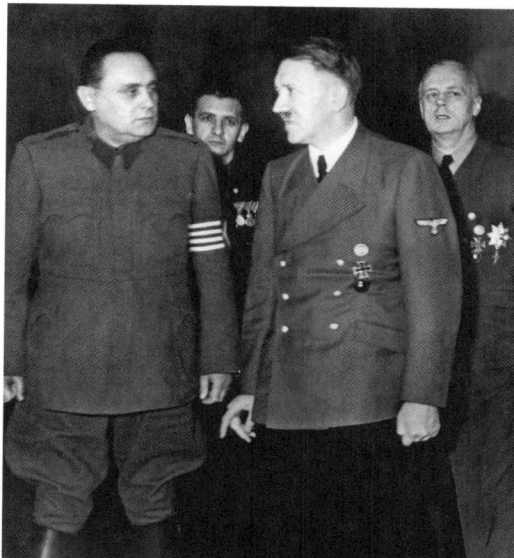

Adolf Hitler and the Hungarian leader Ferenc Szálasi.

Others, such as the members of the overtly Nazi Nyílas – the Arrow Cross Party – under Ferenc Szálasi, strove to implement Nazi rule in Hungary, including the repression of Jews and any other groups of those considered undesirables.

There were also many, ranging from Conservatives to Social Democrats, who had no love for Germany, but found her demonstrations of economic friendship attractive and believed that stronger ties with the German Reich might bring about some revision of the Treaty of Trianon. Thus, Hungarian governments in the late 1930s tried to lie in Hitler's bed without catching his fleas. Inevitably, such efforts were unsuccessful.

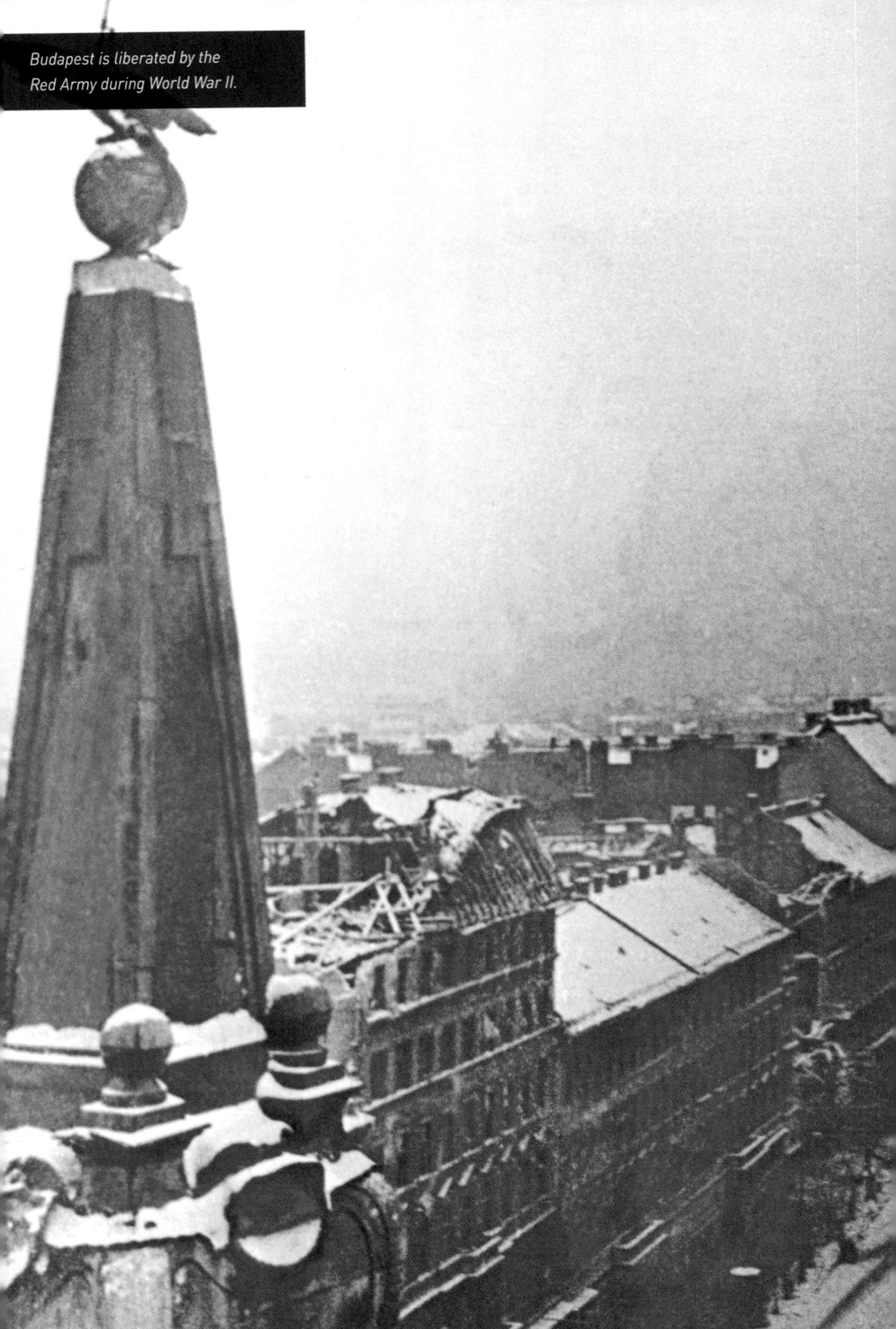

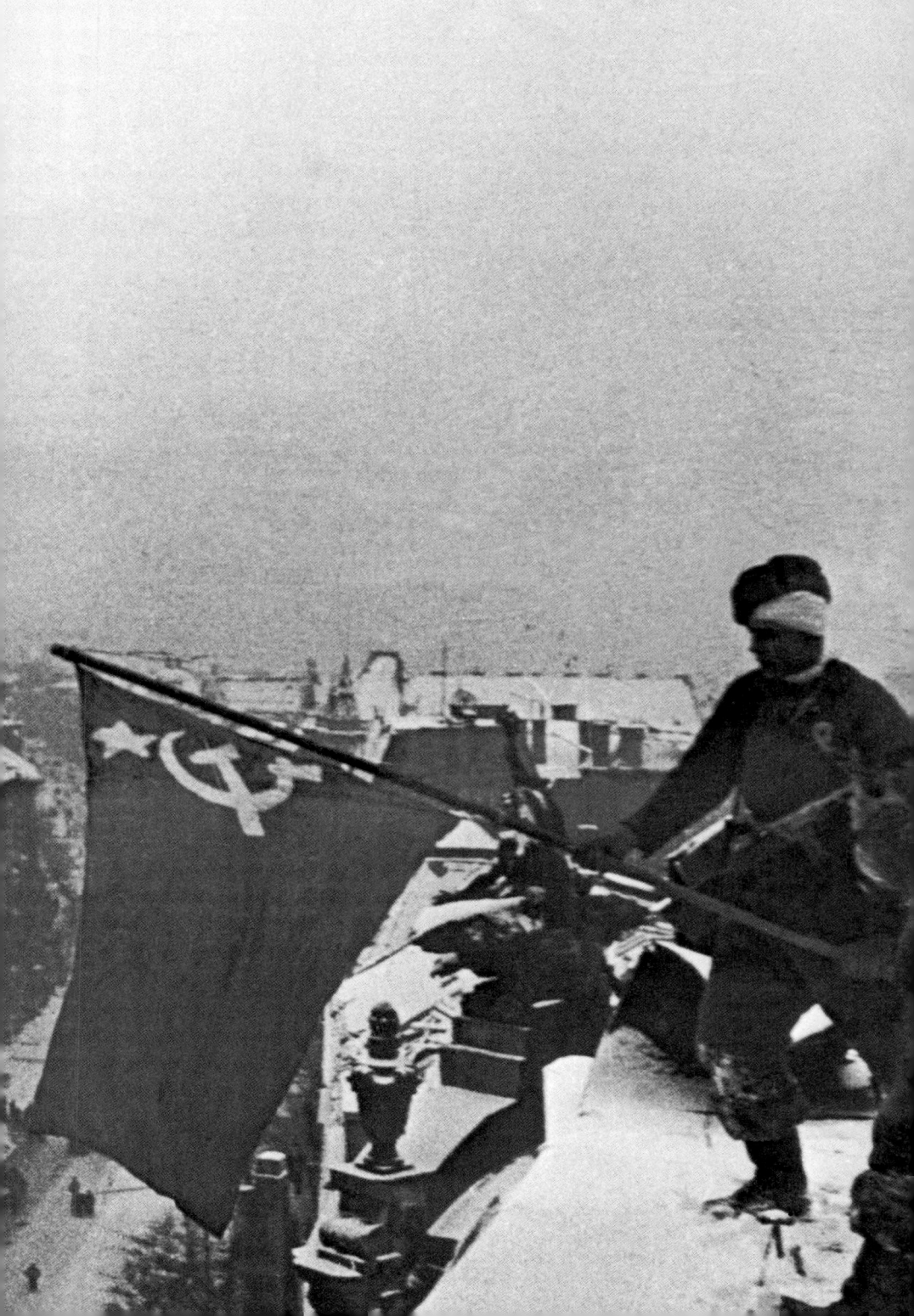

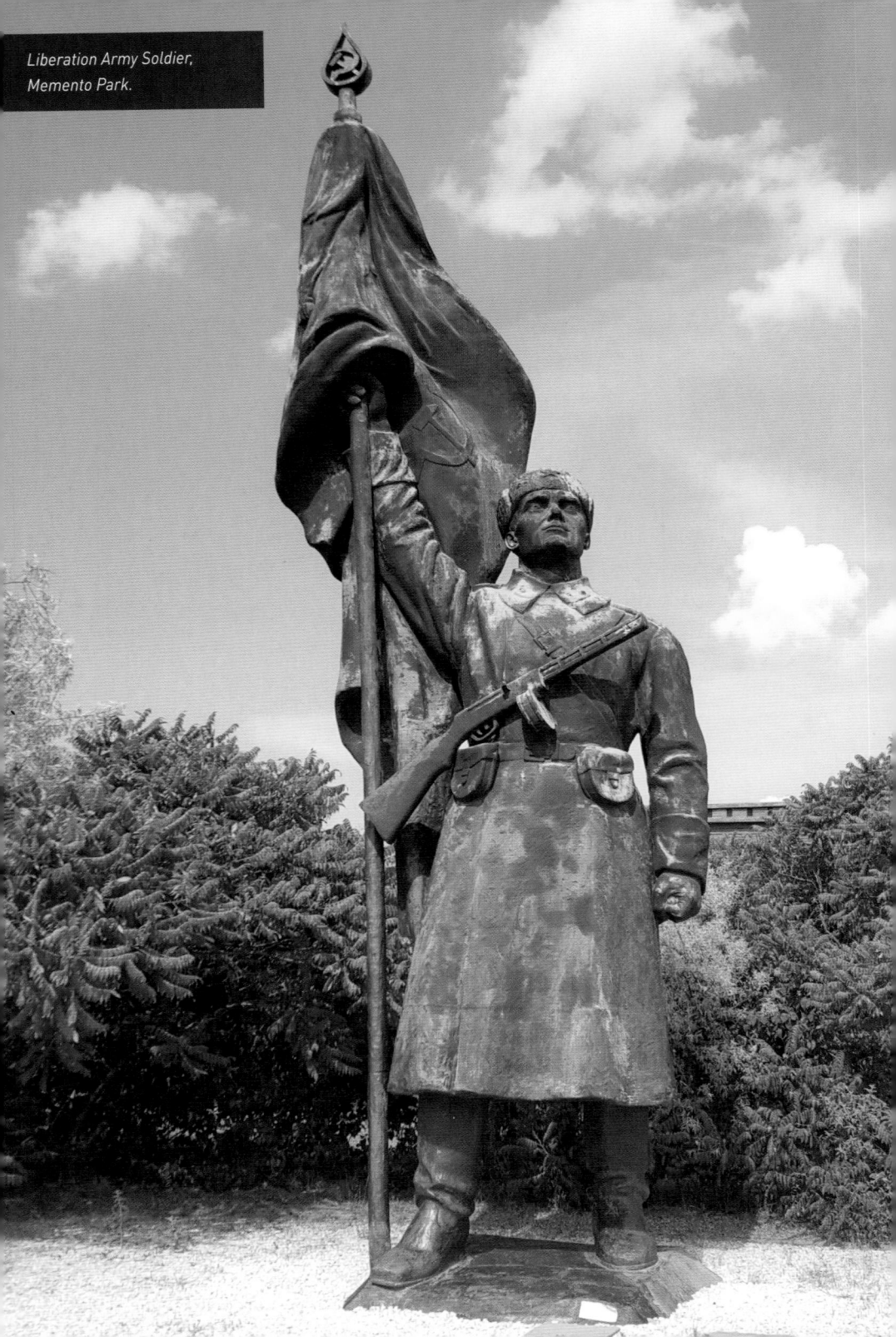

Liberation Army Soldier, Memento Park.

THE PEOPLE'S REPUBLIC AND A NEW DEMOCRACY

Modern Hungary survived reluctant involvement in World War II, Soviet domination and a bloody revolution, and is now coming to grips with democracy.

As World War II approached, Hungary's political situation grew ever more dangerous. The *Anschluss* (occupation of Austria) in March 1938 gave the German Reich and Hungary a shared border, and encouraged the Hungarian government to move politically closer to the Nazis. Under Béla Imrédy (who led the government after the deaths, in quick succession, of Gömbös and his replacement, Kálmán Darányi) a set of anti-Jewish laws was passed, in May 1938, aimed at demonstrating how well the country was adapting to fascism.

Simultaneous attempts to link up with Western democratic powers met with little success. A second set of anti-Jewish laws then came into being, in May 1939, although for the most part they were not enforced. In the elections of that year, the pro-fascist parties did well.

WAR BECOMES INEVITABLE

When Hitler attacked Poland on 1 September 1939, the Wehrmacht was banned from using Hungarian territory and entire Polish regiments sought refuge in Hungary. After Imrédy's forced resignation, the new prime minister, Pál Teleki, tried to keep Hungary out of the war, as a neutral position allowed for possible negotiations with the West. But involvement was inevitable. In November 1938, Hitler had returned to Hungary a large part of its former Slovakian lands. In 1940, he forced Romania to hand Transylvania back to Hungary.

The price was high: the German Army crossed Hungarian territory to occupy Romania. The pattern repeated itself with the invasion of Yugoslavia, only this time Hungary occupied Croatia and Britain threatened to declare war on Hungary. Teleki, seeing his carefully planned compromise collapse, committed suicide in April 1941.

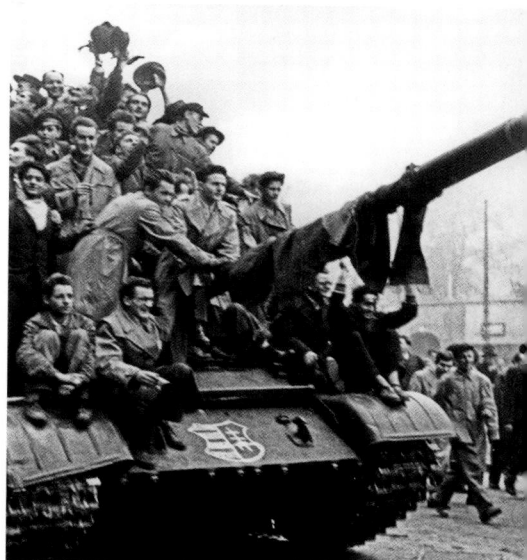

The October Revolution of 1956.

His successor, Lászlo Bárdossy, convinced that Germany could defeat the USSR and that a little commie-bashing would not offend the Western powers, sent a force into Russia to fight alongside the German armies. Britain finally declared war on Hungary in December 1941. A month later, Hitler called in old debts and demanded Hungary's total mobilisation. Horthy – who had acted as regent of the country since 1920, while other political leaders came and went – was still hoping to reach some agreement with the Western powers.

The relationship between Hungary and Nazi Germany was never one of trust, however, and in March 1944 (with or without Horthy's consent is unclear) Germany occupied Hungary. The prime minister, Miklós Kállay, who had presided over the virtual eradication of the Hungarian army near Stalingrad in January 1943, promised unconditional surrender to the Western powers if and when they reached Hungary. He was forced to resign and the Nazis were given free rein by the government of Döme Sztójay. Political parties were suppressed by the Gestapo (the communists had been banned decades earlier), and Jews were removed to concentration camps.

encircled Budapest. On 28 December, a provisional government, made up largely of exiled communists, was set up in Debrecen. On 11 February 1945, 16,000 Germans attempted a desperate sortie from the beleaguered capital. Only a handful managed to ward off the invaders. On 4 April, the last stragglers of the SS and Wehrmacht left Hungarian territory for Austria, destroying the bridges over the Danube as they left Budapest.

In the November elections that year, the Small-holders Party, comprising a motley col-

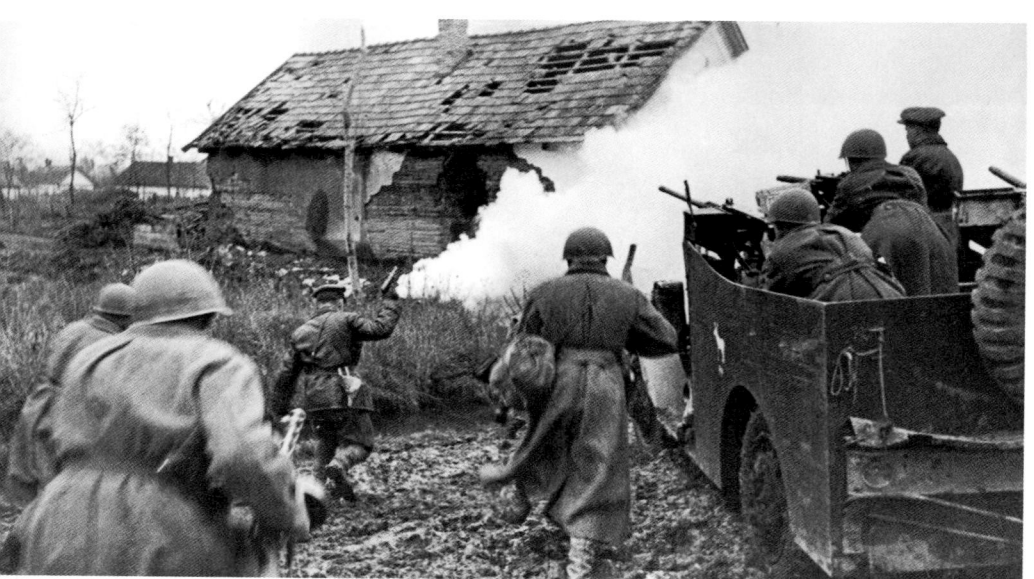

The Red Army approaches Budapest as World War II comes to an end in 1945.

THE RED ARMY MOVES IN

In August 1944, Romania fell to the advancing Red Army. Horthy decided that the time was ripe to make overtures to the USSR. In October he made a speech calling for an armistice and was promptly kidnapped by the Germans. On 15 October, Ferenc Szálasi and his brutal Nyílas (the pro-Nazi Arrow Cross Party) came to power. Efforts to deport Jews and other so-called undesirables intensified.

For the Hungarian right, the moment of glory came too late. On 6 October, the Red Army had begun its offensive to take Hungary. By 29 October, the vestiges of the German Third Army surrendered at Kecskemét. Gradually the Russians

lection of non-aligned politicians, gained an astounding victory, with 57 percent of the votes. The Social Democrats garnered 17.4 percent while the Communist Party came a close third with just 17 percent. Land reform laws were enacted and a degree of democracy prevailed – but not for long.

COMMUNIST CONSOLIDATION

The Soviet response to the communists' electoral defeat was to force the minority parties into a coalition, and to change the electoral rules. Their real strength relied on two main factors: first, they had the backing of the Red Army and the occupation infrastructure; second, László Rajk, an active communist since the early 1930s, was in charge of the Interior Ministry, which allowed him, with the help of the newly founded secret police force ÁVO (changed to ÁVH in 1949), to gnaw away at the opposition, using any means necessary. What is more, they ensured that all the most vital positions were occupied by loyal communists.

A republic was proclaimed on 1 February 1946. In the elections of 1947 absolute power was placed in the hands of Mátyás Rákosi, leader of the communist-dominated coalition

> *In the October Revolution of 1956, angry crowds in Budapest blow-torched the towering statue of Stalin off its feet and dragged it through the city streets.*

ECONOMIC REFORMS

In November 1946 the great Ganz iron works and Weiss steel mills were nationalised, followed in February 1948 by the bauxite mines

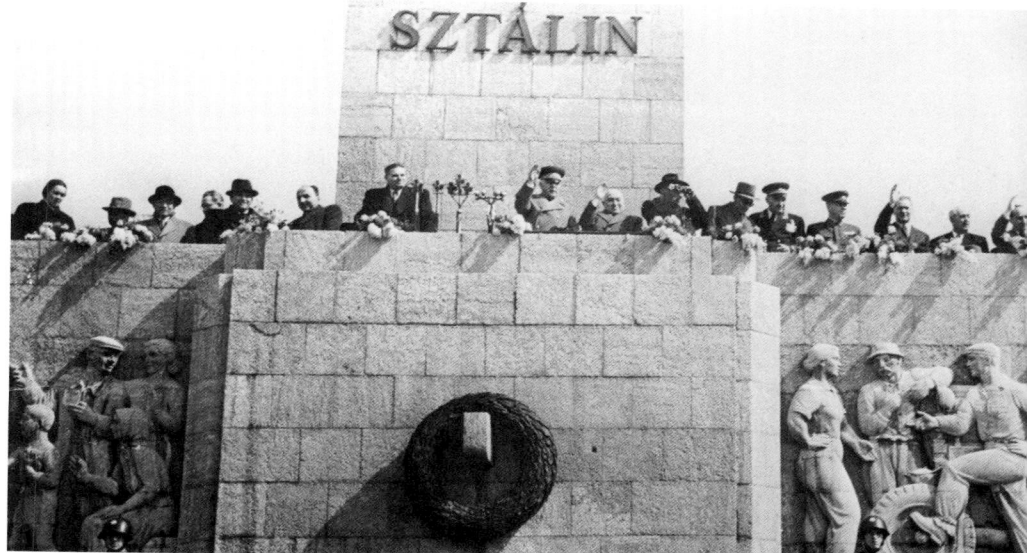

Communist officials watch a parade in a Budapest celebrating 10 years since the Red Army liberated Hungary.

called the Hungarian Workers' Party (Magyar Dolgozók Partjá).

The Paris Peace Treaty, in February 1947, reconfirmed the borders set by the Trianon Treaty, with a little more land removed in the west. Czechoslovakia demanded the expulsion of its 600,000-strong Hungarian minority; about 85,000 of them obeyed.

A strong centralised government was needed to restore the country's economic balance after the spectacular devaluation of the pengö. World War II had steamrollered over Hungary, destroying virtually everything in its wake. Over 500,000 Hungarians were killed in battle, and the retreating German army had confiscated or destroyed anything of value.

and the aluminium industry. In May the banks passed into the hands of the state. In August 1947 a three-year economic plan, concentrating on improving industrial productivity, was launched to put the country back on its feet. In 1948, a plan to collectivise the land was introduced. This widely unpopular scheme resulted in kulaks (peasants with some agricultural land of their own) being forced to join a cooperative, called the kolkhoz.

STALINIST PURGES

By the middle of 1949 the communist stranglehold over the country was complete. Even the powerful religious institutions, notably the Catholic Church, had been subdued, or so it seemed.

Cardinal József Mindszenty put up a vigorous resistance to the nationalisation of education, and was immediately jailed on patently concocted charges.

Mátyás Rákosi, who had spent a good deal of the Horthy years in Moscow, began consolidating the power of the Moscow wing of the party. The first sensational show trial of Hungarian communists – among them László Rajk – began with trumped-up charges of high treason and unlawful representation of imperialist powers. A combination of torture and dedication to his

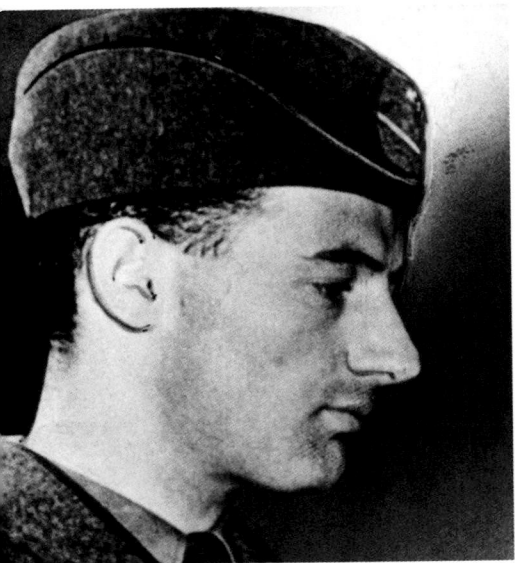

Raoul Wallenberg.

> *The Hungarian pengö set a world record for devaluation. When it was replaced by the forint in August 1945, one forint was worth 400,000 quadrillion pengös.*

party led Rajk to confess to these allegations. He was executed and buried in secret, but in 1956 his coffin was dug up and his bones carried to the Kerepesi cemetery to be laid alongside his colleagues, friend and foe alike.

Around 250,000 people attended the funeral procession on 6 October, 17 days before the revolution. His successor, János Kádár, was

> *Disillusion with the 'free' market economy and nostalgia for the security of the old regime returned the former Communist Party to government just four years after its downfall.*

imprisoned and tortured in 1951, under Rákosi's regime but was later rehabilitated.

Domestic purges continued well into the 1950s, removing party members who before the war had either been stationed in the West, in hiding in Hungary or even fighting Franco in Spain. The ÁVH had a network of informants that kept the state in touch with dissenters. Stalinist paranoia swept the country and prison doors yawned wide. Beneath the Stakhanovichian posters, behind the banners proclaiming the workers' paradise, discontent festered. Peasants were tired of being forced into collective farms; ideological schooling and ÁVH brutality were defeating the purpose of government. After many years of belt-tightening Hungarians were looking for some basic comforts. Consumer goods such as nylons and watches became hot black market items.

During the relative thaw that followed Stalin's death in 1953, the avuncular Imre Nagy took over from Rákosi. Nagy showed a certain willingness to redress the most obvious grievances and adopted a programme of reforms that included allowing peasants to leave the

⊙ A SWEDISH SAVIOUR

In Budapest in 1944, about 100,000 Jews were saved thanks to the intervention of the 32-year-old Swedish attaché, Raoul Wallenberg. This remarkable man was famous for his courageous intervention, in providing Swedish passports and safe houses to Jews who otherwise would not have survived. He disappeared in January 1945, shortly after the fall of Budapest. He is generally believed to have died in custody in the Soviet Union, although this has never been proven. Wallenberg lives on in the hearts of those he saved, and their descendants. A monument to him stands not far from Moszkva tér in Budapest.

kolkhoz. However, his rule did not last long. He was expelled from the party in 1955 and Rákosi returned to power untamed.

REVOLUTION

In July 1956, Khrushchev, who was wooing Yugoslavia, replaced the anti-Tito Rákosi with another unpleasant figure, Rákosi's second-in-command, Ernö Gerö. Earlier that year Khrushchev had denounced Stalinism in a long speech that shook communist parties around the world but apparently had little direct impact

Nagy, who seemed to hold so much promise, was made titular head of Hungary and its improvised revolution.

In an interview with the German journalist Hans-Henning Paetzke, published in 1986, the Hungarian writer Béla Szász summed up Imre Nagy, the man and the politician, whom he knew personally: "He was a friendly man with a great sense of moral responsibility. He wavered between solidarity with the party and solidarity with the people... By the end of the revolution, however, he had come to a firm decision. He saw

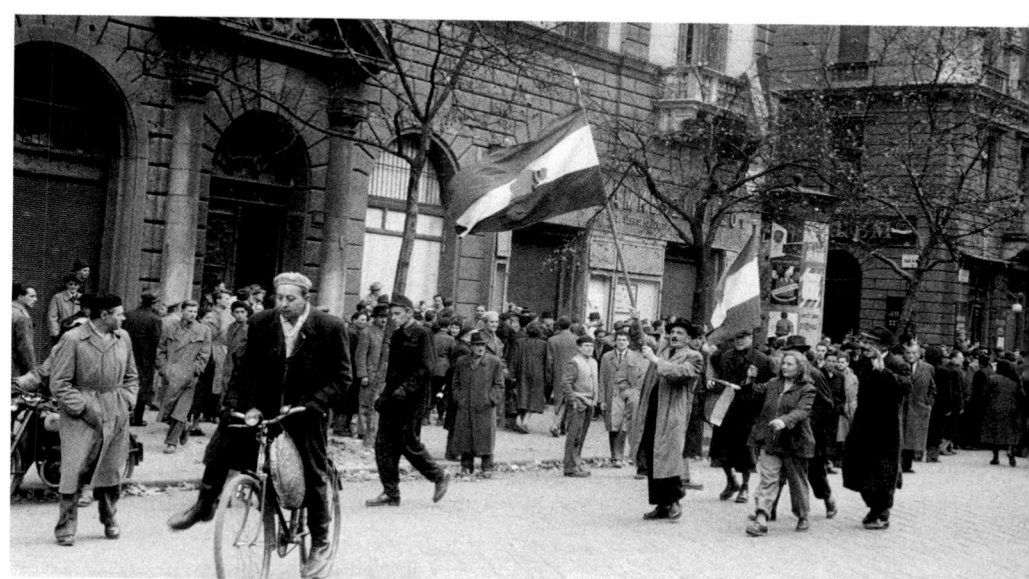

People take to the streets of Budapest during the October Revolution of 1956.

on the Hungarian leadership. On 23 October, a spontaneous demonstration consisting largely of students marched to parliament demanding reforms. Parliament prevaricated, then Gerö (overseas at the time) gave the orders for repression by force.

Two days later, revolution erupted throughout the country. All symbols of communist rule were violently removed from the capital, and the red stars were cut out of every Hungarian flag. Even the soldiers refused to quell the revolution and switched sides. Many members of the ÁVH were executed.

Political prisoners, among them Cardinal Mindszenty, were freed. Old and new political parties crawled out of the woodwork. Imre

himself as the representative of the will of the people and put himself on their side, taking full responsibility for all the consequences." Nagy probably knew that the personal consequences would be tragic.

The decision of Pál Maléter, Defence Minister and leader of the National Guard, to side with the rebellion gave the Soviet Union an excuse to invade, claiming Hungary was illegally breaking away from the Warsaw Pact. The obliteration of the revolution by Soviet tank divisions took only a few days. The cost in human lives was estimated at around 3,000, although the exact number of executions remains a mystery. Thousands were sent to prison; almost 200,000 people fled the country.

Nagy, who had been holed up in the Yugoslav embassy, was promised safe conduct, but was arrested and executed in 1958.

THE KÁDÁR YEARS

The yes-man chosen to lead the country after 1956 was János Kádár, who had been imprisoned by his adversary, Rákosi. Having been hand-picked by the Kremlin, his arrival amid the diesel fumes of the departing Soviet tanks made him suspect from the start. Purges and deportations continued, and Kádár appeased

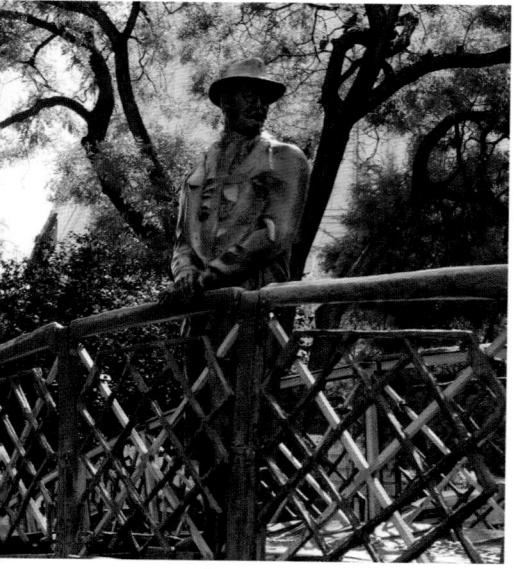

Statue of Imre Nagy in Budapest.

the USSR by faithfully conforming to every one of its foreign policy moves.

At the same time, Kádár pushed for better relations with the Western powers and formed close ties with Austria, under Chancellor Bruno Kreisky. The boost achieved through trade, tourism and industrialisation helped raise the standard of living. In 1977, aiming for reconciliation with the strong Roman Catholic community, Kádár paid a visit to Pope Paul VI. This policy of rapprochement spared Hungary the sharp conflicts between Church and State that characterised other Eastern bloc countries, although it was condemned by Cardinal Mindszenty, who, until 1971, refused to leave the US Embassy where he had taken refuge after the 1956 revolution.

Economically Kádár at first stayed on the old course, pushing through renewed collectivisation and trying to increase industrial production. Poor harvests and an exodus from agricultural work drained Hungary's hard currency reserves. The 1960s were austere years, but Kádár did at least give hope in 1962 with his famous quote: "He who is not against us is with us" – effectively suggesting that he gave some credence to the revolutionaries' claims.

MARKET SOCIALISM

The New Economic Mechanism (1968) allowed for some private sector work and gave various state-run operations a considerable degree of autonomy. Tangible results, rather than political kow-towing, became the determining factor of success. Allowing farmers a certain leeway in the private sector improved food distribution. The soaring price of oil and other raw materials in the 1970s fuelled inflation but, in comparison with other Eastern bloc nations, Hungary fared quite well.

The experiment with market socialism ultimately did not pay off. The country's foreign debt leapt to 18 billion dollars, and while a few people were able to buy Western consumer goods, the final price was unemployment and growing poverty.

AN END IN SIGHT

With glasnost and perestroika loosening up regimes all over the Eastern bloc, Hungary was able to push through reforms unthinkable a few years before. In June 1988, a large demonstration in solidarity with the Transylvanian Hungarians received official sanction. A year later, Imre Nagy and his associates were reburied in Plot 301 of the Kozma Street cemetery, where they had been hastily thrown after their executions. The ceremony was a media event attended by 300,000 people and organised by opposition groups. In September of the same year, the Hungarians opened their borders to let out a throng of East German refugees, precipitating the downfall of the East Berlin Party Secretary Erich Honecker later that autumn.

By the time of the first free elections for 55 years, in spring 1990, several new and prewar parties had emerged. The winner in this tight contest was the centre-right Hungarian

Democratic Forum (MDF), a new party whose ranks included a broad spectrum of conservative forces. (These internal tensions gradually led to its division into several small parties.)

Prime Minister József Antall's coalition government steered a course towards Europe and a market economy. The transition was painful. Inflation climbed to 30 percent and unemployment soared as communist-era industries and agriculture were privatised.

In 1994, the Hungarian Socialist Party (the old Communist Party) was reelected and ran an effi-

democracy, with an orderly change of governments all committed to pushing through the economic reforms required to 'bring the country back into Europe'.

THE WAY AHEAD

Democracy and capitalism have not provided Hungarians (or indeed many of their neighbours) with a quick fix to their political or socioeconomic woes. Since the early 1990s, foreign investors have pumped money into the economy, but little of that investment seems to have trick-

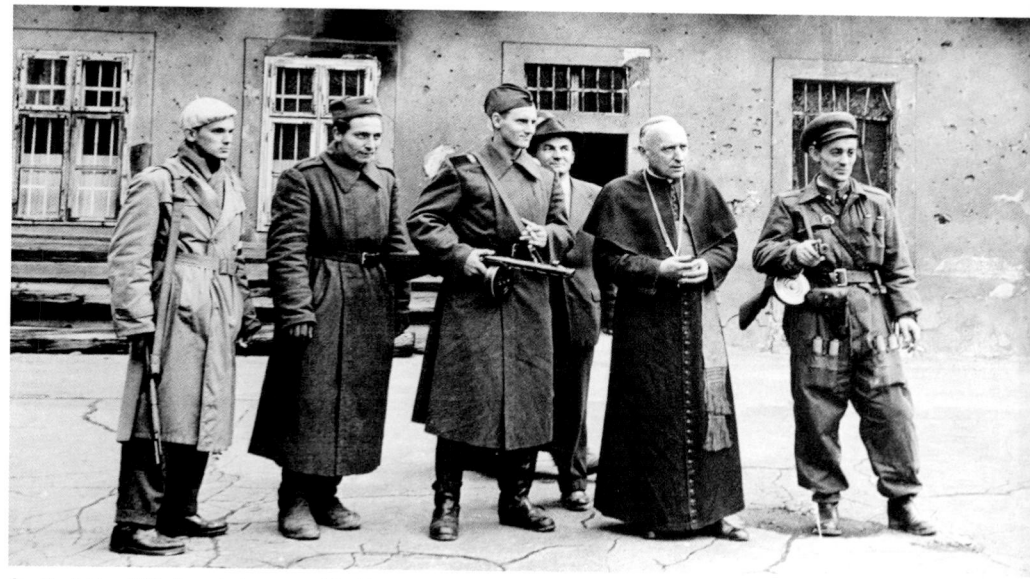

Cardinal József Mindszenty is escorted by his armed liberators in 1956.

cient administration in coalition with the liberal Alliance of Free Democrats (SZDSZ), and continued the necessary economic reforms, allowing the country to continue its recovery from 50 years of communist mismanagement.

In spite of promising economic signs, a slower inflation rate and a general improvement in living conditions, the Socialists were voted out in 1998. Power went to a coalition that included the centre-right Federation of Young Democrats-Hungarian Civic Party (FIDESZ-MPP); the remnants of the Hungarian Demoratic Forum (MDF) and the agricultural-based Independent Smallholders' Party (FKGP).

Since the collapse of communism, Hungary has taken the route of a normal parliamentary

led down as far as the average Hungarian. Even joining the European Union must seem a mixed blessing so far. While there is an emerging middle class, many Hungarians now face considerably higher costs of living, and wages have failed to keep up. Homelessness is on the rise, evident especially in areas like Budapest's seventh and eighth districts. The corruption and culture of backhanders that were so much part of the old system are still prevalent at all levels of business and administration.

But Hungarians are a canny, adaptable and clever nation, and most people still believe, albeit grudgingly in some instances, that by staying the course, they are on track towards a normal, prosperous European existence.

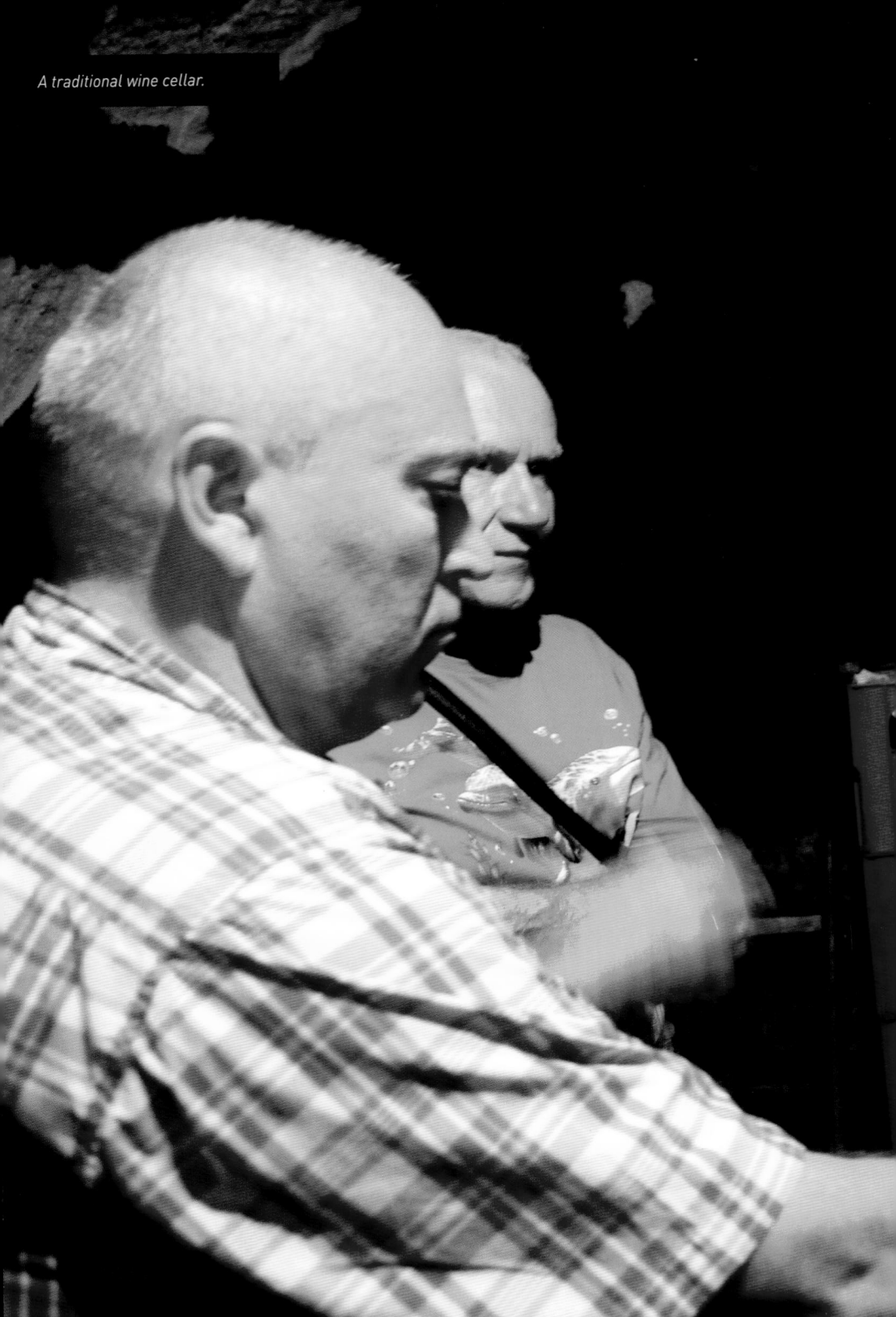

A traditional wine cellar.

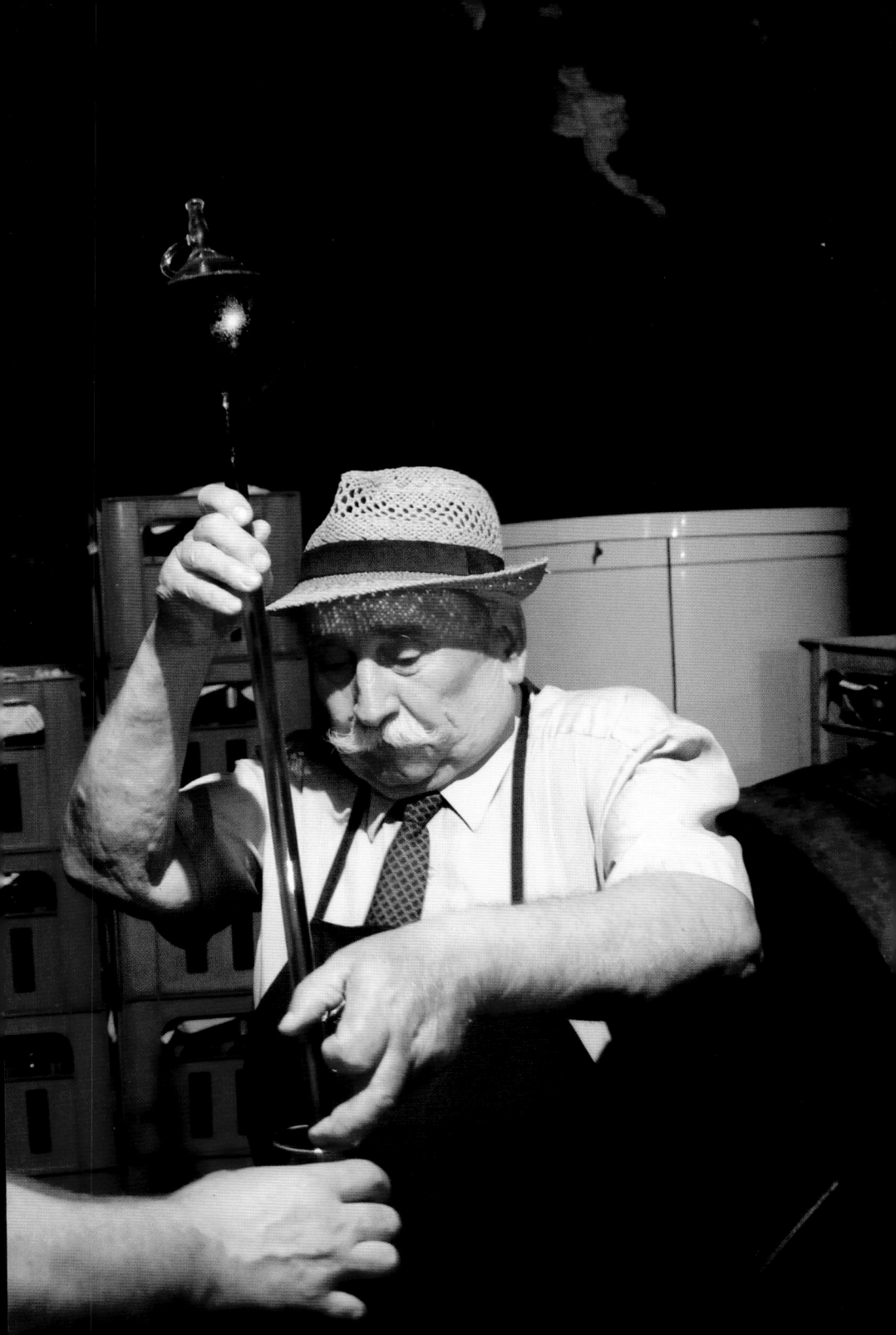

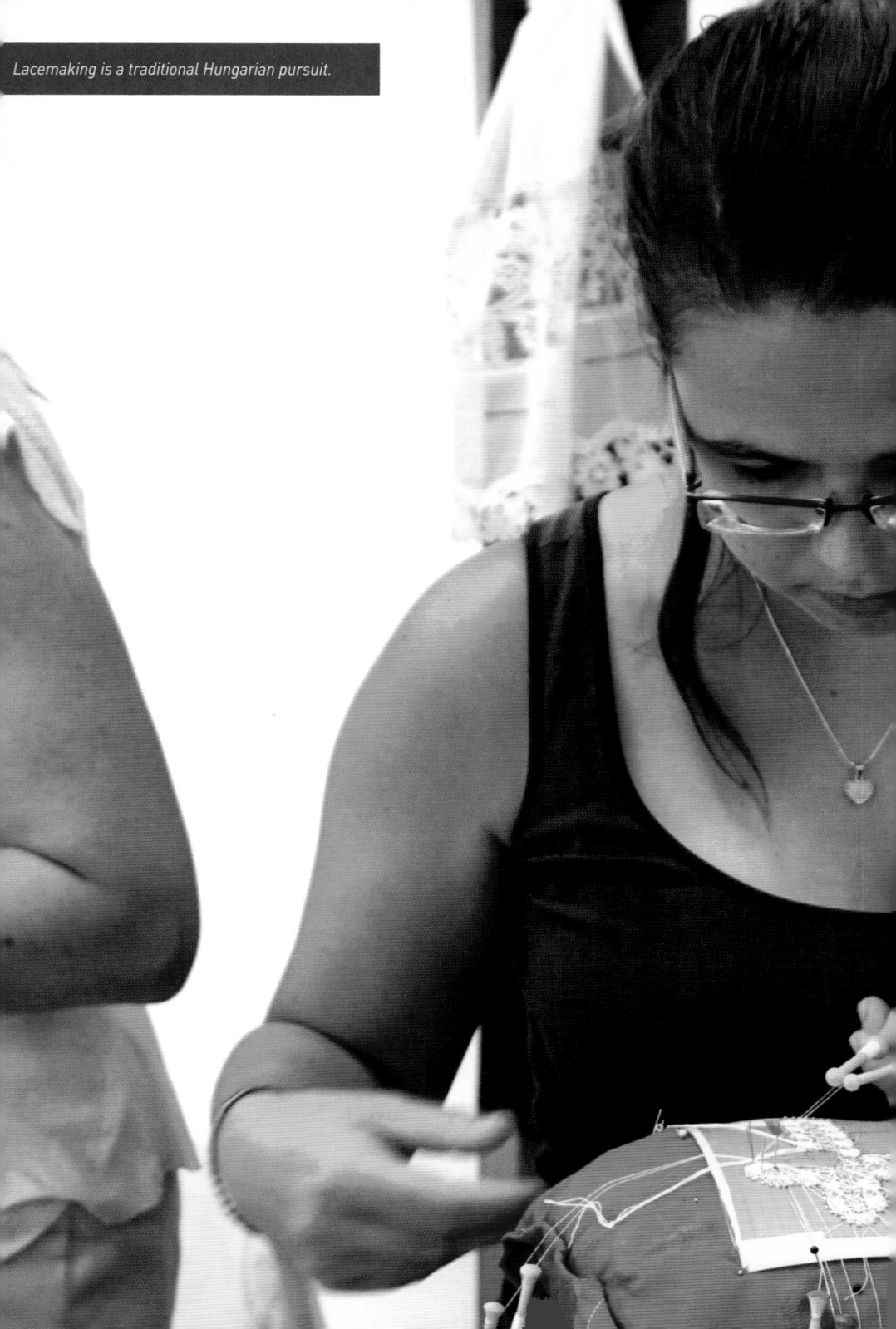

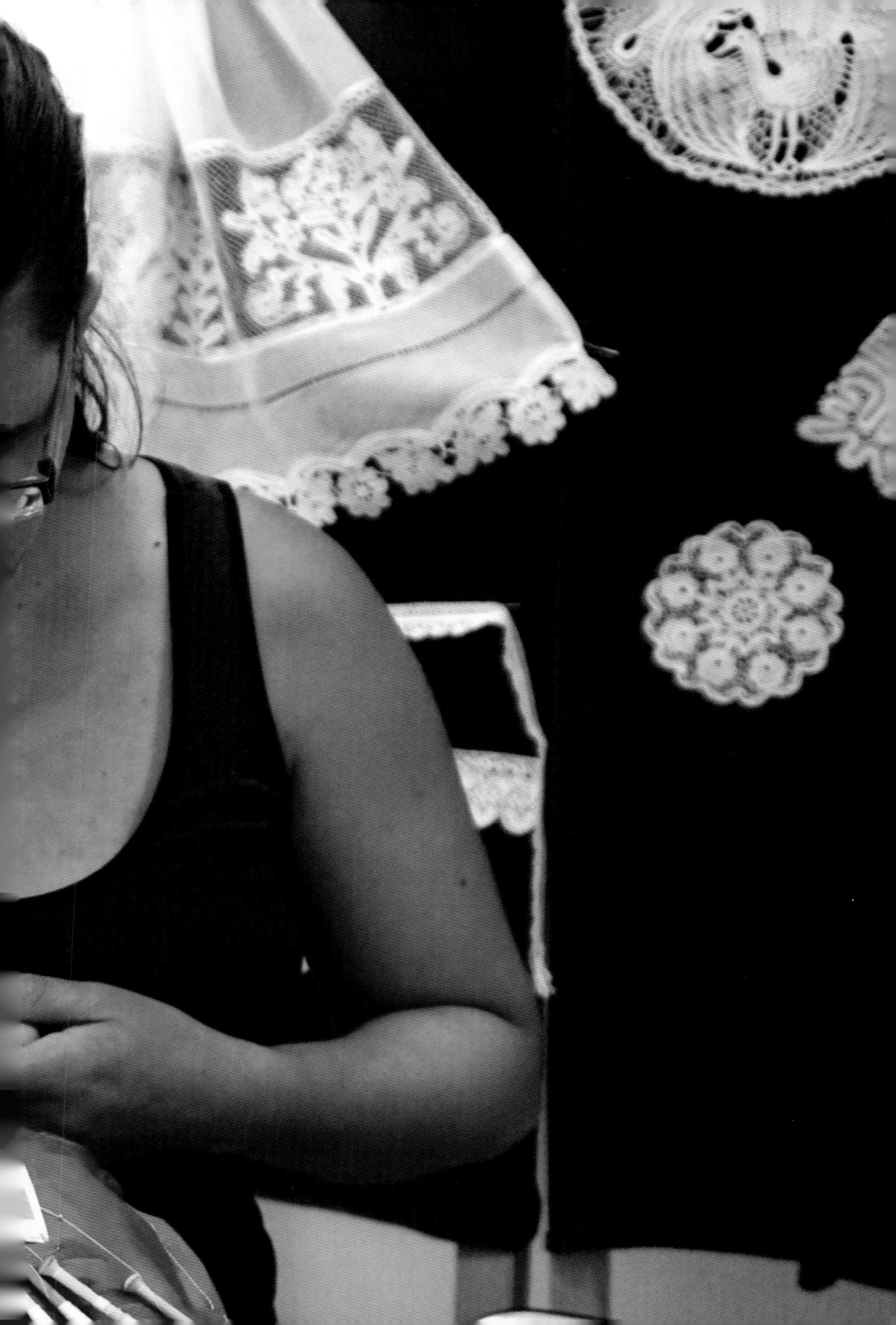

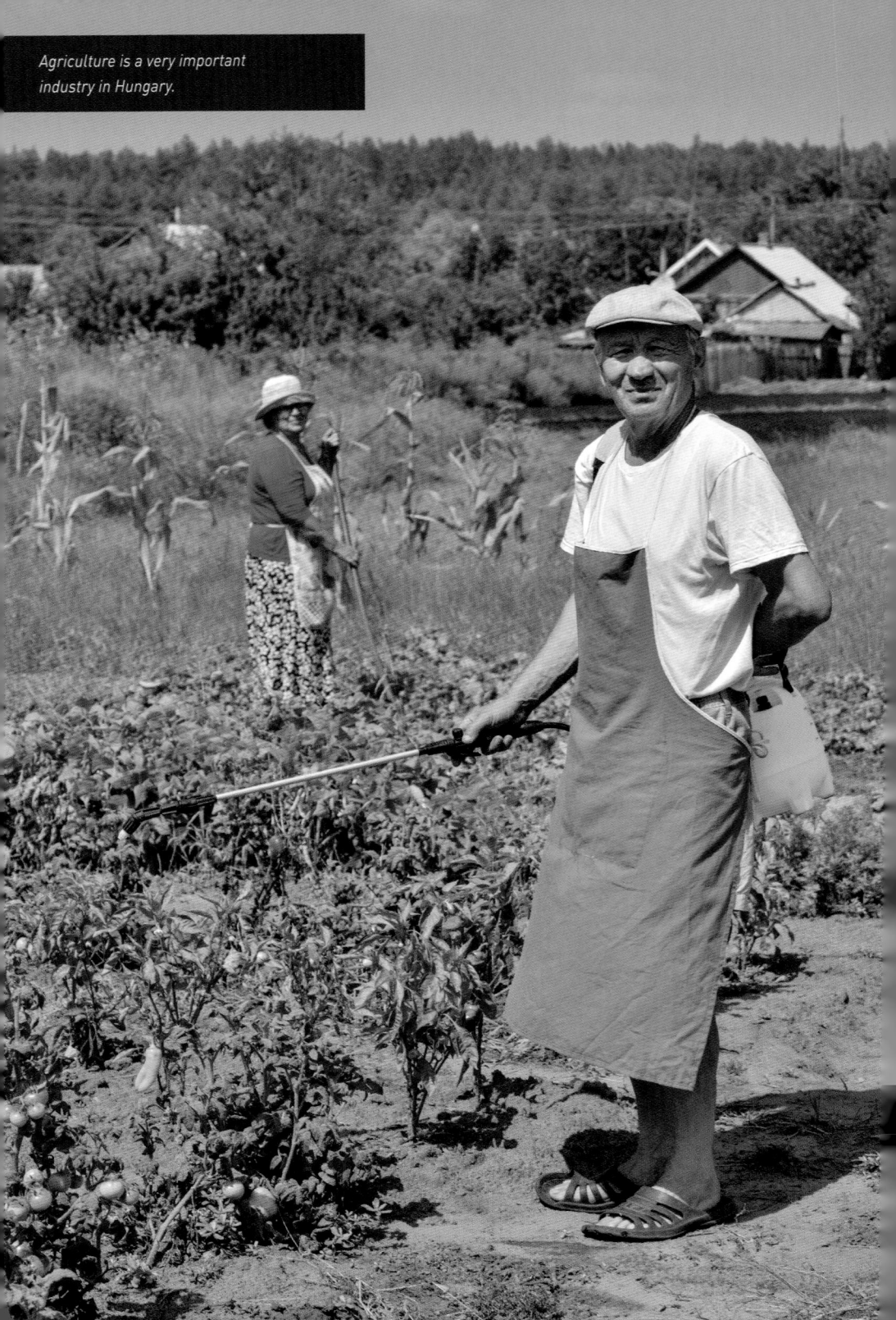

THE PEOPLES OF HUNGARY

Hungary has invited foreigners to settle since the times of St Stephen. Today it is home to Slavs, Germans, Romanians and many others.

What sort of people are the Hungarians? Warring nomadic tribes from the steppes of Northern Asia, extrovert Southern Europeans, mysterious people from the Far East? Are they a people broken by the merciless blows of history, or a people who have proved themselves again and again?

The Hungarian philosopher Béla Hamvas wrote that the Hungarian people comprise five archetypes corresponding to the five geographical regions: the eastern Great Plain, the northern provinces (including Slovakia), western Transdanubia, the south – crossroads of many different civilisations – and finally the former principality of Transylvania, now part of Romania.

DIFFERENT LIFESTYLES

Hamvas believes the ancient Hungarian character is best preserved in the east. Here some people's lives are half nomadic and half settled. Their characters are determined by passion, a desire for freedom, a revolt against anything foreign, vanity, pride, indifference to religion and a concentration on the present.

A provincial lifestyle is dominant in the north, in a culture that remains close to nature. Social ties are loose, and the people tend to be melancholy and impractical.

The west, however, is the home of practicality, civilisation, reason and the everyday work ethic. A stable social order, loyalty, the desire for knowledge and an active life have left their marks on the Transdanubian people, whose lifestyle is strongly influenced by the Western European ideals of progress.

The more contemplative people of the south of Hungary are characterised by their easy-going, peaceful and balanced attitude, together with a great capacity to enjoy life. These people are survivors, who took almost no part in the

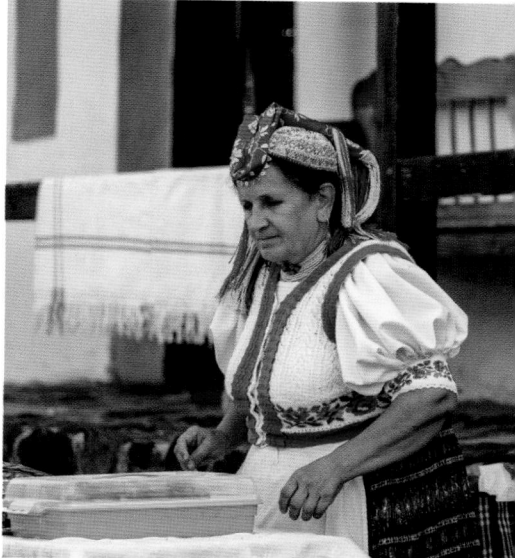

At the Thanksgiving Festival in Hollókő.

country's historic struggles, which they simply allowed to pass them by.

Most of the Hungarians who exemplify the fifth type now are, of course, citizens of a different state. Except for four years during World War II, Transylvania has been part of Romania since the end of World War I. The fifth type is therefore represented within today's Hungary only by those who left Romania.

For 80 years, Transylvanian Magyars have been quitting their mountain homes for the Hungarian plains, fleeing from varying degrees of ethnic, economic and political discrimination. The spiritual baggage they carried with them from their homeland of forests and valleys is shown in their often absurdist humour, with its complexity, wry ambivalence and deeply etched paradoxes. Their experience is one of a history rich in compromises and in rebirth. They have a practical outlook, a high expectation of life, good taste and, when necessary, great cunning.

LEGENDARY HOSPITALITY

Language differences are never great enough to prevent Hungarians from opposite corners of the country understanding one another. Difficulties arise only in making themselves understood by foreigners who don't speak Hungarian. But when

Hungarian tolerance has been put to the test since 1990. Asylum-seekers from Asian countries heading for Western Europe, but failing to cross the border into Austria, are applying for political asylum here. Chinese businesses are mushrooming all over the country, bringing non-Europeans in some of the largest numbers seen since the Magyar conquest.

SLOVENES AND SOUTHERN SLAVS

The smallest – and oldest – ethnic minority consists of the Slovenes (Vend in Hungarian). The con-

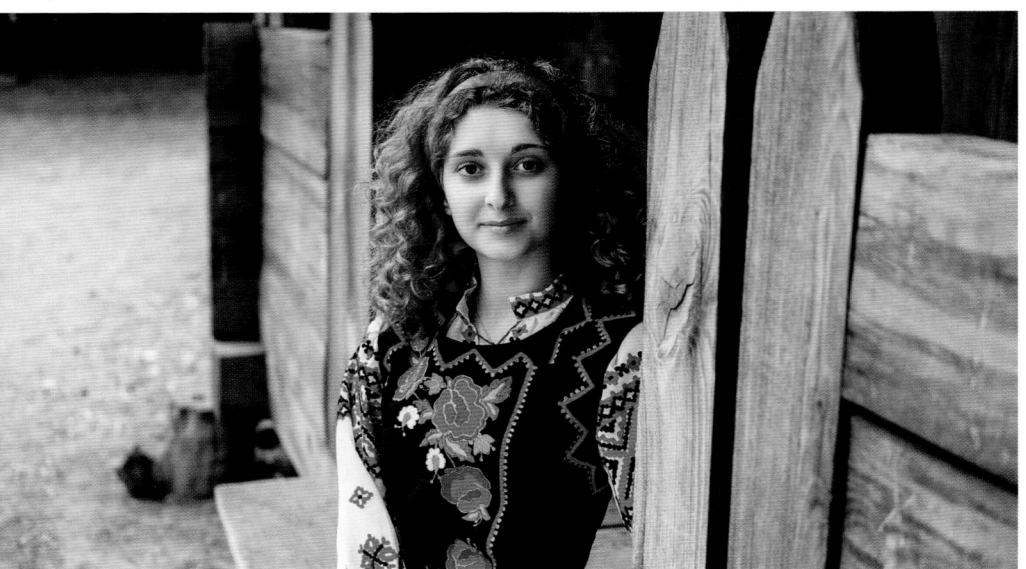

A young woman wearing a traditional embroidered costume.

language fails, the legendary hospitality springs into action. Like most clichés, this one is based on fact. Hungary has never been a country closed to foreigners. Ever since the Magyar conquest, foreign visitors – known in those times as hospes – have been welcome to settle in the country. Paragraph VI of the Exhortations of King István (Stephen) I to his son Imre shows that great value was placed on hospitality towards strangers in the Middle Ages: 'Guests and immigrants are so useful that they well deserve their position as the sixth element of royal dignity. For a country with only one language is weak and easily broken.' Sound advice, that has not always been heeded by Hungarian politicians in later centuries – and particularly not in the mid-20th century.

quering Magyars found an independent Slovenian kingdom in southwestern Transdanubia. Its capital was Mosapurc, probably in the region of modern Zalavár. The original population has not lost its identity, despite being ruled by outsiders for the

Almost 90 percent of Hungary's population is ethnic-Hungarian, but within its borders live 13 ethnic groups: German, Slovak, Romanian, Croat, Serb, Slovenian, Bulgarian, Greek, Ruthenian, Ukrainian, Armenian, Polish as well as Gypsy, or Roma, peoples.

past 1,000 years, probably because of the isolated peasant society in which it has lived for centuries.

The Slovenes were Christians before the coming of the Magyars and spoke a Slavic language. Within the borders of modern Hungary, between the Mura and Rába rivers, there are now nine Slovenian villages with a total population of about 5,000. The Slovenian language is taught in the primary schools of these villages.

A larger grouping is the Southern Slavs, with a population of around 200,000, comprising several ethnic groups. Apart from Slovenes, there are

The Schokats acquired their name because, unlike the Serbs, they cross themselves using the whole palm of the hand (saka means palm of the hand).

are diligent in encouraging the survival of their mother tongue.

Industrialisation and urbanisation have brought about a high degree of assimilation into the Hun-

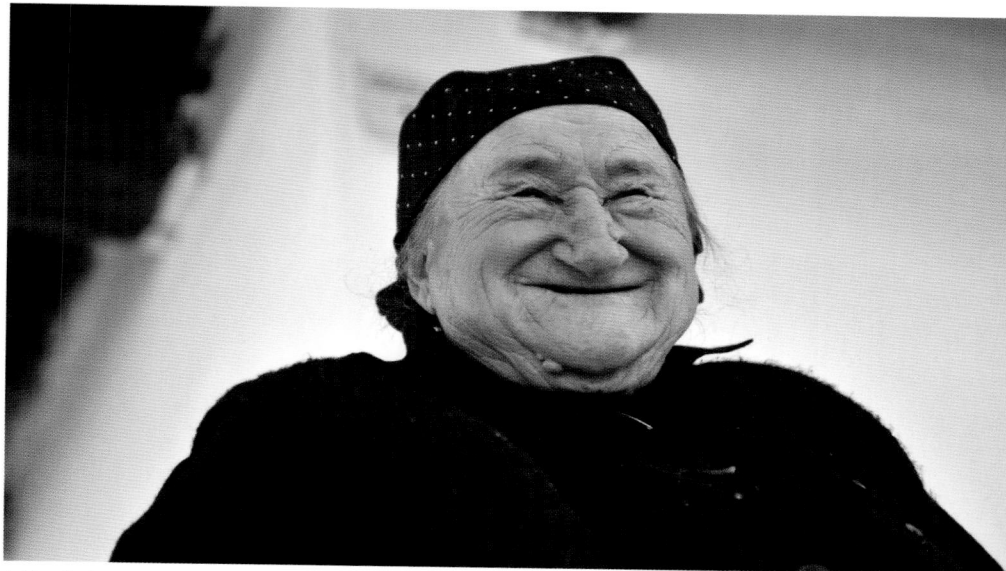

A friendly face.

Serbs, Schokats, Bosnians and Croats, who make up 90 percent of Southern Slavs. Most of them live in the south of the country along the borders with Slovenia, Croatia and Serbia, but you can find Serbian villages along the Danube, even north of Budapest. These settlements date front the time of Turkish expansion and were founded by refugees from the Turkish dominions who came to Hungary in 1690. Szentendre is one example.

While the Serbs live in scattered settlements, the Croat population is largely concentrated on the banks of the Dráva. The Schokats and Bosnians live mainly in the county of Baranya along the Croatian border. The Serbs and Croats are bilingual – as are almost all members of the ethnic minorities, except the very young – and

garian population, and yet the largest number of people who proudly assert their ethnicity belong to this Southern Slav group. There are several reasons for this. One is the proximity and contact with other members of this ethnic group outside Hungary. Many a family gave refuge to friends and relations from across the border during the wars in the former Yugoslavia in the 1990s. Indeed, this influx was a shot in the arm for a community losing its young people to life in the big cities. Another reason is the language classes in both primary and secondary schools and the Serbian and Croatian programmes on the local Hungarian radio stations. Furthermore, the Southern Slavs have always been loyal inhabitants of Hungary, without the burden of collective guilt.

THE GERMANS

The same cannot be said of the largest ethnic minority in Hungary – some 230,000 people – the Germans. Here you cannot help but notice a loss of language and of culture which, despite all the efforts of government and ethnic councils, may be too late to reverse. Over 1,000 years, Germans entered Hungary at different times, from different places and in different numbers. They therefore form a minority that has no economic, political or cultural unity, and have a high degree of assimilation.

of Tolna, Baranya and Somogy were known as Swabian Turkey, and this is where most Germans live today.

A German middle class had been slowly moving into towns almost since the time of the conquest. As a result, the bourgeoisie who lived in the cities of Hungary during the middle of the 19th century were predominantly Germans. They were subject to a continuous process of assimilation, but village communities remained generally intact until the end of World War II.

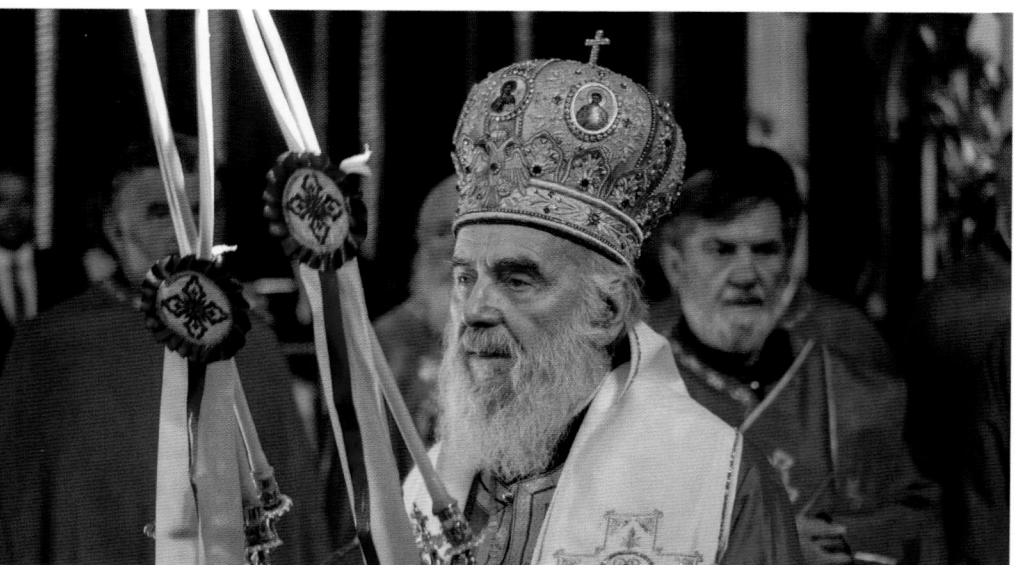

Irinej Gavrilovic, Patriarch of the Serbian Orthodox Church.

PRESERVING CULTURES

The first major wave of German immigration came during the reign of King András II in the 13th century. Most settled in Transylvania and won privileges from the king that allowed them to preserve their culture until well into the 20th century. However, in the mid-1970s they were forced, by the rigorous 'Romanisation' policy of the Ceaușescu regime, to move to Germany.

Germans also came to live in Hungary after the Turks were driven out in the 18th century, arriving with the so-called 'Swabian trains'. The Habsburg emperors settled them in the areas of southwest Hungary that had been devastated by the Turks, in Batshka and Banat. The counties

Ⓞ SLOVAKS

Some 100,000 Slovaks in the northern counties live mostly in villages of mixed ethnic population. Like the Slovenes, they are in a way the original inhabitants of these areas, since Slovakia was part of the Kingdom of Hungary until World War I. The ethnic line between Hungarians and Slovaks cannot be clearly defined. Within modern Slovakia reside about half a million Hungarians, many of them victims of compulsory exchanges of population under the communists. Others dwell in the Békés area of southeast Hungary near the Romanian border, most of them in the town of Méhkerék and the outlying villages.

One-third of the 15 million-strong 'Hungarian nation' lives outside Hungary. Some of them still argue passionately for the restoration of Hungary's pre-1920 boundaries.

A COMMUNITY DIVIDED

The great split within the German population of Hungary came about in the years between the two world wars, and was partly the result of racial ideas

In the autumn of 1942, about 40 percent of Germans were members of the Volksbund, and the number of sympathisers was probably much higher. The German Reich had been recruiting soldiers from among the Hungarian Germans since the beginning of the war, first secretly, then officially. In May 1943, recruitment was sanctioned even among those liable for military service in the Hungarian army. After the Germans entered Hungary on 19 March 1944 all ethnic Germans between the ages of 17 and 62 were obliged to fulfill their military service in the German army.

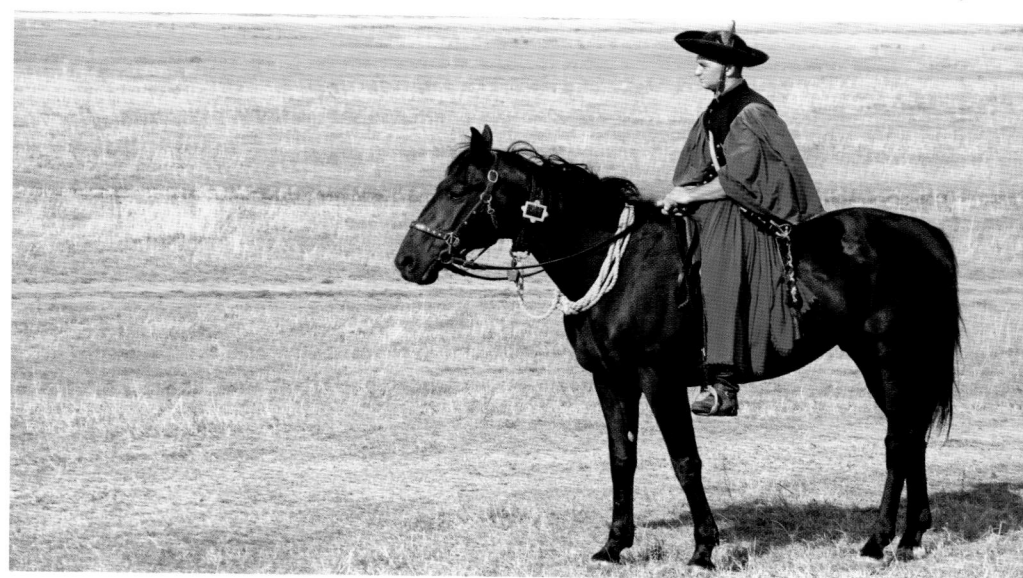

Csikós horse-herdsman near Hortobágy.

imported from Germany. Developments in Germany caused great confusion among the Hungarian Germans. In 1933, Jakob Bleyer, one of the leading figures of the German minority, prophesied: 'What is happening now to the German people is either our last chance of salvation or our final ruin.'

In November 1938, the *Volksbund der Deutschen in Ungarn* (People's Federation of Germans in Hungary) split off from the *Ungarländischer Deutscher Volksbildungsverein* (Hungarian Society for German Culture). The former was a fifth column for the German national *Volksbund für das Deutschtum im Ausland* (People's Federation for German Culture Abroad). The Volksbund spread Nazi propaganda among the rural populace, with considerable success.

Between 1946 and 1948, large numbers of Germans were labelled as war criminals and deported. Those who remained adopted the Hungarian language, both to obey the law and as a means of self-defence. The use of German rapidly declined as a result. Final restoration of full civil rights did not take place until March 1950. However, complete rehabilitation could not be achieved by bureaucratic measures alone, and was hindered by the absence of cultural or political organisations that could have helped the Germans to reaffirm their deeply scarred ethnic identity. Many years would be needed to heal the wounds of the war years.

Since 1990, many German businesses have come to Hungary and with them have come

German managers. Many of those exiled after the war retired to Hungary, while their children and grandchildren are buying holiday homes or even resettling here. They form a growing expatriate community, with its own German-language weekly newspaper – the *Pester Lloyd* (www.pesterlloyd.net).

After English, German is the most popular foreign language taught in Hungarian schools, but community leaders must still work to revive old traditions in the face of widespread assimilation into mainstream Hungarian culture.

ASSIMILATION VERSUS ISOLATION

According to research carried out in 1997–98 by Anne Kende and Eszter Szilassy, assimilation is, for many members of the ethnic minorities, a double-edged sword. It can be the means to secure social and economic equality, and it can also spell the death of their culture.

The communist regime, in its grim pursuit of industrialisation and centralisation, did a very thorough job of eroding cultural identity, which had no place in its ideology. The advent of democracy raised issues that had been smoth-

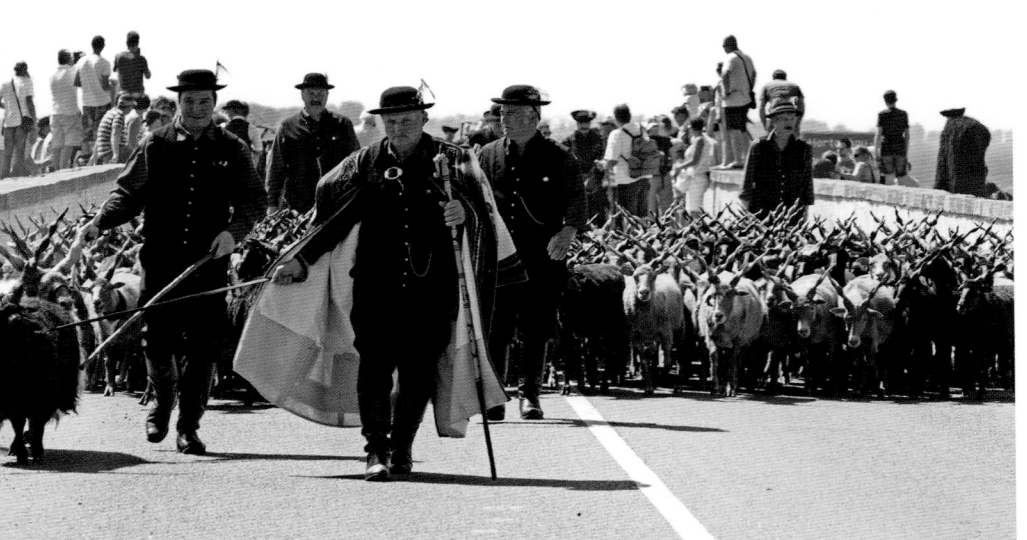

Shepherds and their sheep cross Hungary's famous nine-arched stone bridge, near Debrecen.

MAKING LIFE EASIER

Today, any town or village with a minority group may elect its own ethnic council to deal with any issues specific to it. Since 1979, bilingual signs have been displayed in those Hungarian villages in which at least one-third of the population belongs to an ethnic minority, and the language of the minority can be used in all government departments. In practice, however, these measures are not always fully implemented, partly because of the hostile attitude of some local officials, but partly also because the Serbs, Germans and Slovaks can all speak fluent Hungarian and, indeed, expect to do so when dealing with officialdom.

ered for decades and, in response, parliament passed the Minority Law in 1993 and created the Office for National and Ethnic Minorities in Hungary (http://archiv.meh.hu). But greater political opportunities have brought both benefits and disadvantages.

Generally speaking, the smaller groups (for example Polish, Ukrainian and Armenian) perceive assimiliation as a natural and positive process. The larger minorities, particularly the German and Slovak communities, see the Western ideals of modernisation and prosperity as a direct threat to their language and way of life.

Parents want their children to have a better life than they did, which seems to translate as going to the disco rather than the folk dance and speaking Hungarian rather than their mother tongue, even at home. For many, the sheer pace of change in the post-communist world is alarming: they fear that their language and culture, after surviving in a foreign land for hundreds of years, will be virtually extinct in a matter of decades.

While acknowledging that they are now free to claim their rights as equal citizens, Hungary's minorities know that they must fight a continual battle to keep their culture alive.

The 300,000 Hungarians of Serbia live in the northern region of Voivodina, represented by the Alliance of the Voivodina Hungarians.

The 150,000 Hungarians living in the Ukraine have been suffering more from the dire economic situation than from discrimination, and many of them have chosen to move to Hungary.

In December 2004, a referendum was held to decide whether the government should allow Hungarians living abroad to hold dual citizenship. The proposal was greeted with enthusiasm by ethnic Hungarians in Central Europe as

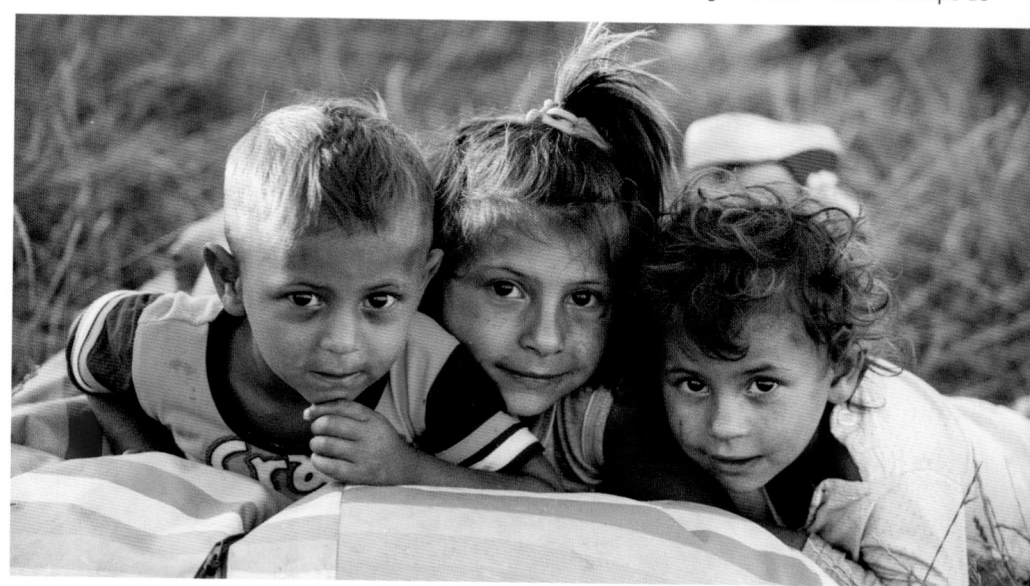

Children of Hungary's Roma community.

HUNGARIAN MINORITIES

The third group of Hungarians are those living outside Hungary – an estimated 2.4 million, most of whom are in Romania. The Democratic Alliance of Hungarians in Romania represents about 6.6 percent of the country's population and has become a desirable coalition partner, wooed by other Romanian political parties, and has used this leverage to achieve better rights for its members.

The democratic changes of the 1990s also brought an improvement in the human rights situation of the 560,000-strong Hungarian minority in Slovakia, where the Party of Hungarian Coalition has played a similarly influential role to that of its sister party in Romania.

it would allow them to live in Hungary and hence within the EU. The governments of the states in which they live opposed the idea, perceiving it, amongst other things, as a chance for Budapest to influence their internal affairs.

Within Hungary, Prime Minister Guyrcsány argued that the potential influx of people would place a huge burden on the social security system – a view which contributed to the proposal's defeat, which was hailed (by some) as a victory of forward-thinking over dwelling on the past. Nevertheless, the episode reveals the unresolved ethnic tensions within the region that could erupt if expectations raised by westernisation and EU membership are not met.

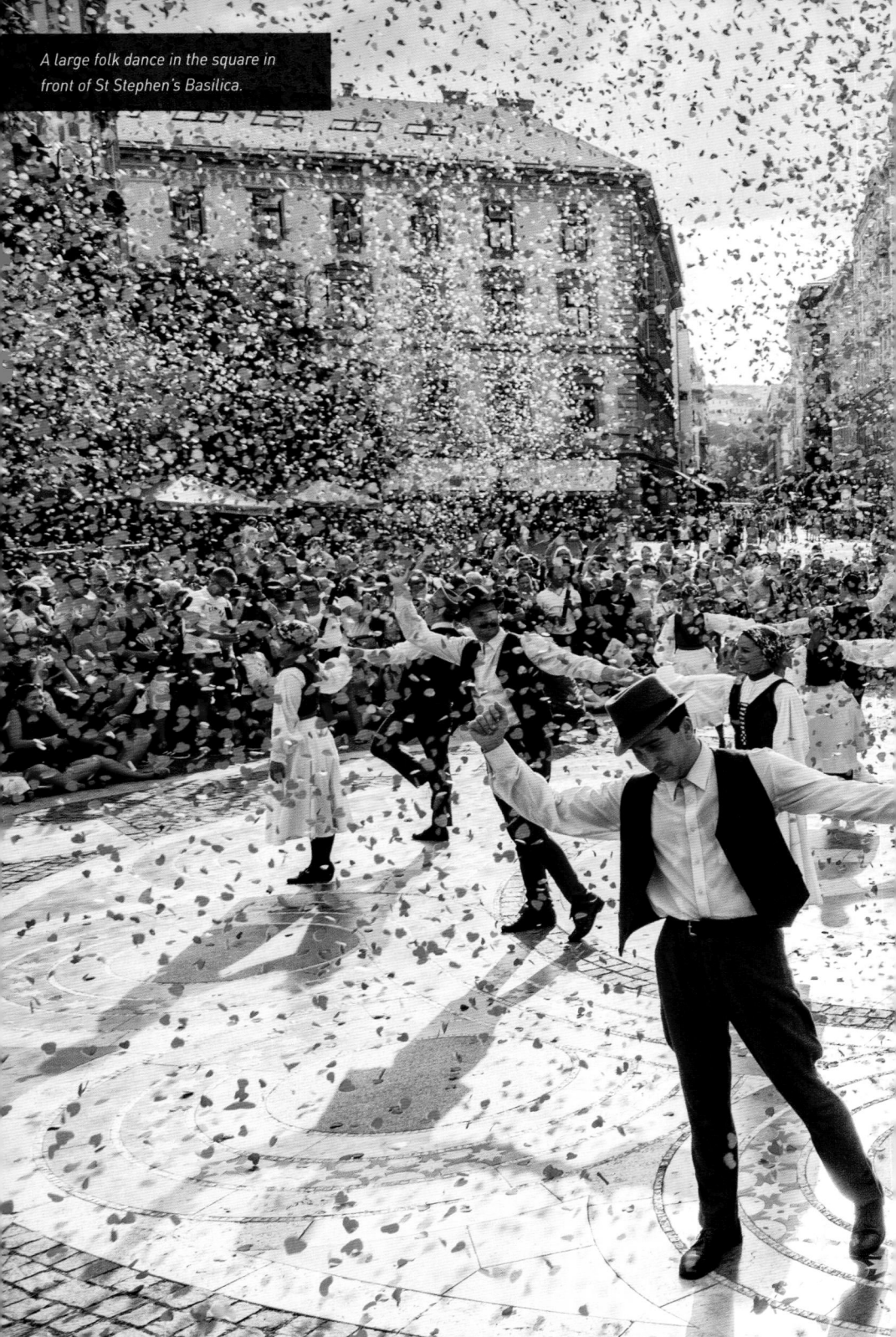

A large folk dance in the square in front of St Stephen's Basilica.

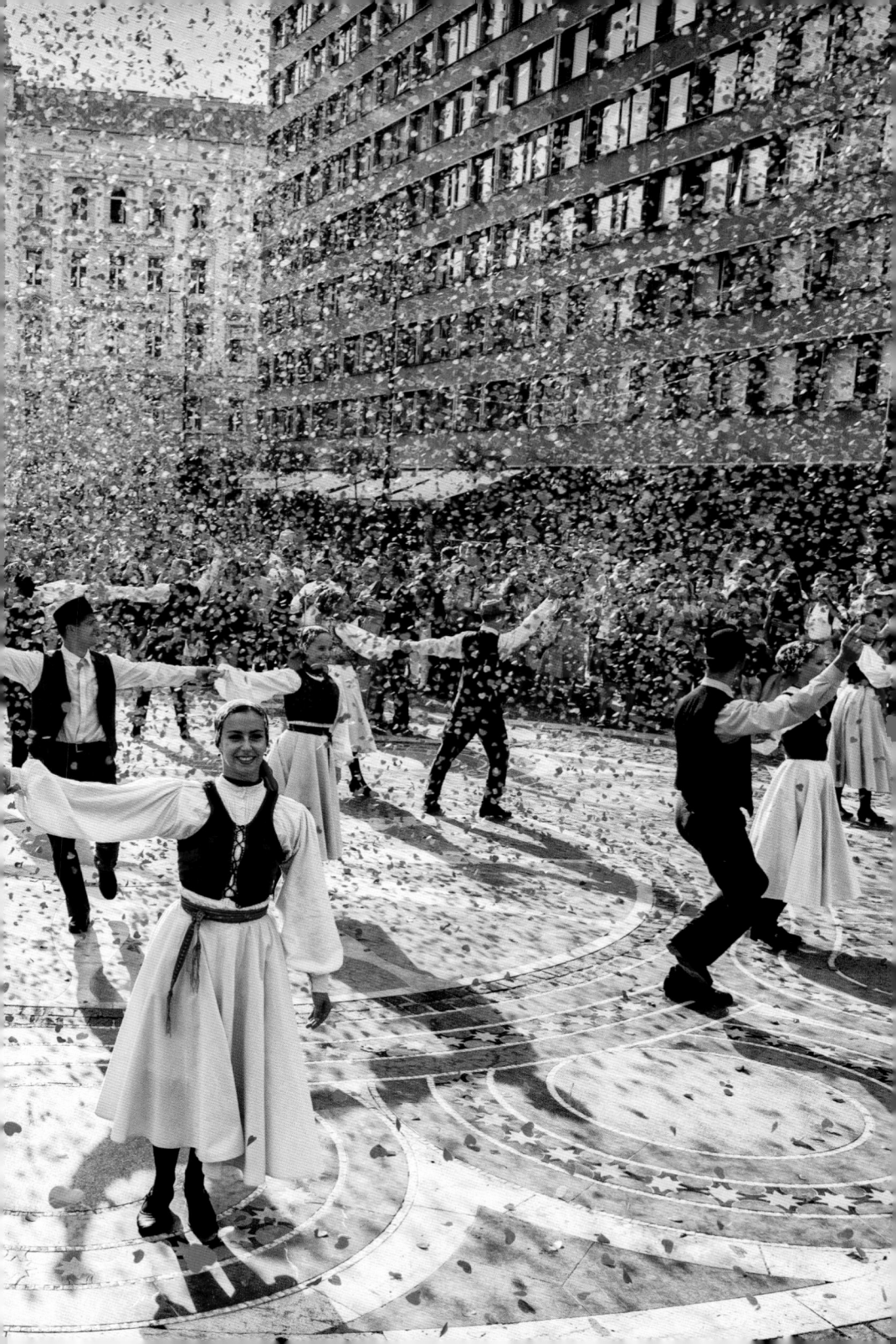

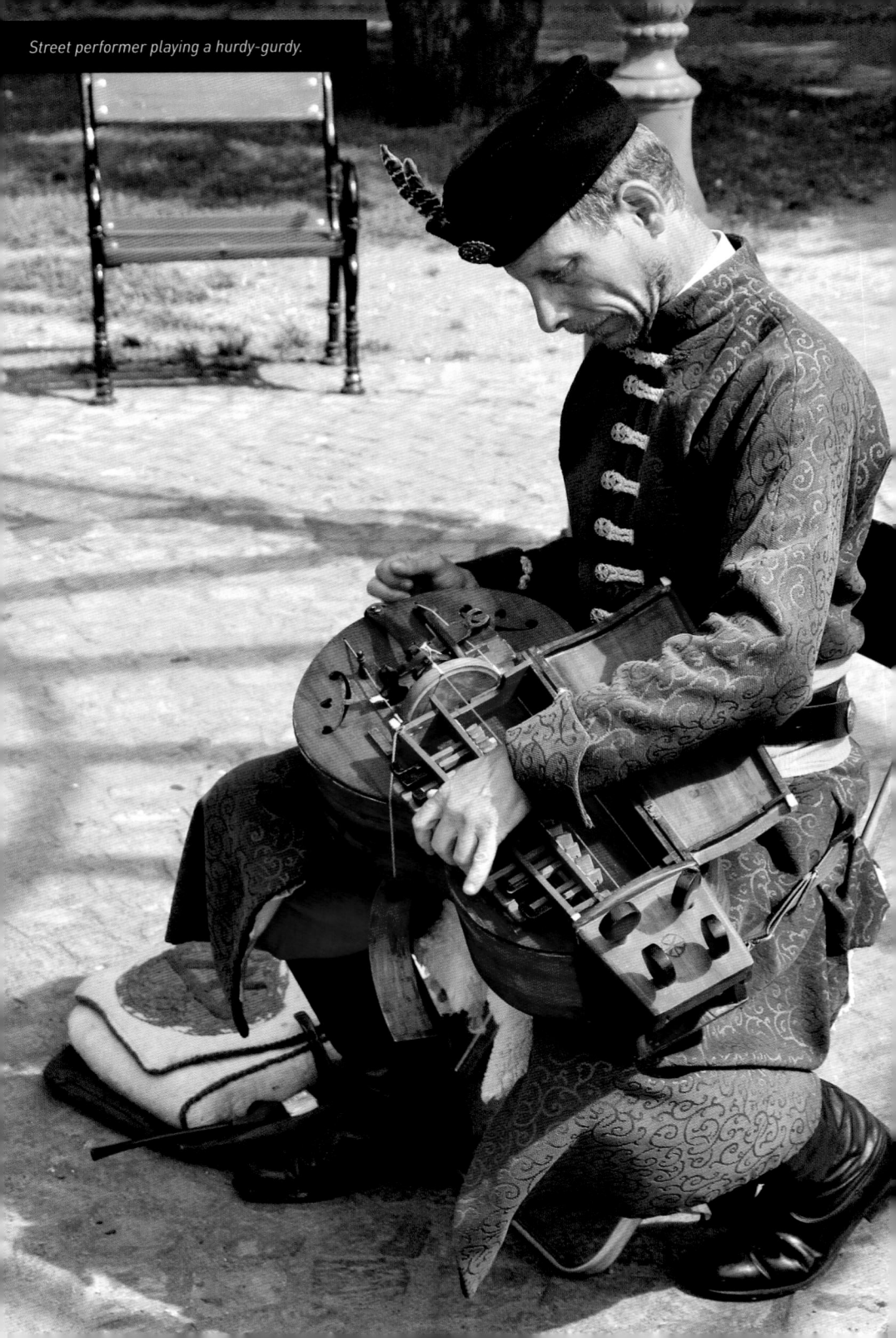

FOLK ART AND TRADITIONS

Despite the increasing urbanisation of Hungary, the country still has rich traditions of folk music, crafts and architecture.

The traveller to Hungary these days will encounter all kinds of folklore and events relating to traditions from every part of the nation, from the modest little tájház (regional museum), to elaborate events featuring marriage ceremonies, dancing and fairs. Since the 1970s, Hungary has been busy renewing its connection to its roots, and folklore provides a form of national identification.

SEARCH FOR IDENTITY

The geographical position of the Magyar ethnic group has meant that its folk traditions have always enjoyed a lively exchange with the people around it, such as the Romanians, Germans and various Slavic groups. However, in the search for its identity and its roots, the Hungarian intelligentsia has always preferred to go back to – or create – a specific, unmistakably Hungarian culture.

This quest, which has been revived time and again for the last 120 years, guided the interests of the intellectuals towards 'the art of simple, uneducated village people'. By the 1880s, the value of collecting folk art had been recognised and many thousands of objects had been gathered from the villages.

In this same vein, the huge celebrations of the 'Millennium', organised in 1896 to commemorate the 1,000-year anniversary of the Maygar conquest of the Carpathian Basin, were a timely opportunity to give plenty of space to the exhibition of folk art. Masterpieces of craft and folk art, as well as examples of early craft traditions, were collected. A gigantic 'folk' village was built, consisting of typical houses from the various regions. Institutes

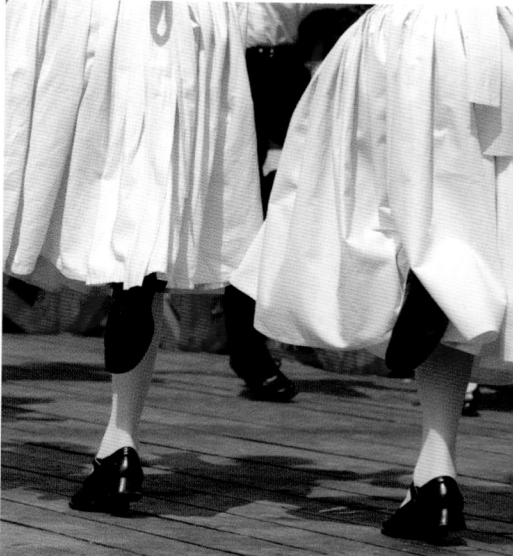

Folk dancers.

for the study of and research into folk art were founded.

Around the same time, Béla Vikár was recording folk songs (see page 104); architects went out and measured farmhouses and drew up plans of their lay-outs, artists drew the costumes of regions rich in tradition, and the inseparable twins of Hungarian culture, Zoltán Kodály and Béla Bartók, set out on their travels in order to collect folk melodies.

However, some intellectuals were of the opinion that anything produced by the peasantry could not possibly be 'refined' enough for polite society, and had to be elevated to the level of the concert hall. Led by the deeply rooted paternalism of the city fathers, these people misguidedly wanted to mould village art to their own image and taste.

In the years between the wars Hungarians became increasingly interested in folk culture, perhaps in response to the huge loss of territory imposed by the Treaty of Trianon (see page 60). Their activities were more enlightened and better planned than those of their predecessors; collecting continued, although at a slower speed. Countless recordings of folk music were made, dances were filmed, and hundreds of photographs were taken.

rich traditions, for instance, in the Matyó area (Matyóföld) east of the capital. At the same time, the colourful costumes, customs and its various textile arts and crafts of this region made seductive advertising material.

A similar fate befell the Puszta in the east of the country, the Hortobágy. Here the cracking of whips can be heard virtually day and night, even if it means that the horses have to gallop tirelessly over the wide-open plain. Thanks to the radio, gypsy music, which was once discreetly played in coffee-houses, became com-

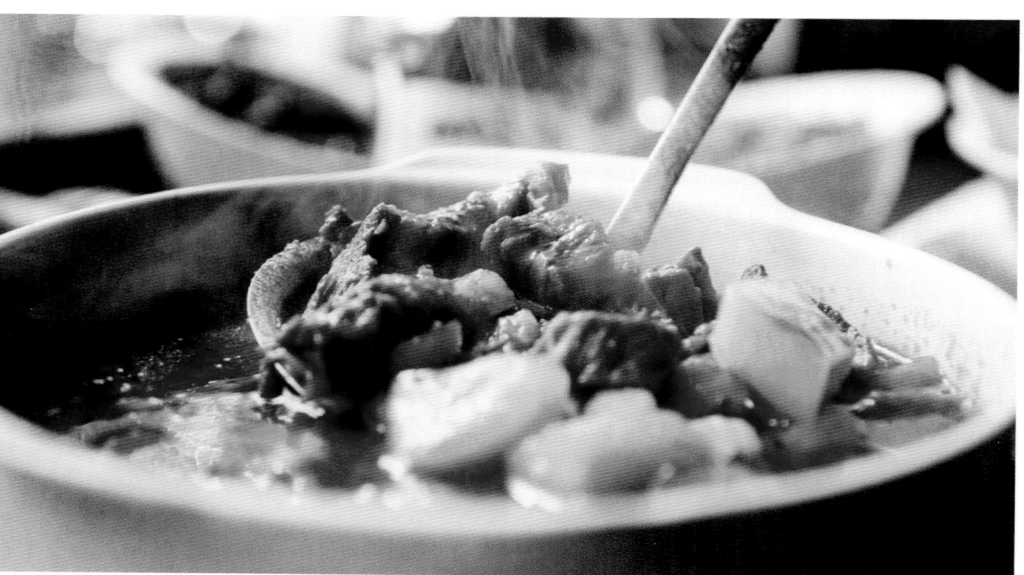

Goulash is a popular Hungarian dish.

ROMANTIC VIEW

This process also took another turn, inspired by visitors from abroad. Once the attraction of folk traditions had been discovered by tourists, the tourism industry concentrated all its energies on this topic and successfully promoted an idealised image of Hungary. This image can be traced back to romantic nationalist ideals current throughout Europe in the 19th century, and was repackaged in the interests of the tourist trade during the 1930s.

As in so many countries, this was a mixed blessing. In some areas of Hungary, the tendency of the tourist industry to take over folk arts undoubtedly encouraged the survival of

mercialised, strengthening the cliché. And thus, the stereotype of the Hungarian cowboy dressed in national costume being serenaded by a gypsy in a *csárda* (inn) was created. This symbolic trademark of Hungary is ubiquitous, yet it almost completely obscures the authentic rural culture that still lives on in the countryside.

At the end of the 19th century, Hungary lured adventurous tourists by promoting itself as the land of 'Csikós, Gulyás and Fogas' (cowboys, goulash and pike).

CULTURAL CHANGES

Within a few years of the end of World War II, the self-contained world of the Hungarian peasant farmer had fallen apart. The collectivisation of agriculture and industrialisation meant that a far smaller proportion of the population was living a traditional rural life. The popular storytellers and singers began to disappear; individual, hand-made objects in daily use were replaced by mass-produced items with all their advantages and disadvantages, and their uniform, sterile style. Taking all these things as a whole, the this passive consumerism virtually paralysed village life, and it was only in the late 1960s that traditional music made a comeback.

REVITALISATION VIA TV

Ironically, it was television, blamed for all the damage in the first place, that played an important role in getting things started. A country-wide television competition for folk music uncovered unsuspected energies. Choirs and dance groups, which until then had more or less existed only on paper, came into the limelight.

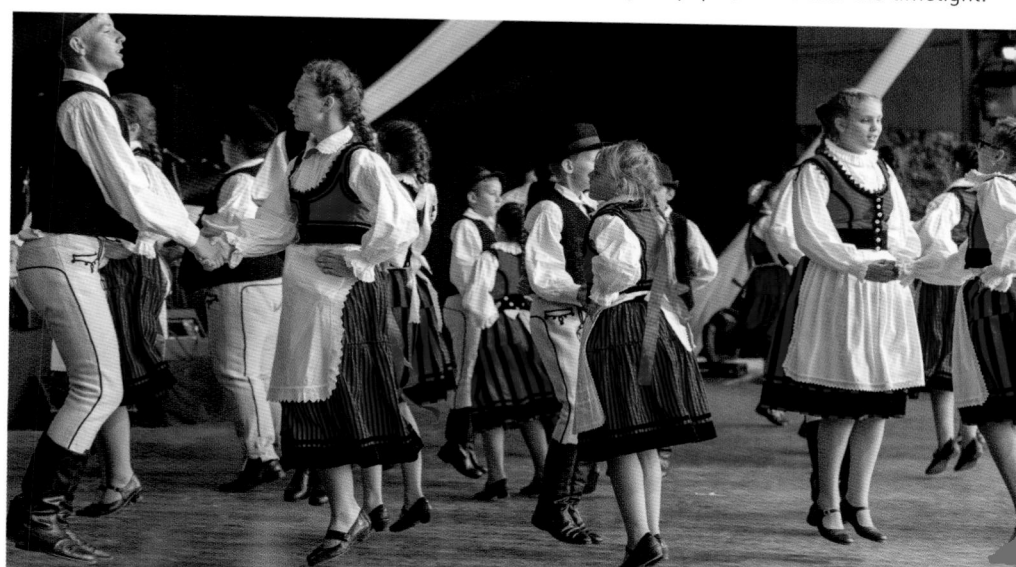

Hungarian children in traditional folk-dancing costume performing.

process was perhaps an unwelcome but inevitable one, dictated by the changing times. The old, traditional communities and their values were slowly but surely dying out; social and family ties slackened or came apart for good, the old village institutions lost their role and their significance. Only the rural singing and dancing groups survived the turbulence of the times.

After 1945, many amateur choirs, orchestras and dance groups were formed in the provinces as a result of individual initiatives. However, they too suffered from the competition of mass culture imported from abroad. It was much easier to sit in front of the TV set, or take advantage of what the city had to offer than to spend time organising live entertainment. For some years,

⊘ DANCE HALLS

In the 1970s, a programme aimed at revitalising village life combined with a vigorous youth culture gave rise to a fascinating sub-cultural phenomenon: the dance hall. The dance hall provides energetic entertainment, a winning combination of 1950s rock'n'roll jamborees and peasant festivals, featuring youthful enthusiasm and straightforward melodies.

At the same time, traditional handicrafts also received much needed attention. Potters and weavers, basket-makers, indigo dyers and blacksmiths all set to work revitalising their age-old crafts.

The performance of Hungarian folk songs and music was a strict requirement for participation, and a number of unknown treasures and talents simultaneously came to light.

FOLK ARCHITECTURE

The harmonious appearance once presented by the typical Hungarian village can today really only be seen in old photographs. Sadly, many houses built in rural areas nowadays are functional but frankly hideous. You can only find farmhouses in the traditional style in the various

the Káli Basin (southeast of the town of Tapolca) constitute probably the most impressive area in terms of Hungarian building tradition.

There are also many beautiful farmhouses in the small villages of the region around Nógrád. Worth a visit, though somewhat museum-like, is Hollókő (see page 222). Its old centre has been on the Unesco list of world cultural monuments since 1988. It consists of 55 small houses and includes a church. Some of the houses have now been turned into bed-and-breakfast accommodation, and one serves as

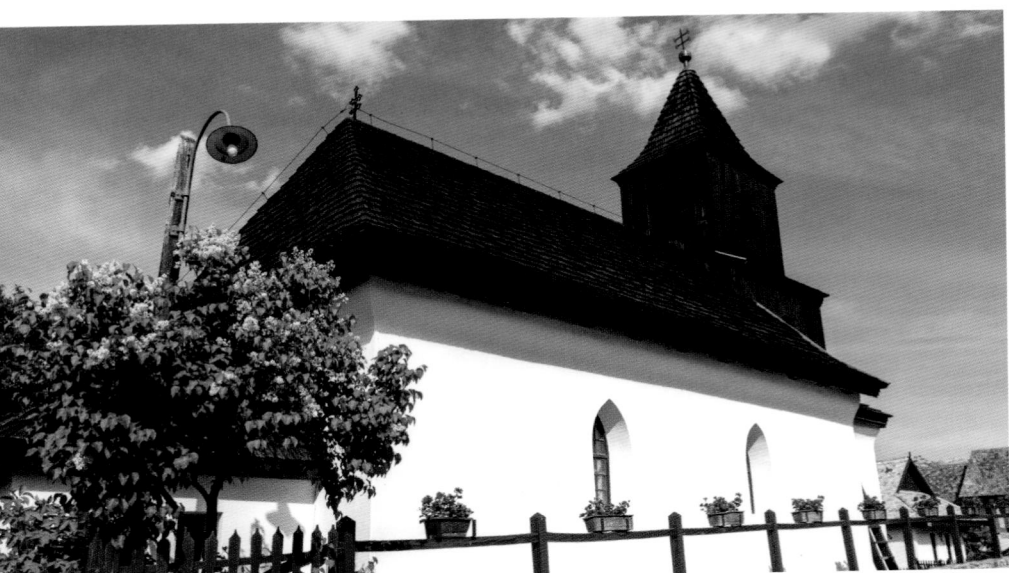

Traditional church in Hollókő.

museum villages (skansen) and in the more isolated settlements. In some villages of southern Transdanubia (such as Adorjás and Kórós), in the small communities of western Transdanubia (Őriszentpéter) and in the villages in the hills above the northern shore of the Lake Balaton region, remnants of the traditional, elongated Hungarian farmhouse with its typical pergola have survived.

It is in these regions that you will probably find the largest number of well-preserved houses, thanks to the influence and the conservation work of intellectuals who have moved out into the country. From an architectural point of view, Szentbékkálla, Salföld, Kékkút, Kővágóörs and the surrounding villages in what is known as

⊘ AN ARCHITECTURAL TOUR

If you enjoy exploring and would like a particularly interesting tour, concentrating on rural architecture, the following route is recommended: start from Budapest and go to Dunaföldvár (Highway No. 6) then to Cece, to Kölesd, Gyönk, Hőgyész, Kalaznó, Bonyhád, Dunaföldvár and back to Budapest. This tour will not only familiarise travellers with some exceptional examples of rural architecture, but will also reveal some of the more typical small, noble country residences (such as those in Gyönk, Kölesd and Hőgyész). Today, they are often used as schools and cultural centres, which generally means that they are well maintained.

a museum displaying artefacts and utensils peculiar to the region that are still in daily use. An ethnic group known as the Palóc (pronounced Palots) lives in this area.

Tourists usually only stray into the inner regions of the counties of Somogy and Tolna and their towns by accident. Here the elongated villages lying at the feet of the gentle lines of hills are often still inhabited by German-speaking people. These villages have little or no tourist infrastructure and no hotels or restaurants. There is, however, usually a village inn or a simple bar that opens from midday onwards.

Way out east along the Ukrainian, Romanian and Slovak borders some original buildings have survived – away from the border crossings – although the flooding of the Tisza in 2001 destroyed a considerable number of old houses, which were traditionally built of mud with no solid supporting structure.

OPEN-AIR MUSEUMS

If you can't get to the more remote villages, you could visit one of the open-air museums. The largest is the Hungarian Open-Air Ethnographical Museum (see page 176) near Szentendre, where planners have gathered together the most characteristic buildings from nearly all the major regions of the country. Eastern Hungary is well represented with a bell-tower, farmhouses, a small Reformed Church and a 17th-century wooden Orthodox Church. About 1.5 km (1 mile) to the west are houses from Transdanubia. Here, folk music concerts are frequently held, as are craft courses for children.

There are also important museum villages in Szombathely, Nyíregyháza and Szenna (south of Kaposvár), which can be visited from spring to autumn. Visitors can obtain information about famous buildings that are difficult to locate and about places worth visiting from books in the inexpensive series *Library of Landscapes, Periods and Museums*, available in several languages. Another useful guide on this topic is the old *Road Atlas of Hungary*, out of print but fairly often found in secondhand bookshops. Any site of special interest is marked by a red star next to the name on the maps and in the index. In the following section of the atlas, the names of these places appear with a brief explanatory text.

RELIGIOUS ARCHITECTURE

In Hungary the Protestant churches (mainly Calvinist Reformed churches) are especially interesting because of their painted, coffered ceilings. The decoration of the galleries, ceilings and pews of these churches combines the rich ornamentation of the Renaissance with naïve floral decoration and other ornamental motifs of folk art. The artists were mainly travelling joiners whose names are unknown. Unfortunately, many of these architectural gems are located on the inaccessible fringes of the country, where public transport is limited.

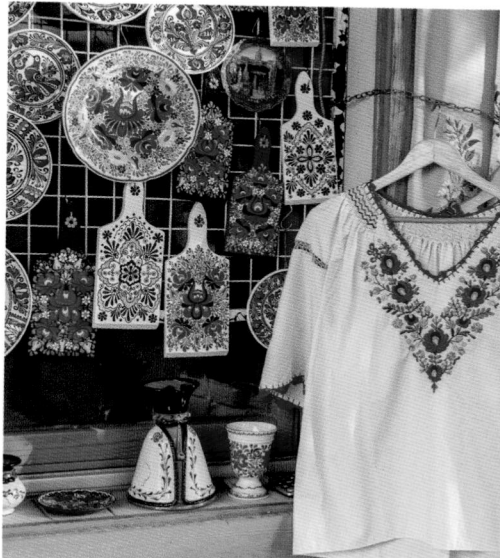

Traditional Hungarian shirts with embroidery, together with decorative painted plates and cutting boards.

The Calvinist churches of the communities south of Pécs, Kórós, Adorjás, Drávaiványi and Kovácshida date from the early 19th century. The churches of Tákos, Vámosoroszi, Gacsály, Tivadar and Milota (in eastern Hungary) are particularly recommended for their coffered ceilings. The ceiling of the Reformed church in Csenger, completed in 1745, deserves special attention. It features a central arrangement of leaves and floral ornamentation featuring tulips, rosettes and wreaths.

A quintessentially Hungarian feature is the wooden bell-tower, where 'Hungarian folk art reaches the heights of great art', to quote one respected academic writer. The superbly built wooden structures are evidence of the high level of Hungarian carpentry skills. The most beautiful wooden bell-towers can be found in the region of the upper Tisza, and among them is the impressive Nyírbátor tower, standing proud at 30 metres (85ft). Another can be seen beside the Avas Reformed Church in Miskolc.

REGIONAL COSTUMES

The rural costumes of Hungary only became colourful in the middle of the 19th century. At that time regional variations began to appear

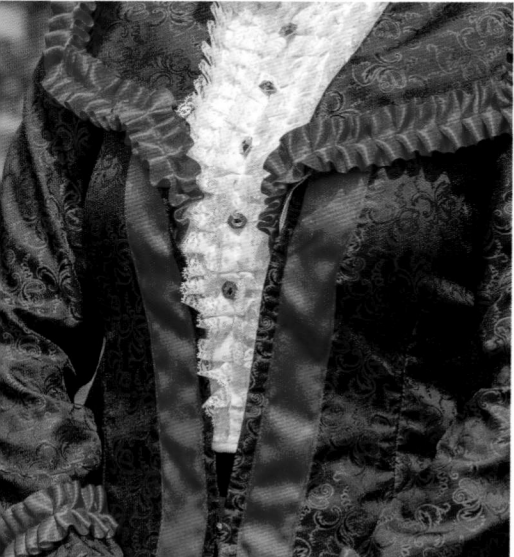

Detail on a woman's folk costume.

in the Hungarian national costume, which was still fairly uniform in its basic features. While the costume of the women changed more noticeably and reflected the fashion of the day, that of the men tended to be more conservative. The most beautiful Hungarian costumes, with their perfect harmony of styles and colours, are now found in the Magyar villages of Transylvania in present-day Romania. Within the borders of Hungary, the prettiest costumes for festivals and holidays are worn by the communities of Transdanubian Sárköz, the swampy area between Szekszard and the Danube.

If national costumes were once commonplace in Hungary, today they are only taken out and dusted off for special occasions. Village life leaves no room for fine dress, yet the old garments are still kept and treasured.

FOLK ARTS AND CRAFTS

The work of rural craftsmen can be seen and purchased in many places. Great masters of their craft, people with skill and formal training, often have large studios that operate as galleries and shops. The untrained eye may not get the feeling for authenticity right away, but a visit to any of the country's many ethnographic or regional museums will help you to distinguish the genuine article from tourist tat.

Many shops are run by the Cooperative of Folk Art and Crafts (Népmüvészeti és Háziipari Szövetkezet). The largest of their stores is located at the corner of Váci utca and Régiposta utca in the Inner City (Belváros) of Pest, but you can find good folkloric shops throughout the country.

You can obtain useful information about workshops from the Folk Art Association (Népmüvészeti Egyesület Szövetsége). In their exhibition rooms, you can from time to time see interesting collections of ethnic products. Both places are located at Corvin tér 8, just off Fö út, Budapest I.

MARKETS AND ANTIQUE SHOPS

There are other places and opportunities for buying original pieces. With a bit of luck, you can still find old items of craftsmanship in the Budapest flea market and antique shops throughout the country. The Esceri Flea Market at Nagykôrösi út 156, 1194 Budapest, is well worth the trip out to this industrial area of the city. You can find antiques of all kinds, paintings, porcelain, clothes, ornaments and household appliances. To get there take the number 54 bus from Boráros Square in the 9th District by the Petöfi Bridge. Get off at the Fiumei út bus stop and walk across the footbridge.

Here the odd piece of genuine folk art can turn up, in the form of traditional clothing, textiles or ceramics. The prices are fairly high and, whereas at one time you could haggle (indeed it was expected that the customer would argue over the price), this is rarely the case today.

Antique shops (for example, the state-owned Folkart Centrum, Váci utca 14, Budapest V) have an extremely wide range of traditional crafts on sale. The shops in the Buda castle district and in Szentendre also have a beautiful selection, but buyers should note that the prices here are sometimes well above what you would pay elsewhere in the country.

Hungarian farmers from Transylvania (mainly from the Székler region) set up stalls in the pedestrian subways of the Pest inner city and offer original woven and embroidered handicrafts such as cushions, tablecloths and skirts. They sell at fairly reasonable prices in the face of stiff competition from other tradespeople selling similar, but mass-produced, wares, and

The Great Annual Market in Pécs, despite its name, takes place on the first Sunday in every month. It is the country's biggest market and has the most traditional wares. If the weather is good, huge crowds squeeze into the market square behind the railway station, where you can buy just about anything from kittens to used cars, old PCs, books and roller-blades. In the southern part of Hungary, many villages still practise their old crafts, and on market day you'll see vendors selling their linen, quaint cutlery, old-fashioned mats and bags.

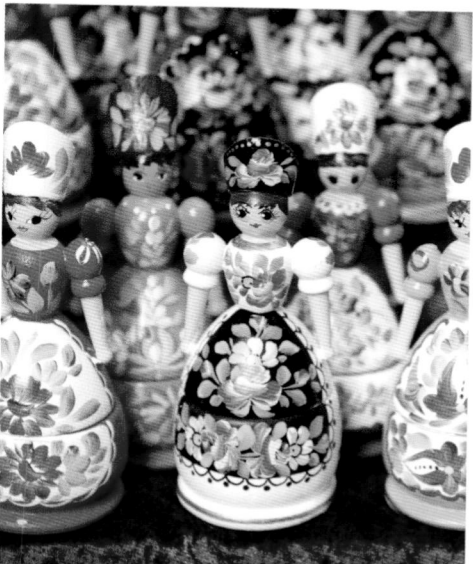

Hungarian folk art puppets.

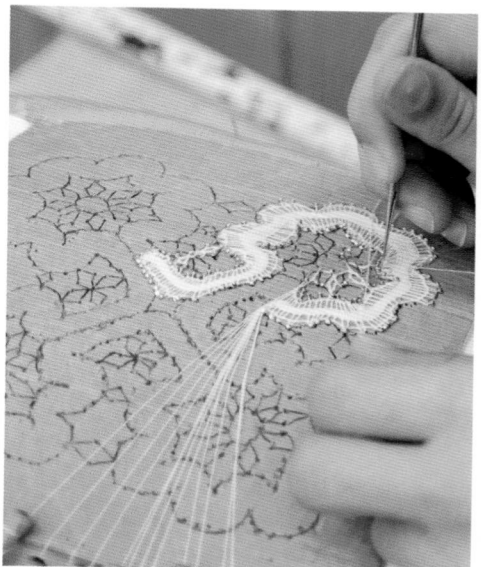

Hungarian lace motif on pillow.

from Roma traders, who build up their basketry wares like barricades.

REGIONAL FAIRS

A special feature of regional fairs is the markets. Once every part of the country had its traditional market places, the more important market towns having developed along the trade routes. Even today, the larger markets still attract tens of thousands of people. The Bridge Market on the Kilenclyukú híd (Nine-Arch Bridge) in Hortobágy (19–20 August) has been held there for a century. Traditional Hungarian singers and dancers entertain the crowds throughout the day, and food stalls ensure visitors have the necessary stamina to shop until they drop.

A NEW GENERATION

The output of the new arts and crafts generation is influenced by established folk art and follows its traditions and patterns. Besides flowery embroidery, Hungary is renowned for its leatherware, lace (from Kiskunhalás), and especially for its pottery, using traditional floral motifs. A speciality inherited from the Turks is black pottery which has been fired in a sooty coal kiln. The designs are etched into the surface using a smooth pebble. Mohács is particularly famous for this type of work, but it is found in the Puszta as well, notably in Nádudvar, a few miles north of Hajdúszoboszló.

You can see these products in the markets all year round, but twice a year the master craftsmen get together for a special occasion. The first date every year is the last Sunday in March, when an exhibition and market of traditional crafts is held in the Budapest Sports Centre (Budapest *Sportscarnok*, Hungária korüt 44–52, Budapest XIV). This is a well-attended event and several hundred exhibitors congregate – puppeteers, leather-workers and saddlers, carvers of wood, bone and horn, to name just a few – to peddle their wares. Groups of dance-house performers provide entertainment, The second major event is the Crafts

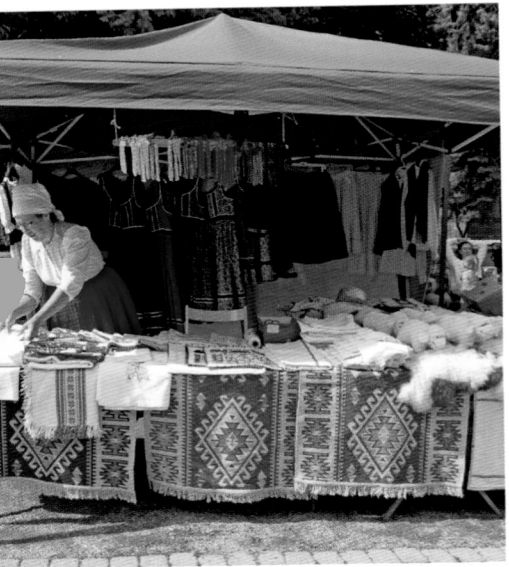

Selling traditional clothes at a folk festival in Eger.

Fair (*Mesterségek Ünnepe*) which takes place around 18–20 August in the old Castle District of Budapest.

It is not always easy to distinguish this relatively recent folk art movement, with its originality and genuine value, from the garish pastiches of folklore aimed at raking in hard cash. Perhaps it's feeling; perhaps the difference lies in the amount of advertising done and the size, number, and national provenance of the coaches that turn up at these events. The horse shows of Bugac, while fascinating and fun, are not quite the same as those in Szilvásvárad. However, the embroidering ladies of Buzsák are originals, as are the painting ladies of Kalocsa. Without denying well organised 'state' folk traditions their

useful role, a visitor to Hungary might find it a positive experience to get to know authentic folk traditions as well.

LEARNING THE CRAFTS

To keep these skills alive, craft courses are held in several places during the summer months. In Velem in Western Hungary, young people staying in a specially built camp can learn wood carving, pottery and weaving. In Zalaegerszeg, you can practise wood carving, and in Magyarlukafa (Baranya district), as well as working with wood, there are courses in basketry and weaving on handlooms.

The Museum Village (Sóstói Müzeumfalu; see page 253 for opening times) near Nyíregyháza also has a broad range of programmes during the summer months, with beautifully restored houses as a backdrop: cooking, dancing and music-making (sometimes with audience participation) are among the activities.

One of the most interesting courses is offered by the famous folk music group Téka (which has been going strong since the mid-1970s) and their friends and supporters, who launched the Foundation for Preserving Hungarian Cultural Traditions. It is held in the second half of June in the eastern Hungarian town of Boldogkőváralja in the Zemplén, in a camp with tents surrounding a huge wooden barn that provides the dance floor. Visitors can take part in singing, dancing and music-making, by all ethnic minorities in Hungary, and learn about various crafts from weaving, pottery and spinning, to carving and pleating. The bagpipe and hurdy-gurdy workshop held here in August is something very special. Téka also has its own dance club in Budapest (see below), where young people can learn the various folk dances, and concerts and other events are held.

Of all the traditional arts practised in Hungary today, folk dance and folk music perhaps offer the greatest variety and are the most accessible to the foreign visitor. Téka is not the only group involved in maintaining and advancing traditions. Almost every town of medium size has a music and dance ensemble, and new ones keep popping up. (In fact, there are many even outside Hungary.) A good source of information is the website: http://hungaria.org/hal/folklor.

Apart from books on the subject, your own ear is not a bad guide here. The Rózsavölgyi record store in Martinelli tér 5 in District V of Budapest has a large selection of recorded folk music and can start you off in the right direction. Note that Hungarian folk music is not the same as Gypsy (Roma) music, although the former is also played by Romani.

One particular type you are likely to hear is folk-rock or eszpresszó-rock, which is very popular in Hungary. Musicians in bars usually play in trios or quartets on electric organ, saxophone and percussion, performing Hungarian songs in a rock style. Another variation on the same theme is the creative use of modern elements with old melodies, as performed by the remarkable group *Ghymes*.

WHERE TO HEAR FOLK MUSIC

Where can you hear genuine folk music and see genuine folk dances? You could try the Téka Club in Budapest (Dagálgu utca 15a in the 13th district, tel: 349 7761). If you go to the bigger dance venues you will almost certainly hear amplified or recorded music, but in one of the city's smaller bars, you may just stumble upon a traditional group of musicians.

However, if they notice a foreign tourist, they may strike up the tune to some international hit, although you can ask them to carry on as before (and perhaps offer a tip). Or you may be lucky enough to get caught up in a country wedding, where you will be able to appreciate the genuine sounds of Hungary.

⊘ DANCE-HOUSE CULTURE

While you are in Budapest, a visit to a dance house (*táncház*) is highly recommended. The dance house is a large room where an old Transylvanian form of entertainment takes place: musicians play their socks off for a modest fee while young people take to the floor.

Some of the dance houses occasionally offer dancing lessons. This is where, at the risk of looking foolish, you can learn the steps to some Hungarian peasant dances, which require serious concentration as well as plenty of energy. Information is available from the Táncház Egyesölet, PF153, 1255 Budapest, tel: (1) 214-3521, www.tanchaz.hu.

FESTIVALS

Some of the festivals and folk music events are very entertaining, although they can seem quite lengthy if you don't understand what's going on. Information about the various events can be obtained from the House of Folk Dance (a branch of the Institute of Folk Culture), Szentlélek tér 8, Budapest I.

One celebration well worth seeing is the Kaláka-EBU Festival, which takes place every year in early July at Diosgyőr Castle in Miskolc and features all sorts of ethnic music as well

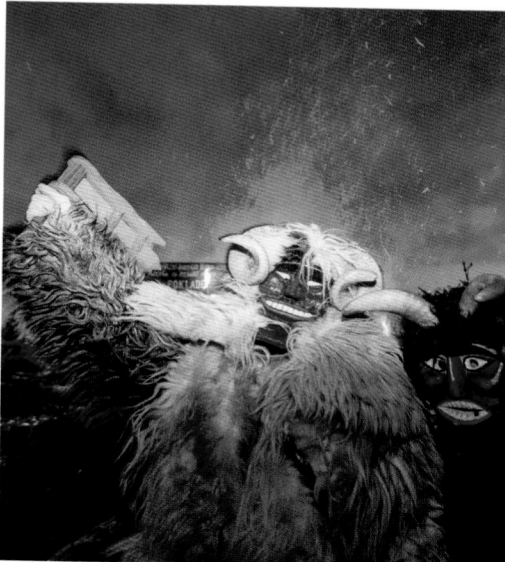

The Busójárás, an annual carnival held in Mohács.

as Hungarian folk. Information about this event is available from the Kaláka foundation, Dániel Gryllus, 1359 Budapest Pf. 655, tel/fax: 36 1 355 9382; e-mail: gryllus@elender.hu

Another special event is the dance-house meeting, which takes place every year at the end of March in Budapest as part of the Spring Festival. An endless procession of folk musicians and dance groups congregate for this Sunday festival, cheered on by the thousands who come to join in.

An even more diverse programme is offered at the European Folkloric Festival, at the beginning of June in the capital, where visitors can listen to the national folk music of Hungary, of the country's ethnic minorities and of guest groups from abroad.

📷 HUNGARIAN ARCHITECTURE

Hungary's architectural legacy compares favourably with any other country in Central or Eastern Europe, owing to centuries of competing faiths and rulers, among them Romans, Ottomans, and Habsburgs – and not forgetting the Communists of course.

The most obvious place to start is Budapest, which embraces all manner of architectural forms and styles, from the ostentatious neo-Gothic Parliament building and Moorish-Revival Great Synagogue, to the city's Ottoman-era bath houses and the zoo's wonderful Art Nouveau animal houses, which are unlike anything else in Europe (see page 143).

Beyond the capital, there's Pécs, with its splendid mosques, and Kesckemét, which showcases some superb Secessionist structures, while both Győr and Sopron are stunning Baroque towns. There's some fabulous vernacular architecture to explore across Hungary too, particularly in the Northern Uplands, such as the museum village of Hollókő, now a Unesco World Heritage Site (see page 222). Close by, in the Western Zemplen region, the picturesque villages of Hollóháza and Fuzér display similarly folksy dwellings.

Like many eastern European countries, Hungary wasn't immune to the worst excesses of Communism, and this is most obvious in elements of its architecture. For one such example, head to the steel town of Dunaújváros (see page 178); a monument to Stalinist economics, its appeal – for some at least – lies in its Bauhaus and Socialist-Realist aesthetic, manifest in its uniform rows of concrete blocks.

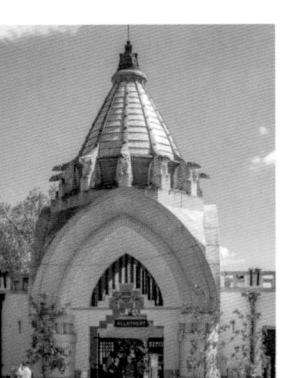

Entrance to Budapest Zoo.

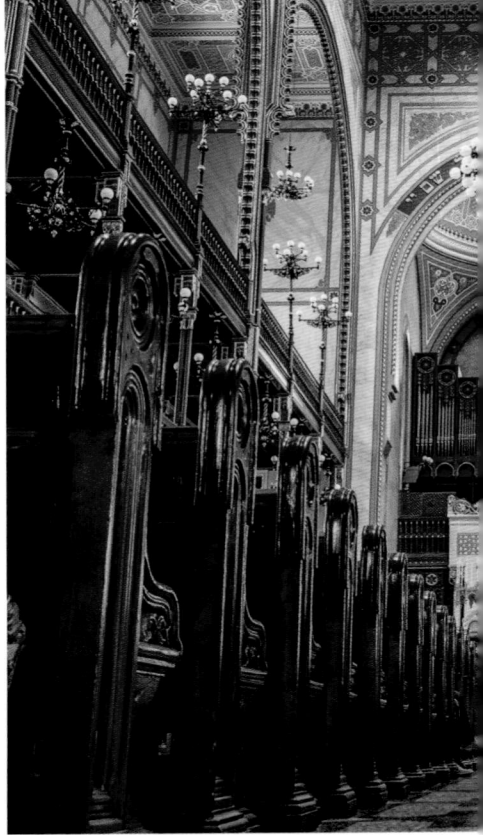

Inside Budapest's synagogue.

Attractive facade of Lutheran Church at Siofok, with modern design by Hungarian architect Imre Makovecz, and angel wings above the main entrance.

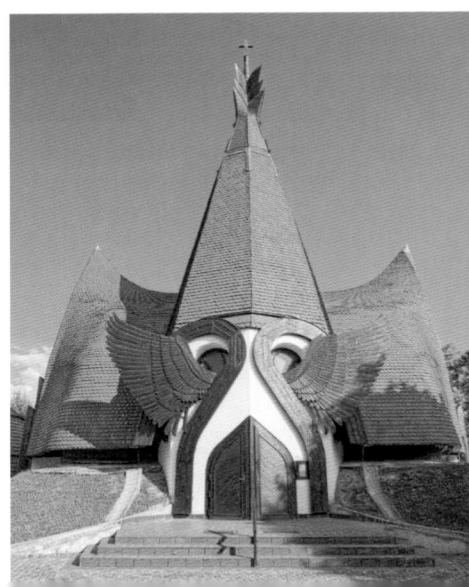

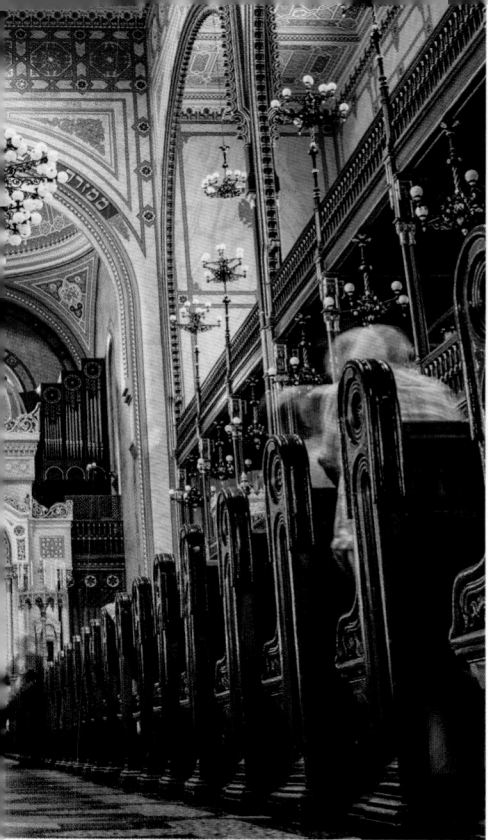

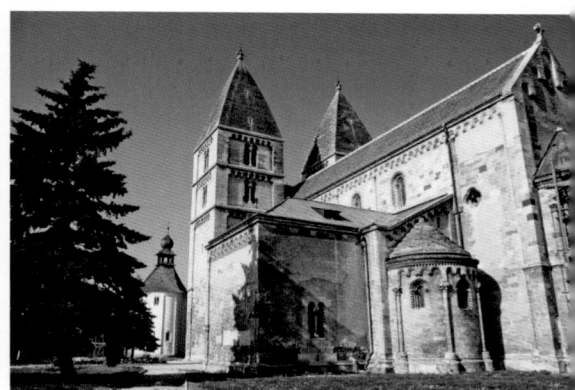

Church in Ják.

Hungary's religious architecture

Hungary boasts some wonderful ecclesiastical architecture, beginning with the abbey church in Ják, one of Europe's finest Romanesque monuments. The most outstanding examples of the neoclassical form are St Stephen's Basilica in Budapest and the colossal Basilica in Esztergom, the country's largest church, while the most impressive example of Gothic is Pannonhalma Abbey near Gyor. Hungary's once formidable Jewish heritage manifests itself most obviously in some superb synagogues, the finest of which are the Moorish-style Dohány utca Synagogue in Budapest – the second largest in the world – and the Secessionist-style Great Synagogue in Szeged, designed by the renowned Jewish Hungarian architect Lipót Baumhorn (see pages 150 & 240).

In unremarkable Paks, you'll find the remarkable Catholic Church, the unmistakeable work of Imre Makovecz, one of Hungary's most controversial architects; a singularly unique, strikingly organic structure made of wood, its bell tower reveals three spires topped by a cross, crescent and a sun sign. Meanwhile, tucked away in the remote northeastern corner of the country are a cluster of enchanting medieval wooden churches of the type more commonly found just across the border in Romania – those in Csaroda and Tákos are two beautiful examples (see page 252).

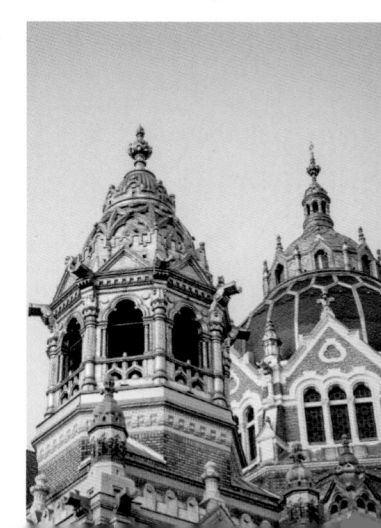

Detail on the dome of Szeged Synagogue by Lipót Baumhorn.

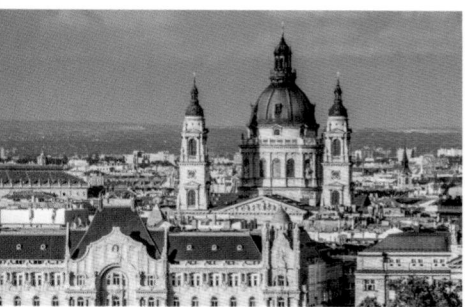

Stephen's Basilica, Budapest.

asha Qasim Mosque, Pécs.

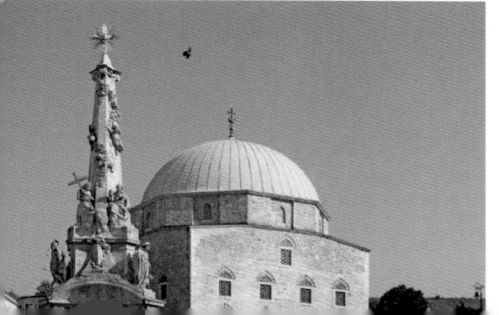

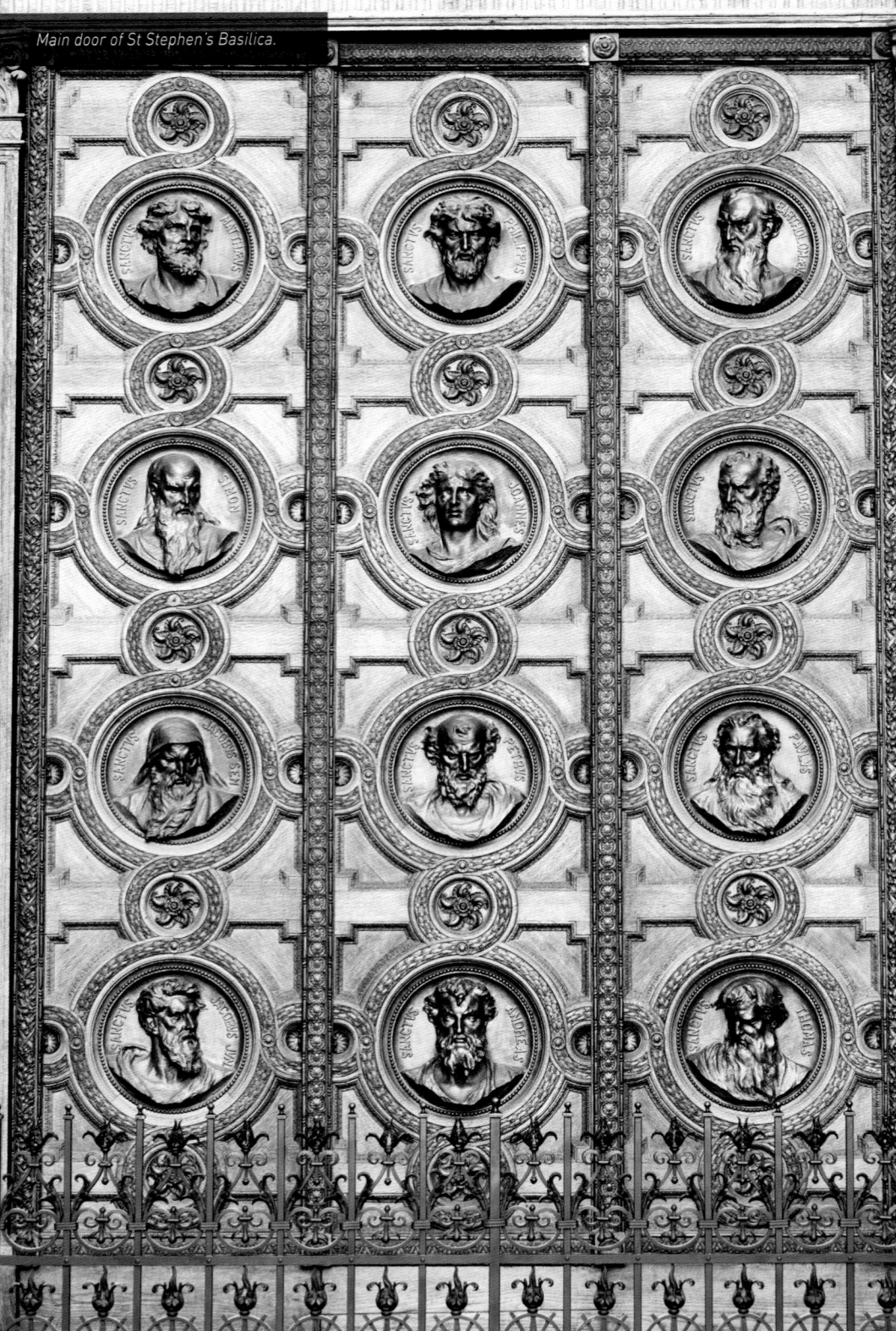

Main door of St Stephen's Basilica.

LITERATURE

The development of literature in Hungary has been repeatedly interrupted by conflict, but is slowly gaining recognition in the rest of Europe.

Within the mosaic of European languages, Hungarian has a colour and shape all of its own. Its only – and distant – European relative is Finnish. Both belong to the group of Finno-Ugric languages, as do Estonian and the minority languages of the Lapps, Vogules, Ostiaks and Samoyedes. Like the language, Hungarian literature has been isolated for centuries. This situation has changed over the last few years, mainly as far as the German-speaking public is concerned, and new works are regularly translated into German. In this way, Hungarian literature is at least partially integrating with European culture.

UNEVEN DEVELOPMENT

Hungarian civilisation came relatively late, but the monarchy's shrewd conversion to Christianity in the early 11th century allowed the country to be a part of progress in Europe. Conforming to European medieval standards offered the Hungarians their only chance of establishing themselves on the Pannonian plain. This pressure to conform did not diminish over the ensuing centuries. A frontier post between the east and west, Hungary faced two directions at once: the eastern face was on the lookout for foreign invasions, while the western one was trying to assimilate foreign influences.

Throughout its history, Hungary's cultural development was blighted again and again by conflict. In peacetime, people tried desperately to fill in the cultural gaps, a process which repeatedly forced authors to use their craft for social and political ends. This sporadic development, caused by the continual need to catch up, explains the ambivalence

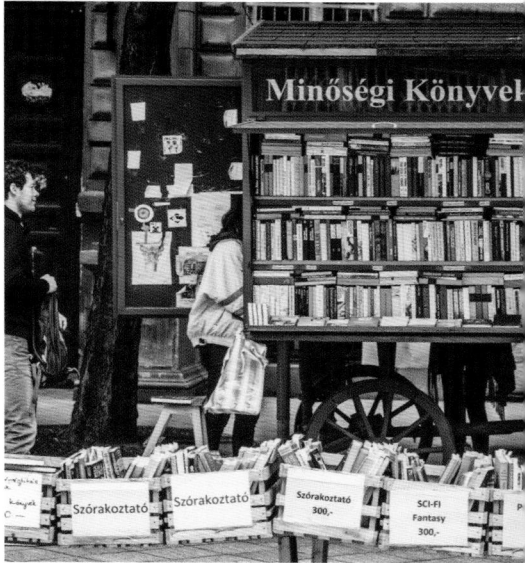

A street bookstore in Budapest.

of the Hungarian literati even today towards the West – on the one hand, bitterness about their isolation and the treachery of the West (although without its support, it is generally believed Hungarian culture has little chance of survival); and on the other, a sense of self-sufficiency, a desire for isolation and a firm belief in national strengths.

LATIN ORIGINS

Until the late 19th century, Latin was the language of the learned and the cultured. The dominance of strict clerical literature is perhaps one reason why texts in the Hungarian language did not appear until the 13th century. The first known Hungarian texts are also religious: a funeral oration, Halotti beszéd, and a lament for the sorrows of the Virgin Mary, Ómagyar Mária siralom.

The chronicles of the time, recounting the ancient history of Hungary and tales of its kings, were written in Latin, as were the poems of the first notable poet in Hungary, the humanist Janus Pannonius (1434–72). With the Reformation, the number of schools, printing presses and publishing houses increased substantially, and the first buds of Hungarian national literature emerged.

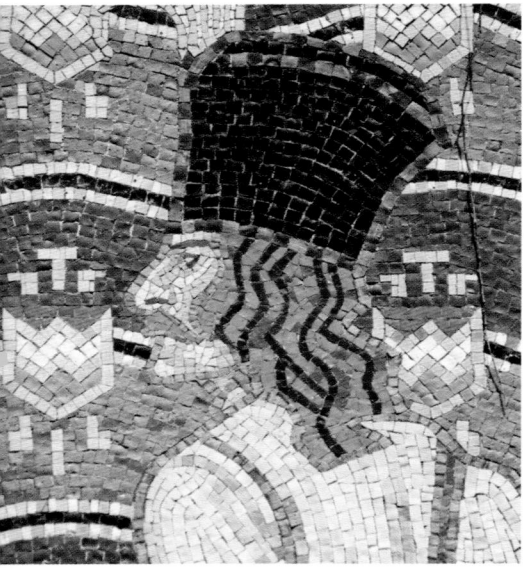

Mosaic of the poet Bálint Balassi, 1554–1594.

In 1590 Gáspár Károli finished the first complete translation of the Bible. Sermons became a popular literary form and continued to be so until the Counter-Reformation. Hungarian literature gained an accomplished stylist in Péter Pázmány (1570–1637), whose works had a decisive influence on the development of modern Hungarian prose. The translation of the psalms by Calvinist Albert Szenci Molnár (1574–1634) encouraged the development of the lyrical form. He also devised a Latin-Hungarian dictionary and a Hungarian grammar, with the aim of making Hungarian accessible to the rest of Europe.

Troubadour and soldier Bálint Balassi (1551–94), wrote lyrical poems about love,

> *The rousing verse of Sándor Petőfi, Hungary's revered national poet, inspired Hungary's doomed 1848 revolution. He died in the fighting, aged just 26 years old.*

valiant knights and God that are still vibrant today. He drew on a well-established tradition of Hungarian poetry, but his skill in form and language makes his work stand out. The promise of this new writing was fulfilled in the 17th century, with the work of such writers as the poet and general Miklós Zrínyi (1620–64), author of the Baroque epic *Szigeti veszedelem* (The Siege of Sziget). The poem tells the story of his forefather, the commander of Szigetvár, whose troops fell under attack from Suleiman the Magnificent (see page 39), and is now considered a masterpiece.

THE ROMANTIC CONTRIBUTORS

The first half of the 19th century saw a revival in language and literature. The work of the poet Mihály Csokonai Vitéz (1773–1805) formed a bridge between the rococo style and the emerging national romanticism. However, the initiator of the decisive movement for renewal in literary circles was the language reformer, publisher, translator and author Ferenc Kazinczy (1759–1831). Writers who previously had worked in isolation found common ground in his intellectual circle, which also opened up channels

⊘ TRANSYLVANIAN TRADITION

A hundred and fifty years of Turkish occupation (1541–1686) severely curtailed literary creativity in Hungary. By contrast, a rich literary tradition of memoirs developed in the Principality of Transylvania, largely due to the fact the area managed to stay out of the war. The memoirs of Prince János Kemény (1607–62), Miklós Bethlen (1642–1716), Péter Apor (1676–1752), the exiled Prince Ferenc Rákóczi II (1676–1735) and his loyal follower Kelemen Mikes (1690–1761), are examples of philosophical and religious soul-searching of an exceptionally high literary standard.

between Hungary's noble houses and contemporary European influences, especially French and German classicism.

This influence was visible in the middle years of the 19th century, in Hungary's golden age of art and literature, in which writers, fuelled by romanticism, embraced the nationalist cause. The historical drama Bánk Bán written by József Katona (1791–1830) was celebrated with wild enthusiasm as part of the national awakening. The themes of universal and national suffering mingled in the poems of Ferenc Kölcsey

(1790–1838), who wrote the words to the Hungarian national anthem.

REALISM

The turning-point to realism came with the works of the novelist, short-story writer and satirist Kálmán Mikszáth (1847–1910). His anecdotal and ironic style was imitated by many, but the world of the gentry that he satirised was coming to an end. Social criticism was developed by Zsigmond Móricz (1879–1942). Móricz belonged to the generation of progressive

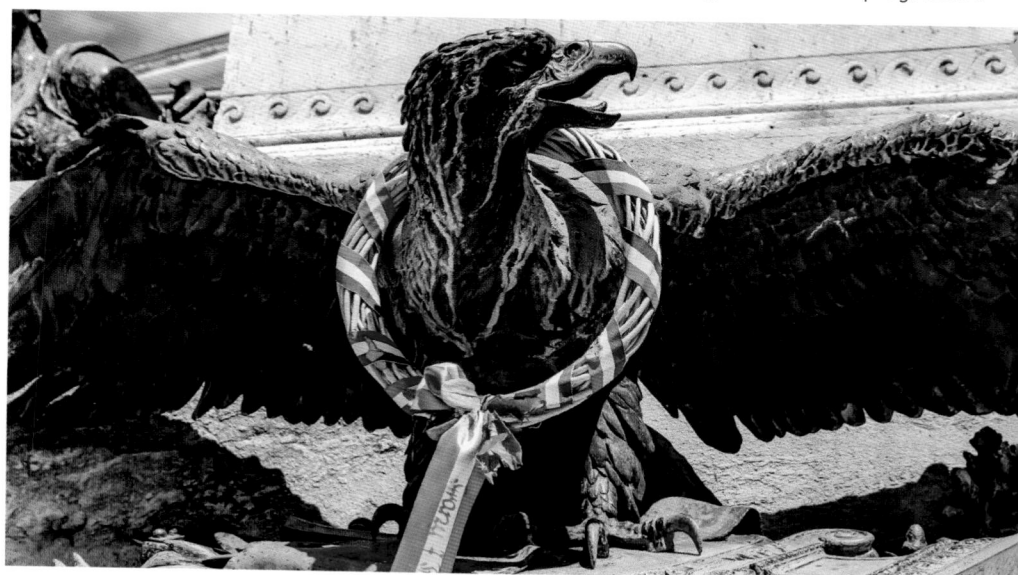

Statue of an eagle on the monument to poet János Arany, in Budapest.

☉ THE RADICAL FOLK SONG

The great master of Hungarian romanticism, Sándor Petőfi (1823–49) utilised the folk song – a simple and direct form for expressing the political and human ideals of freedom. In his poems, the spirit of the revolutions sweeping Europe in 1848 reached the Hungarian reader in familiar nationalist guise. The reading of his radical 'National Song' Talpra Magyar (Rise up, Magyar) triggered the 1848 revolution against Habsburg domination. His friend János Arany (1817–82), who perfected and then transcended the romantic style, was also inspired by folk song lyrics. He was an ingenious manipulator of language, who succeeded in conveying political and philosophical ideas in classic forms. His

ballads and epics are masterpieces, in perfection of form and in their closeness to the language of the people.

During the 19th century, the popularity of prose writing increased. Miklós Jósika (1794–1865) and Zsigmond Kemény (1814–75) wrote historical novels; the adventure stories of the prolific novelist Mór Jókai (1825–1904) are still enjoyed today. Meanwhile, the existential pessimism of the dramatic poem Az ember tragédiája (The Tragedy of Man) by their contemporary Imre Madách (1823–64) pointed the way to the modernism of the 20th century.

writers who established a circle around the journal Nyugat (The West), developing ideas for the radical transformation of society, for a 'new Hungary'.

The guiding light in this progressive thinking was the lyric poet Endre Ady (1877–1919). He radically revised the romantically idealised self-portrait of Hungarian culture. Ady's work also signalled the beginning of modern Hungarian poetry. His audacious verse and radical views provoked vigorous literary, political and moral debates and provided the decisive push that

The struggle against social and cultural backwardness and the conditions of the peasantry was the origin of rich social literature in the years between the first and second world wars. The novel *A Village Adrift* by the brilliant essayist and novelist Dezső Szabó (1879–1945) became a touchstone of this new intellectual movement. The author Zoltán Szabó (1912–84), who died in exile in England, the essayist and novelist László Németh (1901–75), and the poet Gyula Illyés (1902–83) are among the most important representatives of this revolutionary trend.

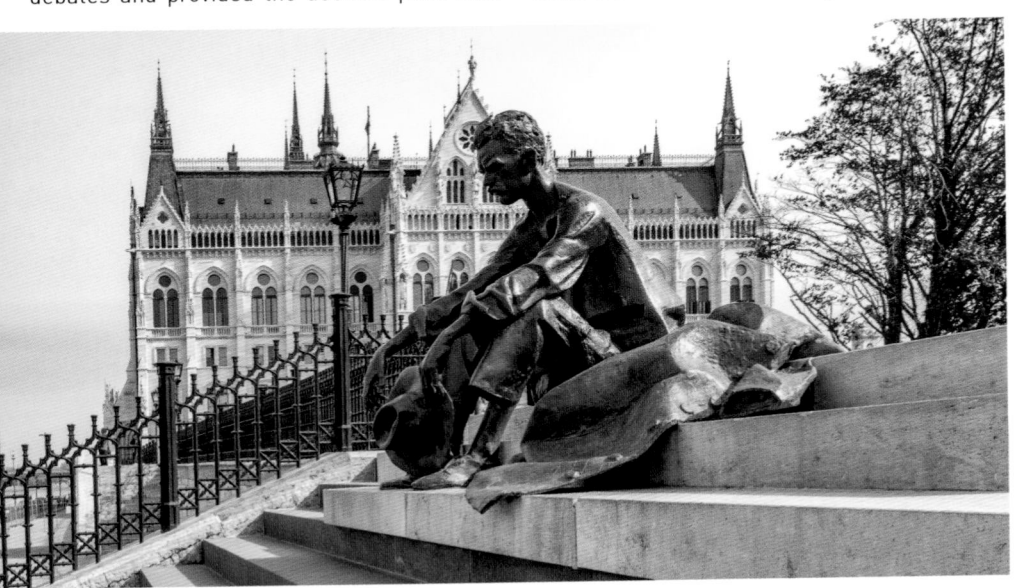

Statue of the poet Atilla József.

raised the standards and popularity of poetry in the years between the two world wars. We only need to look at the finely chiselled masterpieces by Desző Kosztolányi (1885–1936) – who was also an excellent prose writer – and at the explosive dynamism of the language of Attila József (1905–37).

POLITICAL RESPONSIBILITY

By the 19th century, literature had become an important factor in Hungarian politics, and writers often saw themselves pushed into a role of political responsibility for their people. This is a pattern that has persisted over the years and still applies, to a lesser extent, today.

Sándor Márai (1900–89) emerged as the most important and influential prose writer of the mid-20th century. His diaries are still a very rewarding read, enjoyable both for the clarity of the prose and the lucidity of thought.

Responsibility for the community characterises post-World War I Hungarian literature from Transylvania (part of Romania since 1920). The novelist Áron Tamási (1897–1966) recorded the language and attitudes of Transylvanian Szeklers in inimitable fashion. András Sütő (1927–2006) was also influenced by the vocabulary of Transylvania, rich in archaic elements. He creates linguistic jewels out of the Hungarian language, which is at risk of dying out in Romania.

The poets Domokos Szilágyi (1938–76) and Géza Szőcs (b. 1955) convey the besieged situation of the Hungarian minority through a multi-layered, metaphorical language. Its poetic power breaches the bounds of nationalism to express existential and universal human values.

CONTEMPORARY LITERATURE

The post-war years brought a complete reorganisation of the literary world. All publishing houses and journals were nationalised, and anything published had to undergo strict party censorship. Only after the 1956 uprising did a gradual liberalisation come about. Authors who had begun their literary careers before or during the war began to be published once more.

New on the literary scene were the poems of Ágnes Nemes Nagy (1922–91) with their clear, refined language and thought, the frivolous elegance of Sándor Weöres (1913–89) and the diamond clarity and hardness of János Pilinszky's lyricism (1921–81). László Nagy (1925–78) and Sándor Csoóri (1930–2016) were both inspired by the language of folk songs and started to develop a system of metaphors based on images of nature. In the 1960s they became, together with Gyula Illyés, leaders of an intellectual movement that rediscovered national values.

István Szilágyi's (b. 1938) historical novels rediscover a classical genre within the modern context, while the austere prose of Ádám Bodor (b. 1936) deals with the absurdities of the human condition in the modern age.

The prose writers Géza Ottlik (1912–91) and Miklós Mészöly (1921–2001) successfully mingled Western European and Hungarian culture yet without neglecting the responsibility that intellectuals have for their own people.

As an essayist, György Konrád (1933–2019) considered Central Europe to be the cultural and political home of thinking Hungarians. As a novelist, he contributed to the intellectual life of Central Europe with experimental literary records of Hungarian history.

György Petri (1943–2000) – the author of audacious political poems – was the angry young man of modern Hungarian poetry. Both Konrád and Petri published only in the underground *samizdat* press in the 1980s and gained recognition and popularity after 1990.

THE YOUNGER GENERATION

With censorship now a thing of the past, modern Hungarian literature has broken with the tradition of making a political statement beyond the aesthetic one. Some lament that writers are no longer the nation's living political conscience. However, the brilliant experimental prose of Péter Esterházy, Péter Nádas, László Márton or László Krasznahorkai might be regarded as proof that, at least in literature, Hungary is now emancipated into the European norm. The literary scene has

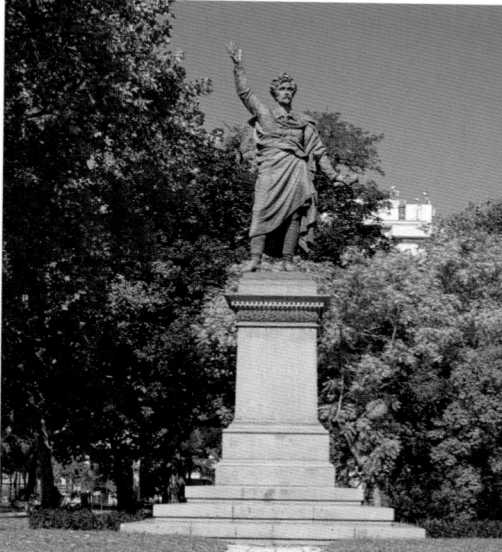

Monument to Sándor Petőfi in Budapest.

opened up; coming to grips with the past 50 years is one of the main issues. Writing itself is a theme for many contemporary authors, who make a critical attempt to shed more light on time, space and history from an individual point of view.

In the last decade, there has been a surge in good translations of modern Hungarian literature into other European languages. Sándor Márai (who committed suicide in exile in the last months of the old communist regime) has been a bestseller in Germany. A breakthrough in English is more difficult, but the excellent *Hungarian Quarterly* magazine provides an insight into Hungarian writing.

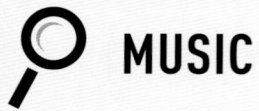

MUSIC

Hungarians are extremely musical. Much of their folk tradition is rooted in music, they eat, drink and talk music, and they populate orchestras and occupy concert stages around the world.

The musical tradition goes back to the 12th century, to the songs of the Chermiss and other Ugric peoples living along the Volga and on the Ob. After the conversion of the Hungarian state (established by István (Stephen) I) to Christianity at the turn of the first millennium, the musical culture of Christendom played a formative role. Under Mátyás Corvinus

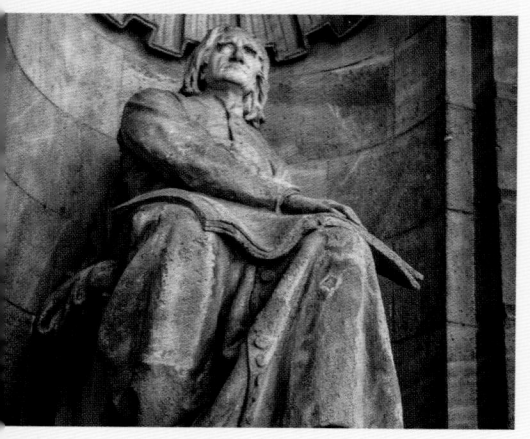

Franz Liszt monument.

(King Matthias), the choral style, influenced by the Flemish school, appeared in Hungary. However, the conquest of Hungary by the Turks in 1526 brought courtly culture to an abrupt end. In the now divided country, the rhymed chronicle became the most common musical genre, and the singing, travelling chroniclers were the sole keepers of the national musical consciousness. Among them was Sebestyén Tinódi (1505–56), known as the Lutist, who told Bible stories and heroic tales of warriors. The most prominent musician was the lute virtuoso Bálint Bakfark Greff (c.1507–69).

CULTURAL CENTRES

In the 16th and 17th centuries the virginal (a type of harpsichord) became the most popular instrument in wealthy bourgeois houses. The best secular music was arranged for this instrument, although religious music was also often included. In cities where bishops resided, most importantly Győr and Eger, the music of the Counter-Reformation, the high Baroque style, reached its peak. In 1711 a collection of cantatas, Harmonia Caelestis by Prince Pál Esterházy, was published. From 1761, Josef Haydn served the Esterházy family as court musical director for 30 years. The towns of Bratislava and Sopron saw the first results of urban, bourgeois musical culture. Debrecen and Sárospatak, where the Reformed Church was strong, were the cradles of Hungarian choral music. The choir founded by György Maróthi (1715–44), the Cantus of Debrecen, still exists today.

In the 19th century, thanks to Ferenc Erkel (1810–93), the Hungarian National Opera was founded. In his earliest stage-works (the two most famous are László Hunyadi, 1844, and Bánk Bán, 1861), he attempted a synthesis of Italian cavatina and military music. Erkel also composed the Hungarian national anthem in 1844. Karl Goldmark (1830–1915) represented the German community in Hungary. His popular opera The Queen of Sheba (1875) was influenced by the music of the synagogue, which he heard as a child.

However, among 19th-century Hungarian composers, only Franz Liszt (1811–86) achieved worldwide fame. He established the Academy of Music in Budapest, and was the founding father of modern Hungarian music. Describing himself as 'part gypsy', his compositions, such as his Hungarian Rhapsodies, drew on traditional Roma music. Despite his patriotism, Liszt's first language was German, and he never fully mastered Hungarian.

FOLK MUSIC

The 'typically Hungarian' music you will hear today developed over the last 150 years from the verbunkos, a traditional dance associated with the recruitment of soldiers. This music is distinct from folk music of peasant origin, which still survives and is celebrated in the dance houses – tánchÁz – in Hungarian (see page 89).

For more than 200 years the fiery rhythms and lilting melodies of Hungarian folk music have stirred the imagination of classical composers. The anthropologist Béla Vikár (1859–1945) made sound recordings in Transylvania, and began research into previously unstudied peasant music. Following the initiative of his colleague Zoltán Kodály (1882–1967), Béla Bartók (1881–1945) decided to travel among the peasants in order to catalogue the rich treasure of folk songs. Peasant music influenced the methods of composition of both men, Bartók most notably in *Bluebeard's Castle* and Kodály in his *Peacock Variations*. Although also a talented composer, Kodály's creative strength was most evident in his role as national musical educator. His ideas have made Hungarian music teaching among the best in the world. Composers such as Sándor Jemnitz (1890–1963), György Kósa (1897–1984) and Pál Kadosa (1903–83), who left a legacy in music and education, have been undeservedly forgotten.

The communist era was not kind to music: contemporary Western music was branded as 'bourgeois decadence', Bartók was castigated as a 'cosmopolitan' and left Hungary in 1940 to die in poverty in the United States. The Békés-Tarhos music school for talented children from farming families was closed in 1954. A conservative folklore style and academic rigidity became the rule. György Ligeti (1923–2006), a musician first influenced by Bartók and Kodály, left Hungary after the failed 1956 revolution to find freedom to develop his ultra-modern, iconoclastic style of composition.

NEW GENERATION

After 1956, some freedom of musical expression was promised. By 1959 the first works in the rediscovered new style were premiered – Six Orchestral Pieces by Endre Szervánszky (1911–77) and the String Quartet by György Kurtág (b. 1926). By the early 1960s, the 'New Wave' of Hungarian opera had arrived with works such as Blood Wedding by Sándor Szokolay (1931–2013).

Jazz, too, began to free itself from ideological pressure and the first clubs were founded; jazz is now popular throughout the country. Beat music was a new wave of unofficial musical culture. New Hungarian compositions such as Szőllősy's *Third Concerto* (1970), *Balassa's Requiem* (1972) and Durkó's oratorio *Funeral Oration* (1975) won international awards. In 1971 the Studio for New Music was founded by young composers reacting against the rigidity of the established New Hungarian Music, and music centres were set up in universities and clubs.

Since the 1990s, the relaxation of constraints on creativity and the reduction in subsidies have left Hungarian composers pondering the same questions as their contemporaries in the West: how to retain artistic integrity and earn a living. The pop sector, meanwhile, has taken off in grand style.

When frizzy-haired balladeer Jimmy Számbó accidentally killed himself in late 2000, it can be said to have marked the passing of an era in Hungarian pop music. Shut off by censorship and the impenetrable language, Hungarian pop and rock developed in a hothouse atmosphere, producing stars such as Számbó and the rock outfit Sziami, who have been compared favourably to Joy Division. The old favourites still tour to packed houses, but the new generation of Hungarian pop aims to imitate Western mainstream pop in everything but language. The nation's favourite TV show has become Magyar Pop Idol. As elsewhere, the career longevity of its winners remains to be seen.

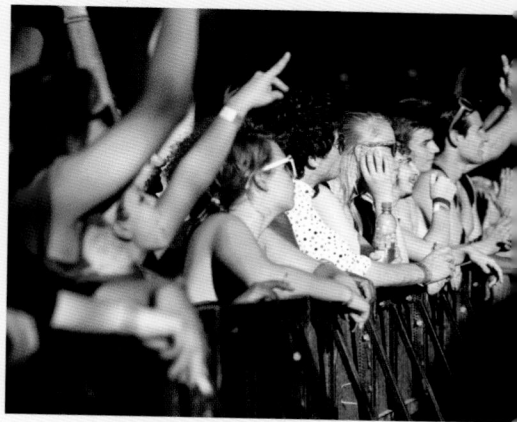

Sziget Festival.

Rap has also taken off, with acts like Ganxsta Zolee making a convincing case that gangster rap exists in Angyalföld. Perhaps due in part to its non-reliance on lyrics, electronica, especially trance beats, is still as popular in Hungary today as in the 1990s. A visit to a dance club or a summer rave can seem like a trip back in time, and generally the atmosphere is just as friendly. DJ Tommyboy aims to stay ahead of the curve, while Anima Sound System, Hungary's answer to Massive Attack, are well worth checking out. To see top international and Hungarian acts, catch the eight-day long Sziget Festival held on Óbuda Island in August.

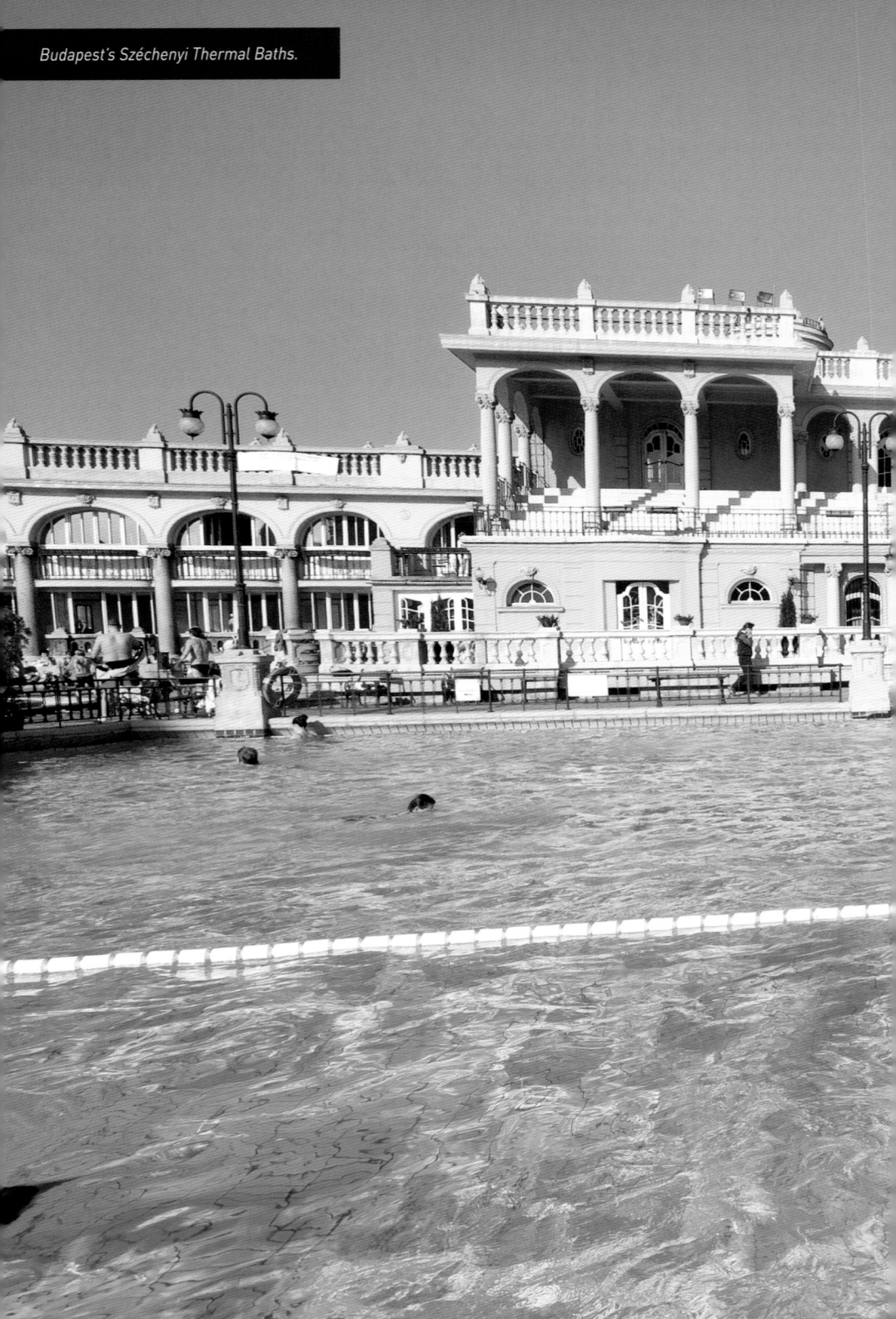
Budapest's Széchenyi Thermal Baths.

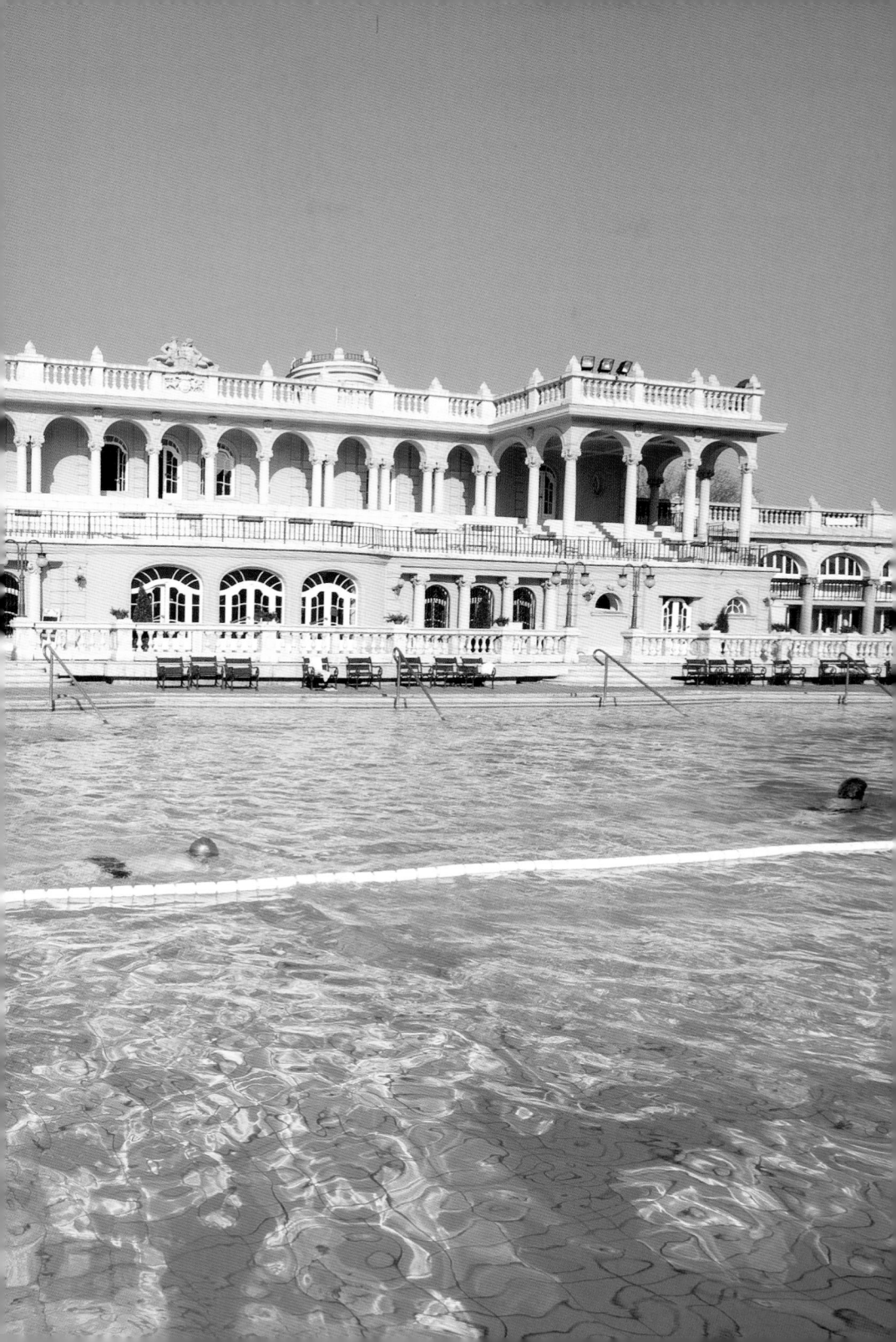

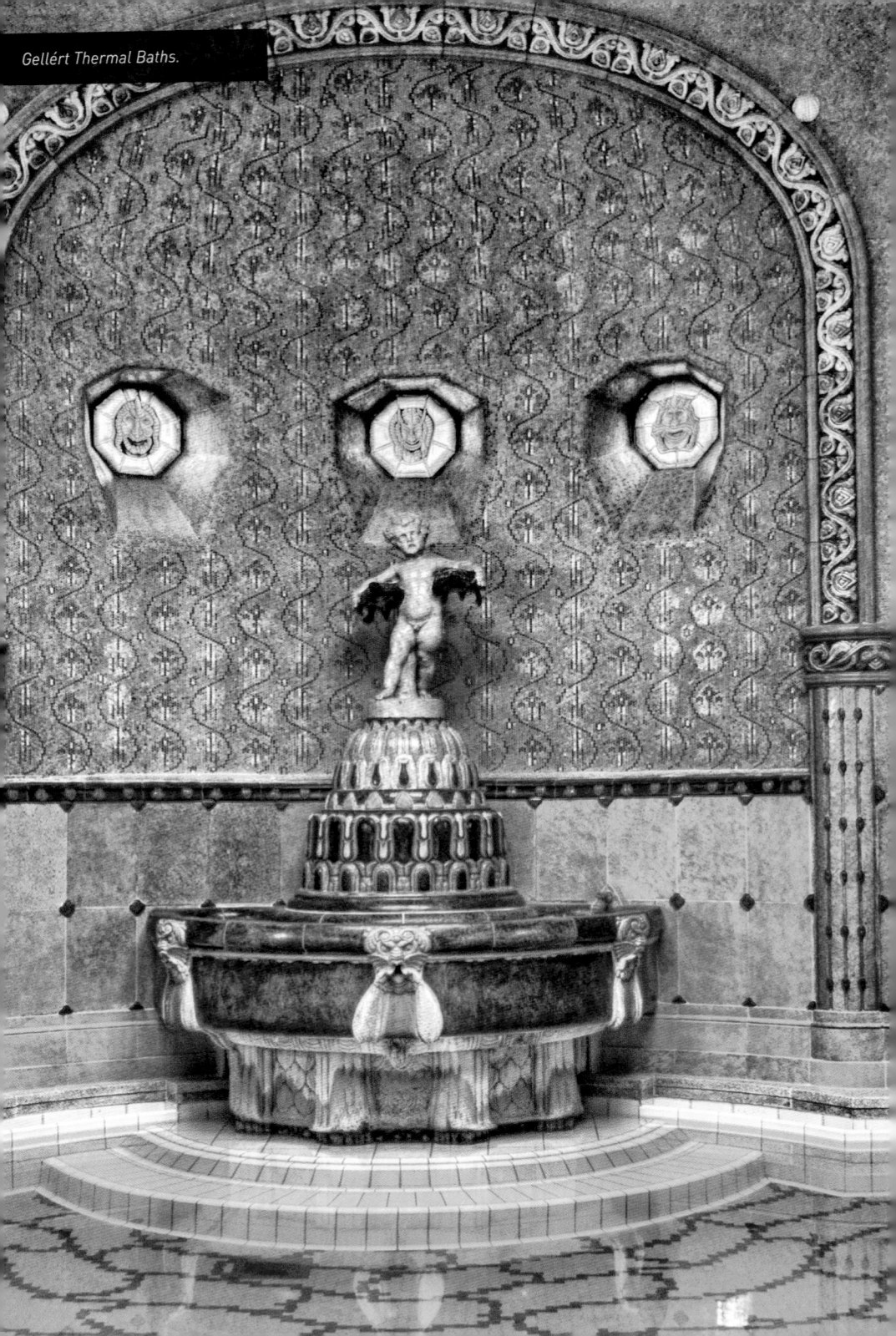

HOT SPRINGS AND SPAS

Hungary has more than a thousand hot springs, prized since Roman times for their medicinal qualities and as places to relax.

Hot springs are to Hungary what oil is to Texas. The land is like a sponge, and hundreds of spas have been built on this ground, like derricks in oilfields. You don't need to go through the country with a divining rod to find water – just stop somewhere and dig, and you'll soon discover a spring. In fact, a number of spas came into being when the government was drilling in search of oil. Zalakaros, to the southwest of Lake Balaton, is one such place.

Healthy people visit the spas on a regular basis, to give themselves a quick 'general overhaul', and to enjoy a longstanding tradition. As well as being favourite meeting places, spas are also frequented by the sick, acting on doctor's orders, since Hungarian spa waters are particularly effective in easing rheumatic ailments, stomach and intestinal conditions and gynaecological problems.

Towards the end of the 19th century, under the rule of the Austro-Hungarian monarchy, the Magyar waters received international acclaim, which spread as far as America, where bathers also followed the call to visit the spas for the sake of their health. In 1907 a brochure introduced Budapest as 'the greatest mineral water spa in the world'. This bold claim was perhaps no exaggeration, and Budapest is still the most important spa town in Europe.

DAILY ROUTINE

For some, a visit to the spa is part of their daily routine. In the spas you meet familiar faces, you can bathe together with your family, neighbours and friends, just as other people might meet at the local bar. The Hungarian people love anything to do with water, whether it's a matter of sport, relaxation or health.

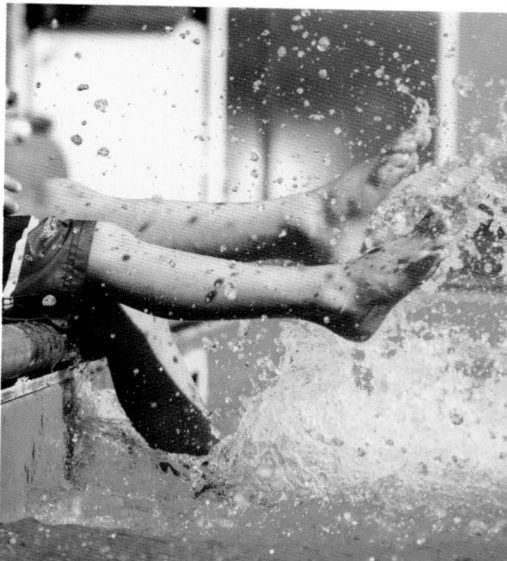

Relaxing at the baths.

The spring water seems to favour humans, too, cleansing their bodies at exactly the right temperature.

Foreigners who really want to become acquainted with the Hungarian way of life should visit a thermal spa at least once during their stay in the country, whether it's a traditional bath house in the Turkish style or the more elaborate type of establishment in the style of Gellért in Budapest, or one of the great spas out in the country, Hajdúszoboszló, Hévíz, Bük, or the Nyíregházi Sóstó. Visitors should be aware, however, that spa treatments are not always suitable for people with heart problems or high blood pressure, or for stroke victims. In fact, it is always advisable to consult your own doctor before having any treatment involving hot springs.

WATERY TRADITION

Bathing traditions are as old as humanity itself. Traces of homo erectus dating back 600,000 years have been found in the vicinity of some hot springs. This was no coincidence; even in prehistoric times people were aware of the beneficial effects of the waters, and since then the history of Hungary has always unfolded around its natural springs.

> *The Széchenyi Baths, located in Városliget (City Park), are the hottest springs in Budapest. Join the locals and enjoy the architecture, the warmth, and a game of chess.*

and personal hygiene. Between 1541 and 1686 they built a dozen bath houses in Hungary, all based on the same pattern, with the Turkish crescent perched on top of the copper dome,

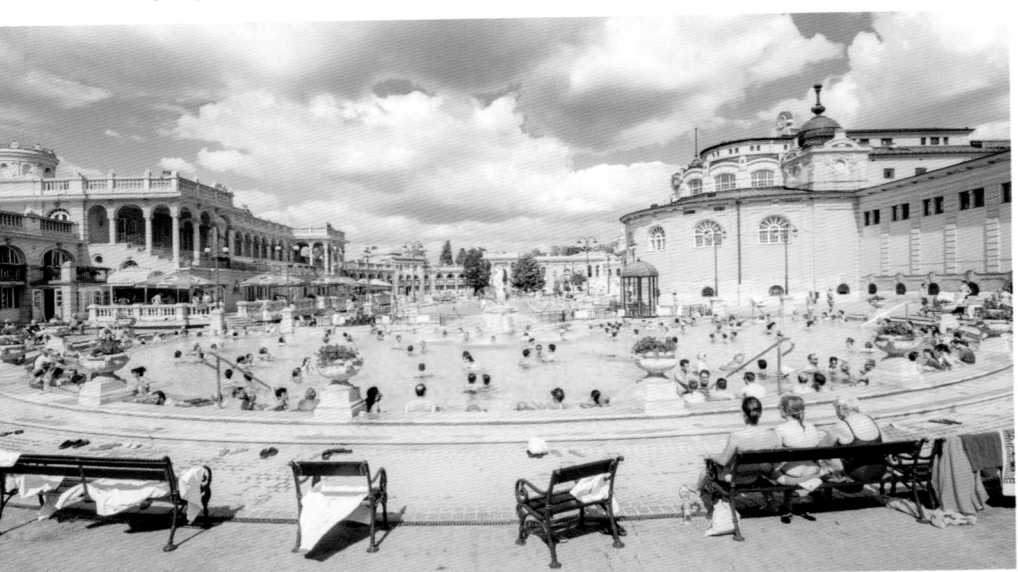

Lukács Baths, Budapest.

The Romans, who occupied parts of Hungary for nearly 400 years, made use of them to recreate the luxury of the baths back home. The ruins in Aquincum (north of Buda on Szentendrei utca No. 139) and in Gorsium (just south of Székesfehérvár) are evidence of this. Later, many of the medieval chronicles tell the story of Saint Elisabeth, who would treat lepers at the foot of the Gellért Hill in Buda, in the baths that were founded by the Knights of St John.

TURKISH BATHS

However, it is the Turks who have left the best-preserved evidence. Like the Romans, they were keen bathers and created a sophisticated social rite out of the process of bathing

similar to those found throughout the Ottoman Empire.

Budapest has five of these Turkish baths, also known as steam baths – Király (II Fö utca 8–10), Császár (II Frankel Leó utca 29–31), Rudas (I Döbrentei tér 9), Rác (I Hadnagy utca 8–10), and Pesterzsébet (XX Vízisport utca 2). These baths are not geared towards foreign visitors and are mainly used by local people, for whom they act as meeting places. That in itself is reason enough to leave the well-trodden path and try them out, if you really want to get to know Hungary and gain a true impression of the traditional and Middle Eastern bathing rituals.

The original Rác baths were built in the 15th century, and were the favourite bathing place of Mátyás Corvinus (King Matthias I), who entered them in private by a covered passage from the nearby royal castle. The baths were rebuilt in 1865 by the Hungarian architect, Miklós Ybl.

Király has the best preserved baths. They were built in 1556 under the rule of Pasha Arslan, and were at that time within the fortifications erected by the Turks around the quarter known as the 'water town' (today known as Víziváros in Hungarian), so they would not miss out on their daily bath when under siege. The dome was damaged by bombs in World War II and has since been rebuilt.

If you go to bathe, watch the time: the sexes bathe separately by the hour, as it is usual to take to the water almost naked. Most people wear a cloth for the sake of modesty when walking around the baths, but it is often laid aside when they get into the water.

THE RIGHT DEGREE OF HEAT

You can choose the sequence of baths to suit yourself, but the usual procedure is to start

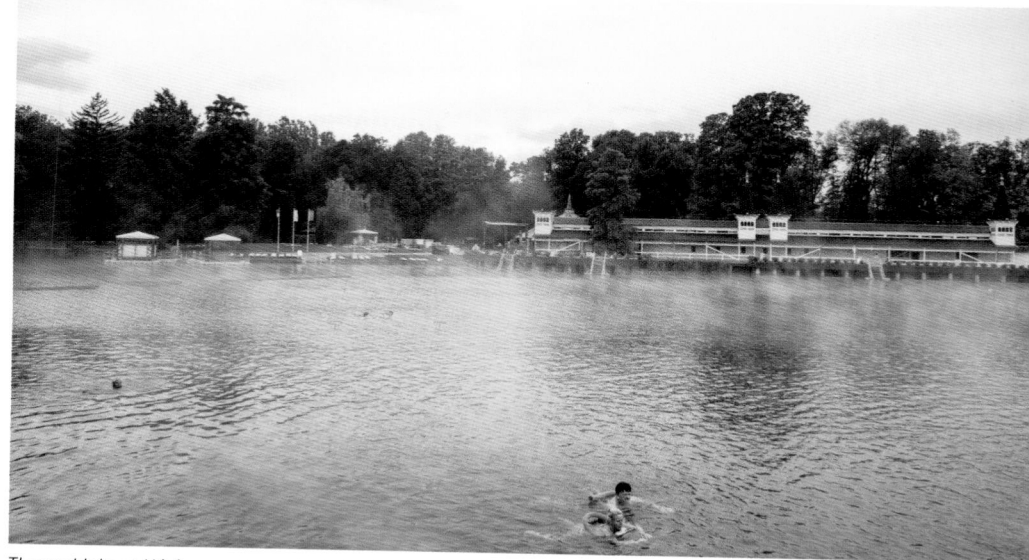

Thermal lake at Hévíz.

⊘ RELIEF FOR RHEUMATISM

The lake at Hévíz is one of the best hydrotherapy sites in Hungary. Close to Lake Balaton and only 65 km (40 miles) from the Austrian border, Hévíz, an attractive resort and the self-styled 'mecca of rheumatism sufferers', has the largest thermal lake in Europe, with a surface area of 4.75 hectares (12 acres).

The sulphurous and slightly radioactive water bubbles up at a constant temperature of 40°C (104°F) from a crater 37 metres (120ft) deep and supplies 86 million litres (19 million gallons) of water a day. The thick layer of medicinal mud at the bottom of the lake is used for treating rheumatism and is exported abroad.

This lake was known to the Romans, but spa facilities were not developed until the end of the 19th century, when bathing pavilions were constructed on piles in the centre. The village was completely rebuilt between 1977 and 1986. The old wooden platforms were replaced by concrete, but the pavilions were reconstructed in the traditional style. Ladders lead down to the water, which is covered in flowering lilies.

The lake itself is a great attraction, and bathing in it is extremely beneficial and relaxing. Swimming is possible even in the winter, as the water temperature never falls below 26°C (75°F) and the rising steam warms the air.

with the warm rooms. One room is heated to 45°C (113°F); in the steam rooms the temperature rises to (55–65°C/131–49°F). A brave leap into chilly (26°C/79°F) water will refresh and revive you, to say the least. Then you can warm yourself in the hot pools, with temperatures of 28°, 36° and 40°C (82°, 97° and 104°F), until you are ready to submit to the hands of the masseur.

The favourite bath is the central pool under the dome, which is at body temperature (36°C/97°F). Here visitors often stay long-

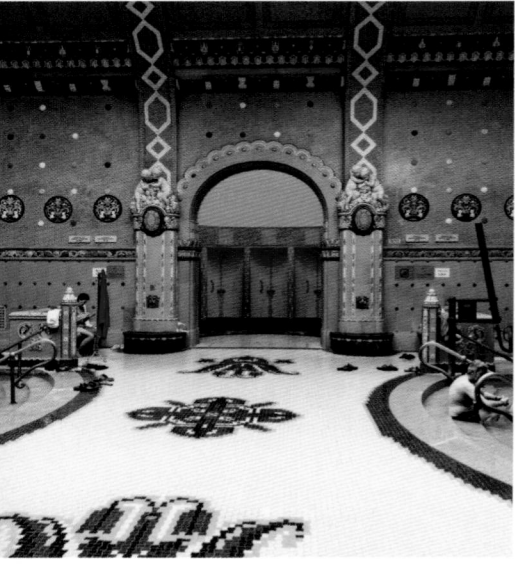

Gellért Thermal Bath.

est, gossiping or discussing current affairs, while veiled in steam. This can be a memorable sight on a fine day, when the sun's rays, fragmented by many panes of glass, stream through the dome in multi-coloured shafts of light.

The Lukács baths (II Frankel Léo utca 25–29) are the most reputable even today for their mud baths, which ease ailments of the joints. Spa treatments, just like ideas, follow fashionable trends. In 1913 the Széchenyi bath (XIV Allatkerti körút 11) was the favoured resort of the 'spa tourists'. The baths are conveniently close to the excellent Gundel restaurant; a good meal is just what's needed to round off a good soak. Széchenyi, with its neo-Baroque building,

its domes and equestrian statues, was in the early 20th century the biggest spa centre in Europe. A dozen baths, from mud to *hammams*, public baths to luxury baths, had something to offer every taste and every purse. The hottest springs in Budapest rise here, which means you can bathe in the gigantic open-air pool even on the coldest days. The main challenge at these times is to get from the changing rooms to the water as quickly as possible. But, of course, you soon forget the cold once you have dived in and your head is enveloped in the warm steam. In a much photographed scene that typifies Budapest, chess players sit in the water conducting their games with serious intent and great concentration.

FASHIONABLE GELLÉRT

From 1981, taking the waters at the Gellért Hotel and its baths (XI Kelenhegyi út 4) became the height of fashion among the jet set. The Shah of Persia, Richard Nixon, Raquel Welch, Luchino Visconti, and even Queen Juliana of the Netherlands were among those who took treatment here. Today, the Gellért is justifiably popular with wealthy Hungarians and foreign visitors. Staying at the hotel is great fun; you can don your complimentary robe and slippers and descend to the baths in a private lift. The facilities consist of beautifully tiled pools and a range of baths and treatments, although finding your way round is something of a challenge if you speak no Hungarian.

The Gellért building is representative of Hungarian art nouveau, with unmistakable Moorish influences. Outside there is a wave pool for more boisterous activity in summer.

More modern and clearly geared towards health is the Thermal Hotel Margitsziget on Margaret Island, which offers state-of-the-art hydro- and physiotherapy, sports facilities and even a small open-air theatre for the patients.

For details of opening hours, prices, temporary closures and special events for all the city's baths, visit www.spasbudapest.com.

The rest of the country is well stocked with thermal and healing baths, too, and they make a restful break when travelling. The days when hotels and facilities tended to be a little rundown are not quite over, but even in the less elegant resorts, bathing is always an interesting experience. Thanks to a modernisation programme drawn up in 1977, Hungary's spas are constantly improving and compare favourably with more expensive sanctuaries in Austria.

AQUATIC PARADISE

Among the newest spas to enjoy increasing popularity is the one in Mosonmagyaróvár, located just inside the Hegyeshalom border crossing with Austria, which offers therapy for rheuma-

Cycling, riding and canoeing excursions to the Szigetköz region along the Danube, cultural programmes, even golf (at the Princess Hotel) make a longer sojourn here an attractive proposition.

Zalakaros (to the south of Lake Kisbalaton) is like the fairy-tale frog kissed by a princess. In 2001 it opened its latest section with landscaped saunas and underwater massages, hot on the heels of its stylish pools with little islands. The waters, discovered during oil explorations, have the highest fluoride content of all the spa waters

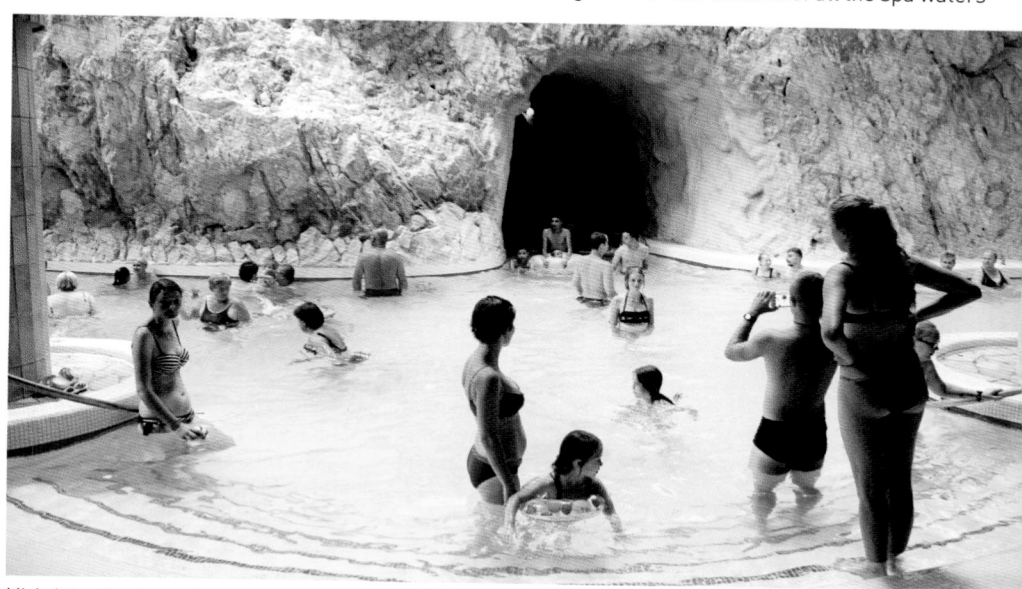

Miskolctapolca thermal pool and cave.

tism and arthritis. Hotels and good restaurants have sprung up around it, and the local authorities and entrepreneurs have understood that sitting around in hot water is not all that a spa should offer.

> *Bük, about 29 km (18 miles) east of Szombathely, is also very popular. The 58°C (136°F) waters contain calcium, magnesium, fluoride and carbonates, and are used in the treatment of a wide range of disorders from post-operative to gynaecological.*

in Hungary. As the waters also contain sulphur, the occasional whiff of rotten eggs cannot be helped, but it's a small price to pay for feeling so wholesome and healthy.

HEARTFELT EASE

Three other spas in the west of Hungary have built a reputation for themselves. Balf, in the foothills of the Alps near Lake Fertö, was known for its curative waters in Roman times. The Roman general Marcus Aurelius sent his battle-weary soldiers here to rest and recuperate. The water even splashes within the sacred buildings in Balf, and the ceiling of the Baroque chapel is painted with a biblical bathing scene.

Harkány has both water and mud baths – the latter are rich in sulphur and fluoride. The area used to be known as Büdösrét (Stinking Meadow) because of the characteristic sulphurous smell, but people decided that the benfits to be gained made it bearable.

Balatonfüred on the north bank of Lake Balaton is not only a hydrotherapy centre, thanks to the medicinal waters of the lake, but also one of the oldest spas in the lake district because of the springs, which contain carbon dioxide.

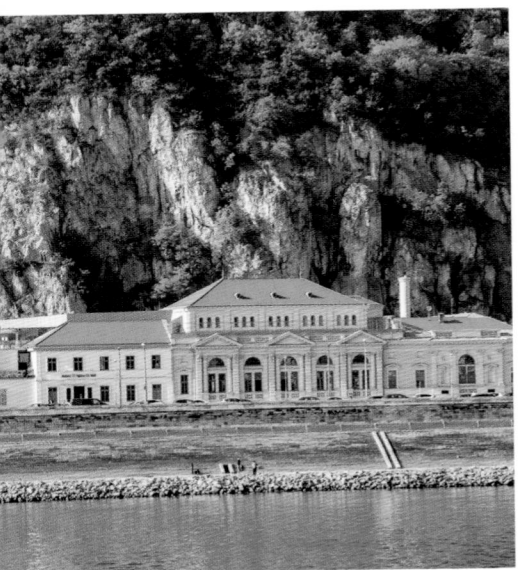

The Turkish-style Rudas Baths in Budapest.

In the modern hospital, research is carried out into heart diseases, and the spa has significant success in treating them. Balatonfüred is also an elegant town, popular with summer visitors, although the medicinal waters are for the use of patients only.

EASTERN HUNGARY

The east, too, has its share of great spas, such as **Gyula** in southeastern Hungary, which specialises in the treatment of chronic rheumatic conditions. Its facilities are set in a protected environment, in a beautiful park just opposite the 16th-century castle.

West of Debrecen is Hajdúszoboszló, which has long been one of the most dynamic spas in Hungary in terms of its advertising and promotion. In 1925, it was oil that was being sought here, but drilling brought something else bubbling up from below – water at a temperature of 72°C (162°F). This water, it transpired, was particularly useful in the treatment of open wounds, and after World War II, when thousands of injured veterans were in great need of help, Hajdúszoboszló became one of the most sought-after spas in the country. This spa treats about a million patients every year and claims a 90 percent cure rate.

Besides the spa, Hajdúszoboszló has added an Aquatic Park to its facilities, which is appreciated by younger visitors. It has a 113-metre (362ft) double slide, a huge 'black hole', a white-water passage and other watery delights. In fact, Hajdúszoboszló is so successful that it has overshadowed the quieter thermal baths in Debrecen, which nonetheless are very enjoyable, especially as a break from sightseeing. The pleasure of relaxing in the soothing waters of a spa after a few days' walking around museums is something to be relished.

WATER, WATER EVERYWHERE

Hungary has some unusual physical features, which can make spa treatments even more interesting. In **Miskolctapolca**, a spa situated just a few kilometres away from the industrial centre of Miskolc, you can bathe in slightly radioactive caves with a water temperature of 30°C (86°F), and you can also inhale wholesome steam if you suffer from asthma. This is a truly spectacular place to bathe, in the half-light of tortuous caves with clear waters and soft lighting.

This chapter has highlighted the more popular spas. But wherever you go – to Pécs, Szeged, Györ, Kecskemét, Nyíregyháza – you will find medicinal waters. Almost every town has hot springs and baths. In fact, there are 1,100 springs in use, with an average water temperature of 25°C (77°F), and 450 hot spring baths, of which a third have been built since 1970. This boundless source of energy has been harnessed for central heating in homes and for various purposes in agriculture and industry – which makes good environmental sense and is no doubt the envy of many other European states.

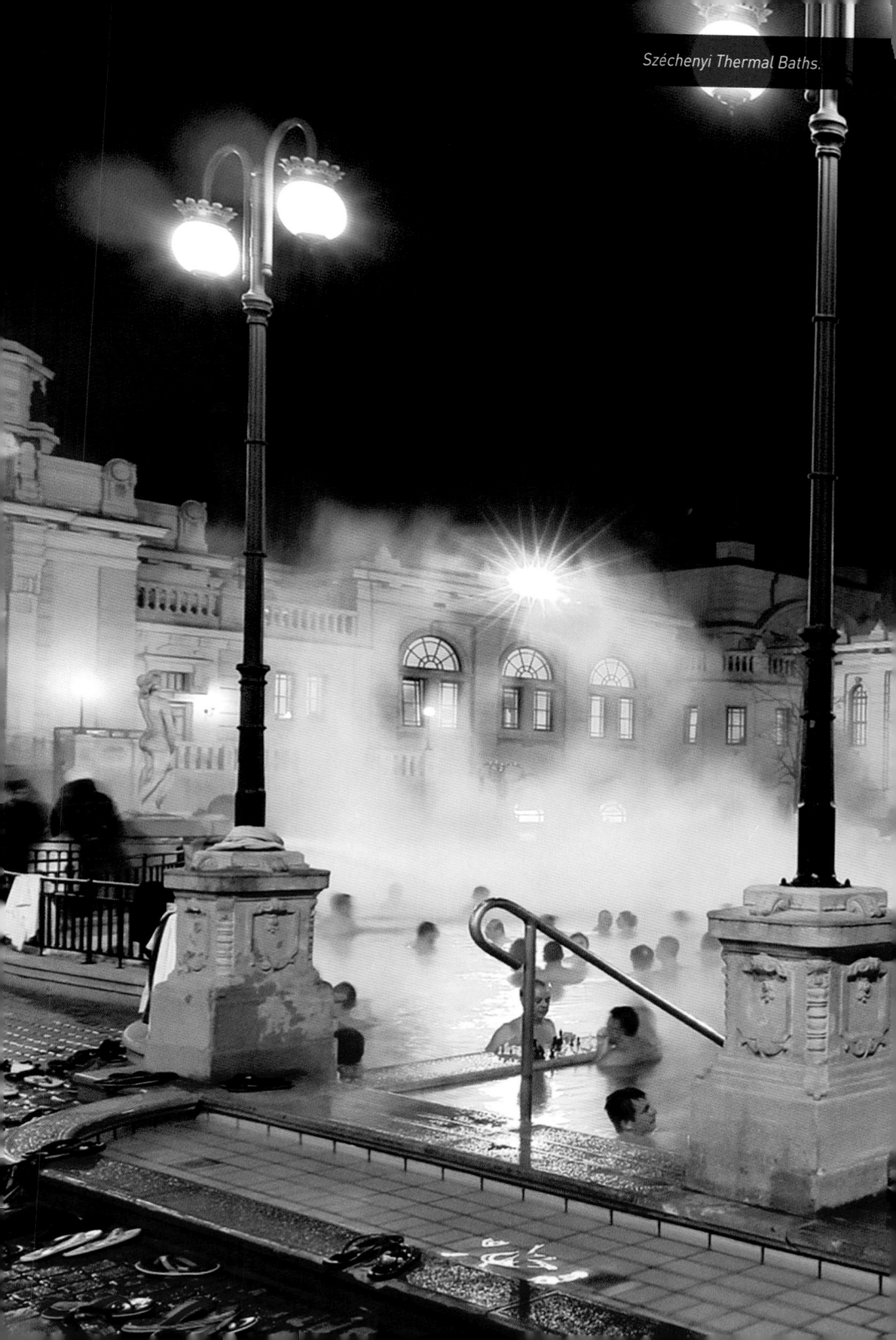

Széchenyi Thermal Baths.

HUNGARY AT THE MOVIES

Though the filming of a millennial parade in Budapest in 1896 marked the official beginning of Hungarian movies, it was not until 1912 that production began in earnest. By the start of World War I, some two dozen film studios were operating and, as no foreign films were imported, production flourished.

It was the beginning of a long love affair between the Hungarians and movies. Going to the cinema quickly became fashionable, and a star cult arose around figures such as Franciska Gaál, Vilma Bánky, Lia Putty, Kató Nagy, Mihály Várkonyi, Pál Lukács and the great Béla Lugosi. The first generation of Hungarian filmmakers included names such as Sándor (Alexander) Korda (who produced The Third Man) and Mihály

Bela Lugosi in 'Dracula', 1931.

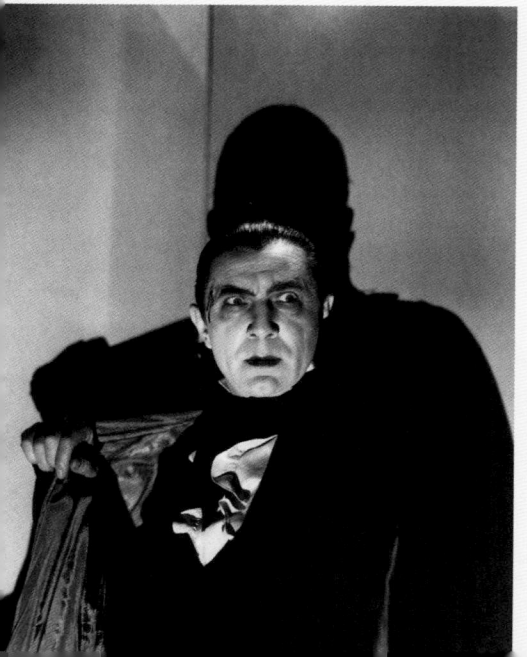

Kertész (Michael Curtiz, director of Casablanca), while Adolph Zukor sired the Famous Players Film Co., which later became Paramount Studios.

Under Béla Kun's short-lived soviet, the Hungarian film industry became the first in the world to be nationalised. Following reprivatisation under the Horthy government, however, its vigour started to fade. The clouds on Hungary's film horizon had a silver lining for western film studios: American, Danish, French and Italian films flooded the market, reducing domestic production to almost nil. Hungarian filmmakers found employment abroad, mainly in Austria and Germany.

THE TALKIES

The birth of the talkies gave the film industry a new lease of life. To promote domestic production, the government granted tax exemption to companies producing films in Hungarian, and the Hunnia Film Studio shot the first Hungarian sound film, *The Blue Idol*, in 1930. The real breakthrough, however, was the highly successful *Hyppolit the Butler* (1931) by István Székely (who, as Steve Sekely, made *The Day of the Triffids* in 1962).

In 1939, the government tightened its grip on film production: all screenplays were examined by the National Committee of Film. In the spirit of anti-Jewish legislation, the Chamber of Moving Picture Art gradually expelled anyone of Jewish origin from the industry. István Székely and Béla Gaál were blacklisted, while Gyula Kabos, the public's darling, could no longer be cast. Scores of actors left for the US, where contracts were forthcoming for those who could disguise their accent. Screen-writers managed to circumvent the decree by ghost-writing into the early 1940s: István Szöts' 1942 melodrama, *Men of the Alps*, won a Biennale of Venice award.

LIVING WITH CENSORSHIP

Made with government assistance in 1947, Géza Radványi's *Somewhere in Europe*, a moving story about children in the last days of the war, won international acclaim. However, following renationalisation of Hungarian film production in 1948, only censored films that were in tune with 'the new spirit of the new era' could be released. József Révai of the Ministry of People's Education single-handedly supervised film production and by 1953 had created a new style – 'schematic film' – which, despite the initial success of *A Foothold of Land* by Frigyes Bán, became synonymous with dull. The political climate eased when Imre Nagy's government took power in 1953 and put József Darvas in Révai's place. Hungarian audiences were able to see Italian neo-realist films, whose influence relaunched Hungarian motion picture art. Instead of propaganda, films now focused on Hungarian private life, highlighted by films such as Zoltán Fábri's *Merry-Go-Round* (1953).

The failed 1956 revolution led to a new political correctness, focusing on literary adaptations, some of considerable merit – among them László Ranódy's *Abyss* (1956), *Stay Good Until Death* (1960) and *Drama of the Lark* (1963), and Zoltán Fábri's *Anna* (1958) and the touching *Boys of Paul Street* (1968).

But change was in the wings: young directors, cameramen and writers were emerging from the experimental Béla Balázs Studio (BBS), established in 1959 and named after one of the world's most important film theorists. Balázs (1884-1949) began as a librettist for Bartók and a screenwriter for Pabst. The BBS produced a wide range of expressive styles, from penetrating documentaries to a pioneering – indeed courageous – break-up of traditional narrative methods. The emerging film directors became world leaders in the art: István Szabó's 1964 *Age of Illusions* won the Silver Sail at the Locarno Festival for Best First Work, while Miklós Jancsó's 1965 film *The Round-Up* was internationally acclaimed.

Péter Bacsó launched another movement, 'grotesque satire', with his 1968 film *The Witness* (banned from release for nine years). It is the story of a simple official who is manipulated into giving evidence at a show trial; while waiting to take the stand, he is given sinecures, one being the development of a Hungarian orange – in fact, a lemon. Ferenc Kardos's *A Crazy Night,* and Sándor Rózsa's *Spider Soccer* followed the new fashion.

Hungarian film had found its niche: artistic, documentary, witty, literary, intellectual, challenging the system. Few artistic genres in the country, perhaps, had such freedom.

The world beyond Hungary knew little of this treasure, however, until István Szabó's *Mephisto* won Hungary's first Oscar in 1982 in the category of Best Foreign Film. Based on Klaus Mann's novel, it is the story of an actor in Nazi Germany who allows his own existence to come second to the popularity of a character he plays. Throughout the 1980s,

Hungarian films, such as János Xantus's *Eskimo Woman Feels Cold* (1983) and Péter Tímár's *Sound Eroticism* (1986) showed increased sensitivity.

MOVIE-MAKING TODAY

Hungarian film seems on the brink of a renaissance. While the older generation are still going strong (such as István Szabó with *Sunshine,* released in 2000, the story of three generations of a Jewish-Hungarian family) it is the young director Antal Nimrod with *Kontroll (a* dark satire set entirely in the city's underground system), who seems, for the moment, to point the new way. Worth watching too will be the next project from the team behind *The District.* Their debut feature plays like the Central European answer to *South Park.* Two Hungarian films to have won Oscars in recent years are *Son of Saul* (2015), a hard-hitting film about the Holocaust by Lászlò Nemes, and *Sing* (2016), a short film by Kristóf Deák that documents a young girl's involvement in a school choir.

Budapest, meanwhile, has long been a favourite destination for film producers, both for its cheapness and its atmosphere; among the many films to have been shot (or partially shot) here include *Evita* (1996), *The Boy in the Striped Pyjamas* (2008), *A Good Day to Die Hard* (2013) and *Blade Runner 2049* (2017).

Klaus Maria Brandauer starred in 'Mephisto', 1981.

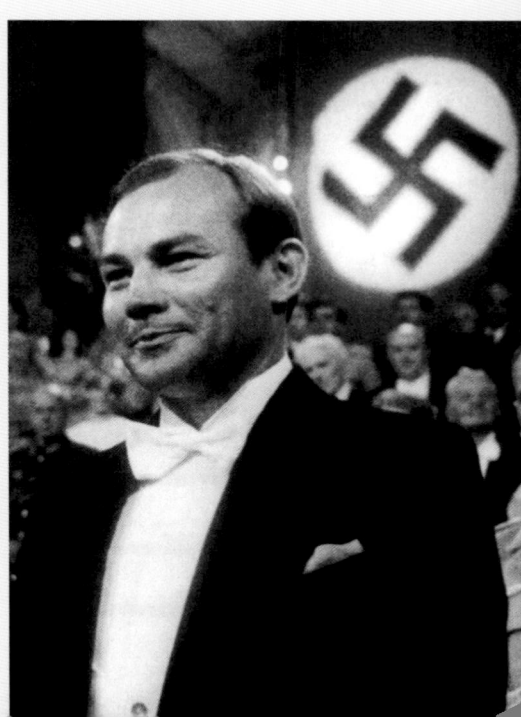

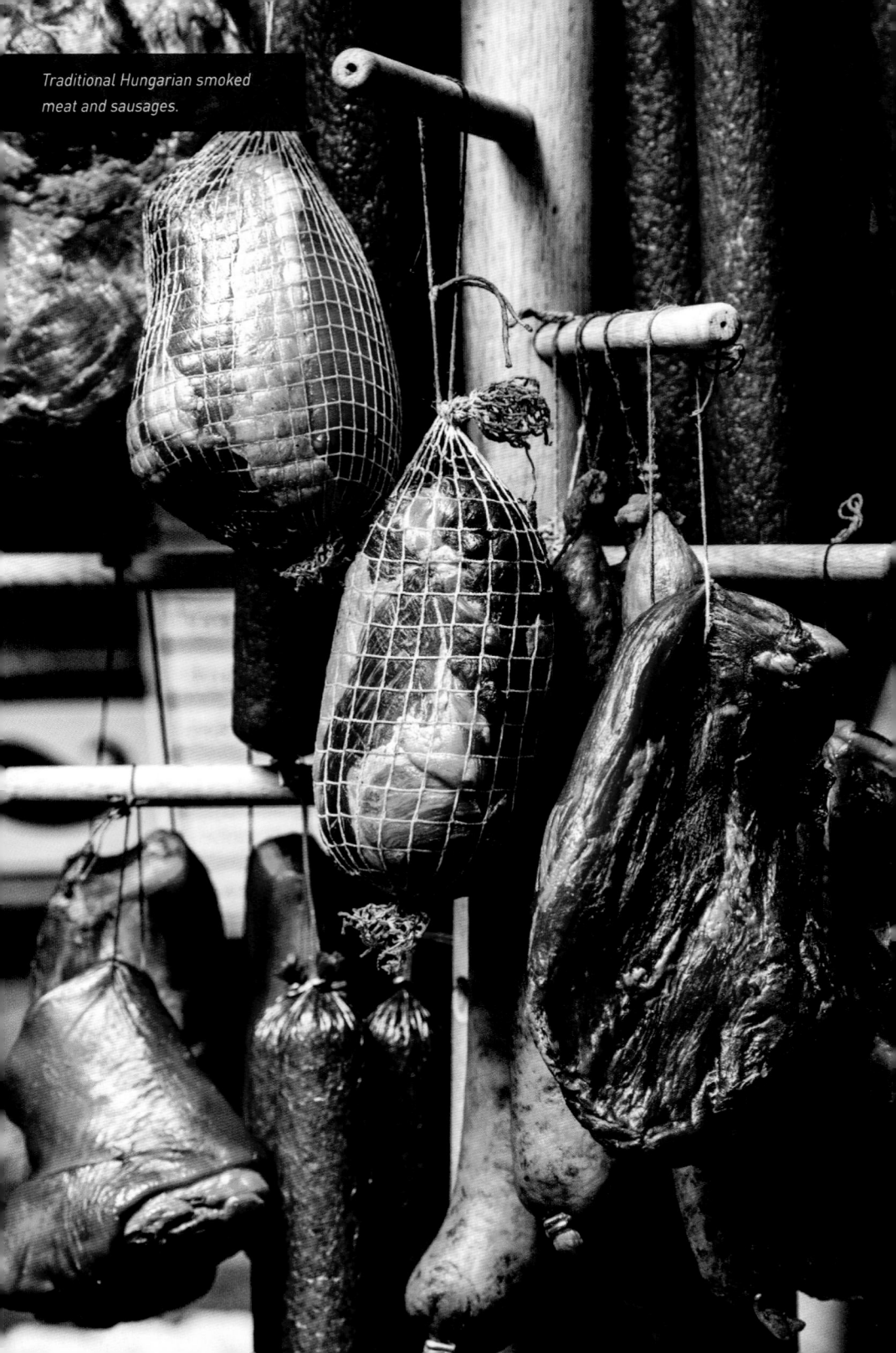
Traditional Hungarian smoked meat and sausages.

FOOD AND DRINK

Hungary is home to the famous gulyás, and its food is richly flavoured with cream, paprika, onions and horseradish.

If the Hungarian dishes you taste and savour during your visit bear little resemblance to the 'Hungarian' cooking you have sampled elsewhere, don't be surprised. Some of the ingredients are found fresh only in Hungary, and not all restaurants abroad succeed in recreating the authentic tastes and textures. Hungarian food today is quite different from that of a hundred years ago, and the early 20th-century influence of France has left its mark on many dishes. However, some traditions still hold sway in the preparation and enjoyment of food in Hungary.

CULINARY ROOTS

Traces of early Hungarian cuisine are present in the hearty soups, rich in grains, and cabbage-based dishes. During the Great Migration (9th–10th centuries), nomadic Magyars experimented with different ways of preserving food, including a recipe for kneading a paste and rolling it into balls which could later be cooked in boiling water. These *tarhonya* (dumplings) are made with flour and eggs, and the small balls can be browned in lard with onions and paprika, and then served with meat.

Nomads since early times, Hungarians developed and refined their culinary skills by assimilating recipes and techniques from the lands they visited as friends or enemies. Their travels brought them into contact with Bulgarians and Turks on the Black Sea. Later, King Mátyás and his Italian wife Beatrix introduced Western habits into the royal kitchen. It was Mátyás who brought the turkey to Hungary, and historical documents reveal that his royal feasts included up to 10 dishes per course.

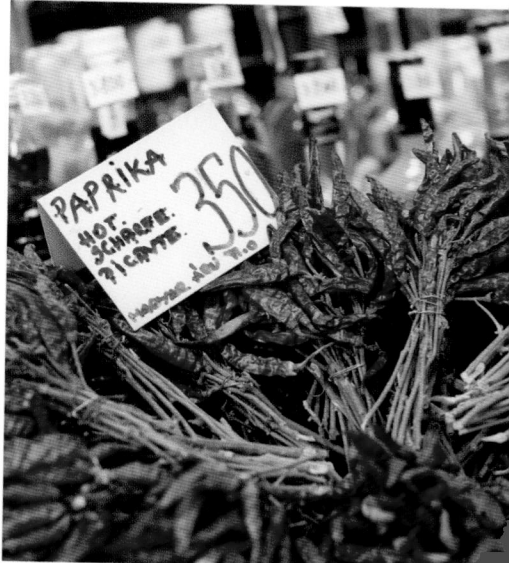

Dried bunches of red paprika.

FAVOURITE SPICE

The best-known ingredient of Hungarian food today is paprika. Paprikás is a general name given to dishes seasoned with paprika and served with sour cream sauces, especially fish, fowl and veal dishes. Red meat, pork and fatty fowl such as goose or duck are not prepared as often with this spice. Hungarian goulash (gulyás), probably the most famous Hungarian creation (and the most misunderstood in foreign kitchens), uses plenty of paprika in a meat soup or stew containing onions and small potatoes.

Onions are a mainstay ingredient, cooked to a glassy state, flavouring soup (but removed before serving), or raw and sliced in rings on top of salads or grilled meat. Fresh spring onions

One of Hungary's best-known fishy delicacies is the pike-perch (fogas). Its firm, almost boneless white flesh is best tasted fresh on the shores of Lake Balaton.

silvery Lake Balaton pike-perch (*fogas*), weighing 8–10 kg (18–22 lb) at maturity. Because the pike-perch is quite delicate, it cannot be transported alive, so if you eat it anywhere other than near the lake it's probably frozen. Another of the regional fishes is sturgeon (*tok*) from the Tisza, which is delicious and has very few bones. Trout is also found in Hungary, particularly a variety with red and black spots, which is a favourite in restaurants.

The many varieties of carp are popular and commonly served fried in breadcrumbs or 'Ser-

are very popular in a sandwich filling made with sheep curd, butter and paprika. Parsley is a common seasoning ingredient in Hungary, and bay leaf, dill, caraway, marjoram and tarragon

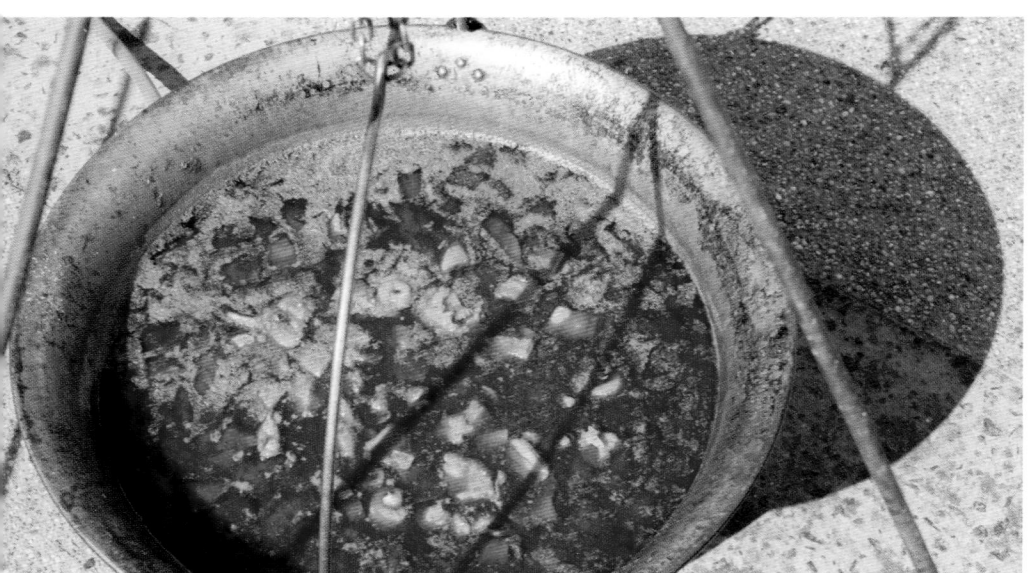

Szeged-style fish soup, also known as halászlé, is a hot and spicy paprika-based dish made with freshwater fish.

are used in many recipes. Some rarer spices such as saffron and ginger are found in special dishes. Finally, there is cream, cream and more cream. Cream in the soup, in the sauce, in the dessert – always delicious, with a flavour that is never quite matched outside the country. There is little regional variation in cooking, perhaps because the country is too small, but you will sometimes find regional ingredients; pumpkin-seed oil, for example, is used in the Őrség.

CATCH OF THE DAY

Some of the most flavoursome and authentic Hungarian dishes are made with local fish, many varieties of which are only to be found here. The best-known – and possibly the tastiest – is the

bian' style (rácpaprikás). Carp, bream and razor fish from Lake Balaton are also delicious when served sliced in two, sprinkled with paprika and grilled until crisp. They are best enjoyed in this way in the open air, washed down with a good bottle of Hungarian wine.

Hungarian fish paprikás, or fish soup, has some loyal fans. Look for it on the menu as az igazi halpaprikás. It is traditional to taste this dish at its best along the banks of the Tisza River at Szolnok or Szeged, in the middle of the Puszta at Tiszafüred, by the Danube at Komárom or on the shores of Lake Balaton. Some restaurants prepare it in a giant cauldron suspended over an open fire, and let the aroma lead you to your seat.

Halpaprikás should contain at least three kinds of fish, including catfish, carp and a locally caught variety (sturgeon or pike-perch), and is even better with small fry added. The fish is layered in a big pot, with the best on top, then simmered in onions, paprika and water, unstirred. The smaller fish at the bottom of the pot often remain there, serving only to flavour the dish. The dish is usually eaten with spaghetti or túróscsusza (cottage cheese noodles).

There are a small number of variations on this theme, including halpörkölt (fish stew flavoured with onions and lard), halleves (fish soup with vegetables), ikerás (fish soup with roe – highly recommended), halragu (fish ragout flavoured with mushrooms, wine and sour cream), barátleves (friends' soup) and halleves ikrafelfújttal (fish soup with roe soufflé).

THE FESTIVE TABLE

The end-of-the-year holidays in Hungary, as in many other countries, are times for good eating and for the renewal of traditions. If you are in Hungary at Christmas or New Year you will

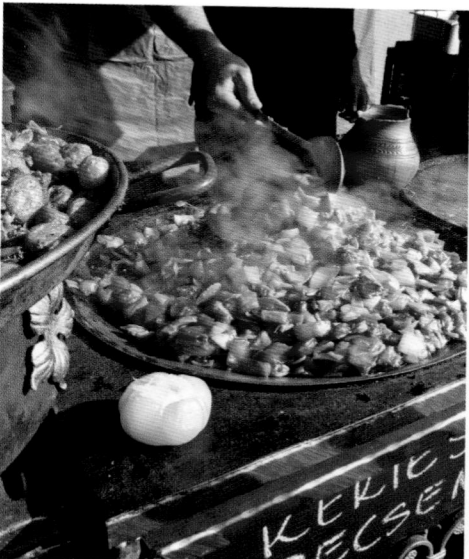

Traditional Hungarian food served at a carnival.

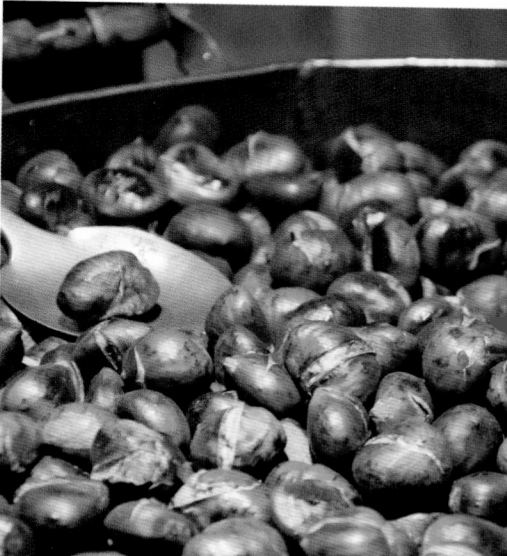

Freshly roasted chestnuts.

⊘ GOULASH

Hungarian goulash (gulyás) is probably the most-maligned and most-loved meal to come out of Hungary. Maligned, because outside the country any old meat dish made with paprika is referred to as goulash. The real thing has several forms – gulyás, pörkölt, tokány. Strictly speaking, goulash is a meat soup prepared with onions and paprika, to which cubed potatoes and noodles are added. Pörkölt is a ragout made with meat and minced onion, the strong flavour of which predominates. The sauce is thick and smooth. Tokány is similar, using small strips of meat, mushrooms, sour cream, peas and other vegetables. Paprika is sometimes replaced by pepper in this dish.

A tasty regional speciality is Székelygulyás, Transylvanian goulash, which combines different types of meat with sour cream, paprika and cabbage.

Most of these stews are thickened with sour cream, though egg yolks are also used. In finer cooking, flour is avoided as a thickener, but you may find its rather unpleasant flavour (and lumps) in thick sauces served in cheaper restaurants. Sometimes pasta is boiled into a dish at the end of cooking to give it a thicker consistency. In any event, goulash has earned its reputation as a filling meal, and remains a perennial favourite in Hungary.

be able to sample the seasonal customs and cuisine first-hand, especially if you are lucky enough to be invited into a Hungarian home. There you are likely to be served walnut-fattened turkey, stuffed with chestnuts and prunes, poppy-seed rolls, Bishop's Bread and much more.

A typical dish for this time of year is roast suckling pig, although a real suckling pig is a rarity and the usual victim is more likely to be a young hog. Crisp and golden, with an apple stuck in its mouth, suckling pig is

carniverous tourists, who arrive en masse to witness the feast. This is the only way to taste orja soup, made on the spot with spicy spare-ribs. The soup is typically followed by boiled meat and horseradish, and by festive stuffed cabbage, making use of the different parts of the pig. The meat is also used to prepare Hungarian sausages, of which many varieties exist, salami and the sharp csabai from Békésecaba being the most famous.

Black sausage or blood pudding is made by stuffing the large intestine with pig's

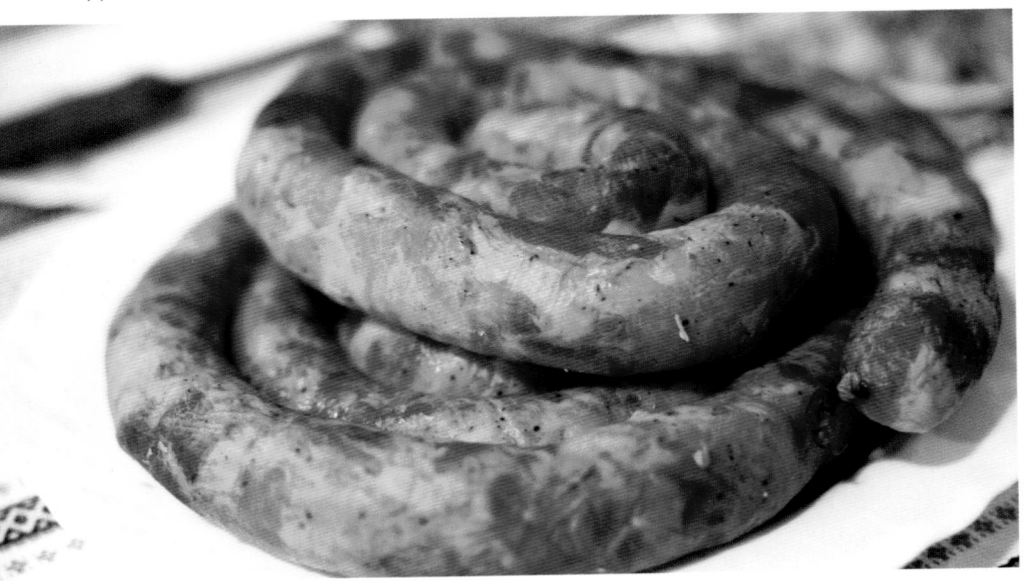

Handmade sausage.

served with vinegary red cabbage, caraway seeds for flavouring and sour gherkin pickles. Tradition has it that the suckling pig on New Year's Day brings good luck all year round. If you are not game enough to enjoy tackling part of a whole suckling pig, conjure good luck instead with a hearty pörkölt made of the same meat, served with tarhonya in red paprika gravy. Carnival doughnuts (fánk) are a popular winter dessert served piping hot and sugary.

HUNGARIAN SAUSAGES

Pig-killing and sausage-making time is still an important winter tradition in rural Hungary. Some of the bigger farms welcome busloads of

blood diluted with milk and vegetable stock, pork and bacon, onions, black pepper and marjoram. White puddings are made with a liver base using lemon, garlic, paprika and marjoram.

If partaking in one of these feasts, leave room if you can for the supreme delicacy on the menu, tenderloin roast in caul. The caul, or veil, is a fatty membrane covering the large intestine. It allows the tender pork to be stewed in its own aromatic juices. The feast continues with yet more courses of cottage cheese noodles, crackling, salads, plums pickled in spiced red wine, strudels, cakes and cream – all served with Hungarian wine and topped off with fresh fruit and coffee.

A slurp of Krambambuli, a spicy punch served flaming on New Year's Eve, is the traditional way to usher in the new year. The list of ingredients can include chopped fruit, stoned dates, raisins, candied orange peel, dried plums, walnuts, sugar, rum and brandy, all of which are flambéed before white wine, cinnamon, lemons and oranges are added.

SEASONAL FOOD

One traditional Easter meal in Hungary is Easter ham, spiced, pickled or smoked, served in slices spring chicken, a favourite dish in Hungary and one which, though quite simple, is delicious when prepared with care. Fresh kohlrabi and chilled cucumbers are also heralds of spring, along with tender young goose, sorrel sauce, fresh dill seasonings and May asparagus.

Strudels (rétes) are the pride of Hungarian cuisine. It is the quality of Hungarian flour that makes them so distinctive. The dough, made from fine flour, sour cream, lard and egg yolks, is rolled out as thin as tissue paper. The filling

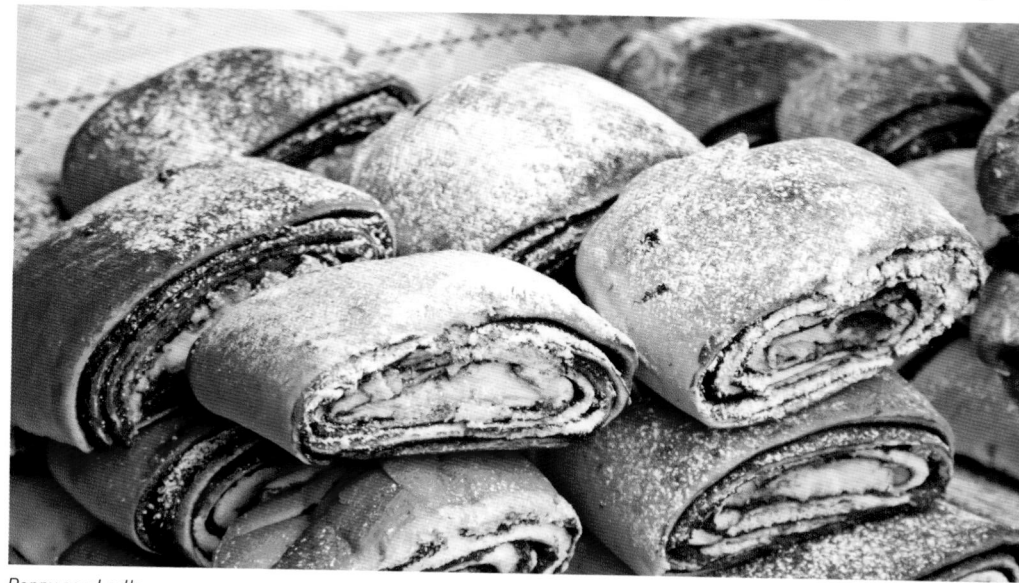

Poppy seed rolls.

with fresh spring vegetables, such as spinach, onions, radishes, peas. The ham is left to cool in the cooking water (along with Easter eggs) and should never be served re-heated. It is either eaten warm just out of the boiled juices or cold with horseradish and aspic.

Easter lamb is another seasonal favourite. Methods of serving include lamb's head soup, Transylvanian tarragon lamb, lamb paprika stew, paprika lamb with sour cream and a variety of cutlets, chops and leg of lamb dishes.

Horseshoe cakes are festive pastries sprinkled with walnuts or poppy seeds that are associated with Easter celebrations. Easter Monday is traditionally reserved for breaded

is spread over the pastry, which is rolled up and baked. Rétes are delicious when served hot with cream and powdered with sugar.

In summer, fruit soups (cherry, plum or gooseberry) are refreshing, as are cold meats garnished with salads of cucumber, cauliflower, tomatoes, mushrooms, beans, celery, lettuce and peppers.

At harvest time, you can enjoy ripe, delicious fruit. Chestnuts and walnuts are roasted and sold in paper bags in the parks and on street corners. Csája, a warming grog, is a favourite drink for this time of the year, and has taken the place of honigli, the traditional tipple made from the first pressings of newly harvested grapes.

A RICH HARVEST

Autumn is the time for harvesting grapes, which brings us to the wines of Hungary. Though the selection is not as broad as in France or Italy, Hungarian wines are enjoyable and some are excellent. Grapes have been grown in the Buda region since ancient times, and under the Habsburgs the drink became more common as vineyards spread south and east. Its growth in popularity, as well as that of wine taverns *(borozó)* was halted by phylloxera – a disease-spreading grub that destroyed vineyards all

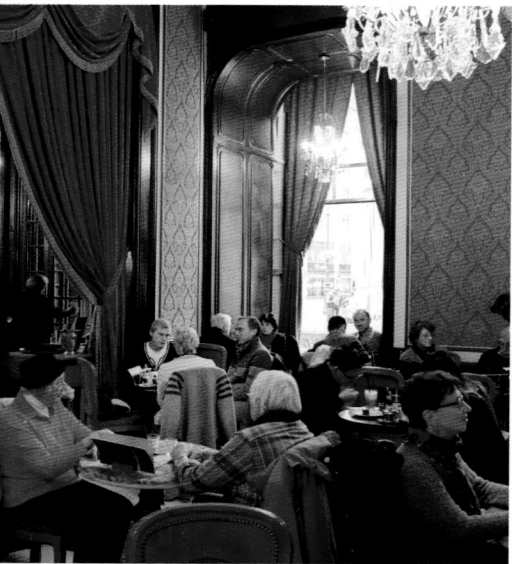

Budapest's Café Gerbeaud.

If you're in Hungary at harvest time, it's worth sampling honigli, the white wine made from the first pressings of newly harvested grapes from Buda.

over Europe in the late 19th century. Thanks to new, pest-resistant vines imported from the US, wine production resumed.

Vines are grown in many parts of the country. Some areas, such as the warm volcanic slopes of the northern coast of Lake Balaton (Badacsony and Bakony) are particularly fertile. The dry, white Olaszrisling is worth looking out for.

In southern Transdanubia, Szekszárd (see page 259) produces good reds, as does Villány (see page 266). However, there are two wines that are internationally known. The first, Egri Bikavér (Eger Bulls' Blood), owes its name to its beautiful deep red colour and to its strength and aroma. It is made from various grape varieties, not always in the same proportions. The centre of production is Eger (see page 224).

The second comes from the area to the northeast of Eger, from the confluence of the Tisza and Bodrog rivers – Tokaj, which is the centre of a high-quality wine-producing area (see page 229). The Tokaj grape itself contains a lot of sugar, which affects the alcohol content of the wine. The sweetest and heaviest Tokaj wine is Aszú. Its grapes are harvested at the end of October, by which time they have almost shrivelled up to raisins and become very sweet. The selection of grapes for pressing is very strict, and the number of baskets (puttony) it takes to produce each barrel is carefully monitored – the more baskets, the better the grade.

MENUS AND MUSIC

The average menu usually has the following sections: *levesek* (soups), *köretek* (vegetables and side dishes), *saláták* (salads), *tésztak* (cakes), *készételek* (prepared meals), *frissensültek* (freshly fried dishes), *különlegességek* (specialities). *Saláták* may mislead the customer into expecting something green and fibrous, but the word applies mainly to pickled vegetables; they help to cut through heavier foods but are rather lacking in roughage. Thus, life as a vegetarian here is difficult, unless you are willing to believe that the Hungarians use butter and oil instead of *zsír* (a grease made from pork fat that lubricates every cooking utensil and shortens every pastry dough).

Music plays an integral role in restaurants. Indeed, the romantic vision of sweltering, dancing Budapest hasn't vanished completely, and you'll still find a few Gypsy musicians plying their trade; their repertoire is international, from Strauss waltzes to German folk songs, and even the odd Beatles number, but all played gypsy-style – *alla zingara*. In many other places, however, music is piped in from above, and it can get a little wearing.

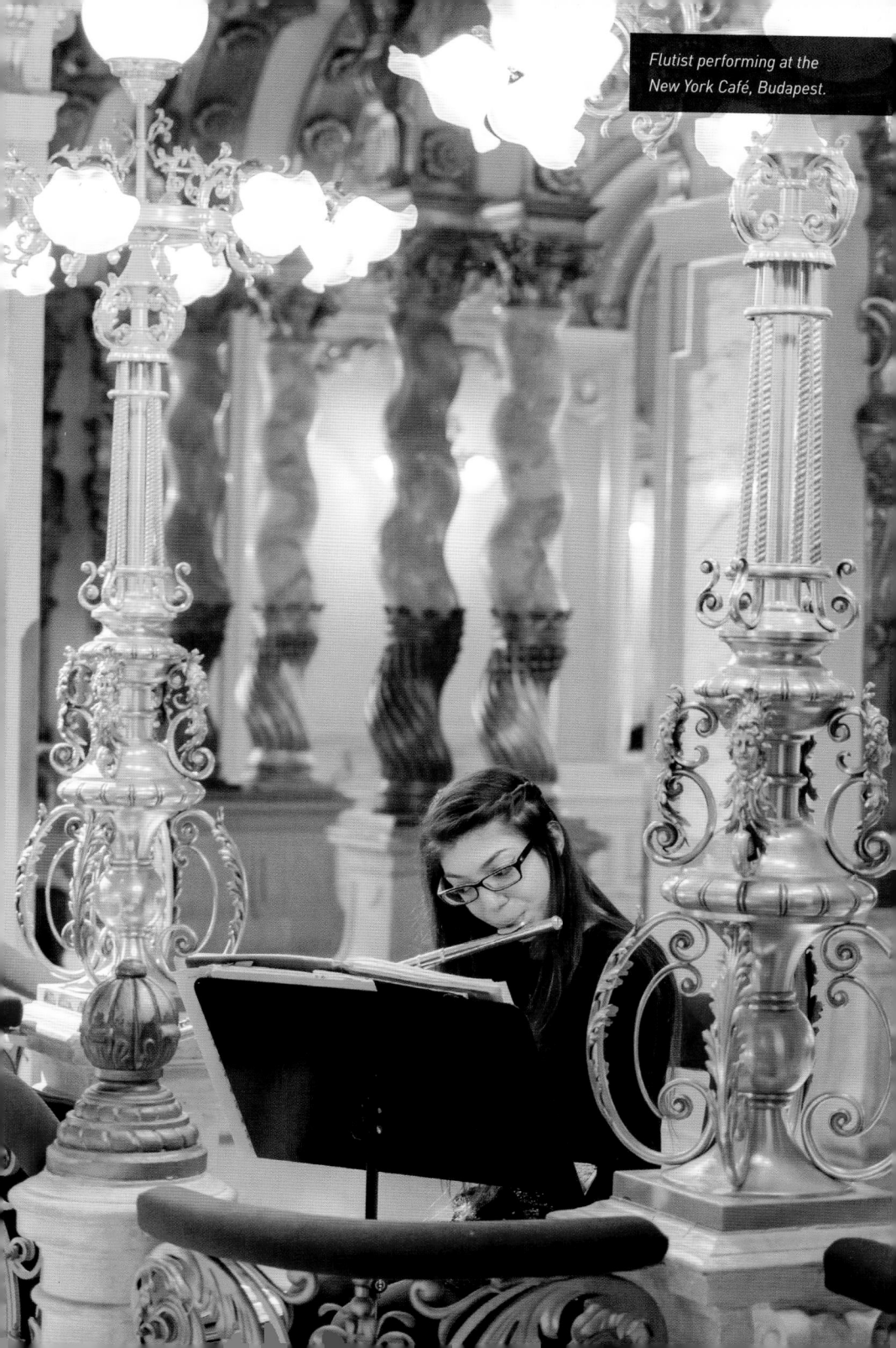

COFFEE HOUSES

Before 1945, Budapest was known as the 'city of coffee houses'. At the end of the 19th century, astute business people opened one coffee house after another, and coffee merchants, speculators and adventurers were all keen to invest their money in such enterprises.

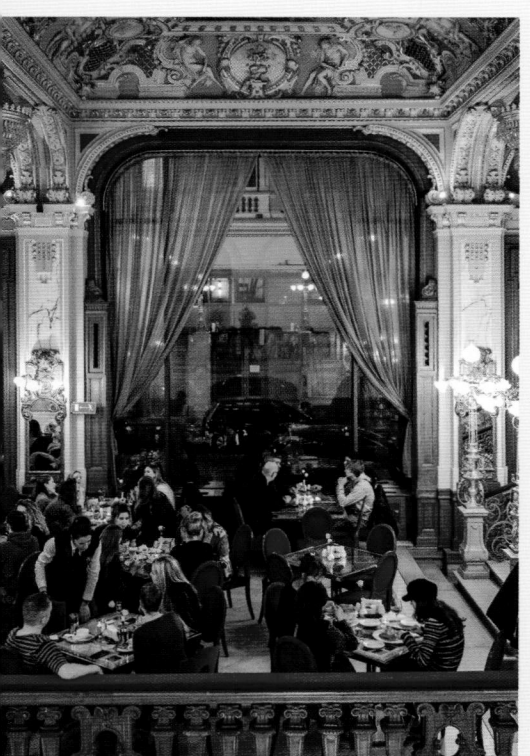

New York Café in Budapest.

This was where the literary circle congregated and debated. To escape their cramped, freezing apartments, poets made their way to the warm, smoke-filled cafés and penned their verses, joined by journalists, actors, small-time singers and operetta starlets. Southern cattle-traders and street-walkers came to listen. On the tables, in bamboo racks, were dozens of newspapers and journals. Friendly and efficient waiters served coffee, soda water, and eggs for breakfast.

PEST'S COFFEE HOUSES

Despite the massive social upheavals and fluctuations in fortune of the last 100 years, something has been retained of the glimmering world of opulent and eclectic Art Nouveau cafés that characterized the city's golden age. The most splendid is the New York Café, downstairs in the New York Palace Hotel, Erzsébet körút 9-11. It opened in 1894, and 110 years later was closed for renovations that have restored the café to its former glory, complete with frescoed ceilings, marble columns and gilded mirrors. The walls are adorned with portraits of the artists who patronised the place and drawings of the literary society that once met here.

Something of the same feeling can be found in the spacious surroundings of the Art Nouveau café in the venerable Astoria Hotel (open daily 7am–11pm) at 19–21 Kossuth Lajos utca, once the haunt of political plotters and shady functionaries.

At 29 Andrássy út is Café Müvész (open daily 8am–9pm), the most splendid of the coffee houses that have survived along the lower part of the radial road, and the one with the most atmosphere. Artists from the opera house opposite, elderly retired bankers and respectable old ladies visit the rooms of this small coffee house, furnished with sculptures and adorned with mirrors. The Müvész also has an outdoor terrace for people-watching on sunny days.

If you reach Vörösmarty Square, haunt of street musicians, via the old Metro route, you will arrive at the entrance to one of the most elegant and historic coffee houses in the city – the Gerbeaud (daily 9am–9pm). The first coffee house by this name was founded in 1858. Now it's been restored, come to admire the splendid examples of art and craft, plus masterpieces of interior decoration and period furniture.

Often spelled 'Zserbó' In the Hungarian fashion, this coffee house and pâtisserie is a popular meeting place for what's left of the former upper middle classes, for the new entrepreneurs with their sharp suits and mobile phones, for Hungarians from the West who return for a visit or to live, and foreigners in search of local colour.

The service may not always match up to the atmosphere or the utterly delightful cakes, but an afternoon in the Gerbeaud is a revealing glimpse into Hungarian life. Full meals are served in the two restaurants. Another distinguished old coffee house is the Centrál (daily 8am–midnight) at Károly utca 9. Originally opened in 1887, this was Budapest's most lively literary café in the early 1900s, and has managed to retain its wonderful ambience.

ACROSS THE RIVER

Buda, too, has its share of classic coffee houses. Ruszwurm (open 10am–6pm), rather too close for comfort to the Hilton Hotel, is a tiny establishment dating from 1827, in an old building on Szentháromság utca. Inevitably, because of its location, Ruszwurm has become something of a tourist trap, living on the reputation of its pastries, which were once delivered to connoisseurs in far-off Vienna. Nevertheless, it's a pleasant place to stop and recharge the batteries on iced coffee and strudel.

ESZPRESSÓS

In the 1930s, the increasing tendency towards functional architecture was reflected in a series of elegant and generously proportioned cafés, but over the years they have been either redecorated or closed. When the heyday of the coffee houses drew to a close, fancy new eszpressós took their place, and Budapest was full of them. From the 1930s to the 1950s, one eszpressó, after another opened its doors. They included chic venues with names like Mocca, American, Parisien, Joker, Intim and Darling, and they gave the city a cosmopolitan flair. Eventually, the trend of using decadent Western names came to an end: in neon lights above the new eszpressós revolutionary names loyally echoing radical slogans – Plan, Prosperity, Spartacus – appeared to take their place.

A NEW GENERATION

More recently, new cafés are popping up all over with the same look and feel of any number of similar places in London, Paris, or Amsterdam. The music is usually a barely audible background beat and the crowd is cool. At the foot of Castle Hill, in the parish room of St Anne's Church on Battyhány tér, is Angelika (daily 9am–11pm). Although relatively modern, the low vaulted ceilings, stained-glass windows and marble floors create an inviting atmosphere.

These days, there's been the rapid rise of the artisan, or craft-coffee, movement in Budapest, the result of which has seen the introduction of a number of contemporary, beautifully-designed cafés run by local, enthusiastic baristas who really do know their beans. A few worth seeking out include Espresso Embassy (Mon–Fri 7.30am–7pm, Sat & Sun 9am–5pm), at Arany János utca 7, Tamp & Pull (Mon–Fri 7am–7pm, Sat 9am–

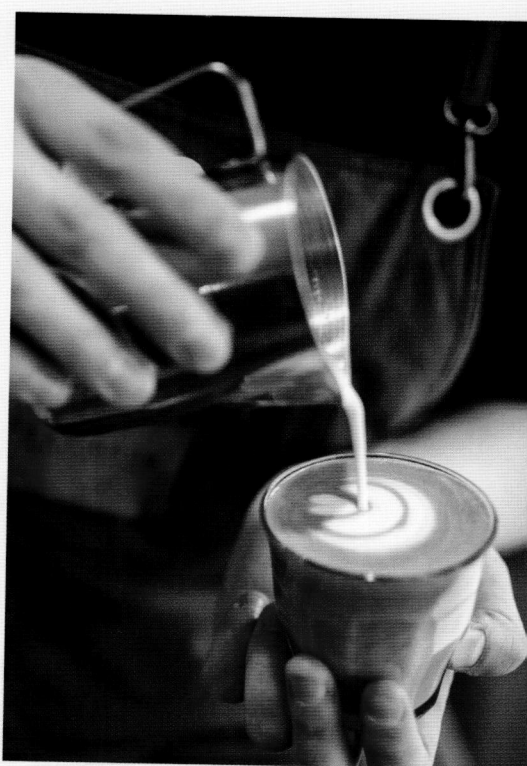

Making a fresh coffee.

5pm, Sun noon–4pm), at Czuczor utca 3, and the London Coffee Society (daily 8.30am–6pm), at Dohány utca 27. These certainly seem to be the way forward for the capital's coffee houses.

📷 BATHHOUSES

Across Hungary countless hot springs lurk beneath the surface of the relatively thin Carpathian basin – hence there are now more than 80 towns or settlements throughout the country boasting in excess of 120 baths.

While the earliest remains of baths date back to the Bronze Age, the first major advances were made by the Romans who established the town of Aquincum, now a suburb of Budapest, with its assortment of pools. But it wasn't until the Ottomans pitched up in the sixteenth and seventeenth centuries that a culture of bathing became truly established, before the fashion for high-end spas swept across central Europe in the late nineteenth and early twentieth centuries. As well as being an important social hub, bathhouses have always been highly regarded for their medicinal and therapeutic properties, reputedly able to help cure myriad ailments, from rheumatism to respiratory problems.

Beyond Budapest – which has a monopoly on the country's grandest bathhouses (see opposite) – the countryside is teeming with all manner of bathing possibilities, from Hévíz, near Lake Balaton, which is reputedly the world's second largest thermal lake (see page 212); and a unique thermal water cave in Miskolc, to more modern waterparks like those in Nyiregháza and Debrecen (see pages 252 & 246).

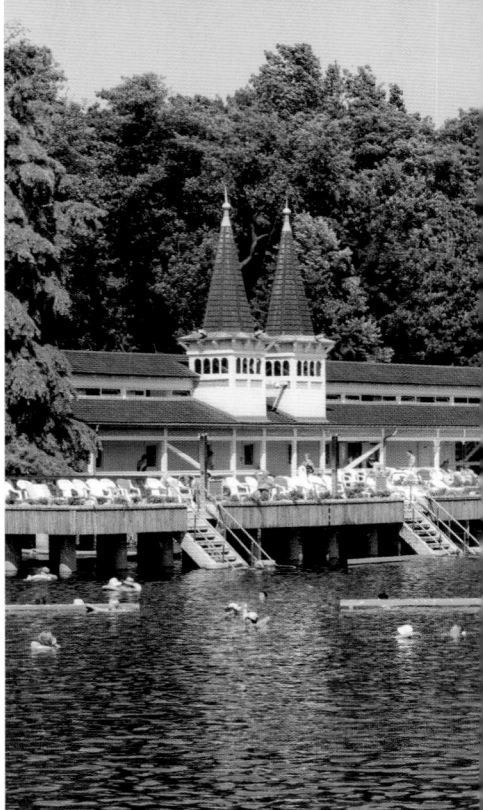

Thermal lake at Hévíz.

Hot spa at Miskolctapolca.

Aerial view of Széchenyi Thermal Baths.

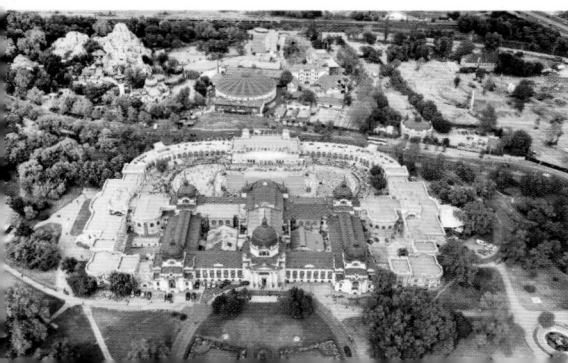

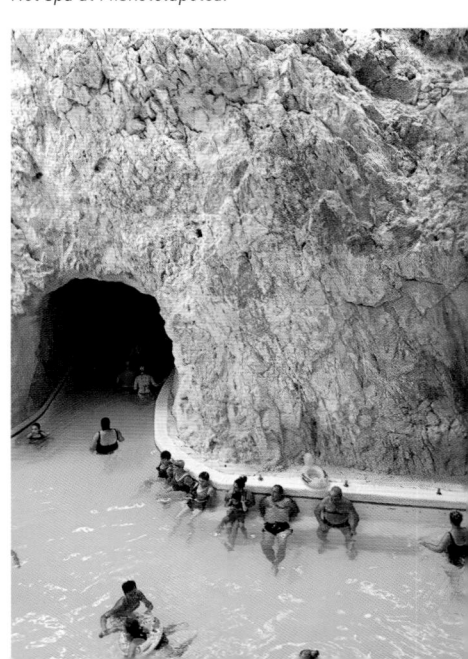

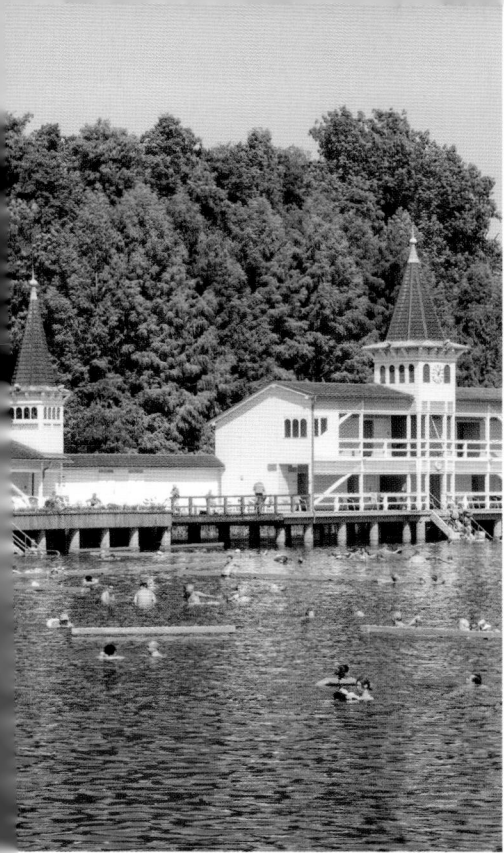

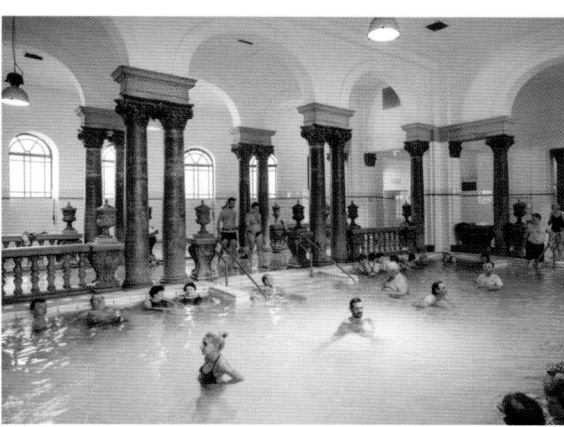

Relaxing in the baths.

Budapest's bathhouses

Some of Europe's most iconic bathhouses are to be found in Budapest and a visit to the Hungarian capital is simply not complete without taking to the waters. The most popular of them all is the Gellért Baths in Buda, an Art Nouveau masterpiece complete with a main pool, hot pools and steam baths (see page 112), though for atmosphere you can't beat an hour or so wallowing in the sixteenth-century Király or Rudas baths, whose layouts – a central bathing pool surrounded by smaller pools set beneath light-filled cupolas – are of classic Turkish design (see page 110).

Meanwhile, over in the Városliget at the enormous, neo-Baroque Széchenyi baths (there are sixteen pools here; see page 154), you're quite likely to witness the somewhat surreal spectacle of elderly gentlemen playing chess on floating boards while immersed chest-high in steaming water. In recent years, the city's bathing scene has been given an exciting new dimension, thanks to the advent of night-time parties, complete with music, laser discos and even films. The baths are not especially cheap – expect to pay 3500–5000Ft – but you'll find the experience an immensely rewarding one.

Playing chess in the bath.

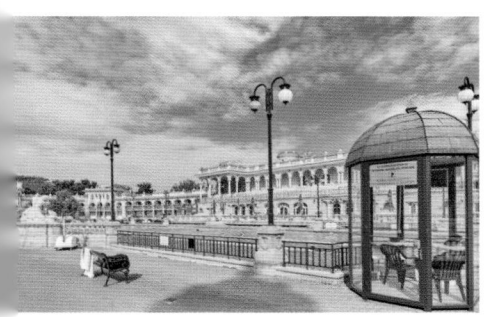

...échenyi Thermal Baths.

...tail of a statue at Széchenyi.

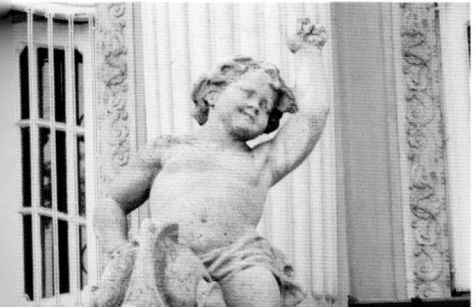

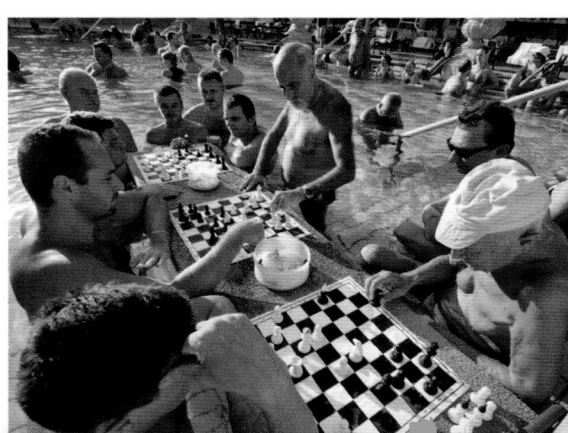

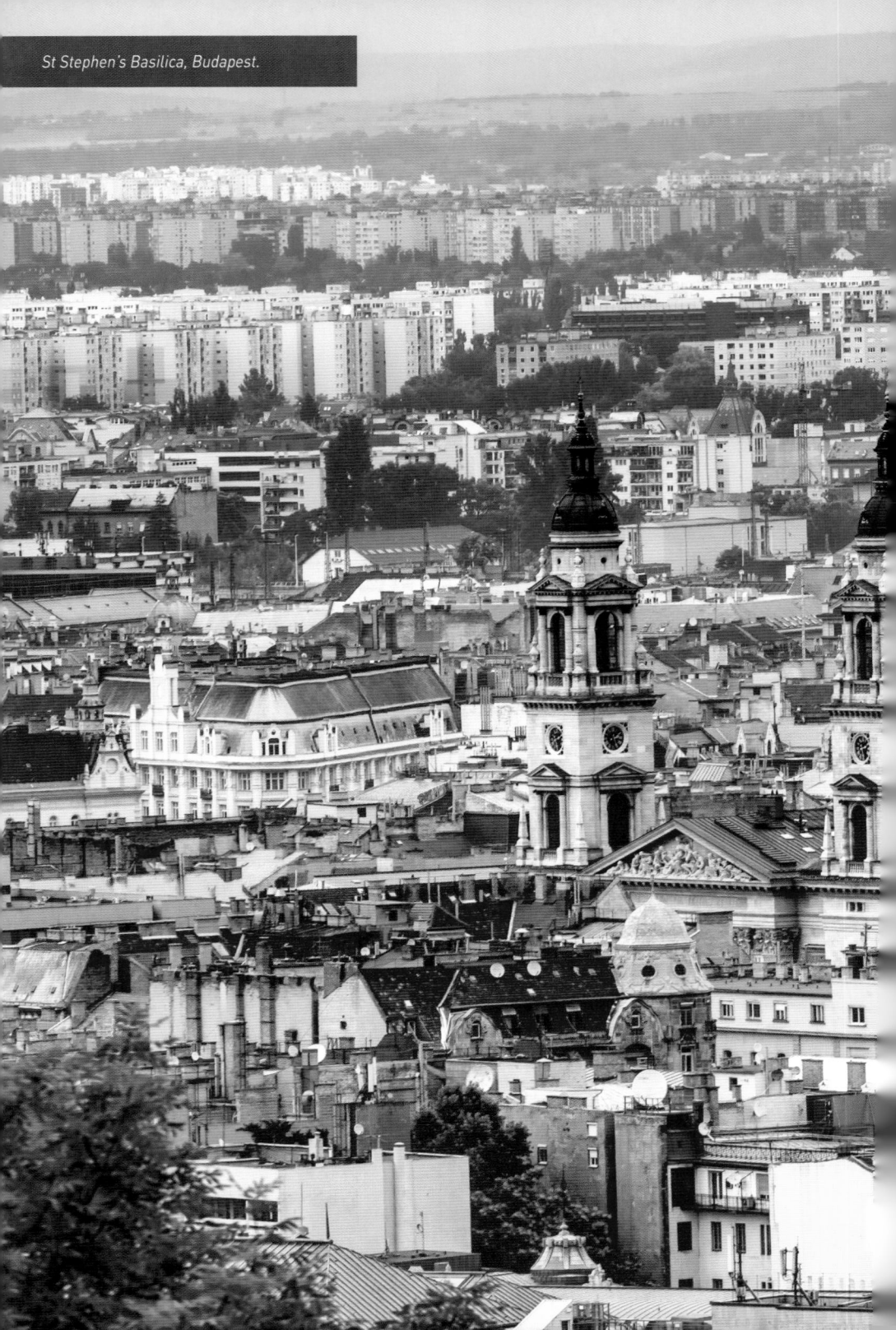

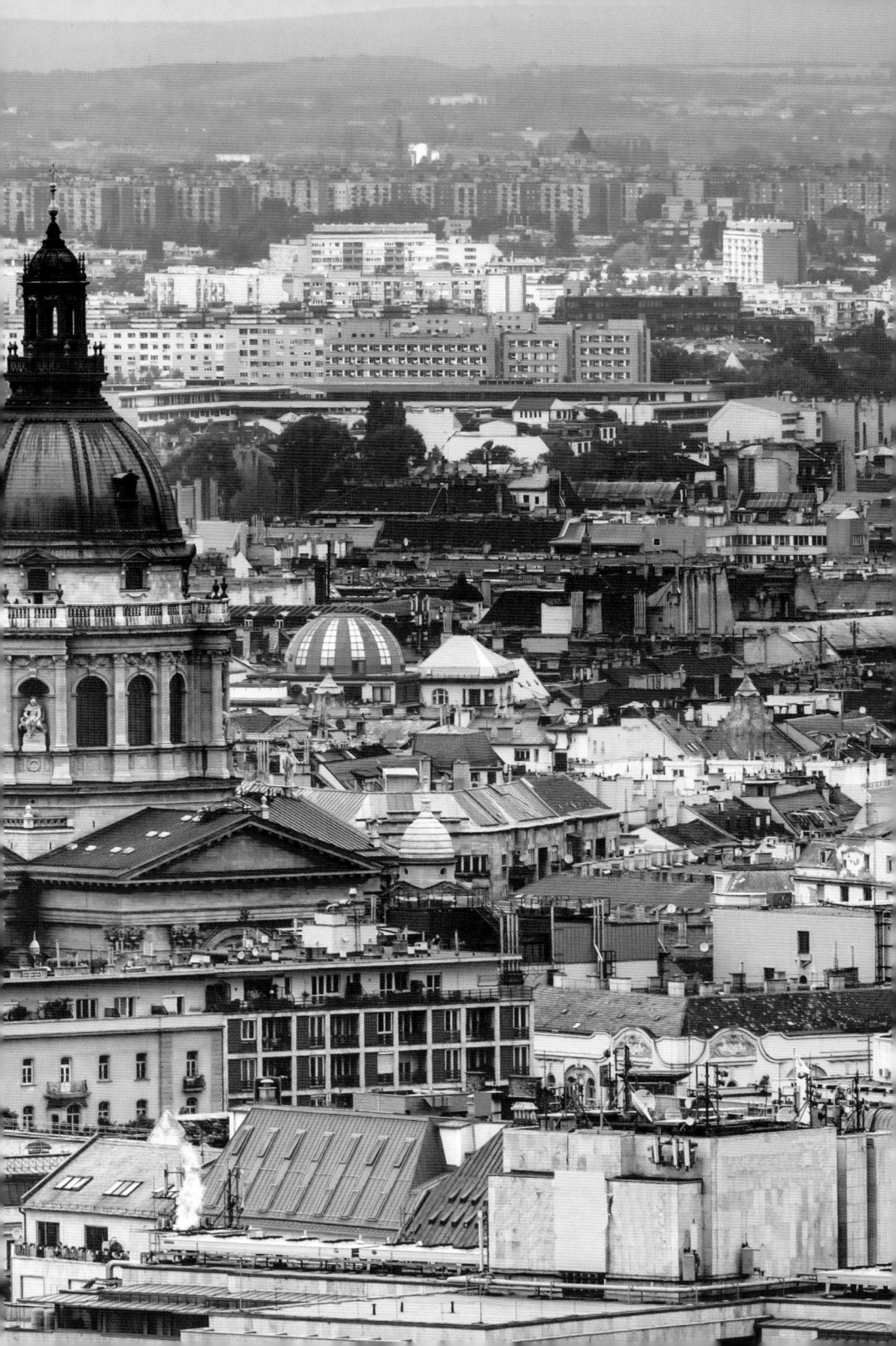

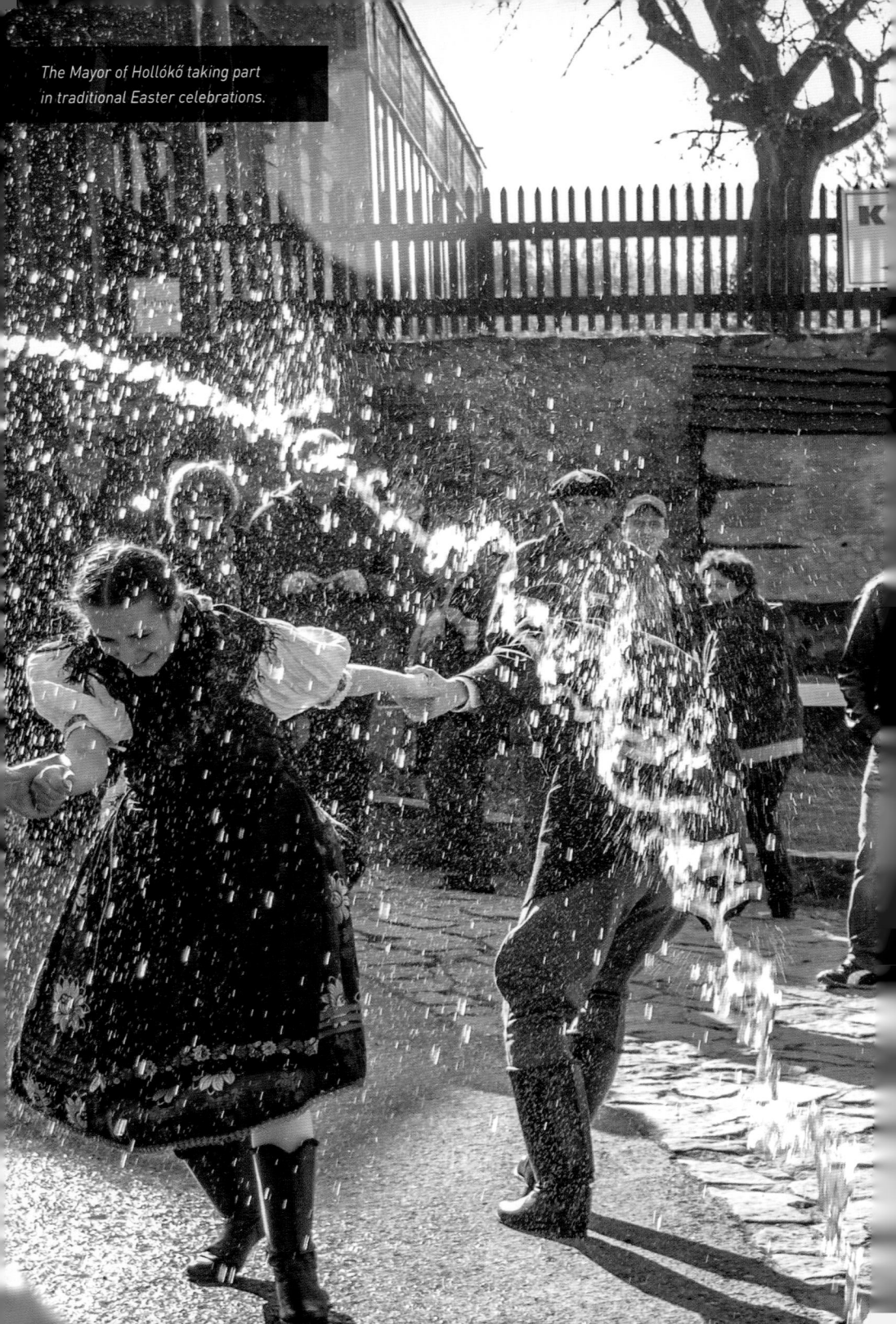

The Mayor of Hollókő taking part in traditional Easter celebrations.

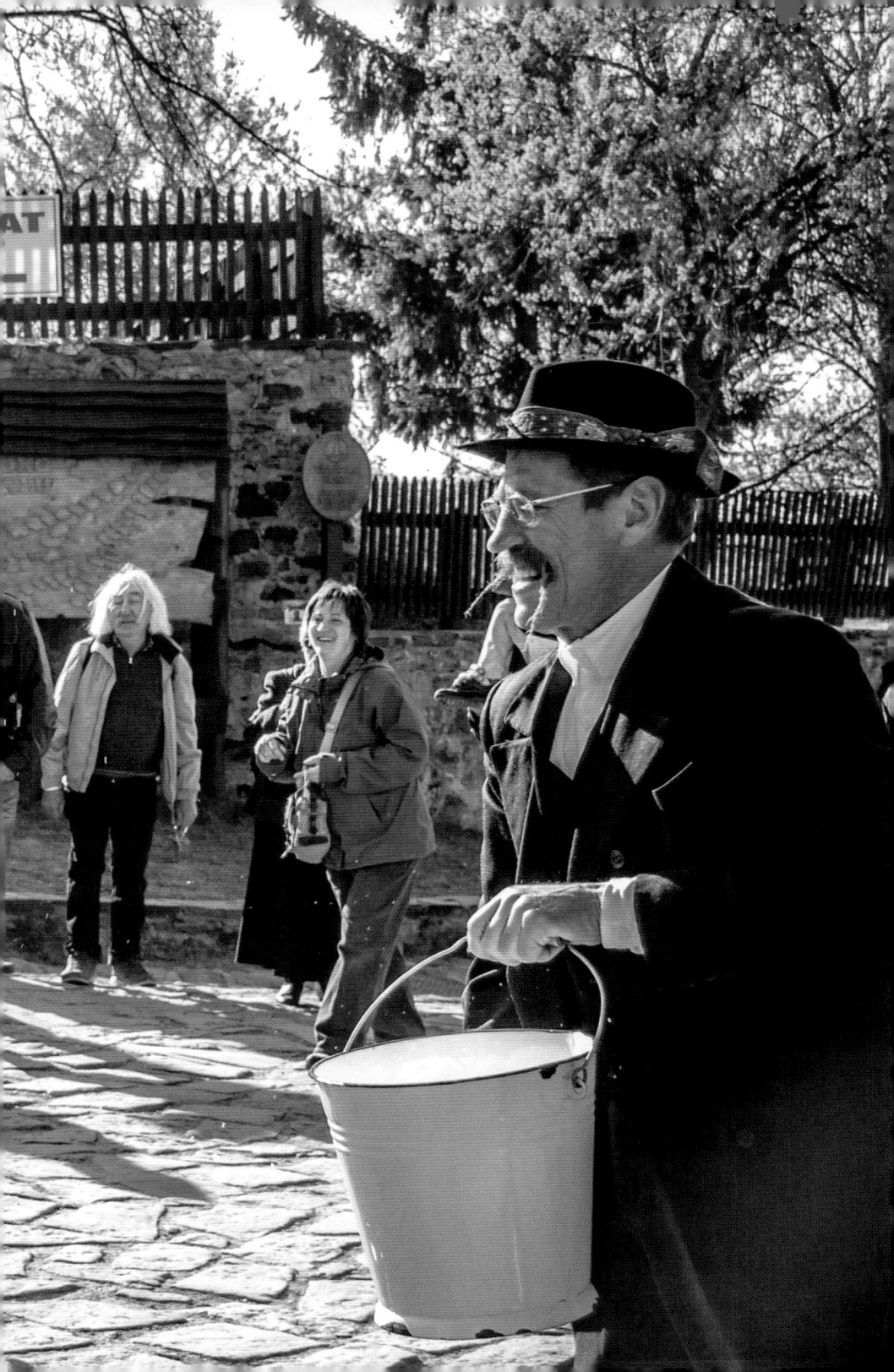

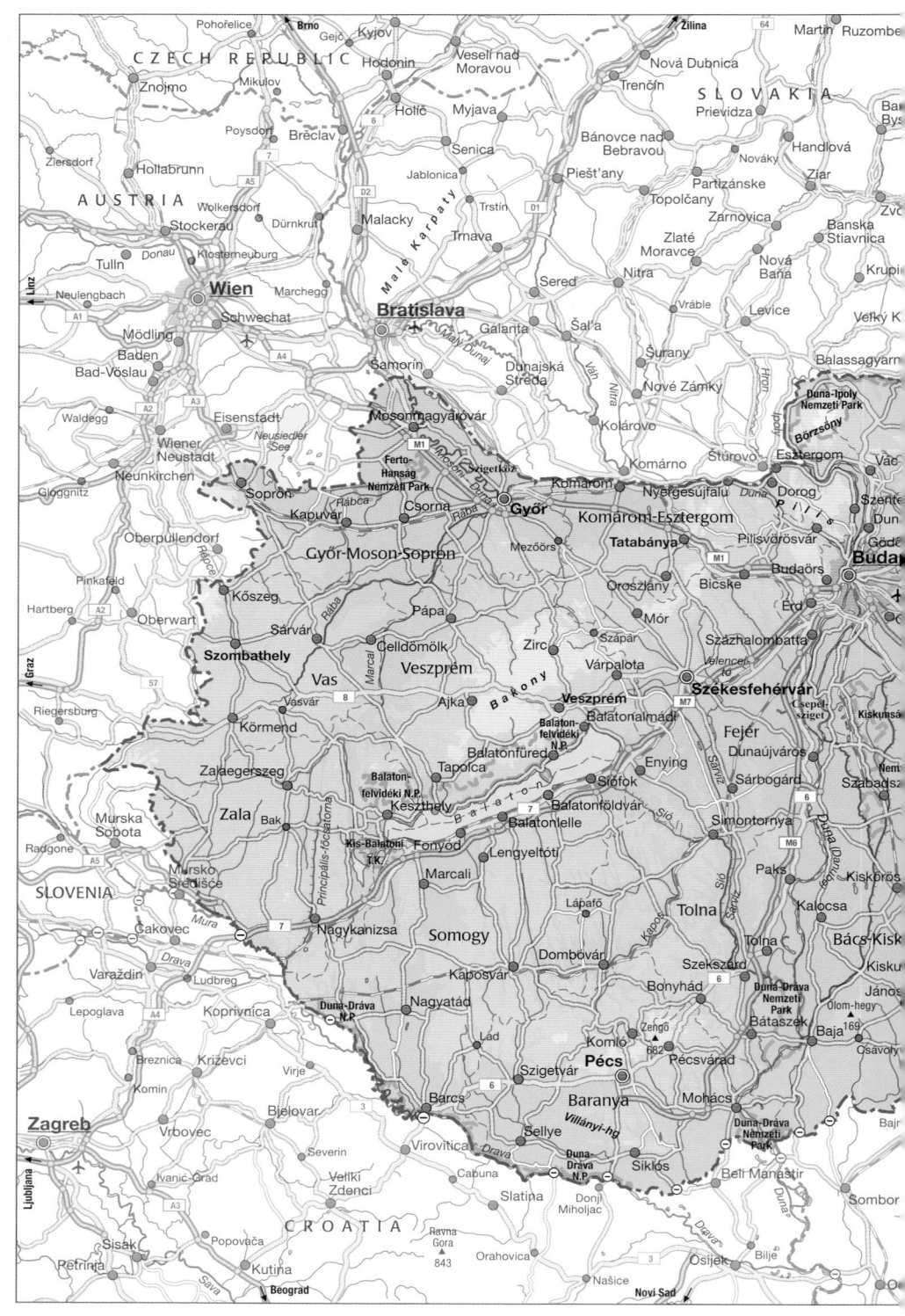

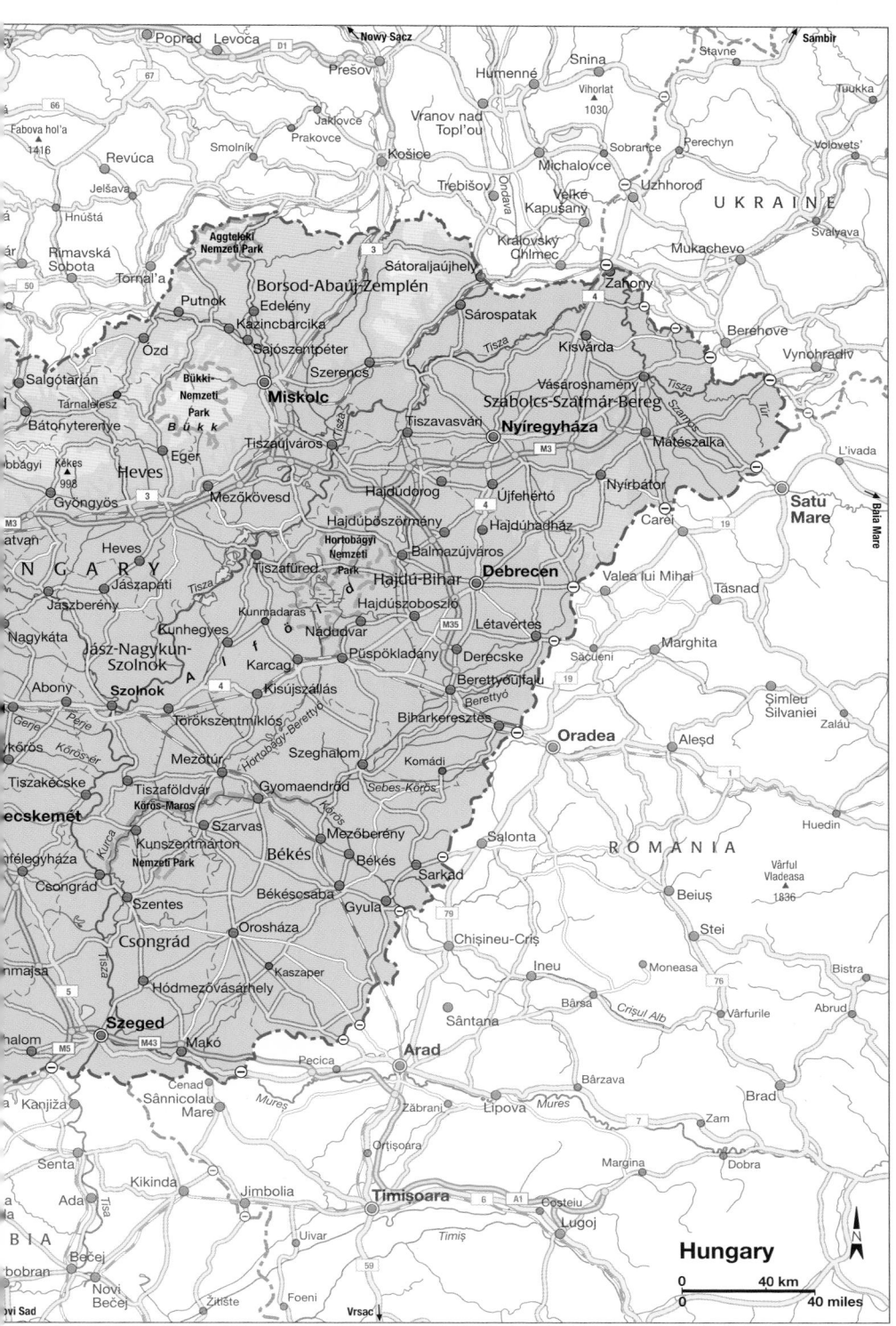

Hungary

0   40 km
0   40 miles

N

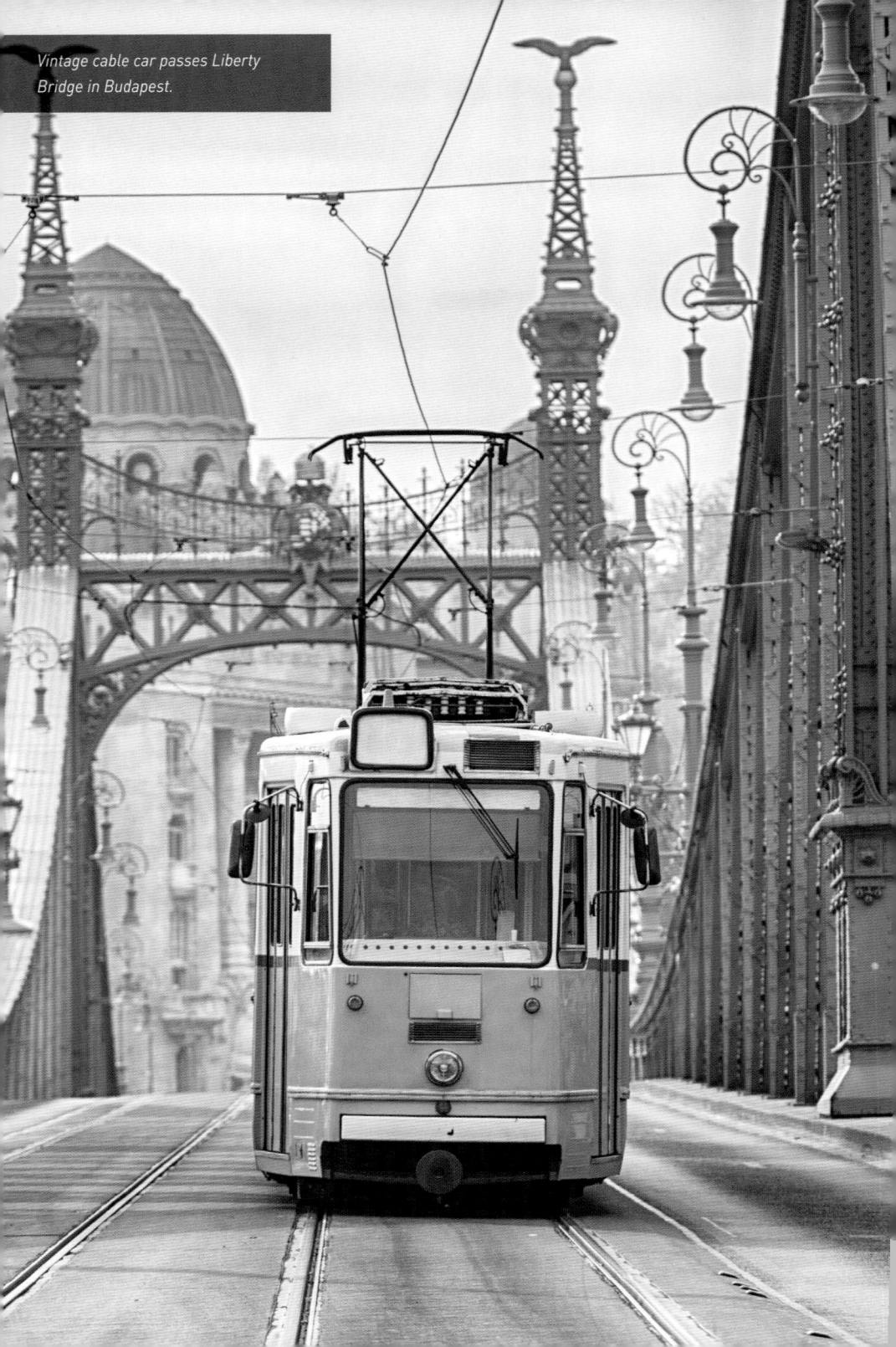

INTRODUCTION

A detailed guide to the entire country, with principal sites clearly cross-referenced by number to the maps.

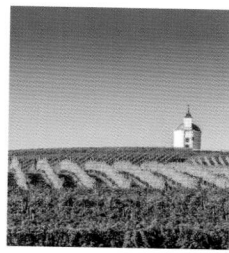

Vineyards and a chapel.

Hungary is a relatively small nation covering 93,030 sq km (35,910 sq miles) and with slightly under 10 million inhabitants, a fifth of whom reside in the capital, Budapest. A land-locked nation, it shares borders with Slovakia in the north, the Ukraine and Romania in the east, Serbia and Croatia in the south, and Slovenia and Austria in the west. The Danube flows south through Hungary and divides the country into two unequal parts: the smaller Transdanubia in the west, and a wild eastern region defined by the immense flatness of the Great Plain (Nagyalföld) and the rugged remoteness of the northern mountain ranges. The climate is shaped by steppe, Mediterranean and even Atlantic influences, and guarantees plenty of sunshine and rain. The winters can be harsh, especially on the vast eastern plain.

Apart from the obvious cultural wealth of its cities, such as Budapest, Szentendre and Pécs, it is not easy to pinpoint the exact source of Hungary's beauty. There are few natural wonders on the Grand Canyon scale, and few castles come close to the grandeur of those in Bavaria, for example. Hungary is, rather, a collection of subtle experiences: a purplish sun hanging over the baked plain, delicate stucco work on simple houses, horses pulling a load of coal along a shimmering road, an organist practising in a remote chapel.

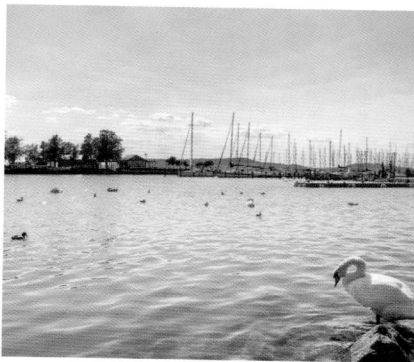

Lake Balaton.

A trip through Hungary – whether by car, bus, or train – can be a memorable experience, even more so if some of it is explored on foot, by bicycle or on horseback. In some areas where there is a high concentration of tourists, such as around Lake Balaton, Hungarians tend to see Westerners as a source of hard cash and treat them accordingly. However, compared to the service culture found in much of Europe, the tourist industry in Hungary is often refreshingly relaxed, not to say lackadaisical.

The following chapters explore the entire country, starting in Budapest, the Danube and Transdanubia and then covering the lesser-known attractions that are to be found in the wide open spaces of the Great Plain.

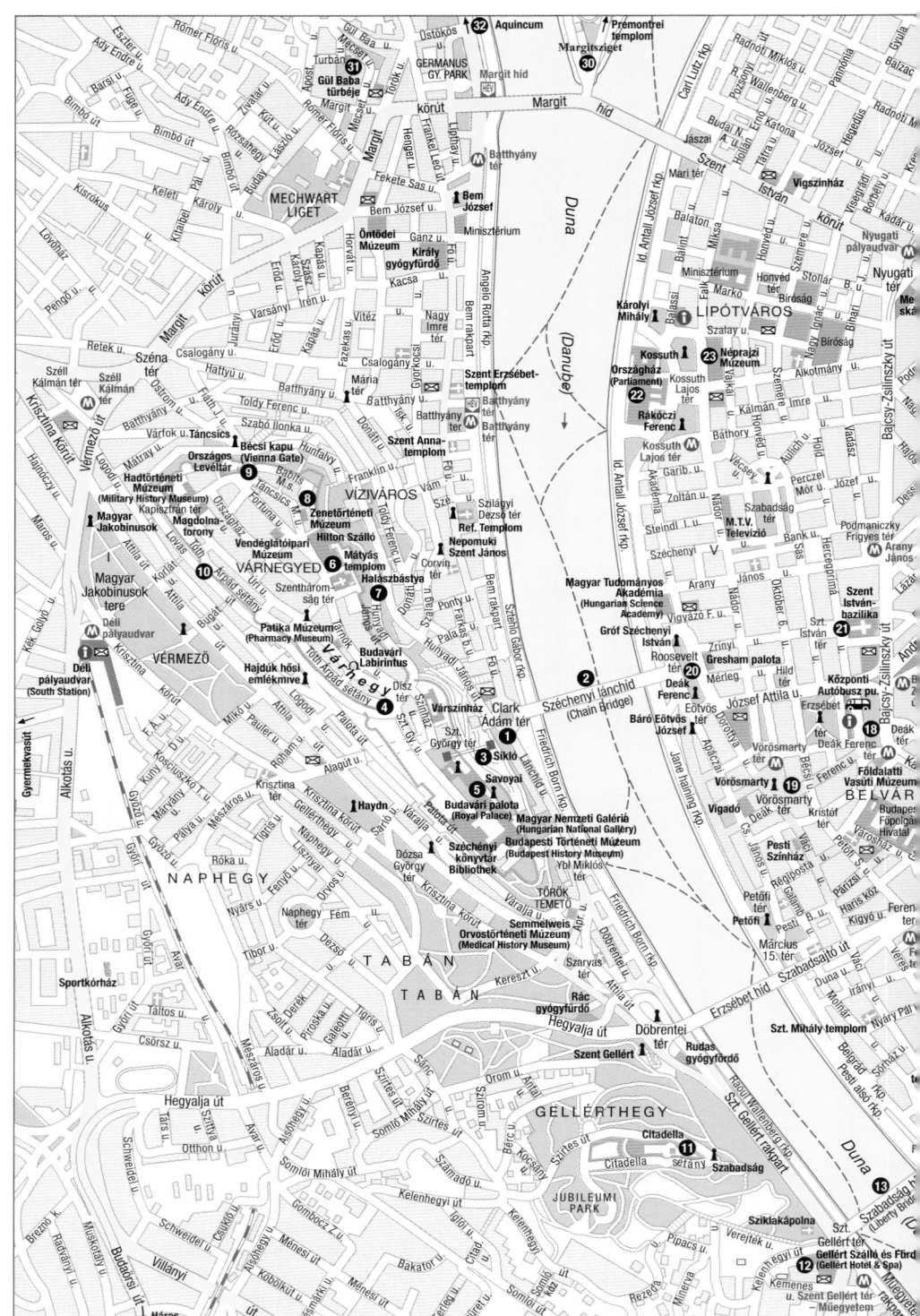

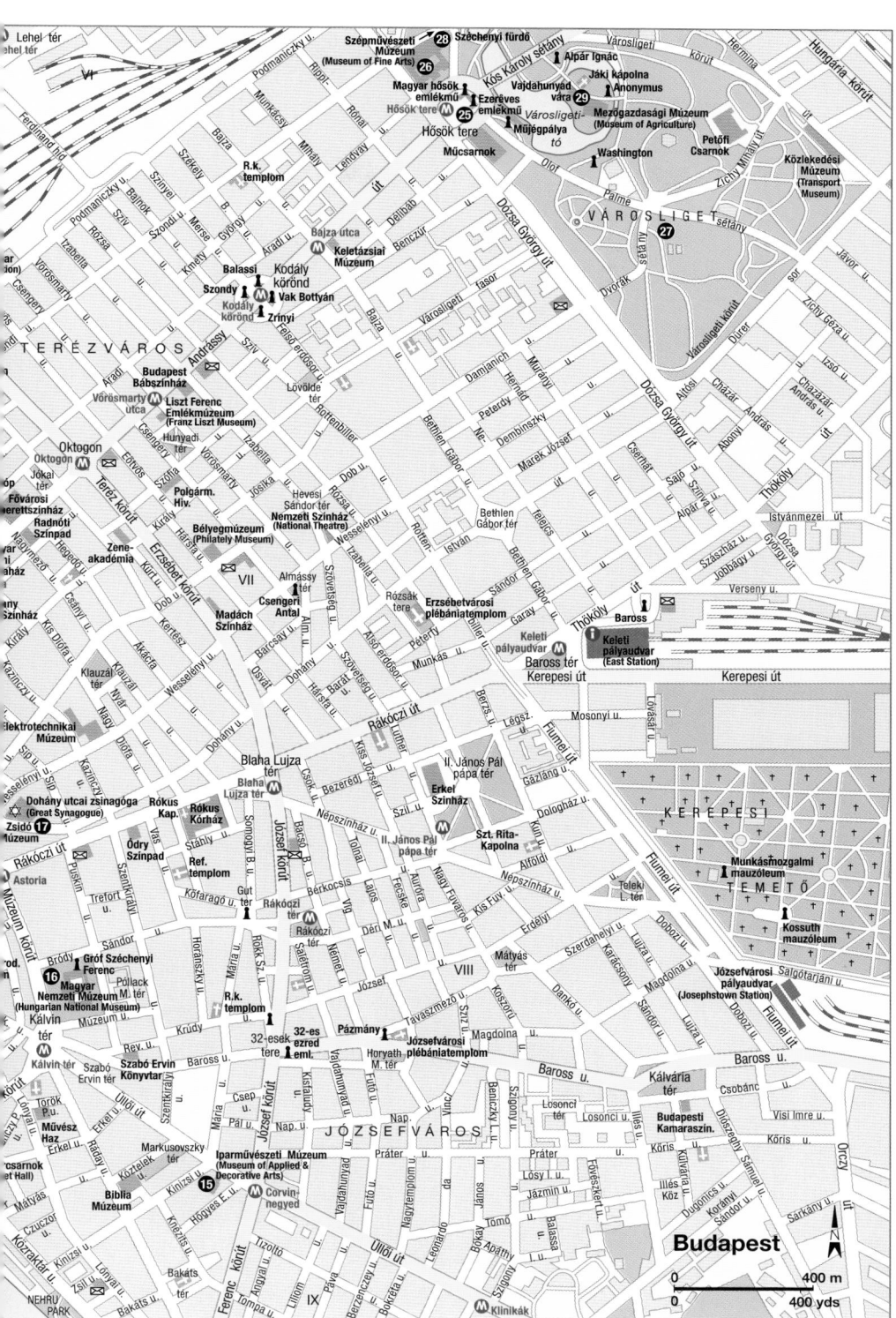

Budapest

0   400 m

0   400 yds

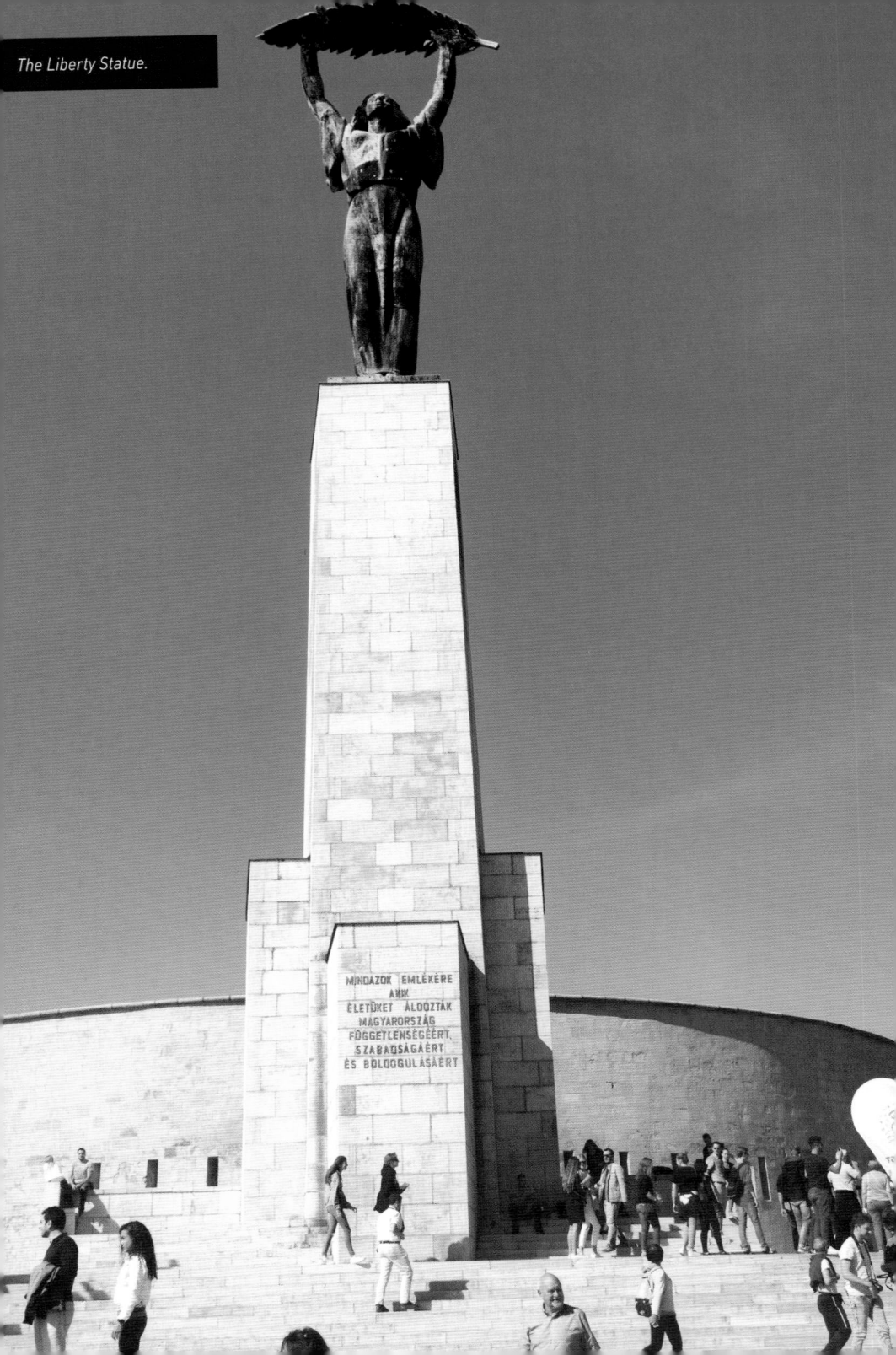

The Liberty Statue.

BUDAPEST

With a wealth of culture, splendid architecture and sumptuous coffee houses, Budapest, the Pearl of the Danube, is an ever-changing city that demands repeated visits.

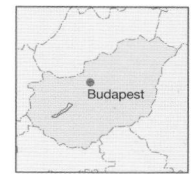

Those halcyon days when Budapest was romantically compared to Paris, and every Western tourist could afford a meal in the best restaurants, are long gone. The fall of the Iron Curtain and the triumphant march of capitalism has turned most of the old stereotypes upside down, and nowadays Budapest has its fair share of 24-hour shops, luxury hotels, animated street vendors and wild honking traffic – just like any other wealthy Western city.

The restaurant scene is unrecognizable from just a few years ago, while the city's nightlife is now among the most exciting in Europe, with the famous ruin bars of the seventh district the go-to venues of choice for locals and tourists alike. Alternative music is big business, while theatre, opera and classical music all offer first-rate experiences.

Some things, however, never change: Budapest is the seat of government, the centre of Hungarian industry and commerce, the great turbine that powers the country. It continues to attract provincial Hungarians looking for gold on its weary pavements. It is the cultural heart of the nation and a city of international standing, yet it still possesses some of the late 19th-century flair that attracts nostalgic Westerners. Artists of all varieties still frequent its famous coffee houses, and, as the grime of 40 years of neglect

Embracing the city's café culture.

is removed from one monument after another, the great city of former days has re-emerged big time.

The city has been occupied many times: the Mongols came raging through the country in 1241, followed by the Turks in 1541 and the Habsburgs in 1686. In 1919, the Romanians marched in. During World War II, invasion came from Nazi Germany, followed by the Russians, whose tanks returned in 1956 to crush the popular uprising. However, there were times when peace prevailed, when the city flourished economically

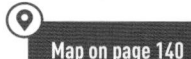

⦿ Main attractions
Royal Palace
Matthias Church
Vienna Gate
Gellért Hill
St Stephen's Basilica
Parliament
Széchenyi Baths
Margaret Island

Map on page 140

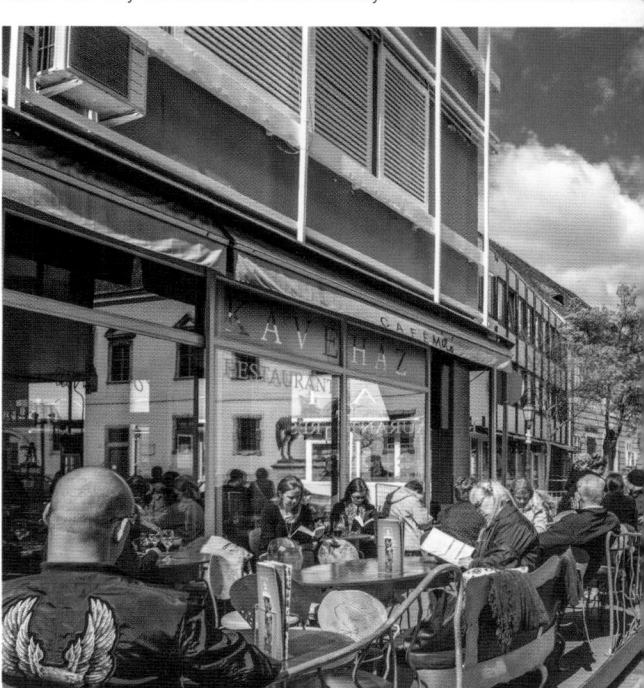

and culturally, for example under Mátyás Corvinus (1458–90) and after the Great Compromise of 1867 that established the Austro-Hungarian Dual Monarchy (see page 55).

BUDA

Budapest is in fact composed of three historically independent communities, which were united in 1873: Pest on the east bank of the Danube (Duna) and Buda and Óbuda on the west.

The motorway route from the West to Budapest leads you to the Buda bank of the Danube, where Castle Hill and Gellért Hill rise up steeply from the city. If you follow the road at the foot of these hills along the Danube, you will reach **Clark Ádám tér ❶**. All distances in the country are measured from the oval '0 km' stone just to the south of this roundabout, which absorbs the flow of traffic crawling across the **Chain Bridge ❷** (Lánchíd). This proud landmark was the first solid bridge to be built over the Danube, between 1842 and 1847, to connect Buda and Pest. The undertaking was financed

by Count István Széchenyi, who invited builder William Clark and (unrelated) architect Adam Clark from Britain to design and construct the masterpiece.

A quaint, antique **funicular railway** (Budavári sikló) ❸ scales the difference in height between the river bank and the top of **Castle Hill** (Várhegy) ❹ – a Unesco World Heritage Site and from where the views are excellent. Alternatively, if you're feeling energetic you can climb the countless steps to the top.

From Castle Hill, the eye is drawn to the Danube and its bridges (you can see almost all of them from here), Margaret Island on the left, the imposing Parliament building with its greenish-brown dome on the Pest bank and the Danube Promenade (Duna-Korzó). Pest spreads east across the plain to the usually misty horizon.

THE ROYAL PALACE

The **Royal Palace ❺** (Budavári palota), commonly known as the castle, is the logical place to begin a tour of Budapest. The city's first royal castle was built on the southern part of the Castle

Chain Bridge.

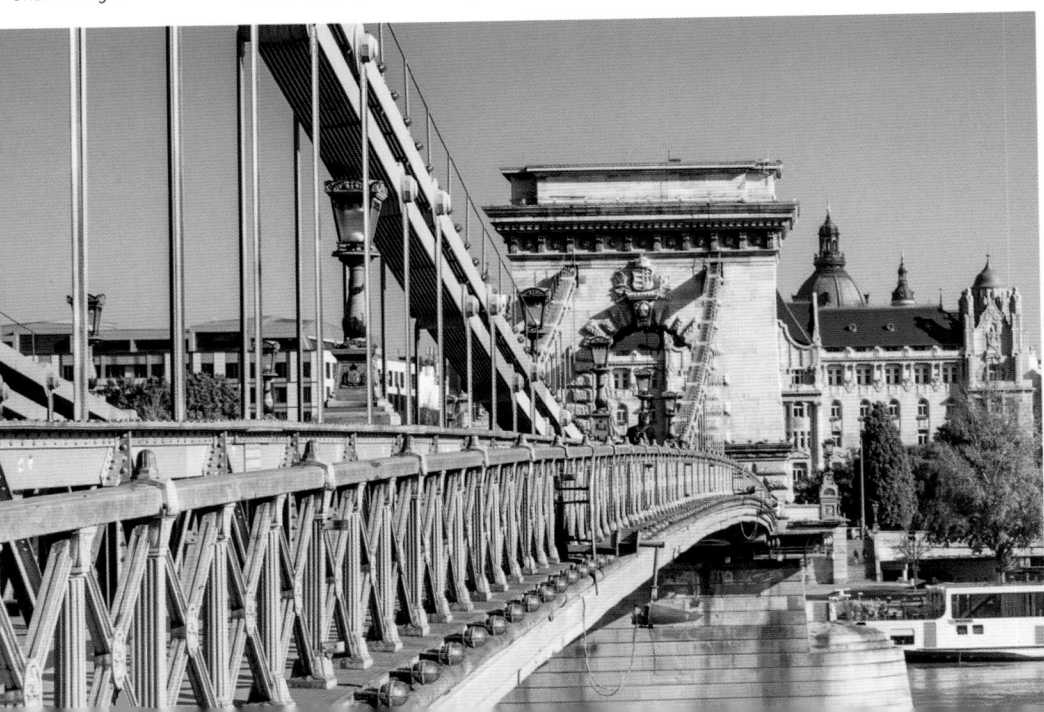

Hill in the early Middle Ages (*circa* 1255) by King Béla IV, after Pest had been ravaged by the Mongols. Like many of the country's buildings, the castle has been destroyed several times – in the Turkish wars, during the revolution of 1848–49 and in World War II – but always rebuilt. Even the gates surrounding this enormous building – a mixture of styles, including Baroque – are remarkable. The castle houses two notable museums: the Hungarian National Gallery in wings A, B, C and D; and the Budapest History Museum in wing E.

The **Hungarian National Gallery** (Magyar Nemzeti Galéria; Tue–Sun 10am–6pm; www.mng.hu) presents a grand overview of Hungarian art from the Middle Ages to the present. An exhaustive collection, some of the highlights include the Gothic altarpieces on the first floor, an entire wing (B) devoted entirely to arguably Hungary's greatest painter, Mihály Munkáscy – look out for *Storm on the Puszta* – and, on the second floor, a series of paintings by artists from the Nagybánya School, including Károly Ferenczy.

In the **Budapest History Museum** (Budapesti Történeti Múzeum; Tue–Sun, Mar–Oct 10am–6pm, Nov–Feb 10am–4pm) you can see remains of the medieval royal castle. The exhibition spans an impressive two millennia of history, from prehistory – including the Avars – through to Budapest in modern times, covering urban planning, fashion and trade, among other things.

The view from the castle terrace – the same one enjoyed by Eugene of Savoy, the general who finally ousted the Turks in 1686 – has an enduring appeal.

The northwest courtyard of the castle is adorned by Alajos Stróbl's King Mátyás Cascade, a grand fountain depicting the king hunting.

MATTHIAS CHURCH

The centre of Castle Hill is dominated by **Matthias Church ❻** (Mátyás templom; Mon–Fri 9am–5pm, Sat 9am–noon, Sun 1–5pm; www.matyas-templom.hu), built 1255–69. Originally called the Church of Our Lady, its popular name comes from King Matthias (Mátyás), who extended and decorated the building and

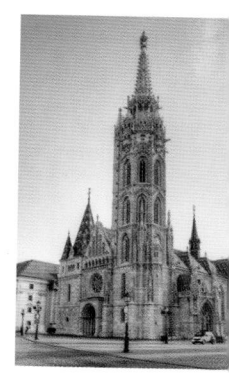

Matthias Church.

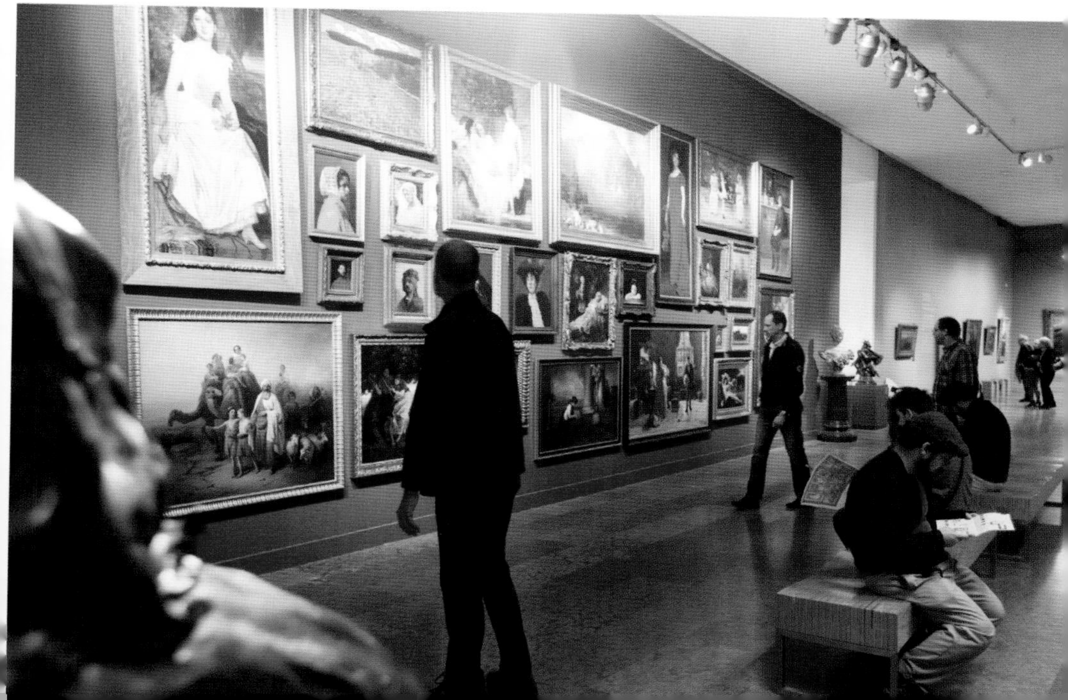

Inside the Hungarian National Gallery.

was twice married in it during his reign (1458–70). The church's present-day appearance dates from the renovation of 1873–96 and, like the Fishermen's Bastion monument (see below), was the work of Frigyes Schulek.

Once your eyes have adjusted to the dim light inside the church, you can admire the stunning decorations on the pillars, walls and ceilings. At the back of the church is a fresco depicting the 1456 siege of Belgrade by the Turks, which was won by the Christian armies under János Hunyadi, Mátyás' father (see page 37). The robe embroidered by the Empress Sissy (1837–98), wife of Emperor Franz Josef, on the death of her son, can be seen, as can a small piece of her platinum-embroidered wedding veil. Outside the church is a statue of King István (St Stephen), the revered founder of Hungary.

FISHERMEN'S BASTION

A wonderful panorama of the city can be enjoyed from the **Fishermen's Bastion ❼** (Halászbástya), built in 1905 as a monument to the fishermen who

Fisherman's Bastion.

courageously defended Buda against the Turks in the Middle Ages. Behind the Fishermen's Bastion, the Miklós Tower, a late-Gothic remnant of a former Dominican church, forms part of the glass façade of the Hilton Hotel. The successful, and initially controversial, integration of this historic monument into a modern hotel complex results in a delightful contrast, heightened by the reflections and distortions of the Fishermen's Bastion in the shining glass.

The streets and alleys to the north and east of Castle Hill are decidedly peaceful compared to the lively crowds around Matthias Church and the Fishermen's Bastion. The houses here, painted in lovely pastel colours, are almost all jewels of classical or Baroque architecture, with many attractive doorways and courtyards.

At Fortuna utca 4, the **Hungarian Museum of Commerce and Catering ❽** (Kereskedelmi és Vendéglátóipari Múzeum; Tue–Fri 10am–5pm, Sat–Sun until 6pm) is much more interesting than it sounds and should appeal to anyone interested in social history and

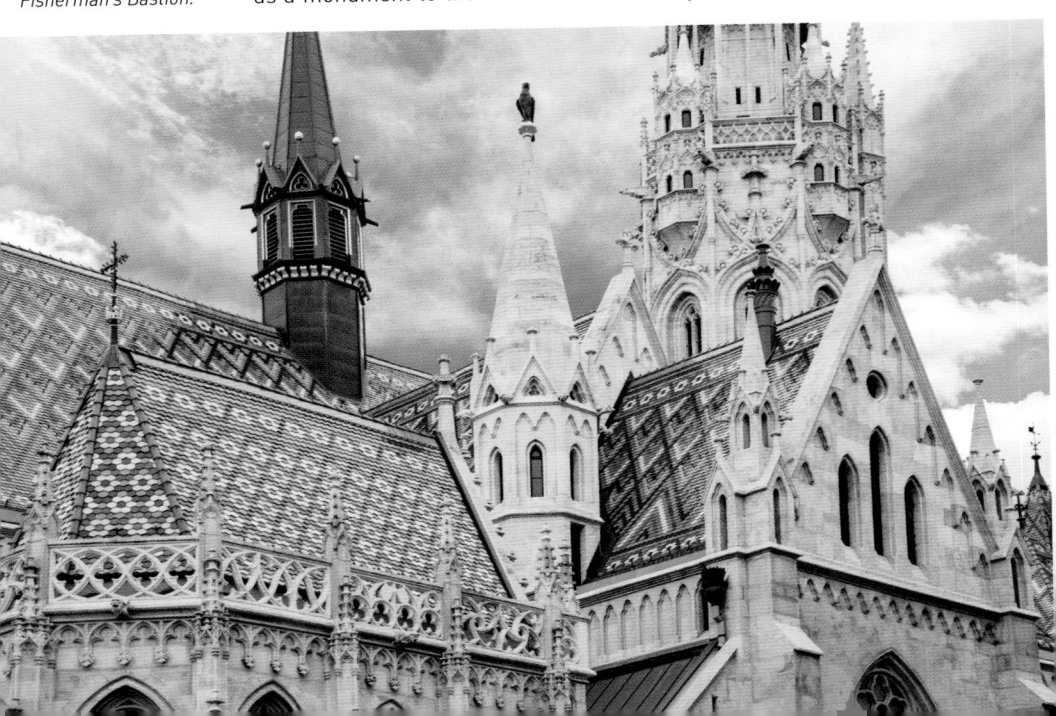

design from the early 20th century. The museum is divided into two sections. The catering part looks at the life of the famous confectioner, Emil Gerbeaud, and displays exhibits from the elegant 19th-century Budapest coffee houses, restaurants and hotels. The commerce section features shop fronts, period advertising (including an innovative model dog that rapped on shop windows to attract customers' attention), early lighting displays and other items of bygone charm.

If you head north past a statue of Pope Innocent XI you will come to the **Music History Museum** (Zenetörténeti Múzeum; Táncsics Mihály utca 7; Tue–Sun 10am–4pm), home to an exhibition on the Hungarian composer Béla Bartók who once had a workshop here. Also on display are numerous instruments, notably a beautifully carved and painted 1790 Parisian pedal harp.

VIENNA GATE

Further north is the **Vienna Gate** ❾ (Bécsi kapu), which offers good views of the Buda hills. The square in front of it (Bécsi kapu tér) is dominated by the mighty building of the **Hungarian State Archives** (Országos Levéltár; Mon & Fri, 8.30am–5.45pm, Tue–Thu 8.30am–2pm), which holds Hungary's most important national historical documents. In nearby Kapisztrán tér is the Gothic **Magdalene Tower,** from the former Church of Mary Magdalene, heavily damaged by Russian bombs in 1944–5.

On the western edge of Castle Hill is the **Bastion Promenade** ❿ (Tóth Árpád sétány), the site of the **Museum of Military History** (Hadtörténeti Múzeum; Tue–Sun 10am–4pm, until 6pm Apr–Sept), which offers particularly illuminating coverage of the two world wars, and the Siege of Budapest.

There are many cafés and restaurants in the area, the most famous of which is the **Ruszwurm Pâtisserie** (Ruszwurm cukrászda) at Szentháromság utca 7. The dining room, decorated throughout in 19th-century Biedermeier style, is small, but with a bit of luck you should be able to find a seat, and the prices are reasonable.

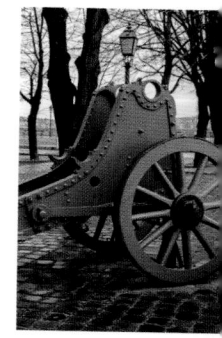

Artillery at Buda Castle.

Vienna Gate.

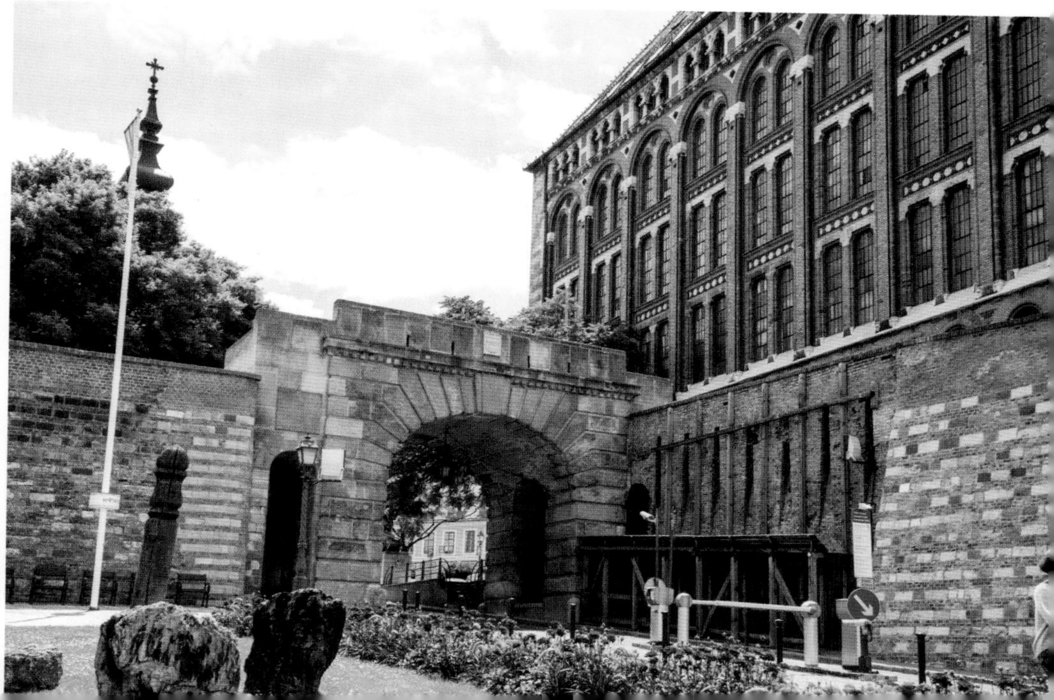

Alternatively, you can have refreshments in the quirky, cavernous limestone **Labyrinth** (Labirintus; daily 10am–7pm) situated beneath Buda Castle and opening onto Úri utca 9. You could also grip your mobile and head for the **Telephone Museum** (Telefonia Múzeum; Úri utca 49; Tue–Sun 10am–4pm), a small museum documenting the history of this most popular means of telecommunications.

GELLÉRT HILL

The next hill towards the south on the Buda embankment is **Gellért Hill** (Gellérthegy), which can be easily identified by the enormous statue holding a palm frond at its summit. The statue may be reached by bus, taxi or via steps and snaking paths, which bypass the 1902 monument to Bishop Gellért, who in 1046 was said to have been thrown by pagans from this point into the Danube in a barrel pierced through with spikes.

The summit is crowned by the **Citadel** ⑪ (Citadella), built by the Habsburgs after the suppression of the revolution

of 1848–49. The barracks, where German troops made a desperate last stand in 1945, now contains a café/restaurant and the large yet unobtrusive (and inexpensive) Citadella Hotel.

The **Liberation Monument** (Szabadság szobor), the hallmark of Budapest, rises before the walls of the Citadel. This reminder of the liberation of Hungary from German occupation was originally commissioned by Regent Horthy in memory of his son, who died in an accident, but was actually erected by the communist government. Some of the communist sections of the monument are now missing; these have been relegated to the Statue Park along with the rest of the unwanted Lenins and Red Army memorabilia. The stars, however, are etched in the verdigris that sank into the soft sandstone pillar.

At the foot of Gellért Hill, right by the Pest entrance to the Liberty Bridge, is the venerable **Gellért Hotel and Spa** ⑫ (Gellért Szálló és Fürdő). This is a luxurious establishment, overlaid with the comforting patina of years of service, and the impressive spa facilities are in art nouveau style.

The embankment north of the Gellért, Hill can be reached on foot. Pass the Pauline Church (Sziklakápolna) on the left, with its interesting grotto chapel, then continue to two old Turkish baths, the Rudas and the Rác, both situated near the Elizabeth Bridge (Erzsébet híd). The Rudas (see page 110), which is open to men only, is situated on the embankment, while the Rác is located a little further inland. Both baths are fitted with steam rooms and hot pools beneath a cupola.

ACROSS THE DANUBE TO PEST

To continue the visit, walk up the Pest side of **Liberty Bridge** ⑬ (Szabadság híd), which leads to the University of Economics. In the vicinity, the **Market Hall** ⑭ (Vásárcsarnok), between

The Citadel.

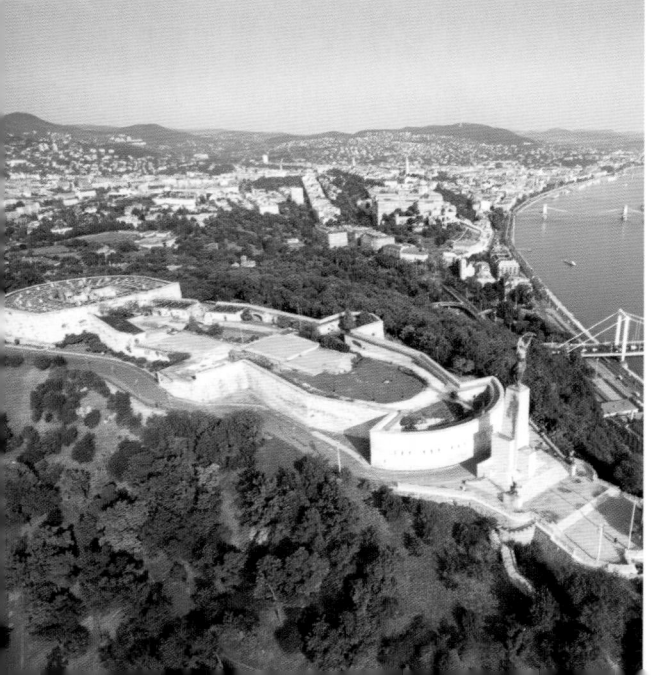

Vámház körút and Sóház/Pipa utca, is an attraction in itself; its steel-framed brick building dates from the end of the 19th century and was renovated in the 1990s. Here you will find all kinds of fresh vegetables, pulses and meat, and diverse articles from brooms to local crafts.

Vámház körút bends to the left at Kálvin tér and becomes Múzeum körút. Note that Üllői út goes off to the right, and a short distance away on this road, at No. 33, is the **Museum of Applied and Decorative Arts ⓕ** (Iparművészeti Múzeum; Tue–Sun 10am–6pm; www. imm.hu). The museum, an architectural jewel of the turn of the 20th century built by Ödön Lechner, has a good selection of Hungary's handicrafts, from faïence and ceramics to embroidery, leatherwork and marquetry.

Back on Múzeum körút you come to the most important museum in Budapest: the **Hungarian National Museum ⓖ** (Magyar Nemzeti Múzeum; Tue–Sun 10am–6pm; www.hnm.hu), which was founded by Ferenc Széchenyi in 1802. The current neoclassical

building was designed by Viennese architect Michael Poliak (Mihály Pollák in Hungarian) and built between 1837 and 1847. Its gigantic pillared hall, massive chandeliers and grand, wide staircases make the building worth a visit for the architecture alone.

The museum is home to a wonderfully rich and varied collection. Start with the archaeological exhibition, featuring some stunning animal figurines and anthropomorphic urns from the Copper Age, and magnificent bronze-spoked wheels. Upstairs, highlights include Beethoven's Broadwood piano (acquired by Liszt), the ceremonial trowel used to lay the foundation stone of the Chain Bridge, and the right hand and left ear from the statue of Stalin, which was torn down in 1956.

The museum's most prestigious items, however, are St Stephen's crown, the coronation mantle, the royal sceptre, the orb and the sword. Having being smuggled out by the Germans at the end of World War II and eventually resurfacing in the United States, the crown and insignia, powerful

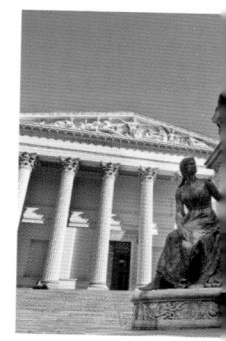

Hungarian National Museum.

Market Hall.

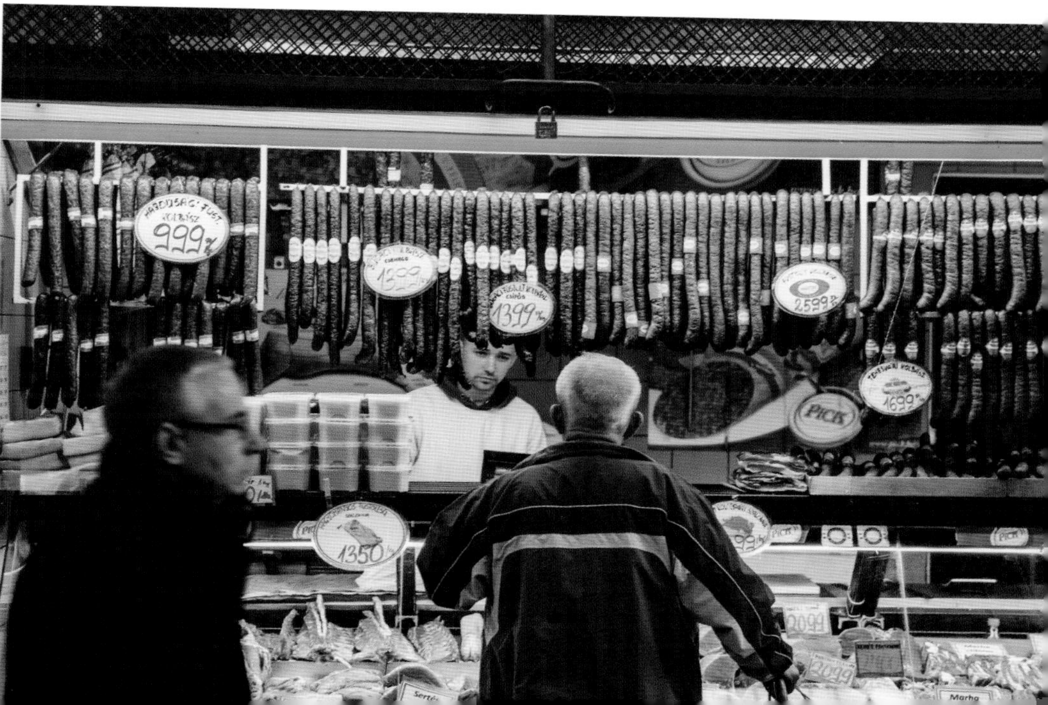

Tip

A moving memorial to the victims of Nazism – a metal weeping willow, the leaves of which are engraved with the names of the dead – stands behind the synagogue.

symbols of Hungarian nationhood, were returned to their rightful home by the US government in 1978.

Múzeum körút crosses Rákóczi út, a wide, busy artery that heads up to the Eastern Train Station (Keleti pályaudvar). On this corner is the **Hotel Astoria,** a 19th-century café and restaurant, whose faded charm and traditional menu make it a good stop for lunch or dinner.

THE JEWISH QUARTER

At the intersection of Rákóczi út and Múzeum körút is Budapest's wonderful Jewish quarter. Hungary's once-flourishing Jewish community was devastated during World War II and now numbers a mere 80,000 people, most of whom live in the capital. At the fringes of the quarter, on Dohány utca, is the spectacular **Great Synagogue** ⑰ (Dohány utcai zsinagóga; May–Sept Mon–Thu & Sun 10am–8pm, Fri 10am–4pm; Oct–Apr Mon–Thu & Sun 10am–4pm, Fri 10am–2pm; www.greatsynagogue.hu), which was built in the 1850s by the Viennese architect Ludwig

Förster and has a seating capacity of 3,000. The small Jewish museum in the front section documents Jewish life in Budapest, from everyday practice and religious festivals, to the Holocaust.

THE HEART OF THE CITY

Károly körút continues to **Deák tér** ⑱. This is the city's public transport hub and, appropriately, the site of the **Underground Railway Museum** (Földalatti Vasúti Múzeum; Tue–Sun 10am–5pm), which displays exhibits on continental Europe's first underground railway system. Between Károly körút and the Danube is the Inner Town (Belváros), the heart of the capital and the main area for shopping and people-watching.

Leaving Deák tér by way of Deák Ferenc utca, you will head past the simple Lutheran church, and on to **Vörösmarty tér** ⑲ This spot is dedicated to the country's most important romantic poet, Mihály Vörösmarty (1800–55), and the area surrounding his statue teems with locals, tourists and street artists.

Great Synagogue.

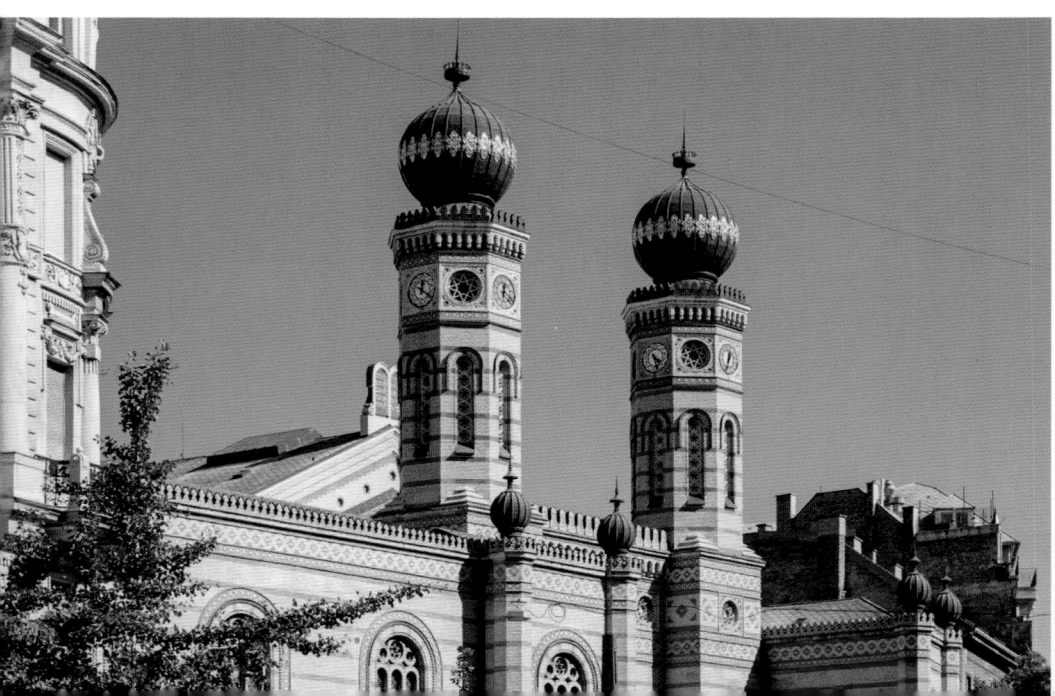

Gerbeaud, the grand coffee house that has occupied No. 7 on the square since 1858, is still frequented by prosperous Hungarians in need of coffee and cake or a meal at the restaurant below, which brews its own beer.

Váci utca, the centre of the Budapest shopping district, starts at the southern end of Vörösmarty tér. Along with travel agents, cafés and restaurants, you'll find several Hungarian temples to consumerism here: elegant department stores, high-end fashion boutiques and designer shops.

Just south of Vörösmarty tér is the neo-Byzantine **Pesti Vigadó** (daily 10am–7pm), one of the city's best-loved concert venues that once played host to the likes of Dohnányi, Bartók and Kodály. Recently refurbished, the guided tours are well worth considering.

Join the throng for a stroll along the **Danube Promenade** (Duna-Korzó) on a warm summer evening to savour the view of the Castle district opposite. Heading south you'll pass **Petőfi tér,** a square named after the poet whose words inspired the 1848 revolution against the Austrians. The square remains the focal point of demonstrations. Note the 13th-century **Inner City Main Parish Church** (Belvárosi plébániatemplom), an interesting synthesis of various styles including Romanesque, Baroque and even Turkish.

Back at the northern end of the Korzó is **Roosevelt Square** ⑳ (Roosevelt tér). On its northern edge is the **Hungarian Science Academy** (Magyar Tudományos Akadémia), another brainchild of István Széchenyi, built in neo-Renaissance style in 1862–65, after the count's death. In pride of place on the square is the **Gresham Palace** (Gresham palota), an art nouveau treasure by Zsigmund Quittner, built for the Gresham Life Insurance Company in 1903 and now a Four Seasons Hotel.

THE BASILICA

Take the narrow Zrinyi utca to the left of the palace to reach **St Stephen's Basilica** ㉑ (Szent István bazilika; Mon–Sat 9am–7pm, Sun 1–6pm; chapel:

> **⊙ Fact**
>
> By night, Váci utca comes alive with bars, restaurants and gambling dens. It's a bit of a hotspot for pickpockets though, so be vigilant.

Danube Promenade.

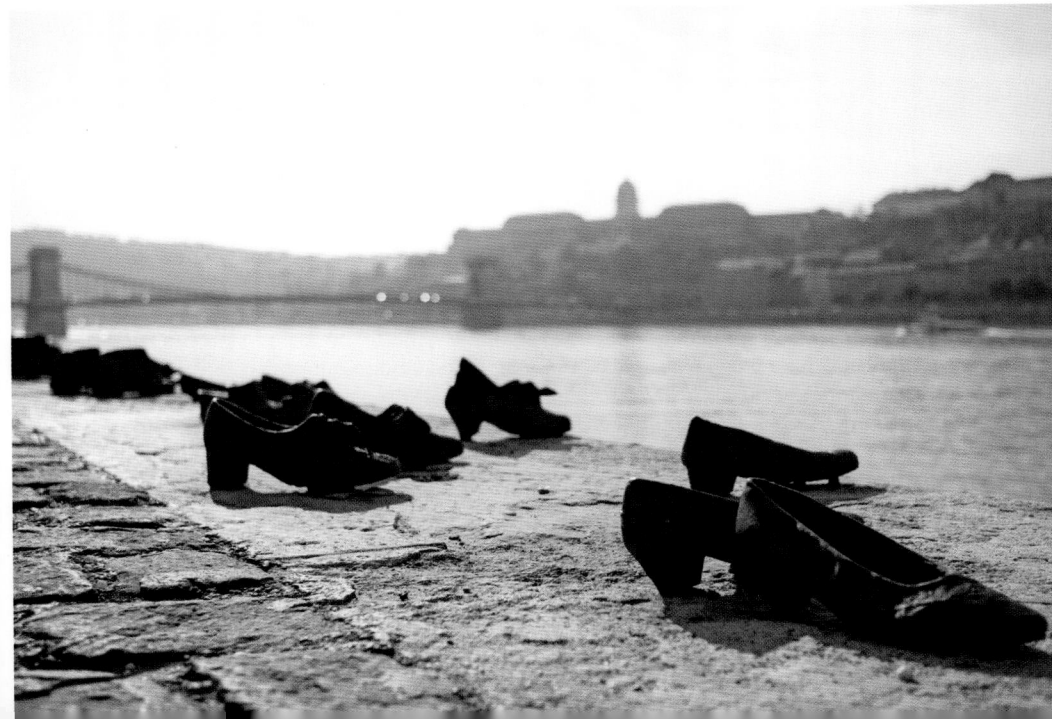

⊙ Tip

To see the Holy Right, head to the Sacred Right Chapel, which can be found at the front of the Basilica, on the right. The hand is kept in a miniature golden monument: insert a 200Ft coin in the slot into the machine and a light will illuminate the Holy Right for around one minute.

Mon–Sat 9am–4.30pm, Sun 1–4.30pm; www.bazilika.biz). Although building work was begun in 1851, the dome collapsed in 1868 and construction was only completed between 1873 and 1905 under the direction of Miklós Ybl, of State Opera House fame. The mosaics in this gigantic dome, which may be reached by a lift and steps, are by Károly Lotz, and the figure of St Stephen on the high altar is by Alajos Stróbl. Rather gruesomely, the church is home to one of St Stephen's 100-year-old mummified hands, known as the Holy Right.

LEOPOLD TOWN

Continuing north through the quieter streets of Leopold Town (Lipótváros) takes you to Szabadság tér, home of Hungarian Television and the American Embassy (where the rebel Cardinal Mindszenty lived in exile between 1956 and 1971). Just beyond the latter looms the central dome of Hungary's **Parliament** ㉒ (Országház; guided tours in English daily 10am, noon, 1pm, 2pm and 3pm; www.parlament.hu), which, at 96 metres (315ft), is the same height as

the cupola of the basilica, perhaps representing equality of secular and religious power in the country. Designed by Imre Steindl and completed in 1904, this neo-Gothic edifice is immense: 268 metres/yds long and 116 metres/yds at its widest point, with some 20km (12 miles) of staircases inside. The exterior walls feature 233 statues, and the numerous frescoes were executed by some of Hungary's most notable artists, such as Mihály Munkácsy and the indefatigable Károly Lotz.

Highlights of the interior include the Dome Hall – with its star exhibit, the revered crown of St Stephen – and the magnificently gilded Lord's Chamber. At the end of the tour take time to enjoy the exhibition, complete with the oversized red star that was removed from the dome following the end of communism.

Opposite the Parliament, on Kossuth Lajos tér, is the neo-Baroque **Ethnographic Museum** ㉓ (Néprajzi Múzeum; Tue–Sun 10am–6pm; www.neprajz.hu), built between 1893 and 1896 as the seat of the Royal Court. The museum's

Leopold Town.

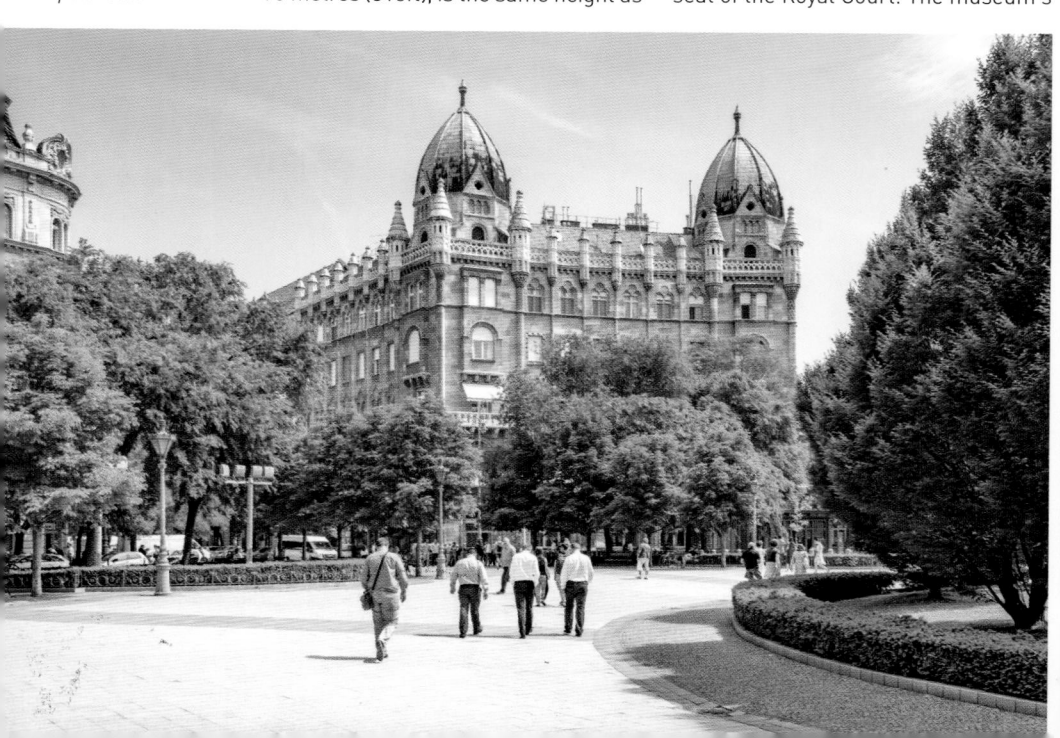

remarkable architecture includes a pil-lared hall several storeys high, stained-glass windows and a grand ceiling fresco, also by Lotz, depicting Justice and recalling the building's former function as the Palace of Justice. The collections cover village life through the ages and prime the visitor well for a trip through the country.

Kossuth Lajos tér is itself an impres-sive sight. Two statues in the middle of the square honour the heroes of two of Hungary's many failed bids for inde-pendence: Lajos Kossuth, leader of the Hungarian Revolution of 1848, on horseback; and Ferenc Rákóczi II, who led the ill-fated War of Independence (1703–11). To the south of the Parlia-ment is a fine statue of József Attila, one of Hungary's finest poets, and the Holocaust Memorial, which marks the spot where hundreds of Jewish adults and children were gunned down by the Arrow Cross before being thrown into the Danube.

THEATRELAND

Back towards Deák tér is the broad, tree-lined **Andrássy út,** on which the **Hungarian State Opera House** 🄬 (Magyar Állami Operaház) was built from 1844–75. Opposite the entrance to the opera are statues of the Hun-garian composer and pianist, Franz Liszt, and Ferenc Erkel, composer of the 'national' opera *Bánk Bán.* There are numerous small, independent theatres in the vicinity of the Opera House, including the Mikroszkóp, Thalia, Vidám and Radnóti theatres, and the well-regarded Budapest Operetta.

Continue along Andrássy út until you reach busy **Oktogon tér.** Take a right here and you'll come to one of the most traditional coffee houses in Budapest, the **New York Café** (Erzsébet körút; daily 8am–midnight) with its superb, painstakingly restored interiors. At one time the cream of Budapest soci-ety used to meet here; some of them

are reunited in the Kerepesi Cemetery, east of the city centre.

The **Millennial Monument** (Ezeréves emlékmű) in **Heroes' Square** 🄬 (Hősök tere) marks the end of Andrássy út. The 'Millennium', as it is commonly known, was built in 1896 to commem-orate the conquest of the Carpathian Basin by the Magyars (see page 27) and depicts the Archangel Gabriel, surrounded by tribal chiefs, with their leader Árpád in the centre. The signifi-cance of the monument is underlined by the Tomb of the Unknown Soldier and the statues of Hungarian kings, princes and statesmen right behind it. They stand in a semicircular row of col-umns, from St István to János Hunyádi and Lajos Kossuth, and look down sternly on the square filled with tour-ists, acrobatic roller-bladers, skate-boarders and cyclists.

The area around the Millennial Monument offers many opportuni-ties for entertainment and relaxation. On the north side of Heroes' Square, the excellent **Museum of Fine Arts** 🄬 (Szépművészeti Múzeum; Tue–Sun

⊙ Fact

The Holy Right, St Stephen's mummified hand, gets an annual outing on 20 August, St Stephen's Day. On this day, the Holy Right is paraded through Budapest, celebrating the life of the first Hungarian king.

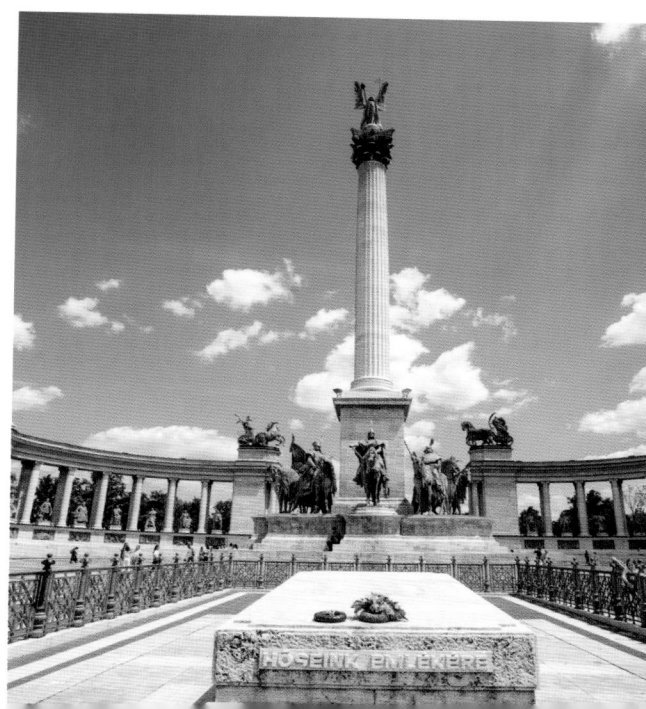

Millennial Monument.

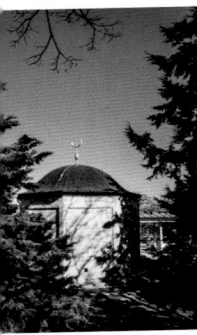

Tomb of Gül Baba.

10am–6pm; www.mfab.hu) is housed in a building by Albert Schickedanz and Fülöp Herzog and contains Egyptian, Greek and Roman collections, as well as modern sculpture and drawings. The first-floor paintings include works by the major European artists from the 13th to 19th centuries, including Raphael, Brueghel and El Greco. Opposite is **Műcsarnok** (Tue, Wed & Fri 10am–6pm, Thu noon–8pm), an art gallery which holds temporary modern art exhibitions.

A WALK IN THE PARK

Located behind the Millennial Monument is the **City Park** ㉗ (Városliget), the biggest park in the city and a great place to unwind. At its northwestern edge is the city's famous **Zoo** (Állatkert; 9am–6pm, Fri–Sun until 7pm; www.zoobudapest.com), renowned above all for its Art Nouveau pavilions, including the remarkable Elephant House. Next door, the **Gundel** restaurant retains a touch of the elegance of times past. The birthplace of pancakes à *la Gundel* (covered in nuts, cream and chocolate sauce), you can find this dish all over the country, but it is best tried here or at the Bagolyvár, a Gundel offshoot, next door.

Many visitors head for the sensuous pleasures of the **Széchenyi Baths** ㉘ (see box). The romantic **Vajdahunyad Castle** ㉙ (Vajdahunyad vara) stands on an artificial island in the middle of the Városliget pond, where you can boat in summer and ice-skate in winter. The castle houses a **Museum of Agriculture** (Magyar Mezőgazdasági Múzeum; daily 10am–5pm). The building is a copy of the former palace of János Hunyadi in Vajdahunyad, now in Romania, but all the other parts of the castle are copies of historic Hungarian buildings, creating a quirky mixture of kitsch and opulence.

MARGARET ISLAND

Another sanctuary from city stress is **Margaret Island** ㉚ (Margitsziget), an oasis of greenery between the Margaret and the Árpád Bridges. You can reach the island by car from the Árpád Bridge, but it is closed to motorists

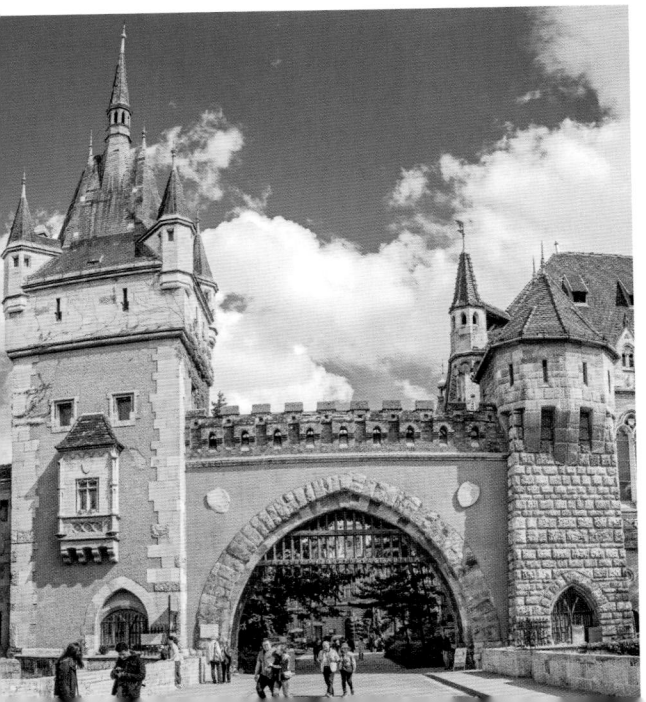

Vajdahunyad Castle.

⊘ SZÉCHENYI BATHS

The Széchenyi Baths (Széchenyi fürdő; daily 6am–10pm) are a stupendous neo-Baroque complex built in 1913 with an outdoor pool and full spa facilities (see page 129). Outside the palace-like structure is a statue of the Hungarian geologist Zsigmondy Vilmos, who, in 1878, discovered the thermal spring that would come to feed the Széchenyi Baths when they finally opened in 1913. The water rises from a depth of 1,256 metres (4,120ft) and feeds steam baths, hot baths and saunas. Inside, expect to witness the surreal yet quintessential sight of grown men, fully submerged in the hot water, playing chess with one another. The Széchenyi Baths are open all year round and are an essential Budapest experience.

beyond the two hotels at the north of the island. Buses are the only motorised traffic; if you don't want to walk, you can hire a horse-drawn trap, bicycle or 'bicycle car' for four people.

The most prominent building on the island, at a height of 57 metres (187ft), is the **Water Tower** (Víztorony) above the open-air stage. In the tower of a restored **Premonstratensian church** (Premontrei templom), the south wall and windows of which date from the 12th century, hangs one of the oldest bells in Hungary (14th/15th century), which was found in 1914 under a tree uprooted by a storm.

A little further to the south, you'll find the ruins of a convent of Dominican nuns, which King Béla IV had built after the Mongol invasion of 1241. He placed his daughter Margaret there, to be brought up as a nun fulfilling a vow for deliverance from the Mongol purge. The island, previously known as Hare Island, was named after her. Near the centre of the island, south of the Rose Garden, are the ruins of a 13th-century Franciscan church.

Sports enthusiasts will find swimming pools, tennis courts, boathouses and jogging tracks here. More sedate pleasures are to be had in the Japanese Garden, with its carp pools, hot spring and Rose Garden. North of Margaret Island, **Óbuda-Sziget** hosts the marathon eight-day long Sziget Festival each August, featuring some of the world's biggest and best rock and pop acts.

TURKS AND ROMANS

Leaving Margaret Island at its southern end via the Margaret Bridge (the one with the elbow in it), you'll reach **Óbuda** and its reminders of Hungary's Turkish past. Near the Buda bridgehead, on Turbán út and Mecset utca, is the **Tomb of Gül Baba** ③ (Gül Baba türbéje), a dervish known as 'Father of Roses' because legend has it that he introduced the flowers to Hungary. A rose

garden now surrounds his simple tomb; there is also a pleasant café overlooking the city. At Fő utca 82–4, are the **Király Baths** (Király gyógyfürdő; daily 9am–9pm), built by the Turks in 1556. Under the four squat green domes, the tallest crowned by a golden crescent, is an octagonal pool at the top of four flights of steps; formerly men only baths, they are now unisex.

Beyond Árpád híd you'll find the **Imre Varga collection** (Tue–Sun 10am–6pm) of works by the prolific contemporary sculptor, who is now well into his nineties. Close by are the ruins of the once bustling Roman civilian town of **Aquincum** ③ and its museum (Szentendrei út 139; Tue–Sun 9am–5pm; www.aquincum.hu), which was built on the site of a Celtic settlement in 1 BC (named Ak-Ink, or ample water). The museum houses finds from the excavations, including the bronze parts of a water organ and some outstanding mosaics. Do not miss the **civilian amphitheatre,** just across the railway embankment, and, at Meggyfa utca 18–20, **Herkules Villa** with its remarkable mosaic.

☉ Tip

You can trace Buda's Roman past with a visit to the **Military Amphitheatre** (Római katonai amfiteátrum) on Pacsirtamező utca, which was once larger than the Coliseum in Rome.

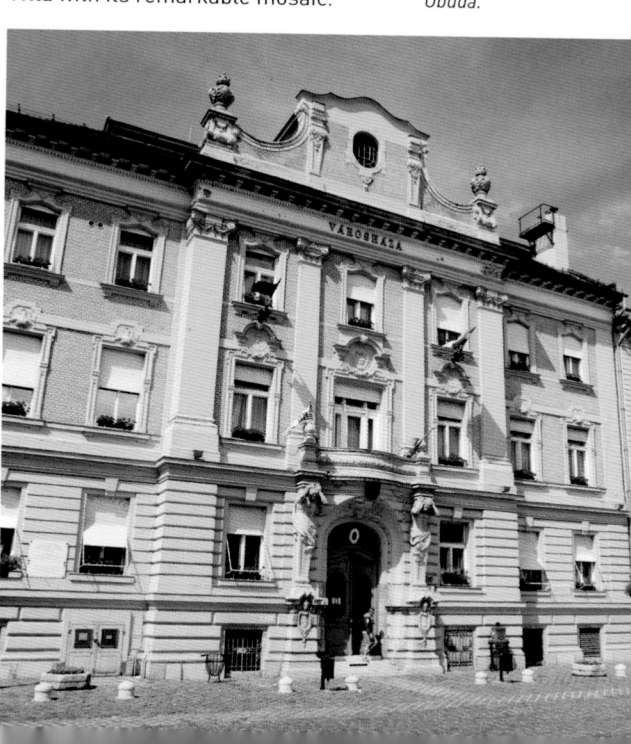

Óbuda.

Royal Palace of Gödöllő.

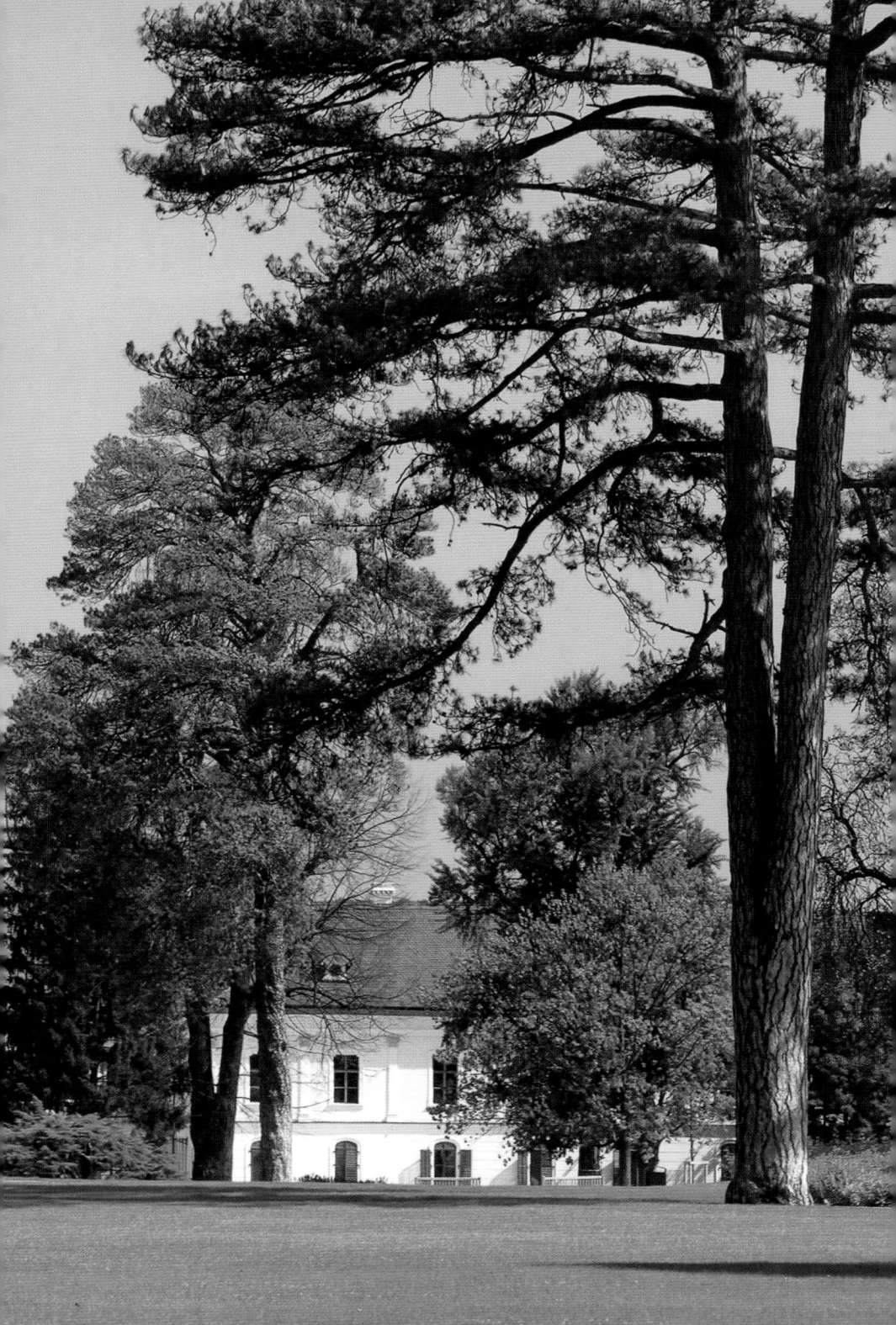

AROUND BUDAPEST

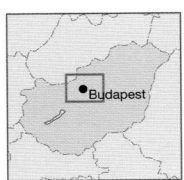

The area around Budapest offers a range of sights, from Roman remains and Baroque castles to nature reserves and a variety of traditional villages.

⊙ Main attractions

Martonvásár
Székesfehérvár
Tata
Gödöllő

Map on page 159

If you want a break from city sight-seeing, why not head out to the area around Budapest, which has much to attract the visitor in the way of scenery, wildlife, art and culture. This chapter includes several excursions, which radiate from Budapest. Although we have indicated travel by road, Hungary has a good rail network (see page 274), which can take you to most of the destinations in this chapter.

LAKE RESORTS

Follow highway No. 70 southwest from Budapest towards Székesfehérvár and Velencei-tó, through undulating countryside, meadows, orchards and vineyards. In Érd, on the outskirts of Budapest, you can see one of three minarets, evidence of the Turkish occupation of Hungary (1543–1688).

Martonvásár ❶, 30km (19 miles) from the capital, is a beautiful palace, to which Beethoven was a frequent visitor – he was in love with one of the daughters of the Brunswick family, who resided here. The park (or perhaps the love affair) is believed to have inspired the *Moonlight Sonata*, which Beethoven wrote at Martonvásár, and a blackbird is said to have 'whispered' the theme of the third movement of his *Violin Concerto* into his ear here. There is a small museum (Tue–Sun 10am–noon and 2–4pm) dedicated to the composer, and outdoor concerts and recitals are held in the atmospheric surroundings.

Many rare plants are cultivated in the lovely 70-hectare (170-acre) gardens, which are open to the public all year round (daily 8am–6pm, winter 8am–4pm; www.martonvasar.hu).

Just before Székesfehérvár, on the right, is **Velencei-tó ❷**. The northern and western shores of this lake are covered in reeds and form a nature reserve to protect the rare water birds that nest here, including white-tailed eagles, marsh harriers,

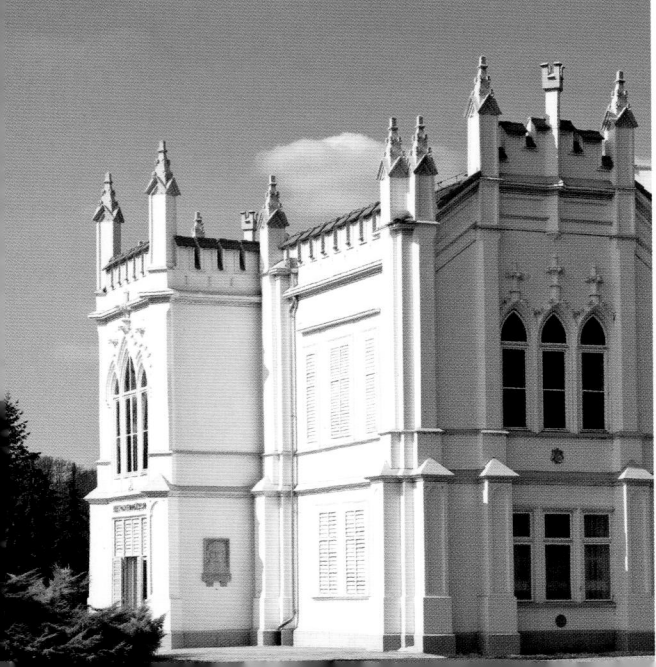

Brunszvik castle.

and great white egrets. The southern shore consists of several adjoining resorts, the most popular of which are **Agárd** and **Gárdony**. Anglers come here to catch carp, eel and sometimes catfish.

HUNGARY'S OLDEST TOWN

Székesfehérvár ❸ (pronounced Say-kesh-fehair-var) at the southwestern end of Velencei-tó, 50km (30 miles) from Budapest, is the oldest town in Hungary. The former Roman settlement of Gorsium, to the south, served as the spiritual centre for Pannonia early in the first millennium AD. Árpád, leader of the conquering Magyars, founded his dynasty here. His descendant, St Stephen (István I), chose Székesfehérvár as his residence (1000–38) and had the royal basilica built here in 1016. For almost 500 years it remained the country's royal city.

After the destruction of most of its medieval buildings in the long Turkish occupation, Székesfehérvár enjoyed something of a renaissance during the reign of Maria Theresa (1740–80), and the town's well laid-out buildings date from this time. Despite destruction, industrialisation and heavy traffic, the shape and size of the old town remain unchanged to this day and Székesfehérvár has successfully retained its romantic aura. The town centre, now almost free of cars, is a pleasant place for a stroll.

In the centre of Székesfehérvár is **Town Hall Square** (Városház tér), once the site of the royal palace and basilica of István I, and still the town's main piazza. The southwestern tower of the basilica stood where the fountain (a representation of the nation by Béla Ohmann) stands today. In the **Garden of Ruins** (Romkert; Apr–Oct Tue–Sun 9am–5pm) behind the square, the apse, several pillars and the tomb of

> **⊙ Tip**
>
> Hungary's founding father is buried in the Garden of Ruins, albeit minus his right hand, which is in St Stephen's Basilica in Budapest (see pages 151 and 152).

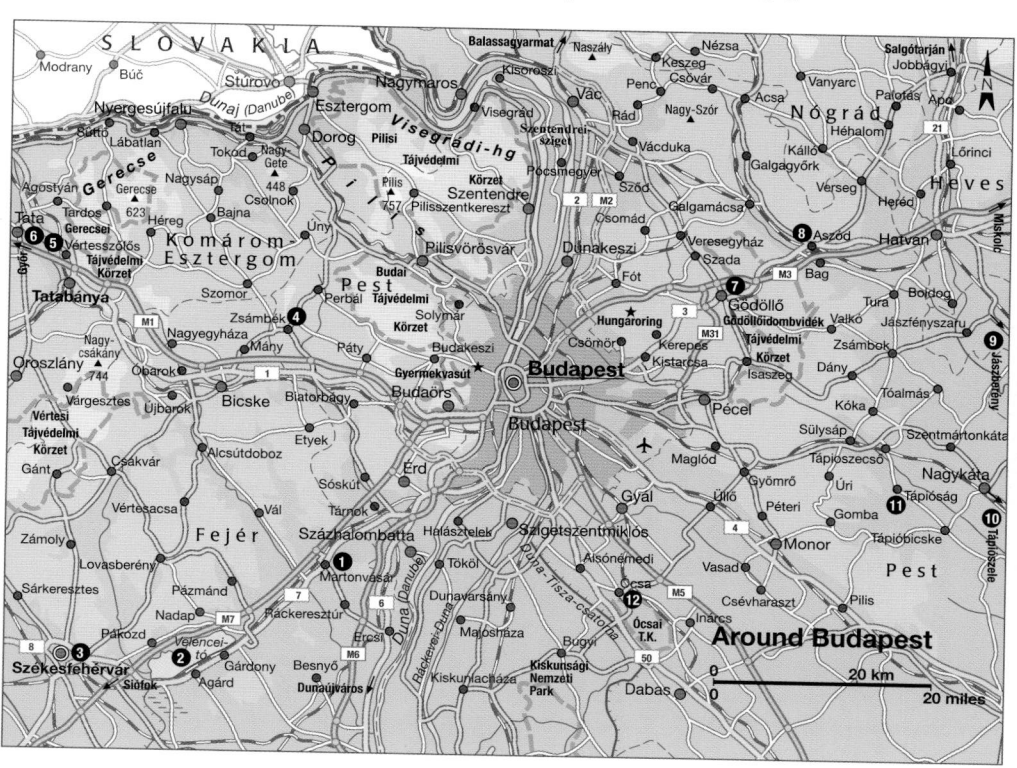

István I (St Stephen) can still be seen. The garden is covered by a large metal-and-plexiglass roof, and the pavement forms an elegant flyover that offers a high vantage point.

At the far side, under the arches, is a small building that houses a busy fresco by Vilmos Aba Novák; the image depicts Hungarian history with some unusual characterisations (note the faces of the priests).

The town hall, its main entrance adorned with the figures of Justitia and Prudentia, stands on the southern side of the square. The unclothed equestrian figure facing it is a memorial to the Hussars, the cavalry regiment established by King Mátyás to fight the Turks. Opposite the town hall is the **Hiemer House** on Jókai utca 1, which has stood here since the beginning of the 18th century. It is decorated with delicate rococo stucco work and features a prominent bay window.

Located close by is a Baroque Franciscan church (1720–42) and its monastery buildings, in which religious artworks are displayed. The eastern side of the square is bounded by the **Bishop's Palace** (1801) one of the most notable buildings of the period, constructed using the old stones of the basilica. The interior is a haven of restrained neoclassicism.

To the north of the square, in Fő utca, is a Baroque **Cistercian Church**, with two towers and monastery buildings. It was built between 1745 and 1751 by the Jesuits and is well worth visiting. Unique in Hungary, the furnishing of the sacristy is carved out of oak and lime. This architectural treasure survived World War II thanks to the parish priest of the time who protected the sacristy with sandbags, even at the cost of damage to the nave. The woodcarver, János Hyngeller, also worked on the **Black Eagle Pharmacy** (Fekete Sas Patika; Tue–Sun 9am–5pm), dating from 1758, which stands opposite the church. The original Baroque fixtures and fittings, including a splendid horseshoe-shaped Empire-style table complete with glass cabinets, remain in superb condition.

From Városház tér, via the narrow, rising streets, you can reach the heart

In the main square of Székesfehérvár.

⊘ ROMAN REMAINS

Not to be missed – especially if you do not have time to go to Tác – is the King Stephen Museum (István Király Múzeum; May–Sept Wed–Fri 10am–4pm, Sat & Sun noon–6pm; Apr & Oct–Dec Tue–Fri 10am–2pm, Sat & Sun 2–6pm; https://szikm.hu/). The museum is located in Székesfehérvár, near where the excavations of the old Roman settlement and the collection of Roman carved stones from the Gorsium settlement can be found.

In the museum, you will find a collection of Roman coins that were excavated at the nearby Gorsium settlement. The upper floor is devoted to a fascinating array of artefacts, including jewellery and tools used not only by the Romans, but also by Celts, Avars and Slavs.

of the town, **Prince Géza Square** (Géza nagyfejedelem tér). Here you'll see the Gothic **Chapel of St Anne** (Szent Anna kápolna), a tiny, unassuming white building that dates from 1470 and is the only surviving medieval building in Székesfehérvár.

Next to it lies **St Stephen's Cathedral** (Szent István székesegyház), founded by Béla IV around the same time as the chapel, although the sections visible today date largely from the 18th century. Parts of the Gothic windows are still discernible in the church's two towers. A Byzantine church once stood in the middle of the square and its outline has been embedded into the pavement.

For a speedy return to Budapest, take the toll-free M7 motorway.

BUDAPEST TO TATA

To reach Tata, head northwest from Budapest on the M1 motorway. En route, you could make a short diversion via the small town of **Zsámbék** ➍, with its Romanesque church and 13th-century monastery ruins. The church's towers are a focal point in the area as cultural events are held here on Saturdays from June to August.

Just before Tata is **Vértesszőlős** ➎, the oldest and most extensive excavation site of a prehistoric settlement in Hungary. It was here in 1963 that Homo erectus remains (c.450,000 BC) were discovered in a former quarry. Their bones, tools, the animals they hunted, and the remains of their campfires are all exhibited in an open-air museum.

Tata ➏, a charming town built around many springs and lakes, was a summer resort for King Sigismund and King Mátyás back in the 14th and 15th centuries. The town was largely destroyed during the Turkish occupation, but its fortunes were revived in the 18th century, when much of it was rebuilt under the eye of architect Jakob Fellner, whose talents account for the town's harmonious Baroque appearance.

Along the **Old Lake** (Öreg-tó), fed by several warm springs, there is a large park containing the remains of the 13th-century church of Vértesszentkereszt. Ruins of the **Old Castle** (Öregvár), dating from the 14th and 15th centuries, can also be seen by the lake. The castle was demolished by the Turks and rebuilt by the Austrians at the end of the 19th century. Its restored rooms now house the **Kuny Domokos Museum** (Tue–Sat 9am–5pm), which has various exhibits illustrating the history of the area, and a collection of ceramics that will appeal to lovers of faïence.

In Kossuth tér you can see a mid-18th-century church with two towers, and off Rákóczi utca are the remnants of a palace dating from 1769 that belonged to the Esterházy family. It now serves as a wing of the municipal hospital.

Relics of Tata's once-productive system of mills, locks and canals can be spotted around the town. The Nepomucenus Mill on Alkotmány utca houses the **German Minority**

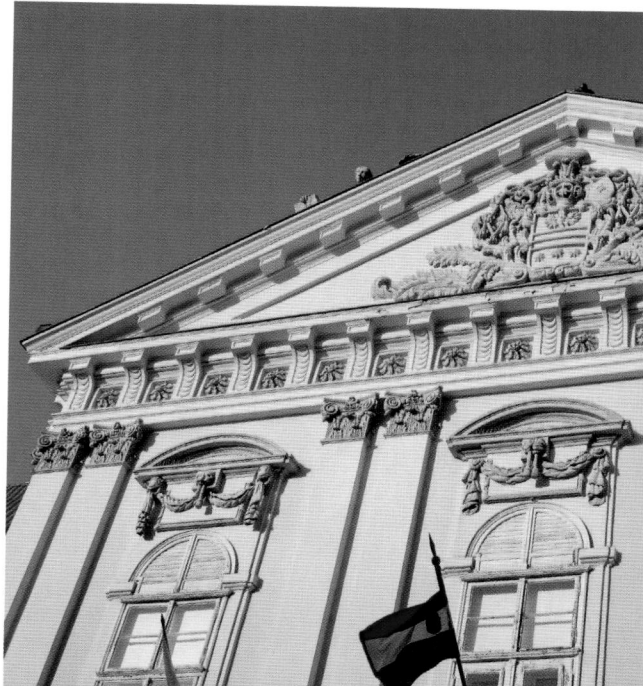

Bishop palace in Székesfehérvár.

Museum (Apr–Oct Tues–Sun 10am–6pm, reduced hours in winter) with an ethnographic collection revealing the life, history and handiwork of the German people who were once a majority in this region. On Ady Endre utca is the Baroque Miklós Mill, dating from 1770 and built by Jakob Fellner.

Öreg-tó is the focus for many activities including swimming, boating, cycling fishing and horseriding. **Angol Park** has its own smaller lake (Cseke-tó) and is a good place for a relaxing stroll. The Water, Music and Flower Festival at the end of June puts the town on the map; the festivities include equestrian displays, boat parades and fireworks. The other big event on the lake is the arrival of the wild geese. Tata and its lake are on their migration path, and twice a year up to 15,000 of these birds take a rather noisy break here.

A TASTE OF THE PUSZTA

No sooner do you get beyond Budapest's eastern limits than you come to the Great Plain (Nagyalföld). The switch is unnerving – from the cosmopolitan bustle of the capital to farming villages, horse-drawn carts, peasant women in rubber boots and the occasional villa built by a Pester or a returning son or daughter.

Just 30 km (18 miles) from Budapest is the town of **Gödöllő** ❼. (Note: **Hungaroring**, the only Formula One racetrack in Central Europe, lies on the M3 between Budapest and Gödöllő, so expect some congestion in the July/August racing season.) In 1867, the Hungarian state, which was then newly incorporated into Austria-Hungary, gave the town and its remarkable Baroque Grassalkovich Palace, also known as the **Royal Mansion** (Királyi kastély; Apr–Oct Mon–Thu 9am–5pm, Fri–Sun 10am–6pm; Nov–March daily 10am–5pm; www.kiralyikastely.hu), to the recently crowned King Franz Josef I and his wife, Elisabeth (Sissi). Their royal presences boosted Gödöllő's economy, but the decision was nevertheless made to turn the palace over to more educational purposes, and it became an agricultural college.

For a few years between the two world wars it served as the holiday home of Regent Horthy, before being left to fall into decay. Following its renovation and reopening in 2011, it's now possible to see the grand state rooms, private apartments – complete with some of Sissi's possessions – Baroque theatre, and the Riding Hall, which hosts temporary exhibitions.

On Gödöllő's main square, **Szabadság tér,** is the **Gödöllő Town Museum** (Wed–Sun 10am–4pm), celebrating not only Queen Sissi but also the sounds of nature, the oceans and, in stark contrast, the work of the Artists' Colony that thrived here from 1901 to 1920. Inspired by the English pre-Raphaelites, the colony had a lasting influence on Hungary's art and architecture.

Garden of Ruins, Székesfehérvár.

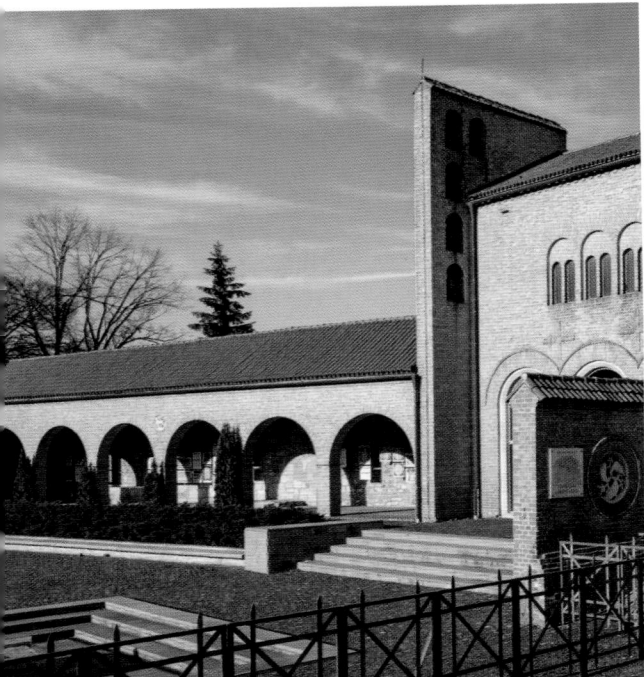

Further east, on the way to Aszód, you will come across a sign to **Máriabesznyő,** a church of pilgrimage up on a hill. At the entrance to the path is a typical Transylvanian gate of carved and painted wood. The venerated statue of the Virgin and Child at Máriabesznyő is of ivory and was discovered during building work on the chapel by Count Grassalkovich.

A short distance northwest of Gödöllő is **Aszód ❽**, whose main square was entirely renovated for the year 2000 celebrations. Among the buildings to be viewed in the town is the **Podmaniczky Palace,** part of which is now used as a school. The Grand Hall on the first floor is a masterpiece of Baroque art, with *grisaille* painting and a large fresco depicting the Virtues.

EASTERN FOLKLORE

From Hatvan, drive southeast on Route 32 to **Jászberény ❾**, the centre of a region called Jászság, after the Jazygen, a people from the Caspian Sea who settled here in the 13th century (the common local prefix Jász-indicates their towns). Their main occupation was sheep-rearing, as suggested by sporadic appearances of votive statues of St Wendelin, patron saint of sheep and shepherds.

The heart of the town is Lehel vezér tér, and nearby is the **Jász Museum** (Apr–Oct Tues–Sun 9am–5pm; Nov–Mar Tue–Fri 9am–4pm, Sat & Sun 9am–1pm; www.jaszmuzeum.hu) on Táncsics Mihály utca. The museum is home to a comprehensive collection of artefacts from the region, including replicas of living rooms, folkloric costumes and the famous Lehel Horn, which allegedly belonged to one of the Magyar chieftains, although its carvings suggest Byzantine work from a few centuries later. Jászberény comes alive with the **Csángó**

Festival and other folkloric gatherings held throughout the summer months.

The well-tended thermal bath in **Nagykáta,** just south of Jászberény, might be the ideal place to wash off some of the dust and do a few lengths in the competition pool before returning to Budapest.

The area southeast of the capital has a wealth of sights: the **Blaskovich Múzeum** (Mar–Nov Tues–Sun 9am–5pm) in **Tápiószele ❿**, with its remarkable antique furniture, jewellery, glass and porcelain, and the traditional houses in the tiny village of **Tápióság ⓫**.

If time allows, it's worth making a detour to **Ócsa ⓬**, which stands in the middle of a protected landscape stretching to the Danube. The three-nave church in town, probably built during the early 1200s, is considered to be the most important Romanesque monument in Hungary east of the Danube. The simple building was renovated in the 1990s. Inside are numerous frescoes, some of them not very well restored but still quite impressive.

Romanesque church in Ócsa.

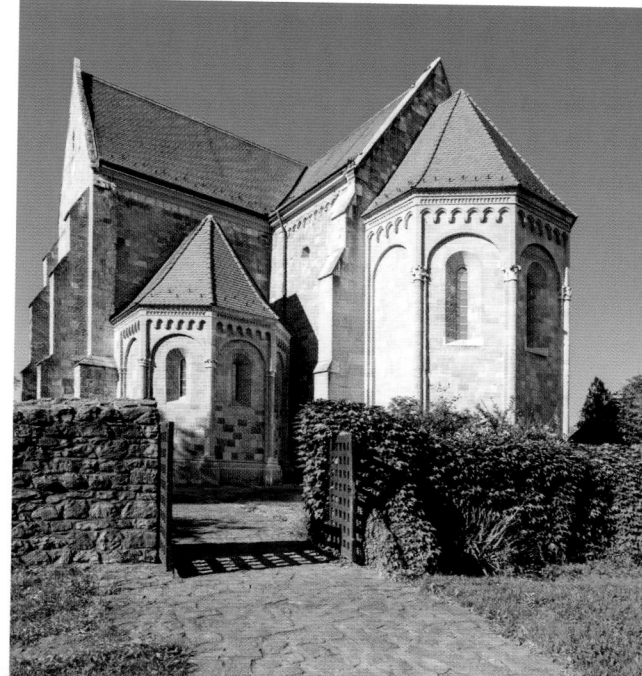

FOOD AND FESTIVALS

Hungary boasts a formidable culinary tradition, combining elements of native and foreign – notably French and Central Asian – cuisine to exciting effect.

The archetypal Hungarian dish is of course goulash (*gulyas*), a thick, soup-like stew comprising beef, potatoes, onion and peppers, and invariably flavoured with a dash of paprika – this ubiquitous, and much-loved, Hungarian spice, known as 'red gold', is the one foodstuff most synonymous with Hungarian cooking. The country may be landlocked, but fish plays a big part in the Hungarian kitchen, in particular a spicy fish soup (*halászlé*) – popular in towns along the Danube and Tisza – and pike-perch (*fogas*), a staple dish in restaurants around Lake Balaton. For those possessed of a sweeter tooth, *dobostorta*, a wicked, chocolate-layered sponge cake topped with caramel, should more than satisfy.

More surprising, perhaps, is the quality and depth of Hungarian wine. An industry revitalized in recent years, there are now 22 wine-growing regions, the most celebrated of which is Tokaj-Hegyalja, home to the eponymous, and world-famous, dessert wine. Other wine roads well worth visiting are Villány-Siklós in southern Hungary which yields a fantastic variety of both reds and whites, and Balatonboglár and Badascony near Lake Balaton, where white wines predominate – by far the most enjoyable way to sample a few vintages is to visit a local wine cellar (*borospince*).

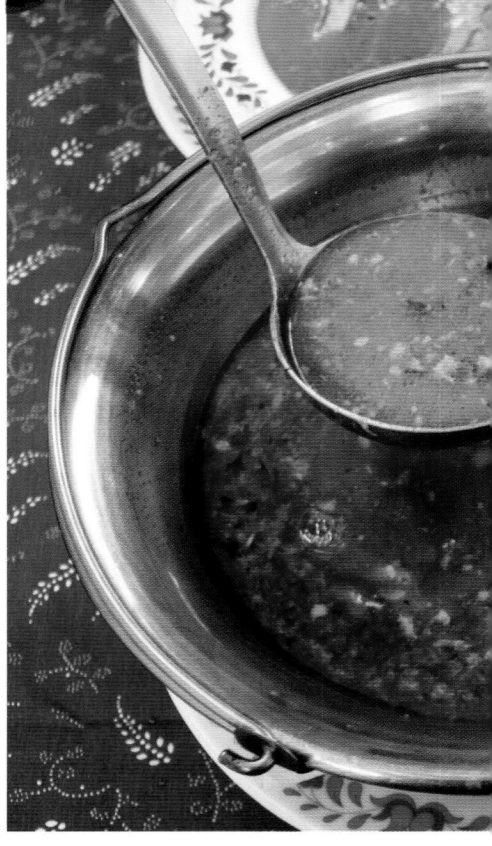

Halászlé is a hot and spicy paprika-based fish soup.

Drying paprika.

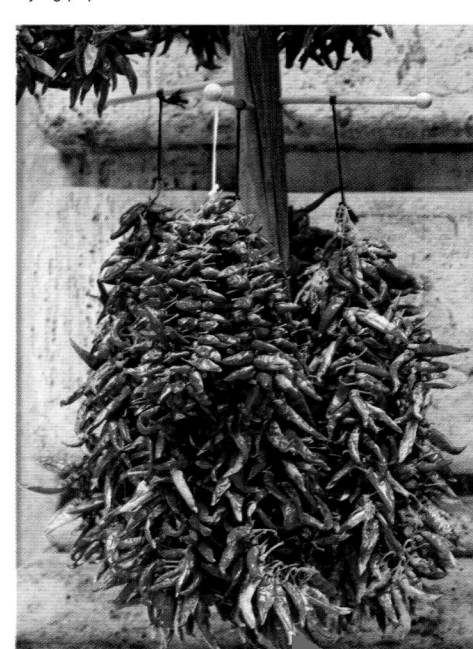

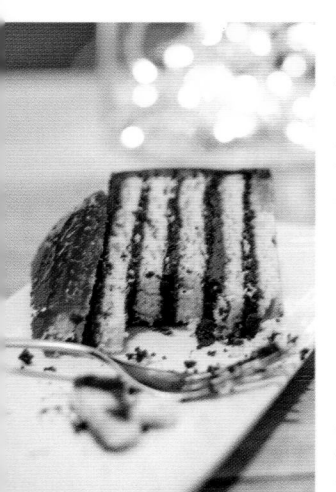

Dobostorta, made with chocolate buttercream and topped with caramel.

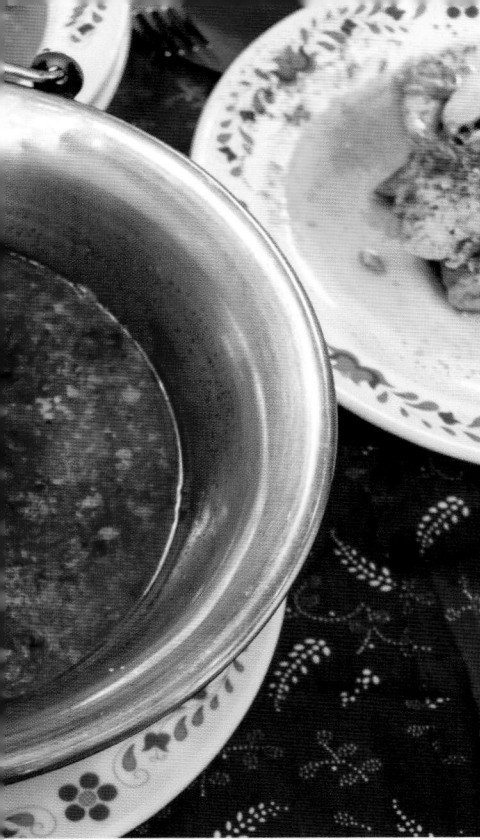

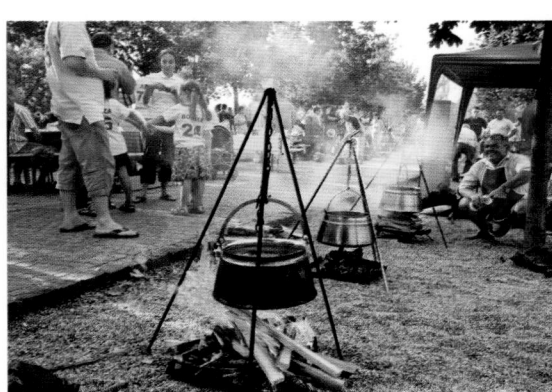

Baja Fish Soup (Halászlé) Festival.

Food festivals

Hungary abounds in colourful gastronomic festivals, most of which are accompanied by music, dancing and, of course, lots of drinking. The highest-profile foodie fests are the Szolnok Goulash Festival, which sees more than seven hundred pots of the stuff prepared over two days, and, in a similar vein, the Baja Fish Soup Festival, where more than two thousand bubbling cauldrons consume the town's enormous main square. Meat gets a look in courtesy of the convivial Békéscaba Sausage Festival, where chefs from all over the country compete to create their own unique version of the mighty banger. A couple of more offbeat foodie festivals include the Onion Festival in Mako and, even more curiously, the Horseradish Festival in the village of Uljeta.

The best of the country's many alcohol-fuelled festivals take place in Budapest, and include the Budapest Pálinka Festival, where distillers from all over the country gather to offer their own take on the fiery national drink, and the Budapest Beer Festival, where there's a choice of more than 200 different brews and loads of scrummy street food. For more details on these festivals, visit www.carnifest.com/country/hungary.

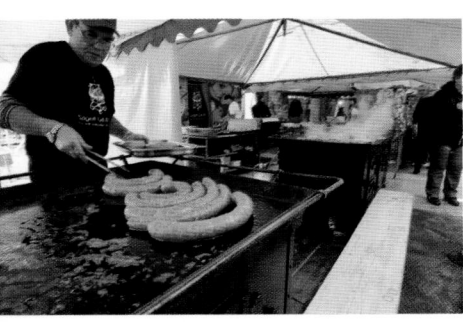

ékéscsaba Sausage Festival.

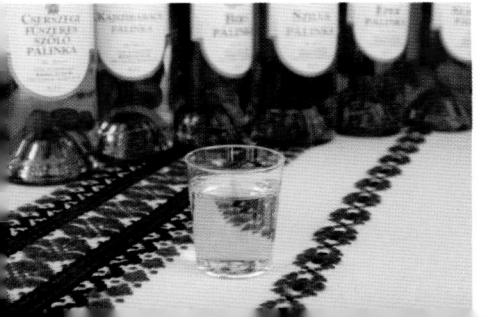

udapest Pálinka Festival.

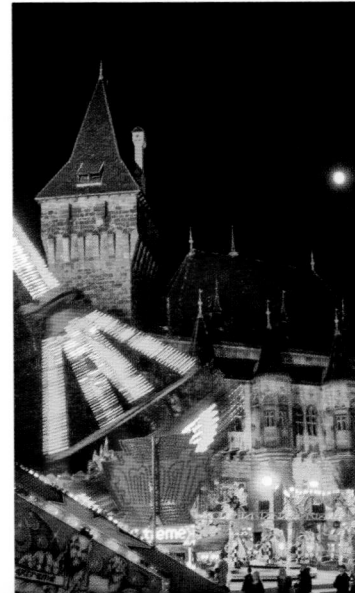

Oktoberfest.

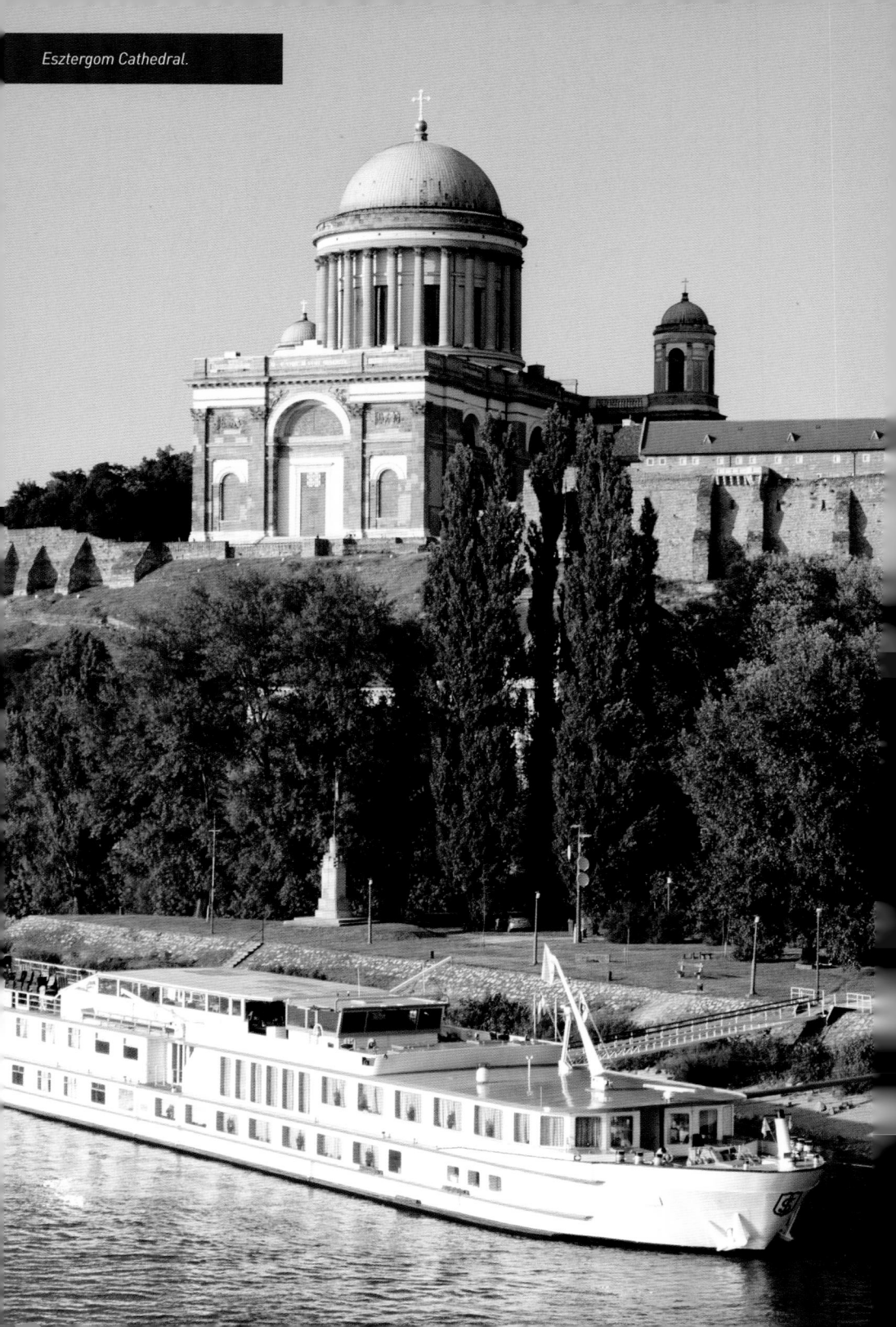
Esztergom Cathedral.

THE DANUBE

A boat trip along the River Danube offers an alternative view of Hungary, and passes through lonely landscapes, historic towns and the site of a disastrous battle.

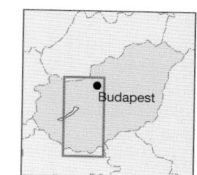

The second-longest river in Europe after the Volga, flowing 2,857km (1,775 miles) from the Black Forest to the Black Sea, the Danube (Duna in Hungarian) commands respect. Fed by more than 300 tributaries from a catchment area of 816,000 sq km (315,059 miles), it has nine nations along its banks: Germany, Austria, Slovakia, Hungary, Croatia, Serbia, Bulgaria, Romania and the Ukraine. Yet it is more than just water, it is a vital artery through which myriad cultures, merchants, warriors and more have passed. The great Hungarian poet, Attila József described it as 'cloudy, wide and great'.

The Danube also has political significance: throughout the centuries, statesmen thought aloud about creating a powerful Danube Federation to resist aggression from east and west. The towns along its banks – Budapest included – have all developed a special connection to the river, and the river has given them a special character, perhaps a little more patience or fatalism, knowing that whatever is now shall pass.

TRANQUIL LANDSCAPES

There are few villages near the river and hardly any people in sight. The only exception on the Hungarian side is **Gönyű** ❶, a sleepy place which

can only with some exaggeration be labelled as the harbour of Győr (see page 189).

Behind the dike, you can see the roofs of low houses, and a few weathered boats on the banks. Elsewhere in this desolate country between water and forest, only the occasional white house or an excavator removing gravel and mud from the riverbed and piling it into whitish-yellow heaps act as reminders of human presence. Here and there, silt deposited on both banks has raised them up, so that the

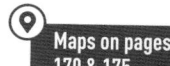

Main attractions
Esztergom
Visegrád
Vác
Szentendre
Kalocsa
Szekszárd

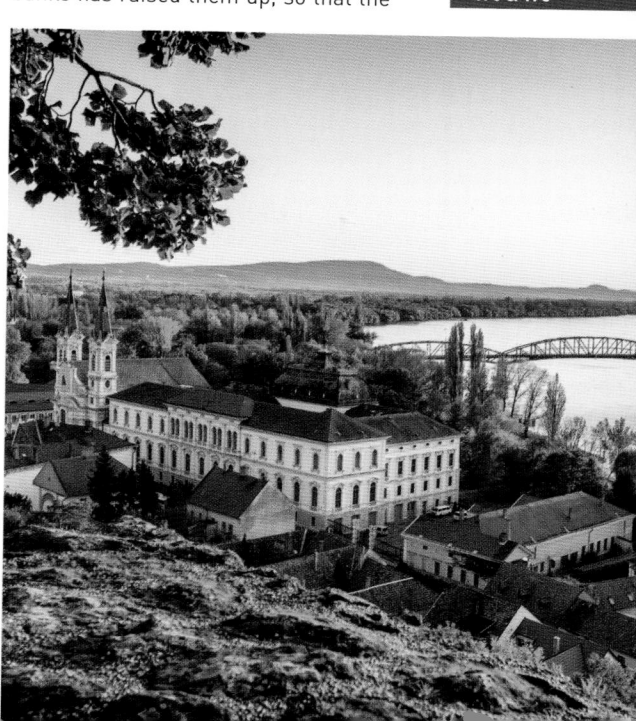

Esztergom's old town.

Maps on pages 170 & 175

surrounding countryside appears to be lower than the river.

You don't reach 'civilisation' again until you get to **Komárom ②** (on the Hungarian side) and Komárno (in Slovakia). In earlier years, the two towns – then unified – belonged to Hungary and played a key role as a defensive fortress in the Turkish wars and in the revolution of 1848–49. Today they are divided into two distinct areas, but joined by a rail and road bridge.

But that is not all this little town has to offer: the ruined fort in the river is just one attraction. Several fortified places are now open to visitors, including the 640-room **Fort Monostor** (Mar–Oct Tue–Sun 9am–6pm; www.erod.hu), built following the Hungarian Revolution of 1848 and consisting of 14 adjoining buildings and 4km (2.5 miles) of underground passages; the well-presented museum relays the history of this and other forts along the Danube. The town also has a pleasant thermal bath.

Just past Komárom, the scenery along the Danube banks changes. On the Hungarian side, the dense woods thin out, the foothills of the Gerecse Hills come close to the river, and villages once again appear. Finally, the great dome of the basilica at **Esztergom** rises from the rocky plateau in front of the Pilis Hills.

ANCIENT CAPITAL

At the time of the Árpád kings **Esztergom ③** served as the capital of Hungary. It was here that István, first king of Hungary, was born in 875, crowned in 1000 and died in 1038. As befits the centre of Hungarian Catholicism, its neoclassical Basilica (Főszékesegyház; daily 8am–6pm; www.bazilika-esztergom.hu) is the biggest church in the country: its dome, supported by four pillars, has an inner height of 71.5 metres (235ft).

This immense building, begun in 1822 and completed in 1856, is 118 metres (387ft) long and 40 metres (131ft) wide, and the roof of the entrance hall, which faces the land, is supported by eight Corinthian pillars, each 22 metres (72ft) high. The

Canoeing on the Danube.

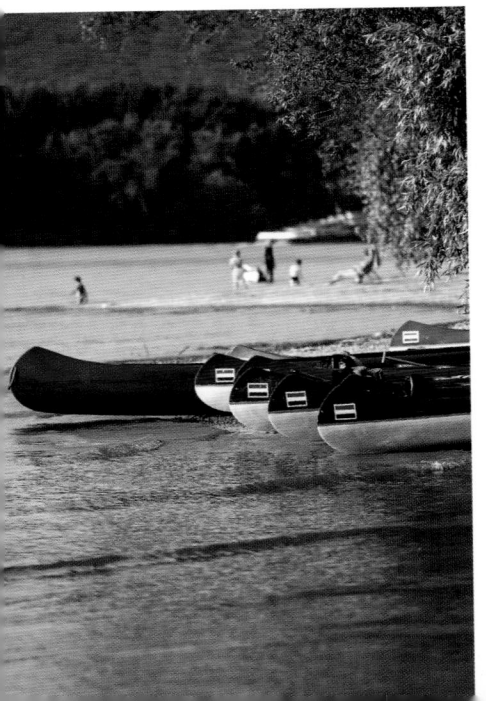

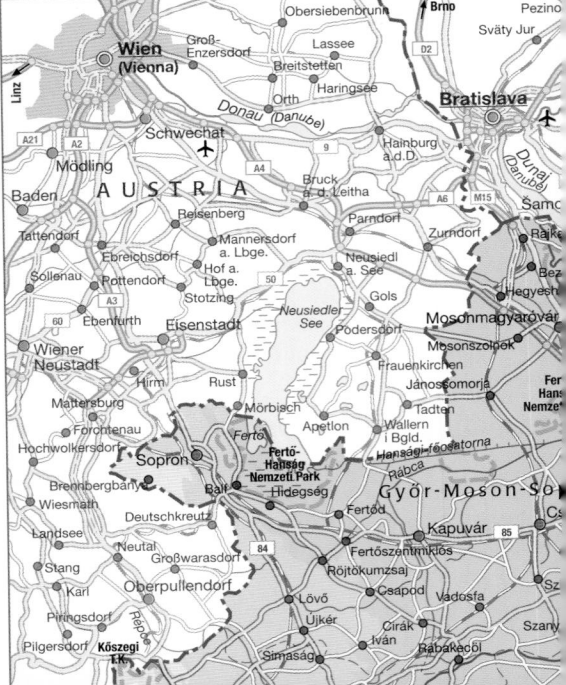

Basilica was consecrated on 31 August 1856, and Franz Liszt composed the Gran Mass for the occasion (Gran is the German name for Esztergom).

The Basilica's main attraction is the older Bakócz Chapel. Originally constructed for Archbishop Tamás Bakócz between 1506 and 1511 as part of the medieval church of St Adalbert, its walls are of red marble. The chapel survived destruction by the Turks during their retreat in 1683, and was taken apart and incorporated into the south wing of the Basilica in 1823. The chilly crypt, meanwhile, holds the tomb of Cardinal József Mindszenty, the leader of Hungary's Catholic church; imprisoned and then exiled for his anti-fascist/anti-communist stance, Mindszenty was finally laid to rest here in Esztergom with state honours in 1991.

The former **Royal Palace,** which was later the residence of the archbishops, fared better than the church of St Adalbert, and archaeologists are constantly unearthing new fragments. These days the **Castle Museum** (Vár Múzeum; Apr–Oct Tue–Sun 10am–6pm, 10am–4pm rest of year; www.varmegom.hu) is housed here. Visitors can admire several beautiful Romanesque portals dating from the 12th and 13th centuries, for instance, at the entrance to the castle chapel. Some of the rooms of the palace have also survived or been restored, such as the Vaulted Hall, which is probably the oldest living space in Hungary.

Apart from Castle Hill (Vár-hegy), the Basilica and the Royal Palace, there are several other interesting sights in Esztergom. The Archbishop's Palace, between Castle Hill and the Danube, houses the **Christian Museum** (Keresztény Múzeum; Mar–Dec Wed–Sun 10am–5pm; www.keresztenymuzeum.hu), one of the most notable art collections outside Budapest. Among its exhibits are valuable paintings and wood carvings dating from the 15th and 16th centuries representing the work of artists from the entire Danube region, including Hungary. Some Italian artists are also featured.

> **⊘ Tip**
>
> A visit to Esztergom is best done as part of a boat excursion from Budapest.

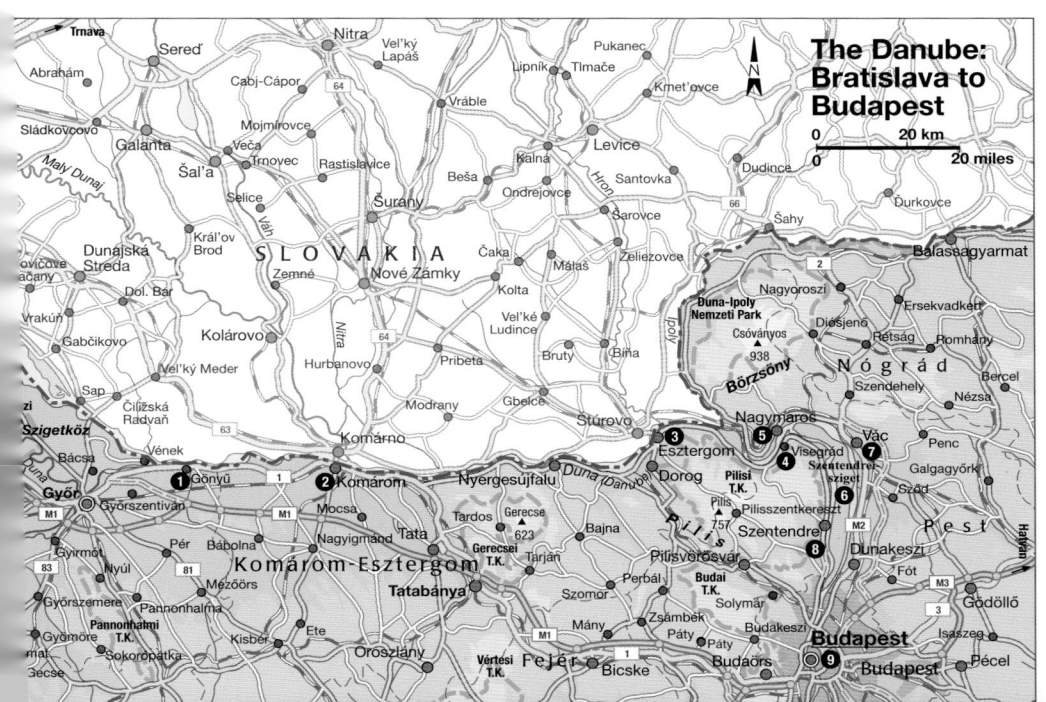

The Danube: Bratislava to Budapest

⊙ Fact

Some 10km (6 miles) below Esztergom, the Slovak-Hungarian border turns north to follow the River Ipoly, which flows into the Danube from the Slovak mountains.

If you have time, take a look also at the **Balassi Bálint Museum** (Balassi Bálint Múzeum; Tue–Sun 9am–5pm; www.balassamuzeum.hu), dedicated to the 16th-century troubadour and poet (see page 100).

The rest of Esztergom, with its 17th- and 18th-century houses, is worth looking at. A small arm of the river forms an island – Prímás Sziget – that is used for all types of leisure activities. Here too is the Mária Valéria Bridge (aka The Friendship Bridge), until 2001 a stump left over from World War II, but which now links Esztergom with Štúrovo in Slovakia. At the bridge-head is an old customs house turned museum.

A ROYAL SEAT

Visegrád ❹ today is merely a small town on the Danube, but in the 14th and 15th centuries it was one of the residences of the Hungarian kings. St Stephen's Crown and the Royal Insignia were kept from time to time in the castle above the town. The kings of the house of Anjou started using Visegrád as a royal residence in the first half of the 14th century. King Sigismund of Luxembourg extended the palace (Mar–Oct Tue–Sun 9am–5pm, rest of year 10am–4pm) at the foot of the castle. However, it was in the second half of the 15th century, under the 'Renaissance King' Mátyás Corvinus and his wife Beatrix of Aragon, that Visegrád had its golden age, when the palace entertained guests in boundless luxury and wine flowed from the fountains.

The imposing **Solomon's Tower** (Salamon torony; May–Sept Wed–Sun 9am–5pm), now restored, was part of the lower castle, and a vantage point from which to control river and road traffic. It is linked to the upper castle by a half-ruined wall, along which you can climb to the castle, although it is easier to follow one of the two roads leading up the hill east and west of the ruins. Both offer a good view of the Danube valley, its villages and the forested Börzsöny hills.

Past Visegrád, the Pilis rise to heights of 750 metres (2,460ft). These hills are largely covered with forest,

Fishing on the Danube.

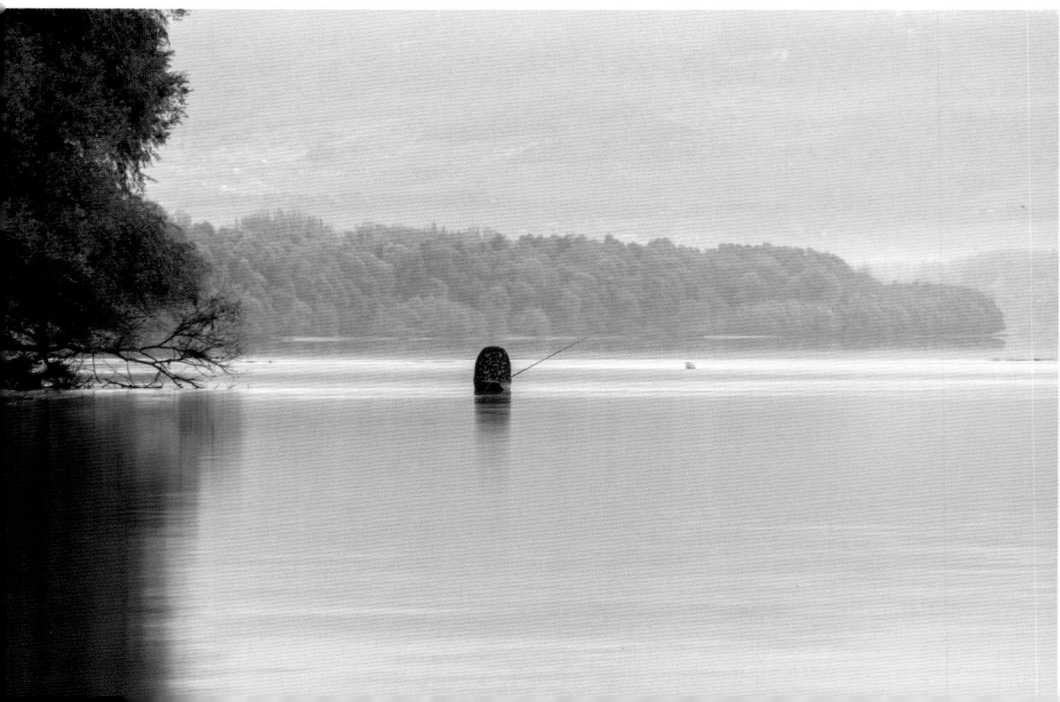

and the valleys are sparsely populated. Once, they served as royal hunting grounds. Today the hunters are mostly well-heeled foreigners who come to shoot stag, deer, wild boar and moufflon. Less bloodthirsty pursuits take place on the artificial lake that has been carved into the bank of the river here.

Diagonally opposite Visegrád, on the other side of the Danube and linked by regular ferries, is the village of **Nagymaros ⑤**. During Visegrád's prime it is believed the nobility had several palaces here, but nothing remains of them today. Nowadays the village is well known for other reasons. In 1977 the Hungarian government under Kádár agreed to build a dam here as part of a joint venture with the Czechoslovak government to generate hydroelectric power. The Slovaks built their power station at Galsčikovo, but Hungarian resistance to the dam galvanised opposition to the communist regime in the late 1980s and contributed to its downfall. The Hungarian government has since pulled out of the project.

Slovakia has pressed ahead and as a result relations between the two – none too cordial at the best of times – have soured. The matter is still before the International Court in The Hague.

A few miles from Visegrád-Nagymaros, the river turns abruptly to the south and splits into two channels. The easterly one, used by international shipping, flows past Vác. On the other, favoured by water sports enthusiasts, lies the picturesque town of Szentendre. Lying between these two channels is **Szentendre Island ⑥** (Szentendreisziget), 38km (24 miles) long and about 3km (2 miles) wide. Many Budapest dwellers have a weekend retreat here, and come to enjoy the sandy beaches.

CITY OF CHURCHES

Viewed from either the river or the island, **Vác ⑦** and its Baroque town centre appear picturesque and unsullied. In the 11th century, István I made it a bishop's seat endowed with a cathedral, which did not survive the Turkish occupation. In the 18th century,

⊘ Tip

The Danube Bend, probably the most beautiful stretch of scenery on its Hungarian course, lies between Esztergom and Szentendre. The landscape is at its most impressive near Visegrád, where the Börzsöny and Pilis hills force the river into a fairly narrow gorge; the view from Visegrád castle over the valley is stunning.

A ferry crossing the River Danube near Vác.

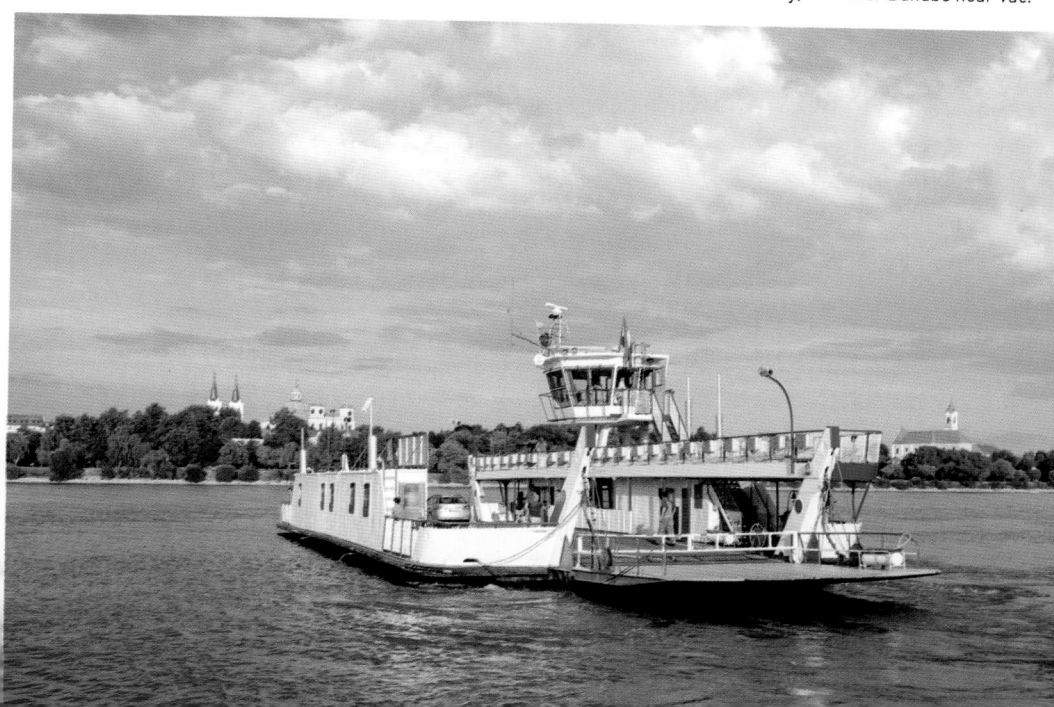

○ Fact

Szentendre was saved
from terminal decline
when, in 1928, drawn by
the lovely surroundings
and the favourable light,
several painters from
Budapest formed an
artists' colony.

Vác's self-aggrandising prelate Bishop Kristóf Migazzi embarked on a building programme that gave the town many of its Baroque buildings.

The **Cathedral** (Vaci Székesegyház) on the broad, tree-lined Konstantin tér was also built on Migazzi's orders. With its mighty Corinthian pillars, it is considered one of the finest examples of neoclassicism in Hungary. The interior features such interesting sights as the frescoes in the choir, the Affliction of Mary and the Triumph of the Trinity in the dome, both by the Swabian-born painter, Franz Anton Maulbertsch.

If you leave Konstantin tér and head north, you will come first to **Szentháromság tér** and then to a two-towered Piarist church. Both date from the Baroque period. The most valuable piece in the church is a tabernacle, adorned with polished Venetian glass.

The centre of the old town is the handsome **Március 15 tér,** surrounded by three of Vác's significant buildings: the Dominican church; the former Bishop's Palace, now a school; and the Town Hall, bearing the coats of arms of Hungary and of Migazzi. From the square it is a short walk down to the Danube promenade, a favourite spot for a stroll at weekends and on warm evenings.

At the northern exit of the town is a late Baroque triumphal arch, which Migazzi had built in 1764 for a visit by Maria Theresa. It looks rather strange today, surrounded by suburban houses, as does the gloomy prison next door, enclosed by high walls and barbed wire. It began life as an academy for aristocratic boys, was later used as a barracks and was turned into a prison in 1859. It became infamous for the incarceration and torture of political prisoners under both the Horthy and communist regimes.

SEVEN CHURCHES OF SZENTENDRE

The most interesting place on the right arm of the Danube Bend, **Szentendre** ❽ is only 18km (12 miles) north of Budapest and easily reached from the city by a commuter rail service. With its atmospheric winding streets,

Szentendre, a town known for its museums, galleries, and artists.

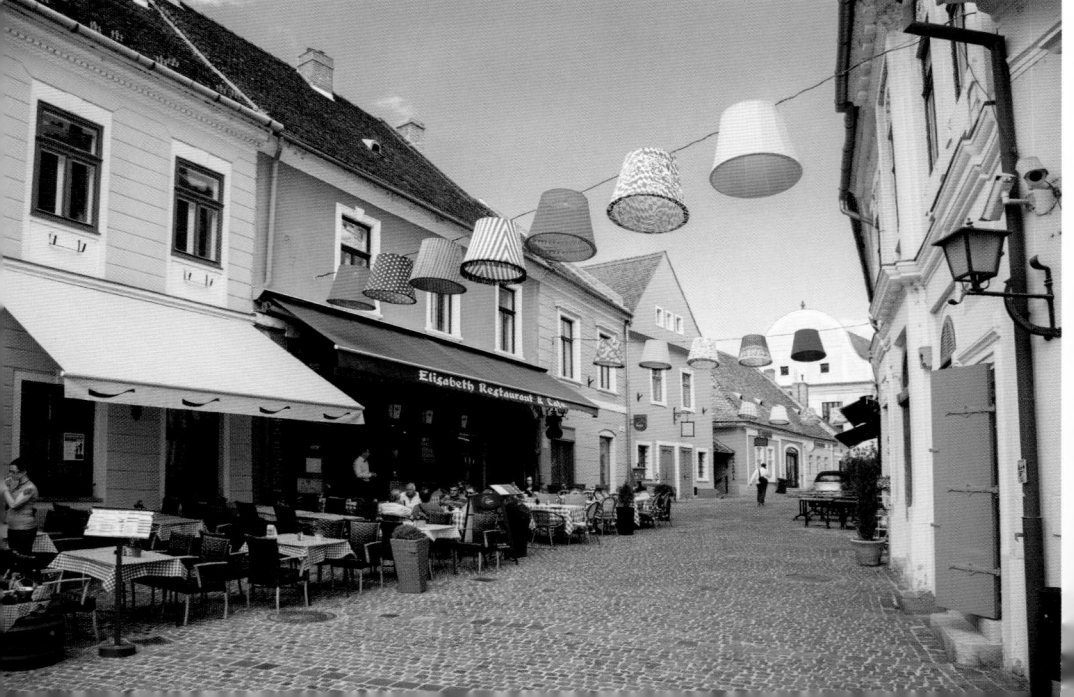

craft shops, churches, museums and a clutch of interesting contemporary art galleries, it's well worth seeing, though it's often overrun with tourists. The best times to visit, therefore, are weekdays in summer, and weekends in winter, when most of the museums and galleries are open. Szentendre's main attractions are generally open mid-Mar–Oct Tue–Sun 10am–4pm, Nov–mid-Mar Fri–Sun 10am–4pm.

Fleeing the Turks, a large community of Serbs settled here at the end of the 17th century and, together with Dalmatian and Greek families, they made Szentendre a thriving trading centre for the next hundred years. Their prosperity began to diminish in the late 19th century, however, and many families returned to Serbia, leaving the town almost deserted (only a fraction of its current population is of Serbian descent).

The town's skyline is dominated by seven churches: four Serbian Orthodox, two Catholic and one Calvinist. Once there were six Orthodox churches here, all with Serbian names, which the surviving ones still bear. Some of the the precious works of art that once adorned them can be viewed at the **Serbian Ecclesiastical Art Collection** (Szerb Egyházművészeti Gyüjtemény; Wed–Sun 10am–4pm), next to Belgrade Cathedral, itself sporting a richly ornamented interior.

The impressive merchants' houses around the main square, **Fő tér**, with their capacious warehouses, are evidence of the vast wealth that was once accumulated here. The Greek Orthodox Merchants' Cross stands in the middle of the square, erected in 1763 by the 'Privileged Serbian Trading Company'.

Numerous museums and galleries around the square display the output of the artists' colony. The most popular is the **Margit Kovács Museum** (daily 10am–6pm) at Vastagh György utca 1, which holds the extensive oeuvre of the

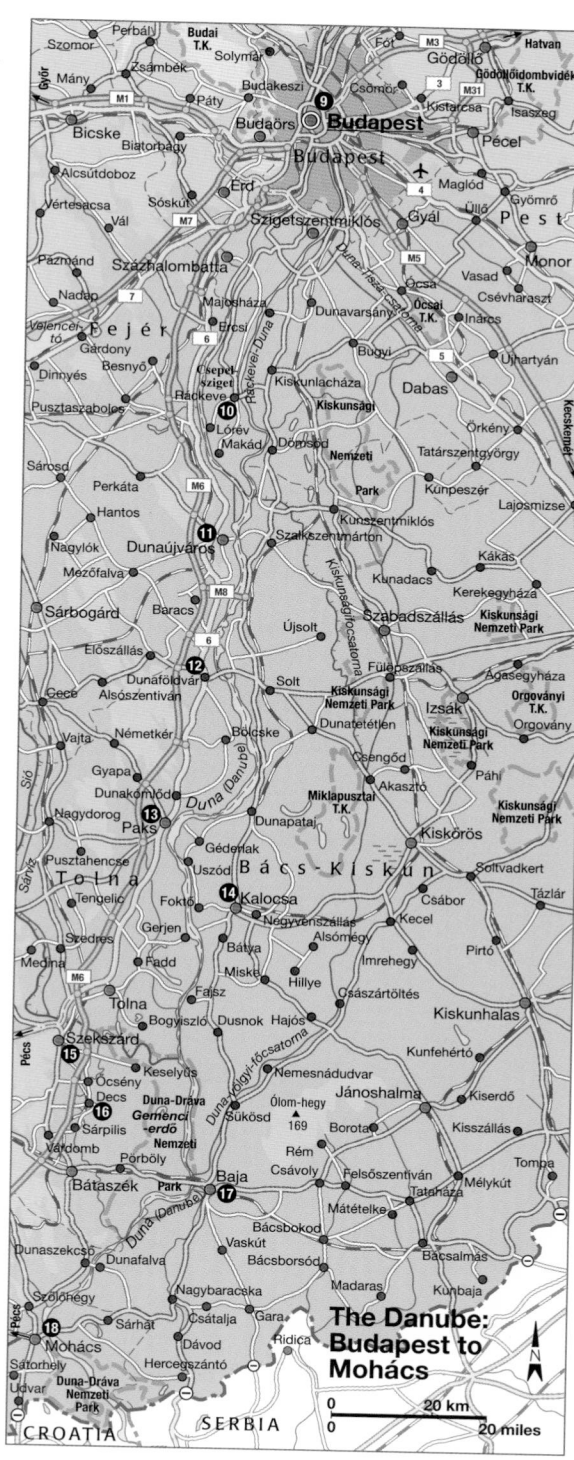

The Danube: Budapest to Mohács

much-loved ceramicist (1902–1977), whose work was greatly influenced by folk art. A more recent addition to the religious and social mix of Szentendre is the **Szánto Memorial House** and tiny synagogue (the first to be built in Europe since the war) on Alkotmány utca. The house recalls the Jewish citizens of Szentendre and their terrible fate in 1944.

There's more superb art in the **Ferenczy Károly Museum** at Kossuth utca 5 (Tue–Sun 10am–6pm; www.muzeumicentrum.hu), which contains pieces by several members of the Ferenczy family, not least Károly, one of the pioneers of the Nagybánya School, established in 1896; look out for the lovely On Hilltop.

About 3km (2 miles) northwest of the town is the enjoyable **Hungarian Open-Air Ethnographical Museum** (Magyar Szabadtéri Néprajzi Múzeum; mid-Mar–Oct Tue–Sun 10am–5pm; www.skansen.hu), which aims to showcase rural Magyar culture with reconstructed buildings and displays of artisan crafts.

CITY APPROACHES

The point where the two Danube channels surrounding Szentendre Island meet again marks the northern boundary of the city of **Budapest ❾**. The right bank is called *Római part* (Roman bank) and *Rómaifürdö* (Roman baths) – indicating that you have reached Aquincum, capital of the Roman province of Pannonia.

Sadly, the view from the river of Óbuda (Old Buda) is obscured by apartments blocks and highways, and the capital only comes into view at **Margaret Island.** In the shadow of the Buda Hills is Castle Hill with Mátyás (Matthias) Church, Fishermen's Bastion, the Hilton Hotel and the castle. Behind it is Gellért Hill, crowned by the fortress and the Liberation Monument, and dropping steeply down to the Danube.

Along the left bank lie the city's official buildings – the massive complex of the neo-Gothic Parliament, the Hungarian Academy of Sciences and Arts, then a bunch of hotels and

Szántó Jewish Memorial House and Temple.

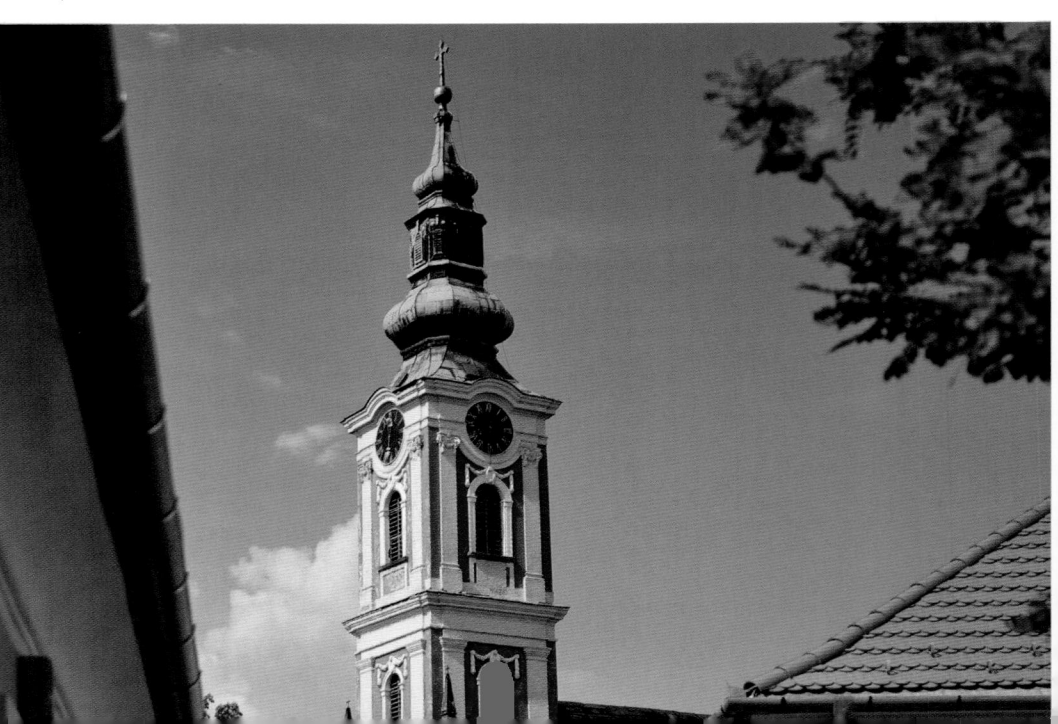

the Vigadó concert hall, and a sea of houses in the background.

After the **Chain Bridge,** the oldest bridge in Budapest, you come to the foot of the castle, in the heart of the capital. On the left (Pest) bank, either side of **Elisabeth Bridge** (Erzsébet híd) is **Belgrade Quay** (Belgrád rakpart), where all boats moor and passengers go through customs and immigration.

Gellért Hill features in one of Germany's legends of the Danube. The beautiful Lau, the water queen, ignored the warnings of her husband, the Danube King Ingold, and joined the witches' feast on Gellért Hill. She was saved from Satan in the nick of time when Dr Faustus wrapped her in his magic cloak.

Csepel Island (Csepel-sziget), 47km (29 miles) long, marks the point where the Danube leaves the city. Only its northern-most point still belongs to the capital. It contains the largest Hungarian heavy industrial concern, the steel and metal works of Csepel, whose workforce has repeatedly taken a decisive part in the politics of the country, including the doomed 1956 revolution.

SOUTH OF BUDAPEST

The river divides in two around Csepel Island. Industrial traffic uses the broader western Danube channel, which winds its way once more through thinly populated riverine landscape.

However, the left-hand channel, which goes around Csepel Island from the east, is far more pleasant. Several bridges lead to the island, and its banks are lined with villas, weekend chalets and well-kept gardens. It is also popular with fishing and water sports enthusiasts.

The town of **Ráckeve** ⑩ lies on the western shore of the island's southern tip. On Kossuth utca stands a Baroque palace belonging to Duke Eugene of Savoy, and designed by Johan Lukas von Hildebrandt; formerly (and not so long ago) a plush hotel, it's now closed, awaiting its fate. The blue church tower that overlooks the town belongs to the oldest Serbian Orthodox church in Hungary, dating back to

⊙ Fact

Only 11km (7 miles) separate Mohács from the border with Croatia.

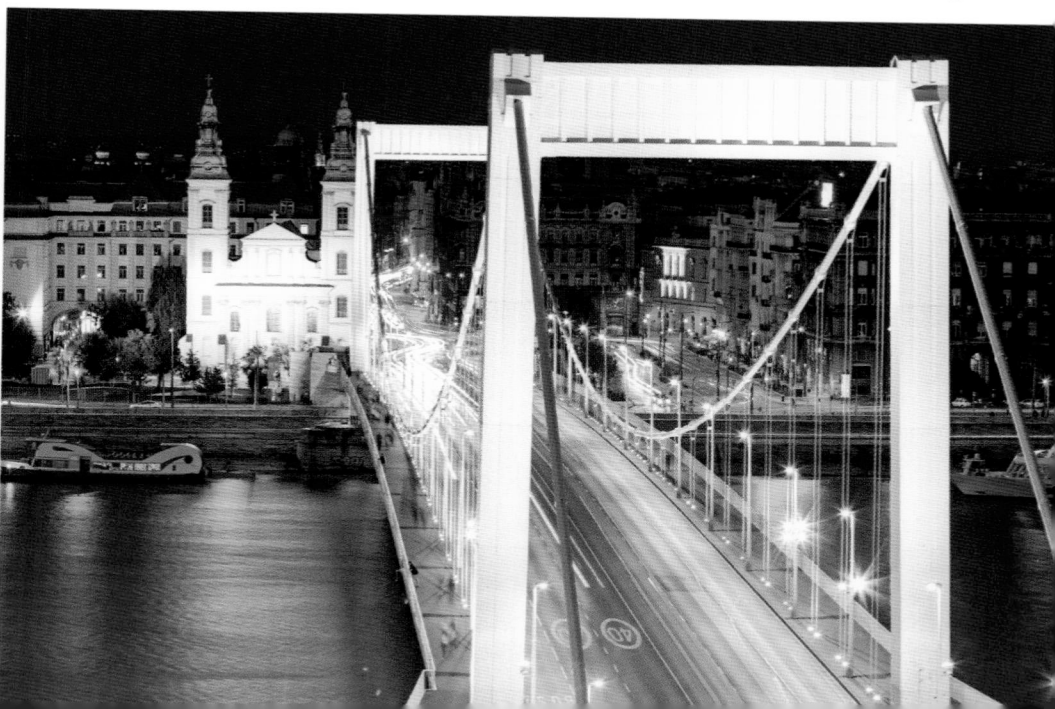

Elisabeth Bridge.

1487. It has a beautiful set of frescoes from the mid-18th century, while the bell tower, a medieval construction, stands apart from the church. Ráckeve also has an art nouveau Town Hall, a legacy of more prosperous times in the early 20th century, when the town also built an iron bridge to replace the old wooden one.

If you're travelling by car you can visit **Szigetbecse,** the birthplace of world-famous photographer, André Kertész (1894–1985). The house where he spent time with his uncle is at Makádi utca 40.

The scenery between Budapest and the Serbian border is not as interesting as that between Vienna and Budapest. The land to the right and left of the river is barely cultivated, and there are only a few towns on the banks. For this reason the Hungarian Danube Shipping Company runs no hydrofoils or hovercrafts on this stretch, either scheduled or chartered. Russian, Romanian and Bulgarian passenger ships travel this way to and from the Black Sea, but they make no stops.

Freight traffic is intensive on this part of the river, as the industries of Csepel Island, the oil refinery and power station at **Százhalombatta,** and the iron and steel works at Dunaújváros still get most of their raw materials via the waterways.

A SOCIALIST PARADISE?

Some 50km (30 miles) south of Budapest is **Dunaújváros ⓫**. Where once the little village of Dunapentele lay, stand iron and steel works surrounded by some 30 other factories and housing developments. It is not pretty, but it is by now a bit of history, with its banks of highrises, concrete pavements and broad streets, and if you enjoy a bit of Bauhaus/Socialist realism, this place will likely appeal. Dunaújváros (originally Sztálinváros) did not pay its way: the coal for the steelworks had to be imported from as far afield as the ore, thwarting the dream of cheap steel.

Infinitely more appealing is **Dunaföldvár ⓬**, another 20km (12 miles) to the south, which deserves a mention for having the only bridge

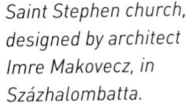

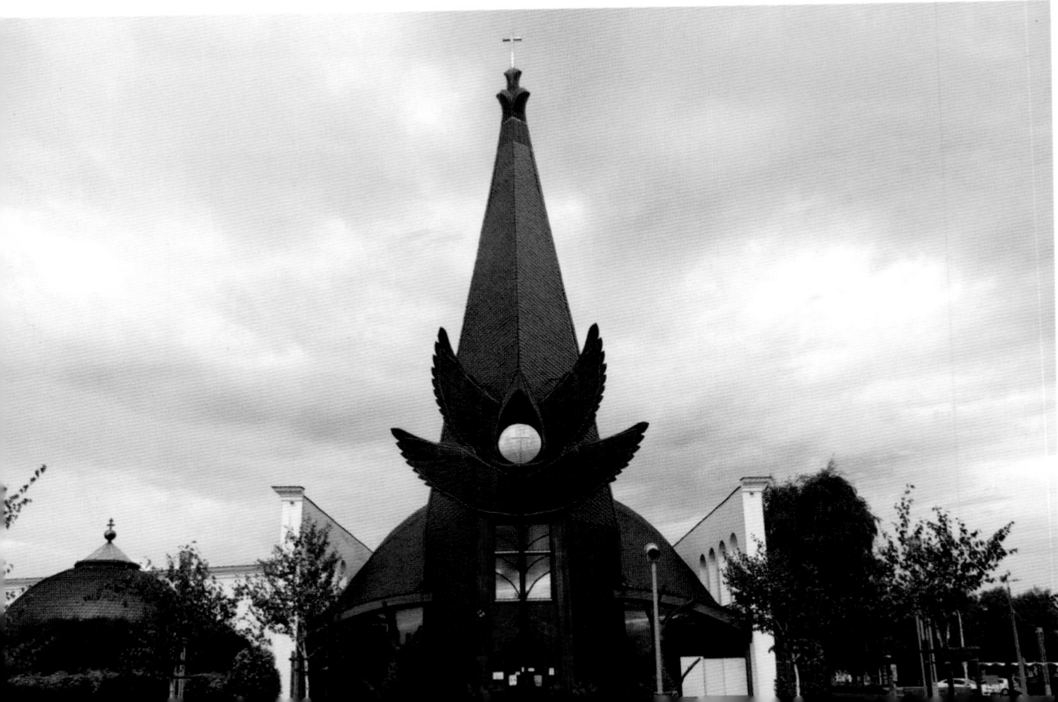

Saint Stephen church, designed by architect Imre Makovecz, in Százhalombatta.

over the Danube between Budapest and Baja, an important link between Transdanubia and the Great Hungarian Plain. It also has a reasonable spread of tourist amenities, including hotels, a spa and campsite.

Beyond Dunaföldvár, the river veers southeast and flows through a landscape almost devoid of people. For 30km (19 miles), with the exception of two small villages, there are no settlements on the riverbank until you reach **Paks ⑬**. This town has a bad name, owing to the atomic power plant that began generating kilowatts in 1982. This doesn't mean that the whole town has been washed away: it has an attractive Baroque town centre, with an unusual row of shops integrated into the foundations of the church. Its art gallery (Paksi Képtár), in a simple classical building, is well stocked with contemporary paintings and sculptures. The **Municipal Museum** (Deák Ferenc utca 2; Tue–Sun 10am–6pm), in addition to the permanent exhibitions on local history, always has unusual temporary displays. The power plant, just south of the town, is something of a tourist attraction in itself, with a visitor centre and even a **Museum of Nuclear Energetics** (Atomenergetikai Múzeum; Mon–Fri 9am–3pm, Sat 9am–1pm; www.atomeromu.hu).

However, Paks' flagship sight is without doubt the remarkable **Catholic Church** on Hősök tere, built between 1888 and 1890 and designed by Imre Makovecz in his typical, stylised, popular way. The interior is simply decorated, entirely in wood. Outside stand the angels of light and darkness, perhaps a reminder of the dualism in life. The tall, narrow separate bell-tower, its slate roof reaching all the way to the ground, is reminiscent of Hungary's eastern churches.

RED GOLD

Some 15km (9 miles) downstream from the ferry at Gerjen, you can make a diversion to the pretty, paprika capital of **Kalocsa ⑭**, an ancient bishopric 10km (6 miles) from the Danube. Red gold is celebrated in the Paprika Museum (Szent-István király utca 6;

Drying paprika.

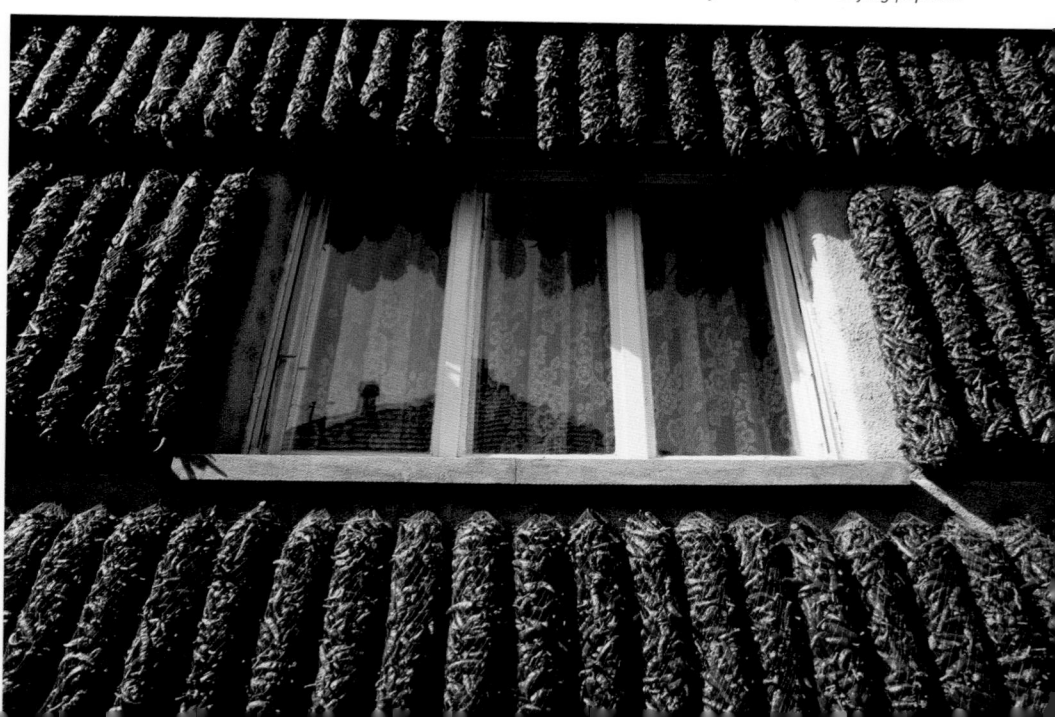

Apr–Oct Tue–Sun 11am–5pm), just a few doors down from the grand library. The annual pepper harvest takes place every September after the fields around Kalocsa fill with farm workers picking bright red peppers. The entire town, its population swelled by busloads of tourists, celebrates the harvest with a Paprika Festival. And all year round, strings of dried peppers festoon store windows and roadside stands, shops sell folk-art gifts adorned with images of paprika, and restaurants and houses are covered in traditional floral motifs, often with red peppers incorporated into the design.

The focus of the town is the **Cathedral** and the adjacent **Archbishop's Palace** (Érseki palota) on Kossuth Lajos utca. The former was designed in Baroque style by Andreas Mayerhoffer and completed in 1735, though there has been a cathedral on this site since the time of St István. The palace has a Great Hall, where Franz Liszt gave recitals. The chapel, too, should not be missed, for its Maulbertsch paintings.

Kaloca's main street, Szent-István király utca, is partly closed to traffic, which makes it pleasant for a stroll. The pedestrian section is adorned with a bevy of bronzes depicting prominent people associated with the town, including Asztrik, who brought King István the crown from Rome and founded the first bishopric of Kalocsa.

THE GEMENC FOREST

Szekszárd ⑮, a town of 35,000 inhabitants, now lies 12km (8 miles) away from the Danube, but was once on its banks (see also page 259). It is the gateway to the Gemenc Forest (Gemenci-erdő), which stretches for some 25km (16 miles) southwards along the right bank of the Danube. It forms part of the Danube-Drava National Park (Duna Dráva Nemzeti Park), which, at more than 49,000 hectares (120,000 acres), is the biggest nature reserve in the country.

Although access to parts of the park is restricted, it is possible to enter this flood-plain, with its network of causeways and quiet lakes surrounded by

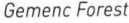
Gemenc Forest.

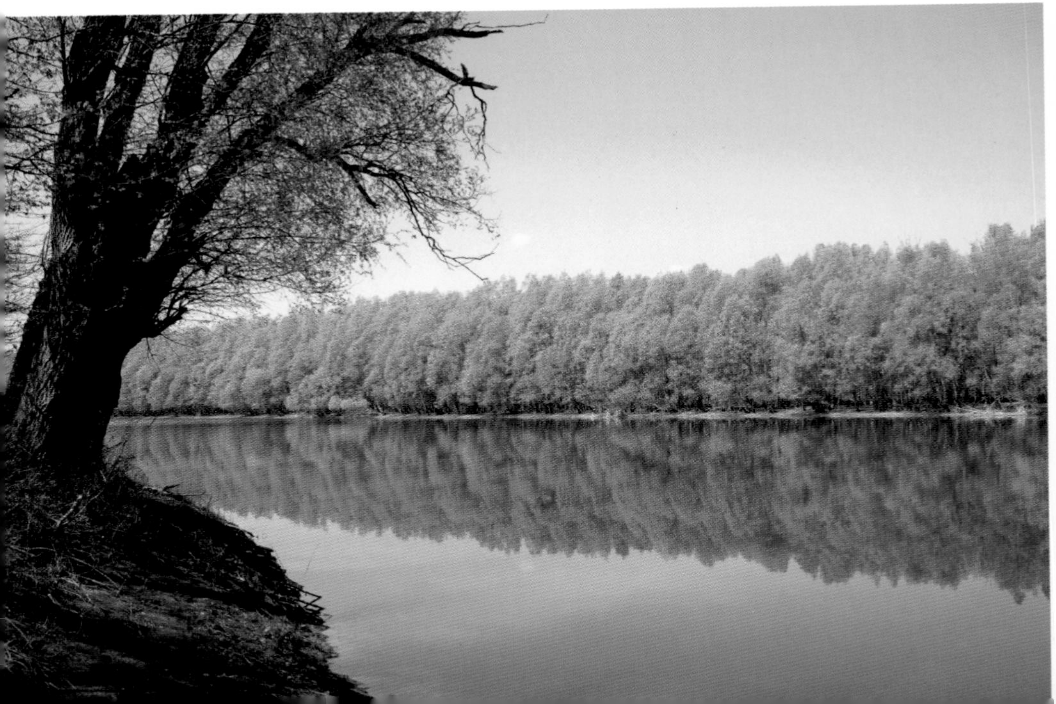

fields of reeds, remnants of the old river course, and bright glades. Ancient willows and poplars, oaks and rowans make up the forest, which is also the habitat of red deer and wild boar. Boat tours of the forest and rides on the narrow-gauge train can be arranged at one of Szekszárd's tour agencies, at the **Gemenc Excursion Centre** in Bárányfok, just east of the town (tel: 74 312 552), and the **Ecotourism Centre** in Pörböly (tel 74 491 483).

For those who like messing about on the water, the **Sió Canal** flows into the Danube here. It comes from Lake Balaton and is only navigable by smaller pleasure boats or canoes.

Between Szekszárd and the Gemenc Forest lies the **Sárköz,** an area that remained isolated and retained its customs longer than most. There are four communities lying on this slight elevation that rises gently up out of the otherwise flat land. Today their colourful traditional costume, with its dominant reds, can only be seen in the peasant house and Regional Museum (Tájmúzeum; Tue–Sun 9am–4pm) in Decs ⑯, or in the workshops of the Sárköz cooperative, which make the clothes for export.

JOURNEY'S END

Baja and Mohács are the last towns through which the Danube passes before it leaves Hungary. **Baja** ⑰, in a restful setting on the banks of the Sugovica, a tributary of the Danube, is renowned for its fish soup, manifest in the colourful Fish Soup Festival on the second Saturday of July – over 2,000 bubbling cauldrons fill the main square, Szentháromság tér, which opens out on to the river. Petőfi sziget, the island on the other side, is somewhat run down, but the town has done a great deal to promote water sports here. The choice of aquatic activities includes fishing, boating, swimming and canoeing, plus tennis and mini-golf.

On the large, cobbled square is the **István Türr Museum** (Wed–Sat 10am–4pm), named after a Hungarian general on Garibaldi's staff in the war for the unification of Italy. This simple, classical building covers every aspect

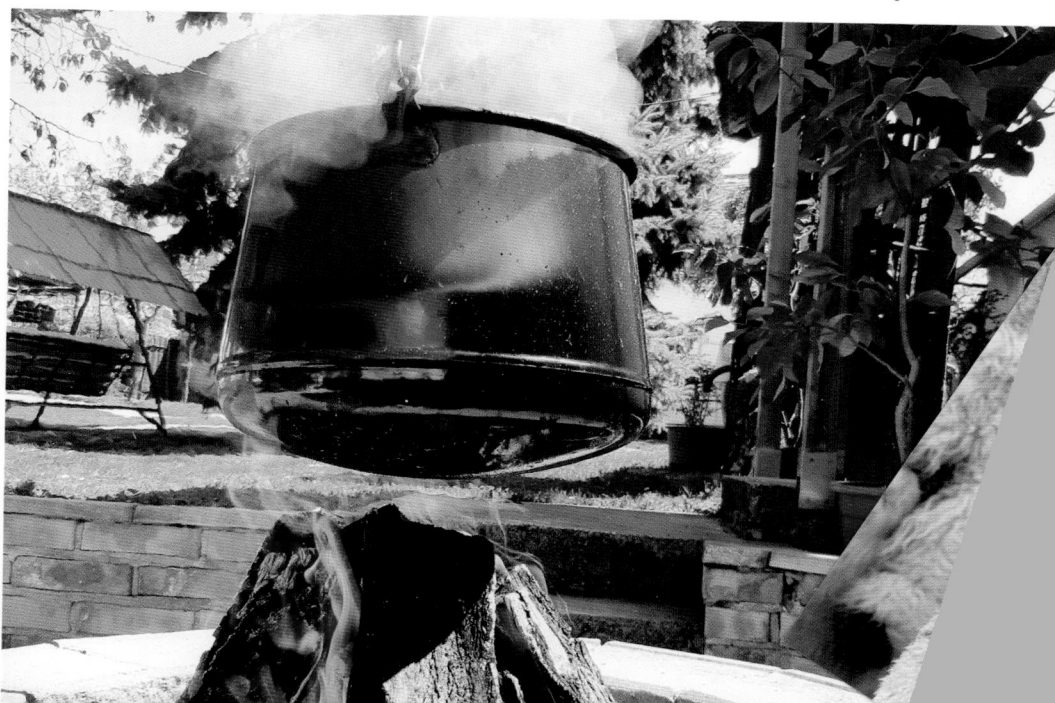

Cooking halászlé.

of life on the Danube, from work to geology, and it has an attractive exhibition displaying the costumes worn by the area's various ethnic groups.

Two of Baja's four churches are Serb Orthodox, and it also has a high school which uses German as its primary language. Once the Turks had been driven out of southern Hungary in the late 17th century, German and Serbian farmers were invited to repopulate the area. The region is still referred to as 'Swabian Turkey' since many of the settlers came from Swabia in southwest Germany.

You can crown your day with a local fish speciality – perch rubbed with paprika, baked and topped with sour cream is a delicacy not to be missed.

Mohács ⓭ is linked to one of the greatest catastrophes in the history of Hungary. Here, on 29 August 1526, the Turks destroyed the Hungarian cavalry and most of the country's leaders. King Lajos (Louis) II lost his life – ignominiously drowned in a brook when his horse fell on top of him. There is a memorial to the event in the tiny hamlet north of Mohács. After this defeat, Hungary became easy prey for the Turkish army, so much so that the Baroque poet Miklós Zrínyi (see page 100) lamented: 'Our land, like a well-tended vineyard, was trampled down by a wild boar.'

The highlight of the year in Mohács is Busójóras, a festival of Serbo-Croat origin that takes place on the last Sunday of the carnival season. The carnival procession features fearsome wooden masks and is accompanied by music, symbolising the passing of winter and also the eviction of the Turks. It is a popular and spirited celebration, fuelled by highly seasoned fish stew and strong drink.

The site of the disastrous battle is at **Sátorhely**, 7km (4 miles) southwest of the town, where a **Memorial Park** (Emlékpark; Apr–Oct daily 9am–6pm, rest of year 9am–4pm; www.mohacsiemlekhely.hu) commemorates the events; each year, on the date of the battle, there's an extravagant wreath-laying ceremony.

Busójárás Festival in Mohács.

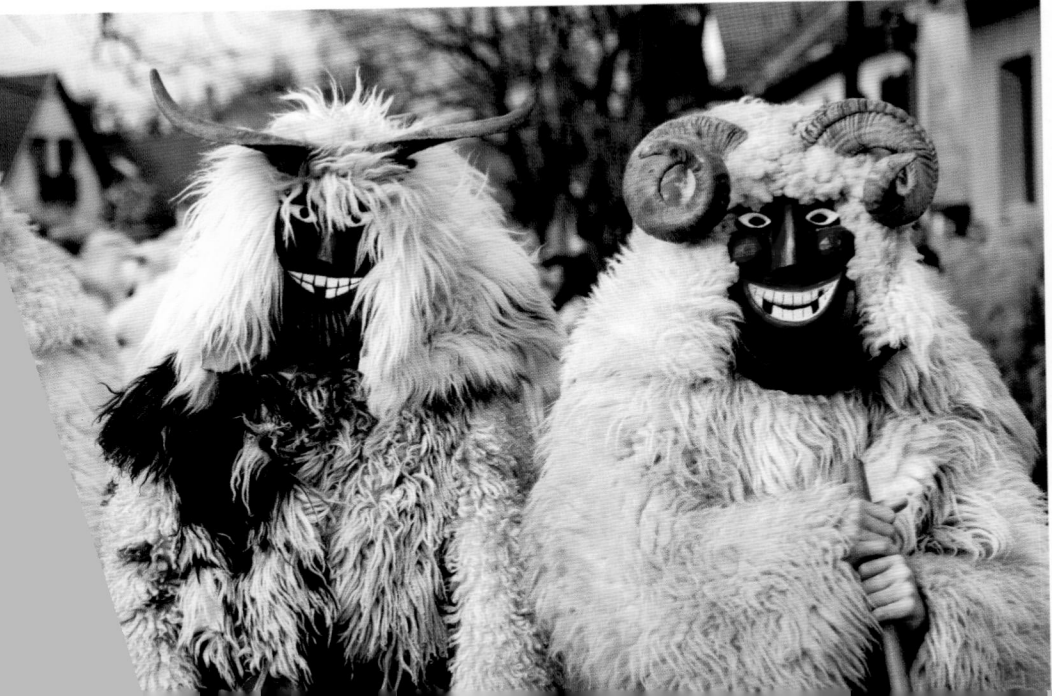

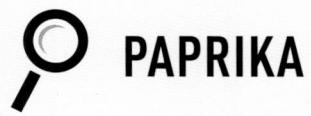

PAPRIKA

Next to the salt and the toothpicks on nearly every Hungarian table you'll find a shaker or a little dish of paprika, the spice that immediately brings to mind Hungary and the Hungarians. In fact, this association is a relatively recent one: the use of paprika in Hungarian cooking only dates back about a century and the plant itself is not native to this country.

It may have reached Hungary from Spain, or from India via the Turks, or from America. The etymology of the name itself seems to be rooted in the Balkans. What is certain is that paprika grows wild in Central and South America, and that Christopher Columbus brought it back to Europe with him in 1493.

Legend has it that a beautiful Magyar maid, confined to a harem for the Sultan's pleasure during the long Turkish occupation of Hungary, succeeded in escaping, taking home some paprika seeds with her.

At first the 'heathen pepper' served as a decorative shrub in genteel aristocratic gardens. As a member of the poisonous nightshade family, it was initially viewed with suspicion, but nevertheless came to provide poor people with a cheap and effective way of making bad food taste edible, especially as its full flavour emerges best when cooked with pork fat. To this day, all southern Hungarian peasants keep a stash of home-grown and ground paprika. The simple tanya (homestead) with its strands of drying peppers has become part of the romantic appeal of the Hungarian landscape.

Paprika's widespread usage in modern Hungarian cuisine is the result of a process of gentrification. The poor man's pepper gradually found its way to the table of both kings and peasants. On top of its savoury qualities, Albert Szent Györgyi discovered in 1938, that paprika is extremely rich in vitamin C, and won the Nobel Prize for doing so. Ask along the way what homeopathic applications exist for paprika, and you may be surprised to learn that it cures everything from the common cold to premature hair loss. According to a 17th-century manuscript, wreaths of paprika and paprika powder are supposed to keep bloodthirsty vampires away.

What makes Hungarian paprika so special is a complex issue. It would appear that cultivation of the spice in the continental climate and the flatness of the Great Plain produces a distinctive flavour in both the sweet and the hot varieties.

Szeged, a beautiful city on the Tisza, close to the border with Serbia, is the capital of paprika (although many suggest that the true capital is Kalocsa on the Danube). The Szegedi Paprikafeldolgozó Vállalat has been growing, hybridising, grinding and packaging the red gold since 1951. Today, as well as production and processing, it has a modern research facility devoted entirely to paprika, where, wreathed in secrecy, new grinding methods are tried and new strains of the spice are tested.

Paprika for sale.

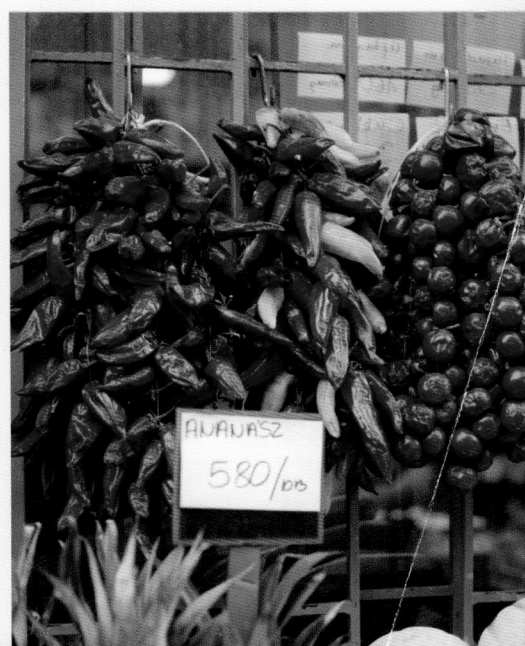

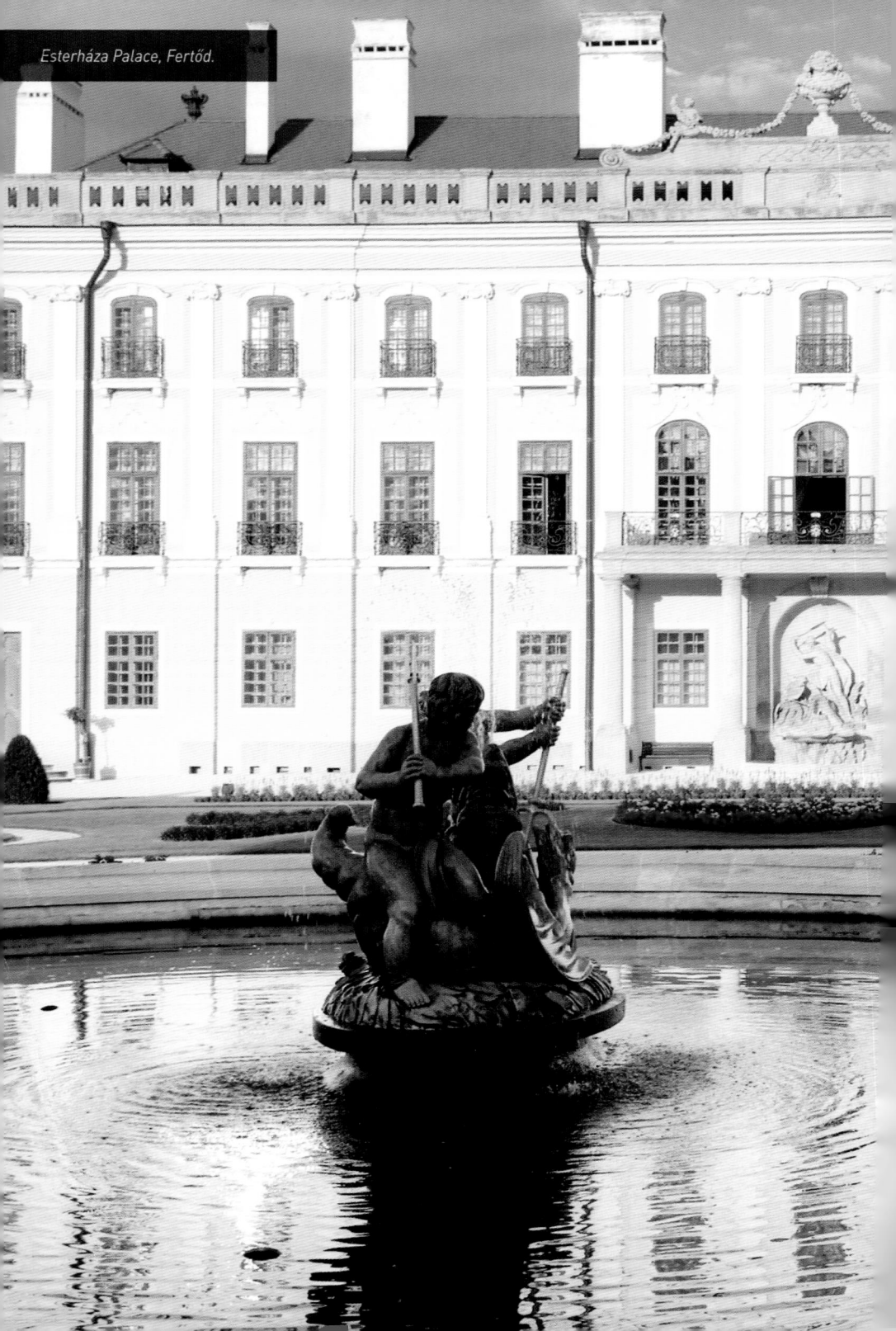
Esterháza Palace, Fertőd.

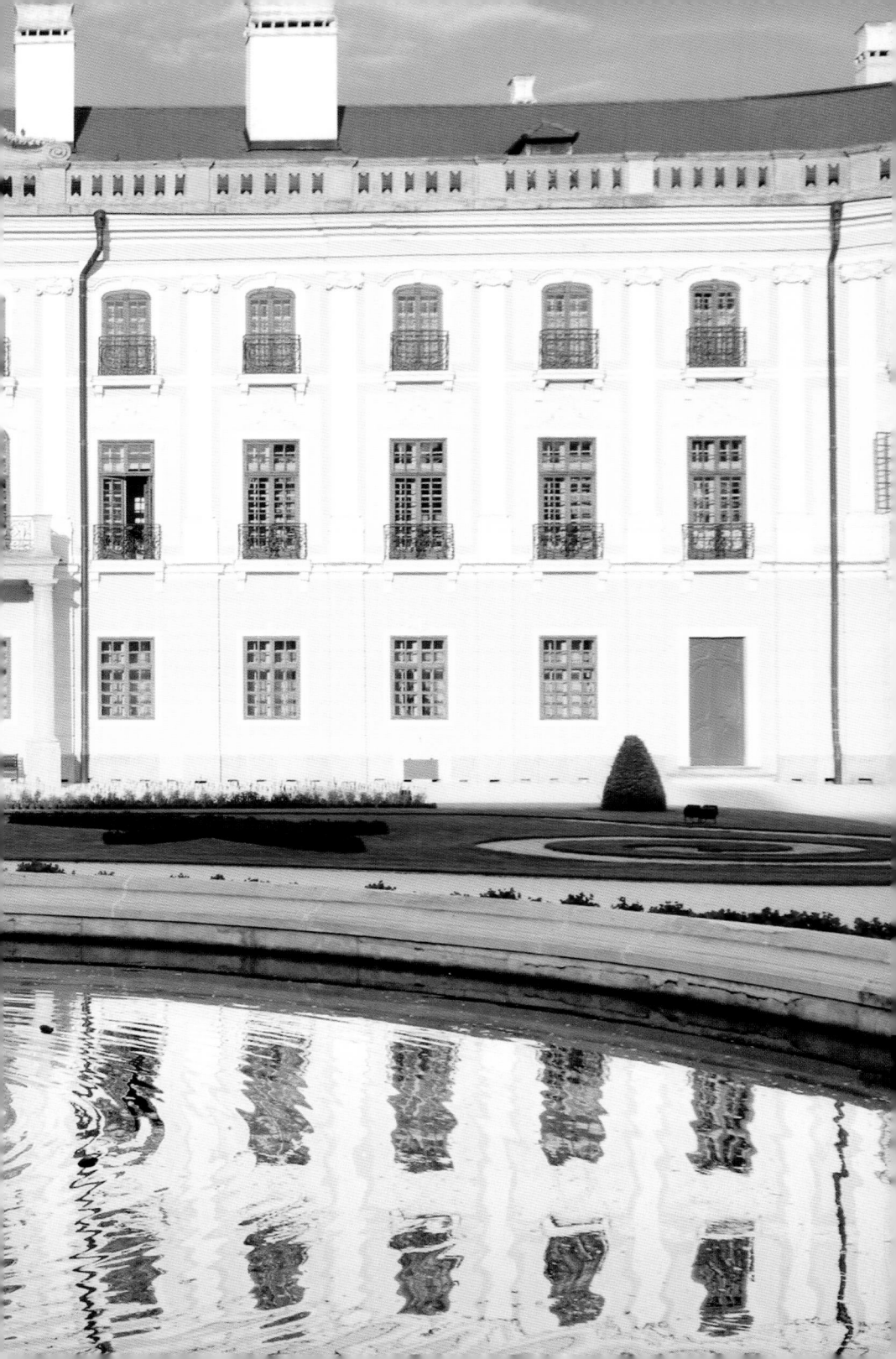

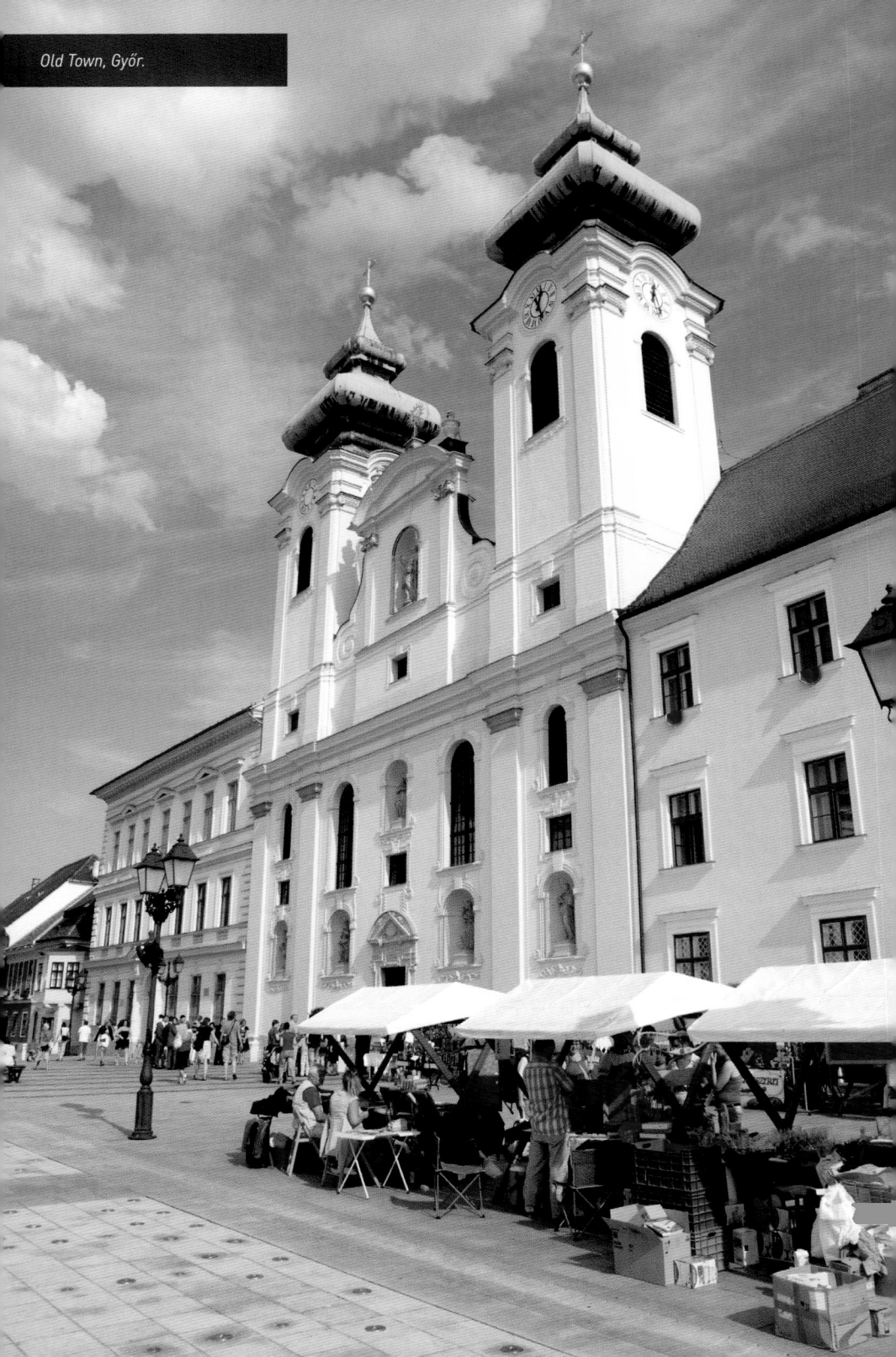

GATES TO THE WEST

Western Hungary is a tranquil region of beautiful landscapes, where Romanesque churches are found in isolated spots and Hungary's turbulent history marks its towns and villages.

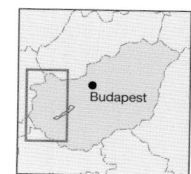

Across the western border of Hungary each year pour millions of visitors, keen to reach their next destination, usually Balaton or Budapest. Relatively few take time to enjoy Transdanubia (Dunántúl in Hungarian), a region that includes some of the country's most beautiful sights, Romanesque churches, grandiose castles, Baroque towns, mysterious lakes and lonely landscapes.

BUDAPEST VIA HEGYESHALOM

The main flow of traffic from the West goes via **Hegyeshalom** ❶, on the M1 motorway all the way from the border to Budapest. Don't forget the matrica, the sticker you need for your car.

There isn't much to see near the frontier, either in Hegyeshalom or in Mosonmagyaróvár. Water enthusiasts, however, may enjoy the amenities of the Mosonmagyaróvár thermal bath (fürdö) complex, which includes a modern hotel.

BETWEEN THE RIVERS

Avoid the main road and make a small diversion north into the **Szigetköz** ❷ ('Between the Islands'), a 275-sq km (106-sq mile) floodplain between the main channel of the Danube and a side channel, the 'Little Danube'. Even after regulation of the main flows of water, the

Historic building in Győr.

area, criss-crossed by numerous waterways, has retained much of its pristine charm. Return to the main highway via Hédervár, Asványráró and Mecsér.

Cross the highway, and 5km (3 miles) further on you will come to the village of **Lébény** ❸ where the Benedictine Abbey Church of St James (Szent Jakab apátsági templom), completed in 1208, is one of the most important Romanesque buildings in Hungary, despite additions in other styles over the centuries.

Main attractions
Fertőrákos
Kőszeg
Szombathely
Ják

Map on page 188

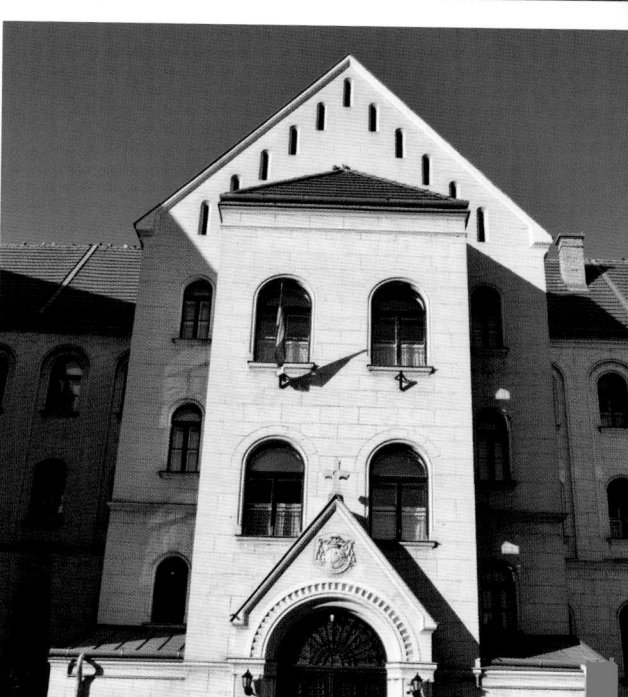

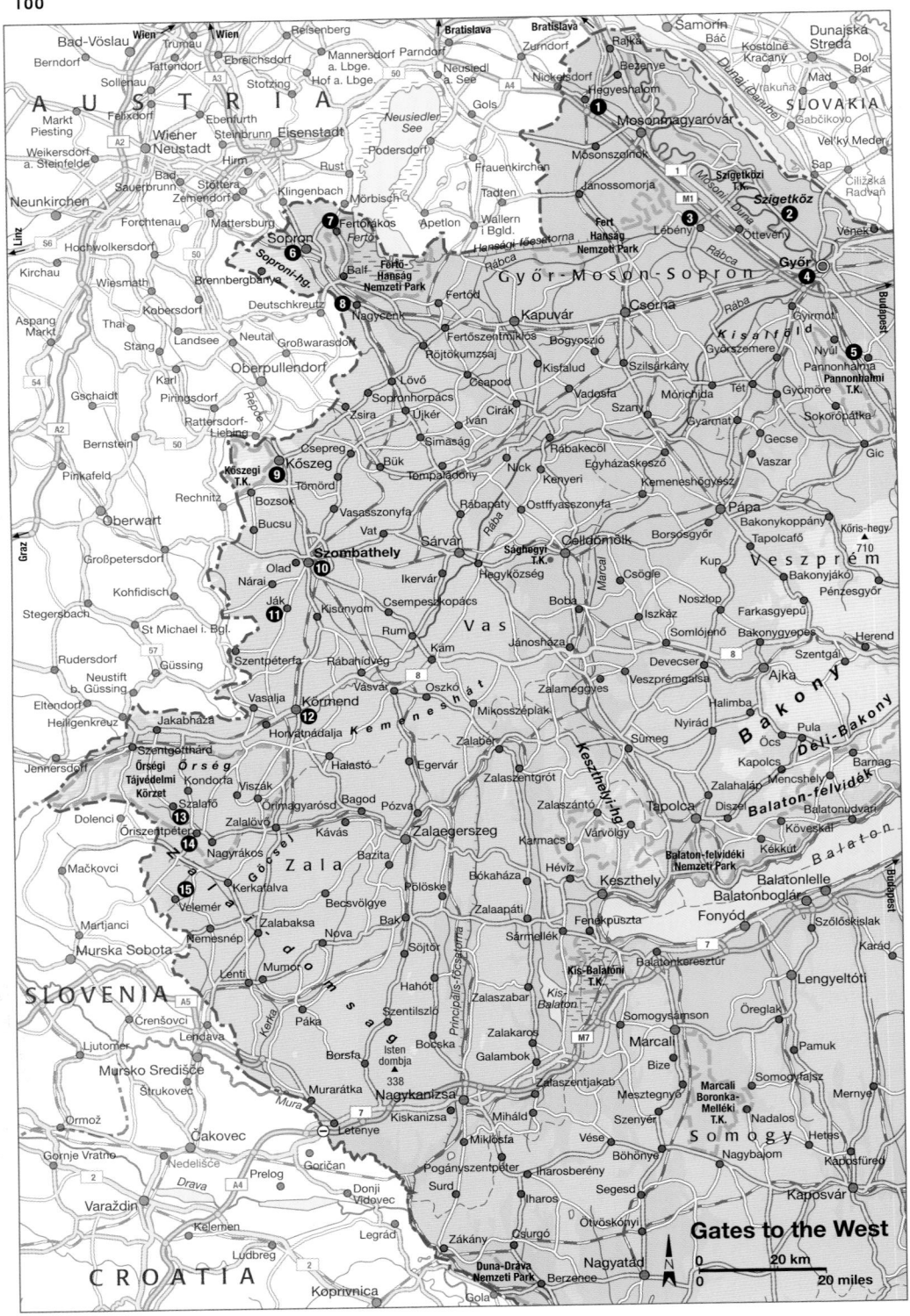

Gates to the West

The three-aisled basilica with semi-circular apses is one of the so-called family churches, built by an aristocratic sponsor and later given to a monastic order. Hungary's turbulent history has left its mark. In the 15th century imperial troops burned monasteries and churches to the ground, and the whole of western Hungary has been attacked time and again by German and Austrian troops. Barely rebuilt, the church fell victim to the Turks in 1529 and again in 1683. The Jesuits took it over and refurbished it in Baroque style, and in the 19th century, the church was restored to its original form.

The western wing is particularly impressive, with two mighty towers and a beautiful portal, which is perhaps surpassed only by the south portal on the side of the former monastery.

CHURCH AND STATE

Back on the main highway, **Győr ❹** is 15km (9 miles) further on. The administrative and economic centre of the Kisalföld (the Little Plain), this large industrial city is the capital of the Győr-Moson-Sopron district, and lies at the confluence of the Little Danube, the Rába and the Rábca, land that has been settled for centuries. After the Celts and the Romans, the Avars built their circular fortress (gyürü), hence the Hungarian name, Győr. The Turks, who razed it to the ground in 1529, called it *janik kula*, or burned town.

The bishopric of Győr was founded in the 11th century by King István, as part of his plan to strengthen the nation's power and identity by converting to Christianity. He also created an independent archdiocese of Hungary.

On the site of an old Roman *castrum* a fortified place was prepared to serve as a bishop's seat – evidence that he had both political and spiritual responsibilities. The newly appointed Hungarian princes of the church made a decisive contribution to establishing the power of the state. This process is clearly visible when standing on Chapter Hill, with the ensemble of cathedral and castle in front of you, symbolising the unity of spiritual and secular power in the Middle Ages.

DOMINANT HILL

Surrounded by industrial suburbs, the old town gathers around **Chapter Hill** (Káptalan-domb), where there are numerous houses with 17th–19th-century façades. At the top of the hill, dominating the scene, is the harmonious castle-cathedral complex. The warren of streets, many closed to traffic, invites you to stroll, do some window shopping or have a good meal at the Hotel Klastrom, a former monastery.

The Cathedral of Our Lady (Székesegyház; daily 8am–noon, 2–6pm) dates back to the foundation of the bishopric of Győr (Raab in German) in the early 11th century. Destroyed several times, it was remodelled in Baroque style in the mid-17th century and received a neoclassical façade in the 19th century. The reliquary of St László, king of Hungary, one of the

⊘ Tip

Győr is internationally known for its ballet, shaped by Ivan Markó, who left the ensemble in 1989. If there's a performance during your visit, try to get tickets.

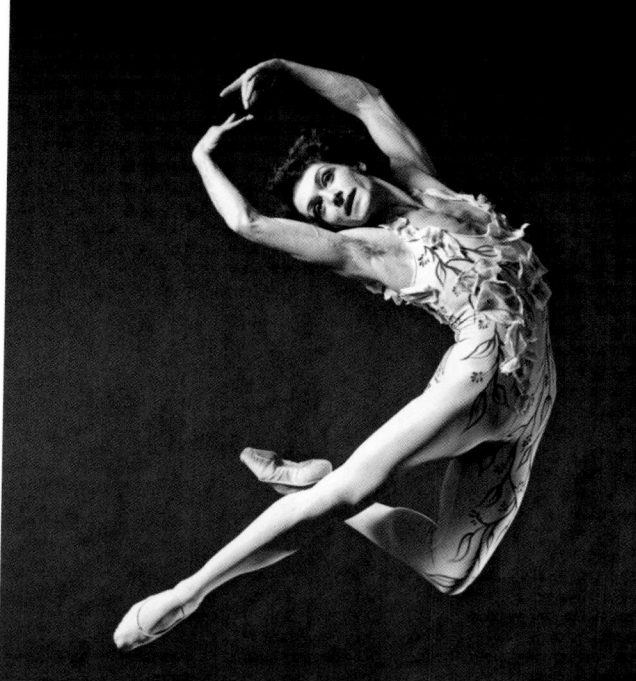

Dancer Ivan Markó in 1972.

greatest masterpieces of medieval goldsmiths' work (c.1405) is kept in the Gothic Héderváry Chapel. Known as the *Weeping Icon of Mary*, it originated in Ireland and is still visited by pilgrims today. The cathedral's treasure chamber contains a wealth of gold and silver objects.

BISHOP'S CASTLE

Next to the cathedral is the fortified **Bishop's Castle** (Püspökvár; Tue–Sun 10am–4pm), which proved its mettle in the turbulent years of the Turkish wars. It changed owners several times, until the Habsburgs finally prevailed around 1600. The castle remained a garrison until 1788.

One tower has 12th-century foundations, and the late-Gothic Dóczy Chapel dates from 1481. Its Baroque makeover was carried out in the 18th century.

The Carmelite Church (1713–25) on Bécsi kapu tér is the most beautiful Baroque building in Győr. Designed by Austrian architect, Martin Wittwer, the light Italianate interior is full of paintings and sculptures and reliefs.

NOTABLE BUILDINGS

Széchenyi tér, the nearby square, is used for open-air theatre and concerts during the Győr Festival Days, from the end of June into July. The square contains several important monuments, one of which is the Jesuits' house at No. 9; this is now a **Pharmacy Museum** (Mon–Fri 7.30am–4.30pm), complete with a beautifully-furnished apothecary that's still in use. Also notable is the 17th-century church of **St Ignatius**, whose principal treasure is the rococo painting of the patron saint by the eminent Viennese artist, Paul Tröger.

The House of the Abbot (No. 5) harbours the János Xántus Museum (Tue–Sun 10am–6pm) with a collection of paintings, furniture and ephemera from the region's past. Note the carved stone mullion on the balcony window in the shape of a crucifix.

THE OLDEST MONASTERY

Some 20km (12 miles) south of Győr, on Highway 82 to Veszprém, is the village of **Pannonhalma ❺**, site of the oldest monastery in Hungary, **Pannonhalma**

Pannonhalma Abbey.

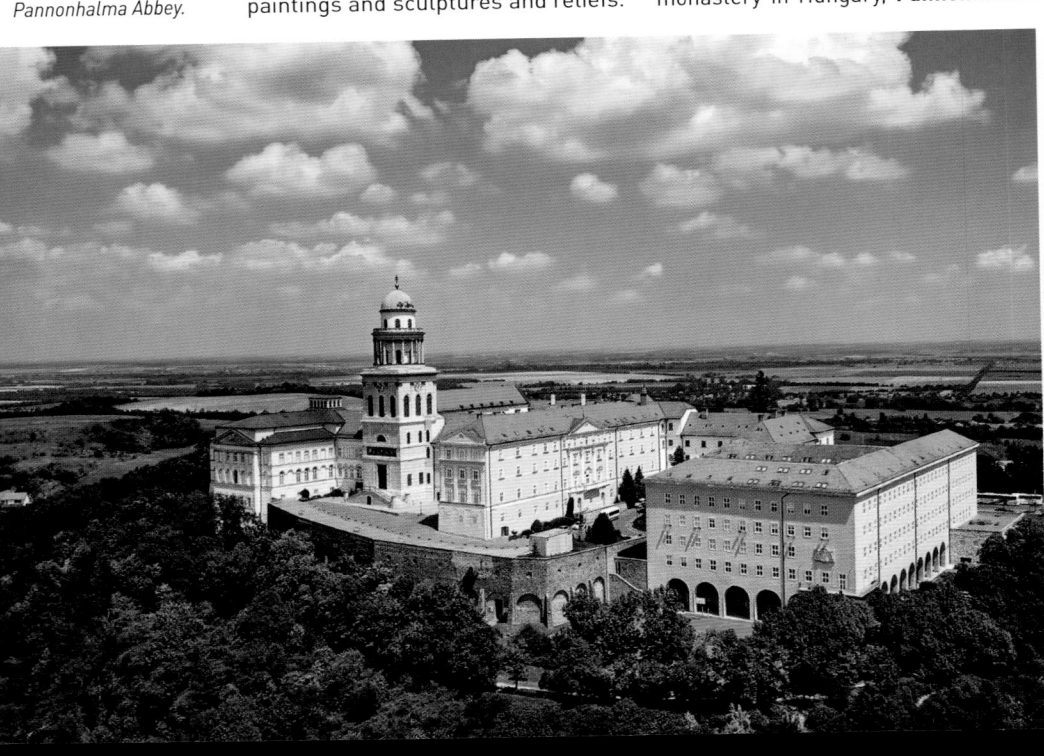

Abbey (Pannonhalmi foapátsád; daily June–Sept 9am–7pm, May & Sept 9am–6pm, Apr & Oct 9am–5pm, Nov–Mar Tue–Sun 10am–4pm; www.bences.hu). Designated a Unesco World Heritage Site, this Benedictine abbey stands on the 100-metre (330ft) St Martin's Hill and was founded in 996 by Prince Géza, father of King István I. It was here that Christianity in Hungary originated.

The monastery is dedicated to St Martin of Tours, patron saint of France, of beggars and of geese, who was born in 317 in the Roman garrison town of Savaria, modern day Szombathely. In the archives is the charter of the Abbey of Tihany on Lake Balaton, dated 1055, the first document containing names in Hungarian.

The oldest surviving part of the abbey church is the 13th-century crypt, with the abbot's throne, known as the seat of István. Buried in the crypt, beside her second husband, the Hungarian Count Lonyay, is Princess Stephanie of Belgium, widow of the Austrian heir to the throne, Rudolf, who killed himself in 1889. You can also visit the monastery's

winery, which produces a surprisingly accomplished tipple, though tours should be booked in advance.

PROTECTED CITY

Some 6km (4 miles) from the Austrian border crossing at Klingenbach, between the Sopron hills in the west and Lake Fertő in the northeast, lies **Sopron 6**, one of Hungary's most rewarding cities. Encircled by rows of 19th- and 20th-century houses, the horseshoe-shaped old quarter lies in the shelter of a wall dating from Roman times (the Roman name for Sopron was Scarbantia) and has the richest collection of historic buildings in Hungary, many of them listed.

The town's hallmark is the Fire Tower (Tuztorony; daily, mid-June–Sept 10am–8pm, Oct–mid-June 10am–6pm; www.tuztorony.sopron.hu), whose foundations are medieval; the central section, with an arcade and a beautiful view, dates from the Renaissance; and the top of the tower and its Baroque copper roof are 17th-century. The statues ensemble on one façade

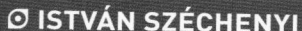

Fire Tower, Sopron.

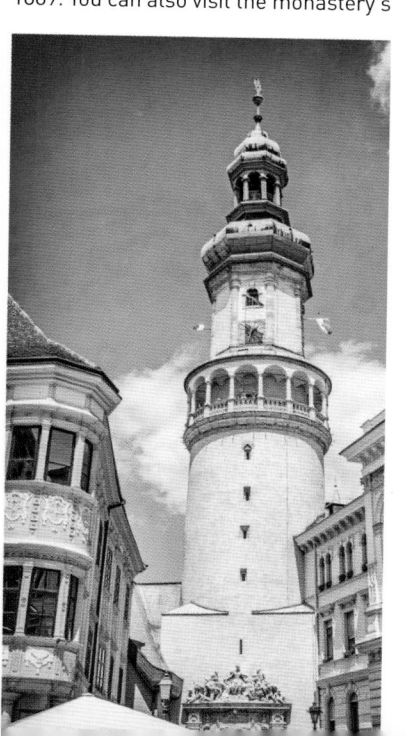

⊘ ISTVÁN SZÉCHENYI

Born in 1791, Count István Széchenyi was a key force in the modernisation of 19th-century Hungary. He travelled widely, including to England, where he was impressed by the level of education and technology.

From around 1820, his programme of liberal reforms encompassed both practical modernisation and social equality, believing that the nobility's monopoly on land ownership should be broken since it stunted economic development. He founded the Academy of Science in Budapest to foster the Hungarian language, scientific research and social progress. His diverse achievements included the Danube River Steamship company, harnessing of the country's waterways, and horse breeding.

Széchenyi is also said to have had the idea for Budapest's Chain Bridge (Lanchíd) after becoming exasperated with the slow boat crossing, declaring: 'I would offer a year's income for a bridge between Pest and Buda!'

His role in 1848's failed revolt against Habsburg domination is still disputed. While he supported radical reform, he remained Catholic and pro-Habsburg, believing that Hungary could not survive without Austrian support. This conflict caused a nervous breakdown in 1849, a symptom of the mental illness that led to his suicide in 1860.

is by Zsigmond Kisfaludy-Stróbl and honours the citizens of Sopron who voted in the 1920 referendum to stay in Hungary.

HISTORIC SQUARE

The tower is at the end of **Fő tér**, the main square, which is lined with beautiful 15th- to 17th-century houses and also boasts a few good cafés and restaurants. In the centre stands the Baroque **Trinity Column** (c.1700), one of the most remarkable in Hungary, behind which is the **Church of St Mary** (Apr–Oct daily 8am–6pm, Nov–Mar daily 8am–4pm), also known as the **Goat Church** for the relief of a goat at the foot of the tower. Dating from 1280, this is Sopron's most impressive sacred building, a three-aisled Gothic church with a slender tower, 43 metres (141ft) high; in the 16th century, three Hungarian queens were crowned here. The frescoes and carvings in the adjoining **Chapter Hall,** part of a former Franciscan monastery, are worth seeing.

Nearby, the Gothic Fabricius House (May–Sept Tue–Sun 10am–6pm, until 2pm rest of year) exhibits restored Roman statue and antique furniture. Immediately next door, the Renaissance Storno House (May–Sept Tue–Sun 10am–6pm, until 2pm rest of year) was formerly a merchant's townhouse and contains fine furniture, splendid frescoes and Gothic altarpieces. On the opposite side of the square, the Angel Pharmacy Museum (May–Sept Tue–Sun 10am–4pm), housed in a Gothic building, displays a well renovated apothecary.

INTERESTING ALLEYS

In Templom utca and the parallel alleys of the old town, Új utca (New Street) and Kolostor utca, nearly every house is worth a closer look. At Nos 2 and 4, a former Esterházy palace houses a museum of mining and forestry (Apr–Sept Mon–Fri 10am–4pm, Sat & Sun 10am–5pm), two industries of major importance in Sopron, though these two exhibitions are possibly for diehards only.

The Middle Ages seem to survive in the narrow, twisting alleys, where

Main square in Sopron.

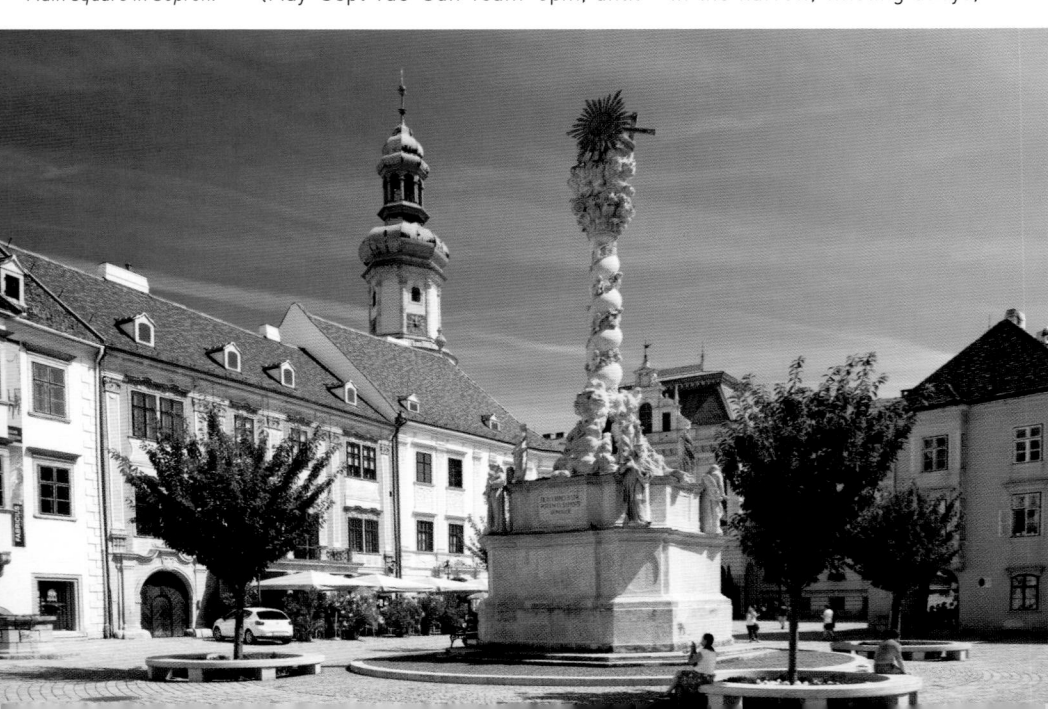

you'll find two medieval synagogues: at Új utca 22 the Old Synagogue (Ózsinagóga; Apr–Oct Tue–Sun 10am–6pm) houses a museum, and at No. 11, the New Synagogue (Új Zsinagóga) has a *mikvah* (ritual bath), but cannot be visited.

BEYOND THE WALLS

There is life outside the old walls, too. At the town's highest point is **St Michael's Church** (Szent Mihály-templom), and in the cemetery is Sopron's oldest sacred building, the Romanesque-Gothic **St James's Chapel** (Szent Jakab-kápolna).

On Bécsi útca, the old road towards Austria, a fascinating Bakery Museum (Pékmúzeum; May–Sept Tue–Sun 2–6pm) explores the traditional craft courtesy of the original kitchen and the baker's modest dwelling spaces.

STONE, SPA AND STATION

Some 10km (6 miles) northeast of Sopron stand the small town of **Fertőrákos ❼** near Lake Fertő, with a delightful little Baroque palace, the former residence of the bishops of Sopron.

The real attraction here is the Roman quarry (Apr–Oct daily 10am–6pm; www.fertorakosikofejto.hu), which was in use until 1945 and whose cut Leitha limestone was used to build St Stephen's Cathedral and the Ringstrasse buildings in Vienna. The mighty limestone blocks standing upright form massive vaults vaguely reminiscent of Egyptian temples. One of these vaults has been turned into a Theme Park, which is actually a cave like area with exhibits pertaining to the history of the quarry; while another has been converted into a cave theatre complete with heated seats – most useful.

ESTERHÁZY FLAMBOYANCE

The great Baroque **Palace of Fertőd** (Tue–Sun 10am–4pm, until 6pm

Apr–Oct) – often called the 'Hungarian Versailles' – was built in the 1760s by the most flamboyant of all the Esterházys, Miklós 'The Magnificent'. With its own opera house, and Haydn as court musician, it rivalled the splendid court at Vienna. Of the palace's 126 rooms, about 25 are on view, the most impressive of which are the panelled and gilded Sala Terrana, and the Banqueting Hall, decorated with J.J. Mildorfer's wonderful ceiling fresco. Other rooms are richly furnished with 18th-century masterpieces, desks, chairs, tiled stoves, chinoiserie and impressive Gobelins.

THE GREATEST HUNGARIAN

About 14km (9 miles) from Sopron on Highway 85, **Nagycenk ❽** was the home of the 'greatest Hungarian', Count István Széchenyi (1791–1860). Built in the mid-18th century and rebuilt in 1834–40, the **Széchenyi Mansion** was the family home until 1945, and was also Hungary's first building to have gas lighting; flush toilets and bathrooms were installed here

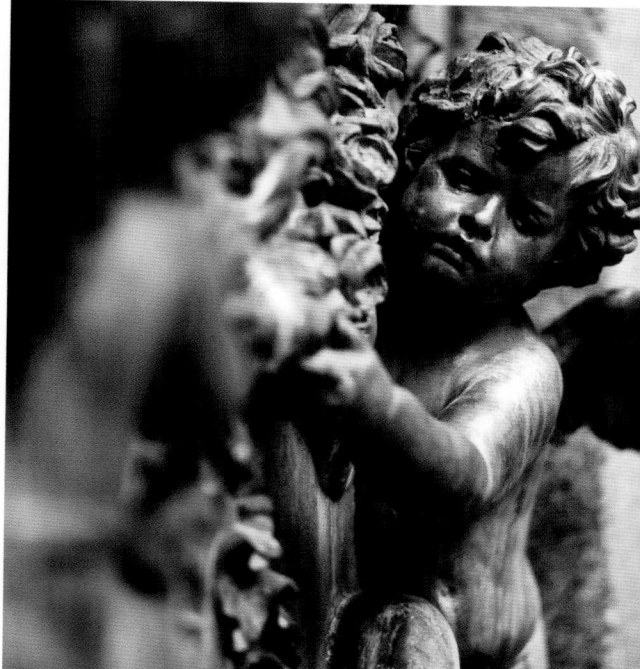

Detail of an angel face, Nagycenk.

20 years before they came to Vienna's Hofburg Palace.

Inside is the István Széchenyi Memorial Museum (Apr–Sept Tue–Sun 10am–6pm, Oct–Mar 8am–4pm; www.szechenyiorokseg.hu), with exhibits charting the family history and the great Hungarian's achievements, all explained on audio guides that can be hired at the door. One wing of the castle is a comfortable hotel.

Some 15km (9 miles) past Nagycenk, the road to Kőszeg turns off to the right. Stop briefly in Sopronhorpács to admire the magnificent entrance arch on the Romanesque church. Inside, you will find paintings by the 18th-century masters Dorffmeister and Maulbertsch.

KŐSZEG

Kőszeg ❾, the old border fort of Güns, is a picture-book medieval town. It has a defiant-looking castle with a moat, and a largely intact town wall. Enter the main square, Jurisics tér, through **Heroes' Gate** (Hősök kapu), built in 1932 to commemorate the town's repulsion of the Turks 400 years earlier. Above it is a replica Gothic tower which offers great views.

The square is surrounded by beautiful houses. One Renaissance building is decorated with 17th-century graffiti, while another, the Town Hall – an exuberant mixture of styles and colours – displays coats of arms and VIPs portrayed on shields.

In the middle of the square are two churches: the 15th-century Gothic St James's (Szent Jakab-templom), remodelled in Baroque style; and early-Baroque St Emery's (Szent Imre-templom).

The oldest parts of Jurisics Castle date from the 14th century, but numerous additions have changed it over the years. It houses the Castle Museum (Vármúzeum; Tue–Sun 10am–5pm; www.jurisicsvar.hu), with many reminders of the heroic defence against the Turks under Miklós Jurisics in 1532. Ever since, the bells in Kőszeg have been rung daily at 11am.

Outside the walls, on Fő tér, is the elegant Sacred Heart of Jesus Church

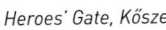
Heroes' Gate, Kőszeg.

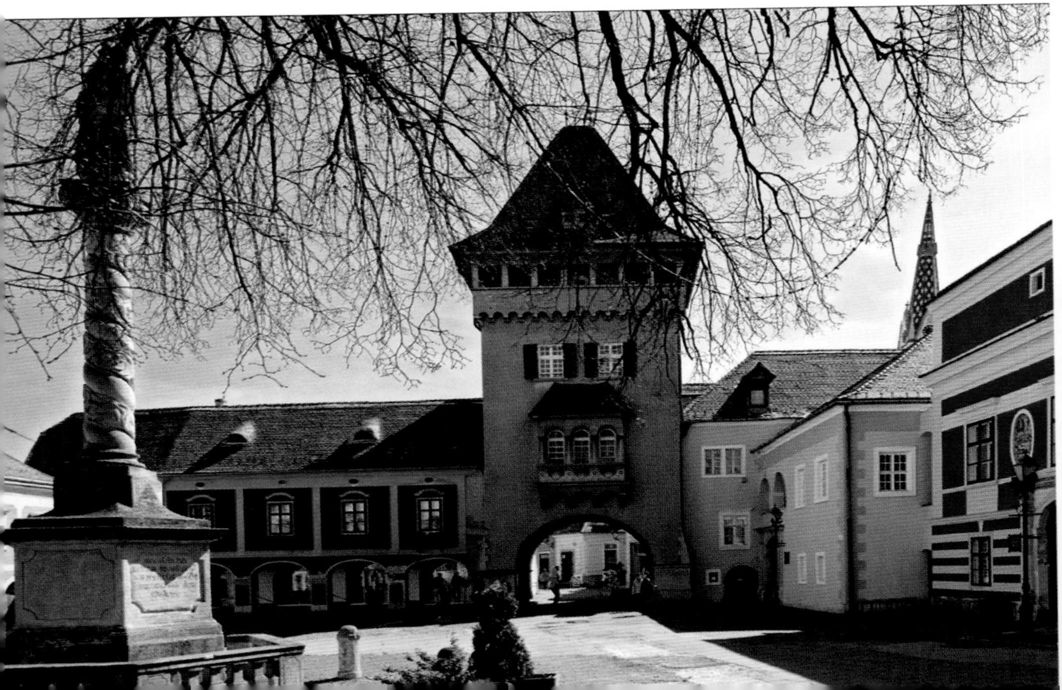

(Jézus Szíve-templom), a white, neo-Gothic apparition with slender spires. It was designed by Ludwig Schöne at the end of the 19th century, with an intensely colourful interior decorated by Viennese artist Otto Kott.

SZOMBATHELY'S ROMAN PAST

From Kőszeg it is not far south to **Szombathely** ❿ (formerly Steinamanger), the capital of the county of Vas and, after Győr, the biggest town in Transdanubia. It is a friendly, well-kept place whose Hungarian name means market place, and the town is still a trading centre for the surrounding area. This was once the site of the Roman town of Savaria, where Septimus Severus was proclaimed emperor in AD 193, and St Martin of Tours was born in AD 317.

You can see some impressive discoveries in the Garden of Ruins (Romkert; Tue–Sun 10am–4pm, until 6pm Apr–Sept) behind the 18th-century cathedral. A splendid Roman mosaic floor has been unearthed, as have the remains of St Quirinus' Basilica, which was built with stones taken from the governor's palace.

The Iseum is a disappointing modern reconstruction of a Temple of Isis on Rákóczi Ferenc utca. It stands next to the Szombathely Gallery (Apr–Oct Tue–Sun 10am–5pm, Thu until 6pm, Nov–Mar Wed–Sat 10am–5pm), which has an impressive art collection, especially of works of contemporary Hungarian artists. Opposite the gallery, the Béla Bartók music school is housed in a Moorish-style synagogue built in 1881.

At Kisfaludy Sándor utca 9, excavated remains are displayed in the Savaria Museum (Tue–Sun 10am–6pm; www.savariamuseum.hu); these include Roman stones, figures from the church in Ják, and prehistoric remains, notably a figure of a fertility goddess from the nearby village of Sé.

BISHOP'S PALACE

During the reign of Maria Theresa (1740–80), Szombathely became a bishopric and a number of religious edifices were built, one of which, the **Bishop's Palace** (Püspöki palota;

Bishop's Palace, Szombathely.

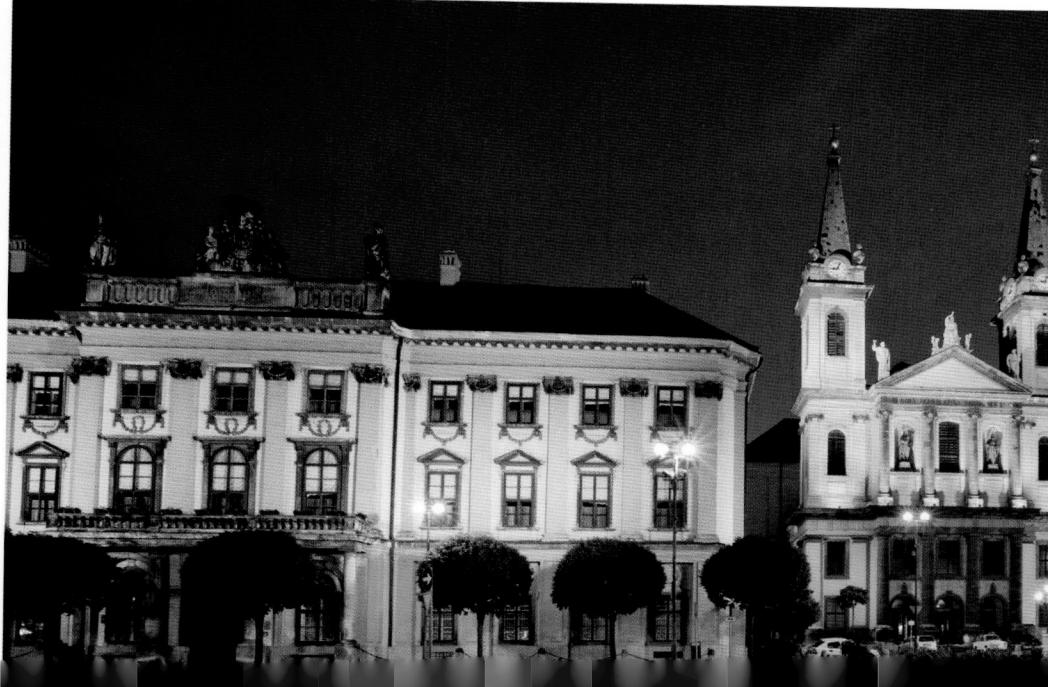

closed to the public) on Berzsényi tér, is especially grand. The frescoes in the Sala Terrena are by István Dorfmeister, who was involved in several other projects, for example the cathedral, whose interior was largely rebuilt after World War II.

In a park on the western edge of town, on Árpád utca, you can visit the Vas Museum Village (Vasi Múzeumfalu; June–Aug Tue–Sun 9am–7pm, Apr, May & Sept–Oct 9am–5pm), where several old farmhouses have been collected and displayed.

SHOPPING AND BATHING

Shopping is still a big thing in the region, as prices here are lower than in Austria. But the spas of the district also offer good value and attract many clients from across the border. The best known are **Bük** (due east of Kőszeg) and **Sárvár** (25km/15 miles to the east of Szombathely on the main Sopron road).

With a long tradition of spa treatments, Bük hot spring is the most prolific in Central Europe (see page 113),

and feeds a small lake; the town also has one of Hungary's few golf courses. By way of contrast, Sárvár is a relative newcomer, its springs discovered as recently as the 1960s.

ROMANESQUE MASTERPIECES

To the south of Szombathely is the most important architectural monument in the region. The 13th-century **Benedictine Abbey Church** (May–Oct Tue–Sun 10am–5pm; free) in **Ják** ⓫ is possibly the finest Romanesque building in Hungary, a great, twin-towered church rebuilt in the original style after fire damage early in the 20th century. Particularly impressive is the great portal with a wealth of figurative decoration, though the exterior decoration of the three round apses is of special interest, especially the stone-framed false arcades.

Ják's influence extended to the building of the tiny, single-nave church in Csempeszkopács (on Highway 87), another jewel of Hungarian religious architecture, with a Romanesque apse.

Benedictine Abbey of Ják.

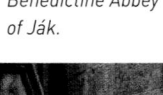

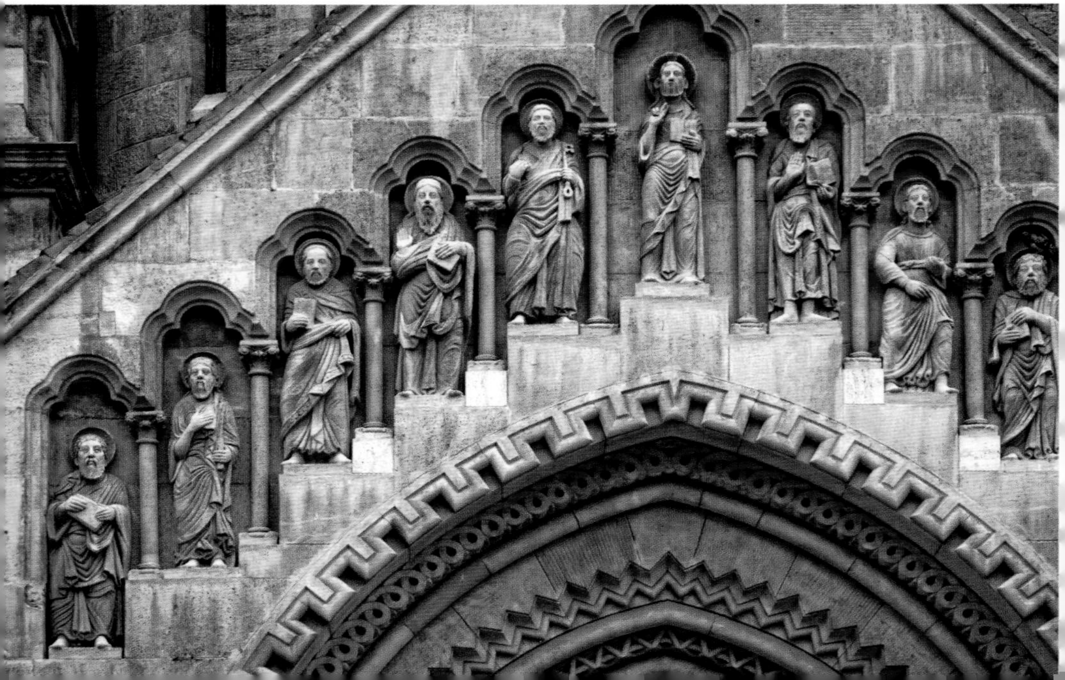

KÖRMEND

Heading south, at the junction of Highways 8 and 86, you reach **Körmend** ⓬. Its **Batthyány kastély,** the palace of the Batthyány-Strattman princes, is a massive Baroque building housing the **Batthyány-Strattman Museum** (May–Oct Tue–Sun 10am–5pm, Nov–Apr Tue–Sat 10am–4pm; www.muzeumkormend.hu), which offers intriguing insight into the family by way of costumes, documents and personal effects. The adjoining shoe collection is more interesting than it sounds, with footwear belonging to the great and good including Empress Elisabeth of Austria and the famous Hungarian actress Mari Jasai (1850–1926).

ON THE WAY TO LAKE BALATON

Compared to the elaborate border posts in Nickelsdorf and Klingenbach, the border crossing at **Heiligenkreuz** is small fry. But even here you can find yourself in a queue lasting many hours. Highway 8 is narrow, but in good condition.

Just inside the border, a road branches off to Szentgotthárd. To the southwest in **Szalafő** ⓭, at the end of a long, winding, narrow road, is an open-air museum (Apr–Oct Tue–Sun 10am–6pm) with a collection of ancient thatched farmhouses arranged around a courtyard.

This region is known as Őrség, and has much the same character as Hungary's far eastern border: small, sleepy villages, rolling hills, little churches, old farmsteads. The main town, **Őriszentpéter** ⓮, has an atmospheric old church and a collection of historic artefacts at the cultural house on Városszer 55. Local restaurants offer excellent food and specialities (such as a kind of gnocchi called *dödölle,* and salads dressed with pumpkin-seed oil).

South of Őriszentpéter in **Velemer** ⓯ is a Catholic church dating back to the 13th century, with walls covered in ancient frescoes. Finally, heading east, you drive alongside a railway track towards Zalalövő, which is in the Göcsej region, but only just. It has a small lake used mainly for fishing, and a regional museum house on the main road.

Traditional rural home in Szalafő.

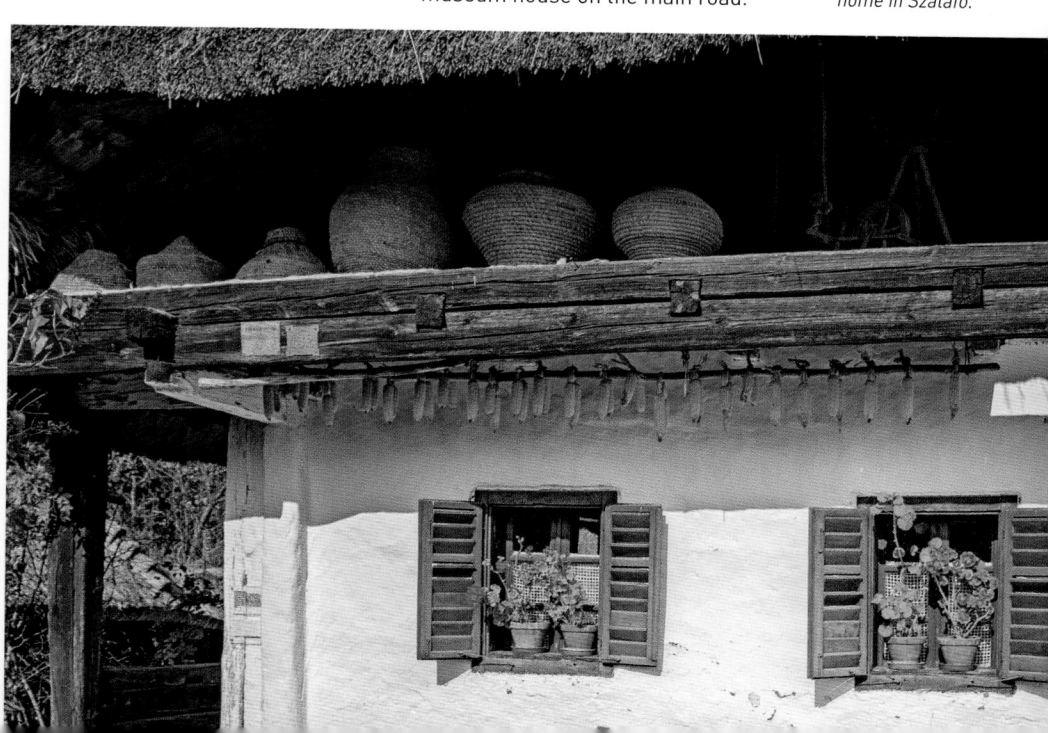

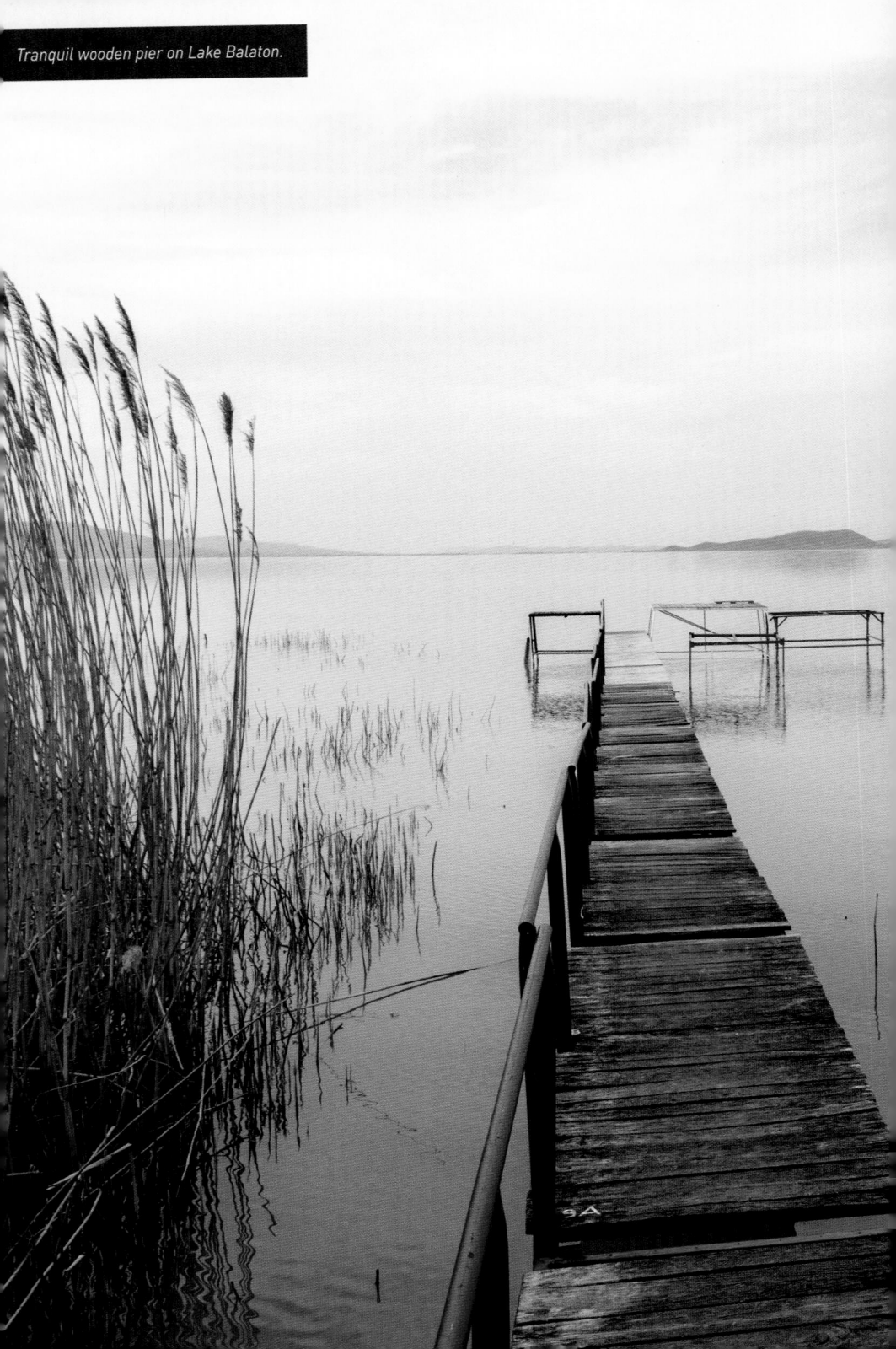
Tranquil wooden pier on Lake Balaton.

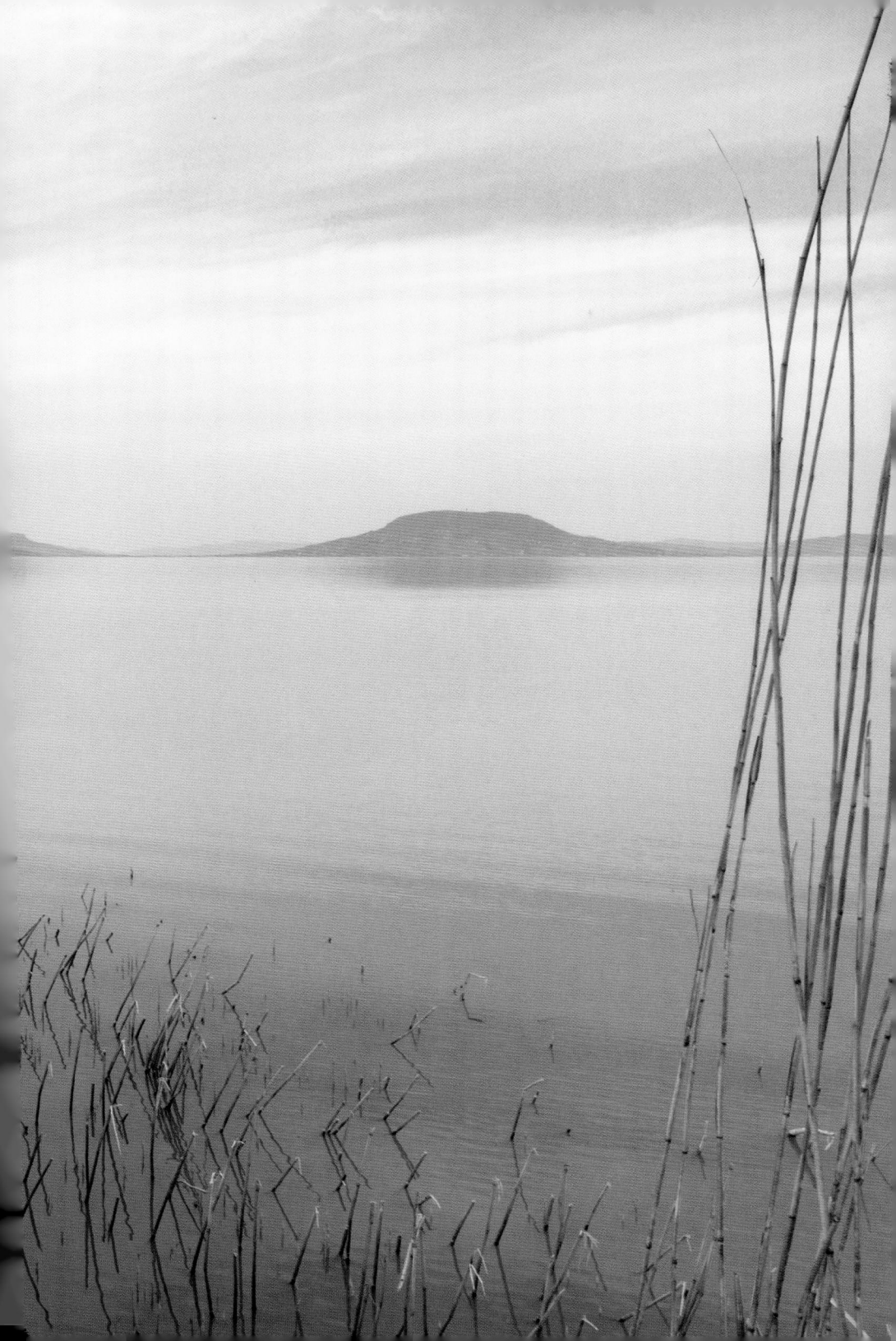

Tihany at Lake Balaton.

AROUND LAKE BALATON

Lake Balaton has some peaceful, picturesque stretches on the north shore, some lively resorts to the south, and a scattering of pretty towns on the wooded hillsides that roll down to the shore.

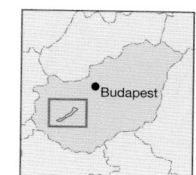

In this land-locked nation, they call Lake Balaton the 'Sea of Hungary'. Its area of 595 sq.km (230 sq. miles) makes it the biggest lake in Central and Western Europe.

It is also Hungary's most important tourist attraction, after Budapest. The heavy influx of visitors during the summer months has the usual side-effects of local price rises and a shortage of accommodation, even at campsites. The ecological consequences can be severe, too, ranging from vehicle pollution to a thin layer of suntan oil on the lake, which has poor drainage. Years of low rainfall are also a problem. However, the slow economy, which hobbled agriculture, has had a beneficial effect on the environment. Coupled with a concerted effort by the authorities, it has helped save the lake from death by pesticides, herbicides and artificial fertilisers.

STORM WARNINGS

Beware, however, of storms: when storm baskets at mooring places are at half-mast, it's a warning. Yellow rockets warn of strong winds, so smaller vessels, rowing boats and yachts alike, should stay near the shore. Red flares warn of a storm approaching and are a signal for all vessels to head for harbour.

The winds also cause a tidal effect in the narrows of Tihany. A strong southwesterly can press the water back into the eastern half of the lake; when the wind dies down, the water flows back.

To reach Lake Balaton from Budapest, use the motorway M7 or Highway 70. The former passes Velencei-tó to the north, the latter goes by Martonvásár and Székesfehérvár, the old city where the kings of Hungary were once crowned (see page 159). Since all trips round the lake are circular, your point of entry is arbitrary.

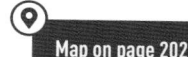

Main attractions
Veszprém
Balatonfüred
Tihany
Badacsony
Szigliget

Map on page 202

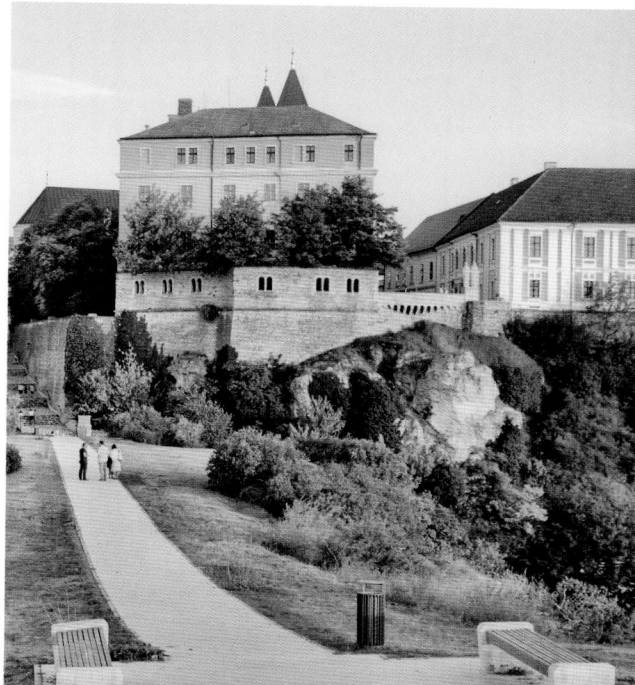

Veszprém castle.

202

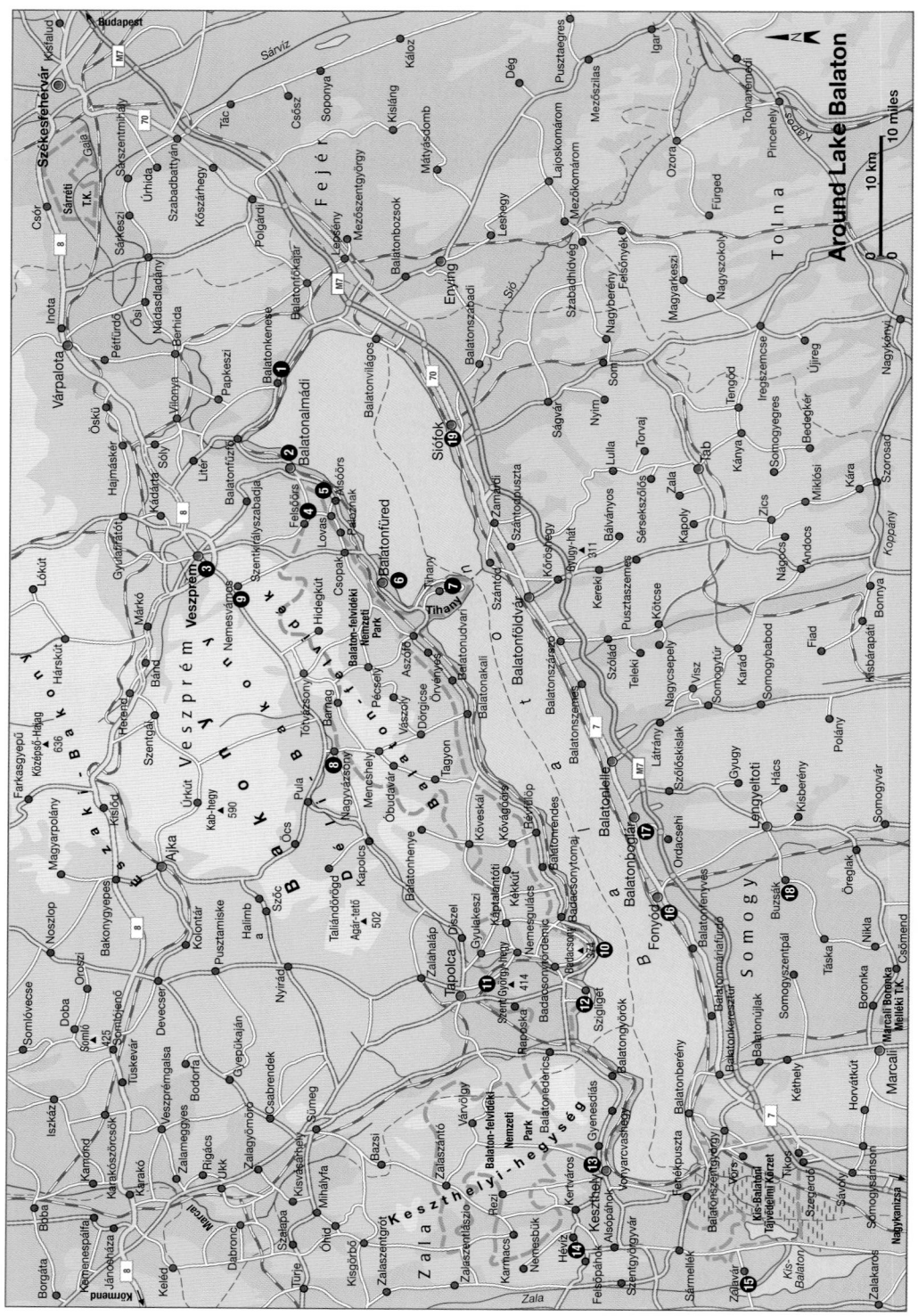

You can enjoy the liveliness of Balaton and the quiet of the countryside by staying a few miles from the shore where it is far less crowded.

THE NORTH SHORE

Coming from Budapest, you will catch your first glimpse of the northeastern part of Lake Balaton between Siófok and **Balatonkenese ❶**. Here, the surface of the water stretches out before you, and in the distance you can make out the outline of the hills beyond Balatonfüred and the Tihany peninsula.

Initially, the northeastern shore is not attractive, though each resort has either a beach eked out of the reeds and loess, or at least a swimming pool (for example, in Balatonfűzfő). Between the towns you come across two peculiarities of the countryside. On the hills above Balatonkenese is a rare plant that produces hanging bunches of white honey-scented flowers in May, and is known as 'Tartar bread' (the botanical name is Crambe tataria). During the 13th-century Mongol invasion, people dug up the roots, which grow 1.5 metres (5ft) deep, and roasted and ate them as a substitute for bread.

The second is the loess ridges, which are up to 40 metres (130ft) high and studded with dark holes, the entrances to the 'Tartar caves' in which the local population sought refuge during the Mongol invasion and later during the Turkish wars.

Balatonalmádi ❷, protected against the north winds by the heights of the Balaton hinterland, has been a bathing resort since the late 19th century. As well as some pleasant lakeside walks, it has two beaches, both of them quite small. On a hill in the Vörösberény district of the town there is a 13th-century Protestant church fortified and surrounded by a stone wall.

VESZPRÉM

Veszprém ❸ is not on the lake itself, but about 13km (8 miles) north of Balatonalmádi. It was founded as a bishopric by King István (Stephen) I; the bishops of Veszprém had the sole right to crown Hungarian queens. Nothing remains of the first castle and cathedral; what the Turks left intact was given the *coup de grâce* by the Austrian army in 1702, during the War of Independence.

The handsomely restored Castle Quarter (Vár) stands on the ridge of a hill that overlooks the rest of the town. Its entrance is marked by the Heroes' Gate, a neo-Romanesque portal built in 1936 on the site of the old town gate to commemorate the dead of World War I. In the neighbouring courtyard stands a pretty fire tower (daily 10am–6pm), as well as a Gallery of Modern Art (same times) with mostly abstract pieces.

Beyond is the Piarist Church (Piarista templom; Tue–Sun Apr–Oct 10am–5pm), a simple, neoclassical structure now used for temporary exhibitions. You are now in the main square, Szentháromság tér, in the centre of which stands the **Baroque Trinity Column**, erected in 1750. The square's

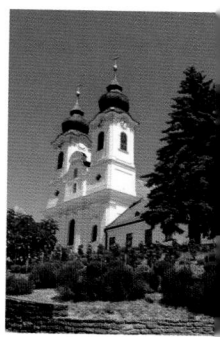

Tihany Abbey.

⊘ LAKE BALATON

Lake Balaton is 77km (48 miles) long and is 14km (9 miles) wide at its widest point; the lake runs from southwest to northeast, bisecting the region of Transdanubia, and is located around 135km (84 miles) southwest of Budapest. The peninsula of Tihany divides the lake in two: the eastern section is smaller, but broader and deeper, whilst the western part of it is longer and narrower. On the opposite bank, between Tihany and Szántód, where there is a car ferry, the lake is less than 1.5km (1 mile) wide. If you want to drive around the entire lake, it's a total distance of 197km (122 miles). The scenery on the northern bank, with volcanic mounds, vineyards and wide bays, is very picturesque; whilst the sand dunes and shallow waters of the south bank are perfect for families with children.

Technically, Lake Balaton qualifies as a 'shallow water' lake. The average depth throughout the lake is a mere 3.5–4 metres (12–13ft). Even at its deepest point – located at the narrow part near Tihany – Lake Balaton is only 11 metres (35ft) deep. Because the lake is so shallow, it warms up relatively quickly in the sun. It cools down just as quickly when the weather turns cold however; but in summer you can be sure that the water will be warm enough to swim in and the beaches densely packed.

⊙ Tip

At Felsőörs and Alsóörs you reach the part of the coast known as the **Balaton Riviera.** The vegetation is lush by Central European standards, and narrow paths wind uphill into vineyards from whose grapes popular white wines are made.

single most impressive building is the **Bishop's Palace** (Püspöki palota; Tue–Sun Apr–Oct 10am–5pm), which reflects the pomp of the Baroque age. Designed by Jakob Fellner, it was built between 1765 and 1776 using stones from a royal castle that once stood on this spot; apparently, Hungary's first flush toilets were installed here.

Fellner also worked on the **Gizella Chapel** (daily May–Oct 9am–6pm) next to the palace, named after the wife of István I and containing Byzantine-style frescoes of the Apostles. Opposite is the Gizella Museum (same hours as chapel), displaying a trove of dazzling ecclesiastical items: chasubles, vestibules, vestments, paintings and suchlike.

Nearby stands **St Michael's Cathedral** (Székeseghház; daily May–Oct 10am–5pm). Parts of it date from the early 11th century, and there is an early-Gothic crypt, but much of it was rebuilt in 1907–10 in neo-Romanesque style. It is used for concerts and exhibitions as well as worship. A glass dome behind the cathedral shelters the excavated remains of St George's Chapel.

The boundary of the Castle Quarter is marked by the old bastions, which offer a splendid view over the rest of the town and its surrounding area, in particular the viaduct of Veszprém, built in 1938. István and Gizella are honoured here with statues erected in 1938, the 900th anniversary of István's death.

Some 9km (6 miles) west of Veszprém on Highway 8 is **Herend**, where world-famous porcelain has been manufactured since 1826. Exporting over 75 percent of its products to the likes of Japan and America, some of its most distinguished buyers have included Tsar Alexander II, the Shah of Iran, and the British royal family. Visitors can take a tour of the mini-factory (daily Apr–Oct 9.30am–6pm, Tue–Sat Nov–Mar 10am–4pm; www.herend.com) – observing clay basket weavers, glazers and painters along the way – and find out more about Herend's history in the museum (same times). At the café you can sample drinks and snacks from authentic Herend tableware.

Ceramacist at work in Herend.

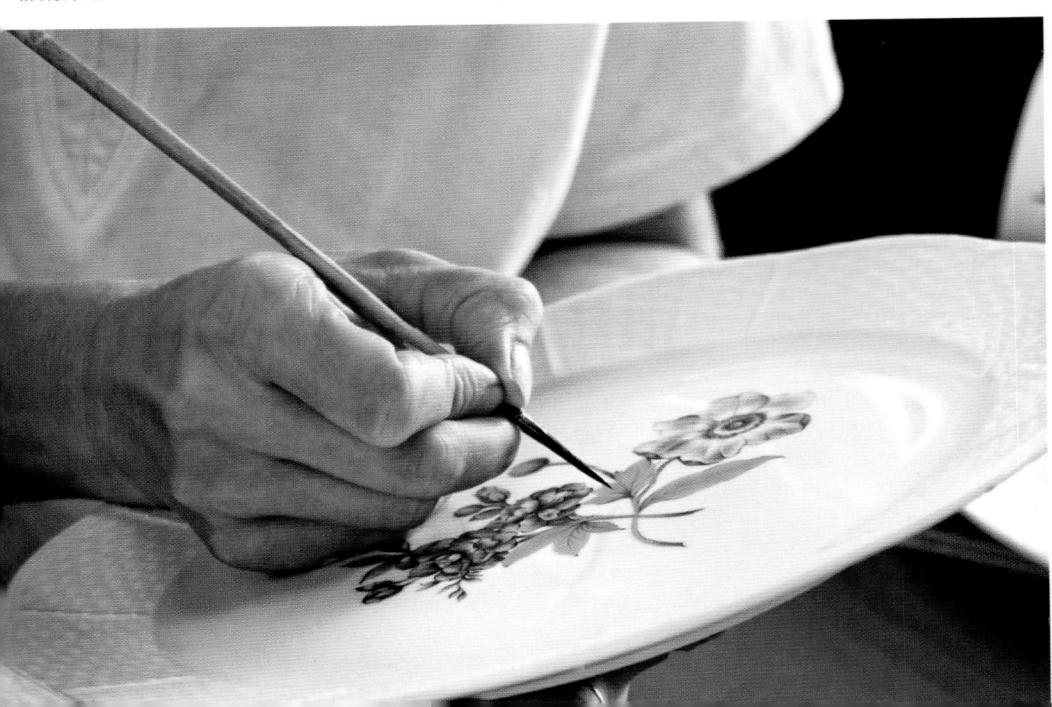

FELSŐÖRS AND ALSÓÖRS

In **Felsőörs** ❹ you can see a medieval church built of red sandstone, with a richly decorated portal and a somewhat bizarre tower with an impressive roof. The façade has an interesting design with three windows separated by great carved knots to ward off evil spirits.

Alsóörs ❺ is the site of an important fish-breeding farm. There are said to be 42 different kinds in the lake, but the most famous is fogas (a kind of pike or perch), with a delicate taste and firm flesh. In the fogas breeding season, twigs are tied to ropes 610 metres (2,000ft) long, which are laid out in the lake. The fish lay their eggs on them and the ropes are then drawn out and the eggs transferred into pools; as soon as the young hatch, they escape into the lake via a special channel.

Also in Alsóörs is the oldest stately home on the shore. Built around 1500, it is called the House of the Turkish Tax Collector, maybe because of its turban-shaped chimney, or because a tax collector lived there during the occupation.

THE CAPITAL OF LAKE BALATON

Some 9km (6 miles) further west, **Balatonfüred** ❻, officially a 'National City of the Grape and Wine', is the most traditional resort on Lake Balaton. The section of Balatonfüred stretching along the main road is modern and not very attractive but all along the waterfront the atmosphere is relaxed and laid-back thanks to its promenades, busy piers, sailing boats and old-fashioned ships.

The town owes its reputation to the hot springs that contain carbon dioxide. Their medicinal powers were discovered in 1632 and in the 18th century the first permanent bath houses and pavilions were built; the sanatoria followed in the 19th century. The biggest, built in Secessionist style, was named after the Empress Elizabeth and is today one of the best-known hospitals for the treatment of heart and circulatory diseases.

The hospital is flanked on the east by Gyógy tér, the town's central square, on the northern side of which is the former sanatorium. In July every year, in the great hall, the Anna Ball takes place. It is the social event of the season and

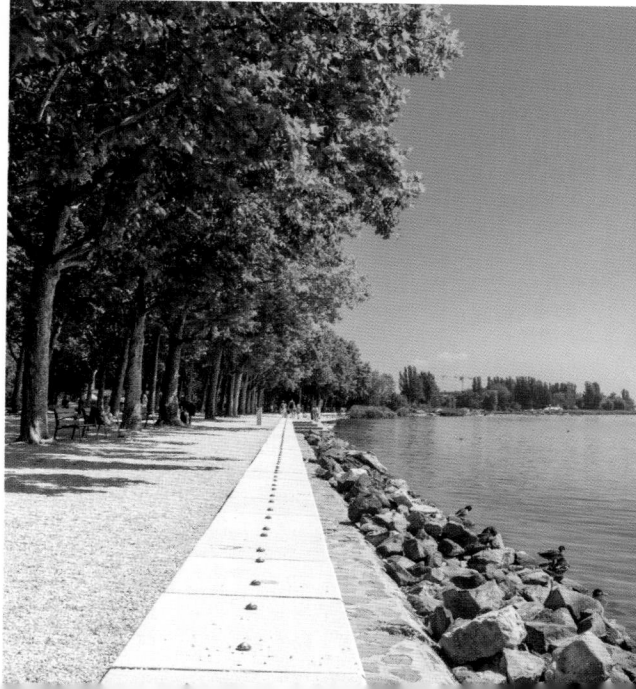

Balatonfüred.

⊙ SAILING CENTRE

Sailing on Lake Balaton is a long-standing tradition, thanks to the trailblazing Széchenyis. These days, Balatonfüred is the centre of sailing on the lake, although there are several other sailing schools located in Siófok, Balatonszemes and Tihany. You can see almost every type of boat you can imagine on the lake, from small dinghies to large yachts.

Around the mid-19th century, steamships began to make pleasure trips around the lake. Today, similar vessels still make the same trip, although they are now fuelled by diesel. A trip around Lake Balaton takes about 25 minutes from the eastern end of the lake, and 40–50 minutes from the western section.

dates from 1825, when it was held as a coming-out ball for the daughter of the Szentgyörgyi-Horvoith family.

In the centre of the square is the 19th-century Kossuth Pump Room, fed by one of five hot springs. If you are interested in late-Baroque and classical architecture, take a stroll along Blaha Lujza utca between Gyógy tér and the neoclassical Round Church. You will also find a pharmacy (1782); the Kedves pâtisserie (1795); and a villa (now a hotel) that belonged to the 'Nation's Nightingale', singer-actress Lujza Blaha, darling of Hungarian audiences around the turn of the 20th century.

FAMOUS FIGURES

There are numerous memorial statues to prominent figures between Gyógy tér and the shore promenade. The great reformer István Széchenyi (see page 191), the Hungarian poet, Sándor Kisfaludy (see page 209) and the Indian poet, Rabindranath Tagore are all remembered here. Not only did Széchenyi help revive the economy of the region in the 1840s, but he also pioneered steamship travel on Lake Balaton in 1846 and made sailing fashionable. The Blue Ribbon competition that takes place every two years is held in his honour.

Kisfaludy's work was strongly influenced by the Balaton landscape. As for Tagore, who spent some time in Balatonfüred having treatment for a heart condition, he is remembered both in the memorial and in the Tagore sétány (promenade) along the lake. Until 1972 it was lined by rows of poplar trees, but they were all felled by a sudden whirlwind. The poet left some lines of his verse next to a lime tree that he planted:

When I am no longer on this earth my tree,

Let the ever renewed leaves of spring
Murmur to the wayfarer
The poet did love while he lived.

TIHANY PENINSULA

Tihany ❼ offers the most picturesque scenery on Lake Balaton. This peninsula runs far out into the lake, its verdant slopes occasionally broken by bizarre-shaped rocks, the

Swimming in Balatonfüred.

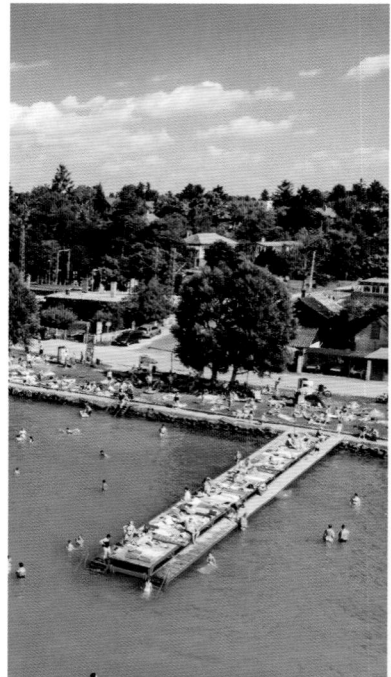

⊘ ROYAL BURIAL GROUND

Tihany is old ground, not only geologically, but also historically speaking. Here King András I, the 'most Christian bearer of the sceptre', as the charter calls him, founded a monastery in 1055. It was supposed to be the burial ground for all Hungarian kings. However, only the founding king is buried in the Romanesque crypt, the sole surviving part of the building. The inscription in the crypt reads: 'This is the only royal tomb in the 1,000-year-old Kingdom of Hungary that was passed down to us in its original form.' The squat, unadorned pillars bearing the massive vault are impressive and the narrow tomb of the king also has a touching quality. The tombstone is cut from white limestone, with a twisted staff and a simple cross, chiselled out at one end.

The village's Baroque church, which is above the crypt, has two towers that can be seen from a considerable distance, was built between 1719 and 1754, after the Turks had been driven out of Hungary. The first building was destroyed by fire in 1736, but the abbot, Agoston Lécs, persevered. The church's splendid, harmonious interior is most effective. The pulpit, the altars, organ and choir and the decoration of the sacristy are the work of Austrian artist, Sebastian Stuhlhoff, a woodcarver who worked here for more than 25 years in the 18th century.

whole crowned by the twin towers of a Baroque abbey church, surrounded by little farmhouses and fishermen's cottages, although most of these are now shops, cafés and restaurants.

In order to appreciate the view fully, you should approach from across the lake, on one of the boats from Balatonfüred, or by ferry from the opposite shore.

Evidence of Tihany's volcanic past is the geyser mounds – petrified remains of the activities of hot springs half a million years ago. The only other places where you will find so many mounds are in Iceland and Yellowstone Park in the US. Another distinct reminder of the peninsula's prehistoric past is the Belső-tó (Inner Lake), which is 26 metres (85ft) higher than Lake Balaton, in an extinct crater. To the south of it is the Hármashegy, Tihany's highest mountain.

The history of Tihany at the time when Hungary still had close contact with the Eastern churches is reflected in the hermits' cells in the basalt-tufa cliffs that drop down to the lake to the east of the church. They date from the abbey's foundation, when King András invited monks from Kiev to settle here. The king had spent part of his youth at the court of the Prince of Kiev, Jaroslav the Wise, and married his daughter, Anastasia.

In 1921, the last emperor of the house of Habsburg-Lorraine, Charles I, spent his final night on the soil of his former empire in the abbey. Following the failure of his second attempt to retain at least the title of king of Hungary, he was interned in Tihany then taken to the Danube harbour of Baja. He boarded the British warship hms *Glowworm*, which took him into exile on Madeira.

THE UPPER REGIONS OF THE LAKE

During 150 years of Turkish rule in central Hungary (1541–1699) the border between the Ottoman and the Habsburg empires ran through the hills of the northern shore of Lake Balaton. During the anti-Habsburg revolt under Ferenc Rákóczi in 1703–11 the border

Just outside Tihany, near Lake Balaton.

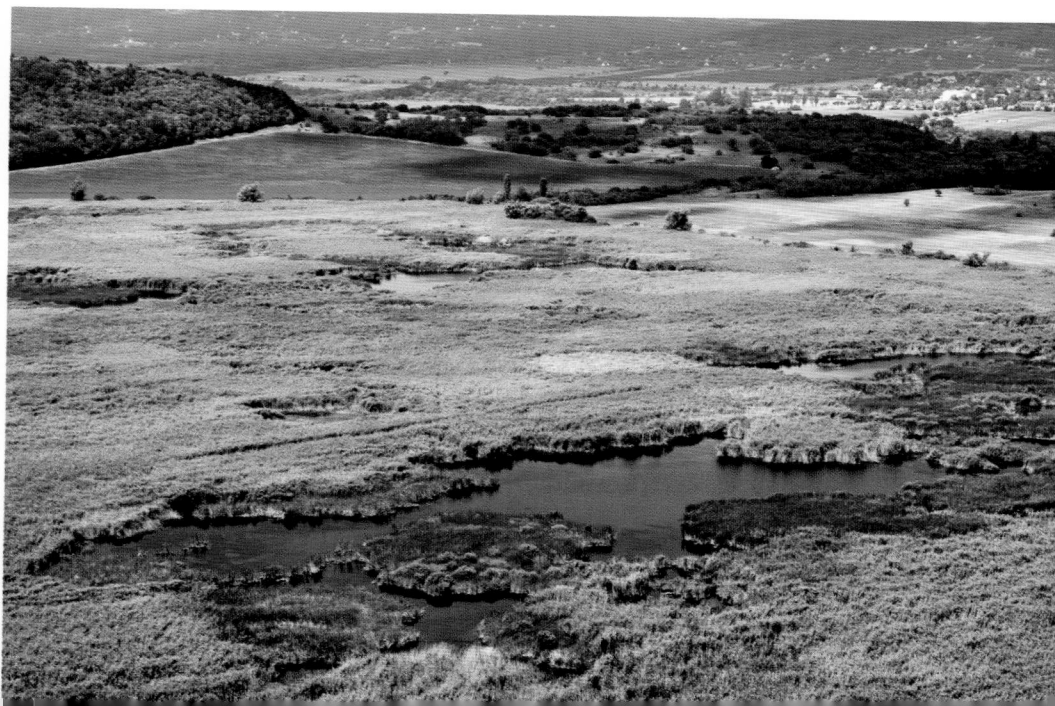

forts served as bases for rebel troops, before imperial forces destroyed them during and after the collapse of the revolt. **Kinizsi Castle** (daily, June–Aug 9am–7pm, Mar–May & Sept–Oct 9am–5pm, Nov–Feb 9am–4pm) at **Nagyvázsony ⑧**, about 25km (16 miles) to the northwest of Tihany, was one of them. Its horseshoe-shaped barbican, whose mighty outer fortifications once kept the castle well protected from attack, and the 28-metre (92-ft) high fortified tower are still in good condition.

The castle is named in honour of Pál Kinizsi, a general under Mátyás Corvinus, and the fact that Hungary was relatively untroubled by the Turks during the second half of the 15th century is due to his military skills. Locally, he is remembered chiefly for his brute strength. A picture in the Kinizsi Castle Museum (hours as above) portrays him lifting a burly Turk with his teeth and, with a sword in each hand, performing a kind of warrior dance.

Held at the end of July, Kinizsi Days is three days of medieval festivities, featuring jousting, craft fares and the like.

NEMESVÁMOS

Between Nagyvázsony and Veszprém is the *csárda* (inn) of **Nemesvámos ⑨**. Lying on the border between two districts, it was a famous 'Betyár *csárda*' at the end of the 18th century, Betyárs being people who had either escaped military service or were in some way on the wrong side of the law. They earned their living by highway robbery and as they usually robbed the wealthy and left the poor alone, they were very popular – numerous songs and stories sing their praises. In the Nemesvámos inn they were fairly safe, for when the police from one district approached, they escaped to the other. With its open-arched passages on the ground and upper floors, the csárda is a good example of late 18th-century rural architecture.

BADACSONY

To the west of Tihany the bays are mainly full of reeds, the beaches

Kinizsi Castle.

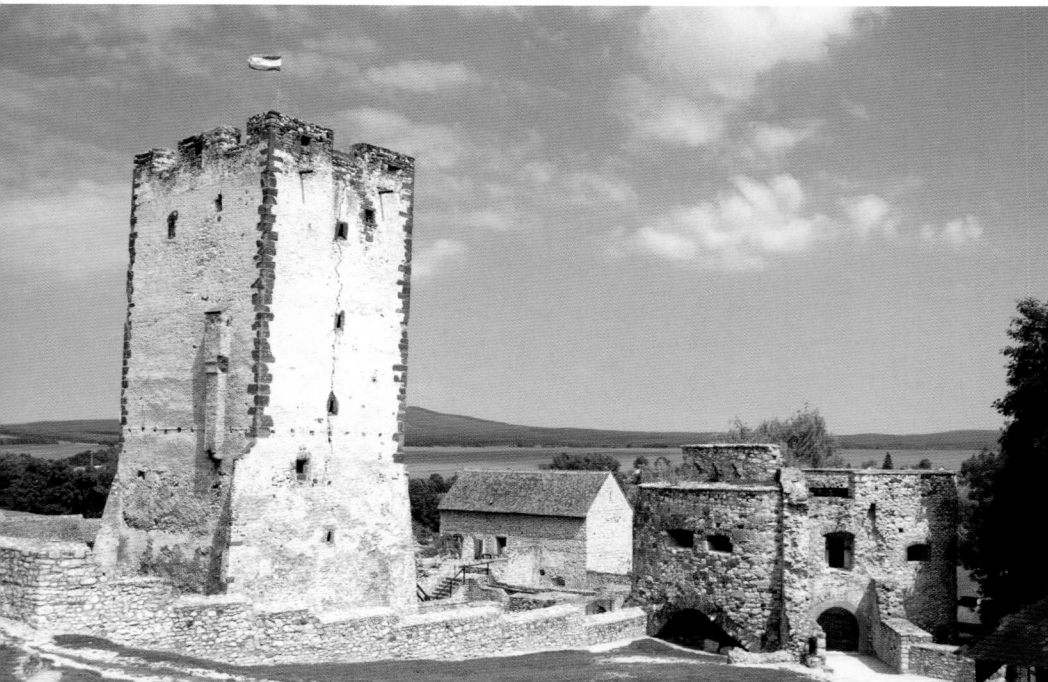

narrow, and the railway and Highway 71 run parallel to the shoreline in several places. There are a few unusual sights between Tihany and Badacsony, including some strange heart-shaped tombstones of white sandstone in the churchyard of **Balatonudvari.**

Approximately 30km (19 miles) to the west of Tihany, the landscape suddenly takes on a dramatic appearance. The massive hill of **Badacsony ⑩** rears up and protrudes into the lake like the foothills of a mountain range, standing like a sentinel at the entrance to Tapolca plain, out of which rise more bizarre-looking volcanic hills.

On the gentle lower slopes of Badacsony grow the vines which produce several respectable white wines drunk both in and outside Hungary – among them Sylvaner and Riesling.

Further up the gentle slope becomes rocky, with basalt cliffs looking like organ pipes stretching steeply towards the plateau on the summit, which is thickly covered with a dark crown of forest. Viniculture has a long tradition on the slopes of Badacsony, and there is a legend that no vintner could become mayor of any of the villages on the slopes if he had let a stranger pass by his cellar without offering a glass of wine.

ARTISTS AND WRITERS

In the little lakeside resort of Badacsony, the **József Egry Museum** (May–Oct Tue–Sun 10am–6pm) exhibits the work of local lad and one of Hungary's foremost painters (1883–1951), whose beautiful Balaton landscapes and family portraits are a joy. Two houses on the hillside stand in memory of the poet Sándor Kisfaludy (1772–1844) and his actress wife, Róza Szegedy, who spent many years here.

The Kisfaludy House, today a popular restaurant offering a magnificent view of the lake, once housed the poet's wine press. A path from the parking lot leads up to the Kisfaludy Lookout (437 metres/1,400ft) for more fine views. The Róza Szegedy House, meanwhile, contains a literary museum that celebrates her husband's work and

⊙ Tip

A number of pleasant country houses nestle among the vineyards and of Badascony, and marked trails through the hills make it a great place for walkers.

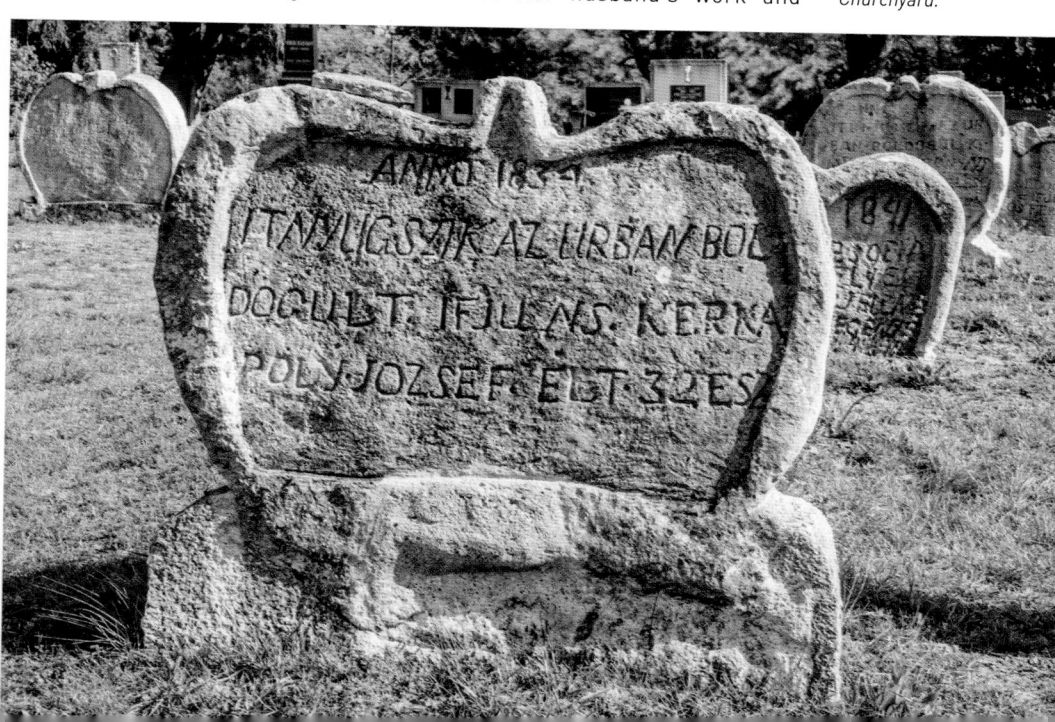

A grave in Balatonudvari Churchyard.

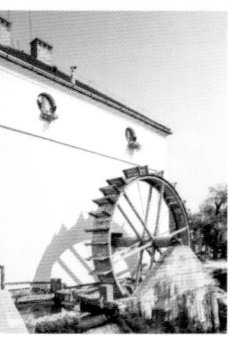

Mill house, Tapolca.

Vineyards on the shores of Lake Balaton.

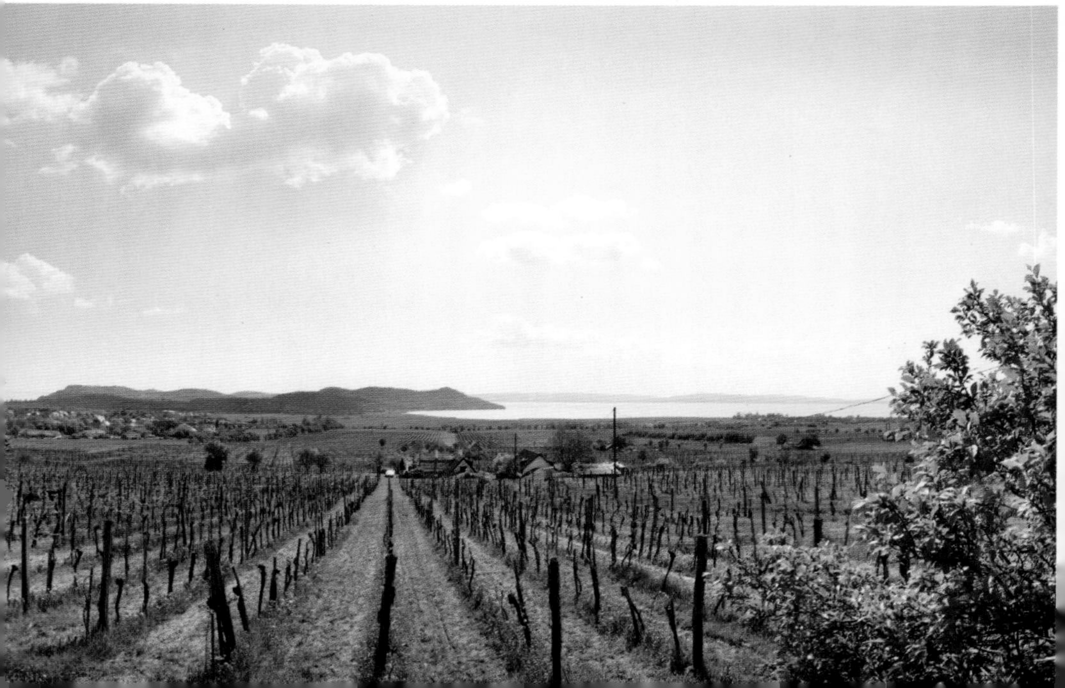

that of other Hungarian literary figures, alongside some of her personal effects.

The castle in nearby Szigliget, which formerly belonged to the wealthy Esterházy family, is now an artists' retreat. In Badacsonytomaj, one of four villages that make up the Badacsony region, there is a church built of basalt with two bell-towers, near Highway 71. It was erected in 1932 and is said to be the only one of its kind in Europe.

Another interesting excursion in the Badacsony area is to **St George's Mountain (Szent György-hegy)** ⓫, 414 metres (1,358ft) high. Its main attraction is the 'great organ' on the eastern edge of the hill, a wall of basalt columns up to 40 metres (130ft) high.

ON THE WAY TO KESZTHELY

En route to Keszthely, make a quick stop in **Balatongyörök** to see its lovely beach and the **Belvedere** (Szépkilátó). This promenade offers a splendid view of everything this part of Lake Balaton has to offer: the vineyards and the bay of Szigliget, the castle ruins on the

former volcanic mounds on the plain of Tapolca, the massif of Badacsony and the fine lines of the southern shore.

Szigliget ⓬ comes alive in early August with a programme of folk dances, concerts and equestrian shows. Tapolca used to be maligned as an industrial centre whose bauxite and manganese mines poured pollution into Hévíz Lake (see page 212). The closing of the mines simultaneously saved Hévíz and filled **Tapolca Lake** Cave (Tavasbarlang; daily Jun–Aug 10am–6pm; Tue–Sun Apr–May, Sept–Oct 10am–5pm) with clear water; its 4km (2.5-mile) system can be navigated in little rowing boats.

THE PALACE AND THE TOWN

In the town of **Keszthely** ⓭, sloping gently down to the lake, the first thing you will notice is the **Festetics Palace** (daily July & Aug 9am–6pm, May–June & Sept 10am–5pm; Tue–Sun Oct–Apr 10am–5pm; www.helikonkastely.hu) with its generous proportions. The Baroque southern wing dates from 1745, but most of it was created between 1883 and 1887 and the town has developed outwards from it.

In front of the palace is the statue of Count György Festetics (1755–1819), a man of the Enlightenment and to whom both the palace and the town owe much. The palace contains a museum (mostly furniture and portraits) and the Helikon Library, containing one of the most valuable collections in the country, though the library hall with its classical coffered ceiling is the star attraction.

In 1797 Count György founded the Georgikon, the first advanced agricultural institute in Hungary, from which a modern agricultural college developed. The excellent **Georgikon Farm Museum** (Georgikon Majormúzeum; Apr–Oct Tue–Sun 10am–5pm) has a voluminous collection of dairy and viticultural equipment, tractors and ploughs. Embued with the spirit of Ancient Greece, Count György initiated the Helikon meetings of poets, which made a major contribution to Hungary's cultural rebirth, inspired by the nationalist ideals sweeping Europe in the early 19th century.

Kossuth utca, which leads down to the lake, is an interesting street. At No. 22 is a medieval house with a double row of arcades, in which Karl Goldmark, composer of the opera The Queen of Sheba, was born in 1830. Close by you'll find a trio of minor attractions (daily May–Sept 9am–6pm, Oct–Apr 10am–5pm): firstly the Panopticum, featuring waxwork figures from Hungarian history ranging from Attila the Hun (who was not really Hungarian) to Cardinal Mindszenty, who took refuge in the US Embassy in Budapest in 1956 and refused to leave until 1971; secondly the Doll Museum (Babaés Néprajzi Múzeum), with some 7,000 china dolls and 40 wax figures in Hungarian national dress; and thirdly the peculiar Csiga Parlament, a replica of the parliament building in Budapest, made of about 4.5 million snail shells (Pannonian) of different sizes.

Finally, for a concentrated introduction to the Balaton, its geology,

> **⊘ Tip**
> There are two beaches in Keszthely, one near the Hotel Helikon, and one further west, called Várois Strand, which is popular with windsurfers.

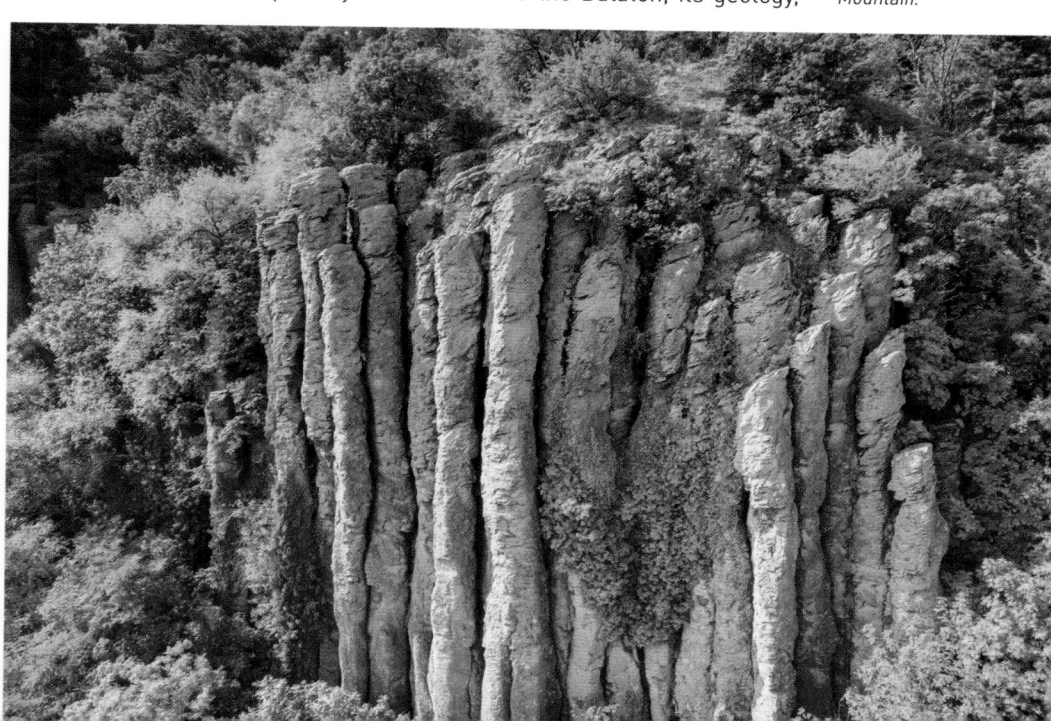

Natural basalt columns on St George's Mountain.

⊙ Tip

An oddity awaits in Zalaszántó (on the way to Sümeg): a Buddhist stupa in the Human Rights Park. Its cupola has a diameter of 24 metres (80ft).

sociology, history, and fauna and flora, visit the well-stocked **Balaton Museum** at Múzeum utca 2 (Tue–Sun May–Oct 10am–6pm, Nov–Apr 10am–5pm).

FENÉKPUSZTA AND HÉVÍZ

In **Fenékpuszta,** 8km (5 miles) south of Keszthely, stand the ruins of the Roman fortress of Valcum. Among the attractions are the foundations of an ancient Christian basilica and the classical stables and accommodation of the Festetics stud farm.

About 6km (4 miles) northwest of Keszthely lies the spa of **Hévíz** ⓓ, whose reputation, extending far beyond Hungary's border, rests mainly on its gigantic thermal lake, the largest in Europe. In summer the water temperature rises to 34°C (93°F), and in winter it seldom falls below 26°C (78°F). The changing rooms and bath houses, which are built on stilts extending out into the lake, were originally conceived by Count György Festetics at the end of the 18th century, although they have been rebuilt since.

ZALAVÁR

For anyone with a strong interest in local history, a visit to **Zalavár** ⓔ is recommended. It is about 20km (12 miles) south of Keszthely, in the (nowadays mainly drained) marshland around the Kis Balaton (*Kis* means small) and the little River Zala. There isn't much to see here, apart from the foundation walls of a small 9th-century church, but the area has great historical significance. Zalavár is where the Slavs of Pannonia were converted before the invasion of the Danube region by the Magyars.

This is where the historic confrontation took place between the missionaries of the Archdiocese of Salzburg, who proclaimed the teachings of Christ using the Latin language and liturgy, and the Slav apostles Cyril and Methodus, who preached in the Old Slavic language and celebrated the Mass according to the Byzantine liturgy. The later schism of the church between East and West, between Byzantium and Rome, and between the Orthodox and Papal churches – with all its secular

Old church at Hévíz.

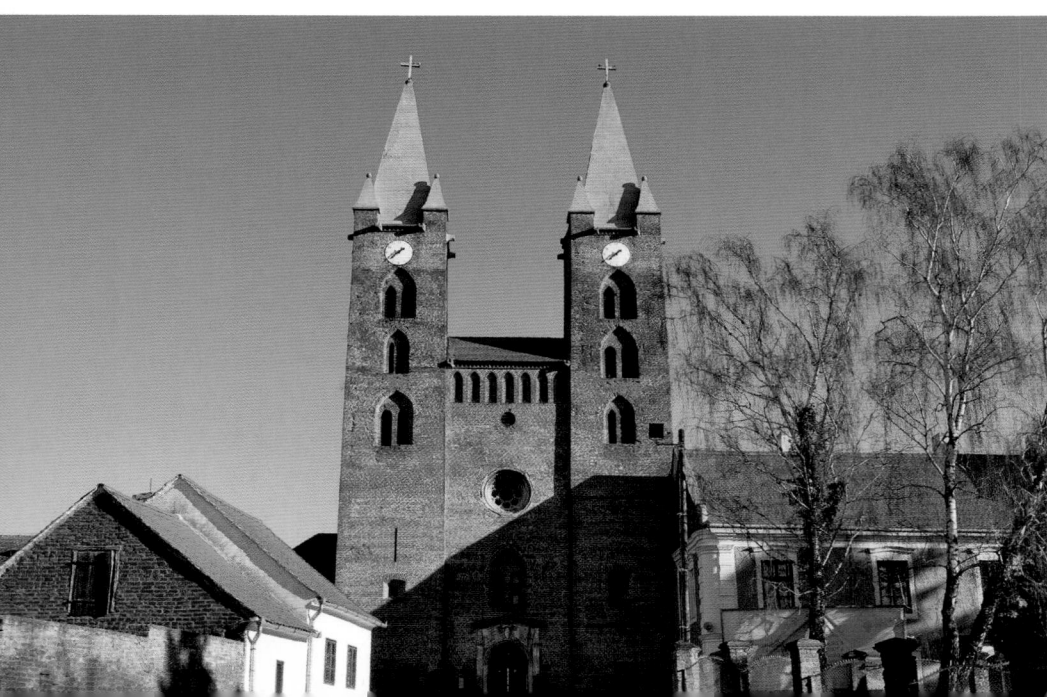

consequences – originated in Zalavár, a sleepy little place today.

More lively is the modern bathing facility at the Zalakaros spa. The waters are said to be very good for you – despite the powerful smell of sulphur.

THE SOUTHERN SHORE

The landscape of the southern shore is generally flat and the cultural sites are not as diverse as on the northern shore, but it does have its advantages. The northeast winds blowing down from the Bakony hills stir up the shallow water, and the waves wash sand and silt to the shore, creating long sandbanks which are a delight for children.

A string of bathing resorts has developed behind the sandbanks. Between Siófok and Balatonberény (a stretch of some 65km/40 miles), one resort practically runs into the next. In recent years, any open spaces that remained between the old farming and fishing villages, with their attractive villas and summer houses, have been developed.

Countless eszpressós, ice-cream bars, csárdas (inns) and other tourist haunts fill the streets. The atmosphere in summer is always lively, to say the least – and completely dead at the end of the season.

The southern shore has one further attraction: in clear weather, it offers a splendid view of the bizarrely shaped hills and basalt cliffs of the north shore, evidence of the region's volcanic origins.

TRADITION LIVES ON

Apart from its beach, **Balatonberény** has a notable 15th-century village church, and in the surrounding villages there are still some pretty, traditional farmhouses with thatched roofs and pillared verandahs. Take a look, for instance, at the farmhouse in **Balatonszentgyörgy,** just back from the shoreline, at Csillagvár utca 68. This little house, built in 1836, houses a collection of exhibits illustrating the local way of life in times past. Further along the street, in the grounds of a bird sanctuary, is Csillagvár Castle,

Excavation of the church of the Holy King Stephan in the 11th century in Zalavár.

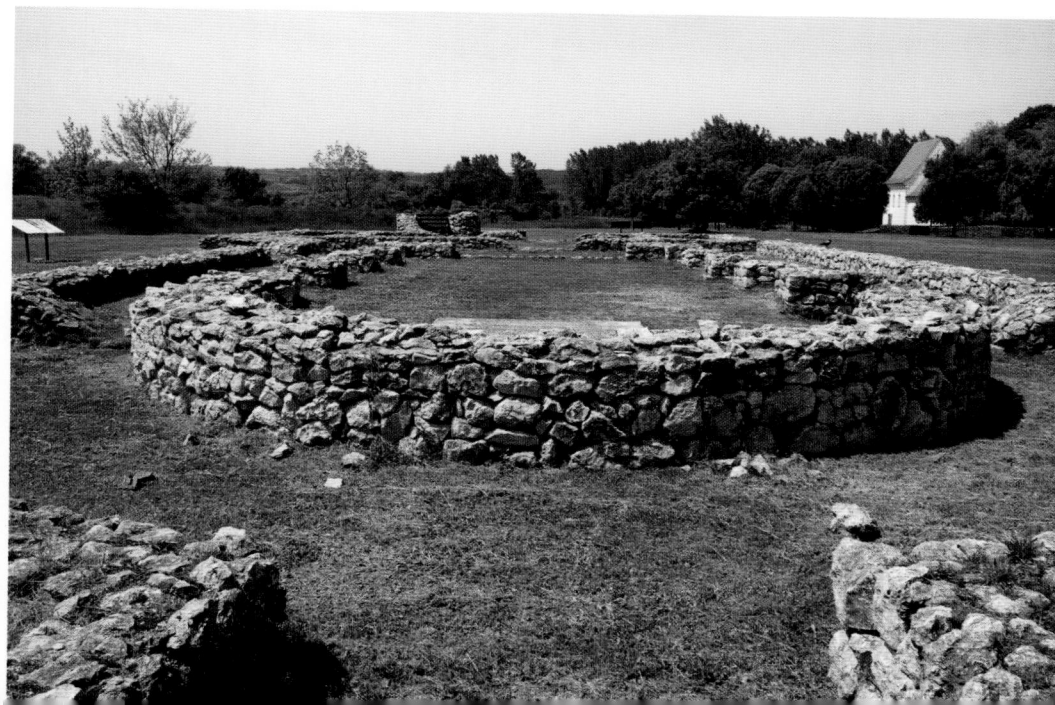

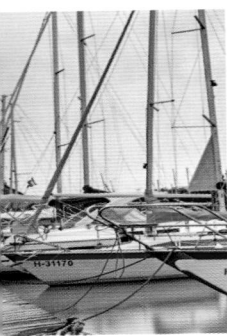

Fonyód harbour.

Fonyód pier.

where the rich local history is well documented.

The 7km (4-mile) stretch between Balatonmáriafürdö and Balatonfenyves (where there is a shady pine wood behind the beach) is a recreation park.

Fonyód ⑯, the town before Balatonboglár, also has its small hill and the old village lies between the two peaks. Fonyód has the second largest harbour on Lake Balaton, with a pier, and the second longest beach (after Siófok, see below).

Balatonboglár ⑰ is one of the oldest resorts on the south shore, with a lookout point over the lake, in the shape of a globe. From the tower on the Várhegy you have a view of the vineyards and orchards.

In the cemetery behind the (surprisingly) Bauhaus-style Catholic church are two 19th-century chapels, one red, the other blue, which are used as exhibition halls. The park in front of the red chapel is often the venue for concerts.

The village of **Buzsák** ⑱, some 20km (12 miles) southwest, is worth visiting if you would like to see people in the traditional costumes that are often worn in the summer. The women of Buzsák are also renowned for their embroidery, while the Village House (Faluház) in the centre of town has an exhibition on the folkloric arts of the region.

The neighbouring village, Szölöskislak, has a wine museum celebrating one of the Balaton's major industries. Balatonlelle's modern, red sandstone Catholic church is the site of occasional concerts. If time allows, make your way up to the sleepy village of Zala, where the aristocratic artist, Count Mihály Zichy, used to live. The big white palace, a simple affair, sits in an imposing park. Zichy painted the altar in the local church; in the small memorial museum, among other items, are some of the erotic miniatures he painted on the covers of pocket watches.

SIÓFOK

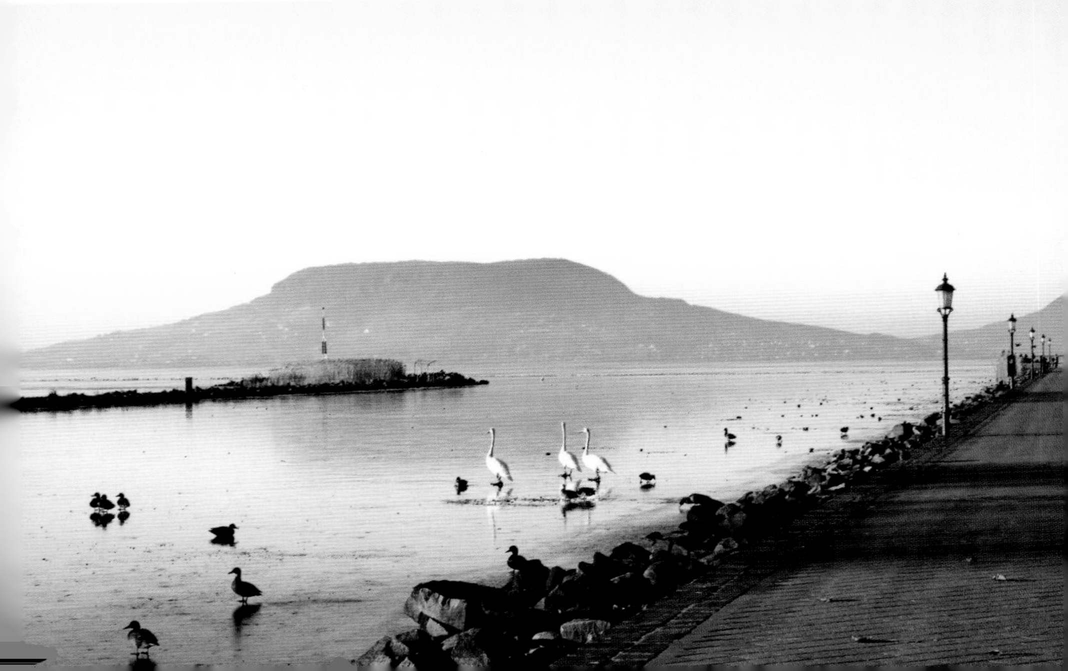

Further east you will reach **Siófok** ⑲, the largest, and brashest, town on the southern shore. It also has the longest stretch of beach on Lake Balaton, which follows the shoreline for 16km (10 miles). This beachfront is divided by the mouth and locks of the Sió canal, which was originally built by the Romans (around AD 290) and connects with the Danube away to the southeast. Right beside the locks is the Nagy Strand beach. The stretch to the east of it is called the Arany-part (Gold Beach), while the western section is known as Ezüst-part (Silver Beach). You have to pay a small charge to use some sections of Gold and Silver beaches, but Nagy Strand, lined with bars and cafés, is free.

The large and often unattractive hotels that line the lakeshore (most of them in the Gold Beach area – Silver Beach is somewhat less developed) should not deter anyone from visiting the town or enjoying the waters. The promenades have improved enormously in recent years and there are boats and bikes to hire and plenty of things to do.

Siófok was an elegant resort in the 19th century, made accessible by the coming of the railways. There are a few surprises to be found in the town, such as the eccentric Evangelical Church in Oulu Park, designed by Imre Makovecz in his typical 'Magyarist' style. There is also a memorial to the steamboats that once plied the waters of the lake. The 45-metre (144ft) water tower on Szabagság tér, constructed in 1912, has become the town's symbol and trademark.

A FAMOUS SON

Imre Kálmán, who was born in Siófok, in 1882, became famous as a master of light entertainment in the golden age of operetta. The house where he was born no longer exists, but on the site, in Kálmán Imre sétány 5 (just east of the canal locks), the **Imre Kálmán Museum** (Tue–Fri 10am–5pm, Sat 9am–1.30pm) is devoted to him. It contains exhibits on the life and work of the creator of such popular Hungarian standards as *Countess Mariza* and the *Csárdás Princess*, and there is a statue of him by Imre Varga.

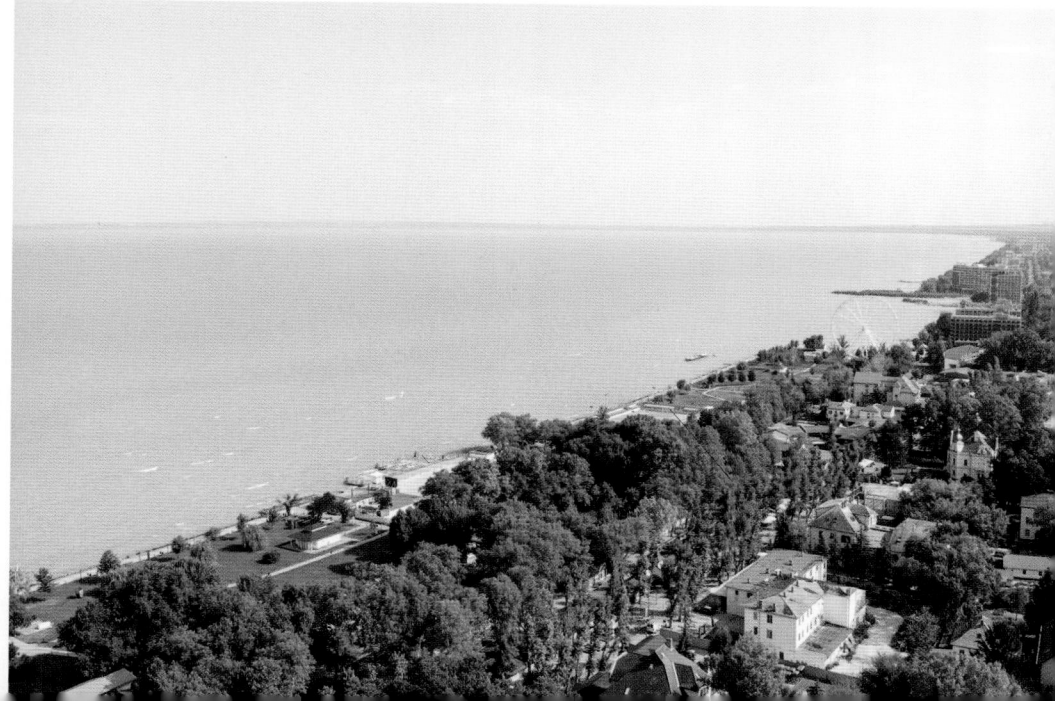

Siófok.

The Unesco-protected village of Hollókő.

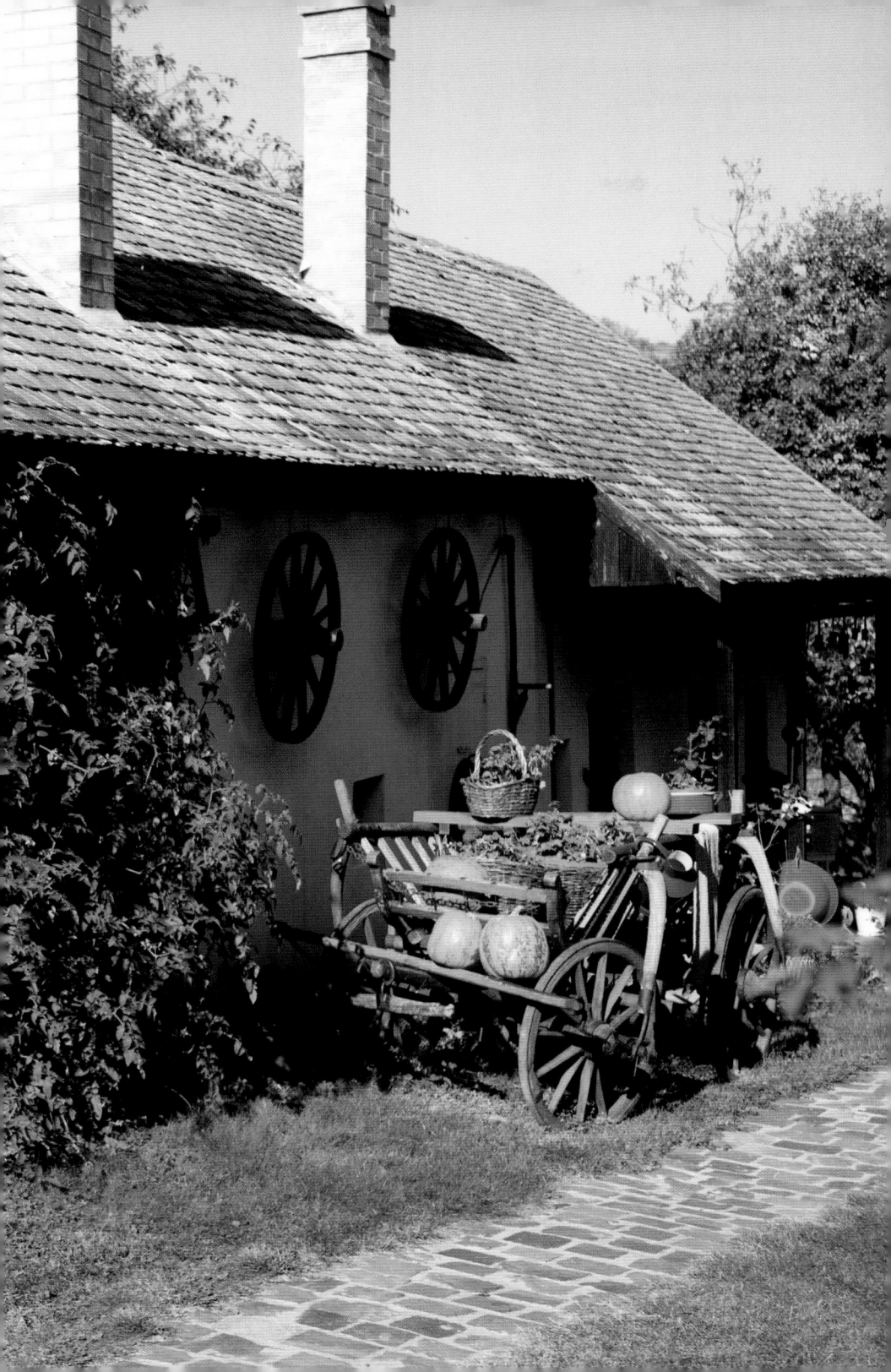

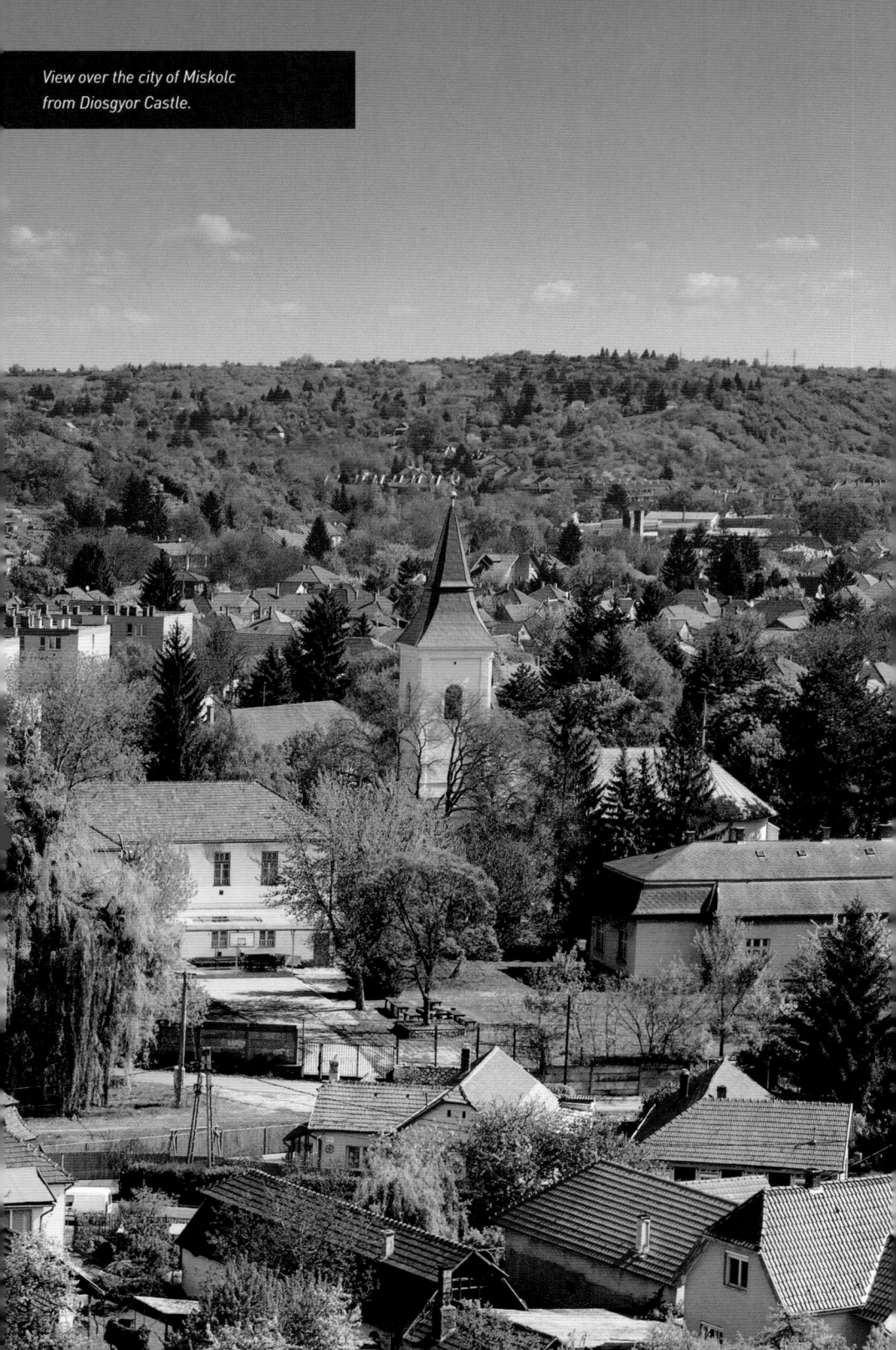

View over the city of Miskolc from Diosgyor Castle.

NORTHEAST HUNGARY

Mountain walks, cave tours, Baroque palaces and villages where traditional ways of life are preserved are just a few of the delights to be discovered in this relatively unexplored region.

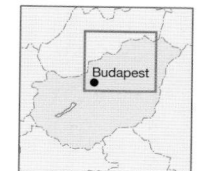

The wooded hills and fertile valleys of the northeast provide a popular escape from the hot summers of the plain. Yet they are not well known to foreign tourists, possibly because many people perceive this part of the country, with its ranges of fairly low mountains, as not 'typically Hungarian'.

In fact, this region has delightful scenery and historic towns and castles such as Eger and Sárospatak, as well as natural phenomena such as the stalactite caves of Aggtelek and the geyser of Egerszalok. It also produces the world-famous Tokaj wine.

Vác is a good launch pad for visiting the Börzsöny, the most westerly of the hill ranges radiating from Budapest. The town lies on the left bank of the Danube, 34km (21 miles) to the north of the capital, and is linked to it by the first railway ever built in Hungary.

The towers of Vác's many churches rise above the single-storey Baroque and classical houses on the slope of the Danube's bank. The cathedral on Konstantin tér seems excessively large for the small town, but its severe classical façade is relieved by a round cupola and the six statues on the portico. Inside are frescoes by the great Franz Anton Maulbertsch. The origin of the old saying 'rich as the Bishop of Vác' is clear from the size of the

building and its richly decorated interior (see page 173).

THE BÖRZSÖNY HILLS

Seen from the river promenade of Vác, the **Börzsöny Hills** look impressive, although they barely reach 900 metres (3,000ft). The hills are sparsely settled apart from the villages on the southern slopes facing the Danube, which are frequently visited by tourists and day-trippers from Budapest.

To find out more about the traditions and the history of this isolated region,

Main attractions
Vác
Hollókő
Szécsény
Eger
Diósgyőr
Tokaj

Map on page 220

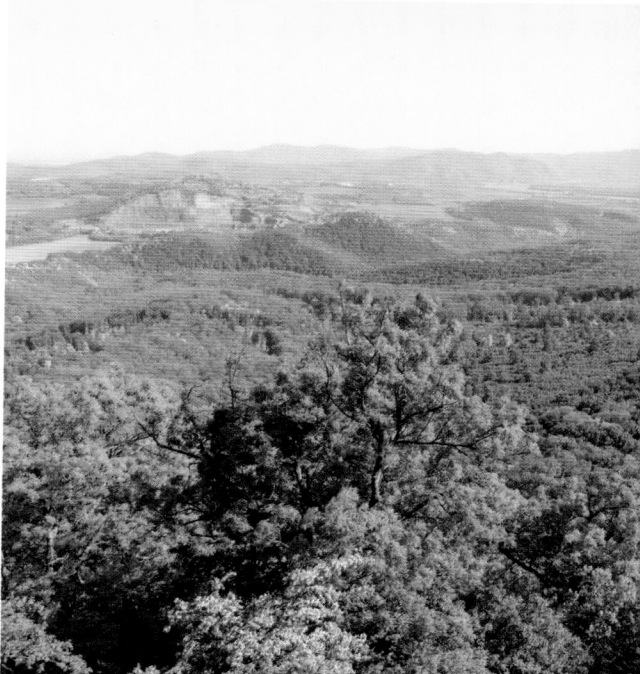

The Börzsöny Hills.

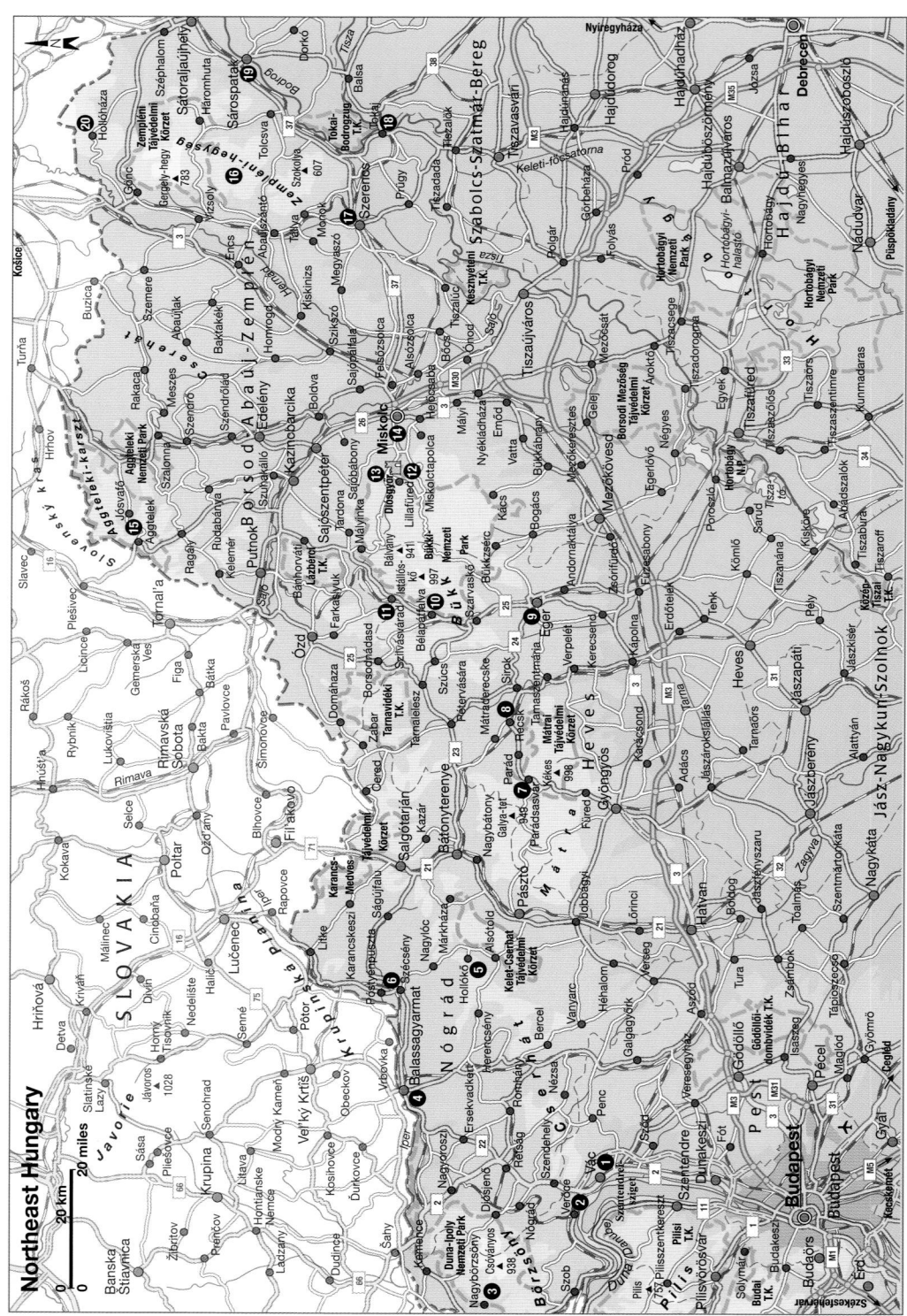

Northeast Hungary

visit the Börzsöny Museum (Tue–Sun 9am–5pm) at Hámán utca in Szob, 30km (19 miles) to the west along the Danube.

Before you arrive, you will come to **Verőce ②**, where there is a **Ceramics Museum** (Gorka Géza Kerámia Múzeum; Mar–Oct Tue–Sun 9am–5pm) devoted to the award-winning artist Géza Gorka (1894–1971), who lived and worked in the house in Királyrét. From here, you can also travel about 10km (6 miles) into the forest on a narrow-gauge railway. From the railway terminus, several paths lead to the surrounding summits.

AROUND NAGYBÖRZSÖNY

In the Middle Ages, **Nagybörzsöny ③** was the centre of a flourishing mining industry, belying its present sleepiness. Gold, copper and iron were dug out of the surrounding hills by Saxon miners, who built their simple, white church in the middle of the town. The water mill on Széchenyi tér, now a national monument to traditional crafts, used to keep Nagybörzsöny well supplied with flour.

At the entrance to town stands St Stephen's Church (Szent István templom), surrounded by a picturesque, defensive stone wall. Built in the 13th century, it is one of the few surviving Romanesque buildings in the country and one well worth an excursion to see.

The Börzsöny range is shared by two counties: Pest in the west and Nógrád in the east. Only a tiny, bumpy road connects the two sides directly, crossing from Kemence to Diósjenő, where on hot summer days locals and visitors enjoy the cooling waters of a little lake, which has a view of the highest peak in the region, the Csóványos.

Nearby is the village of Nógrád, a busy market and military town in the days of King Mátyás I (1458–90). The castle overlooking the area was ruined by lightning striking the arsenal in 1683 while the Turks still held it. That heavenly act spelled the end of Nógrád's greatness, although the county still bears the name.

UNDULATING CSERHÁT

To the east of the Börzsöny range lie the hills of the **Cserhát,** an undulating landscape rising to a mere 652 metres (2,139ft), with valleys that are broad, fertile and densely populated. Inhabitants of this part of Hungary are known as the Palóc (pronounced Palots), who some ethnographers believe to be remnants of a people that came here before the Magyars; others consider them Hungarians with their own customs, influenced by Slovak culture.

The traditional art, both past and present, of this ethnic group is best seen in the **Palóc Museum** (Tue–Sat 9am–5pm; www.palocmuzeum.hu) in Palóc Park in the little town of **Balassagyarmat ④** on the Slovakian border. The collection traces the traditional way of life of the Palóc from cradle to grave, with crafts, customs, routines and rituals.

Traditional costume here is colourful, and the towering headdresses of

⊙ Tip

If you're bored of Baroque, stop in Zebegény for a look at the Art Nouveau parish church. Overlooking the town is a modest memorial to the Trianon Treaty that divested Hungary of two-thirds of its territory in 1920.

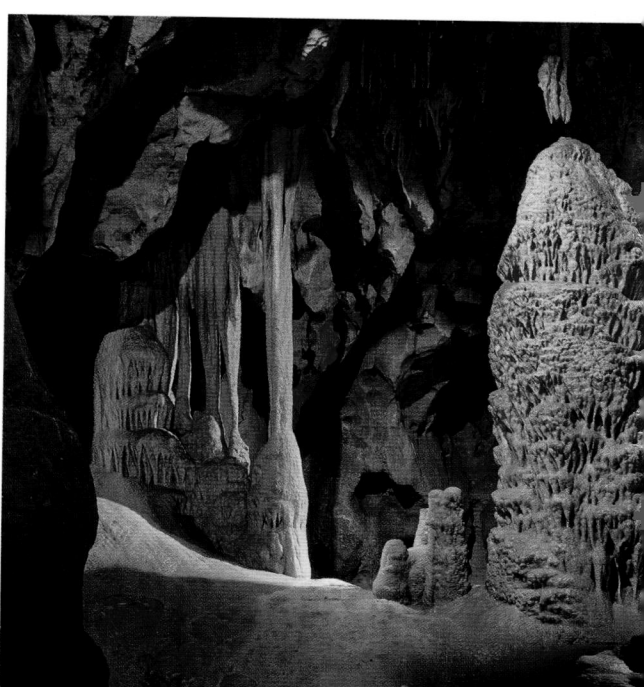

Baradla cave.

⊙ Tip

On the hills above Hollókő are the remains of a 13th-century castle (daily 10am–6pm; free), with wonderful views over the area.

the girls are often decorated with glittering beads. Worth seeing, too, are the 18th-century Palóc houses in the museum garden, spacious, wooden buildings on stone foundations, covered by a densely thatched roof.

THE PALÓC VILLAGE

One complete village of Palóc houses still exists. It is called **Hollókő** ❺ and lies at the foot of a ruined castle some 35km (22 miles) southeast of Balassagyarmat. A Unesco World Heritage Site, the structure of this little village is unchanged since the Middle Ages even though most of the houses were rebuilt after a fire in 1909.

Many of the original residents have sold their houses to incomers from Budapest, and moved to the outskirts. Some of the houses offer simple accommodation to visitors at reasonably low prices while there are also small restaurants with fine, basic fare, and several potters plying their trade. The little church at the fork in the main street has simple interior decor.

One building houses the **Village Museum** (Falumúzeum; daily 10am–4pm, until 6pm mid-Mar–Oct), which is almost as interesting as the one in Balassagyarmat. There's also a **Museum of Dolls** (Babamúzeum; Apr–Nov daily 10am–4pm) wearing the traditional costumes of Nógrád county.

SZÉCSÉNY

Between Balassagyarmat and Hollókő, you pass through **Szécsény** ❻, a pleasant little town with a church rebuilt in Baroque style but retaining a Gothic sacristy. Of the castle, only one corner tower and the wall of a bastion remain, both included in the 18th-century **Forgách Palace** that stands on the same site. In 1705 the Hungarian Diet was held on this spot, and the assembly chose the Transylvanian Ferenc Rákóczi to be the ruling prince. He was to lead them in the desperate and ultimately futile battle against Habsburg domination. The building now houses the **Ferenc Kubinyi Museum** (Tue–Sun 10am–6pm; www.kubinyimuzeum.hu)

Forgách Palace.

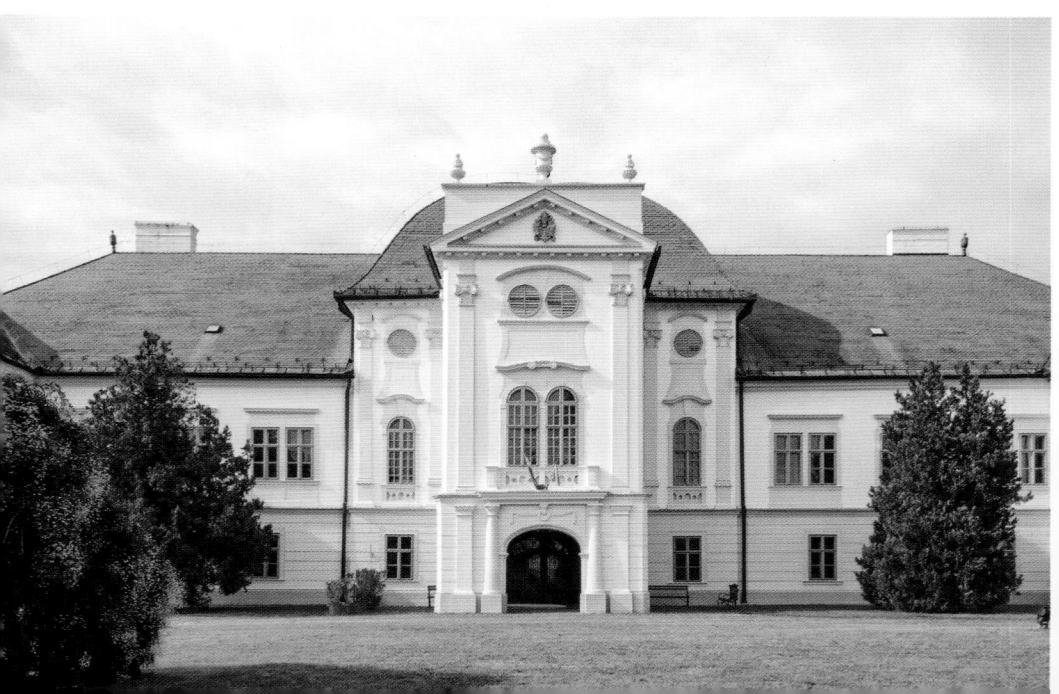

with agricultural, archaeological and hunting exhibits.

SALGÓTARJÁN TO PARÁDSASVÁR

There is little of historical significance about **Salgótarján,** the centre of the Nógrád district. Some 43km/27 miles east of Szécsény in a narrow valley of the Karancs hills, this was a 'model socialist town' of 40,000 inhabitants and an important industrial centre with lignite mines, steelworks, glassworks and high-rise apartments. Much of this history is recalled in the **Mining Museum** (Bányászati Múzeum; Apr–Sept Tue–Sun 8am–4pm) which also has a real mine to visit, and great fun it is too.

To the south of Salgótarján in the Mátra Mountains, is the highest peak in Hungary, the 1,014-metre (3,327ft) high Kékes (Blue Roof), close to the village of Kékestető. From the tower of the Institute of Telecommunications on the peak you have extensive views, including a good portion of Hungary's Great Plain.

Highway 24, which connects Gyöngyös to Eger runs through some of the more important sights of the Mátra range. The grand old Károly dynasty ruled the area for centuries, its most prominent member being Mihály Károly, who headed Hungary's short-lived republic in 1919.

In **Parádsasvár** ❼ the eclectic and playful Károly Castle, designed by Miklós Ybl in the late 19th century, has been turned into a luxurious hotel – the Sasvár. At the end of the town (Rákóczi utca 46) is a glassworks that produces Parád crystal. The factory has a shop and a free gallery displaying artistic glass objects, and in the little house opposite you can visit the small glass museum, see a crystal cutter at work, enjoy refreshments, and purchase souvenirs.

In Parad, close by, the Károlys' former stables have been turned into a delightful **Coach Museum** (Koc-simúzeum; Apr–Oct daily 9am–5pm, Nov–Mar Tue–Sun 10am–4pm), with a number of interesting exhibits covering various types of coaches, from

Waterfall in the Bükk Mountains.

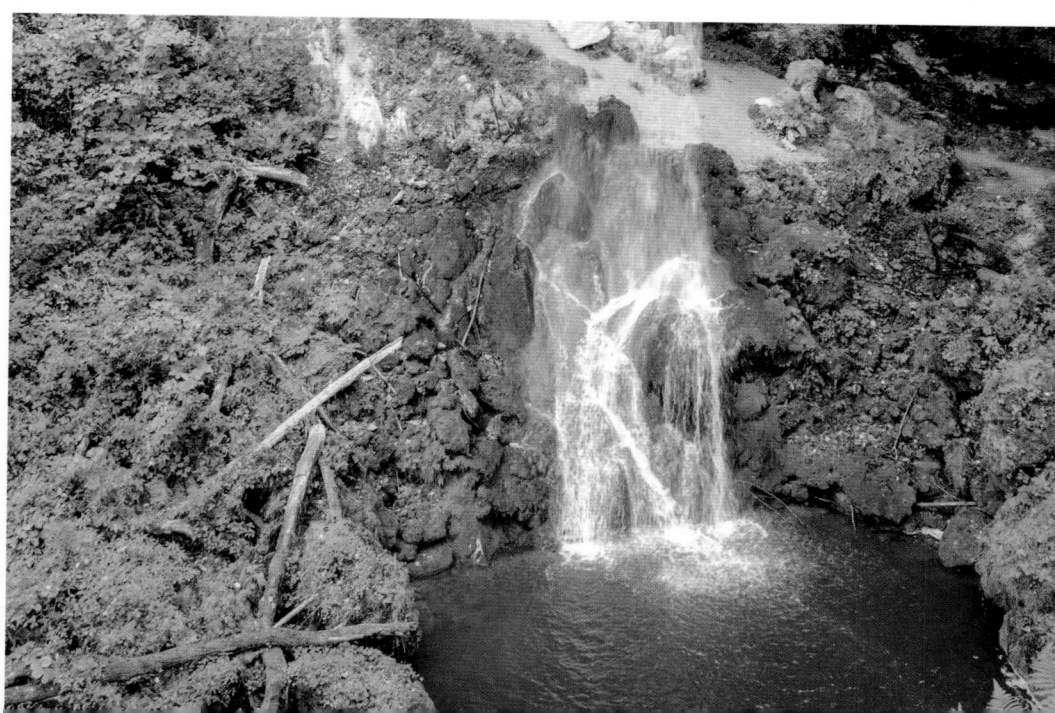

the noble to the popular. There is also a little Palóc house on Sziget utca that brings to life the living conditions of ordinary people years ago.

TRAGIC HISTORY

Highway 24 snakes its way through an alley of horse-chestnut trees, traversing Parádfürdö, where the old bath house was entirely renovated in 2001. The non-descript village of **Recsk** ❽ has an unfortunate reputation: up in the mountains, the Hungarian Stalinists established a labour camp in the nearby stone quarry to re-educate recalcitrant citizens.

In 1953, after Stalin's death, the camp was dissolved and all traces removed. Throughout the communist era, Recsk could not be mentioned, but following the collapse of communism, an organisation of former Recsk prisoners put up a memorial to those who died. The view over the Mátra is wonderful, further underlining the tragedy of the place.

More upbeat is Mátraderecske, a village which holds a parade, with participants in folk costumes, on the last Saturday in June. Besides the soothing waters of its spa, it offers the Mofetta, a unique dry bath of carbon dioxide that issues naturally from the ground and is used to alleviate skin ailments, neuralgia and arterial and joint complaints.

BULL'S BLOOD TOWN

Between the Mátra Mountains and the Bükk range is **Eger** ❾, the most interesting and attractive city in northeast Hungary. It has a turbulent history, varied architecture, and produces a famous red wine: *Egri Bikavér*, Eger Bull's Blood (see box below).

Eger appears in literature, too. The Stars of Eger, by Géza Gárdonyi, which deals with the heroic defence of Eger Castle in 1552 against a superior Turkish force, is one of Hungary's more famous literary efforts (though full of late-romantic pathos). Under the command of captain István Dobó, 2,000 men, bravely supported by their womenfolk, defended the citadel against a Turkish army of nearly 100,000 soldiers.

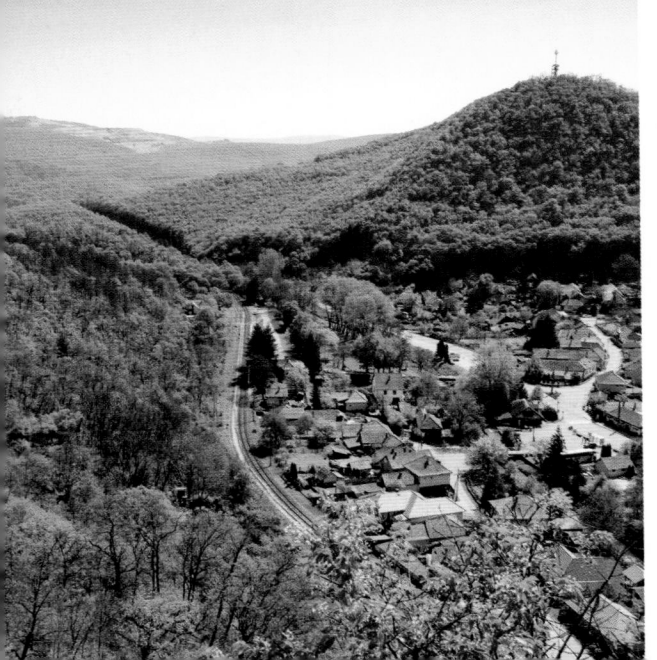

Szarvaskő, a small village near Eger.

⊘ LOCAL WINES

It would be foolish to leave Eger without spending some time in the local wine bars and cellars, located on the outskirts of the city, about 2km/1.5 miles southwest of the cathedral. Here, private vintners will pour you generous measures of local Riesling, muscatel, a dessert wine called Leányka, and the local specialty, Eger Bull's Blood, known locally as Egri Bikavér.

The origins of the name of Eger's famous wine date back to the 16th century. It is said that 2,000 Hungarians, under the command of István Dobó and under the influence of the local wine, fought off a much larger Turkish force at Eger. After their unlikely victory, rumours began to spread that the wine had been mixed with bull's blood to give the soldiers courage and strength.

The Turks captured the town in 1596 and stayed for 91 years, leaving behind a 40-metre (131ft) minaret, the most northerly in the former Ottoman Empire. A climb to the top offers a fabulous view of the town and surrounds. There is also a bastion of the castle and the walls of Pasha Arnaut's baths, which have been incorporated into the modern spa facilities on Fürdő utca.

The castle courtyard contains the restored Bishop's Palace with a Gothic arcade on the ground floor. Inside, the **István Dobó Museum** (museum Tue–Sun 8am–6pm; castle 8am–8pm in summer) has reminders of the castle's defenders, among them the tombstone of István Dobó, whose statue stands in Heroes' Hall. Eger was one of 10 bishoprics founded by King Stephen at the beginning of the 11th century, and the museum also contains a revised version of the founding charter of the bishopric, dating from the 13th century.

Of the former diocesan church, the three-aisled 12th-century Romanesque St John's Cathedral, only stumps remain. The castle yard is used for performances of medieval games and dances.

BAROQUE CENTRE

The true centre of the town is István Dobó tér at the foot of the castle, dominated by the beautiful Baroque **Minorite Church.** Its main façade, with a pair of pillars flanking a curved central section and a curved gable, together with twin towers reaching towards the heavens, displays an extraordinary harmony, which is reflected in the interior. The painting above the high altar is the work of the Bohemian painter, Johann Lukas Kracker.

Dobó tér was the medieval market square. The square's peaceful lines and regular tiling are enlivened by two statues; one (by Alajos

Stróbl) nearer the fort depicts Dobó and the men and women of Eger in allegory; the other (by Zsigmon Kisfaludy Strobl) shows a Hungarian and a Turkish rider locked in battle.

Dobó tér and the surrounding streets are closed to traffic, which makes them ideal for strolling, window shopping or stopping at one of the numerous cafés and restaurants.

Apart from the huge, neoclassical Cathedral on Esterházy tér, designed in the 1830s by József Hild, Eger is predominantly Baroque. The **Archbishop's Palace** (Éseki palota; Apr–Sept Tue–Sun 10am–6pm, Oct–Mar Tue–Sat 10am–4pm; free) nearby is a U-shaped Baroque building with an interesting collection of ecclesiastical items on display in its museum.

The **Lyceum** (Mar–Dec, Tue–Fri 9.30am–12.30pm; Sat–Sun 9.30am–noon), now a teachers' training college, is a square complex of buildings, built between 1765 and 1785 by Jakob Fellner, the great master of the late Baroque. Art historians consider it the most

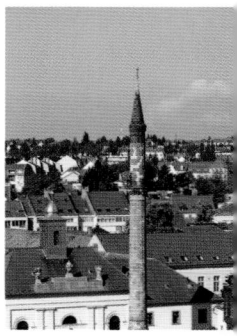

Turkish minaret, Eger.

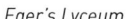

Eger's Lyceum.

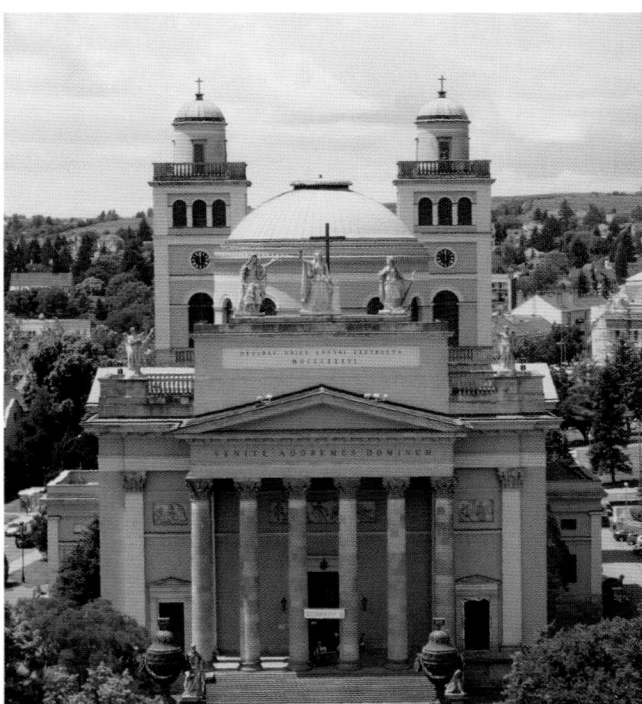

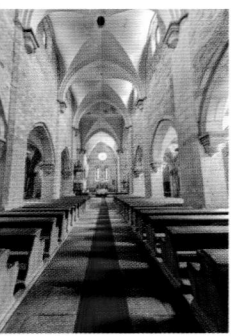

Cistercian abbey at Bélapátfalva.

Beech forest.

important mid-18th-century building in Hungary.

The size of the place is impressive, but the showpiece is the library, with the lively ceiling fresco by Johann Lukas Kracker. It depicts the Counter-Reformation Council of Trent with 132 figures, including Emperor Charles V, and a bolt of lightning striking heretical books. The ceiling in the north wing of the former chapel has a fresco by Franz Anton Maulbertsch.

In Kossuth Lajos utca the Grand Prior's House (now the district library) at No. 16, the offices (No. 9) and the Lesser Prior's House (No. 4) are worth mentioning, for their design and for their magnificent wrought iron gates and balconies.

THE BUKK MOUNTAINS

At **Bélapátfalva** ⑩ is the sole surviving monastery church in Hungary (Ciszteri apátság; Tue–Sun 9am–4pm). Surrounded by lime and chestnut trees, it lies wholly isolated on the western fringe of the Bükk range. French Cistercian monks began the

building in 1232; its main façade, with its Romanesque portal, dates from this period, as do the stocky pillars that divide the three aisles, the vault and the rose window.

Szilvásvárad ⑪ is a popular centre for excursions into the Szalajka Valley. Among its attractions is the **Lipizzaner Stud** (Lipicai Ménes; Tue–Sun 8.30am–noon, 2–4pm) where the horses bred for the Spanish Riding School in Vienna can be seen. There is also the **Lipizzaner Museum** (Lovas Múzeum; Tue–Sun 8.30am–3pm, until 5.30pm May–Sept), which illustrates the history of these splendid creatures.

The beautiful Szalajka valley lies to the east of Szilvásvárad and can be accessed on the popular **Szalajka Forest Railway** (Apr–Oct; regular departures daily). The line winds its way through beech and alder woods, past the trout ponds and the szikla-forrás spring before arriving at the beautiful grassy glade at Fatyolvizesés. Get off the train here and walk back down to Szilvásvárad on forest

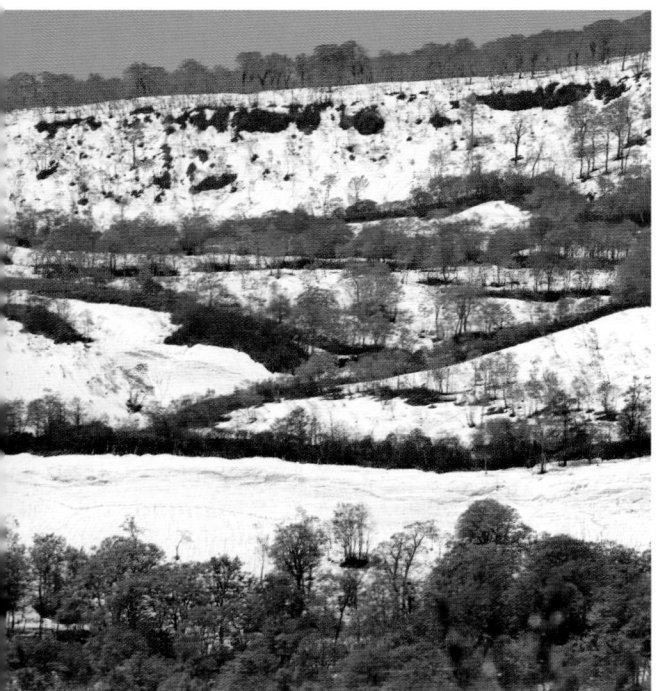

Ⓒ KOSSUTH'S BIRTHPLACE

Another great Hungarian rebel came from this area: Lajos Kossuth (1802–94), the leader of the 1848–49 revolution against the Habsburgs. He was born in the village of Monok, 13km (8 miles) north of Szerencs and his birthplace is now a small museum (June–Aug Tue–Sun 10am–6pm, Mar–May & Sept–Oct Tue–Sun 9am–5pm). Kossuth was the eldest of four children, and part of a noble Lutheran family that was of partial Slovak origin. The tri-lingual Kossuth went on to become a solicitor and then later, a successful politician, known for his rousing and excellent speeches.

Politician Miklós Nemeth, who steered the nation through the transition from communism at the end of the 1980s, was also born in Monok.

paths, pausing at the open-air forest museum en route.

The scenery can also be appreciated along the narrow road from Szilvásvárad to Lillafüred and Miskolc, which twists and turns uphill to the high plateau of the range. The landscape is stern and lonely, made up of meadows and dense beech and oak forests (bükk = beech), juniper bushes and limestone rock, with no trace of human habitation.

Lillafüred ⑫, on the eastern side of the range, is a popular resort dominated by the grand Hotel Palota. Lying in a large park bordered by thick forest, it functioned as a trade union hostel in communist times but is now one of the country's classiest hotels. There are three stalactite **caves** that can be visited (Apr–Oct daily 9am–5pm, until 4pm).

Nearby is Lake Hámori, where you can row on the waters and walk the many footpaths around its perimeter. On the right bank of the lake is a strange building, resembling three piled up limestone cubes. This is the original ironworks (Öskohó) of Ujmassa, the core of the Lenin Metalworks, which turned Miskolc (see below) into the centre of Hungary's most important industrial region.

NEGLECTED CASTLE

On the way to Miskolc, you pass **Diósgyőr** ⑬, where the four massive corner towers of the castle, **Diósgyőri vár** (Apr–Oct Tue–Sun 9am–6pm, July & Aug until 8pm, Nov–Mar 9am–4pm), are almost hidden behind high-rise apartment blocks. This was one of the castles built by King Béla IV after the Mongol invasion of 1241. Successive Hungarian kings used the castle as a kind of pied-à-terre but during the Turkish occupation it became a fortified border post once more. As the Turkish threat faded, tensions between Austrians and Hungarians intensified. Diósgyör stood near the dividing line

between Habsburg Hungary and Transylvania (under Count Thököly and his Kuruz armies) and the emperor finally had it 'and all the people in the immediate surroundings' destroyed.

The ruins were neglected for over 200 years. In the 1930s excavations began, were interrupted by war, then resumed in the 1950s. Too much had been plundered and destroyed to warrant restoring Diósgyőr to its former glory but the huge crenellated towers and walls are testament to its dramatic story.

THIRD CITY

The industrial town of **Miskolc** ⑭ (population 210,000), Hungary's third city, has few interesting sights. The oldest building is the **Avas Calvinist Church** on the slopes of Avas hill, a Gothic building dating from the 13th century which has a more recent coffered wooden ceiling and a free-standing bell-tower with a wooden Renaissance gallery.

Miskolc used to have a large Greek community, hence the Baroque

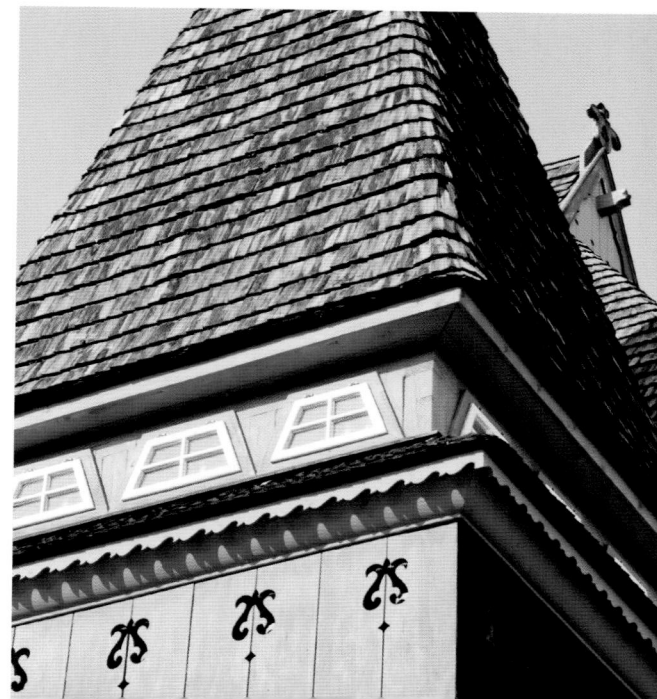

Avas Calvinist Church, Miskolc.

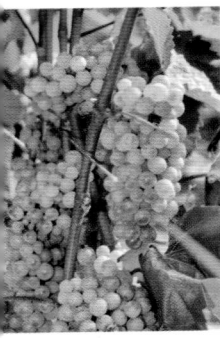

Hegyalja grapes.

Vineyard in Tokaj.

Orthodox Church and Ecclesiastical Museum (Tue–Sat 10am–4pm, until 6pm May–Sept).

The springs of Miskolctapolca (7km/4 miles from the centre) are radioactive and maintain a temperature of 29–31°C (84–88°F). Hot springs also supply a cave-basin, which is the second largest in Europe after Badgastein.

UNDERGROUND LABYRINTH

The industrial areas of Kazincbarcika and Ózd are not particularly appealing to tourists, but the limestone caves in the *karst* of **Aggtelek-Jósvafő 15** 55km (35 miles) northwest of Miskolc near the Hungary–Slovakia border are a great attraction. Their underground passages are among the most complex structures of limestone caves in Europe, and stretch for 22km (14 miles) well into Slovakia.

The biggest cave on Hungarian territory is **Baradla Cave** (daily 8am–3pm, until 5pm Apr–Sept); it is connected to the Domica Cave across the border. Baradla Cave contains the biggest stalagmite in the world – 25 metres (82ft)

high, known as the Observatory. Concerts are held in the caves during the summer months.

THE ZEMPLÉN RANGE

The Aggtelek range and the hills of Cserehát (where Hungary's biggest artificial lake, Lake Rakaca, lies) together form a bridge to the **Zemplénihegység 16** (Zemplén Hills), the last link in the chain of the northeast ranges. The Cserehát and Zemplén ranges are divided by the Hernád River. In the extreme north the hills reach the modest height of 894 metres (2,933ft), while, along their southern and southeastern slopes lies the vine-growing region of **Hegyalja,** where the grapes for Tokaj wines are cultivated.

On your way from Miskolc to Tokaj, you will pass through **Szerencs 17**, a small, rather uninteresting town. That said, it had a key role in the history of Hungary during the period when the people frequently rebelled against the Habsburgs.

At the end of the 16th century, Szerencs castle fell to Zsigmond Rákóczi, a political ally of István Bocskai, who led a revolt against the Habsburg emperor in 1604. In Szerencs both Bocskai and Rákóczi were elected as princes of Transylvania, and Rákóczi was buried here – his red marble sarcophagus is in the Calvinist church. Szerencs is a centre of chocolate production, with a small **Chocolate Museum** (Sat–Sun 9am–1pm).

WINE, WINE, WINE

Táliya, 8km (5 miles) to the east of Monok, competed from time to time with Tokaj to give the regional wine its name, but Tokaj finally won. Over a side altar in the Catholic parish church is a painting (by Franz Anton Maulbertsch) which is especially appropriate to the spirit of the place: the wine harvest of St Wendelin, where even God's angels are helping the saint.

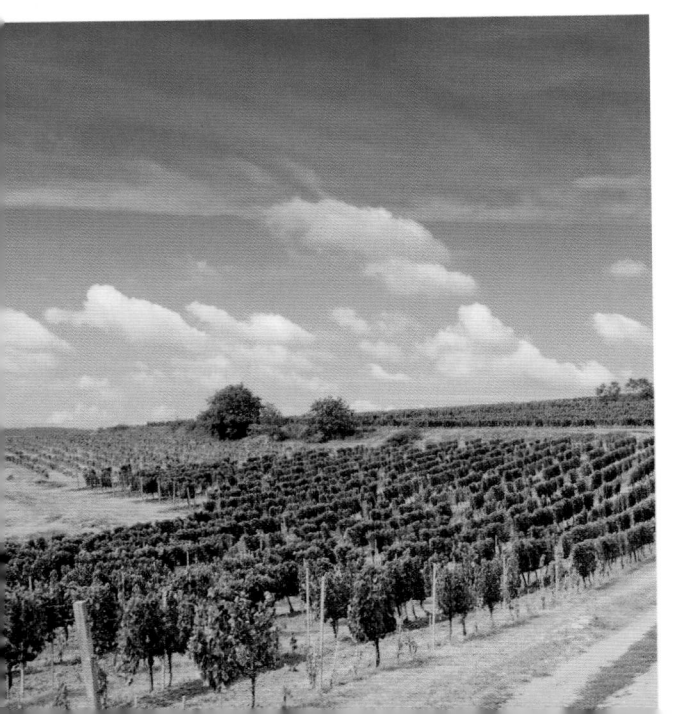

Tokaj ⑱ lies at the end of a hill of loess, pushed out by the Zemplén Hills like a peninsula into the Great Hungarian Plain. However, Tokaj wine doesn't come just from the vineyards close to town, but from the entire wine-growing region of Tokaj-Hegyalja, which covers an area of some 5,000 hectares (12,350 acres).

French and Italian vintners settled here in the Middle Ages, though it is said that even the Celts had vineyards here. Tokaj wine was described on Louis XIV's wine list as the 'wine of kings and king of wines' (some marketing clichés never change). It is served in Auerbach's tavern in Goethe's tale of Faust; Schubert sang its praises, as did Voltaire and Beethoven.

RENAISSANCE LANDMARK

Some 45km (28 miles) to the northeast of Tokaj lie a noteworthy town – **Sárospatak** ⑲. **Rákóczi Castle** (Rákóczi vár; Tue–Sun 10am–6pm) is considered to be the best-preserved Renaissance castle in the country. In 1616 it fell into the hands of the house of Rákóczi, from which several princes of Transylvania were chosen, up to the time of Ferenc Rákóczi II, who led the War of Independence against the Habsburgs from 1703 to 1711.

The castle museum traces its history. The oldest part of the building is the Red Tower, a massive, five-storey structure, dominating the site on the steep bank above the Bodrog River.

The **Protestant College** (Református Kollégium; Mon–Sat 9am–5pm, Sun 9am–1pm), founded here in 1531, was the spiritual centre of Calvinism in Hungary and Transylvania, where young Protestant noblemen received their training. From 1650 to 1655, the great Moravian teacher and humanist, Johann Amos Comenius, whose ideas influenced education and schools until the 20th century, lived and worked here.

The Comenius Exhibition, housed in the single-storey Baroque building in the courtyard, illustrates the history of the college and of student life.

The Library, with a huge collection of works, a wooden gallery and a trompe l'oeil ceiling, is especially worth visiting (guided tours on the hour).

The buildings grouped around the trapeze-shaped courtyard do not blend architecturally, as the wings date from different centuries, but the remaining Renaissance elements are particularly beautiful, especially the stairs and the loggia.

The huge, **Gothic Castle Church** (Vártemplom; Tue–Sat 9am–5pm, Sun noon–4pm) with its Baroque altar and beautiful tombstones is also worth a look.

End your trip through northeastern Hungary with a visit to **Hollóháza** ⑳, 38km (24 miles) northwest of Sárospatak and close to the Slovakian border, where a small **museum** (Apr–Sept Mon 10am–2pm, Tue–Sat 9.30am–4.30pm) relates the history of the town's important porcelain industry.

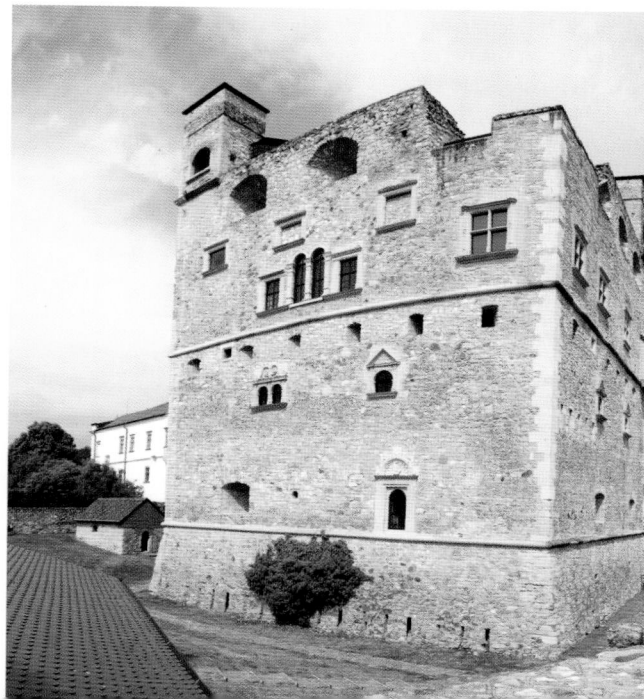

Rákóczi Castle.

📷 LAKE BALATON

Affectionately known as 'Balcsi'
(the 'Hungarian Sea') by millions of
Hungarians, Balaton is the nation's
number-one summer playground.

Balaton is incredibly popular with Austrians and Germans too – indeed the lake can be bursting at the seams come July and August. The largest freshwater lake in Europe – measuring 80km (50 miles) long and anywhere between 1.5km (1 mile) and 14km (9 miles) wide – this is all that remains of the ancient Pannonian Sea that once covered this region. First inhabited during the Iron Age, Balaton later formed the front line between Turkish and Habsburg-ruled Hungary, before the Communists began promoting the lake as a mass holiday destination after World War II, since which time it hasn't looked back.

The lake's low lying southern shore boasts an endless procession of *strand* and a multiplicity of brash resorts, none more so than Siófok, Balaton's undisputed number-one party town (see page 214). Scenery and sightseeing take precedence over on the northern shore, thanks to a sprinkling of picturesque villages like Tihany and Badascony. Meanwhile, the delightful university town of Keszthely, perched at the lake's western fringe, offers plenty of cultural excitement. Venture further inland and you'll encounter vine-filled forest hills, offering superb walks too, one of the world's most famous porcelain manufacturers at Herend, and a superb hilltop fortress at Sümeg.

Benedictine Monastery of Tihany.

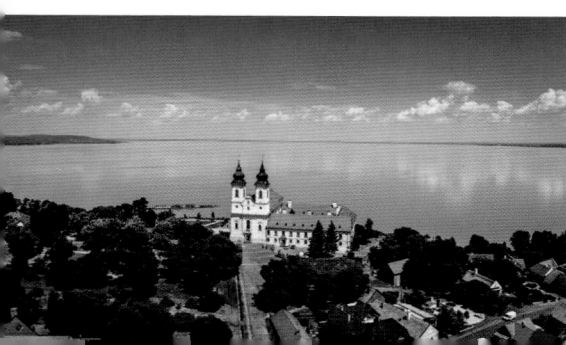

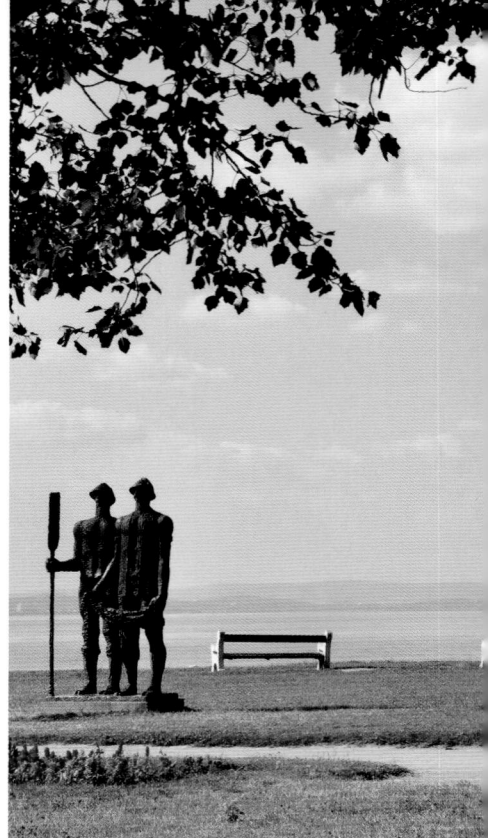

Siófok, Lake Balaton.

Tihany Abbey, and a sailboat, seen from Lake Balaton.

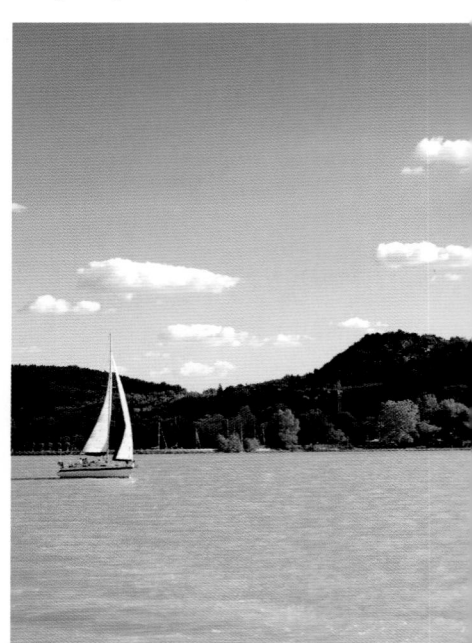

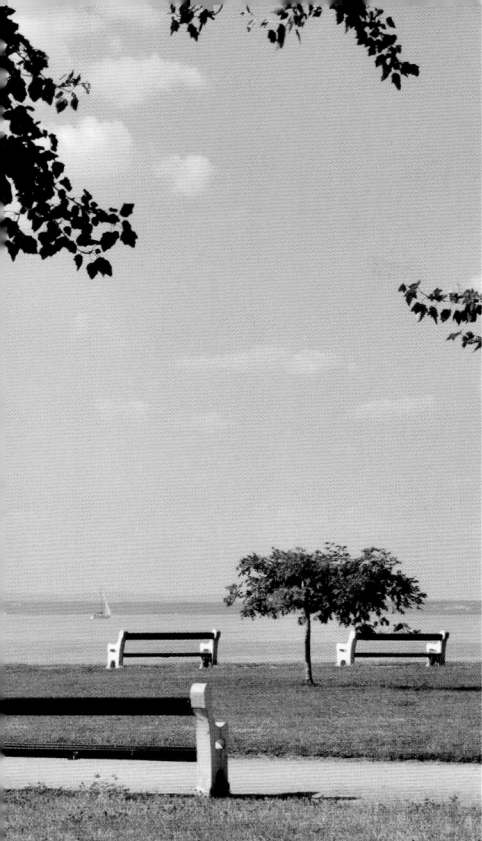

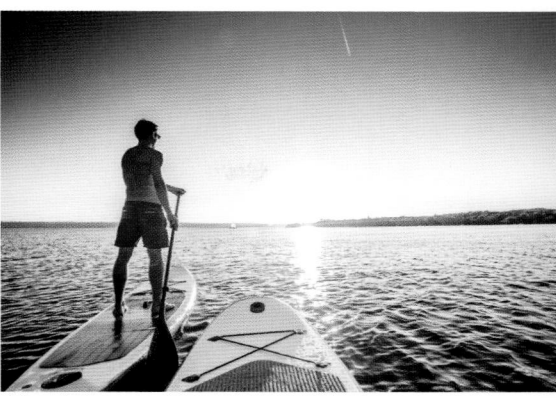

Paddle-boarder on Lake Balaton at sunset.

Lake Balaton activities

Lake Balaton's clean and shallow waters – the average depth is just 3 metres (10ft) – provide ample opportunities for all manner of leisurely pursuits, first and foremost of course, swimming. Indeed one event not to be missed is the annual Cross-Balaton Swim each June, when thousands of hardy souls brave the chilly waters to make the 5.3km (3.3 mile) crossing between Révfülöp on the northern shore and Balatonboglár on the southern shore – the event is open to anyone so feel free to have a crack yourself.

Otherwise, the lake's calm waters make it perfect for stand-up paddle-boarding. That said, the wind can really get up here – indeed, the lake is prone to some ferocious storms – so when it does, it becomes the ideal setting for windsurfing and sailing. Equipment can be hired at many campsites and *strands* along the southern shore, while there are also many schools dotted round the lake if you fancy a lesson. And if you've got the time, energy and inclination, you could always have a go at the 210km-long (130-mile) Balaton cycle path.

Windsurfing on the lake.

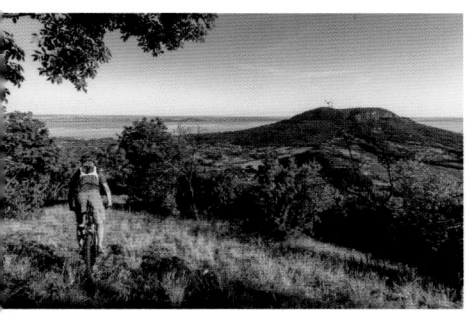

cyclist near the lake.

camping near Lake Balaton.

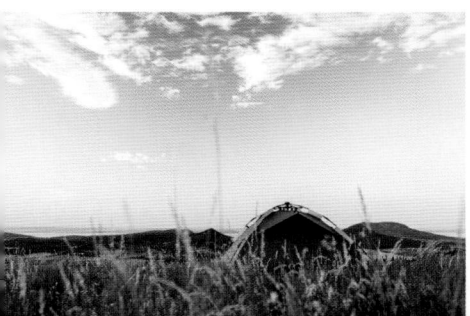

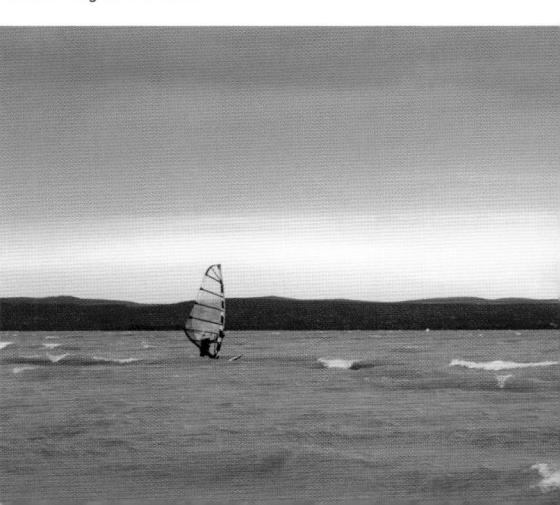

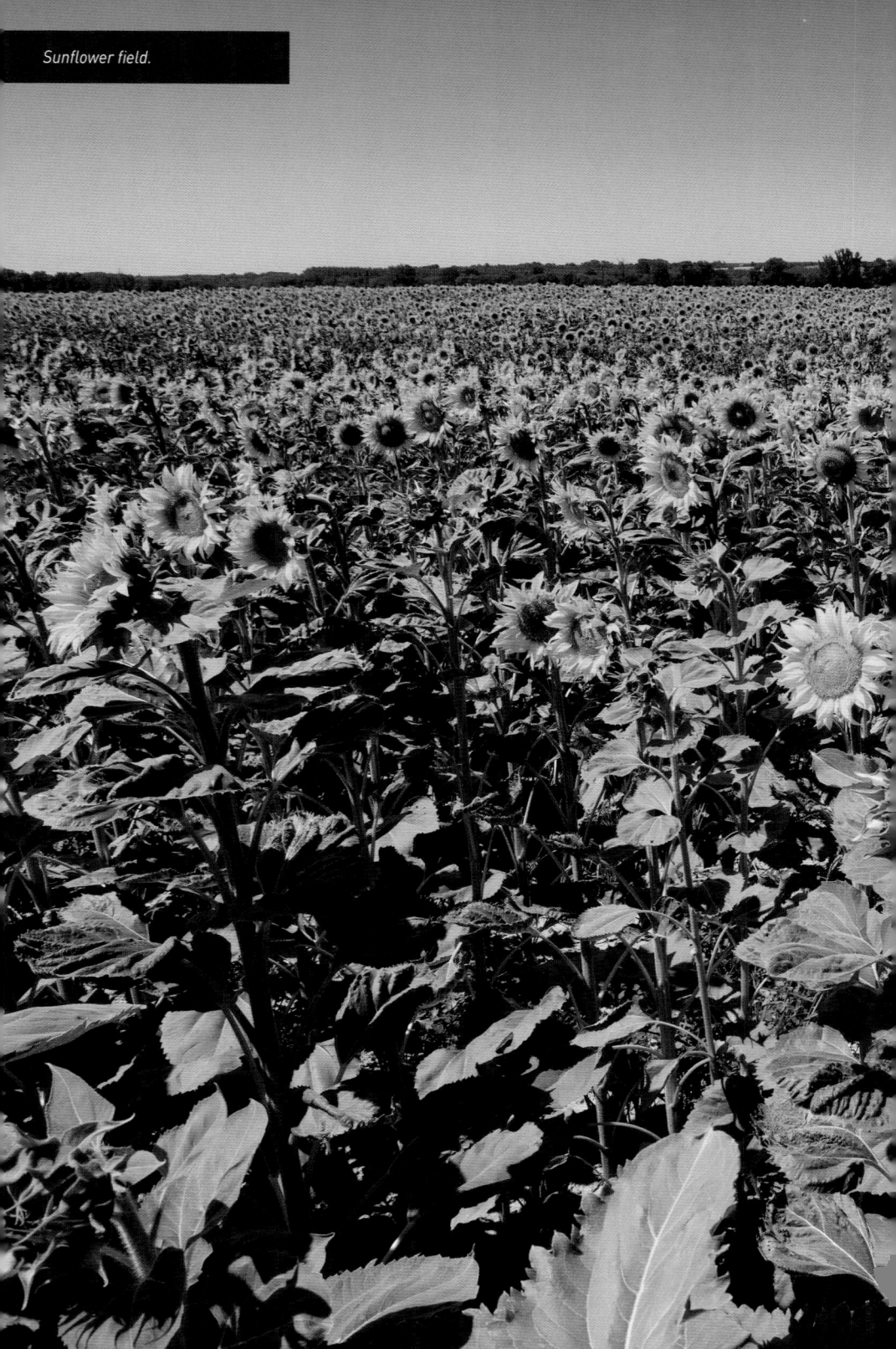

Sunflower field.

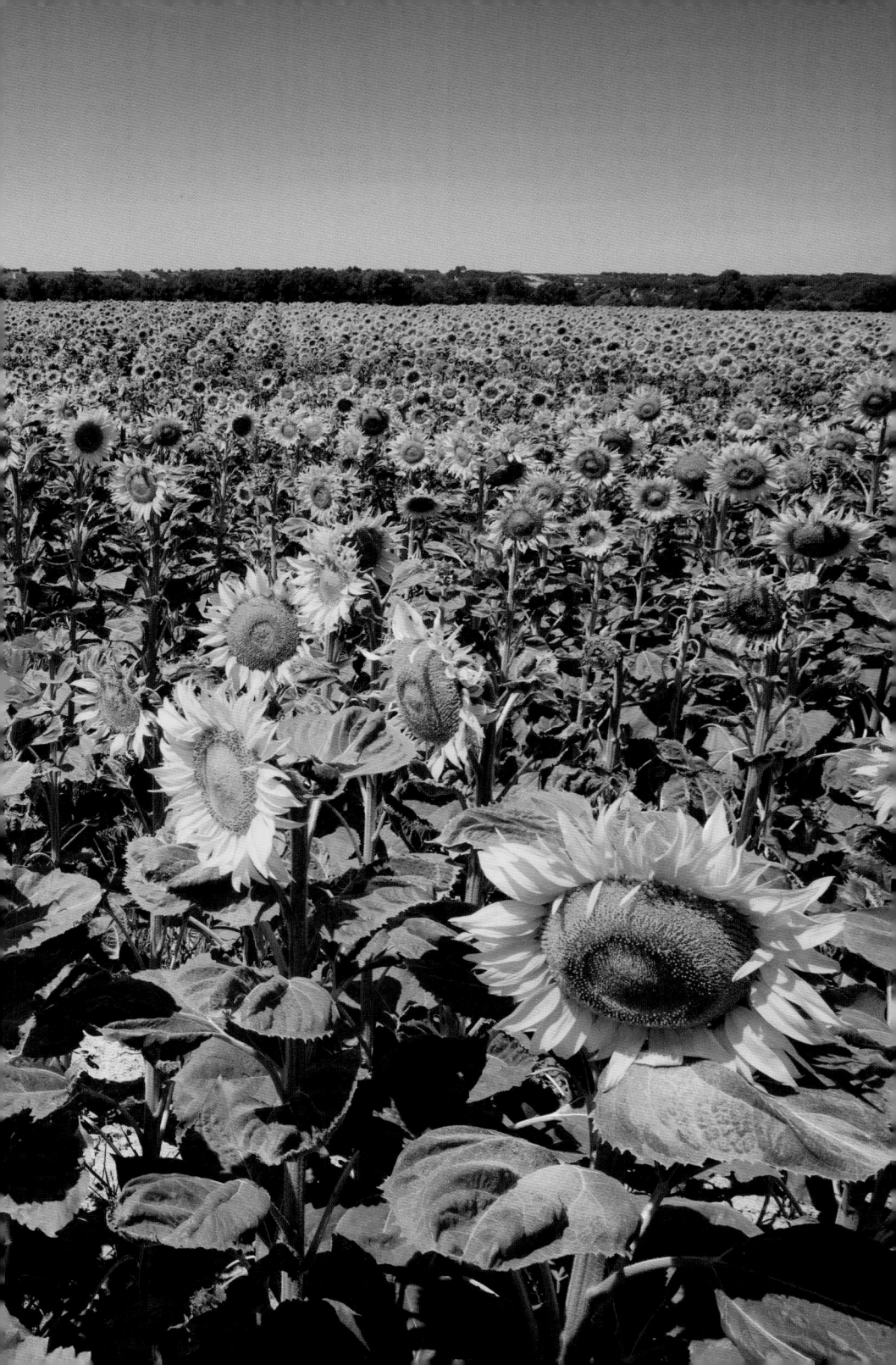

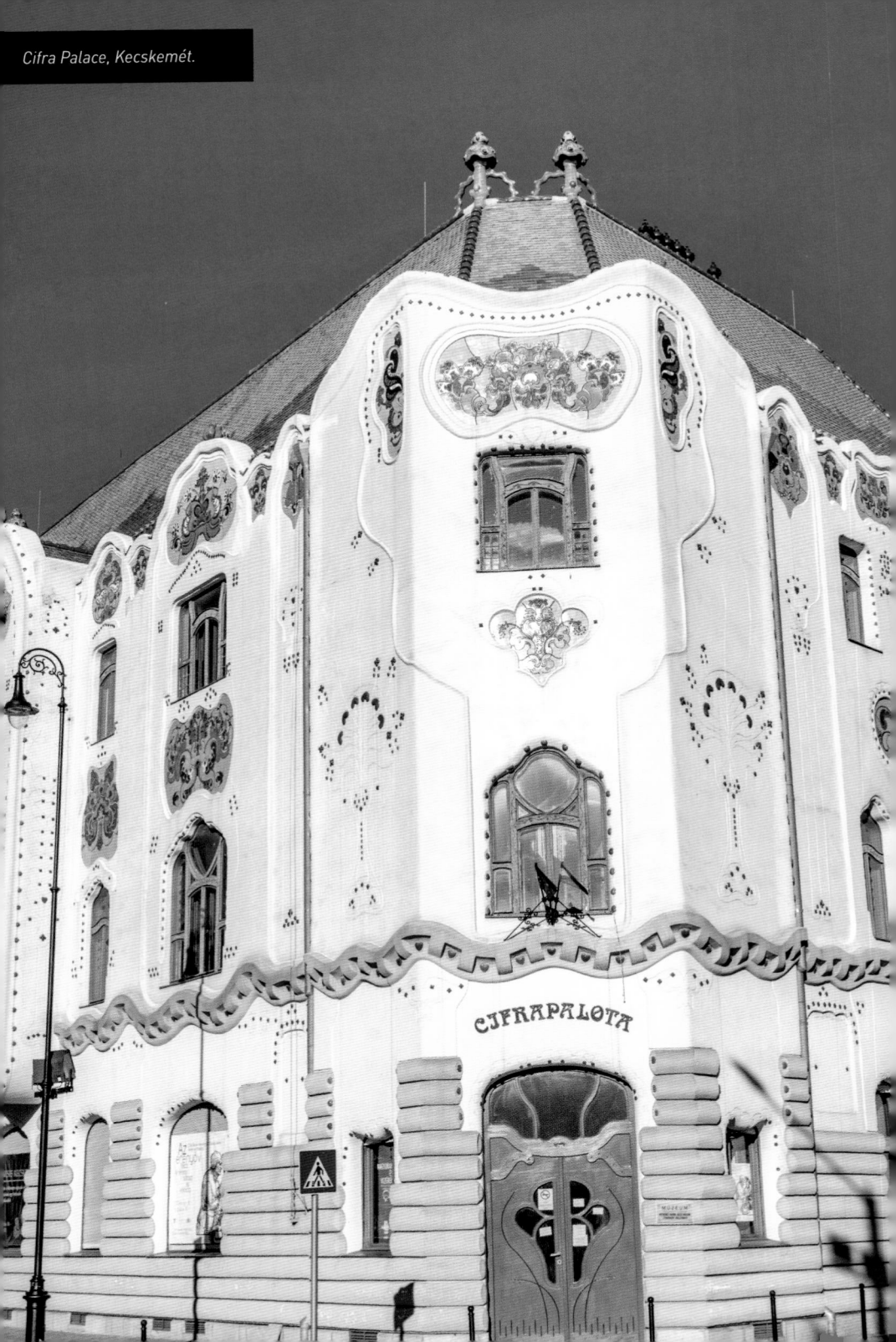

CIFRAPALOTA

THE GREAT PLAIN

The Great Plain sounds like a wild and desolate area but, along with wide-open landscapes, the region also contains two of the most beautiful and culturally interesting towns in Hungary.

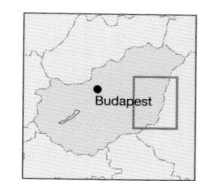

The **Nagyalföld,** the Great Plain, occupies more than half the area of Hungary. Its highest point (182 metres/597ft) lies in the northeast, near Debrecen; the lowest (72 metres/236ft) in the south, near Szeged. The Tisza, the largest tributary of the Danube and the second most important river in Hungary, divides the plain in two as it flows from north to south.

BRAHMS'S FAVOURITE

'The most beautiful town in the world,' said Johannes Brahms of **Kecskemét** ❶, which lies 86km (53 miles) southeast of Budapest. Whilst that may be overstating it a little, this regional capital, between the Danube and the Tisza and with a population of around 110,000, is not an unattractive place. It received its town charter in the 14th century and during the years of Turkish rule was under the Sultan's protection and therefore escaped destruction.

THE CENTRE

Two large squares, Szabadság tér and Kossuth tér, together with the smaller Kálvin tér make up the lively, tree-shaded centre of town, and peddlers use the space to sell anything from books to animal hides. The former synagogue stands where Rákoczi út

Kossuth Square in Kecskemét.

joins Szabadság tér. Built in 1864–71 in a Moorish-Romantic style with a tower and cupola, it now houses a small exhibition devoted to technology and science.

On the other corner of Rákóczi út is one of the most beautiful buildings in town: the **Cifra Palace** (Cifrapalota), adorned with Majolica tiles bearing colourful, stylised flowers, was designed by Géza Márkus, a student of Hungary's great Secessionist architect Ödön Lechner (see below) and is a fine example of Hungarian

---

⊘ **Main attractions**

Kecskemét
Bugac
Ópusztaszer Heritage
  Park
Szeged

◉ **Map on page 236**

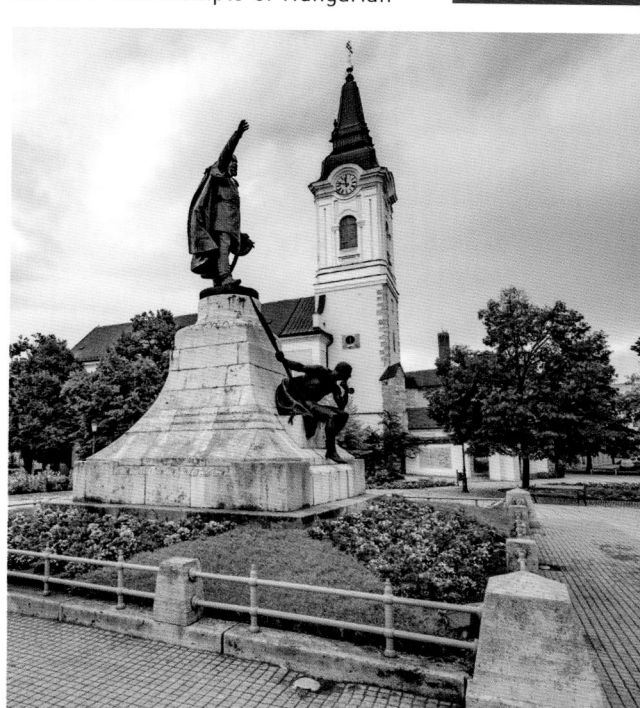

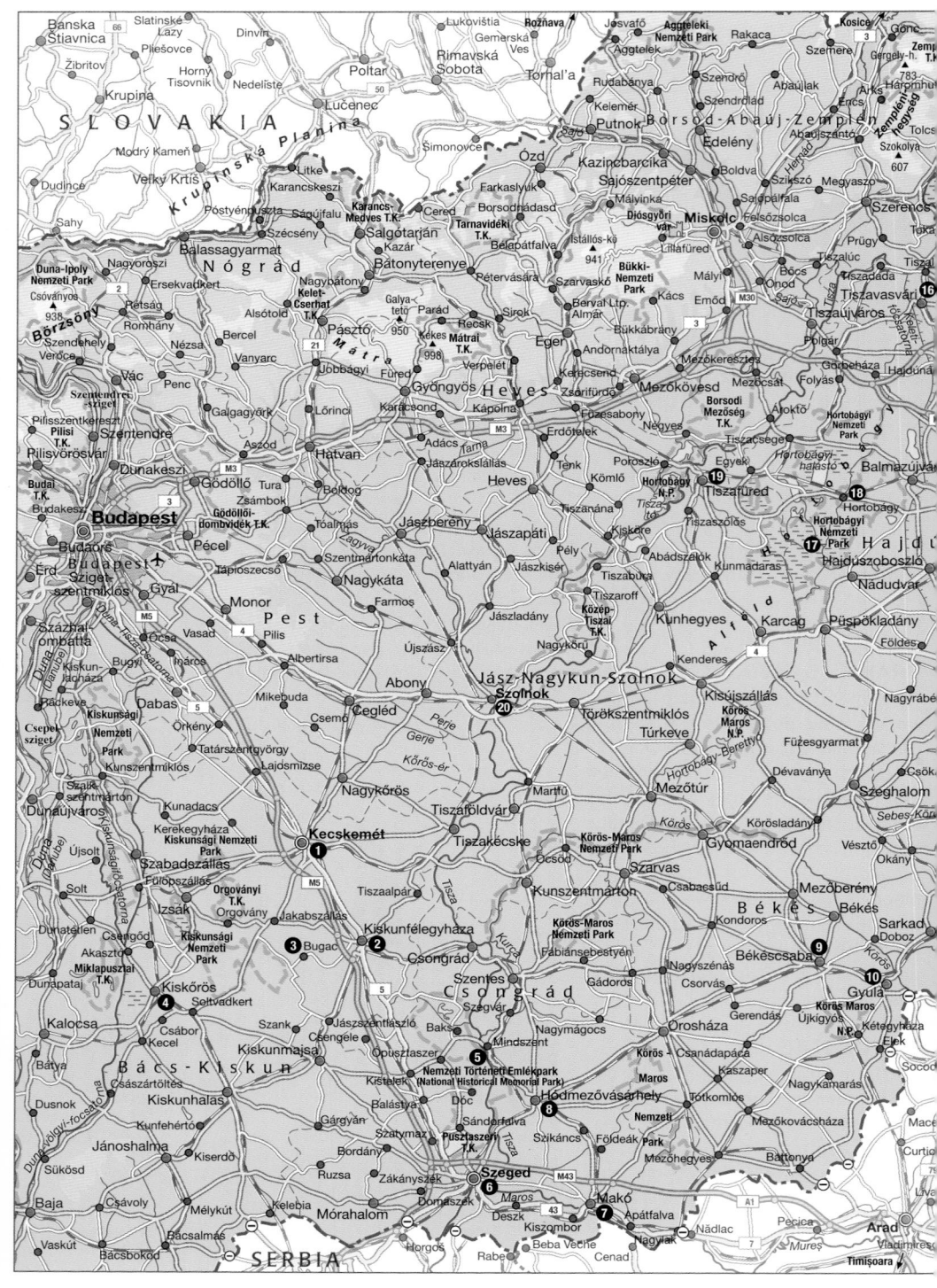

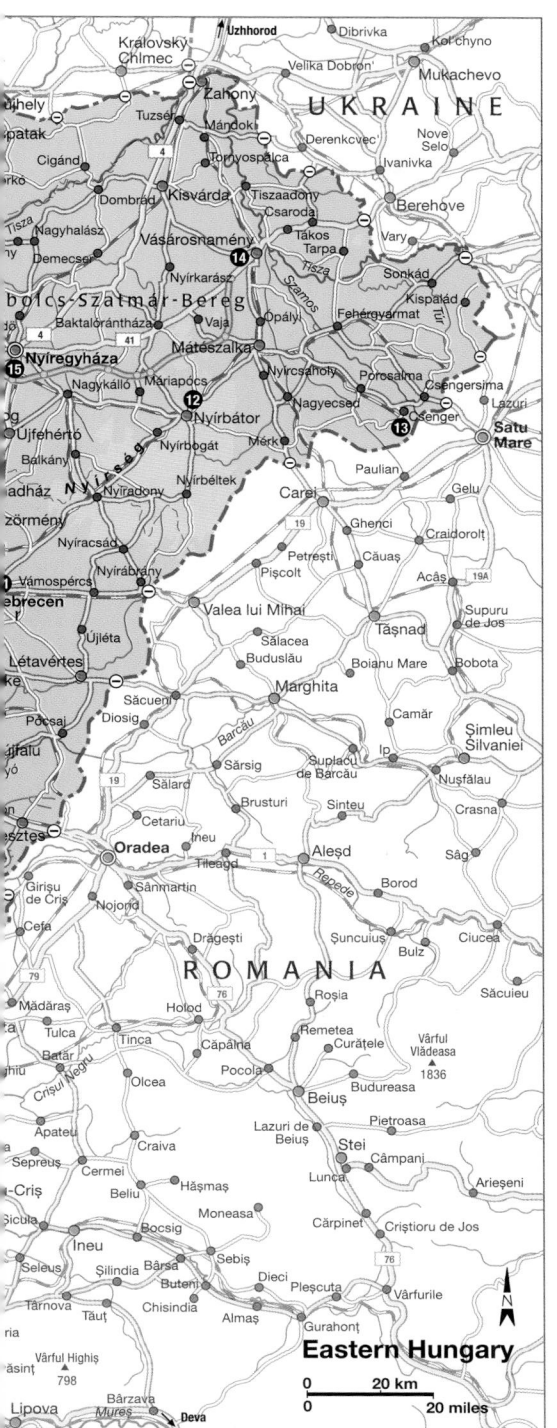

Eastern Hungary

0 — 20 km
0 — 20 miles

art nouveau style enriched with traditional ornamentation.

The Cifrapalota houses the **Kecskemét Art Gallery** (Kecskeméti Képtár; Tue–Sun 10am–5pm), which has a good collection of drawings and paintings, but the best reason to go inside is to see the splendidly decorated former ballroom on the first floor.

In the southwestern corner of Szabadság tér is the **Reformed Church** (Református újkollégium), built in 1680–84 and crowned by a Renaissance tower. The interior, in late-Baroque style, dates from 1790, but the pulpit is pure rococo.

KOSSUTH SQUARE

Kossuth tér, with a monument to the great man (see page 49), joins Szabadság tér. It is dominated by the **Town Hall** (Városháza), designed by Ödön Lechner (1845–1914) and Gyula Pártos, Built in the 1890s, and reflecting Lechner's earlier, more subdued style, the building sparkles with majolica tiles and has a beautiful wrought iron gate. The carillon on the Town Hall, visible from the square, plays works by Zoltán Kodály, the city's most famous son (see page 105), as well as by Mozart and Handel.

The **Katona Theatre** is named after the poet József Katona, who was born in Kecskemét in 1791 and died of a heart attack in this square; there is a memorial to him on the spot where he fell. The **Trinity Column** on the square was erected in gratitude by the citizens who survived the plague in 1739.

The **Zoltán Kodály Institute** (Kodály Zoltán Zenepedagógiai Intézet) keeps alive the name of the composer who was born here in 1882 and who, together with Béla Bartók, did much to pave the way for modern Hungarian music. The building was designed by architect and stage designer József Kerényi.

The **Museum of Naïve Art** (Magyar Naiv Müvészek Müzeum; Tue–Sun 10am–4pm), on Kölcsey utca, is also also Kerényi's design and has some fascinating works and a good shop. The **Toy Museum** (Szóénusz Játék múzeum; Tue–Sun 10am–12.30pm, 1–5pm), on Aponyi tér (another Kerényi design) has lots of delightful 19th- and 20th-century toys, and arranges children's workshops.

⊙ Tip

Perhaps the most important building in the Kossuth Square is the **Church of St Nicholas** (Szent Miklós templom) opposite the Town Hall. Some of it dates from the 13th century, but there are Baroque additions.

The **Hungarian Photography Museum** (Magyar Fotográfiai Múzeum; Tue–Sun noon–5pm; www.fotomuzeum.hu) on Katona I tér, is worth a quick look for its superb collection of Hungarian photos from the second half of the 20th century. The last museum on the list is the **Hungarian Folk Craft Museum** (Magyar Népi Isparm Üvészet Múzeum; Tue–Sun 10am–5pm) with its array of furniture, embroidery and tools.

KISKUNFÉLEGYHÁZA

Heading south, the first town on the way is **Kiskunfélegyháza** ❷. Hungarian place names containing the syllable kun relate to the nomadic Kuman families that Béla IV (1235–70) brought into the country as a reserve force against the Mongols. They settled here, were converted to Christianity and founded towns, but were not very effective as a defence force in the decisive battles of 1240–41 (see page 33).

Kiskunfélegyháza was razed during the Turkish wars, but regained some of its importance thanks to Maria Theresa's policy of resettlement in the 18th century.

Today it is a lively and colourful town, with lines of shops and several sights worth stopping for. The Secessionist-style **Town Hall** (Városháza), a riot of towers and majolica tiles, is the pride of Petőfi tér. Also worth a look is the **Kiskun Museum** (Mar–Oct Tue–Fri 10am–4pm, Sat 9am–5pm) on the main street. Its exhibits relate to the region's history and founders and in the courtyard is one of 80 windmills typical of the area.

BUGAC

The road from the west of town to the village of **Bugac** ❸ is a 14km (9-mile) concrete track. This ancient village (first chronicled in 1381), lying just to the east of the **Kiskunság National Park,** is partly covered by high dunes, shaped by the constant wind into a sea of sandy waves. The area covers 17,000 hectares (42,000 acres) and is cultivated for forestry, orchards and vineyards. In summer, you can get here from Kecskemét by

Kiskunság National Park.

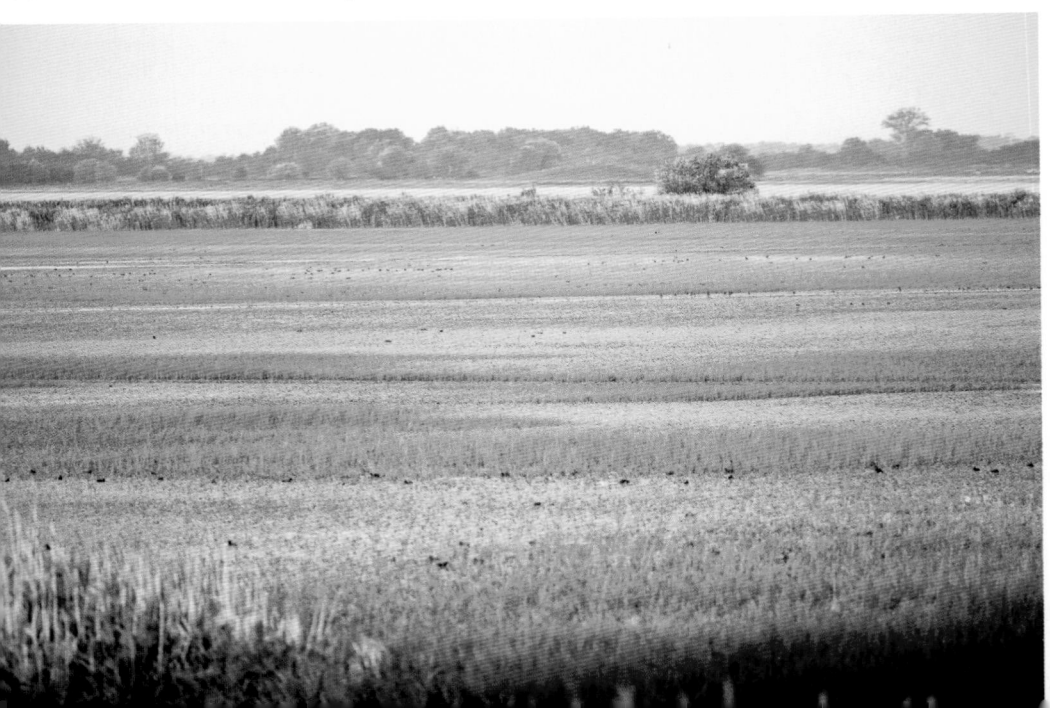

bus, or on the narrow-gauge train (from Kecskemét KK station to Bugac felső station) to see demonstrations of expert horsemanship and old breeds of farm animal, or visit the yurt-shaped **Herdsmen's Museum** (Pásztormúzeum; Mar–Oct Tue–Sun 10am–6pm). After you're done with that, head to the straw-thatched csárda (inn) with good music and food.

BIRTHPLACE OF A POET

A small detour west via Route 54 and Soltvadkert takes you to **Kiskőrös** ❹, the birthplace of Hungary's national poet, Sándor Petőfi (see page 49). The little thatched cottage in the middle of town is now a museum (Tue–Sun 9am–5pm) containing two furnished rooms with a few paintings and a Petőfi family tree. A number of statues of writers from around the world stand outside. There is also a series of bronze busts of the leaders of the 1848–49 rebellion executed after the last cavalcade of the Hungarian troops, in which Petőfi died.

You can now head west to Kalocsa (see page 179), or southeast towards Szeged (see page 240), which takes you through **Kiskunhalas,** with its **Lace Museum** (Csipkeház; Tue–Sun 9am–5pm).

A PICTURESQUE DRIVE

East of Kistelek near the village of Ópusztaszer, the **Nemzeti Történeti Emlékpark** ❺ (Ópusztaszer Heritage Park; Tue–Sun 10am–4pm, until 6pm Apr–Sept; www.opusztaszer.hu) is an impressive yet bombastic memorial to Hungarian history and national sentiment. On display in the park is an extraordinary 360° panoramic painting entitled The Arrival of the Hungarians showing the proud Magyars taking possession of the land that was to become Hungary. The site now includes a natural history museum, old farmhouses and tools, and a 'machine park' featuring farm vehicles, an aeroplane and rolling stock of all kinds.

A final detour could be made to **Csongrád,** which is of Slav origin. The

⊘ Tip

The regional wines, Kadarka or Sylvaner, are specialities of the sandy soil here and were praised by Petőfi himself: 'In the glow of wine I couldn't care less about the coarse world.' There is a lively Grape Harvest Festival in September.

Al fresco dining in Szeged.

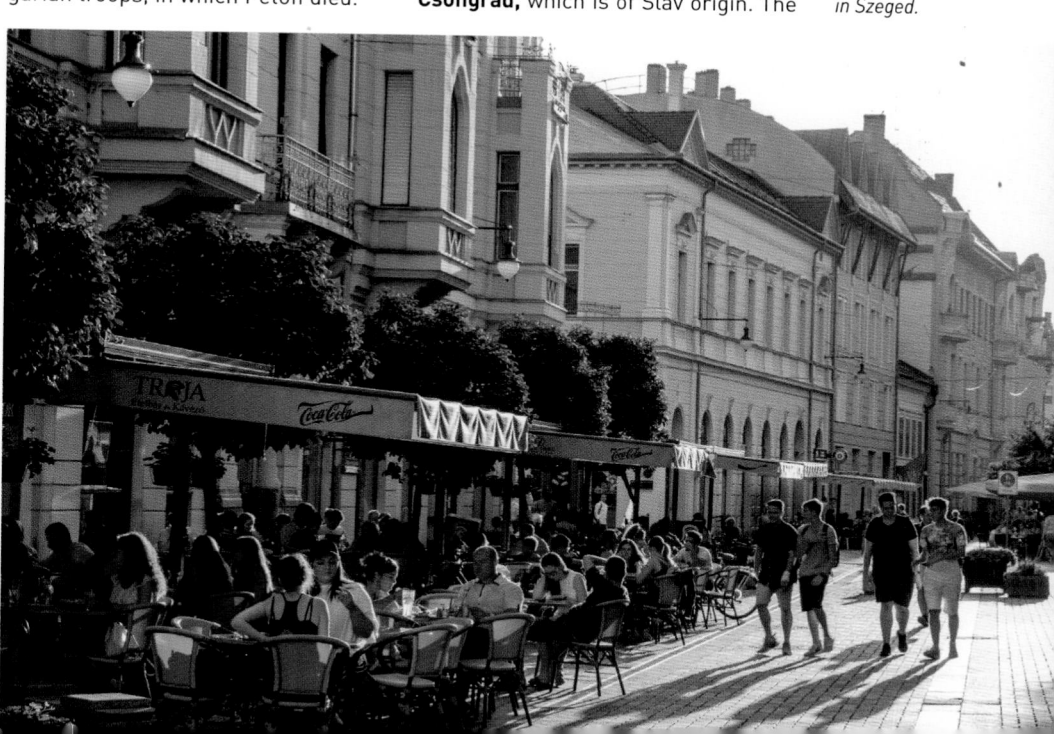

◷ Tip

Kiskunmajs, a medicinal and mineral springs, spa and hydrotherapy centre, is just a few miles east.

old town (Öregvár) has been well preserved behind the dike of the Tisza (where there are sandy beaches). The low, white, thatched houses are a delight; rooms are available in some of them and there are restaurants and cafés for refreshments. The **Village Museum** (Tájház; Mon–Fri noon–5pm, Sat 8am–noon May–Sept; free) provides a glimpse into the past.

SZEGED, THE SUNSHINE TOWN

A narrow road through agricultural countryside takes you south to **Szeged ⑥**, one of Hungary's 'paprika towns'. Archaeological finds show that people have lived here since the Stone Age. Szeged is first mentioned, as a salt trading post, in 1183, but was destroyed by the Tartars in 1241. The town was rebuilt and became a vital trade centre, later a focal point of the peasants' revolt led by György Dózsa in 1514, the Turkish Wars, the struggle for independence under Ferenc Rákóczi II (1703) and the 1848–49 revolution. In Kárász utca is the house where Lajos Kossuth delivered a flamboyant speech that inspired the citizens of Szeged to revolt.

The flood of 1879 destroyed most of the town, but it was rebuilt with international help and the names of towns that donated funds were given to sections of the peripheral road marking the inner city. Much of the city centre has been refurbished, creating pleasant pedestrian streets lined with shops, and agreeable plazas cooled by fountains. However, the most beautiful square is **Széchenyi tér,** with a fountain bearing an allegorical portrayal of the Tisza as bringer of both destruction and blessing.

Architects Ödön Lechner and Gyula Pártos extended what was left of the old **Town Hall** (Városháza), two buildings linked by a bridge and an ornamental tower. Heading west along Hajnóczy utca you come to the restored **Old Synagogue** (Ózsinagóga; closed to the public) bearing a high-water level mark in Hebrew, and then to the glorious **New Synagogue** (Újzsinagóga; Apr–Sept Sun–Fri 9am–noon

New Synagogue, Szeged.

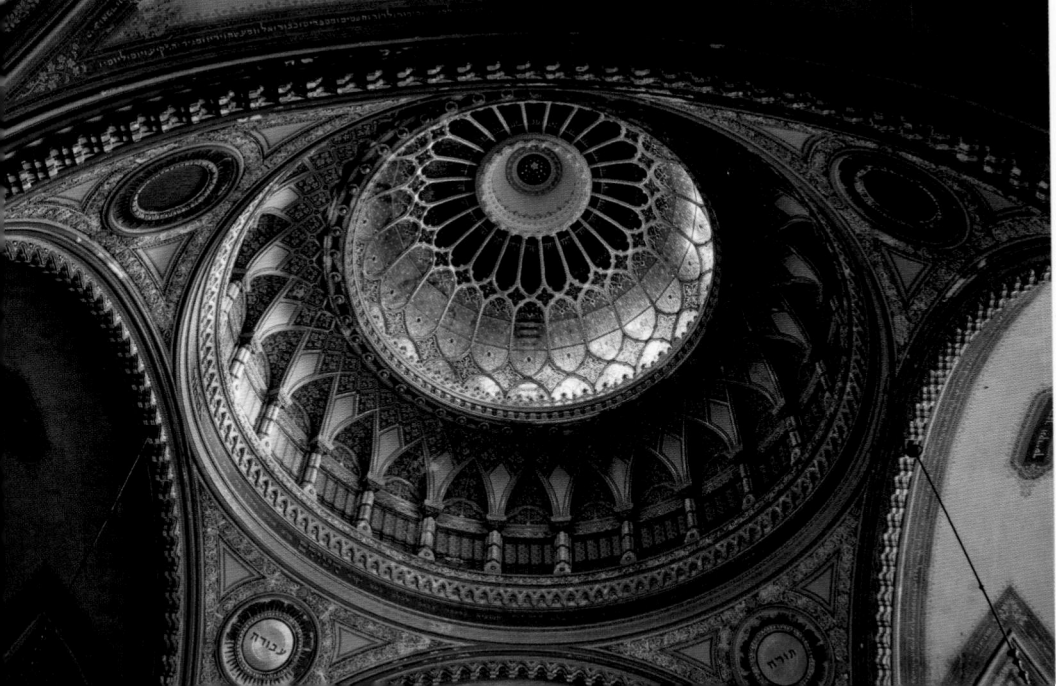

& 1–5pm), designed in 1903 by Lipót Baumhorn and restored in 2001. The stained-glass windows feature flowers from *The Flora of the Jews*, by Szeged's Rabbi Emmanuel Löw (1854–1944). If you continue walking westwards, you will arrive at Szeged's lively marketplace.

ALONG THE RIVER

Most cultural sights are located along the bank of the River Tisza, adorned with statues, notably of Queen Elisabeth, the wife of Franz Josef II. The grandiose, neoclassical **Ferenc Móra Museum** (daily 10am–6pm) concentrates on local history and culture, from handicrafts to art.

Next along the river is **Cathedral Square** (Dóm tér), which marks the entrance to the university quarter. The octagonal (12th–13th-century) Demetrius Tower in front of the cathedral is the oldest building in town; restored in 1985 it now serves as a baptismal chapel. The square is dominated by the red-brick cathedral, a mighty neo-Romanesque building, built between 1913 and 1920. Frigyes Schulek, of Budapest's Mátyás Church fame, had a hand in the design. The interior of the cathedral has marble statues, gilded tabernacles and a grandiose altar while the ceiling fresco in the choir portrays the Virgin of Szeged, wrapped in a peasant's cloak, with embroidered Szeged 'butterfly slippers' on her feet. The organ has 11,000 pipes and is nearly as big as that of Milan.

The cathedral and arcaded square become a marvellous theatrical setting for the Szeged Open-Air Festival of opera, dance and theatre. The folk song praising the town that opens the festival each year is also played every midday on a glockenspiel housed in Dóm tér.

The southern section of the inner city is alive with shoppers and students and there are numerous restaurants offering excellent fish specialities, notably the spicy Szeged fish soup. The Heroes' Gate, a memorial to the soldiers of World War I, leads out of the inner city.

FURTHER AFIELD

About 1km (roughly half a mile) out of Szeged's city's centre, in Mátyás király tér, you'll find the town's most beautiful church, the **Church of the Lower Town** (Alsóvárosi templom). One Romanesque window in the sacristy aside, the church is Gothic. The last stone was laid in 1507 but the Baroque high altar and the pulpit date from around 1700. The Black Madonna, a replica of the statue of Mary from Czestochowa, is an object of pilgrimage and the focus of the annual melon-harvest festival.

Móra Park, with its cultural centre, lies near the northern bridge-head. It is bounded by the ruins of a castle, built by Béla IV (1235–70) after the Tartar invasion, that for many years served as a prison. The town's most prominent citizen is Albert Szent-Györgyi, who was awarded the Nobel Prize in 1937 for his discovery of vitamin C in paprika.

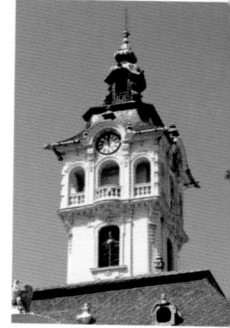

City Hall, Szeged.

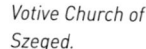

Votive Church of Szeged.

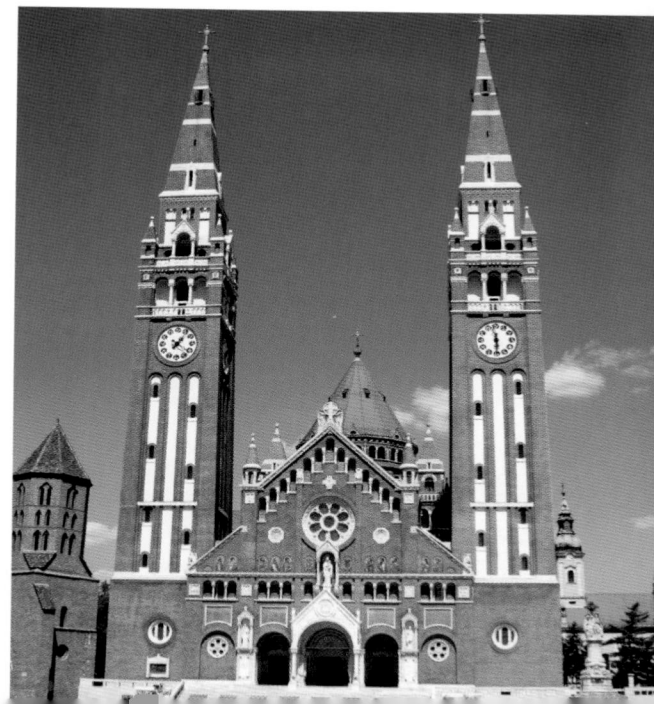

Great Church, Debrecen.

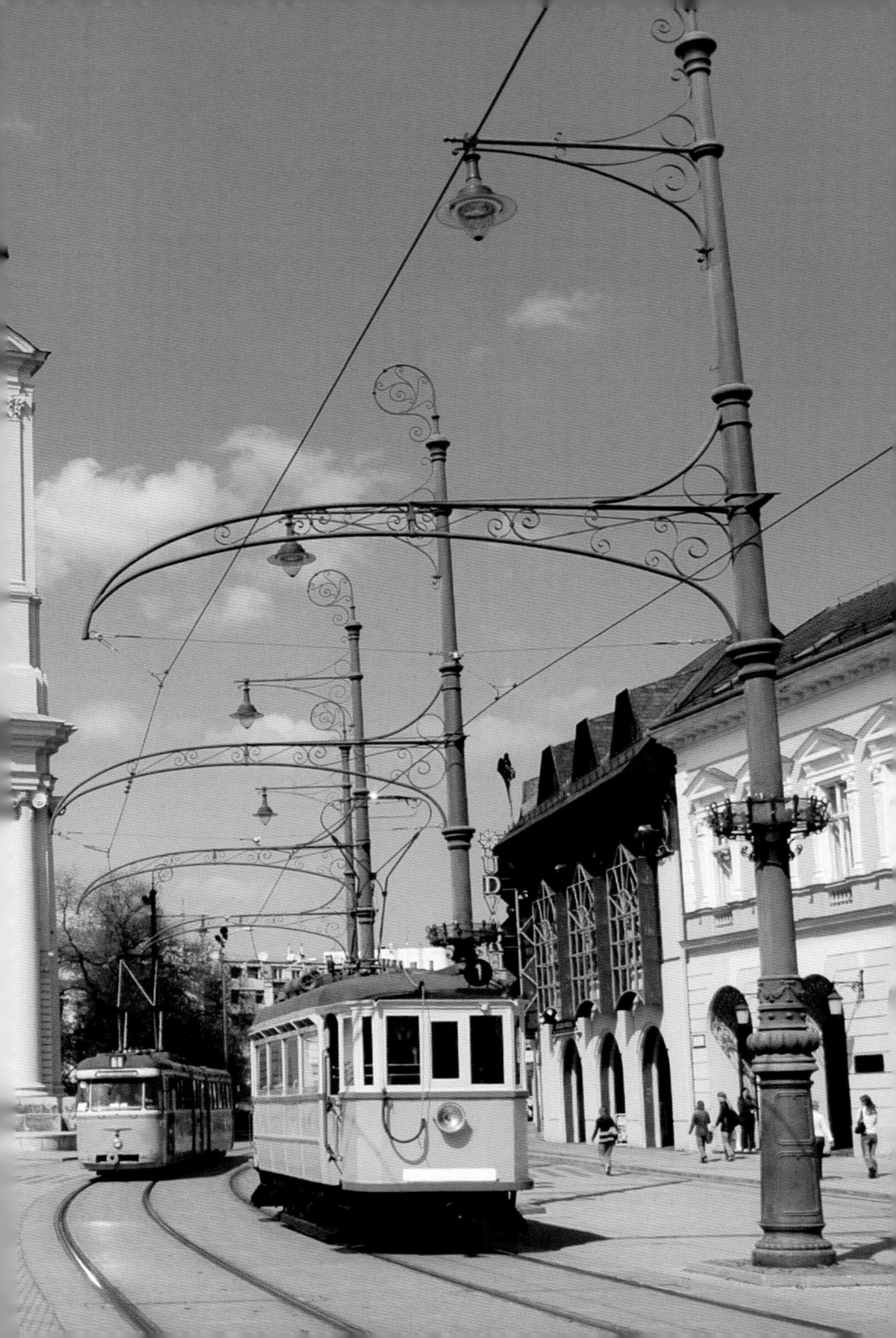

GOING EAST

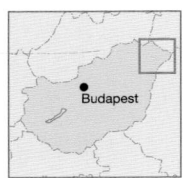

East of Szeged, you can discover local ceramics and distinguished paintings, and explore Hungary's cultured second city, which played a major role in the Reformation.

○ Main attractions
Békéscsaba
Gyula
Debrecen

Map on page 236

Two towns off the beaten track to the east of Szeged are worth mentioning: for example, **Makó ❼**, 30km (19 miles) away on Highway 43, is Hungary's onion capital; here, the Town Hall has been one-upped by the 'Onion House' designed by Imre Makovec. Further east is Mezőhegyes, where there is a stud farm for Nonius horses, a breed introduced from Normandy that helped to make Hungarian horse breeding a world-famous industry.

POTTERY TOWN

The more familiar road northeast from Szeged is Highway 47, which passes the oil refinery and heads into the flat, dusty plain towards **Hódmezővásárhely ❽**. Founded in the 13th century, this town of 54,000 inhabitants is named after the beavers *(hód)* that once lived in Lake Hód. The lake dried up because of the regulation of the river and its bed is now a recreation park, to the south of town.

More interestingly, Hódmezővásárhely is an important pottery town; in the mid-19th century more than 400 potters worked here. Ceramics can be seen in the **Csúcs Pottery House** (Csúki Fazekasház; Tue–Sun 10am–5pm), while there is pottery and painting on display at **Tornyai János Museum** (Tue–Sun 10am–5pm; www.tornyaimuzeum.hu) at Szánto Kovács utca, which also explores the history, ethnography and geology of the area.

On the south side of the main square, Kossuth tér, is the **Town Hall** (Városháza; Mon–Fri 8am–3pm; free), built in classical style, with a lofty tower and bearing an uncanny resemblance to Szeged's town hall. Outside, a bronze Hussar on horseback whirls his sabre, charging to the attack.

The west side of Kossuth tér is bounded by the Hotel Béke, a classical building with attractive wrought

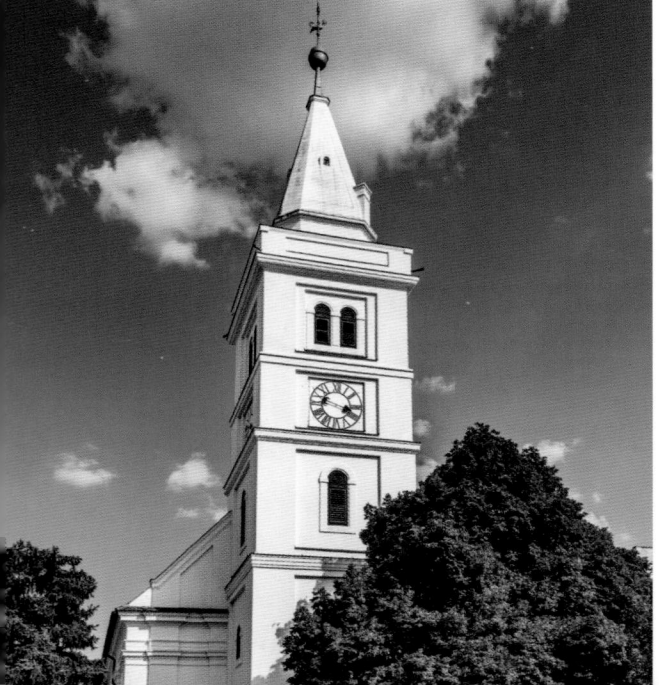

Baroque church, Hódmezővásárhely.

ironwork. The Old and the New churches, and the Greek Orthodox church, are all Baroque. The **Alföld Gallery** (Alföldi Galéria; Tue–Sun 10am–5pm), just off the square, is filled with tableaux extolling the beauty of the Great Plain.

SAUSAGES AND SLOVAK TOOLS

Highway 47 carries on through the nondescript town of Orosháza, by-passes Csorvás, which has nicely restored houses and a good system to slow down through-traffic, and reaches **Békéscsaba ❾**, which is known for its fiery sausage (csabai). This provincial capital has several fine buildings, such as the Town Hall (Városháza) in eclectic style on Szent-István tér, the Hotel Fiume and the Jókai Theatre.

Just off the town centre, on Széchenyi utca, is the **Mihály Munkács Museum** (Tue–Sun 10am–6pm), largely devoted to the works of this 19th-century landscape painter (1844–1900), and undoubtedly one of Hungary's greatest artists.

Another sight worth seeing is the little **Slovakian Village House** (Slovák Tájház; Tue–Sun 10am–noon, 2–6pm) on Gáray utca, which features furniture, costumes, tools and utensils from a traditional Slovak farm.

Before leaving town, visit the **Grain Museum** (Gabonamúzeum; Apr–Oct Tue–Sun 9am–5pm). There are lots of agricultural instruments, and a fine windmill stands outside.

NATIONAL COMPOSER

A detour along Highway 44 takes you to **Gyula ❿** on the banks of the White Körös (Fehér-Körös). Albrecht Dürer's ancestors came from this town; in the garden of **Gyula Castle** (Gyula Vár; Tue–Sun 10am–6pm; www.gyulavara.hu), stands Erkel's Tree, a sycamore in whose shade the composer worked.

Gyula is Europe's only complete brick castle, a massive, imposing fortress with battlements, arrow slits and a square central tower – for 130 years it was in Turkish hands. It is now one of the region's major tourist attractions,

☉ Fact

Ferenc Erkel, composer of the Hungarian national anthem, was born in Gyula in 1810.

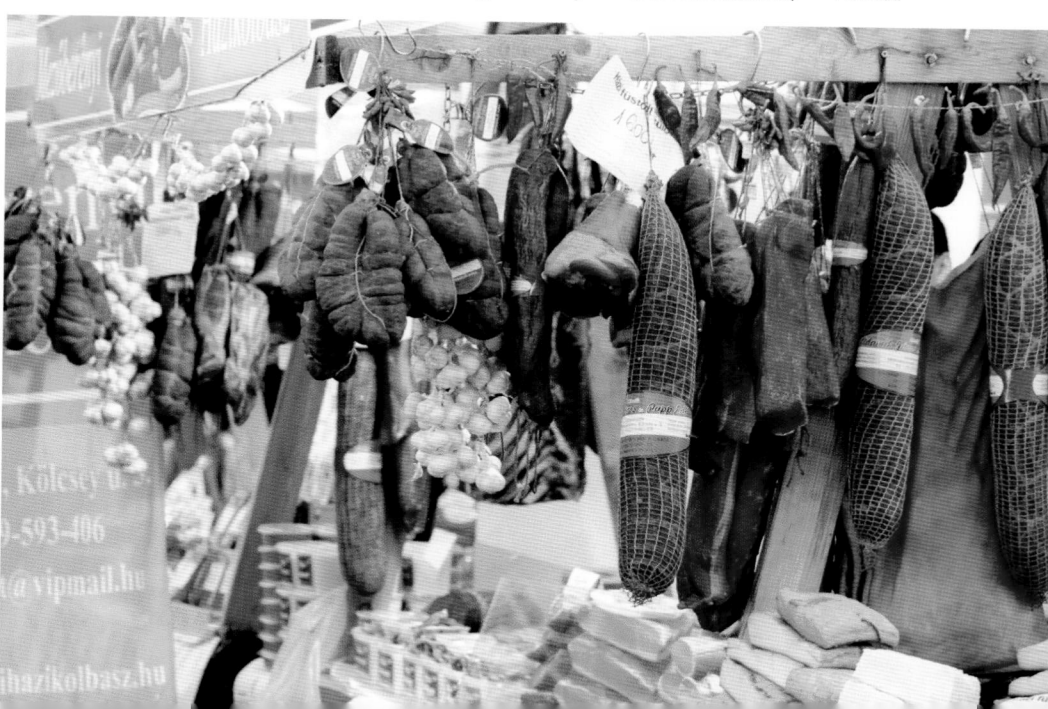

Békéscsaba Sausage Festival.

Tip

There is a spa in Gyula, too – the Castle Baths (Várfürdö; outdoor pools daily in summer 8am–8pm, indoor pools all year).

and every summer between 1 July and 15 August, the home of Gyula Castle Theatre Festival.

Once you have seen the Town Hall, the Greek Orthodox and Roman Catholic churches – all built between 1775 and 1825 in Baroque style – head for the venerable **Százéves** pâtisserie on Jókai utca, housed in a beautifully furnished old building.

CENTRE OF PROTESTANTISM

Head back north along Highway 47, which takes you to **Debrecen ⓫**, which has developed gradually to its present position as the second-largest town in Hungary and a major centre of culture. Once a federation of villages, it was united under a charter in the 14th century. It has always been a major trading centre and the extensive settlement of huge shops and malls that dot the outskirts show that it still is.

When Hungary was divided into three parts by the Turkish wars, Debrecen, a border town, kept its autonomy and its people were free citizens of a

Brick-built medieval fortress in Gyula.

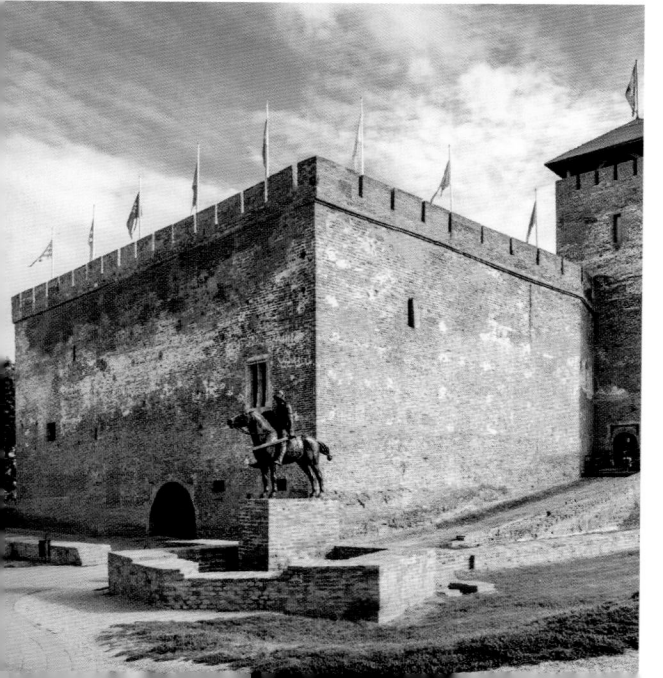

city republic. This was fertile ground for the anti-feudal spirit of the Reformation and became a centre of Protestantism.

The Reformation spread rapidly in the region, despite a law passed by the Hungarian Assembly in 1521 stating that 'Lutherans are to be exterminated'. Debrecen withstood reconversion to Catholicism, which came with the Habsburgs, who seized power after the retreat of the Turks. Not even hard labour in the galleys could shake the conviction of the people of Debrecen. They held on to their faith, and a memorial in the garden of the Reformed Church honours them.

The main street, Piac utca, is lined with grand houses that survived the 12-day tank battle that raged around Debrecen in 1944. On the corner of Béke útja is the former district house, adorned with stained glass windows and Zsolnay tiles. The oldest church, the **Little Church** (Kistemplom), is in Révész tér; built in the 1720s on an oak foundation, it was reconstructed in neo-Romanesque style in 1876.

Opposite the church is the classical **Town Hall** (Városháza). Kossuth tér is the northern extension of the main street and has wisely been turned into a large pedestrian zone, with fountains and benches.

It is bounded by the **Great Reformed Church** (Nagytemplom; Mon–Fri 9am–4pm, Sat 9am–1pm, Sun noon–4pm), a mammoth building in classical style (1814–21). Ionic wall pillars divide the main façade, which is bordered by two square towers. Within its austere interior hangs the Rákóczi-harang, the largest bell in Hungary – forged from cannons used in the unsuccessful war of independence (1703–11) led by Ference Rákóczi II against the Habsburgs. It was here too that Lajos Kossuth proclaimed Hungary's independence on 14 April 1849. Its simple interior is an ideal venue for the groups, choirs, bands and orchestras that perform at Debrecen's numerous musical festivals.

Just behind the church stands the rectangular, two-storey **Reformed College** and its museum (Református Kollégium; Tue–Sat 10am–4pm, Sun 10am–1pm), looking like an impenetrable fortress of the faith. Its history goes back to the 14th century when it was the Latin school of the Dominican Order. In the 16th century it became one of the first Calvinist schools in Hungary and around 1750 it became the Reformed Theological College.

The library, with its old codices and valuable manuscripts, is the second largest in Hungary. The printing press founded in 1561 by Gál Huszár has survived, while the present Alföld Printing Press, a huge concern, is its successor.

Two important political events took place in the college oratory. In 1849, the National Assembly met here, under Kossuth's leadership, and on 12 December 1944, the provisional government convened here while the Red Army was driving the German forces out of Hungary.

There is a rare object in the permanent exhibition of the college – a meteorite that landed southwest of Debrecen in 1857.

MORE CITY SIGHTS

In the **Déri Museum** (Tue–Sun 10am–4pm, until 6pm Apr–Oct; www.derimuzeum.hu), which can be reached via Perényi utca, is an ethnographic and folkloric collection that is well worth a visit. But *The Jesus Trilogy* by Mihály Munkácsy is the greatest attraction here: three huge paintings depicting Jesus and Pilate, Ecce Homo and the Golgotha.

On the western side of the square is the opulent **Hotel Aranybika**, a grand yet simple Secessionist building designed by Alfréd Hajós, twice Olympic swimming champion (1920–24). The great Glass Hall, covered by a huge cupola of coloured glass, hosts a very good restaurant, and there's also an excellent coffee house on site.

If you have time, take a look at the Baroque and Classical houses around Kálvin tér, and at St Anne's Church (1719–46), pure Baroque in style, in Béke útja. Don't overlook the **Csokonai Theatre** in Liszt Ferenc utca, with its Moorish-Byzantine elements. In Széchenyi utca is Debrecen's oldest surviving house, dating from 1710 and a post station in the days of horse-drawn coach travel.

Debrecen's water reservoir is under the **Great Forest**, the Nagyerdő, in the north. This is the city's leisure park, with thermal baths (outdoor pools May–Sept daily 9am–7pm, indoor pools all year), a zoo, boating pond, a restaurant-cum-dance hall and an amusement park. Even the imposing university (Kossuth Lajos Egyetem) is located here.

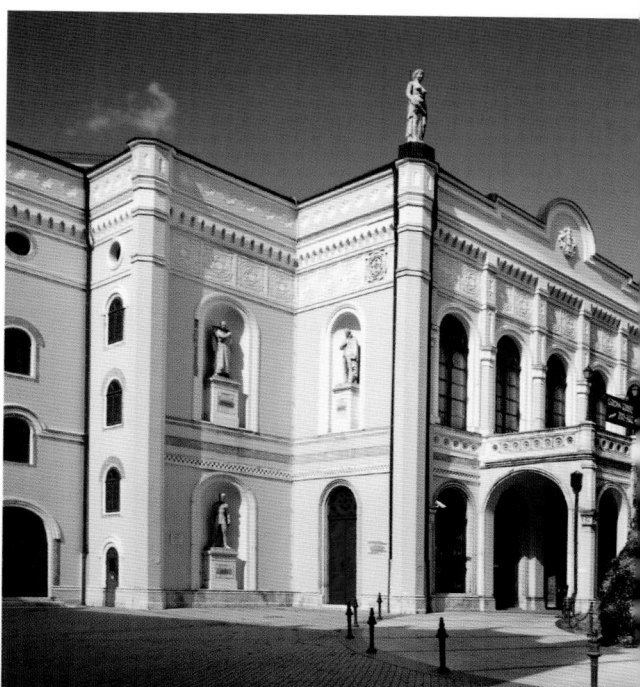

Csokonai Theatre.

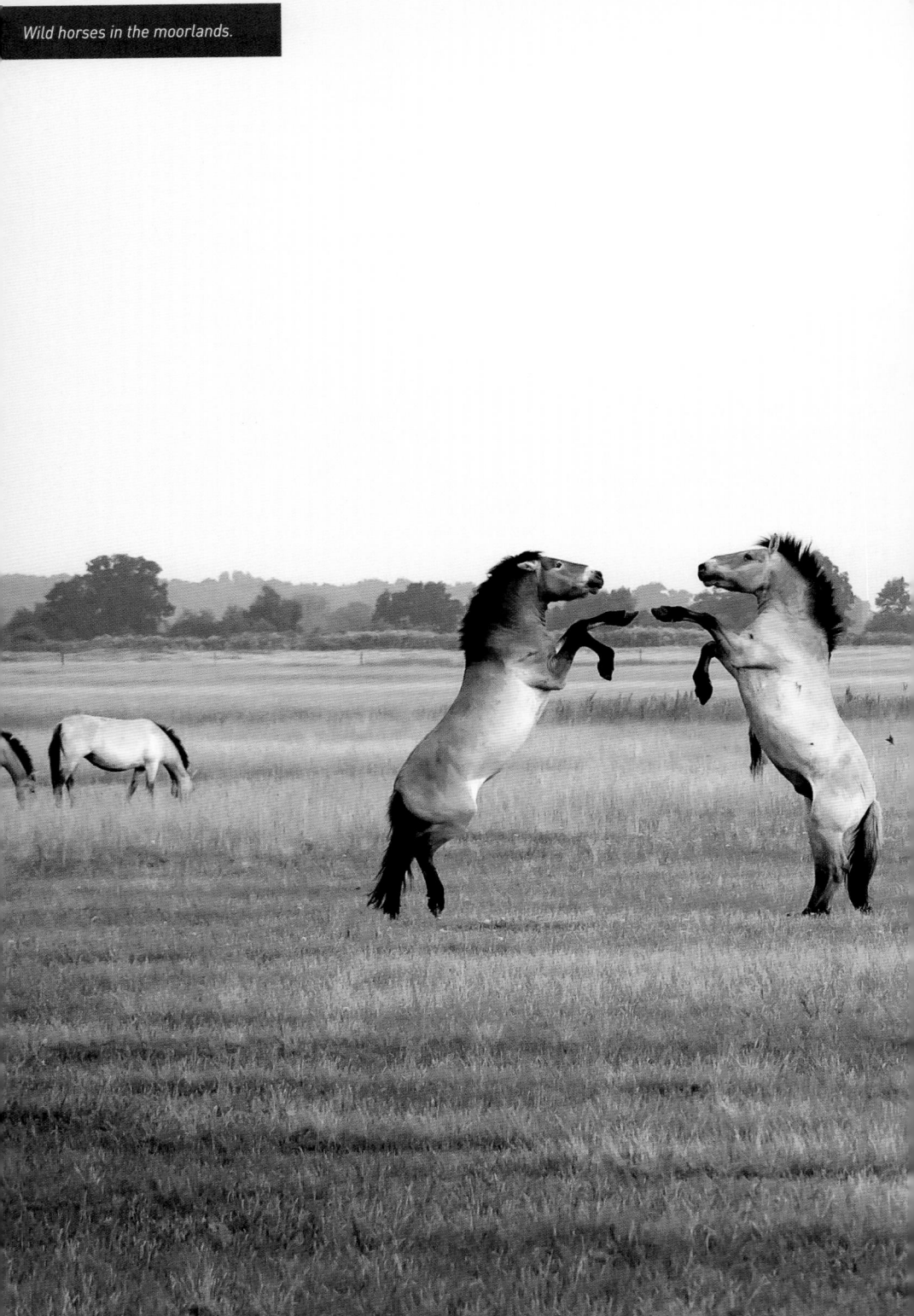

THE PUSZTA

This wild region, containing the biggest area of steppe grazing land in Central Europe and peopled with traditionally dressed herdsmen, exerts a powerful hold over the popular imagination.

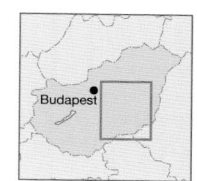

The existence in Hungary of two cultural poles – East and West – was clearly demonstrated in the 19th and 20th centuries in Debrecen, the capital of Calvinism, and Pannonhalma, the capital of Catholicism (see page 190). This division originated in the two spheres of religious and cultural influence that were united in the 9th and 10th centuries – Greek-Slavonic in the east of the country, Latin and the Holy Roman Empire in the western regions.

István (Stephen) I (970–1038) introduced Catholicism to Hungary and was crowned as the first Christian king. However, when Béla IV settled heathen Kumans in the Tisza region southeast of Budapest 200 years later, many Catholic converts readily reverted to paganism. Contemporary chronicles supported the eastern connection and declared the Huns to be ancestors of the Hungarians. An eastward-looking movement was thus born. Debrecen subsequently became known as the 'Rome of Calvinism' – Calvinism being a symbol of rebellion against Habsburg (and therefore Catholic) encroachment.

THE 'REAL' HUNGARY

The two most important politicians of the 19th century, Count István Széchenyi and Lajos Kossuth, represented this dualism. Széchenyi came from the upper echelons of the

Catholic Hungarian nobility and, while he wanted to modernise the country and achieve reforms in the 'backwoods of Hungary' through education and enlightenment, he remained loyal to the house of Habsburg.

Kossuth, who came from an east Hungarian, Protestant family of the lesser nobility, fought 'with word and sword' for his ideal of severing Hungary from the Habsburgs. His aim was a Danube Federation, a project that fitted well with the revolutionary atmosphere current in Europe at the time and

Main attractions
Nyíregyháza
Hortobágy National Park
Hortobágy

Map on page 236

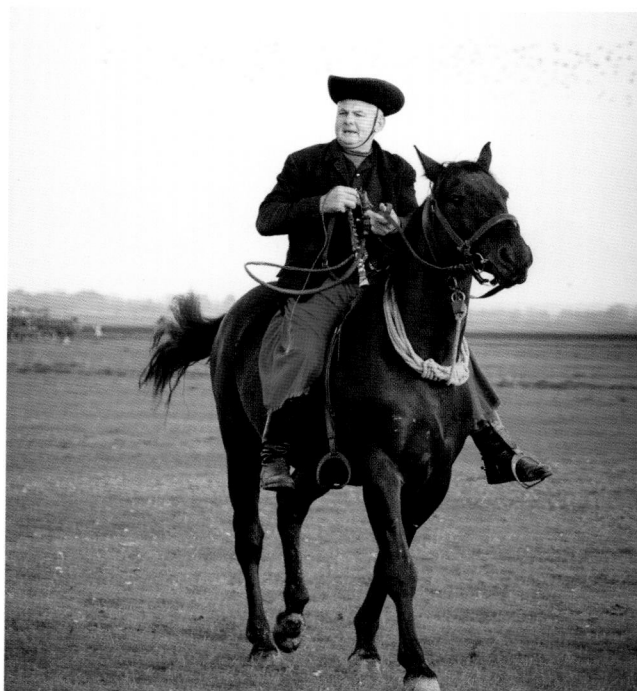

Csikos herdsmen on the Great Hungarian Plain.

⊙ Tip

A trip by car to the **Nyírség** (Birch Country), the sandy regions reclaimed for agriculture, is recommended; picturesque fields of grain, sunflowers and sugar beet are interspersed by woods and apple orchards.

which might well have avoided several European wars in the 20th century, had it been realised.

As discussed in the previous chapter Debrecen has long played an important role in Hungary's political and religious development. This makes it an ideal spot for those who want to find out more about the 'real' Hungary, while using it as a base for exploring the Puszta. For those who want to immerse themselves fully in the culture, Debrecen university offers summer courses in the Hungarian language.

This area remained almost untouched during the Turkish occupation (1541–1699) and, as a consequence, many medieval settlement patterns, old village plans and buildings from the 13th to the 17th century have survived.

NYÍRBÁTOR

Some 55km (34 miles) along Highway 471 from Debrecen is **Nyírbátor ⑫**, a name associated above all else with the 13th-century Báthory dynasty. The Báthorys (*bátor* means brave) have *voivodes*, princes and a Polish king (crowned in

Krakow in 1576) in their family tree, as well as the infamous 'Bloody Countess' Elizabeth, who was said to bathe in the blood of maidens in order to preserve her fair complexion. After several young women had been murdered for this purpose she was condemned to 'perpetual imprisonment' and walled up inside her castle, where she died in 1614. This scandal (and its sexual overtones) has been the subject of many stories, books and films over the centuries, although whether Elizabeth really committed these crimes remains unclear.

The town is worth a visit to see its two beautiful churches, and the place comes alive every July for the Music Days festival, when troubadours and wandering theatrical groups perform in front of the museum.

The **István Báthory Museum** (Tue–Sun 10am–6pm) is at Karoly Mihály utca 21 in the former Minorite monastery, a Baroque building dating from 1737–44. It contains various family mementoes, and a large ethnographic collection. Also on display are finds from the ancient bogland of **Báthoryliget,** a nature reserve

Tourists in Hortobagy National Park.

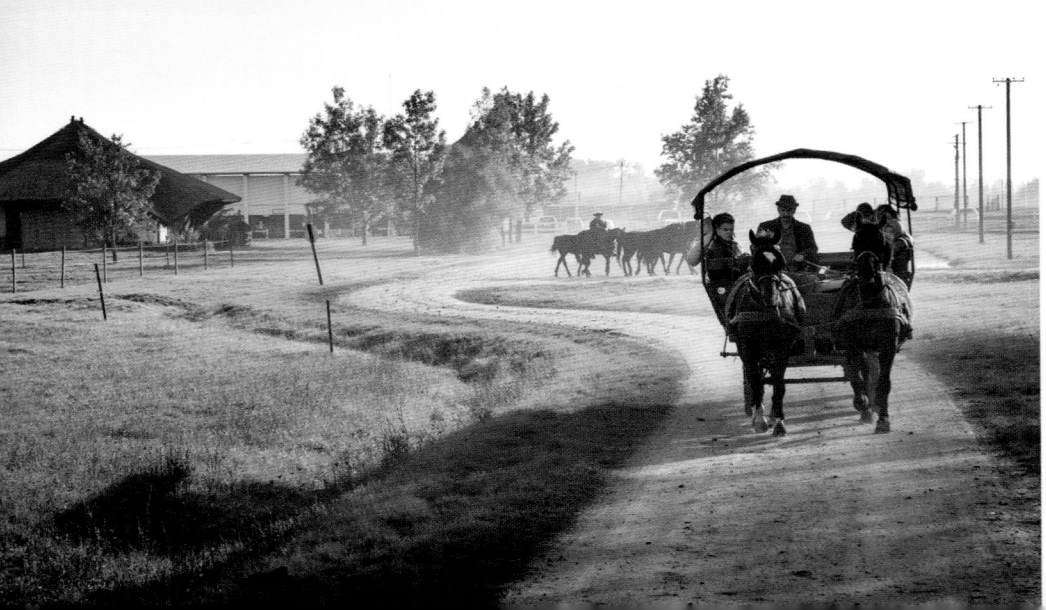

with 30-metre (98-ft) tall oak trees and viviparous lizards. To protect this fragile habitat, visitors must obtain a special permit to enter.

Two churches and a wooden bell-tower adorn the town. The **Calvinist Church** (daily 8am–noon, 2.30–4pm; keys from the pastor's house next door) just off István Báthory utca, was financed by the Báthory family with booty taken from the Turks. It was built between 1484 and 1488, largely destroyed by Austrian troops in 1587, and restored in 1958.

The ribbed vault above the nave and choir, supported by wall pillars, is very beautiful. Set apart from the church is the square, wooden bell-tower with a narrow gallery and four little corner towers, added in the 17th century; this was where non-conformists were made to worship during the Counter-Reformation.

In contrast to this cool beauty is the **Minorite Church** (Mon–Fri 9am–5pm, Sat 9am–7pm, Sun 8am–6pm) on Karoly Mihály utca. Built by István Báthory and destroyed in 1587 by the Turks, it acquired its Baroque splendour in the early 18th century – its most impressive feature is the Altar of the Passion in front of the organ loft.

RELIGIOUS HERITAGE

Religion played a major role in eastern Hungarian culture, and diversity was assured thanks to István Báthory's explicit Tolerance Edict. Some 10km (6 miles) west of Nyírbátor is the ornate Greek Catholic pilgrimage church of Máriapócs, which attracts the faithful from far and wide, especially in September, on the Day of the Virgin. The original painting of Mary by István Pap, which is said to have shed tears on three occasions, was taken to St Stephen's Cathedral in Vienna. The present one was painted by an unknown artist.

Some 22km (14 miles) further along Highway 471 from Nyírbátor you will reach **Mátészalka.** Here, the Calvinist Church, with its painted wooden ceiling, is a vehicle for traditional Hungarian art. The wagons, coaches and sledges in the museum illustrate

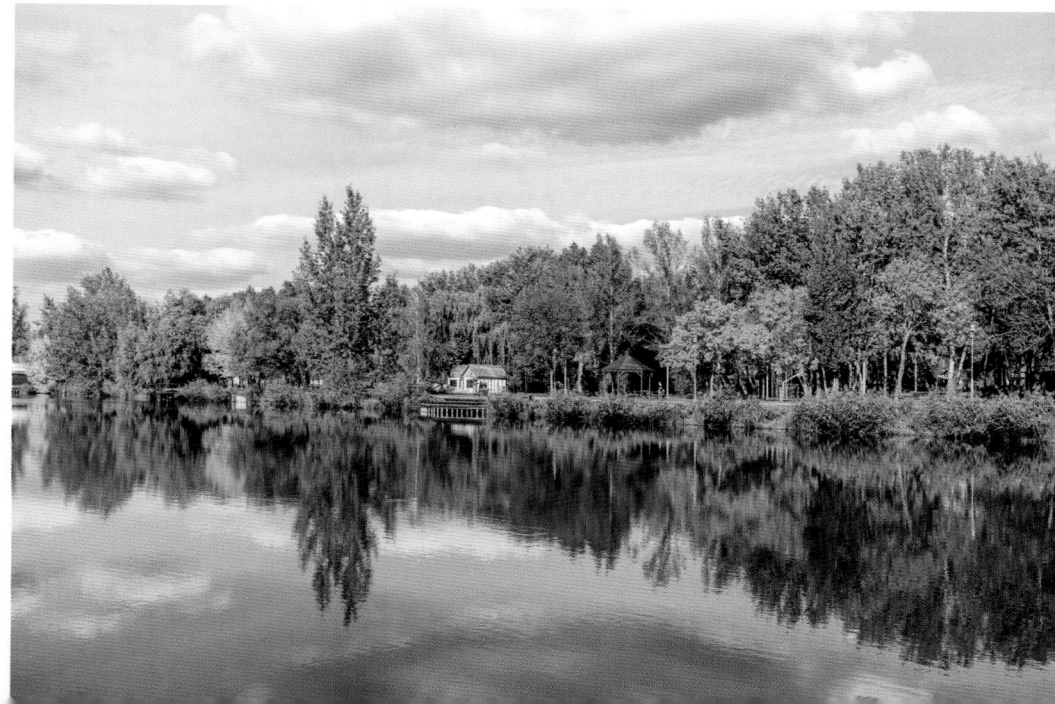

Salt Lake, Nyíregyháza.

the difficulties of transport in earlier times: the chronicles tell of 30 oxen being needed to draw a wagon through mud and snow.

From here, head for the northeastern tip of Hungary, in the Tisza, Szamos, Kraszna and Túr region. It is mainly reclaimed swamp and provides fertile farmland.

BORDER TOWN

If you follow Highway 49 which branches off to the east, you will come to **Csenger** ⑬ on the Romanian border. A town that firmly embraced the Reformation in 1540, its Protestant Church is decorated with glazed tiles, and has a coffered ceiling painted with pretty flower patterns. These 'peasant churches' are an important expression of the Hungarian soul, much like folk songs and tales.

There is another one in **Csenger-sima,** 7km (4 miles) northeast. On the way back towards Mátészalka, turn off onto Highway 491, then use the side road going north from **Fehérgyarmat,** where there is a Calvinist Church,

rebuilt and enlarged several times in contrasting styles.

There are several interesting buildings along this route (Highway 41 heading west). Among them is the Romanesque church in **Csaroda** built in the mid-13th century with 14th-century wall paintings, a painted wooden ceiling dating from the 18th century and a wooden bell-tower. The oldest church in eastern Hungary, it unfortunately suffered some damage from the floods in spring 2001, though it has since been repaired.

In fact, just about every little village in the eastern region has something special: at Túristvándi, there's a watermill; Szatmárcseke is the birthplace of the poet Ference Kölcsey, who wrote the words to the Hungarian national anthem. It also has a cemetery with unusual wooden tomb markers shaped as boats.

The town of **Vásárosnamény** ⑭ offers modest accommodation for those wanting to explore these delights in greater depth. On Rákóczi utca it also has the remarkable **Beregi Museum** (Mar–Oct Tue–Fri 8.30am–4.30pm, Sat–Sun 8am–4pm; Nov–Feb Mon–Fri 8am–4pm), which features, among other exhibits, a fascinating collection of cast-iron stoves from the foundry in Munkács (Mukačevo in the Ukraine).

NYÍREGYHÁZA AND TISZAVASVÁRI

Nyíregyháza ⑮ is the county town of Szaboles-Szatmár-Bereg. Destroyed by the Mongols in the 13th century, it came into its own towards the end of the 19th century as a prosperous agricultural centre. The resulting wealth can be seen in the fair number of stately private houses dating from the 18th and 19th centuries, the County House and the Protestant church in eclectic style.

Several important architects worked here: Ignác Alpár (of Budapest Zoo fame) designed the theatre; the synagogue on Síp utca is the work of Lipót

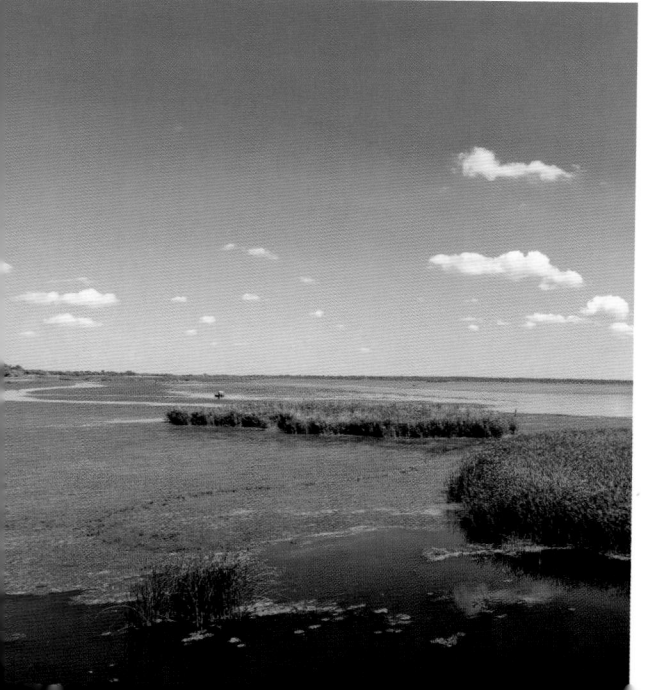

Tisza Lake National Reserve, in Hortobágy National Park.

Baumhorn (as is Szeged's synagogue). The **András Jósa Museum** (Tue–Sun 8am–4pm; free) on Benczúr tér is dedicated to the painter Gyula Benczúr, who was born here, and exhibits works by other local artists.

More modern art is on display in the town's simply named **Art Gallery** (Mon–Fri 10am–6pm, Sat 9am–1pm) at Bocskai utca 5.

Nyíregyháza's other main attractions are the spa and museum at **Sóstófürdő** (meaning 'salt lake bath'), 6km (3.5 miles) away in a heavily wooded area north of the town. The **thermal baths** (May–Sept daily 9am–8pm) have pools containing alkali and iodine.

The **Museum Village** (Sóstói Müzeumfalu; daily Apr–Sept 10am–6pm, Oct 9am–5pm) illustrates the ethnic diversity of the region with a reconstruction of a 19th-century village; craft demonstrations and folkloric programmes are held in the summer. There's also a **zoo** (Állatpark) nearby.

A short detour via Highway 36 to **Tiszavasvári** ⑯ is more pleasant than the main road back to Debrecen. Here a country road, running parallel with the railway and partly with the main canal, crosses the Hajdú ridge. Place names containing the suffix Hajdú indicate towns once peopled by the Haiduks, an army of herdsmen, mercenaries and brigands. István Bocskai (1556–1606), Prince of Transylvania, elevated them to the nobility and granted them land in recognition of their bravery in war. Bocskai also forced an agreement, in the Peace of Vienna of 1606, on religious freedom for Transylvania.

THE PUSZTA

A special travel experience lies in wait for you when you leave Debrecen and travel west on Highway 33 through the Hortobágy Puszta towards Tiszafüred, to the dam on the Tisza. *Puszta* here means barren, or desert land, although some parts of the region are swampy wetlands. Somewhat confusingly, it can also mean 'homesteads that were the property of a nobleman'. In the Alföld, it also refers to the vast grazing grounds and sandy steppes. The two

Nine-arched Bridge, Hortobágy.

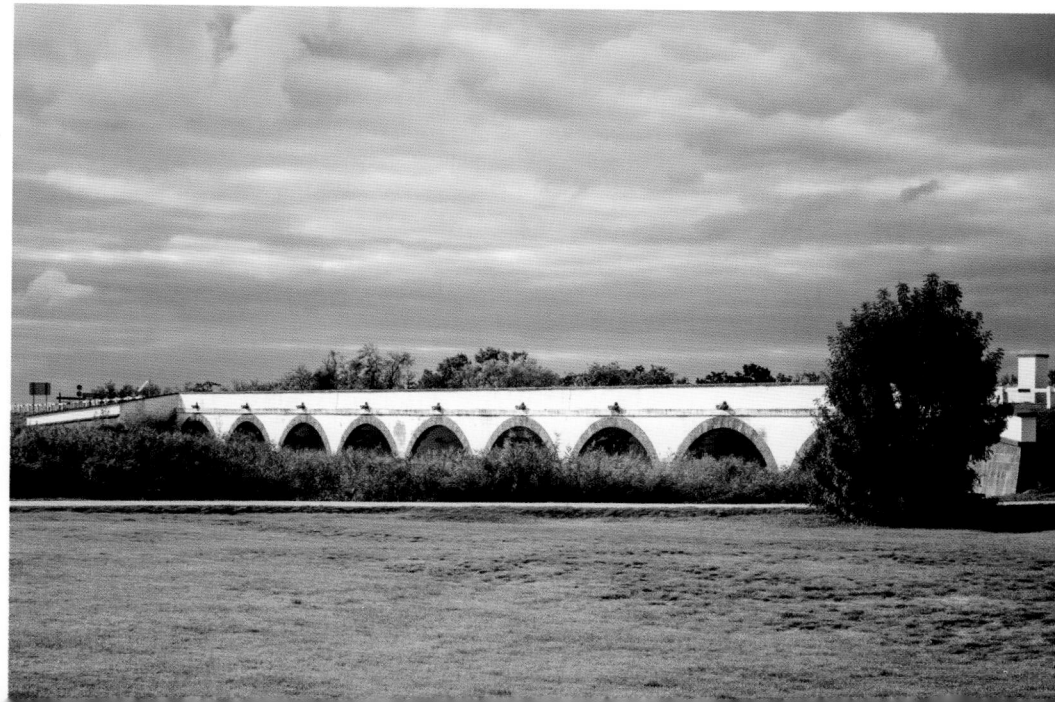

⊙ Tip

These days Lake Tisza is used for water sports and fishing, and sunbathers stretch out on its banks during fine weather. Although it's a fairly popular resort, it doesn't attract the noisy crowds of Lake Balaton.

areas that are now nature reserves are the Hortobágy National Park and the Kiskunság National Park, south of Kecskemét (see page 238).

There were attempts in the 17th century to hold the drifting sand by planting acacias, but it is only since 1945 that there has been a systematic planting of forests, with preference given to broad-leaved trees over conifers, along with a canal-building programme. Underground lie medicinal and hot springs as well as oil and natural gas. With the exploitation of these reserves in the south and east of the region, industrialisation is moving fast.

Due to these developments and to the progressive agricultural exploitation of the Puszta, the character of the landscape has changed considerably. Today it is dominated by machines, not by the vast herds of animals that were here when German statesman, Bismarck, travelled through the region in 1852. He wrote to his wife about the 'very eastern, but beautiful world' which was quite untouched. Modes of travel have also changed with the

times. Bismarck was accompanied by a troop of imperial Ulans 'as a protection against the Betyárs, robbers on horseback, wrapped in great furs, whose leaders wear black masks.' Today, visitors usually arrive in tourist buses, accompanied by informative guides.

The Puszta was once a wild, deserted place. Herdsmen and their animals would head for home in December once snow fell. The csikós, the horse-herder, was the highest in the hierarchy of herdsmen. Next came the gulyás, the 'cowboy', and finally the juhász, the shepherd, whose animals were forbidden to cross a grazing ground before the cattle.

THE NATIONAL PARK

In spite (or because of) these changes, the Hungarian Puszta was inscribed on Unesco's World Heritage List in 1999 as 'an outstanding example of a cultural landscape shaped by a pastoral human society'. The **Hortobágy National Park ⑰** (Hortobágyi Nemzeti Park) 'represents the harmonious

A farm near Hortobágy.

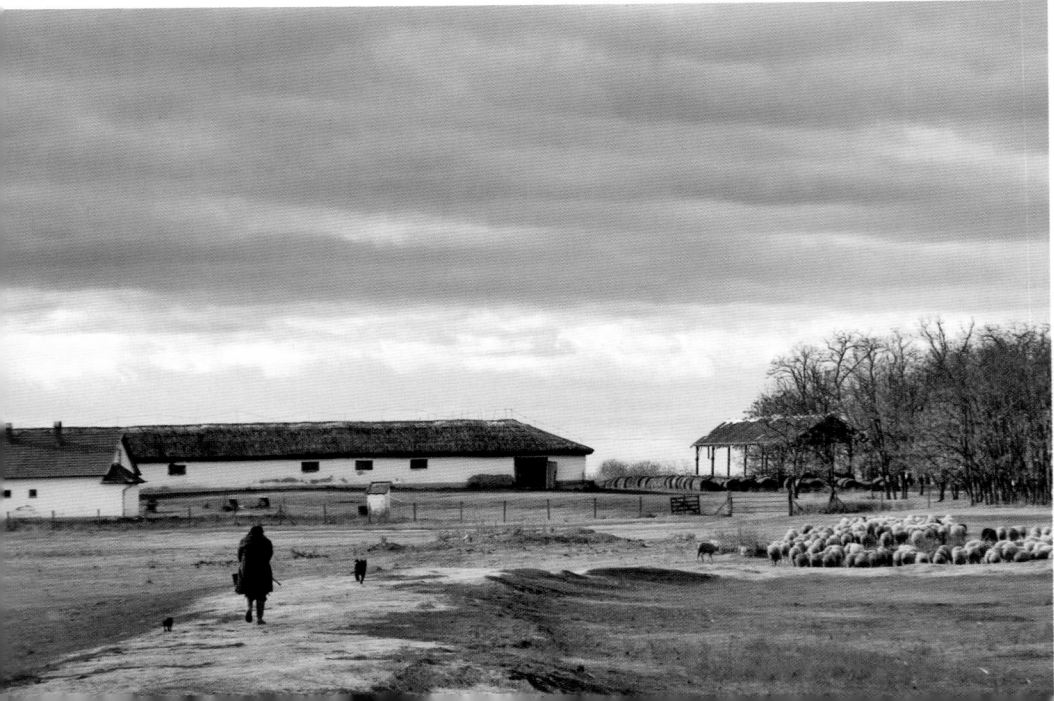

interaction between human beings and nature', it continued.

The **Hortobágy Puszta,** at 70,000 hectares (173,000 acres) the biggest single area of steppe grazing land in Central Europe, certainly fulfils these criteria. Here horses graze in vast herds, and the herdsmen in traditional clothes – white linen shirts with wide sleeves, wide ankle-length trousers, broad-brimmed flat hats – display their elegant horsemanship before groups of admiring visitors.

This is still the home of the grey cattle with their wide, sweeping horns, tough animals that can endure great hardship. From the early Middle Ages until the 19th century, huge herds were driven in long treks to distant slaughterhouses. The herdsmen's dogs are still working today: the little, agile puli sheepdog with its dark ragged fur; the komondor that looks like a large mop; and the smooth-haired white-and-brown kuvasz, the faithful companion of earlier cattle herds, said to be capable of fighting off wolves.

Birdwatchers will find an organised trip, which can be arranged with Tourinform in Debrecen and Hortobágy, the best way to explore the park. Apart from the many kinds of waterfowl (duck eggs provided welcome variety in the otherwise monotonous diet of the herdsmen), herons, cranes and bustards, now rare in Europe, live here.

In the woodlands there are hares, red deer and boar. And finally, at the end of the observation chain, there is the special flora of the region, endless grasses and reeds, tiny flowers, myriad water growths that can only exist in these pristine and protected regions.

HORTOBÁGY

Hortobágy ⑱ is the centre of this region. Its landmark is the 168-metre (551ft) Nine-Arch Bridge (Kilence lyukú híd) built between 1827 and 1833. Every 19–20 August the famous Bridge Market (at the same time as the

Debrecen Flower Festival) is held here, where you can buy just about anything from soup to nuts, as well as tacky mass-produced souvenirs, of course. Otherwise, there are numerous shops in Hortobágy near the bridge, though the prices are fairly steep.

The group of statues entitled People of the Alföld is surrounded by the market and its activity. A csárda (inn) has been here since the 18th century, and is one of a series of eating houses that were sited a day's journey apart on the cattle trail. It offers good food and accommodation.

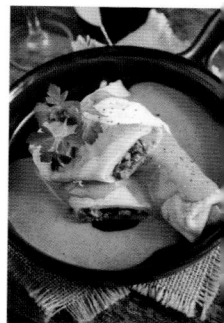

Hortobágyi palacsinta.

There is also a **Herdsmen's Museum** (Pásztormúzeum; daily, mid-Mar–Apr & Oct 10am–4pm; May–June & Sept 9am–5pm; July & Aug 9am–6pm), housed in a former barn and whose many exhibits give information about the herdsmen's lives long ago.

Some of the healing waters beneath the Hortobágy bubble to the surface in the thermal baths at **Hajdúszoboszló** (see page 114). But for unbuttoned outdoor recreation it is best to head west again.

Ecumenical Church in Hortobágy.

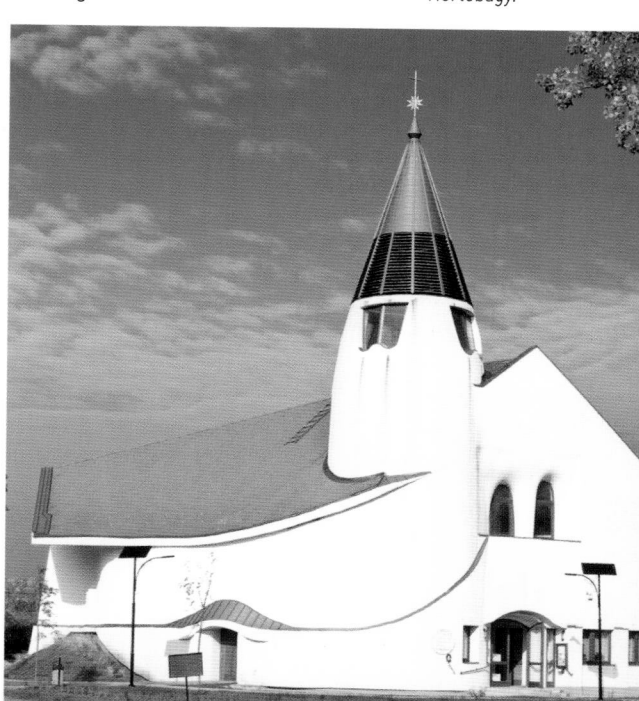

☉ Tip

There are two churches in Szolnok worth seeing: the Trinity Church in Koltói Anna utca and a Baroque Franciscan church on Templom ut that is a venue for summer concerts.

THE TISZA REGION

On Highway 33, you'll reach **Tiszafüred** ⓳ and the dam on the Tisza in 20 minutes. Not even the Danube has had to submit to so much in the name of profitability as the Tisza, having been regulated, shortened, embanked and dammed into a lake of 110 sq km (42 sq miles). In 2000, leakage of cyanide and other heavy metals from a Romanian gold mine caused massive damage to its waters and wildlife, which resulted in Hungary claiming £72 million (US$103 million) compensation from Aural, the mining company.

Leaving Tiszafüred, Highway 34 joins the E60 near Kenderes. After passing fields growing grains and sunflowers, you will reach Hungary's rice-growing region.

Szolnok ⓴, the most important bridgehead on the Tisza, is the next stop on the itinerary. In prehistoric times there was a ford at Szolnok, and the Romans set up a military camp. Under the reign of the Árpáds (900–1301), the city flourished as a trading place for the salt shipped up the Tisza from the eastern Carpathians.

The castle that had stood here since 1506 was destroyed by the Habsburgs after the War of Independence (1703–11). Szolnok played an important part in the 1848–49 revolution and in the workers' movement in the late 19th century. Aided by the Pest–Szolnok railway link, opened on 1 September 1847, industrialisation rapidly increased its prosperity. Partially destroyed in World War II, Szolnok developed into a busy trade and shipping centre with its harbour on the River Tisza.

EXPLORING THE TOWN

At first glance Szolnok is not a pretty sight, owing to the modern buildings constructed by the post-war regime along the traffic-beaten main street. However, on the main square, Kossuth tér, the János Damjanich Museum (Tue–Sun 9am–4pm, until 5pm May–Oct), in a late-Classical former hotel, is a diamond in the rough. Its collections explore the region's Kuman and prehistoric past with models, handicrafts and costumes, as well as the more bourgeois aspects of 19th-century life in Szolnok, such as a typical drawing room and a tobacconist's shop.

The picture gallery reflects the work of the town's well-known artists' colony which flourished in the late 19th and early 20th centuries, and offers more transcendent views of the city and region, such as the Chicken Market by Deák- Ébner.

Szolnok offers plenty of opportunities for relaxation. Down on the banks of the Tisza is the **Tisza Szálló,** a traditional hotel with a nice adjoining spa adorned with frescoes. The elegant ballroom that now serves as a dining room is a good choice for a meal on a summer evening, when you can sit on the terrace watching the river flow. On the opposite bank is the large Tisza Park, with thermal pools and water sports.

Platform at the Szolnok Train Station.

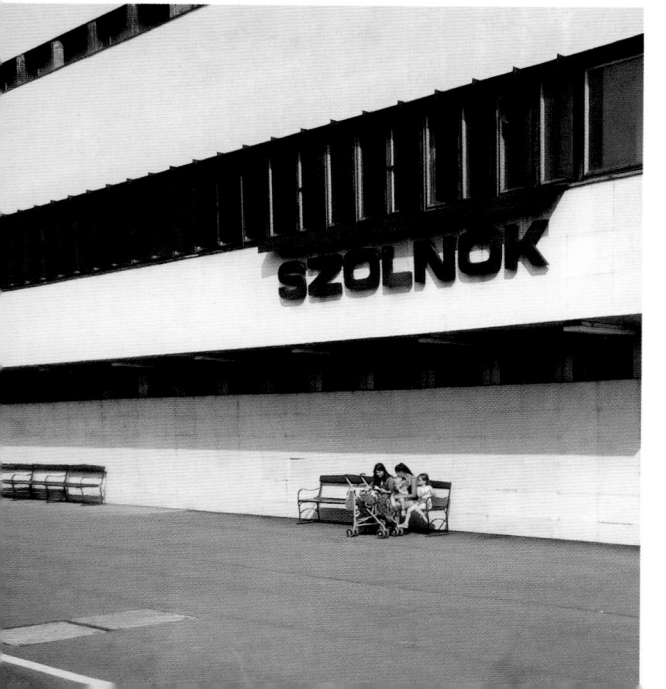

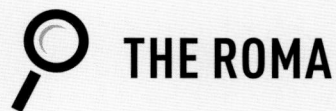

THE ROMA

> 'Who has not seen in the dominions of our fatherland those wandering hordes, travelling from village to village in their covered wagons drawn by wretched nags?

Who does not know of the dark strangers who live out their wretched lives in mud huts on the fringes of our villages? Whose heart has not been overcome by deep emotion on hearing these "new Magyar" musicians strike up their walling melodies? Surely each one of us has noticed how the dark olive, elongated faces of these guests from Hungary differ from those of all the other peoples of Europe, as do their dark, restlessly glittering eyes, their well formed lips, the wiry, dark curly hair, the slender supple forms, the delicate hands and feet, and their ever cheerful and jocular natures.'

This portrait, sympathetically drawn in 1902, is the work of Archduke Josef of Austria, a pioneer of research into the Roma people, Hungary's largest and most disadvantaged ethnic minority, which numbers around 600,000 people. This picture is in some ways still accurate, but the mud huts are now slums, and those who are still nomadic travel in ramshackle vans rather than covered wagons.

After World War II, the traditional Roma occupations (begging, door-to-door selling, horse trading, small businesses) were either prohibited or redundant. Most were forced into unskilled industrial work. Large-scale privatisation in the 1990s left most casual labourers without a job, and the great majority of Roma live off meagre state welfare.

Contrary to popular perception, only about three percent of Roma are musicians, playing to tourists in the cities. The vast majority live in the countryside in conditions of chronic social deprivation: high birth rates, low life expectancy, unemployment and poor housing. Cultural differences and racial prejudice further divide the Roma from the rest of the population. About 70 percent have Hungarian as their mother tongue, the others speak a Romani dialect or Romanian. Within these groups are divisions along ethnic, tribal and cultural lines, which can hinder progress.

Poverty and racial conflicts have led some Roma to seek political asylum abroad, although most do not see emigration as the answer. The European Roma Rights Centre (www.errc.org) campaigns for justice for Roma people throughout Europe and was involved in a case that in 2004 forced certain Hungarian authorities to pay damages to Roma families whose children had been segregated at school. Education is crucial, not only of the Roma people, but also of the rest of Hungarian society, to combat deeply ingrained prejudices.

Unlike other ethnic minorities in Hungary, the Roma community is less concerned with preserving its culture than with catching up socially and economically. The Hungarian government is committed to the 'Decade of Roma Inclusion', but there is a long way to go.

A Roma playing accordion.

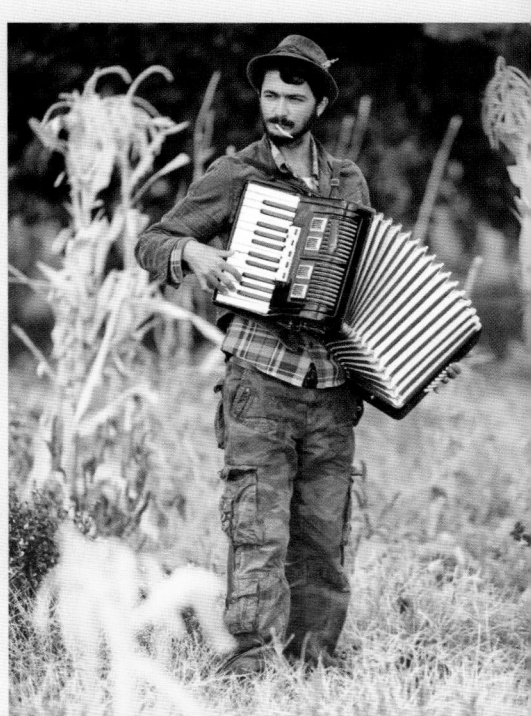

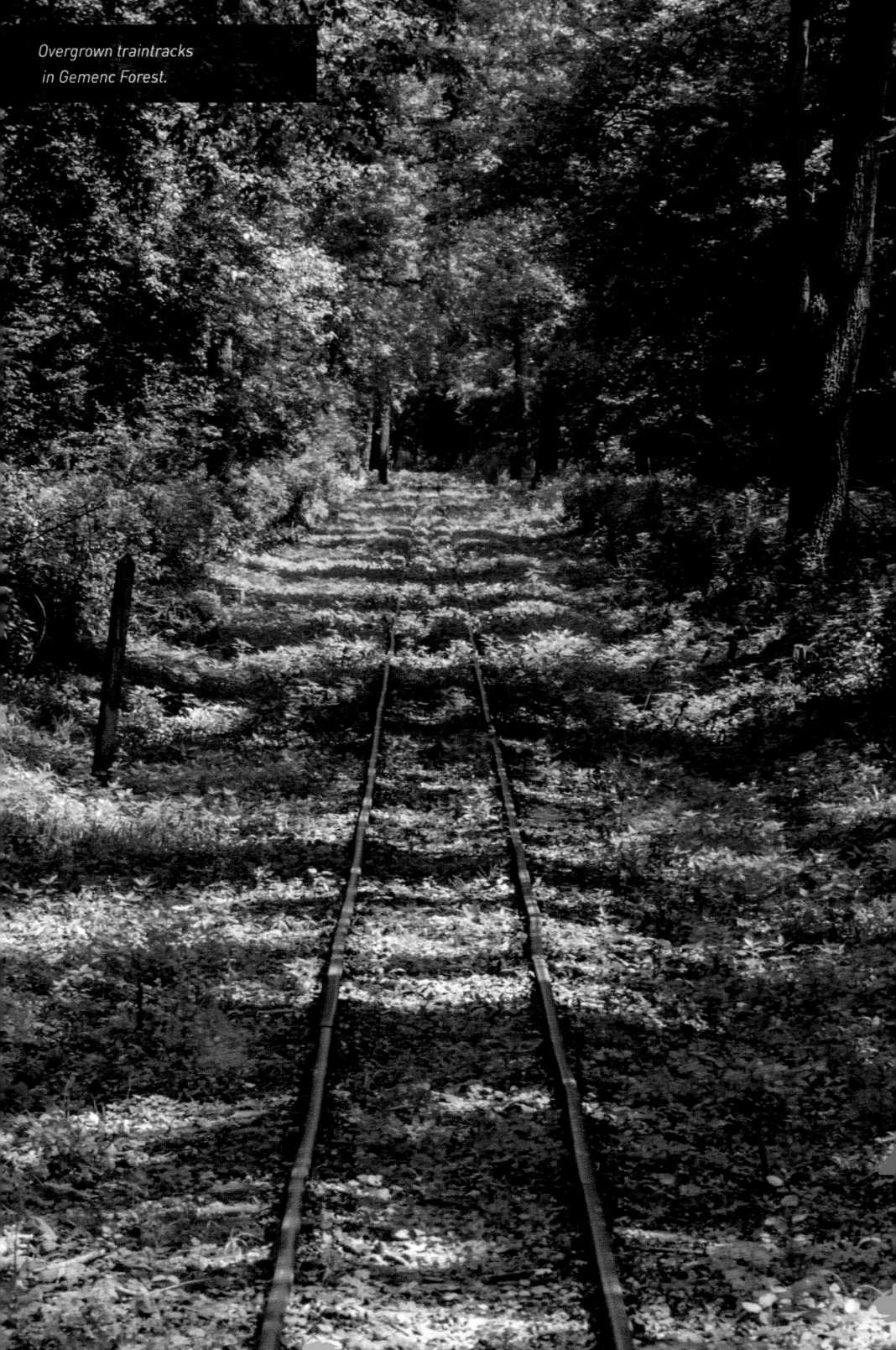
Overgrown traintracks in Gemenc Forest.

SOUTHWEST HUNGARY

Blessed with a mild climate, the southwest offers outdoor activities in its forests, art and architecture in the beautiful city of Pécs and wine tasting in Villány.

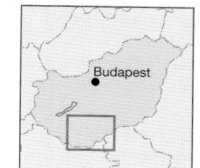

From Budapest, a 160-km (100-mile) drive through the former floodplain of the Danube on Highway 51 brings you to the southerly town of **Baja ❶**, a major riverside settlement since the Middle Ages (see page 181).

ACROSS THE DANUBE

West from Baja, Highway 55 crosses the Danube and the southern part of the Gemenc Forest and the Sárköz, an area criss-crossed by waterways. Many of the high-gabled farmhouses with decorative façades are protected by law. During Roman times this region was known for its wines, though the Turks destroyed all the vineyards for religious reasons after taking the town in 1541 (they had passed this way before, in 1526, after their victory at Mohács).

Szekszárd ❷, a town on the Danube before the river was diverted, is known as the 'town of seven hills'. The hilly landscape and the woods in the nearby flood-plain make it a peaceful holiday resort.

The buildings worth seeing bear the hallmark of the 18th century, as the wrath of the Turks left nothing of old 'Sagard' standing. It had been built on a Roman settlement and was mentioned in documents as both a town and the seat of a Benedictine abbey in the 11th century.

The remains have been restored somewhat heavy-handedly and are in the great white **County Hall** (Megyeház) on the central square, Béla tér. The building also houses the Franz Liszt **memorial room** and an **exhibition** of the paintings of Eszter Mattioni (both Apr–Oct Tue–Sun 9am–5pm). Outside the gates of the town, in the former floodplain of the Danube, is the **Gemenc Forest ❸** (Gemenci-erdő), one of the most beautiful nature reserves in Hungary (see page 180).

The road north out of Szekszárd joins Highway 6 (if coming from

⊙ **Main attractions**
Szekszárd
Gemenc Forest
Pécs
Siklós

Maps on pages
260 and 264

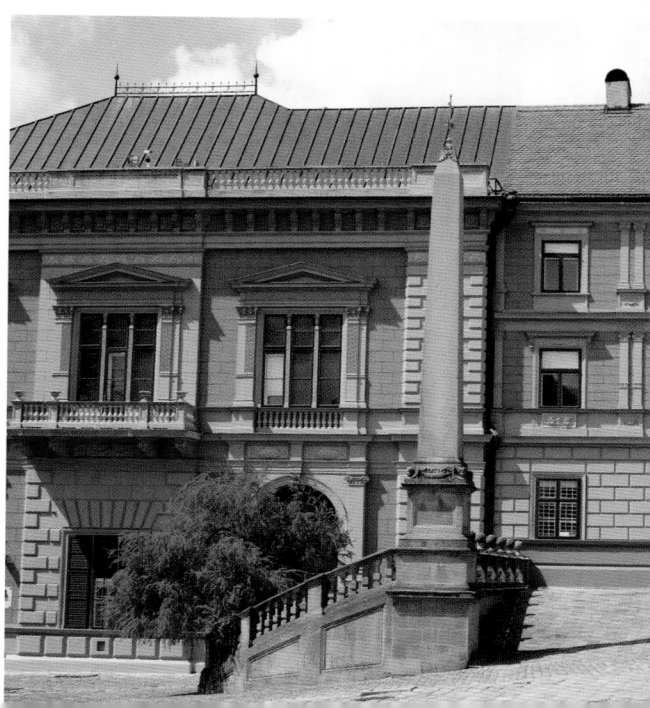

County Hall, Szekszárd.

⊙ Tip

Today, the best-known wine produced in the area is Szekszárd Kadarka, which was introduced in the 18th century by German and Southern Slav settlers. You can sample this wine – a favourite of both Franz Schubert and Franz Liszt, who gave many concerts here – in one of the many cellars around town and the surrounding countryside.

Budapest) after just over 2km (1 mile); join this road and turn south and you will pass through the Mecsek range on the way to Pécs.

AT THE FOOT OF THE MOUNTAIN

This journey of 58km (36 miles) takes you through Bonyhád, Hidas and Pécsvárad, which lie at the foot of Zengő **Mountain**. At 682 metres (2,237ft) its summit is the highest point of this range of forest-clad hills running from southwest to northeast. Here the climate is almost Mediterranean, and almond and fig trees, introduced by the Turks, flourish in gardens and by the roadside. The summers here are warm, but not scorching as in the Alföld, and the winters are mild.

The castle at **Pécsvárad** ❹ started life as a Benedictine abbey, founded by István I. In the 14th and 15th centuries, it was developed into a fortress, which was later demolished by the abbot, Brother Georgius, when it could no longer be defended against the Turks. The Archbishop of

Cologne, Konrad Zinzendorfer, later took over the monastery and rebuilt it in Baroque style. The Romanesque church by the castle wall, with its Byzantine frescoes in the apse, survived, as did the massive gate tower dating from the 15th century, with a Renaissance well-house.

CITY OF ART

A few kilometres along Highway 6 brings you to **Pécs** ❺, contender for Hungary's most beautiful city. Its gentle climate, open, friendly people, architecture ranging from Roman through to the Habsburg period, prestigious art collections and museums, all make it a great place to visit. With the inner city now largely freed of cars, it's a pleasure to stroll along the streets and relax in the pavement cafés.

Originally a Celtic settlement, Pécs became an important Roman town at the time of the Emperor Hadrian, when it was called Sopianae. Before the Hungarians settled here in 899 it was inhabited by Germans and Franks

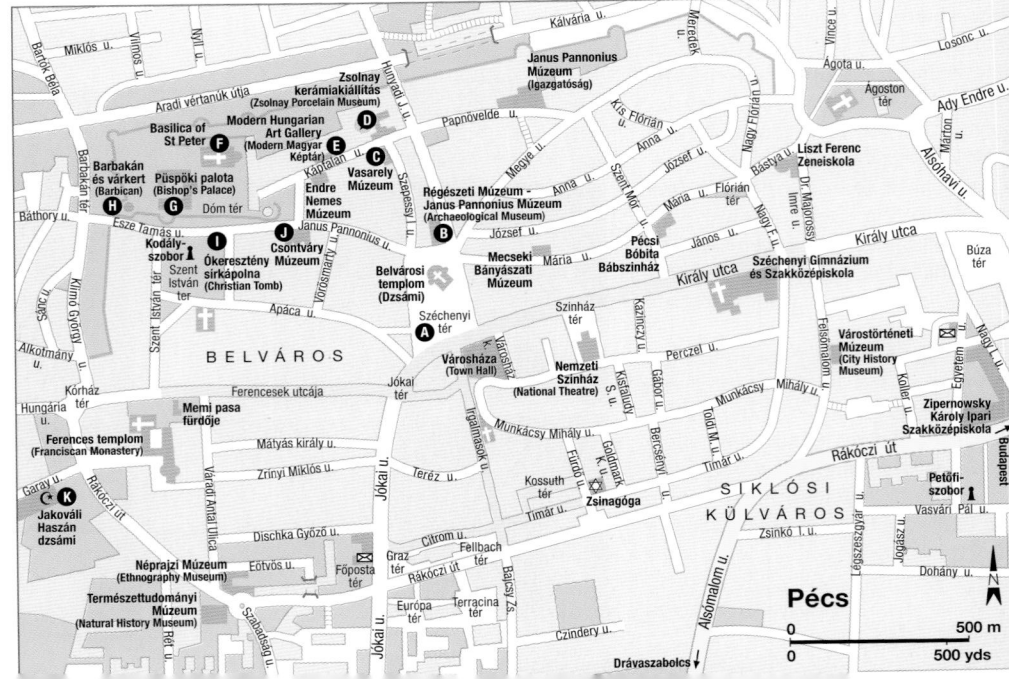

and known as Quinque Ecclesiae (Fünfkirchen in German), after the five Christian churches built here in the 4th and 5th centuries.

The town of Pécs was chronicled for the first time in the reign of King László I in 1093 as a diocesan town and a centre of trade with Byzantium. King Lajos (Louis) I founded the first Hungarian university here in 1367. The Turks conquered the town in 1543 but, instead of demolishing it in their usual fashion, they developed it to reflect their faith and lifestyle, constructing mosques, prayer houses, minarets and an Islamic monastery. In 1686 the city fell to the Habsburgs, and rebuilding took place again – this time in Austrian Baroque style.

MIGHTY MOSQUE

Széchenyi tér Ⓐ, the main square, is dominated by the mighty dome of the former mosque of Pasha Kassim Gazi, the largest surviving building from the Turkish occupation. It was built on the foundations of St Bartholomew's Church.

In 1686, it was given to the Jesuits by Margrave Louis of Baden, who liberated the city from the Turks. The minaret was removed and the mosque was given a Baroque make-over. Following pressure from 20th-century art historians, it was freed from these unsuitable impositions, but most importantly, the Turkish dome was exposed and covered with copper.

Today this building, with both crescent and cross on its tower, serves as the Catholic **Inner City Parish Church** (Belvárosi plébánia-templom), and no one seems to mind the ogives, the fretted stone screens, the mihrab (prayer niche) facing southeast, or the Koranic inscriptions on the wall. In front of the church, there's a Trinity column and an equestrian statue of János Hunyadi, the father of King Mátyás Corvinus (Matthias I), who made a name for himself after ending the Turkish siege of Nándorfehérvár (Belgrade) in 1456 (see page 37).

The streets surrounding the square are all worthy of exploration. To the southeast of the square is

⊙ Tip

For some peaceful walking, head for the hills surrounding Pécsvárad. The hiking trails are marked in yellow and for miles around there is nothing but acacia groves, copses and the occasional farmhouse.

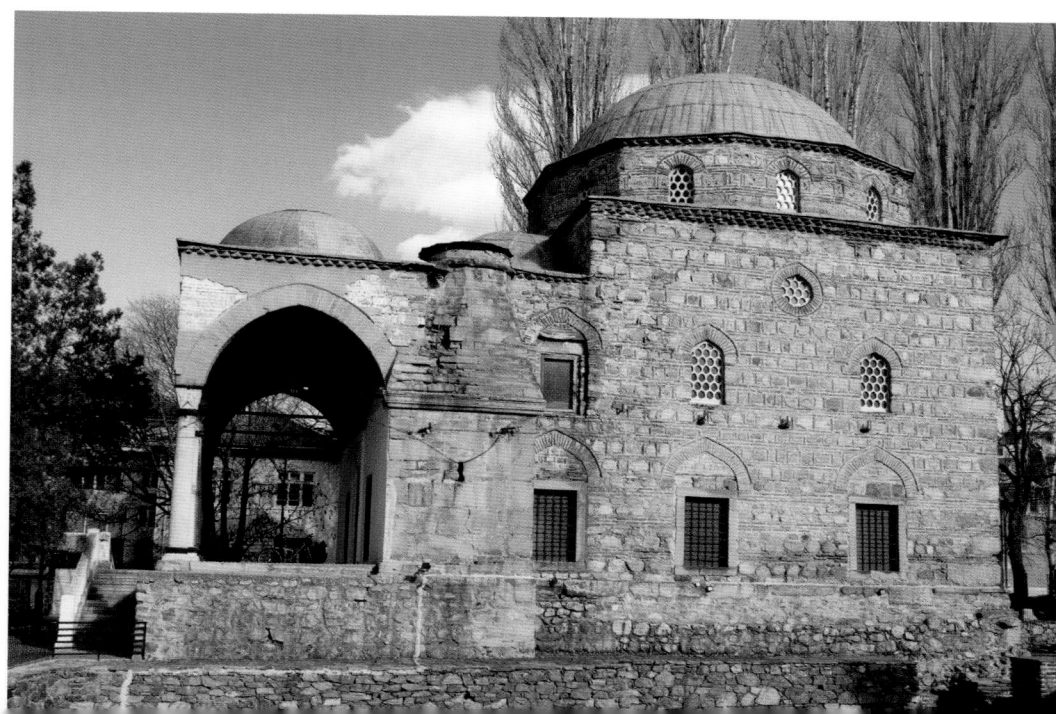

Mosque of Pasha Qasim.

⊙ **Tip**

Pécs' oval-shaped old town is easily negotiated on foot and is enclosed by roads that follow the line of the former city walls, built in the 13th century after the Mongol invasion.

pedestrianised Király utca, which is devoted to restaurants and the beautiful art nouveau Pannonius Hotel. The street opens up onto a square where the National Theatre (Nemzeti színház) is located.

The lively Ferencesek útcaja leads down towards the 16th-century baths of Paska Memi, which stand beside the Franciscan church. Finally, to the south is Kossuth tér where, as well as a car park, you'll find the synagogue (completed in 1865), which stages occasional concerts featuring its rare Angster organ.

Housed in a mid-18th-century building north of Széchenyi tér is the archaeology department of the **Régészeti Múzeum–Janus Pannonius Múzeum B** (Tue–Sun 10am–6pm), which displays archaeological finds dating from Roman times until the Middle Ages. It was named after Janus Pannonius (1434–72), one of the greatest poets of his time. In 1459, King Mátyás made him Bishop of Pécs and royal representative at the papal court, although this did not stop him from joining his uncle, the Primate of Hungary, János Vitéz, in a conspiracy against the king.

UNUSUAL MUSEUMS

A steep street leads up the hill into Káptalan utca and its clutch of interesting museums. At No. 3 is the **Vasarely Múzeum C** (Tue–Sun 10am–6pm), dedicated to the work of Pécs-born Victor Vasarely (1908–97), originator of Op Art, the use of simple shapes to create the illusion of movement. The geometric use of space in his work is impressive.

Just opposite, at No. 2, the oldest surviving house in the city today contains the **Zsolnay Porcelain Museum D** (Zsolnay kerámiakiállítás; Tue–Sun 10am–6pm). The building itself is worth a second look: enter through a Gothic gate and then pass a Gothic wall niche with a seat that was probably used by the coachmen of wealthy citizens waiting for their masters. The stone Renaissance window frames and the neoclassical wrought-iron grilles bear

Zsolnay Fountain, Pécs.

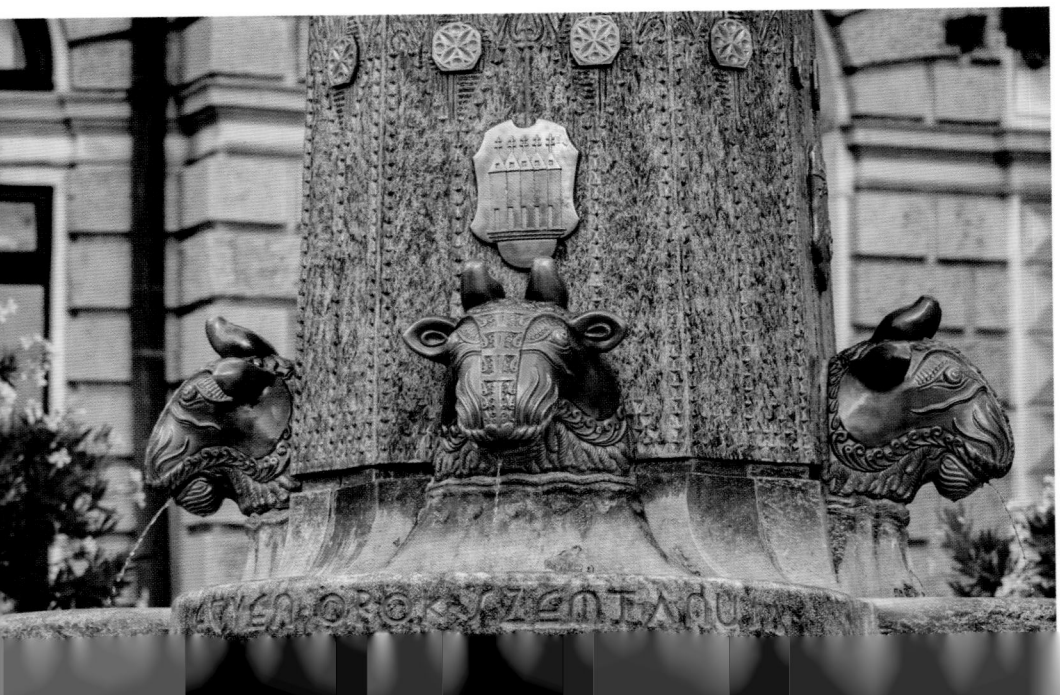

witness to successive repairs and improvements undertaken in whatever style was fashionable at the time.

The ground floor of the museum shows some of the stark works of the sculptor Amerigo Tot. The upper floor illustrates the history of the Zsolnay tile factory with a great many exhibits. Zsolnay majolica, which uses strong, almost metallic colours, was a favourite decorative material for Secessionist (Art Nouveau) architects in Hungary and can be spotted throughout the country, not least in Pécs itself: the tympanum of the post office, for example, or the Zsolnay memorial fountain featuring the four bull heads by Andor Pilch that stands at the southernmost corner of Széchenyi tér.

If you would like to buy some of the ceramic ware, there is a Zsolnay outlet shop near Jókai Mór tér.

Next door to the Zsolnay Museum, at No. 4, is the **Modern Hungarian Art Gallery E** (Modern Magyar Képtár; Tue–Sun 10am–6pm), a good place to get a broad overview of Hungarian art from 1850 to the present day.

THE CATHEDRAL

Continuing west brings you to the sloping Dóm tér, a broad cobblestoned plaza accessed by a flight of steps. The layout of the entire ensemble is one of the most successful bits of city planning in Hungary. At the back is the cathedral, to its right the archives and parish house, and to the left the Bishop's Palace, in classical style and with an amusing modern statue featuring Franz Liszt, by Imre Varga. The intricately designed entrance gate depicting Pécs receiving the keys to the city was installed on 30 December 2000.

The great square is dominated by the **Basilica of St Peter F**, otherwise simply known as the **Cathedral** (Szent Péter Székes-egyház; Mon–Sat 9am–5pm, Sun 11.30am–5pm). Pécs's hallmark, with four mighty square towers and an ornate interior, work on the cathedral began in the 11th century, not far from the foundations of a

Inside the Basilica of St Peter.

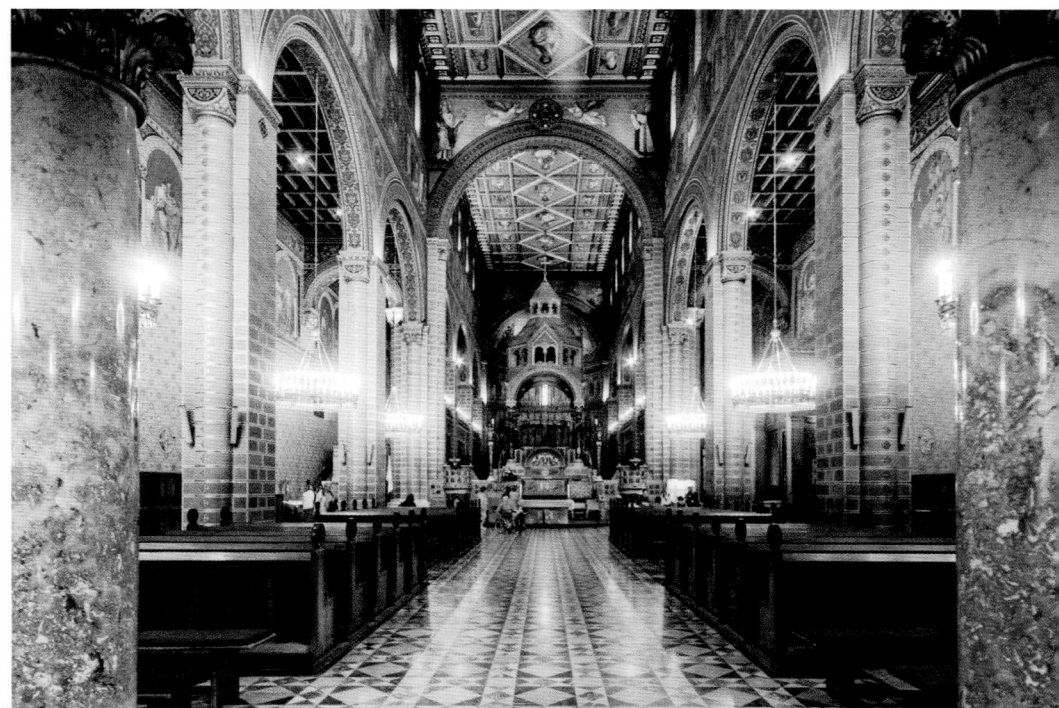

4th-century basilica. More work took place in every subsequent century, until the final phase was completed in the 16th century. The building was thoroughly renovated in 1881, which explains its neo-Romanesque appearance. The unearthed Roman stonework has found a home in the lapidarium of the Janus Pannonius Museum (see page 262). The western towers of the cathedral date from the 11th century, the eastern towers from 100 years later. During the Turkish occupation, part of the cathedral served as a mosque, and the crypt was turned into an armoury.

The red marble Renaissance altar in the **Corpus Christi Chapel** deserves special mention, as does the rich marble decoration in the main choir. The ceiling paintings are by Károly Lotz (1835–1904) and Bertalan Székely (1845–1910).

AROUND THE CATHEDRAL SQUARE

The **Bishop's Palace** Ⓖ (Püspöki palota) in Dóm tér has irregular opening hours (check at the tourist office on Széchenyi tér) and houses some 17th-century Gobelins tapestries from Brussels, a gift to the bishopric of Pécs from Maria Theresa.

Next door is the former **Barbican** Ⓗ (Barbakán és várkert), a medieval construction that was once part of the fortified wall and defended the city gate. You can walk along parts of the city walls, beyond which lies modern Pécs. The circular road here is lined with busts of the 13 leaders of the Hungarian anti-Habsburg rebellion of 1848–49. They were executed at Arad (now in Romania), and this ensemble was unveiled in 1999 to commemorate the 150th anniversary of the event.

Just south of Dom tér is shady **Szent István tér** (also known as Séta tér), whose cooling fountain is a favourite meeting place in hot weather. The 1st-century AD **Christian tomb chapel** Ⓘ (Ókeresztény sírkápolna) near the eastern obelisk is similar to the Roman catacombs, a rarity outside Italy. Much of the opulent painting is preserved; no wonder

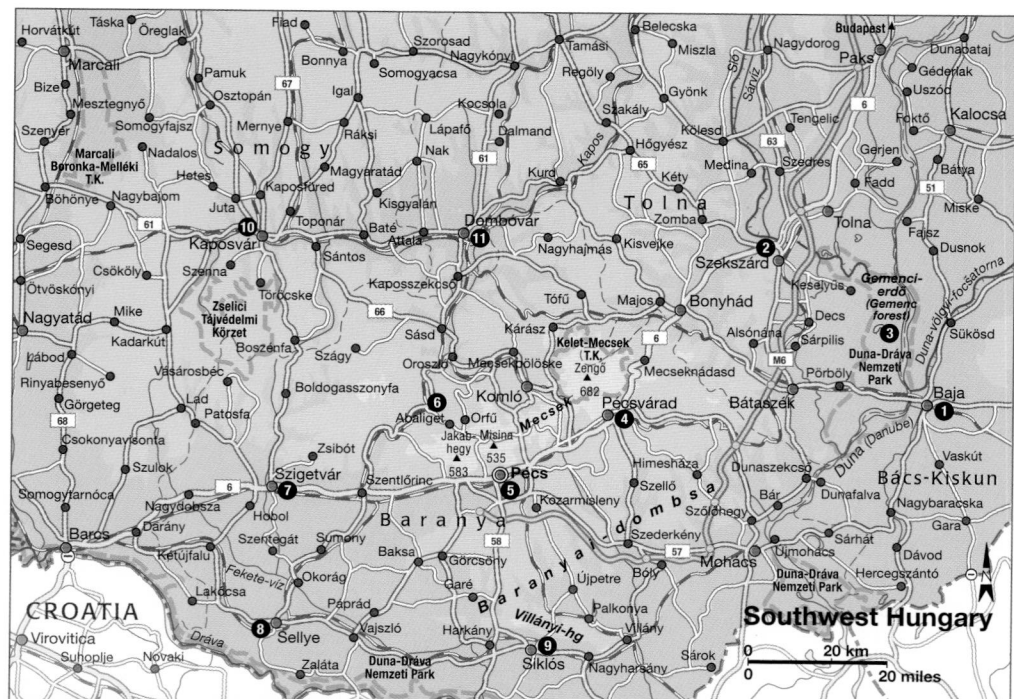

that Unesco gave these tombs a place on the World Heritage List as exceptional illustrations of early Christian sepulchral art.

One of Hungary's well known artists, Kosztka Tivadar Csontváry (1853–1919), is celebrated at the excellent **Csontváry Múzeum** ❶ (Tue–Sun 10am–6pm) on Janus Pannonius utca. In contrast to Vasarely, Csontváry received no recognition in his lifetime, and his tortured genius has been compared to that of Van Gogh. He was wrongly pigeonholed by contemporaries as either Naïve or surrealist, and not until after his death was his work admired by Picasso, among others, and awarded the Grand Prix at the World Fair in Brussels in 1958. The inspiration for many of Csontváry's visionary, even hallucinatory, pictures, came from the Middle East.

OUTSIDE THE CITY WALL

Walk from the centre of town along the pleasant pedestrianised Ferencesek utcája. Just outside the western city wall is the religious centre of the Turks in Pécs, the **Pasha Hassan Jakovali Mosque** ❷ (Jakováli Haszán dzsámi), crowned by its octagonal dome. This building, the most intact Turkish mosque in the country, has been stripped of all additions and restored to its original form. From its high gallery, protected by screens, there is a good view of Pécs. Behind the entrance, with its stalactitic ornamentation, is a small museum (Apr–Sept Thu–Tue 10am–6pm) containing some of the surviving relics and documents from Turkish Pécs.

Two museums on the outer edge of the old town deserve a mention. At Rákóczi út 15, the **Ethnography Museum** (Néprajzi Múzeum; Tue–Sun 10am–6pm) documents Hungarian, Slav and German folk culture, while a journey into Pécs's past can be made at the **City History Museum**

(Várostörténti Múzeum; same opening hours), Felsőmalom utca 9.

FOREST TRAILS

As an antidote to all this culture, you could take a number of walks through the forested Mecsek hills north of Pécs, where the landscape varies between steep gradients and gently rolling meadows. The lower slopes are accessible on foot if you leave Széchenyi tér and head north on Hunyadi János út; towns and villages further afield can be reached by bus or car.

A marked forest trail runs from Egervölgy past the Illyrian fortifications – at a height of 3 metres (10ft) they're impossible to miss, and offer a wide view from the top. The ruins of a monastery dating from the 13th century were rescued from oblivion by archaeologists and the excavations can be visited.

The highest point of the range is the summit of **Misina** (535 metres/1,755ft), from where you can enjoy a beautiful view of the town,

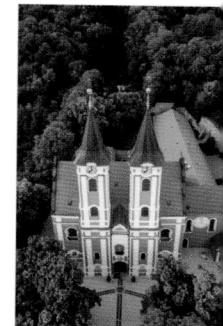

Mary's Congregation, Siklós.

Széchenyi Square, Pécs.

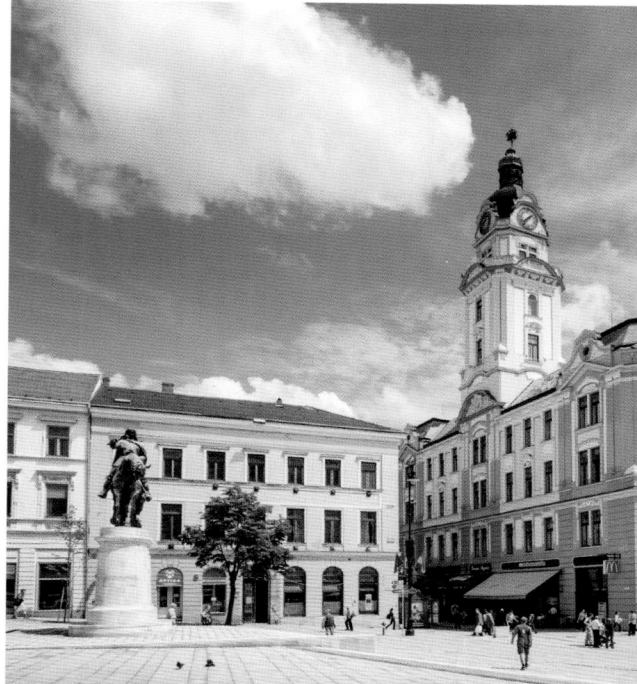

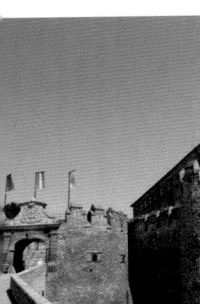

Siklós Castle.

Village of Orfű, on the shores of Lake Pécs.

its tall towers, the green dome of the mosque and the red roofs of the houses.

Abaliget ❻ (daily mid-Mar–mid-Oct 9am–6pm; mid-Oct–mid-Mar 10am–3pm), with its limestone caves, is also popular for excursions. It lies some 20km/12 miles northwest of Pécs and if you are not travelling by car, a bus will take you from Pécs in around 30 minutes along the winding roads through the hills to Orfű, the 'town of four lakes', from where you can take a refreshing 3km (2-mile) walk to the 500,000-year-old limestone caves.

Like all caves, those at Abaliget are cool inside and warm clothing is recommended on the 460-metre/yd walk past the bizarre limestone figurations. The peculiar air in the caves is said to be beneficial for bronchial problems. **Lake Orfű** (Orfűi-tó) has good facilities for water sports and has become quite an attraction over the years as a place to cool off from the city heat. It maintains a friendly, unspoiled atmosphere.

SZIGETVÁR'S CASTLE

Back on Highway 6, heading west from Pécs takes you to **Szigetvár** ❼, a small town all but forgotten by the tourist trade. Its fame rests on the mighty castle surrounded by (now dilapidated) brick walls and bastions. It allegedly took a 100,000-strong Turkish army 33 days of siege to take this castle in 1566 against a tiny Hungarian force led by Miklós Zrinyi, a Croat nobleman.

All 2,500 Hungarians and Croats defending the castle died, but 25,000 Turks also lost their lives in the battle, and Suleiman died on 5 September, before the fort was taken. Despite their victory, the Turks were so weakened that they gave up their planned attack on Vienna. Instead, they rebuilt the castle and the town, recognising the importance of this fortification in the marshes of the Almás River.

Today, the mosque in the castle courtyard contains the **Castle Museum** (Vár Múzeum; May–Sept daily 9am–6pm; Oct–Apr Tue–Sun 9am–4pm) with an exhibition illustrating the history of the town and the castle. Note

⊙ WINE COUNTRY

This entire region is known for its German population – the German (and sometimes Croat) names of the towns are prominently displayed – and for its high-quality wines, typically full-bodied reds. The village of Villány (Wieland in German) is the main centre for tasting and buying wine; look out for the respected Gere and Bock labels. Wreaths hang over the doors of private cellars offering tastings. The Wine Museum (Bomúzeum; Tue–Sun 9am–5pm) on Bem utca provides insights on the industry as well as wine-tastings.

The road back to Pécs leads through more wine villages, whose cellars are rows of quaint-fronted houses along the hillsides. **Palkonya** also has an unusual church that was once, visibly, a mosque.

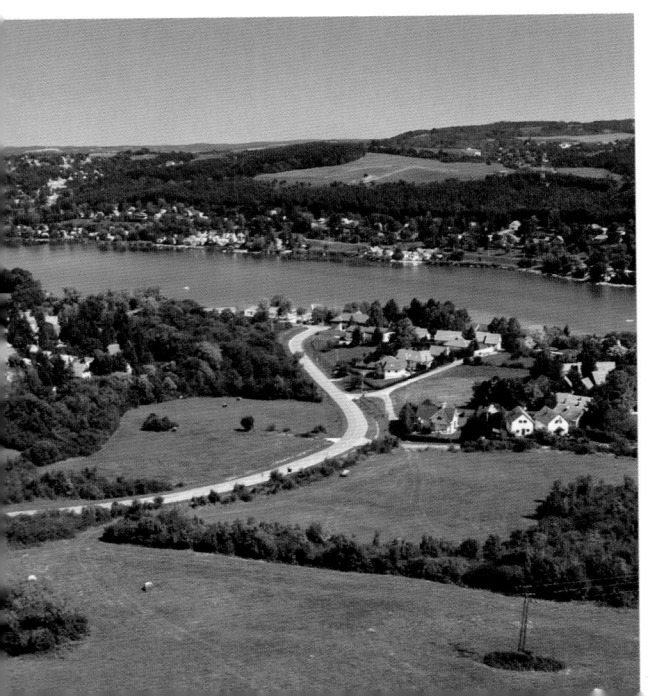

the splendid wrought-iron gate and the screens in front of the windows.

Contrasting bizarrely at the entrance are two modern sculptures, one commemorating the millennium, the other honouring Soviet soldiers who died in local battles in World War II.

The Roman Catholic parish church in Zrínyi tér, the centre of the town, was also once a mosque before being altered to form a single-nave Baroque church. A fresco depicts the battle at the castle. Many Turkish elements – ogive arches, a stalactite vault and two red marble holy water fonts (formerly washbasins for the Turks) – are evidence of the church's Islamic origins. The little house in Bástya utca, built of brick, was once a caravanserai, and is now a **small museum** exhibiting Turkish miniatures (May–Sept daily 10am–4pm).

To the north of town is the small **Park of Turkish-Hungarian Friendship** (Török-Magyar barátság parkja), which was sponsored by the Turkish government as a gesture of reconciliation and inaugurated by President Demirel in 1997, the 500th anniversary of Suleiman's birth. It is dominated by two bronze reliefs, of Miklós Zrínyi and Suleiman the Magnificent, by Metin Jurdanur.

SOUTH OF SZIGETVÁR

To the south of Szigetvár is a low-lying region known as Ormánság, which is distinctive for two reasons. First, to minimise pressure on land and resources, local peasant families generally had only one child. Second, houses were ingeniously built on rollers so that they could be wheeled to dry land when the nearby Dráva River flooded. The Géza Kiss Ormánság Museum (Tue–Sun 10am–2pm, until 4pm Apr–Oct) sheds light on the local way of life in a little peasant house in **Sellye ❽**. Another feature of this area is that some of the churches, notably those in Drávaivány, Kórós and Kovácshida, have painted, coffered ceilings.

Further east, **Harkány** is the site of a well-developed thermal spa. The weather in this part of Hungary is generally hot and dry in summer, so taking a dip at this point is one of the best

Harkány Thermal Bath.

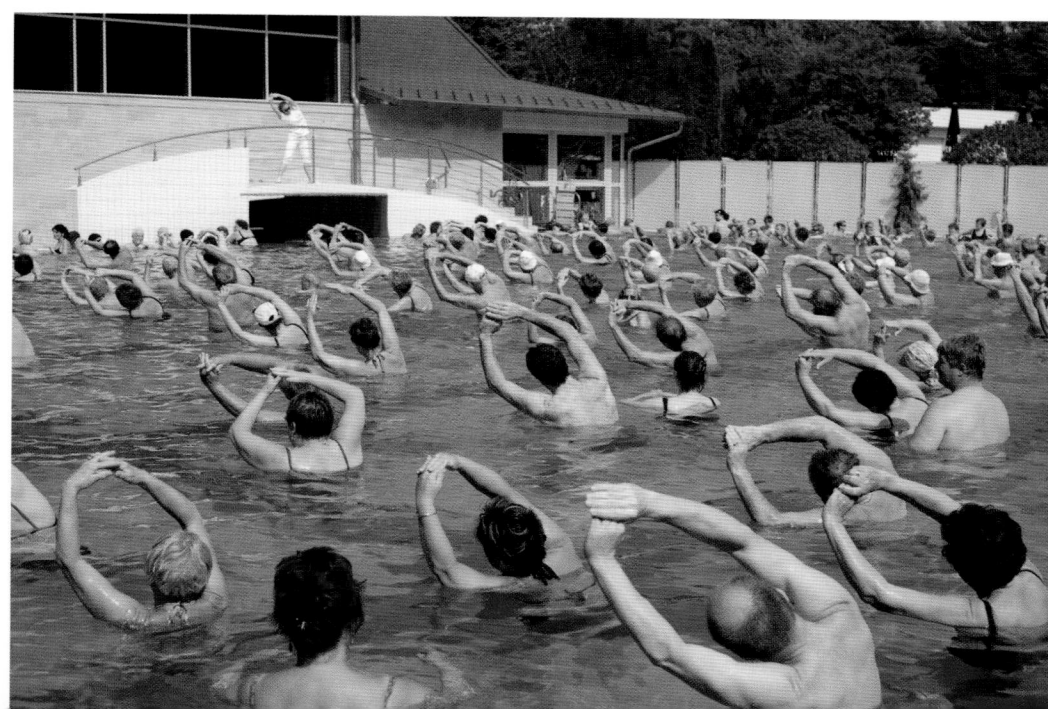

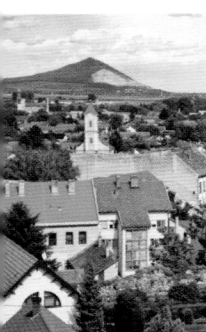

Siklós.

antidotes to the heat. The pretty town of **Siklós** ❾ also has a thermal bath, but its most prominent sight is the ancient castle, and the **Castle Museum** (Vármúzeum; Apr–Oct daily 9.30am–6pm; Nov–Mar Tue–Sun 9.30am–5pm), which houses various exhibits and a modern art gallery.

The church at **Máriagyűd,** just north-west of Siklós, is a Baroque edifice with kitschy votive trappings for pilgrims in search of miraculous healing. More interesting is the little church in **Nagyharsány,** a few kilometres east of Siklós, which has Gothic frescoes; and the nearby Sculpture Park, where one can occasionally catch a sculptor in full creative frenzy.

BACK TO SZIGETVÁR

Highway 67 leads northwards from Szigetvár to **Kaposvár** ❿, a small town surrounded by hills and greenery. The journey takes you 40km (25 miles) straight through the Zselic conservation area (Zselicség, the highest point, is 357 metres/1,171ft), with huge oak forests in which swineherds put their

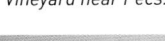

Vineyard near Pécs.

pigs out to pasture in earlier times. Its rolling hills are now criss-crossed by hiking trails that make pleasant walks (maps can be bought in Kaposvár). The village of Ibafa has a pipe museum, the main reason, apparently, being that an old Hungarian tongue-twister claims that the local priest owned a wooden pipe: *Az ibafai papnak fapipája van.*

Kaposvár used to be a purely agricultural town, specialising in wheat, cattle and sunflowers. With the processing of cotton and wood products it has become increasingly industrialised, but keeps its industry within bounds.

The **parish church** in Kossuth tér dates from the mid-18th century but was later covered with so many neo-Gothic elements that the Baroque origins can hardly be recognised. Next to it is a beautiful, limestone votive pillar to the Virgin Mary. Fő utca, which is closed to traffic, is a lively place through which to take a stroll.

The former County House is now occupied by the **Somogy County Museum** (Somogy Megyei Múzeum;

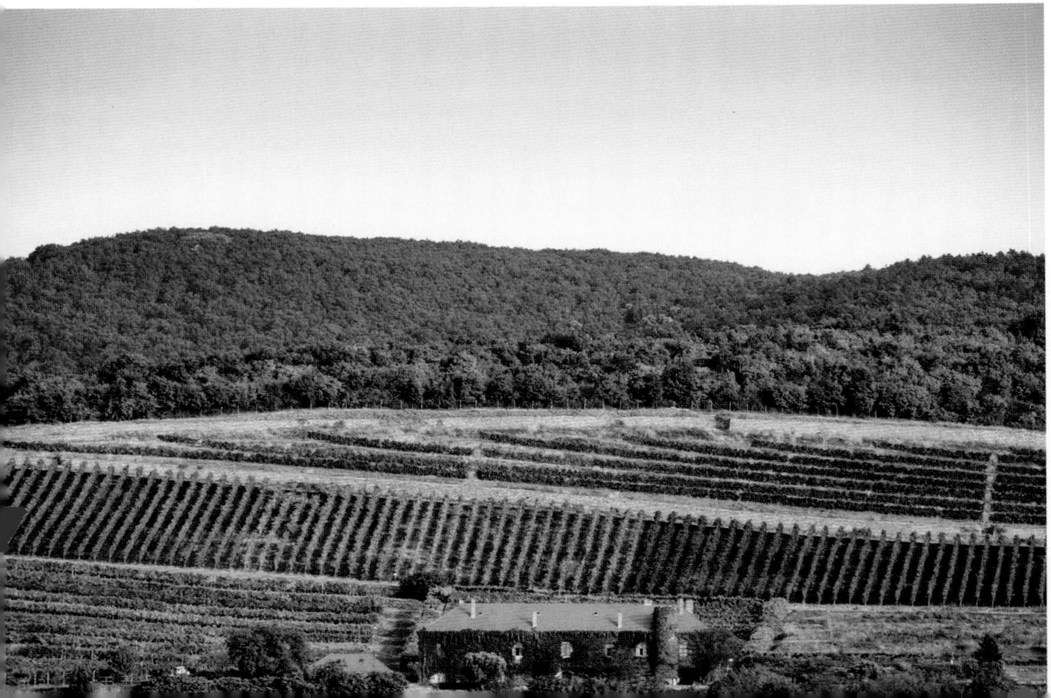

Tue–Sun 10am–6pm), which contains an extensive ethnological collection as well as exhibitions on archaeology and civic history. In front of the building (intended as a prison when it was built in 1828) is a bust of József Rippl-Rónai, the great Hungarian painter, who was born in Kaposvár, and is represented in the museum.

However, the main collection of his work can be found 3km (2 miles) southeast of town at Rómahegy 88 in the **Rippl-Rónai Memorial Museum** (Rippl-Rónai Emlék-múzeum; Tue–Sun 10am–6pm), the house in which he lived from 1906 until his death in 1927. His son, Ferenc Martyn, was born and raised here and went on to become one of Hungary's leading modern artists.

Off to the left (when coming from Kossuth tér) is a passage leading to a small park, where there is a statue to Imre Nagy, the leader of the failed 1956 insurrection (see page 69). End the tour by heading right towards the wonderful Secessionist Gergely Csiky Theatre, a great place to enjoy an opera in this small but extremely civilised city.

The town of **Dombóvár** ⑪, which lies some 31km (19 miles) to the east of Kaposvár, is not a great tourist attraction in itself. That said, it has some well-restored houses, a 19th-century Trinity statue, and a few remnants of an old fort, though most people come here to avail themselves of the benefits of nearby Gunarus, whose waters are used in the treatment of gall bladder and other digestive tract ailments. Proximity to Pécs and Kaposvár makes this little spa town an ideal base for a holiday combining health cure and culture.

Some 8km (5 miles) south of Kaposvár is **Szenna,** famous for the **Skansen** (Tue–Sun 10am–4pm, until 6pm Apr–Oct), an open-air museum with old farmhouses, ancient graves and old agricultural tools. Above all, it is the **Calvinist Church** at Rákóczi utca 2 that makes a visit worthwhile. Built in 1785, its interior is that of a genuine 'peasant church'. There are painted pews, a beautifully carved wooden altar and a coffered ceiling with 117 panels, all glowing with colourful flower patterns.

Inside Szenna's Calvinist Church.

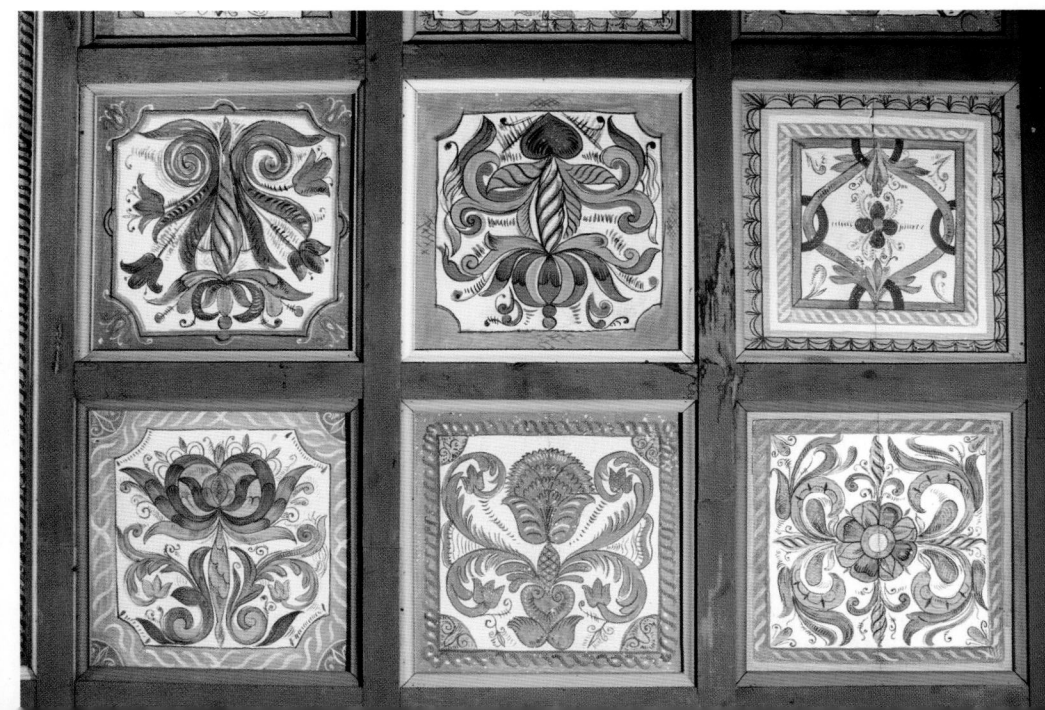

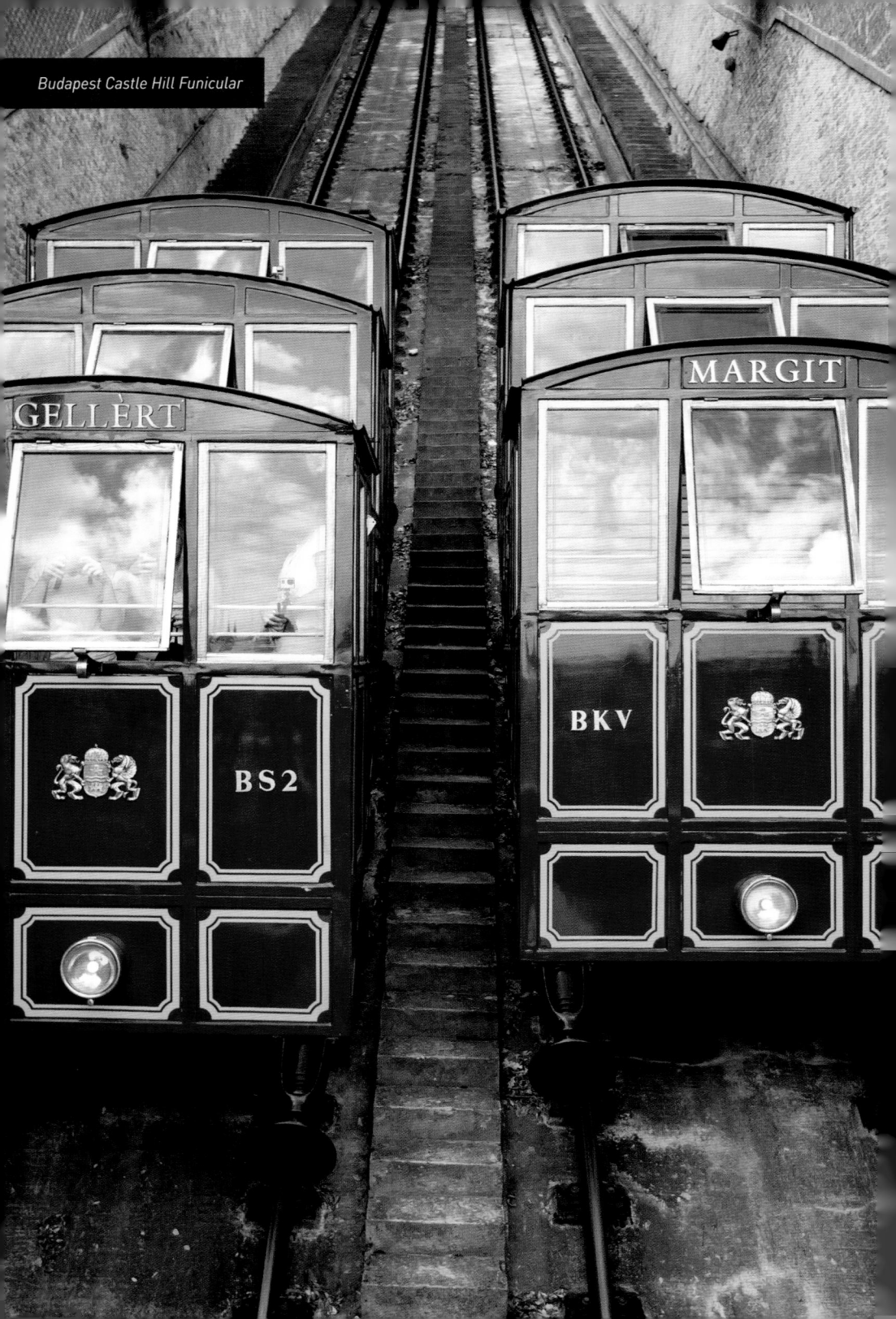

Budapest Castle Hill Funicular

HUNGARY

TRAVEL TIPS

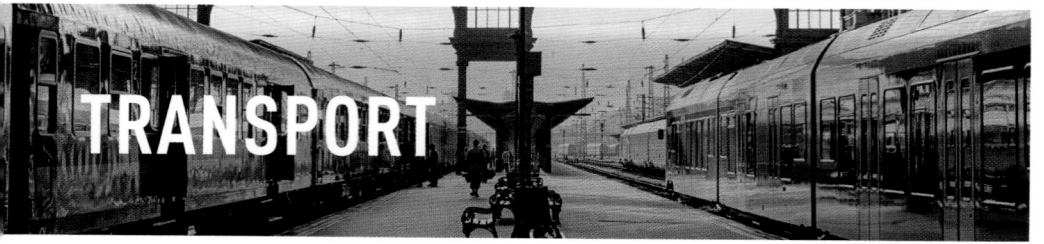

TRANSPORT

GETTING THERE

By air

Budapest's Ferenc Liszt International Airport is served by numerous European and non-European airlines. A host of airlines (British Airways, Ryanair, easyJet, Norwegian Air and WizzAir) now fly direct from several UK airports to Budapest, though there are currently no direct flights to Hungary from North America or Australasia. With the demise of the national carrier, Malév, Budapest-based WizzAir is now the main airline operating out of Hungary.

For the journey into Budapest from the airport, you can take a taxi for around 6,500 Ft, or there's the miniBUD airport shuttle service (tel: 550 0000) which will take you to any address in the city for about 4,800 Ft. Cheaper still is the public bus (#200E), though you will have to transfer to the metro at Kőbánya–Kispest station; the cost is 400 Ft.
Airport, tel: 296 7000; 296 8108 (lost and found), www.bud.hu.
WizzAir, www.wizzair.com.

Budapest Metro station.

By rail

Direct trains run from Germany, Austria and Switzerland to Hungary and usually arrive at Budapest's Eastern Railway station (Keleti pályaudvar). In general, reservations are required for long-distance international trains during the high season and for sleeping cars. Reservations for your return journey can be made before leaving home, or in Budapest with Hungarian State Railways (MÁV):
máv Customer Services,
VI, Andrássy út 35.
Tel: 461 5400 (international travel)
Tel: 461 5500 (domestic travel). The office is open Mon–Fri 9am–5pm, but the information lines operate 24 hours a day, usually with English speakers present.
There are various reduced fares for young people under the age of 26, such as the InterRail card, which is valid in Hungary.

Railway Stations:

Budapest has three main railway stations, which serve both international and domestic routes:
Déli pályaudvar
Southern Railway Station XII, Krisztina körút, tel: 375 6293
Keleti pályaudvar
Eastern Railway Station VIII, Kerepesi út, tel: 313 6835
Nyugati pályaudvar
Western Railway Station VI, Teréz körút, tel: 349 0115
This station mainly serves destinations within Hungary.

Connections

The railway stations in Budapest have good connections to the rest of the public transport system (Metro, buses, trams). There is a direct Metro link between the Southern and Eastern railway stations.

Picking up a taxi outside the railway station will result in one of the most expensive fares you'll pay in Budapest. Ignore the touts inside (and outside) the station and walk until you find a rank or hail a taxi bearing a phone number and a company name, not just a sign saying 'Taxi'. Alternatively, if you're not too tired after your journey, use this as a chance to get acquainted with Budapest's Metro service (see page 273).

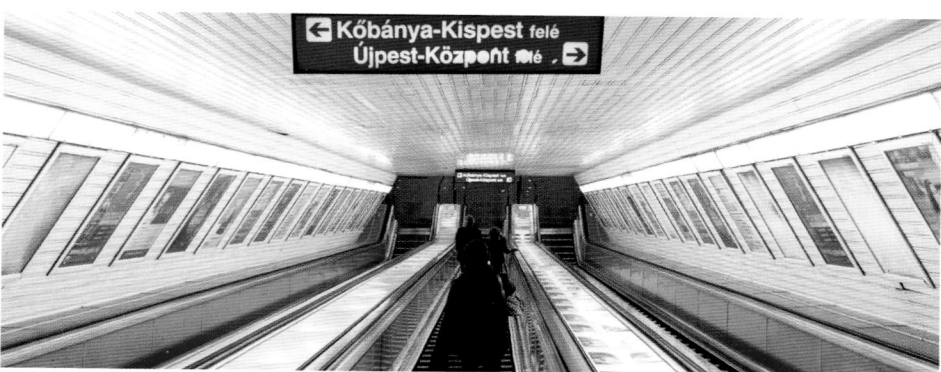

By coach

There are regular long-distance coach connections between southern Germany and Austria and Budapest; visit www.eurolines.com for schedules and fares.

By taxi

Apart from those outside Budapest's main railway stations (see above), taxis are fairly well priced, although cabbies with Western cars may charge more. Don't take taxis that are unmarked or without meters. Also be aware that some drivers alter their meters, so it's a good idea to ask the driver roughly how much it will cost to get to your destination before you get in. Fares are fixed with a starting fee of around 450 Ft, and a price per kilometer of around 280 Ft.

By car

Travel Documents

Motorists arriving in Hungary require a driving licence, a nationality sticker on the car and the correct insurance documents. Also take out an insurance policy which, in the event of an emergency, will guarantee the return of the damaged vehicle. Further information is available from national motoring associations.

Crossing the Border

The most popular route into Hungary is via Vienna and the Nickelsdorf/Hegyeshalom crossing, which then allows easy access to Budapest or Lake Balaton. In summer, however, the wait for customs clearance can be several hours, so choose a minor crossing point, e.g. Deutschkreuz/Sopron a few kilometres further south. This should not be confused with Klingenbach/Sopron, where customs clearance also requires a long wait.

Another alternative is to cross into Hungary via Bratislava. No visas are needed for entry into Slovakia, although making this detour from Vienna involves many extra miles and an additional frontier crossing. To enter southern Hungary, the best crossing point is Heiligenkreuz beyond Graz. The road to Pécs runs through pretty countryside but it is narrow and winding in places, so allow yourself plenty of time.

☉ Distances to Budapest from:

Debrecen 266 km/165 miles
Győr 123 km/76 miles
Miskolc 179 km/111 miles
Pécs 198 km/123 miles
Sopron 210 km/130 miles

Szeged 171 km/106 miles
Zalaegerszeg 224 km/139 miles
See also Driving in Hungary (page 274)

GETTING AROUND

Public Transport

Public transport in Budapest is good, rapid and cheap. An integrated network of trams and buses, the underground railway (Metro) and the suburban railway (HÉV) provide access to all parts of the city in any direction. In the Buda Hills there are also the rack railways, the Children's Railway and the chair lift, the cable railway up Castle Hill and the minibus in the Castle Quarter. The ferries crossing the Danube also belong to the public transport system.

Tickets (best bought in bulk in advance) can be obtained from train and metro stations (from vending machines or staffed counters), as well as news kiosks and tobacconists. Each ticket is only valid for one journey; a single journey costs around 350 Ft, and a transfer ticket around 530 Ft. Don't forget to validate your ticket once aboard. If you are caught fare-dodging – and there are plenty of (often plain-clothed) inspectors doing the rounds – you will have to pay a 8,000 Ft fine. Services (metro, buses or trams) generally run between 5am and 11pm, though there are

Liberty Bridge, Budapest.

an increasing number of night-time buses.

Information about the public transport system can be obtained from www.bkv.hu or www.bkk.hu.

Buses & trams

The Volánbus Company operates a comprehensive transport network which includes smaller towns throughout Hungary. Contact Tourinform Downtown, V, Sütő utca 2 (Deák tér), tel: 438 8080, fax: 356 1964.

In Budapest there are about 30 tram and over 200 bus routes. Express buses have red numbers and only stop at certain points. The 14 trolley-bus routes mainly link up with the Metro routes; route 73 is a direct link between the Western and Eastern Railway Stations. To reach the airport from the city, the Volánbus departs every half-hour from the central bus station at Erzsebet tér.

Metro

The Metro system is by far the quickest way of getting around Budapest. There are four lines: Line #1 (yellow) links the city centre with Mexikói út; line #2 (red) runs west–east, from the Southern Railway Station (Déli pályaudvar) under the Danube to

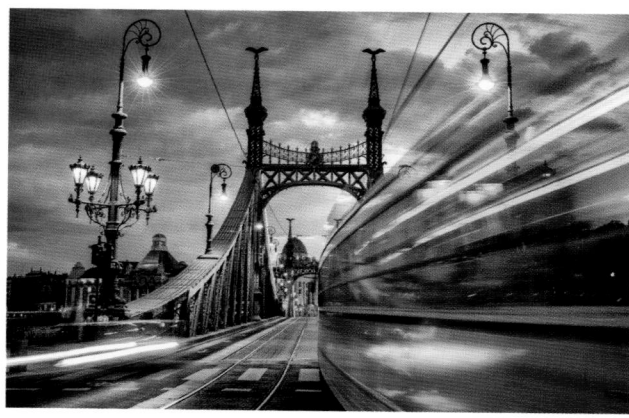

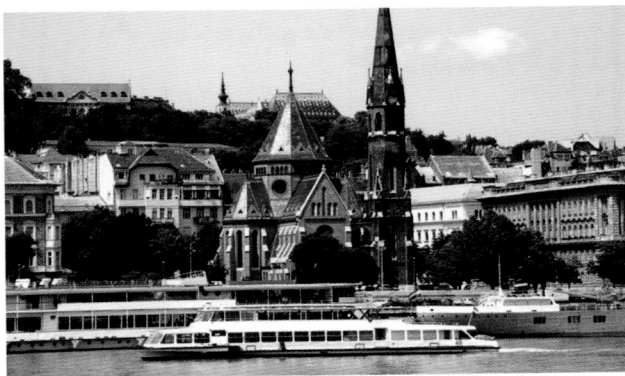
On the River Danube, Budapest.

the other bank, passing the Eastern Railway Station (Keleti pályaudvar) and on as far as Örs vezér tere; line #3 runs north–south on the Pest bank from Újpest központ to Köbánya-Kispest. The three routes intersect at the busy downtown hub of Deák tér. Line #4 (green) runs between Keleti and Kelenföld stations.

Suburban railway (hév)

The HÉV is a rapid overground link with the immediate surroundings of the capital. Within the city boundaries the yellow tickets are valid. For longer journeys tickets can be bought from the ticket offices of the individual stations. The suburban railway has four routes, all of which run from around 4.30am to 11.30pm:
Batthyány tér (M2 station) via Obuda (Acquincum) to Szentendre (the most interesting route for tourists).
Örs vezér tere (MZ terminus) to Gödöllő.
Boráros tér to Csepel Island.
Vágóhíd to Ráckeve at the southern end of Csepel Island.

Trains

One of the more pleasing relics of the communist era is the country's extensive and reliable railway network. There are train connections between most of Hungary's towns. Contact MÁV Customer Services, Budapest VI, Andrássy út, tel: 461 5400, (international information) or 461 5500 (domestic information).

Taxis

Taxis are fairly reasonably priced, providing you make sure to take one bearing a phone number and a company name, not just a sign saying 'Taxi'. Though most taxi drivers are honest and hardworking, it is always advisable to note name, number and company. Whilst it is acceptable to hail a cab, it's slightly less expensive (and safer) to order a taxi to your pick-up address, and there's nearly always an English-speaking operator to take your call. When ordering a cab from the street, look for one of the following:
City Taxi tel: 211 1111
Fő Taxi tel: 222 2222
Volantaxi tel: 433 3322
For getting around major cities like Budapest and Debrecen, you might find using an app-based Taxi service like Taxify (https://bolt.eu) more convenient.

Water transport

There are ferry services from both banks of the Danube to Margaret Island, with departure points for tourists at Batthyány tér and Géllert tér on the Buda side; and in Vigado tér on the Pest side. Contact: bkk, tel: 235 1040, www.bkk.hu.
Mahart operate sightseeing cruises and music cruises on the Danube between Budapest and Szentendre (with some continuing to Visegrád and Esztergom), and hydrofoils between Budapest, Vac and Esztergom, tel: 484 4013, www.mahartpassnave.hu.

Other forms of transport

Cable Railway (Sikló): This nice little ride runs from Clark Adam tér opposite the Chain Bridge up Castle Hill. Every 5–10 minutes, 7.30am–10pm.
Rack Railway: From Városmajor up Széchenyi Hill. Every 15 minutes, 5am–11am.
Children's Railway: From Széchenyi Hill to Hüvösvölgy (Cool Valley) covering 12 km (8 miles). Apart from the driver, the train is manned by children and young people. Tickets are available at stations and fares vary according to length of journey.
Nostalgia Trips: MÁV offers trips in restored trains, with buffet dining. For information, contact the Nyugati (Western) Train Station at Teréz körút 55, tel: 269 5242, www.mavno sztalgia.hu/.
Chair Lifts: From Zugligetu út up János Hill. Terminus near the viewing tower. Operates 8am–4pm (winter), until 5pm (summer).
Microbus: Runs on Margaret Island. Tour guide (in Hungarian).
Horsedrawn Omnibus/Carriage: A horsedrawn omnibus dating from the turn of the 20th-century runs through Óbuda.
A special tourist attraction for those who like such things is a trip through the Castle Quarter in a carriage drawn by two horses. The journey time is around 30 minutes and the fare 5,000–10,000 Ft. Carriages are available outside Mátyás Church.

Driving in Hungary

The accident rate on the roads in Hungary is among the highest in Europe, and Hungarian driving habits leave much to be desired. Driving at high speed and overtaking on blind curves is a major problem so you just need to be aware and stay out of trouble. Moreover, driving at night is

⊘ Driving to Lake Balaton

Coming from the west, if you want to travel directly to the lake, the best approach is to cross the Austrian–Hungarian border at Klingenbach-Sopron and then follow the Hungarian Highway 84 south via Sárvár and Sümeg. To avoid weekend traffic jams at Klingenbach, try using the Mannersdorf–Köszeg crossing, then you can continue to Keszthely via Szombathely and Zalaegerszeg. If you want to approach Lake Balaton near Tihany and Balatonfüred, you can cross the border at Nickelsdorf-Hegyeshalom and continue your journey via Győr and Veszprém.

⊙ Streetwise

The most common street is an *utca*, commonly abbreviated to u. It simply means "street". An *út* or *útja* is different and is a big, wide, straight road or avenue. A *körút* is a ring road. A *tér* or *tere* is a square, and a *körtér* is a roundabout. Other less-used terms are *rakpart* (embankment, sometimes referred to by the initials rkp), *sétány* (parade), *köz* (lane), *fasor* (alley) and *udvar* (passage, arcade or courtyard).

especially dangerous as pedestrians, cyclists and horse- or ox-drawn carts tend to be on the road without any lights. Be especially careful around evening when people come in from the fields or factories.

Driving in Budapest is pretty much a waste of time, energy and nerves. Parking is difficult, jams are frequent, especially in the inner city, and the risk of having one's car broken into is high. The best thing to do is take everything out of your vehicle, find a safe spot (secure car park or hotel garage) and use the city's efficient public transport.

In Budapest, cars are not allowed into the Castle Quarter. Exceptions are made for guests of the Hilton Hotel; parking spaces between the top of the hill and Mátyás Church are rare. You can drive to the hotels (but not beyond them) on Margaret Island via the Árpád Bridge.

For traffic reports, tel: 332 2733.

Driving Regulations

The Hungarian road network – especially the trunk roads – is well developed and, generally speaking, in satisfactory condition.

The most important rules to bear in mind are: seatbelts must be worn at all times; you must drive with dipped headlights at all times, even during the day; and drinking and driving is totally prohibited, as is the use of a hand-held mobile phone. There are strict rules and harsh penalties if you are over the limit. Up to 0.8 milligrams, there are high fines, with possible confiscation of your driving licence; over 0.8 milligrams, prison sentences can be imposed, and foreigners are not exempt.

In court, you have the right to be heard in your mother tongue. For more information, tel: 343 8473.

Maximum Speed Limits

Take care – these are lower than in some parts of Western Europe. Breaking the speed limit is not tolerated, even if the drivers are foreigners.
Built-up areas: 50km/h (32mph)
Country roads: 90km/h (55mph)
Trunk roads: 110km/h (68mph)
Motorways: 130km/h (80mph)
If you are towing a trailer, these speeds are 50, 70, 70 and 80km/h (32, 43, 43 and 50mph) respectively.

Toll Roads

To travel on Hungary's motorways you will need a sticker (vignette or *matrica*), available at petrol stations and at the borders, though you can also order online from www.hungary-vignette.eu. Failure to display a valid sticker on your car can result in a fine up to 100,000 Ft.

Fines

Should you be stopped by the police and fined for some misdemeanour, pay in forint, and request a receipt or a ticket. Police apply the rules strictly.

Fuel

All types of fuel are available in Hungary, including lead-free petrol and diesel. As well as international companies like Shell, the main petrol companies are Hungarian-owned MOL and Austrian-owned OMV; many filling stations are now open 24 hours.

Parking

Opportunities for parking in Budapest are limited, but if you do wish to park in the centre, the best options are the underground car parks in Szent István tér by the Basilica, and underneath Szabadsag tér, both in Lipótváros. Parking on the street typically costs anywhere between 130–450 Ft per hour. Take note that towing and wheel clamping are used to counter illegal parking.

Accidents

If you are involved in a road accident, even if no one is hurt, you must inform the police (tel: 107), who will make a report. You should get a statement of any damage to the car, which can be shown on leaving the country. The accident must be reported within 24 hours. **Hungaria Insurance** (car damage claims), 1087 Kerepesi út 15. **Hungarian**

Automobile Club Emergency Service, tel: 345 1744. 24-hour service by the yellow angels. Foreign languages are spoken at this number. Domestic members of the Hungarian Automobile Club can call 188, but the operators only speak Hungarian.

Insurance claims made against Hungarian citizens must be made through the central office of the state insurance association:
Hungária Biztosító, V, Vadász utca 23-25, tel: 301 6071.

Car Hire

Hungary has branches of all the usual international car hire firms, in major towns and at airports; expect to pay around €35–40 for a day. To hire a car you must be at least 21 years old. All the companies below have a branch at Budapest's Liszt Ferenc International Airport.
Avis: V, Arany János utca 26, tel: 318 4240, www.avis.hu
Budget: I, Kassák Lajos utca 19–25, tel: (70) 931 8000, www.budget.hu
Europcar: V, Hotel Kempinski, Erzsebet tér 7, tel: 505 4400, www.europcar.hu
Fox Autorent: XI, Corinthia Hotel, Hársfa utca 53, tel: 455 4041, www.foxautorent.com
Hertz: Apáczai Csere János utca 4, tel: 296 0997, www.hertz.hu
Sixt: V, Váci utca 141 tel: 451 4200, www.sixt.hu

Cycling

Budapest is striving to become more cycle-friendly and there are now about 200km (125 miles) of cycle lanes in the city; however, take extra care as drivers are still not used to (and don't really care much for) cyclists. Things get better outside the capital: the landscape is fairly flat, and the number of cycle paths is increasing every year. There are three Eurovelo routes in the country: No. 6 (Atlantic to the Black Sea) which follows the Danube, No. 11 (East Europe Route) which (in Hungary) tracks the Tisza, and No. 13 (The Iron Curtain Route) which tracks a course from Sopron and then heads southeast to Szeged before entering Romania. Cyclists can take their bicycles on trains for a small surcharge but are banned from riding on motorways and national highways.

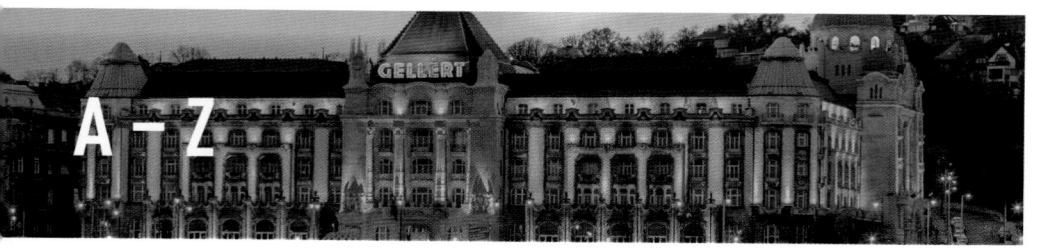

A

Accommodation

Accommodation in Hungary isn't what it used to be – and that's a good thing. One of the most palpable signs of all the changes since the fall of communism is Budapest's hotel boom where visitors can now find accommodation to suit most budgets and tastes. From hulking glass monoliths and beautifully-designed boutique hotels to finely preserved relics of Habsburg hospitality and homely budget accommodation, the Hungarian capital pretty much has it all and often at reasonable prices (except at hotels where it is presumed price is no object). As ever, travellers are advised to book ahead.

Every year the Hungarian Tourist Office publishes a register of accommodation, the *Hotel & Camping Handbook*, which is available free in Tourinform offices in Budapest (see page 282) or check out their website: www.tourinform.hu.

The two most resplendent jewels in the crown of the Hungarian hotel scene are both refurbished 19th-century mansions. One is the old Gresham insurance building, now the magnificent Four Seasons Hotel, which faces directly onto the Danube on the Pest side of Erzsébet híd (Elizabeth Bridge).

The other is the splendid New York Palace on bustling Erzsébet körút, whose glittering café is well worth a visit even if you aren't staying here. Not quite as glamourous, but not far off, is the refurbished is the late 19th-century Corinthia Hotel, also on Erzsébet körút. Yet even with all these additions to the Budapest accommodation scene, the city can be booked out in mid-summer.

Parking and hotels: Car theft and break-ins are widespread in Hungary.

It is therefore important, if you have a car, to choose a hotel with a guarded car park or garage. This can be expensive, anywhere up to an extra 2,000 forint per night. In some cases your car is picked up by a security company and brought back whenever you need it.

Hotel Websites

There are several websites that provide details on where to stay in Hungary, including:

www.hotels.hu – has links to the various hotel chains as well as listings of campsites, spas and apartments.

www.gotohungary.com – the official Hungarian Tourist Office site. Hotels and other types of accommodation throughout the country are listed, but not their rates; for this you need to follow the links.

www.hungarianhotels.com – this is a reservation service, concentrating on Budapest, but does give a few places outside the capital. It also lists flats available for rent on a daily or monthly basis.

Note though that prices are ramped up massively for peak events, such as the Grand Prix weekend at the end of July and at Christmas and New Year. Conversely, there are considerable price reductions to be had out of season. Both reductions and surcharges will be around the 20 percent mark. The rooms are all with bath or shower, except in the case of budget hotels, where your bathroom may be separate but on the same floor. Breakfast is almost always included in the room price but do check beforehand.

Addresses

The Roman numeral at the start of Budapest addresses indicates one of the city's 23 districts. For visitors, the most relevant are: I – the Castle district of Buda (Vár); and V – the Inner City of Pest (Belváros).

Admission Charges

Museum admission charges are reasonable, the typical fee being around 500–600 Ft (€2–3), although some of the major attractions (such as the Esterhazy Palace in Fertod or the Festetics Palace in Keszthely), and many of the Budapest museums, charge in excess of 1000–1500Ft (€4–6).

The Hungary Card allows the user numerous discounts throughout the country on public transport and in a wide range of restaurants and hotels. Further details can be found on www.hungarycard.hu.

If you're doing a lot of sightseeing in the capital, the Budapest Card (www.budapestinfo.hu) represents great value. It's available for 24hr (4500Ft), 48hr (7500Ft) or 72hr (8900Ft), and grants free public transport in the city, free entrance to eight museums, free entry to the Lukács Baths, and two free guided walking tours. In addition, there are discounts of between ten and fifty percent on lots of other attractions, including some of the baths, plus shops and restaurants. The card is available online, from tourist offices, hotels, central metro stations and at the airport.

B

Budgeting for your trip

On the whole Hungary represents great value, though do expect to pay around a third more for goods and services in Budapest. Expect to pay the following in most places: a glass of beer or wine (450Ft; €1.40); restaurant: budget (1800Ft; €6), moderate (3500Ft; €10) and expensive (7000Ft; €20); hotel: cheap (10,000Ft; €30), moderate (20,000Ft; €60) and luxury (33,000Ft; €100); airport taxi transfer (1600–4800Ft; €5–15);

single bus ticket (350Ft; €1.10) and a one-day pass (1650Ft; €5).

C

Children

From a practical point of view travelling with children will present few problems. Most of the better quality hotels are well-equipped, though you'll find very few – even in Budapest – that offer a babysitting service. Many restaurants should be able to provide high chairs. Quite a few restaurant menus now incorporate dishes for kids, albeit these can be quite predictable; a child's portion is *kisadag*. All supermarkets are well stocked with the requisite nappies, baby food and other essentials.

In terms of entertainment, Budapest offers much for kids, with the likes of the Children's Railway, the wonderful Zoo, and puppet theatres to keep them going – and there are loads of city parks too. Outside the capital it's a little trickier. The most obvious destination is Lake Balaton, which, with its clean and shallow waters, is ideal for those with young ones; there are parks with water slides here too. On the same theme, an increasing number of Hungarian spas now incorporate aquaparks, always a sure fire hit. Otherwise, Hungary's many wonderful narrow-gauge railways are great fun.

Children under the age of 6 get to travel free on public transport, with further discounts offered to those between 6 and 14. Children under the age of 12 are forbidden to ride in the front seat of a car. Some museums offer discounted entry rates to children.

Climate

Hungary has a continental climate, although this is moderated by Atlantic troughs. Winters can be very cold and the summers are hot. The warmest region is in the south around Pécs, which enjoys an almost Mediterranean climate. Hungary has an average of 2,015 hours of sunshine per year, which is above the European average. Mean temperatures range from -2°C/28°F in January to 23°C/73°F in June, but can often be much colder and much hotter. To avoid these extremes,

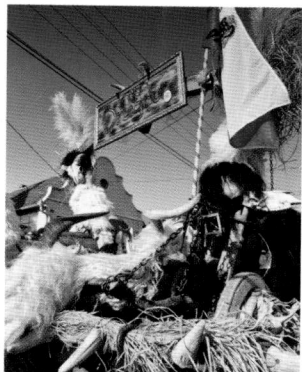

Busójárás Carnival, Mohács.

the best times to visit Hungary are spring or autumn.

Crime and Safety

Hungary is one of the safest European countries, though petty theft is common, particularly in downtown Budapest. To this end, do not carry purses and cameras too obviously; empty your vehicle of any valuables; and do not take valuables to the baths, as lockers are sometimes targeted by thieves.

Ignore any offers to exchange money on the streets (though this is much rarer now) and politely, but firmly, decline any offers of a service – typically a room or a taxi – from anyone approaching you at a train or bus station.

A couple of well-worn scams still persist in Budapest, yet amazingly visitors still fall for them: the first (aimed at men) is to be accosted by an attractive woman, and invited for a drink. The bill at the end will be very large, and pressure (if not something more sinister) is then exerted if you refuse to pay the bill. A milder form is simply being accosted by someone who suggests a particular restaurant, where the prices are high (check the menu first at all times). More generally you'd do well to ignore the persistent pleas of glamorous-looking girls requesting you try out their restaurant, in what is a harmless, but very annoying, practice in certain Budapest streets such as Vaci utca.

In the city, certain localities are known for prostitution, but the business is also practised in cafés, at hotel bars, around discos, and in nightclubs and strip joints. It is very obvious to the casual observer.

Customs and regulations

Cars are generally let through with a cursory glance and maybe a question or two as to what the passengers are carrying. However, from time to time you will be asked to open the boot and pull out a suitcase for inspection.

On entering the country, people over 16 are allowed 250 cigarettes or 250g of tobacco or fifty cigars, two litres of wine and one litre of spirits as travel luggage. In addition, there is a duty-free allowance of one litre of wine, one litre of spirits, 5 litres of beer, 500 cigarettes (or 100 cigars or 500g tobacco) and 1 kg of coffee, tea and cocoa. Up to 5 kg of food are allowed, but it may not contain raw meat. There is no import duty on personal effects such as bicycles, cameras and TV sets, but items with a high resale value such as laptop computers and video cameras are liable to customs duty and 25 percent vat unless you can prove that they are for personal use.

Exporting goods: goods to the value of 303,000 forint may be exported, but licenses are required for gold and silverware, works of art, antiques and objects of historic or archaeological interest. You can export five kilos of foodstuffs which may include two kilos of processed meat products, for example salami and canned meats. Duty-free export limits for tobacco and alcohol are the same as the import limits.

VAT: Hungary has 25 percent vat (Áfa) imposed on many goods. A traveller can claim it back if no more than 90 days have elapsed between purchase and export and the value exceeds 50,000 forints. Customs officials must confirm that goods are in original condition. No more than 183 days may elapse between purchase date and refund. Travellers must bring the refund to the attention of the customs official or subsequent requests will be invalid. No refund will be made for goods used within Hungary.

For more information ask your local Hungarian tourist office or contact Global Blue, www.globalblue.com.

E

Eating Out

When To Eat

Breakfast (7am–10am): It's hard to find an English or American breakfast outside of the big hotel buffets. Try the more modern restaurants/cafés such as Vista.

Lunch (noon–2.30pm): This is considered the main meal of the day in Hungary, and traditionally has three courses: soup, meat and vegetables, dessert. This is often followed by a strong espresso.

Dinner (7–10pm): Hungarians tend to eat early, even when dining out.

What To Eat

Hungary has the most interesting, and arguably the best cuisine in Central Europe, with the spice of paprika enlivening the heavy, rustic food of the region. *Pörkölt* is what foreigners know as goulash. It is unusual, for a national cuisine so reliant on pork, in that it is generally made from beef or veal. *Gulyás* is more of a thick soup.

The Hungarian fish soup *halászlé* is definitely worth trying. There are several other paprika-seasoned dishes apart from *pörkölt* and *gulyás*: *Székler* (also known as *Szeged*), paprika chicken and paprika potatoes. Stuffed paprika, such as *lecsó* (sautéed paprika pods with tomatoes and onions), is a Balkan import. Preserved and stuffed cabbage come from Transylvania.

Boiled potatoes or a form of pasta called *tarhonya* often accompanies the main dish.

Paprika is also partly responsible for the flavour of *Liptauer*, a spread made from sheep's cheese mixed with butter, mustard, caraway and chives.

Vegetarianism hasn't reached much beyond Budapest, where there are a few speciality restaurants. Outside Budapest it is hard to find meatless dishes, and even those that might appear to be so are usually prepared with pork fat. Salads, by and large, are still usually pickled in some way. However, there are excellent fruits and vegetables (particularly the paprika and tomatoes) available in markets throughout the country. See www.budaveg.com.

For dessert, you'll often be offered pancakes. These are mostly made with sweet fillings such as jam. Meat (*Hortobágy*) pancakes are also popular.

Electricity

The Hungarians system runs on 220 volts. Round two-in plugs are used. A standard continental adapter enables the use of 13-amp, square pin plugs.

Embassies and Consulates

Embassies in Budapest Australia, XII, Kiralyhago tér 8–9, tel: 457 9777. **Canada,** II, Ganz utca 12–14, tel: 392 3360. **Ireland,** V, Szabadsag tér 7 (in Bank Centre), tel: 301 4960. **New Zealand** (Consulate), VI, Nagymező utca 47, tel: 302 2484. **United States,** V, Szabadsag tér 12, tel: 475 4400. **United Kingdom,** V, Harmincad utca 6, tel: 266 2888.

Emergencies

Emergency Numbers

These key numbers can be dialled from any telephone:

Ambulance, Emergency Rescue Service: 104 (or 311 1666 for an English-speaking operator)
Fire Brigade: 105
Police: 107

Dentists

One feature of the medical scene in Budapest is the very cheap dental treatment. Even including hotel costs, dental treatment in Budapest can work out cheaper than in some other Western cities.

Bi-Dental
IV, Berzeviczy G. Utca 13, tel: 369 0355, www.bi-dental.hu.

SOS Dental Clinic
VI, Király utca 14, tel: 333 8888, www.smilistic.com.

VitalCenter Dental Network
Danubius Hotel Thermal Margitsziget, tel: 340 4518, www.vitalcenter.hu.

Pharmacies

Medicines can only be obtained in pharmacies, and most are available only on prescription. Payments must be made in cash. Keep receipts for insurance purposes. Opening hours are Mon–Fri 8am–6pm, Sat 8am–2pm.

In every pharmacy there is a notice indicating the nearest pharmacy offering emergency cover at night and on holidays.

Emergency pharmacies can provide medicine 24 hours a day, but you must ring the doorbell for attention after normal opening hours.

Emergency pharmacies:

Deli Gyogyszertar, XII, Alkotas utca 1/b, tel: 225 0602. Open 24hrs.
Terez Patika, VI, Terez körút 41, tel: 311 44 39. Open 24hrs.

F

Festivals

February

Budapest
13 February: Unofficial memorial day to mark the end of the siege of Budapest on 13 February 1945. Mid-February: Hungarian Film Festival.

Mohács
Busójárás Carnival: Hungary's biggest winter festival sees masked revellers re-enact ancient spring rites.

March

Budapest and countrywide
Spring Festival: Four weeks of classical music, ballet and opera, even jazz and rock. The festival also extends to Kecskemét, Szentendre, Sopron, Győr and Szombathely.

April

Budapest
Mid-April: Titanic International Film Festival; independent films from all over the world.

Hollókö
Traditional Easter festival in a village in the Cserhát Mountains.

May

Budapest
1 May: Labour Day celebration in Tabán Park; bands and puppet theatre.

Veszprém
Gizella Days: concerts, folk dancing and medieval markets in honour of Hungary's first queen.

June

Budapest
Danube Carnival: music, dance and exhibitions at venues all over the city.
Last week of May to first week of June: Book Fair. Publishers set up

kiosks on Pest city streets to display newly released titles. There are also authors' signing sessions on Vörösmarty tér. Most books are in Hungarian but there is usually an abundance of coffee-table books on art, architecture, and the like.

Esztergom

International Guitar Festival: Featuring performers from around the world. Classical concerts are performed in the Basilica.
Miskolc-Diósgyör: Dixieland festival in the castle ruins.
End of June: National Folklore Festival at the castle.

Szeged

Open-Air Festival: A summer-long series of cultural events (ballet, opera, rock opera and open-air theatre). June through August.

Sopron

Volt Festival: Heavy rock music festival featuring some big international names.

Zsámbék

Theatre performances and concerts in front of the Premonstratensian church run until August.

July

Baja

Fish Soup Festival: the main square is taken over with hundreds of cauldrons of fish soup.

Balatonfüred

Anna Ball: open-air events and cultural programmes culminating in a spectacular ball.

Gyula

Festival of Shakespeare's plays in the castle.

Visegrád

International Palace Games: Renaissance festival with jousting and lots of pageantry.

August

Aggtelek-Jósvafö

Aggtelek: Summer concerts in the caves.

Budapest Óbuda Island

First week: Sziget Festival, Óbuda Island in the Danube. This week-long festival draws people from all over Europe to see big international pop and rock acts and enjoy the island's unique atmosphere. Fun and games in the Castle District; open-air craft market on Tóth Árpád sétány (Castle Hill). Mid-August: Formula One in the Budapest suburb of Mogyoród.
20 August: Festival of Guilds in honour of St Stephen. Parade in front of Parliament building; music and folk performances; firework display.

Debrecen

International flower carnival with a final grand procession on 20 August.

Fertöd

Eszterházy Baroque Food Festival: Food plus opera, ballet and plays in Eszterházy castle.

Hortobágy

Bridge Fair: Traditional jousting and other events.

Tokaj

Wine festival with open cellars all over the village, plus music and dance.

September

Budapest

25 September: Béla Bartók's birthday marks the start of the Budapest Festival, with concerts, theatre productions, contemporary music series and exhibitions.
Jewish Cultural Budapest International Wine Festival: This festival, in Budapest's Castle District, features wine tastings, displays and auctions, with live entertainment each day.

Szilvásvárad

Lippizaner Festival: Horse show and other events.

October

Budapest

23 October: Anniversary of the 1956 revolution.
Autumn Festival: Experimental art of all kinds.

December

Christmas is celebrated everywhere (reserve restaurant tables well in advance; many places close).

Budapest

New Year's Eve: Gala evening in the Vigadó; fireworks display.

G

Geography

Hungary lies at the heart of Europe, in the Carpathian Basin. It is bordered in the west by Slovenia and Austria, in the north by Slovakia and the Ukraine, in the east by Romania, and in the south by Serbia and Croatia. The River Danube flows north to south through Hungary and divides the country roughly in two: the plains to the east and Transdanubia to the west.

The country can be divided into four distinct geographical regions. The Small Plain (Kisalföld) lies in the northwest near Györ at the centre. In the east, the Great Plain (Nagyalföld) lies between the Danube and the Romanian border and covers almost half of Hungary. (The Puszta, grassless steppe now mainly used as agricultural land, is at the centre of this region. Only in the protected Hortobágy region west of Debrecen has the Puszta been preserved in its original form.)

The Northern Highlands, in the northeast of the country, are not particularly high – 1,015 metres (3,330ft) at their peak.

The fourth region, hilly Transdanubia (Dunántúl), lies between the Danube and the River Dráva on the border with Croatia, with the Mecsek Hill (682 metres/2,237ft), its highest peak. About 18 percent of this area is woodland, mainly deciduous.

Of all the Hungarian rivers, the Tisza (579km/359 miles on Hungarian soil) and the Danube (420km/260 miles) are the longest. Balaton, covering an area of 492 sq km/190 sq miles, is the largest of the country's many lakes. Lake Fertő is second-largest with 320 sq km (124 sq miles) on Hungarian soil.

H

Health and Medical Care

The standards of health treatment and hygiene in Hungary vary considerably. The **European Health Insurance Card** gives EU citizens access to Hungary's national health service (OTBF) under reciprocal agreements. While this will provide free or reduced-cost medical care in the event of minor injuries or emergencies, it won't cover every eventuality – so travel insurance is highly recommended. With the United Kingdom's exit from the European Union currently scheduled for October 31 2019, it is still unclear what the situation with regards to reciprocal healthcare will be afterwards. For up-to-date information, check https://www.gov.uk/visit-europe-brexit.

For emergencies, the ambulance number is **104** or **112** is the central number for emergencies. For lesser problems ask your hotel to call a doctor, or go to a pharmacy (gyógyszertár), and explain as best you can what the problem is. Medical aid is available around the clock from **First Med**, I, Hattyu utca 14, 5th floor, tel: 224 9090. A 24-hour emergency service for members only.

Sunburn (napszúrás) and insect bites (rovarcsípés) are the most common minor complaints for travellers, so take plenty of sunscreen and repellent.

Articles of personal hygiene, from condoms to tampons, are readily available in supermarkets and chemists.

Public toilets in Hungary can be something of an adventure. If there is an attendant, you will be given toilet paper for a small fee ranging from 50–100 forints and given a receipt. Otherwise, as a precaution, bring your own.

Beware of the food, too: it can be very heavy at first for the untrained stomach. Lard is widely used for cooking, vegetarianism is still a mystery outside the capital, and off-season often means few fresh items such as salad or fruit. What the Hungarians call salad is usually pickled vegetables. A mild laxative could help to keep the digestive system moving at first.

I

Internet Access

Internet access throughout Hungary is excellent and just about every hotel and hostel will have Wi-fi (though it may be patchy in more rural areas and/or less accomplished establishments). Most restaurants, cafés and bars will also have Wi-fi, though you will be obliged to buy a drink for using this facility. You may also find some towns and cities have hotspots in the centre. Internet cafés are now few and far between.

L

LGBTQ Travellers

Like much of Eastern Europe, Hungary maintains largely conservative views when it comes to homosexuality, though attitudes are changing (very) slowly. As you might expect, Budapest has a fairly healthy LGBTQ nightlife scene, which culminates in June's Gay Pride Festival, one of the biggest in this part of Europe. There are, though, few manifestations of openly LGBTQ life outside the capital. The Hátter Gay and Lesbian Association (tel: 238 0046; www.hatter.hu) is the best source if information on all aspects of LGBTQ life in Hungary.

Lost Property

For items left on public transport go to the BKV office at VII, Akácfa utca 18, tel: 258 4636 (Mon 8am–8pm, Tue–Thu 8am–5pm, Fri 8am–3pm). For belongings lost on an intercity bus (rather than a metropolitan BKV bus) call 318 2122. For items lost on a MAV train or in a railway station, tel: 312 0213. If you lose your passport, report this to the police station in the district where it was lost.

Budapest Pride.

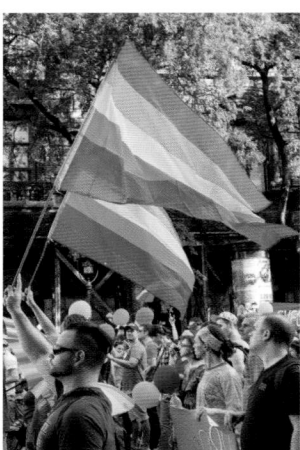

M

Media

Newspapers & magazines
Budapest Business Journal: covering business, finance and politics, the bbj is part of a chain of Central European business papers, www.bbj.hu

Budapest In Your Pocket: useful city directory with some advertising but also impartial reviews of restaurants, hotels and the like. www.inyourpocket.com/budapest/

Budapest Sun: owned by Britain's Associated Newspapers, and catering to the expat community. www.budapestsun.com

Budapest Times: weekly rag offering a fairly comprehensive run-down of current affairs. www.budapesttimes.hu You can also find good English-language news and entertainment listings online at www.xpatloop.com and www.welovebudapest.com.

Radio & television
There are three state-run stations:
Kossuth Radio (540 MW) Talk and music.
Petőfi Radio (98.4 FM) Light Hungarian pop music, sport and some political discussion.
Bartók Radio (105.3 FM) Classical music and literature, including poetry and drama.

The FM band is home to most of the radio stations born in the post-communist era.
Danubius (103.3) mainstream pop music, news.
Roxy (96.4) Pop and dance music.
Tilos (98) Once a pirate radio station, now licensed to broadcast alternative sounds and chat.
Radio Bridge (102.1) Easy listening.

There are five television stations in Budapest that broadcast principally in Hungarian: Duna TV, MTV1 (Maygar TV, not Music TV), MTV2 (ditto), rtl Klub and TV2. Cable and satellite TV, featuring stations such as CNN, BBC, Euro News and MTV (as in Music TV this time) is available in most of the larger hotels.

Money

The unit of currency in Hungary is the forint (Ft), with 1, 2, 5, 10, 20, 50, 100 and 200 forint coins.

Notes are issued to the value of 200, 500, 1,000, 2,000, 5,000, 10,000

and 20,000 forints. Approximate current conversions are:
£1 = 360 Ft
US$1 = 290 Ft
€1 = 320 Ft

Currency Restrictions/Changing Money

There are no limits on the amounts of currency which may be imported and exported, but large sums of money should be declared to the authorities in order to guarantee re-export without hitches.

Most banks (generally weekdays 8am–5pm, and some on Saturday mornings) will change money, especially branches of the OTP, the Hungarian savings bank, though it's much easier to do it at one of the ubiquitous bureaux de change, which are open for longer and at weekends. ATMs accepting most major debit/credit cards are to be found in every corner of the country.

Hotels, travel agencies, tourist offices and campsites will also change money, though the rates are unlikely to be as favourable.

Most restaurants, businesses and petrol stations in Budapest and the major cities accept the main credit cards, but few outlets in rural areas will be familiar with them.

O

Opening Hours

Most shops and department stores in town centres open Mon–Fri 10am–6pm and Sat 9am–1pm, while shopping malls are generally open Mon–Sat 9 or 10am–9pm and Sun 10am–6pm. An increasing number of convenience stores now stay open around the clock. Even in rural areas you can find some shops open until late in the evening. Many of the hypermarkets on the outskirts of Budapest, most notably Tescos, are open 24 hours.

P

Postal Services

In general, post offices are open Mon–Fri 8 or 9am–5pm. However, the following post offices have longer opening hours:

Main Post Office, V, Városház utca 18. Open Mon–Fri 8am–8pm, Sat 8am–2pm.
Keleti Train Station Post Office, VIII, Baross tér 11/c. Open Mon–Fri 7am–9pm, Sat 8am–2pm.
Nyugati Train Station Post Office, VI, Terez Körút. 51–53. Open Mon–Fri 7am–8pm, Sun 8am–6pm.
Address for poste restante: 1364 Budapest IV, Petőfi Sándor utca 13–15.
The Magyar Posta website www.posta.hu has further details of post offices and mailing costs.

Stamps can be bought at tobacconists, which is useful, as a visit to the post office is best avoided: service can be very slow indeed and English is seldom spoken.

Planning your Trip

What To Bring

The continental climate can result in very hot summers and cold winters, so be prepared. In Budapest in summer light clothing is suitable by day, but in the evening you may need another layer. Expect some rain all year round. If planning a trip on the Danube, Tisza, or any other river, bring insect repellent.

Public Holidays

1 January New Year's Day
15 March National Day
March/April, variable Easter Monday
1 May Labour Day
20 August St Stephen's/Constitution day
23 October 1956 Republic Day
25/26 December Christmas
If the holiday falls on a Thursday or Tuesday, the Friday or Monday will be taken off as well and added to the weekend. (See also Festivals page 278.)

R

Religious Services

The services listed below are held in English, unless otherwise indicated.
Anglican, VII, Almássy utca 6. Tel: 269 5161, www.anglicanbudapest.com. Services are on Sunday at 10.30am.

International Baptist Church, II, Torokvesz út 48–54 (Moricz Zsigmond Gimnazium). Tel: 319 8525, www.ibcbudapest.org. Services Sunday 10.30am.
Jewish Information Center, VII, Síp utca 12. Tel: 342 1335 for information on services in Hebrew.
Roman Catholic Pesti Jezus Szive Templom, VIII, Maria utca 25. Tel: 318 3479 Mass Saturday 5pm.

S

Shopping

What & Where To Buy

The huge malls and shopping centres that line the country from east to west are not necessarily the place to look for local crafts and interesting wares. Simple, attractive glassware (mugs, pitchers, soup bowls) or those little enamel soup bowls for goulash can be had at any household shop throughout the nation at very reasonable prices, especially if you purchase Hungarian or eastern products. Buda's Castle Hill and Pest's Váci utca are lined with gift shops.

Shops selling crystal are also widespread. The best place to buy is at the crystal factory in Parádsasvár in the Mátra mountains. Colourful pottery and porcelain from these outlets make for excellent souvenirs or presents, as do indigo print clothing, embroidered shirts, and the like.

Note that the prices for embroidery and lace (from Kiskunhalas, for example) can be quite steep. Bear in mind that lacemaking and embroidered place mats or tablecloths represent a great deal of work that can only be done by hand. In hotels, there is a commission business that also pushes up prices.

Herend (the most famous Hungarian porcelain manufacturer) has shops throughout the country. Up in the northern Zemplén mountains is Hollóháza, with another traditional porcelain manufacture.

Mezőkövesd, where the Matyó ethnic group is centred, sells folk-loric ware at the central department store (Áruház) in the middle of town: Mátyás király utca 8.

In Kalocsa, where the 'painting ladies' work, there are several shops selling local products.

Black pottery (in a coal-fired kiln) is available in Mohács and in Nádudvar near Hajdúszoboszló.

Leatherwork and riding equipment is another Hungarian speciality, as is hunting and fishing gear. Shops with *Vadász, Halász* or *Lovás* in their titles sell such things.

Eatables are another excellent export: salamis (from Pick or Herz, for example) make nice presents, though they may well contain donkey or horsemeat. Hungary also has several excellent wine regions, notably Tokaj, Villány, Balaton, Kecskemét, Szekszárd and Sopron, where you might pick up some special wines. Finally, there is paprika. The rival towns are Szeged and Kalocsa, but whichever it is, pay attention to the words *csípős* (meaning hot, as in peppery) and *csemege*, which means sweet.

T

Telephones

To dial from public phones abroad: 00 + country code + area code + number. To dial outside Budapest: 06 + area code + number. Within Budapest numbers have 7 digits and elsewhere generally six digits. Hungarian mobile numbers have nine digits, and begin with 06 20, 06 30 or 06 70, depending upon the network.

If you want to use your home mobile phone in Hungary, check with your phone provider whether it will work in the country, and what the call charges will be; US cell phones need to be tri-band to work. If you plan on staying in Hungary for a while, you might want to consider buying a Hungarian pay-as-you-go SIM card; T-Mobile or Vodafone are the most ubiquitous outlets. Both have pay-as-you-go offers. Note, though, that roaming charges within the EU were abolished in 2017, meaning that you can use your phone within Hungary as you would do at home; that said, it remains to be seen what the effects of Brexit might be for UK visitors.

Useful Telephone Numbers

Domestic directory enquiries: 198
International directory enquiries (English spoken): 199
International operator (English spoken): 190

Time Zone

Hungary is one hour ahead of GMT, six hours ahead of Eastern Standard Time and nine hours ahead of Pacific Standard Time.

Tipping

In restaurants and bars a tip of 10 percent is expected, depending (naturally) on the service, though do check first to see whether a service charge has been added. The same 10 percent applies to services rendered by taxi drivers, hairdressers and porters.

Tourist Information

Tourist information abroad is available from either a travel agent specialising in Eastern European travel, a branch of ibuzs, or the nearest Hungarian embassy or consulate.

United Kingdom

Hungarian National Tourist Office, 46 Eaton Place, London SW1X 8AL, tel: 020 7823 1032, www.hellohungary. com

United States

Hungarian Tourist Board, Embassy of the Republic of Hungary, 150 East 58th Street, 33rd floor, New York, NY 10155, tel: 212 355 0240, www.hello hungary.com.

Tourist Offices

There are about 120 Tourinform offices in Hungary; these are the addresses of the offices in the main towns. A complete nationwide list can be found on www.tourinform.hu or from one of their offices in Budapest (known as BudapestInfo):

Budapest info points:

V, Deák tér, Sütő utca 2, tel: 576 1401.
XIV, Hosok tere, tel: 30 779 4880
Budapest Liszt Ferenc Airport, terminals 2A and 2B, tel: 576 1402/3

Tours and Tour Operators

Tours in Budapest

To get your bearings in the city, a guided coach tour is not a bad idea, especially the open-topped bus tours. Otherwise, there are numerous operators offering city walking and biking tours, ranging from a couple of hours to half a day.

Detailed programmes are available from hotel receptions, travel agencies and the various organisers. If you're doing a lot of sightseeing in the capital, the Budapest Card (www.budapestinfo.hu) represents great value. It's available for 24hr (4500Ft), 48hr (7500Ft) or 72hr (8900Ft), and grants free public transport in the city, free entrance to eight museums, free entry to the Lukács Baths, and two free guided walking tours. In addition, there are discounts of between 10 and 50 percent on lots of other attractions, including some of the baths, plus shops and restaurants. The card is available online, from tourist offices, hotels, central metro stations and at the airport. The following is a small selection of tour operators in Budapest:

Giraffe Hop-on Hop-off
V, Andrassy utca 2
Tel: 374 7070
www.citytour.hu
Hop-on hop-off bus tours taking in all the main sights on four lines, including a hop-on hop-off cruise.
Absolute Tours
VI, Lázár utca 16
Tel: 269 3842
www.absolutetours.com
Walking, biking and Segway tours.
RiverRide
V, Széchenyi István tér 7/8
Tel: 332 2555
www.riverride.com
Floating bus taking in the main city sights before hitting the Danube.
IBUSZ
V, Ferenciek tere 10
Tel: 501 4908
www.ibusz.hu
Hungary's largest travel agency.
Wasteels
VIII, Kerepesi út 2–6 (Keleti Train Station)
Tel: 343 3492
www.wasteels.hu
Discount railway tickets.

Excursions

For details of boat trips to and from Árpád Bridge, Margaret Island, Szentendre, Visegrád, Esztergom, and to see Budapest by night, contact:
Mahart
Mahart PassNave Shipping Company, V, Belgrád rakpart, tel: 484 4000, www.mahartpassnave.hu.
Budapest Cemetery
If your interests lie in Budapest society of bygone days, you could visit

the Kerepesi Cemetery (Kerepesi temető, situated on Fiumei út just south of the Keleti Train Station). Here you can see the mausolea of numerous vips, including Kossuth, Deák and Andrássy and other actors, writers, statesmen and chess players who have left their stamp on the nation and, in some cases, the world.

Statue Park
After the fall of communism in 1989, the city had to decide what to do with all its Soviet statuary. Coupled with a hatred of the old regime was the feeling that obliteration of the statues would be anti-democratic and a denial of the past. The dilemma was resolved by the opening of the Statue Park in 1993 in the southwest of Budapest. Passing through the red-brick entrance, you'll find gigantic statues of pre-World War II Hungarian communists and assorted Soviet heroes arranged in six groups. A fierce flag-waving soldier based on a call-to-arms poster issued by the communist government in 1919 typifies the style favoured by Soviet aesthetes. Revolutionary music blares out of the ticket office, from which you can also buy drinks and kitsch souvenirs.

To reach the park, take metro line #4 to Kelenföld then bus #101E, #101B or #150. It is open daily 10am–dusk; tel: 424 7500; www.mementopark.hu.

The Children's Railway
High in the hills above Budapest is the Children's Railway (Gyermekvasút), a narrow-gauge line that trundles through the woods between Széchenyi-Hegy (accessed by funicular railway from near Moskva Tér in Buda) and Huvösvölgy.

The Pioneer Railway, as it was known until 1990, was set up in the late 1940s to encourage children to develop an interest in railways, and is still run by 10- to 14-year-olds, with smart uniforms and serious attitudes. The trains are driven by adults, however. The cute red and white trains cover the distance of 11km (7 miles) in about 40 minutes, with stops en route at halts in the forest.

From mid-March until mid-October trains run on a daily basis (departures every 45 minutes); in the winter months there are fewer departures and the railway is closed on Monday. From the halt at Janos-Hegy a path leads to the hill of the same name, with tremendous views – at 529 metres (1,735ft) the highest point around Budapest. From here you can take a chair lift back down to the city. After seeing the museum at the Huvösvölgy terminus, take a bus for the short ride downhill to Budapest. For full details of routes and timetables, see www.gyermekvasut.hu.

Boat Trips on Lake Balaton
There is a wide choice of ferry cruises: afternoon-tea cruises, dinner-dance and disco cruises, and so on. Ferries and cruise ships also run at short intervals between the three harbours of Siófok, Balatonfüred and Tihany. These trips are very popular, so during the peak season, refreshing drinks and a good deal of patience are vital.

Boat trips on Lake Balaton are handled by Balaton Shipping Co. (Balatoni Hajózási), Krúdy sétány 2, Siófok, tel/fax: (84) 310 050, www.balatonihajozas.hu

V

Visas and passports

To enter Hungary, you will need a valid passport. Citizens of the EU, as well as those of the US, Canadian and New Zealand citizens can stay visa-free for up to 90 days. Romanians may stay for 30 days without a visa. Citizens of many other countries, including Australia, need a visa before entering Hungary. In some instances however, these can be purchased at the border. If you're unsure, check with your nearest Hungarian diplomatic mission.

Travellers with disabilities

Access to most of the older sights such as museums, palaces and castles was not designed with wheelchairs in mind. Newer attractions are sometimes better, and spas are fairly well-equipped for people with disabilities. Many of Budapest's older hotels are poorly equipped for disabled travellers, but with so many new hotels springing up in the city, this is changing.

On public transport, there are a growing number of low-floor buses and trams in the city – in particular most of the #4 and #6 trams on the Nagykörút. On the metro, only line 4 has lifts at all stations. On bus and tram timetables, accessible services are underlined. If you want help finding a wheelchair-friendly route, go to the route planner www.bkv.hu/en, which has an accessibility setting.

For more detailed information on accommodation, transport and tourist sites, you can contact the Hungarian Disabled Association (MEOSZ) at: III, San Marco utca 76, 1032 Budapest, tel: 388 2387, www.meosz.hu.

W

Websites

Hungary National Tourist Office: www.hellohungary.com
Tourinform: www.tourinform.hu
Hungary Museums: www.museum.hu
Budapest by Locals: www.budapestbylocals.com

Weights and measurements

Hungary uses the metric system.
In the shops, weights are measured in kilograms (kg) and decagrams (dkg). One "deka" = 10 grams.

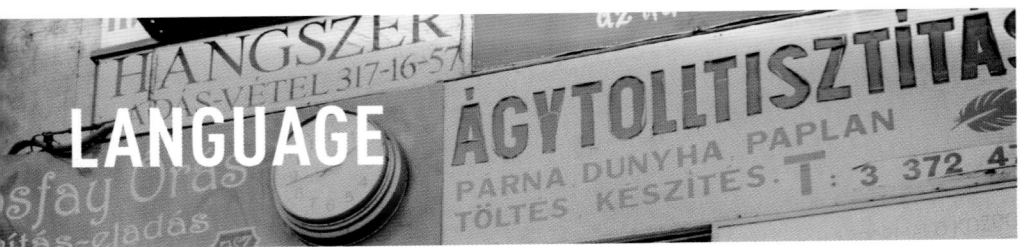

LANGUAGE

Even for foreign visitors who are skilled at languages, Hungarian usually remains a sealed book. Learning Hungarian is different from learning most other European languages. There are no similarities, no opportunities for comparison, no short cuts to understanding this language. The reason is that Hungarian has nothing whatsoever to do with the great Indo-European family of languages: it belongs to the Finno-Ugric group. Its only relatives within Europe are Finnish and Estonian, and its only other relatives are certain languages and dialects in Siberia and Central Asia.

Hungarian is an agglutinative language, i.e. grammatical forms are made by adding suffixes to the root syllable.

PRONUNCIATION

Stress is always on the first syllable of any word. The accent (') does not mark the stress but indicates a long vowel (and occasionally changes its pronunciation). In all syllables the vowels are sounded clearly and fully.

In the Hungarian language the difference between 'stressed' and 'unstressed' syllables is slight.

Two vowels together (ai, ei, eu, etc.) are always pronounced separately.

Pronounced *as in*
a short, deep o as in *on*
á long a as in *larder*
b short, voiced as in *boy*
c short, unvoiced ts as in *Ritz*
cs short, unvoiced ch as in *change*
d short, voiced as in *down*
dz voiced ds as in *Godzilla*
dzs voiced j as in *jungle*
e open e, higher than as in *pet*
é long, drawn-out as in *crayon*
f short, unvoiced as in *coffee*
g short, voiced as in *go*
gy voiced fricative as in *adieu*
h as in English as in *hot*

i long as in *feel*
j as English y as in *yes*
k unaspirated as in *cat*
l as in *English*
ly short voiced fricative as in *Goya*
m short, voiced as in *am*
n short, voiced as in *an*
ng, sounded separately, as in *mankind*
nk not run together not as in *tanker*
ny short voiced fricative as in *vineyard*
o short, open as in *top*
ó long, closed as in *corner*
ö short, open as in *turn*
ő longer than *ö*
p unaspirated as in *stop*
r rolled r, as in *Scottish*
s short unvoiced sh as in *fresh*
sz short unvoiced s as in *sun*
t unaspirated as in *batter*
u short, as in *put*
ú long as in *coop*
ü short as in *mule*
ű longer than *ü*
v short, voiced as in *veto*
z short, voiced as in *doze*
zs short, voiced j as in *pleasure*

USEFUL WORDS & PHRASES

English-speaking visitors should have few difficulties being understood in Budapest. German, however, is more widely understood elsewhere. It might be a good idea to learn a few phrases of Hungarian, if only in order to be polite to your host nation.

good morning *jó reggelt*
hello, good day *jó napot*
hello (fam.) *szia, szervusz*
good evening *jó estét*
good night *jó éjszakát*
goodbye *viszontlátásra*
goodbye (fam.) *viszlat*
how are you? *hogy van?*
how are you? (fam.) *hogy vagy?*
good, well *jó, jól*
sorry *elnézést*

my name is... *a nevem ....*
I speak... *beszélek...*
...English *angolul*
...German *németül*
...French *franciául*
...doesn't work *nem működik*
help *segítség*
big *nagy*
small *kicsi*

LANGUAGE COURSES

For anyone who fancies grappling with the seemingly impenetrable Hungarian language, there are language schools in Budapest, and summer schools at the universities of Szeged and Debrecen. Most courses focus on culture and history as well as language skills. For further information, log onto the following websites:
www.languageschoolsguide.com
1stop-language.com
www.worldwide.edu
www.hls.hu.

ENQUIRIES

what time is it? *hány óra van?*
where is...? *hol van...?*
when? *mikor?*
where to? *hová?*
how much/many? *hány?/mennyi?*
here *itt*
there *ott*
I don't understand *nem értem*
how do I get to...? *merre kell menni...?*
right *jobb*
to the right *jobbra*
left *bal*
to the left *balra*
ahead *előre*
back *hátra*
straight *egyenesen*
pardon me/excuse me *bocsánat*
yes *igen*
no *nem*

please *kérem*
thank you *köszönöm*
of course *persze*

NUMBERS

one *egy*
two *kettő*
three *három*
four *négy*
five *öt*
six *hat*
seven *hét*
eight *nyolc*
nine *kilenc*
ten *tíz*
eleven *tizenegy*
twenty *húsz*
twenty-one *huszonegy*
thirty *harminc*
forty *negyven*
fifty *ötven*
sixty *hatvan*
seventy *hetven*
eighty *nyolcvan*
ninety *kilencven*
one hundred *száz*
two hundred *kétszáz*
five hundred *ötszáz*
one thousand *ezer*

TIME/DAYS OF THE WEEK

today *ma*
now *most*
yesterday *tegnap*
tomorrow *holnap*
later *késöbb*
Monday *hétfő*
Tuesday *kedd*
Wednesday *szerda*
Thursday *csütörtök*
Friday *péntek*
Saturday *szombat*
Sunday *vasárnap*

OUT SHOPPING

open *nyitva*
closed *zárva*
entrance *bejárat*
exit *kijárat*
how much is that? *mennyibe kerül?*
please show me... *kerém, mutassa, meg...*
expensive *drága*

IN THE RESTAURANT

menu *étlap*
waiter! *pincér!*

restaurant *étterem*
inn *vendégiö*
coffee house *kávéház*
traditional inn *csárda*
pastry shop *cukrászda*
cellar *pince*
food *étel*
drink *ital*
breakfast *reggeli*
lunch *ebéd*
supper *vacsora*
appetisers *előetelek*
freshly prepared *frissensültek*
specialities *ajánlatok*
main dishes *főételek*
side dishes *köretek*
desserts *tészták*
warm *meleg*
cold *hideg*
hot *forró*
ice *jég*
red *piros/vörös*
white *fehér*
large *nagy*
small *kis*
I would like *kérek szépen*
the bill, please *kérem a számlát*
enjoy your meal *jó étvágyat*
to your health *egészségedre*
to our health *egészségünkre*
I am vegetarian/vegan *vegetariánus/vegán vagyok*
is there meat in it? *van benne hús?*
without meat *hús-mentes*

FOOD AND DRINK

apple *alma*
apricot *barack*
beer *sör*
coffee *kávé*
espresso *dupla*
fish *hal*
fruit *gyümölcs*
ice cream *jégkrém/fagylalt/fagyi*
juice *lé*
mineral water *ásvány víz*
orange *narancs*
peach *őszibarack*
salads *saláták*
soup *leves(ek)*
vegetable *zöldség*
water *víz*
wine *bor*

ACCOMMODATION

hotel *szálloda*
castle hotel *zastélsálló*
guesthouse *vendégház*
room *szoba*
single *egyágyas*
double *kétágyas*

extra bed *pótágy*
garage *garázs*
parking lot *parkoló*
bathroom *fürdőszoba*
shower *zsuhány*
closet *szekrén*

GETTING AROUND

airport *repülötér*
aeroplane *repülőgép*
main train station *pályaudvar (abbr: pu)*
small train station *vasútállomás*
station (in general) *állomás*
train *vonat*
arrival *érkezés*
departure *indulás*
track *vágány*
boat *hajó*
ferry *komp*
pier *rév*
roadworks *útépités*
petrol station *benzinkút*
car *kocsi*
bus *búsz*
tram *villamos*
baths *fürdő*
thermal bath *thermálfürdő*
medicinal bath *gyógyfürdő*
house *ház*
hill *hegy*
bridge *híd*
gate *kapu*
castle *kastély*
fortress *vár*
palace *palota*
ring road *körút*
park: small wood *liget*
monument *müemlék*
embankment (quay) *rakpart*
island *sziget*
theatre *színház*
church *templom*
city *város*
village *falu*
square *tér*
street/avenue *út*
street *útja (genitive form)*
street/lane *utca (u.)*
town *város*
washroom *mosdó*
toilet *vécé/mosdó/toalett*
ladies *női*
gents *férfi*

EMERGENCIES

police *rendőrség*
doctor *orvos*
dentist *fogorvos*
ambulance *mentőauto*

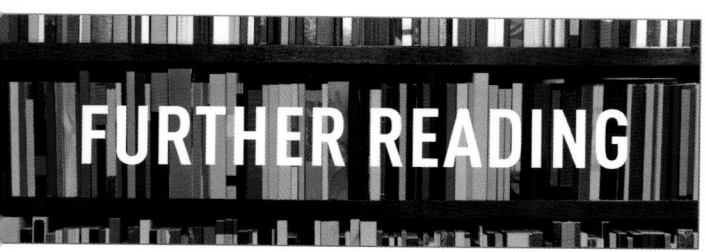

FURTHER READING

GENERAL

Between the Woods and the Water/A Time of Gifts by Patrick Leigh Fermor. In the 1930s this very British adventurer cycled from Holland to Turkey, and spent time where 'east meets west' in Budapest. These are his memoirs of those days.

Budapest 1900 by John Lukács remains one of the best historical books about Budapest or Hungary and evokes the golden era with erudition and a stylish turn of phrase. Probably the best book about the city's history and culture currently in print.

Gundel's Hungarian Cookbook by Károly Gundel is the definitive Hungarian cookbook from the man who defined and popularised Hungarian cuisine.

Homage to the Eighth District by Giorgio and Nicola Pressburger describes the run-down and somewhat seedy eighth district, which was once home to a colourful, pre-war Jewish community. This 'homage' evokes that era.

Hungary: The Rise and Fall of Feasible Socialism by Nigel Swain is a well reasoned analysis of the reasons behind the demise of the more liberal form of 'goulash socialism'.

One Minute Stories by István Örkény. For a taste of modern-day Budapest, try these absurdist despatches from the front line of the Hungarian avant garde.

The Habsburg Monarchy 1809–1918 by A.J.P. Taylor is a gripping account of the demise of the Habsburgs by the master historian.

Under the Frog by Tibor Fischer brings Stalinism, the revolution of 1956 and Hungarian basketball together in a funny and well researched gallop through 20th-century history.

Twelve Days by Victor Sebestyen is an absorbing blow-by-blow account of the 1956 revolution, with detailed coverage of the days leading up to the uprising as well as the aftermath.

Also, **Explosion – Hungarian Revolution** by Jonathan Matthews – a journalist at Radio Free Europe at the time – explores those tumultuous days.

⊘ Send us your thoughts

We do our best to ensure the information in our books is as accurate and up-to-date as possible. The books are updated on a regular basis using local contacts, who painstakingly add, amend and correct as required. However, some details (such as telephone numbers and opening times) are liable to change, and we are ultimately reliant on our readers to put us in the picture.

We welcome your feedback, especially your experience of using the book "on the road". Maybe you came across a great bar or new attraction we missed.

We will acknowledge all contributions, and we'll offer an Insight Guide to the best letters received.

Please write to us at:
**Insight Guides
PO Box 7910
London SE1 1WE**

Or email us at:
hello@insightguides.com

CREDITS

INSIGHT GUIDE CREDITS

Distribution
UK, Ireland and Europe
Apa Publications (UK) Ltd;
sales@insightguides.com
United States and Canada
Ingram Publisher Services;
ips@ingramcontent.com
Australia and New Zealand
Woodslane; info@woodslane.com.au
Southeast Asia
Apa Publications (SN) Pte;
singaporeoffice@insightguides.com
Worldwide
Apa Publications (UK) Ltd;
sales@insightguides.com
Special Sales, Content Licensing and CoPublishing
Insight Guides can be purchased in bulk quantities at discounted prices. We can create special editions, personalised jackets and corporate imprints tailored to your needs.
sales@insightguides.com
www.insightguides.biz

Printed in China by RR Donnelley

All Rights Reserved
© 2020 Apa Digital (CH) AG and
Apa Publications (UK) Ltd

First Edition 1989
Fourth Edition 2020

Every effort has been made to provide accurate information in this publication, but changes are inevitable. The publisher cannot be responsible for any resulting loss, inconvenience or injury. We would appreciate it if readers would call our attention to any errors or outdated information. We also welcome your suggestions; please contact us at:
hello@insightguides.com

www.insightguides.com

Editor: Tom Fleming
Author: Norm Longley
Head of DTP and Pre-Press: Rebeka Davies
Managing Editor: Carine Tracanelli
Cover Research: Tom Smyth
Picture Editor: Aude Vauconsant
Cartography: original cartography Mapping Ideas Ltd, updated by Carte
Layout: Dan May

CONTRIBUTORS

This new edition of *Insight Guide: Hungary* was commissioned by **Tom Fleming** and fully updated by **Norm Longley**.

Norm lived and worked in Eastern Europe for a large part of his working life before returning to the UK and resettling in Somerset. He has written guidebooks on Slovenia, Romania and Montenegro, as well as Hungary and Budapest, which rates as his favourite European city.

This edition builds on the work of previous contributors, including **Márton Radkai**, **Dr Wolfgang Libal**, **Dr Günter Treffer**, **Erika Bollweg**, **Dr Cornelia Topf**, **Grace Coston**, **Philippe Artu**, **Judit Szász**, **István Balázs**, **Ferenc Bodor** and **Pál Csontos**.

ABOUT INSIGHT GUIDES

Insight Guides have more than 45 years' experience of publishing high-quality, visual travel guides. We produce 400 full-colour titles, in both print and digital form, covering more than 200 destinations across the globe, in a variety of formats to meet your different needs.

Insight Guides are written by local authors, whose expertise is evident in the extensive historical and cultural background features. Each destination is carefully researched by regional experts to ensure our guides provide the very latest information. All the reviews in **Insight Guides** are independent; we strive to maintain an impartial view. Our reviews are carefully selected to guide you to the best places to eat, go out and shop, so you can be confident that when we say a place is special, we really mean it.

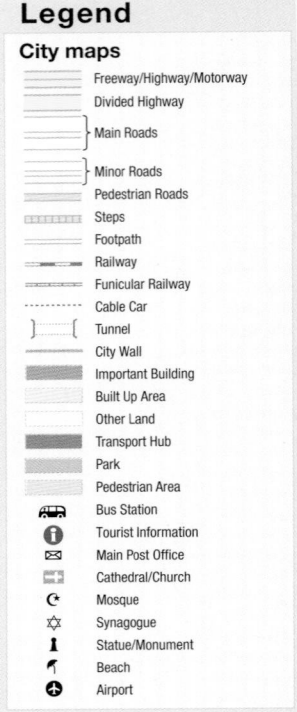

Legend

City maps

	Freeway/Highway/Motorway
	Divided Highway
	Main Roads
	Minor Roads
	Pedestrian Roads
	Steps
	Footpath
	Railway
	Funicular Railway
	Cable Car
	Tunnel
	City Wall
	Important Building
	Built Up Area
	Other Land
	Transport Hub
	Park
	Pedestrian Area
	Bus Station
	Tourist Information
	Main Post Office
	Cathedral/Church
	Mosque
	Synagogue
	Statue/Monument
	Beach
	Airport

Regional maps

	Freeway/Highway/Motorway (with junction)
	Freeway/Highway/Motorway (under construction)
	Divided Highway
	Main Road
	Secondary Road
	Minor Road
	Track
	Footpath
	International Boundary
	State/Province Boundary
	National Park/Reserve
	Marine Park
	Ferry Route
	Marshland/Swamp
	Glacier 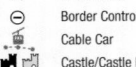 Salt Lake
	Airport/Airfield
	Ancient Site
	Border Control
	Cable Car
	Castle/Castle Ruins
	Cave
	Chateau/Stately Home
	Church/Church Ruins
	Crater
	Lighthouse
	Mountain Peak
	Place of Interest
	Viewpoint

INDEX

MAIN REFERENCES ARE IN BOLD TYPE

N

INSIGHT ● GUIDES

OFF THE SHELF

Since 1970, INSIGHT GUIDES has provided a unique perspective on the world's best travel destinations by using specially commissioned photography and illuminating text written by local authors.

Whether you're planning a city break, a walking tour or the journey of a lifetime, our superb range of guidebooks and phrasebooks will inspire you to discover more about your chosen destination.

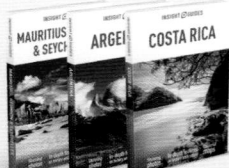

INSIGHT GUIDES

offer a unique combination of stunning photos, absorbing narrative and detailed maps, providing all the inspiration and information you need.

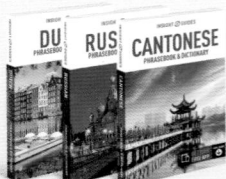

PHRASEBOOKS & DICTIONARIES

help users to feel at home, when away. Pocket-sized with a free app to download, they go where you do.

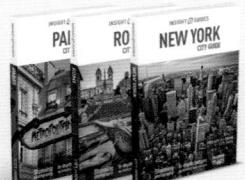

CITY GUIDES

pack hundreds of great photos into a smaller format with detailed practical information, so you can navigate the world's top cities with confidence.

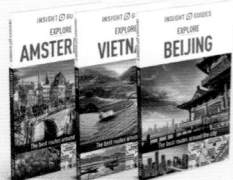

EXPLORE GUIDES

feature easy-to-follow walks and itineraries in the world's most exciting destinations, with our choice of the best places to eat and drink along the way.

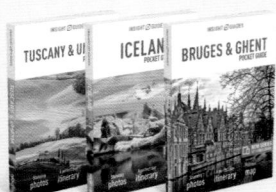

POCKET GUIDES

combine concise information on where to go and what to do in a handy compact format, ideal on the ground. Includes a full-colour, fold-out map.

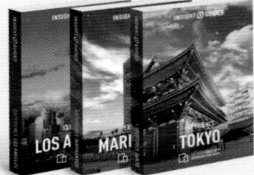

EXPERIENCE GUIDES

feature offbeat perspectives and secret gems for experienced travellers, with a collection of over 100 ideas for a memorable stay in a city.

www.insightguides.com

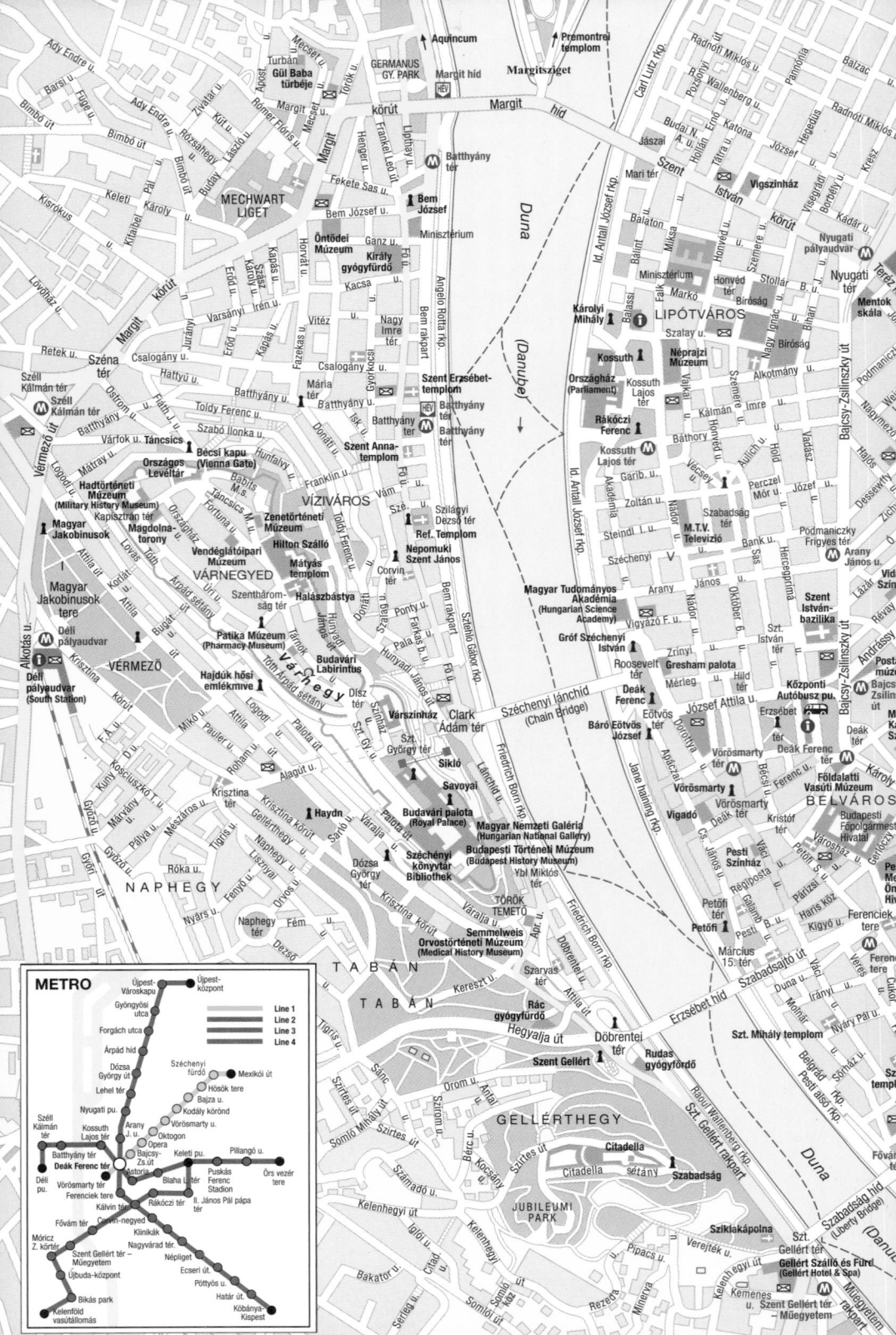